ATTITUDE STRENGT
Antecedents and Consequences _____

The Fourth Ohio State University
Volume on Attitudes and Persuasion

_____

Other volumes resulting from the Ohio State conferences on attitudes and persuasion include:

Greenwald, Brock, and Ostrom: *Psychological Foundations of Attitudes* (1968)
Petty, Ostrom, and Brock: *Cognitive Responses in Persuasion* (1981)
Pratkanis, Breckler, and Greenwald: *Attitude Structure and Function* (1989)

ATTITUDE STRENGTH
Antecedents and Consequences _____

The Fourth Ohio State University
Volume on Attitudes and Persuasion
_____

Edited by
Richard E. Petty
Jon A. Krosnick

LEA LAWRENCE ERLBAUM ASSOCIATES, PUBLISHERS
1995   Mahwah, New Jersey

Lawrence Erlbaum Associates, Inc., Publishers
10 Industrial Avenue
Mahwah, NJ 07430

Library of Congress Cataloging-in-Publication Data

Attitude strength : antecedents and consequences / edited by Richard
    E. Petty, Jon A. Krosnick.
        p.   cm. — (Ohio State University series on attitudes and
    persuasion; v. 4)
    Includes bibliographical references and indexes.
    ISBN 0-8058-1086-2 (hard). — ISBN 0-8058-1087-0 (pbk.)
    1. Attitude (Psychology).   2. Attitude change.   I. Petty, Richard
    E.   II. Krosnick, Jon A.   III. Series.
    BF327.A87   1995
    153.8—dc20   94-45268
                                                         CIP

Books published by Lawrence Erlbaum Associates are printed on acid-free paper,
and their bindings are chosen for strength and durability.

Printed in the United States of America
10 9 8 7 6 5 4 3 2 1

Dedicated to
Thomas M. Ostrom
a founder of the Ohio State Series on Attitudes and Persuasion,
a leading scholar on attitudes,
a good friend and colleague,
and an inspiration to countless social psychologists.

Contents

Foreword

Philip E. Converse

It has been a pleasure for me to read this collection of essays, for at least two reasons: one generic and the other more frankly personal. The generic reason has to do with the importance of the topic. Attitude strength is a crucial concept for the social psychologist. Presented with an individual holding some positive or negative disposition toward an attitude object, the very first thing we want to ask is whether the attitude is held with overpowering conviction, is merely some passing fancy, or lies somewhere in between. For if we can assess the strength of an attitude reliably, then we should possess an important kind of predictive power about the attitude's effects on the holder. Both high theory and common sense converge to say that a strong attitude is one that will endure, will resist attempts at persuasion in contrary directions, will exert influence on the formation of related perceptions and beliefs, and—perhaps most important—will predict behavioral decisions with highest fidelity.

My second and more idiosyncratic ground for pleasure taken in this volume stems from a certain disillusionment I had suffered in the 1960s, 1970s, and even early 1980s with respect to exactly the expectations about the consequences of strong attitudes we have just rehearsed in the preceding sentence. These intuitive expectations about the multiple effects of strong attitudes are so self-evident and clear-cut that I was much bemused, once I had dabbled in the area with the "nonattitude" papers, to encounter in studies reporting from both lab and field on one or more of these phenomena a confusing mix of confirmations, usually weak in magnitude, and full-blown nonreplications. Of course it has never been shown on any persistent basis that attitudes identified as weakly held tend to survive longer and have deeper effects on beliefs and behavior than strong ones. But results, while tilting more often than not in the expected direction, have often in the past had a "now-you-see-it, now-you-don't" quality that was disconcerting. Actual faint reversals of expected patterns did occur now and again, and inconclusive results—failure to reject the null hypothesis—were not at all uncommon. And although outcomes that confirm standard expectations are in the majority, they almost never ring out as loudly and clearly as we feel we have a right to expect. In short, the subject is more complex than meets the eye, and that is of course one reason why this book is substantial in size.

Confronted by such weak and mixed results, I was never quite clear how to set my own mind in order about them. One means of coping is to insist that the theory has to be right, and if test data do not seem to measure fully up to its expectations, there must be something wrong with the empirical observations, because we already know better. Although such a posture scandalizes many, it is not unknown in the history of inquiry, even among top-drawer scientists, and upon occasion has been subsequently vindicated. Albert Einstein, to name one, always preferred a beautiful theory to messy and inconclusive data, and was quite willing to dismiss empirical observations that seemed to disconfirm strong theory, even when he could not put his finger on why the observations might be wrong. In fact, he never did accept the probabilism of quantum mechanics, despite the lengthy sequence of nonobvious but confirmed predictions generated by that formulation of basic physics in the later 1920s and 1930s. On the other hand, various intellectual disasters have been floated on a disregard for observation: The psychologist Cyril Burt was so deeply convinced of his genetic theory of intelligence that he concocted, or at least tidied up, apparent empirical data to fit the theory, and then presented them as proof of its validity. Given such skeletons in the closet, we are generally content in most settings to hearken to the old dictum, "If the map does not fit the terrain, we know which one is wrong." This is as it should be, and is of course the posture throughout the studies that compose this volume. But when theoretical expectations are so strong as to approach the tautological, as with attitude strength, diagnosing mixed findings has often been difficult.

From a personal point of view, then, I take pleasure in the degree to which this volume assures us that a consensus has been building in recent years on the reality of attitude strength effects, and as experience has helped to winnow away various conceptual and experimental confounds, results are now coming through in the expected direction with less equivocation and with sharper effect magnitudes. At the same time, of course, our authors here are helpful in clarifying why past results have often been disappointing, and that is not an unimportant service either.

As it turns out, the very first difficulty to confront us is saying just what "attitude strength" actually means, and especially how it is to be measured. These problems are intuitively surprising: there is nothing in the least abstruse about the notion of attitude strength. A staple of attitude measurement in public surveys involves the type of question, following up a measured attitude, that says "how strongly do you feel about that?" And while researchers dealing with the public at large must be keenly sensitive to terms in questions that will not be commonly understood, the transparency of such attitude-strength questions never seems at issue. Everybody knows what a "strong" attitude is.

However, the more closely we examine the matter, the more elusive the property of attitude strength seems to become. For most lay observers, strength means extremity of opinion pure and simple. There is considerable merit in this view, as chapter 2 of this volume (Abelson) makes clear. But are attitude extremity and attitude strength the same thing? Well, as the saying goes, "not exactly." Most extreme opinions tend to be strongly held, to be sure, but toward the middle of bipolar attitudes we also find some strongly held opinions as well as weak ones (chapter 9: Gross, Holtz, & Miller). This syndrome is well represented by the public official who recently described herself as a "devout, hell-bent-for-leather, card-carrying middle-of-the-roader." Presumably Aristotle, not noted for casual opinions, provides another classic example in his reverence for the Golden Mean as the prudent response to extreme options.

If extremity only makes a partial contribution to what we mean by attitude strength, what else contributes? This volume is rich in further answers, all plausible in their own right, and all advancing beyond the simplistic view of attitude strength that we hold at first blush. But is there nothing left at all of the simpler version?

Most authors here continue to lean conceptually on the notion of attitude strength as something of a latent construct, even though their measurements and experimental manipulations tend to bite off what are recognized to be no more than partial indicators of it. Chapter 10 (Fazio), for example, devotes elegant attention to measurements of cognitive accessibility as one intriguing correlate of the construct of an "attitude/nonattitude continuum," itself unmeasured, but the same dimension as attitude strength.

Having been guilty years back of raising the issue of possible nonattitudes, I would like to make clear my current view of the notion. The relevance to the explication of attitude strength is ridiculously obvious: a "nonattitude" refers to situations where the respondent brings nothing to bear on the terms of discourse displayed in the attitude question, and thus attitude strength on the item stands at zero, whatever response option the embarrassed subject decides to choose. The nonattitude is designed as a limiting case, a "boundary condition." In various scientific inquiries, limiting cases are heuristic to contemplate, quite independent of the question as to whether empirical instances of such an extreme occur in nature.

At the same time, the question of empirical existence is interesting with respect to nonattitudes. Three decades ago, it never occurred to me that there could be any controversy over the proposition that not everybody has preformed attitudes about all possible attitude objects. It does not even strike me as a very profound observation. But as controversy has emerged, it is clear researchers do not like to contemplate the possibility of hidden nonattitudes, especially on the kinds of opinion dimensions they like to measure.

I thought the nonattitude question especially worth raising when I had in hand a body of longitudinal data from a proper sample of a national adult population, the dynamic traces of which were quite unintelligible save by the assumption that the responses sprang from a population that was very heterogeneous in the sense that many members of it had a strongly fixed attitude on the policy issue being tested, while others were responding "as if" randomly in the sequence of repeated measurements over time (Converse, 1964, 1970). The attendant fact that the policy issue involved—bearing on nationalization of the private sector—was at the time (1956–1960) gripping for the politically well informed, but involved abstract relationships that were quite obscure for the politically inattentive, simply lent credence to the possibility of such a rare sharp division of the population into two very contrasting groups, at opposite ends of the attitude strength continuum. Unfortunately, explanation of this unusual case could be read as a proclamation on my part that people in general either have strong attitudes or none at all, regardless of the issue involved, a contention all too easy to rebut. Happily, no authors in this collection have any doubt about the continuous nature of attitude strength between such extremes.

If investigators limit themselves to very widely known issues, nonattitudes may pose little measurement problem, particularly among those relatively well-informed college students constituting most pools of subjects for psychological experiments. But they can always be concealed to some degree in attitudes as measured, insofar as respondents rarely like to confess ignorance if they can rate themselves at some scale score instead.

Furthermore, what "widely known" means can be quite deceptive. In the mass media in France, for example, the ubiquitous measuring stick for describing political candidates, groupings, and policy positions involves the continuum of left–right labels: extreme-left, left, center-left, center, and so on. It seems almost inconceivable that more than a chemical trace of French adults might not understand the symbolism being used here and thereby be unable to relate to the dimension personally. And indeed, if asked to locate themselves on such a left–right scale, anchored with the conventional gradation of labels, very few French respondents reject the task. On the other hand, whether one uses a standard seven-point scale or an enormous one running from 0 to 100, the position most frequently chosen in the French electorate is the exact midpoint ("4" or "50" in the respective scales). Are these all devout centrists? Some undoubtedly fit that description, but it is also true that if we follow the self-location question with further items aimed at what the symbols "left" and "right" refer to in more substantive political terms, surprising numbers of French respondents confess outright that they do not know what these terms symbolize. These "Don't-Knows" scatter themselves to some degree across the range of positions offered. But they cluster very disproportionately at the exact midpoint, an obvious kind of hedge for those uncertain about what the poles refer to (Converse & Pierce, 1986, pp. 128–129).

It is easy to show in this French case that political attentiveness and information are closely associated with both the long-term stability of these self-locations as well as their impact on other political attitudes. Thus, for example, if we remeasure these locations on the same individuals a year later, the temporal correlation (r) within the least politically involved 28% of the sample is only about .30. For the middling 57% of the sample, it is about .60. For the most involved 15%, the value approaches .75. And for a separate sample of deputies elected to the French national legislature—true "experts" with enormous amounts of "working knowledge" in the sense of chapter 11 (Wood, Rhodes, & Biek)—the same r is .93.

This is a rather splendid empirical vindication of the concept of attitude strength, although we must be honest in recognizing that no direct measure of attitude strength per se has been taken. In fact, if we tried to wrench such a measure from these materials by folding together the distribution of self-locations at the midpoint and calling the midpoint *zero attitude strength*, we would be running head-on into what we might call the Problem of the Overstuffed Middle. This is a middle that includes a hodge-podge of attitude strengths, including some true-zero nonattitudes, but also some persons with thoughtful and well-developed centrist convictions. It also includes (and with some attitudes may be dominated by) persons focused on in chapter 14 (Thompson, Zanna, & Griffin) as "ambivalent," reacting in various positive and negative ways to the attitude object that, by their own testimony, net out at about the midpoint.

Thus it is a daunting task to measure attitude strength in any direct or pure way, and our authors here are generally content to leave it as an ideal latent construct. This is essentially the recommendation of chapter 1 (Krosnick & Petty), which defines attitude strength by "characteristics or consequences that strong attitudes are thought to possess," centering in reduced form on the "durability" of attitude positions over time and their "impactfulness" on associated attitudes and behavior.

This definition of attitude strength in terms of its putative effects may seem to put us back to square zero, given our original curiosity as to why efforts to relate measures of attitude strength to consequences such as attitude "durability" and "impact" have often given results that were only weakly positive. But the answer now lies very close to the surface. We have reasonably incisive measures of consequences like attitude durability and impact. We do not have an equally incisive measure of attitude strength. There are instead a remarkable number of concrete measures that obviously bear on attitude strength without reflecting it more than partially. We have seen why attitude extremity falls short of capturing a strength dimension faithfully, because of a muddle in the middle and arguably for other reasons as well. Another obvious measurement tack is to ask respondents directly how important given attitudes are to them personally, on the assumption that positions seen as personally important will also be endowed with greater strength. Chapter 7 (Boninger, Krosnick, Berent, & Fabrigar) reviews evidence from this kind of measure: In a general way, attitudes important to the holder show greater durability and impact than ones not deemed important, and the differences that arise from careful work no longer leave room for question.

All told, about a dozen variables bearing on attitude strength are reviewed over these pages. Beyond some we have already mentioned, these include the reported certainty of the individual about an attitude position (chapter 9: Gross, Holtz, & Miller); variables similar to but differentiable from personal importance, such as "vested interest" (chapter 6: Crano) or personal involvement (chapter 8: Thomsen, Borgida, & Lavine); variables bearing on mental preoccupation or thought devoted to particular attitude objects (chapter 3: Judd & Brauer; chapter 4: Tesser, Martin, & Mendolia; and chapter 5: Petty, Haugvedt, & Smith); and other considerations of underlying knowledge structures (chapter 11: Wood, Rhodes, & Biek) or the congruence of affective, evaluative, and cognitive bases underlying given attitudes (chapter 15: Chaiken, Pomerantz, & Giner-Sorolla; and chapter 16: Eagly & Chaiken).

The face relevance of these variables to attitude strength is for the most part high. On the other hand, the fact that there are so many partial reflectors of the latent construct is a clue to why earlier studies that explored only one of these indicators could not have been expected to show more than limited effects on terms like durability or impact. This is particularly true, of course, in the degree that measures of these separate indicators are not usually very correlated with one another, as is mentioned frequently in these chapters and given a more precise wide-scope demonstration in the important Table 17.3 of chapter 17 (Erber, Hodges, & Wilson). Not only do these variables appear to reflect rather different facets of attitude strength, but chapter 13 (Jaccard, Radecki, Wilson, & Dittus) adduces evidence that even within different ways of operationalizing the same general indicator, correlations are not always very high either. This kind of method-dependence has been another obvious source of mixed or weak results, since most first-generation studies in this area rarely invested in operationalization of more than a single indicator.

It is probably true as well that observed links between attitude strength indicators and consequences like attitude durability or impact have been somewhat attenuated because of the settings which surround most of the research results reported here. While experiments involving randomization of subjects between treatment and control groups must be seen as providing more conclusive testimony about causal relationships than naturalistic observation, several chapters mention the likelihood that experimental manipulations of "treatment" variables are often rather pallid relative to real-life variation. It is also true that college subjects in experimental pools are very unlikely to provide the dramatic variation in attitude strength that can be found in natural populations, where beliefs so intense that holders of them are prepared to kill for the cause can be found in coexistence with true nonattitudes on the same subject.

In any event, the force of all these considerations makes earlier weak findings about the expected effects of attitude strength much less surprising. In the degree that these stem from the multiplicity of useful but relatively independent indicators of attitude strength, we have something of an embarrassment of riches. But it is all in disparate pieces, and the next quest is for some way of putting Humpty Dumpty back together in an intellectually satisfying way.

Numerous chapters address this problem after their own fashion. What these efforts have in common, however, is to take the dozen or so attitude strength indicators or close correlates in the current grab-bag, and try to establish coherent relationships between them. This may involve a logical partitioning, as in chapter 1, or the kind of empirical clustering of these indicators derived from factor analysis, as in chapter 17. Several other chapters, reflecting on the fact that attitudes are strengthened or weakened not only by changes in the environment, but also by complex cognitive and affective processes, assemble at least some of these indicators as tapping different stages in such sequences, thereby suggesting a conjectured temporal ordering for them as well. Some of these factors, such as careful thought about the attitude object or reflections on personal involvement with it, can serve as both antecedents and consequences of attitude strength, interacting causally in a two-way flow, as a kind of positive feedback system.

Most chapters include in their terminal discussions one or more recommendations for future research in their chosen corners of the forest, and while these suggestions are varied, many center upon the importance of a more detailed unpacking of these mediating processes in future work.

I have been away from this subject and this literature for quite a period now. Fifteen years ago I was rather discouraged with the history of results that seemed weak and mixed where I felt they had a right to be clear-cut, and with what I felt to be a general lack of cumulativity in either the problem formation or the conceptual discourse. With the aid of this manuscript, I have been pleased to discover how much serious forward progress of a coherent sort has been made in recent years. The authors are to be congratulated.

REFERENCES

Converse, P. E. (1964). The nature of belief systems in mass publics. In D. Apter (Ed.), *Ideology and discontent* (pp. 201–261). New York: Free Press.

Converse, P. E. (1970). Attitudes and nonattitudes. In E. R. Tufte (Ed.), *The quantitative analysis of social problems* (pp. 168–189). Reading, MA: Addison-Wesley.

Converse, P. E., & Pierce, R. (1986). *Political representation in France*. Cambridge, MA: Harvard University Press.

Preface

This book is the fourth volume in a series of conferences on attitudes and persuasion at Ohio State University. Each volume in this series has appeared when a multitude of scholars in the area had turned their attention to a common problem with broad implications for the field. By the late 1980s, a great deal of research was being conducted on the notion of attitude strength. Social psychologists had long recognized the possibility that attitudes might differ from one another in terms of their strength, but only recently had the profound implications of this view been explored. Yet because investigators in the area were pursuing interesting but independent programs of research exploring different aspects of strength, there was little articulation of assumptions underlying the work, and little effort to establish a common research agenda. The goals of this book are both to highlight these assumptions, to review the discoveries this work has produced, and to suggest directions for future work in the area.

To accomplish these goals, we initially invited a set of scholars to a conference on the beach in North Carolina intended to foster an exchange of ideas on attitude strength. We selected individuals who had already made significant contributions to the published literature and who represented a diversity of perspectives on the topic. At least one author of each chapter in this book attended the conference and contributed to a lively and enriching discussion. Each of the chapters profited from the feedback received from the other participants at the conference.

At a minimum, the chapters assembled here provide an overview of the broad area of attitude strength. Particular chapters deal in depth with specific features of attitudes related to strength and integrate the diverse bodies of relevant theory and empirical evidence. We hope the book is of interest both to graduate students initiating work on attitudes as well as to long-standing scholars in the field. In addition, because of the many potential directions for application of work on attitude strength to amelioration of social problems, the book may be of interest to scholars in various applied disciplines studying attitudinal phenomena.

ACKNOWLEDGMENTS

As usual, there are many people to thank for their contributions to this volume. First, we are grateful to our chapter authors who created a superb conference atmosphere and who accommodated our editorial suggestions. In addition, we are indebted to our colleagues and students at Ohio State who provide a stimulating atmosphere for the study of attitudes and social psychology more generally, our support staff led by Shirley Bostwick, and our editors at Lawrence Erlbaum Associates, who facilitated production of this book in many ways. Finally, we are grateful to our wonderful and amazing wives, Lynn and Cathy, who, as always, were both patient and supportive as the work on this book was completed.

Richard E. Petty
Jon A. Krosnick

1
▼▼▼▼▼▼▼

Attitude Strength:
An Overview

Jon A. Krosnick
Richard E. Petty
Ohio State University

Throughout history, many of the most sensational events and changes have focused public attention on powerful attitudes. From the French Revolution to recent bombings of abortion clinics by right-to-life activists, the incidents that attract our attention are often those associated with strong sentiments. Furthermore, many of the most significant sea changes in U.S. society have involved the shifting of seemingly unmovable and highly consequential attitudes. Among the most notable of these transformations are the shift from the overt racist attitudes of the 1950s to the seemingly more tolerant stance of contemporary society, and the reshaping of traditionalist opposition to a significant role for women in positions of societal leadership into widespread acceptance of such a role. In these cases and various others like them, powerful attitudes were gradually transfigured as the result of intense social pressure and heated public debate. Such concerted efforts at inducing collective attitude change in these instances were inspired partly by the belief that people's attitudes (e.g., prejudice) were responsible for destructive behaviors (e.g, racial discrimination). Therefore, changing the attitudes would change behavior.

Consistent with these informal observations, a number of studies conducted since the 1950s have made it clear that attitudes can be very stable, consequential, and very difficult to change. As Hovland (1959), Hyman and Sheatsley (1947), and others pointed out, most attitudes appear to change only rarely in the course of normal daily life, even when elaborate influence campaigns are mounted to induce such shifts. And some attitudes, such as those toward political candidates, are very powerful determinants of relevant behaviors (e.g., voting in elections; see Schuman & Johnson, 1976).

At the same time, however, social psychologists have accumulated evidence that suggests that attitudes sometimes can be anything but stable and consequential. For example, beginning with LaPiere's (1934) investigation of hotel and restaurant acceptance of Chinese patrons, numerous studies have shown that attitudes are sometimes only very weakly associated with behavior (for a review, see Wicker, 1969). Furthermore, many of the attitude change studies conducted in the laboratory during the last four decades can be viewed as documenting how easy it is to change people's opinions (see, e.g., Eagly & Chaiken, 1993; Petty & Cacioppo, 1981). One especially cogent and influential statement of this view was offered by Philip Converse (1964), who asserted that many people really have "nonattitudes" on major issues of the day, because their apparent preferences are so flexible.

Although these bodies of literature on attitudes may appear to be in conflict with each other, during the last few decades a great deal of research has demonstrated that whereas some attitudes are indeed stable and consequential, others are quite flexible and have few if any important effects. The primary goal of this book is to understand the intrapsychic processes responsible for this variation in the *strength* of attitudes. The various chapters in this volume examine attitude attributes related to attitude strength and the processes by which attitudes attain these attributes. We begin by offering a working definition of attitude strength and outlining a series of attributes of attitudes related to strength that have been the focus of extensive empirical study and that are the focus of the chapters to follow. We also review evidence linking these attributes to the defining features of strength, and we consider the relations among these attributes. Our goal in this discussion is to place the following chapters in a historical and conceptual context.

DEFINING ATTITUDE STRENGTH

Although attitude strength has often been discussed in the social science literature over the years (see, e.g., Raden, 1985; Schuman & Presser, 1981), it has been more of a vague metaphor than a formally defined social scientific construct. For example, when Raden reviewed the literature on attitude strength in 1985, he noted that "attitude strength has generally not been defined with any precision and it does not appear to have any agreed-upon meaning for attitude researchers" (p. 312). Yet the notion that some attitudes are stronger than others has powerful intuitive appeal. But what does it mean for an attitude to have strength? Webster's unabridged dictionary (McKechnie, 1976) provides several meanings for *strength*. Of particular relevance are the notions that strength refers to "the power to resist attack . . . durability . . . force . . . the power to produce a reaction or effect . . ." (p. 1801). That is, just as physically strong people are hard to budge from where they stand and have powerful effects on others and the world around them, so too can it be that some attitudes are harder to change and have more powerful effects on peoples' lives than do others. Thus, it would seem that strong attitudes are ones that possess these two features: They are durable, and they have impact.

In order to formally define attitude strength, we would need to specify its relation to these manifestations. In this regard, we have at least two choices. First, we could define attitude strength as a latent psychological construct that is presumably represented in memory by various attributes of the attitude. From this perspective, durability and impactfulness would be viewed as *effect indicators* of an attitude's strength, because these observable qualities would presumably be results of an attitude's strength (see, e.g., Bollen & Lennox, 1991). If we were to take this approach, we would presume that an attitude's durability and impactfulness covary to at least some extent, and strength would be said to exist only when *both* of these attributes are present in an attitude.

Alternatively, we could treat durability and impactfulness as *causal indicators* of attitude strength, which would be viewed as a *phantom variable* (Bollen & Lennox, 1991; MacCallum & Browne, 1993). In this case, strength itself is not presumed to be a latent psychological construct somehow represented in memory. Rather, it is a heuristic label we attach to certain attitudes as a way of efficiently noting that they possess certain characteristics. Taking this approach, we could assert that an attitude is strong to the extent that it manifests either durability or impactfulness or both. The more of each feature an attitude possesses (i.e., the more durable and the more impactful), the stronger it is. Thus, the two defining features of strength could be said to combine with one another additively or multiplicatively to yield an overall level of an attitude's strength.

Treating attitude strength in this manner allows us to incorporate the most common meaning of the construct and to be consistent with the past work reviewed in this book. Therefore, as a working definition, we are inclined to treat attitude strength as the extent to which attitudes manifest the qualities of durability and impactfulness. Two manifestations of durability have received the most conceptual and empirical attention in past research. The first aspect of durability is the *persistence* of the attitude (or stability, as it is often called). This refers to the degree to which an attitude remains unchanged over an extended period in the course of normal daily life, even if it were never challenged. A second aspect of durability is *resistance*, which refers to an attitude's ability to withstand an attack (Petty & Cacioppo, 1986; see Petty, Haugtvedt, & Smith, ch. 5, this volume). Strong attitudes presumably show persistence and/or resistance.

Likewise, two manifestations of attitudinal impact have been the focus of extensive research. First, attitudes can *influence information processing and judgments*, in the sense that they make it more likely that certain information will come to mind, or that certain decisions will be rendered. Strong attitudes are more likely to impart a bias to information processing activity and judgments than are weak ones. In addition, attitudes can *guide behavior*, and strong attitudes should be more likely to do so than weak ones.

We refer to these four aspects of attitudes (i.e., persistence, resistance, impact on information processing and judgments, and guiding behavior) as the *defining features* of strength. Thus, consistent with common dictionary definitions of strength, we define *attitude strength* in terms of postulated marker characteristics or consequences that strong attitudes are thought to possess. That is, an attitude's strength is the degree to which it possesses these features. The primary goal of this book is to understand how and why attitudes come to have these strength properties, as well as sources of relations among them.

RELATIONS AMONG THE DEFINING FEATURES
OF ATTITUDE STRENGTH

Although the various defining features of strong attitudes can be separated conceptually and empirically, they do seem likely to co-occur, for a number of reasons. First, some of the features appear to influence others in a rather direct manner. For example, an attitude's stability over time is likely to be a joint function of its resistance to overt challenges as well as the degree to which its representation in memory fades naturally over time. Also, attitudes that are expressed frequently in behavior are likely to be reinforced in memory, contributing to persistence. Furthermore, as Schwarz (1978) noted, an attitude assessed at one time is unlikely to predict behavior at a later time if the attitude does not persist over the time interval. That is, the ability of an attitude to predict a subsequent behavior is dependent on the attitude's stability. Similarly, Fazio (1986; ch. 10, this volume) argued that attitudes influence our behavior in part by shaping our perceptions of the world around us. That is, the ability of an attitude to predict behavior is dependent in part on the attitude's ability to bias perceptions of the attitude object and the behavioral context.

In addition to the relatively direct influence of some features on others, there are also likely to be indirect influences of one feature on another. For example, the more a person performs behaviors toward an object that are consistent with his or her attitude toward it, the more committed he or she will be to the attitude (see Kiesler, 1971). The more committed an individual is to an attitude, the more likely he or she is to resist attempts to change it (Hovland, Campbell, & Brock, 1957).

Yet another possible source of commonality among the four features of strong attitudes is shared origins. For instance, factors that might enhance an attitude's impact on information processing also seem likely thereby to enhance its resistance to change. So, for example, the more knowledgeable a person becomes about an attitude object, the harder it will likely be to change his or her attitude toward the object, because there is so much support for the existing viewpoint. In addition, having more knowledge about an object is also likely to enhance the impact of the attitude on information processing, because the person will have a greater ability to interpret events as consistent with the attitude.

Thus, there are a number of reasons to expect that attitudes possessing any one of the four aspects of strength that we have identified will often possess all of them. Yet remarkably little research has been done to date exploring the degree of empirical overlap among these features of attitudes or the degree to which they can reasonably be thought of as reflecting a single underlying construct that might be called strength. We therefore adopt the definition of strength that makes no presumptions about these relations.

STRENGTH-RELATED DIMENSIONS OF ATTITUDES

Numerous studies have investigated the attributes of attitudes (e.g., knowledge) that are correlates of each of the four strength features (e.g., resistance to change). Since the late 1960s, a variety of strength-related attributes have been proposed and investigated. For example, in his chapter on attitude measurement in the *Handbook of Social Psychology*, Scott (1968) described 10 such properties: magnitude (extremity), intensity, ambivalence, salience, affective salience, cognitive complexity, overtness, embeddedness, flexibility, and consciousness. Since Scott's chapter appeared, some of these properties have been the subject of extensive empirical research, whereas other properties have been largely ignored in the empirical literature. In his literature review in the mid-1980s, Raden (1985) expanded Scott's list by examining accessibility, evaluative-cognitive consistency, certainty, direct behavioral experience, importance, latitudes of acceptance and rejection, and vested interest. Since then, a number of other attributes related to strength have been proposed and explored. These specific properties were of interest mostly because they were assumed to relate to an attitude's durability and/or impactfulness.

The chapters in this book focus on some of the strength-related dimensions of attitudes that have been addressed in empirical research extensively since the 1950s. As we describe in the following, these strength-related attributes can be viewed as falling into four categories: (a) aspects of the attitude itself, (b) aspects of the cognitive structure associated with the attitude and attitude object in memory, (c) subjective beliefs about the attitude and attitude object, and (d) cognitive processes by which an attitude is formed.[1]

Aspects of Attitudes

Attitudes are presumed to vary along an evaluative continuum ranging from a strongly positive orientation to a neutral orientation to a strongly negative orientation. This continuum can be decomposed into valence (i.e., positive or nega-

---

[1]Some researchers have recently begun to explore the genetic determinants of attitude strength as well (e.g., see Tesser, 1993). That is, some attitudes may be durable and impactful because they have an inherited component. For example, attitudes such as liking to work may have biological origins that are common to all humans (Arvey, Bouchard, Segal, & Abraham, 1989). Other attitudes (e.g., liking of loud parties) may be tied to inherited individual differences (e.g., introversion/ extraversion; Eysenck, 1967). The chapters in this book focus on aspects of strength that are presumably learned, and thus might be more easily modifiable.

tive) and extremity (degree of favorability). Both valence and extremity might
be related to strength in that, for example, holding extremity constant, negative
attitudes might be more durable or impactful than positive ones. However, most
research attention has focused on extremity. *Extremity* is the extent to which the
attitude deviates from neutrality. The more extreme an attitude is, the more an
individual likes or dislikes the object (see Abelson, ch. 2, this volume; Judd &
Brauer, ch. 3, this volume).

Aspects of Attitude Structure

Many theorists assume that attitudes exist in memory within a network of associative links connecting them to other cognitive elements (e.g., Pratkanis &
Greenwald, 1989). Fazio (1986) proposed that an attitude can be thought of as
a link between the representation of an attitude object and its evaluation in
memory. Attitude *accessibility* is defined as the strength of the object-evaluation
link and is most directly manifest as the ease with which an attitude comes to
mind in the course of social perception (see Fazio, ch. 10, this volume).

Attitudes are also thought to be linked to *knowledge* about the attitude object.
Some attitudes are accompanied by a great deal of attitude-relevant knowledge,
whereas others are associated with little knowledge (e.g., Wood, 1982). In the
attitude strength literature, knowledge has been examined in terms of the size of
the body of information one has about an object, a person's subjective perception
of the amount of information he or she has, and the content of that information
(see Davidson, ch. 12, this volume; Jaccard, Radecki, Wilson, & Dittus, ch. 13,
this volume; Wood, Rhodes, & Biek, ch. 11, this volume). This information can
include memories of emotions and past behaviors that are evoked by the object
as well as more specific attributes of the object.

Furthermore, attitudes vary in the degree to which there is consistency between
evaluations of the object and the information associated with it. Most research
attention has focussed on two kinds of consistency: consistency of the attitude
with beliefs about the object's attributes (evaluative-cognitive consistency), and
consistency of the attitude with emotions associated with the object (evaluative-
affective consistency; Breckler, 1984; Crites, Fabrigar, & Petty, 1994; Rosenberg,
1956; see Chaiken, Pomerantz, & Giner-Sorolla, ch. 15, this volume).

Rather than conceiving of attitudes as single evaluations of objects, it is
possible to view an attitude as the summary of two distinct components: the
degree to which one evaluates an object positively, and the degree to which it
is evaluated negatively (e.g., Kaplan, 1972). *Ambivalence* refers to the degree of
conflict between these two components (see Thompson, Zanna, & Griffin, ch.
14, this volume). Attitudes low in ambivalence involve either mostly positive
evaluation or mostly negative evaluation, whereas highly ambivalent attitudes
involve both positive and negative evaluations.

Subjective Beliefs About Attitudes and Attitude Objects

People hold a number of beliefs about the attributes of their own attitudes and about the attitude object. For example, people perceive some attitude objects to be closely connected to their important personal goals, desires, and wishes (e.g., Petty & Cacioppo, 1990; Petty, Cacioppo, & Haugtvedt, 1992). That is, some attitude objects are high in *personal relevance* and produce a sense of *personal involvement* with the issue (see Thomsen, Borgida, & Lavine, ch. 8, this volume). One particular basis of personal relevance or involvement is *vested-interest* (see Crano, ch. 6, this volume), the extent to which the attitude object is perceived to be instrumental to one's tangible outcomes (see also, Johnson & Eagly, 1989).[2]

In a similar vein, some people consider an attitude to be very important to them personally, and consequently they care deeply and are especially concerned about it (Krosnick, 1988a). Attitude *importance* is thus the degree of psychological significance people attach to an attitude (see Boninger, Krosnick, Berent, & Fabrigar, ch. 7, this volume). Attitude importance is thought to be a manifestation of the degree of personal relevance of the attitude object (Boninger, Krosnick, & Berent, 1995).

Attitude researchers generally believe that people are motivated to hold "correct" attitudes (see, e.g., Festinger, 1954; Petty & Cacioppo, 1986). Yet people are more confident in the correctness of some attitudes than others. Furthermore, people vary in the extent of their confidence that their attitudes toward any given object accurately represent their overall orientations toward it. Attitude *certainty* refers to the degree to which an individual is confident in his or her attitude toward an object, in both of these senses (see Gross, Holtz, & Miller, ch. 9, this volume).

Processes

Rather than focusing on a particular characteristic of the attitude or its structure, some theorists have focused on the cognitive processes by which an attitude is formed. The most notable of these is *elaboration* (e.g., Petty & Cacioppo, 1981; 1986). Elaboration refers to the degree of thinking one does and has done about an attitude object's attributes, its merits and drawbacks (see Petty, Haugtvedt, & Smith, ch. 5, this volume; Tesser, Martin, & Mendolia, ch. 4, this volume).[3]

---

[2]Because links to the self can sometimes be structural (e.g., an attitude that is connected in memory to a self-schema), one might classify personal relevance as a structural feature of attitudes. Although this is reasonable, researchers have emphasized the consequences of *perceived* self-relevance rather than actual self-relevance in the form of structural linkage.

[3]Some other strength-related attitude attributes have been discussed at length in the literature, such as direct behavioral experience (Fazio & Zanna, 1981) and latitudes of acceptance, rejection, and noncommitment (Sherif, Sherif, & Nebergall, 1965). Although these dimensions are not central foci of this book, they are discussed in various chapters.

RELATIONS OF THE DIMENSIONS TO STRENGTH

These attitude dimensions have typically been examined in separate investigations that related each one individually to durability and/or impactfulness (e.g., Fazio, Chen, McDonel, & Sherman, 1982; Haugtvedt & Petty, 1992; Wood, 1982). Furthermore, the key attributes of attitudes related to strength have been defined and operationalized in ways that may make them appear clearly distinct from one another. Thus it is plausible that they may have unique origins and unique effects. As distinct as these constructs appear, however, they all share one feature in common: They appear to be related to the four defining features of strong attitudes.

Studies to date have used a variety of approaches to assess these features. For example, resistance has been gauged most often by exposing people to persuasive messages in laboratory settings and assessing how much attitudes change as a result (e.g., Ewing, 1942). But other studies have employed different change-inducing methodologies. In some, people were asked leading questions about their attitudes that led some to change (e.g., Swann & Ely, 1984). In other studies, people were instructed to think about the reasons for their attitudes, a procedure that also induces change in some of them (Wilson, Kraft, & Dunn, 1989; see Erber, Hodges, & Wilson, ch. 17, this volume). All such manipulations are expected to have more impact on weak attitudes than on strong ones.

Studies of attitude persistence have typically assessed an attitude at one time point, reassessed it at a later time point, and estimated the correlation between the two (e.g., Schuman & Presser, 1981). In some cases, multiple indicators have been collected at each time point, or attitudes have been measured at three or more time points, allowing researchers to estimate attitude stability while correcting for the distorting impact of random and systematic measurement error (e.g., Feldman, 1989; Krosnick, 1988b). In still other studies, stability has been assessed by seeing how much a group's mean attitude is maintained over time (e.g., Chaiken, 1980; Haugtvedt & Petty, 1992). As gauged in any of these ways, the stability of strong attitudes is expected to exceed that of weak attitudes.

A wide diversity of approaches have been taken to assessing the impact of attitudes on information processing. In each case, the valence of attitudes (ranging from favorable to unfavorable) has been used to predict valenced judgments or biases of some sort, based on the assumption that attitudes play a role in determining these judgments. For example, attitudes can bias the evaluation of scientific data: Evidence supporting our attitudes is seen as more compelling than evidence that disagrees with our attitudes (Lord, Ross, & Lepper, 1979). Also, attitudes are presumed to influence attraction to others. We presumably like others who share our attitudes more than those who do not (e.g., Byrne, 1971). Attitudes are also presumed to influence our perceptions of other people's attitudes—we presume that others share our attitudes if we like them, and we presume that they do not share our attitudes if we dislike them (e.g., Heider,

1958). In addition, attitudes are presumed to shape memory for relevant information, such that people are more likely to remember attitude-consistent information than attitude-challenging information (e.g., Festinger, 1957; Roberts,
1985). Conventional paradigms assessing these effects, either in experimental
laboratory settings or via survey questionnaires, have all been used to examine
whether strong attitudes have more powerful effects than weak ones.

Finally, attitude–behavior consistency has been gauged in a variety of different
ways. For example, some studies have measured people's attitudes toward an
object and then given them an opportunity to perform a behavior that is either
favorable or unfavorable toward the object, such as signing a petition advocating
a certain view (e.g., Weigel & Newman, 1976). In other studies, subjects'
behaviors performed in the course of everyday life were measured directly and
compared with attitude reports (Ajzen & Madden, 1986). In still other studies,
instead of observing people's behavior, researchers have relied upon subjects'
reports of their past behavior or upon reports of behavioral intentions regarding
the future (e.g., Davidson & Morrison, 1983; Miller & Grush, 1986). In each
case, strong attitudes were expected to be more consistent with behavior than
weak ones.

Studies to date have not yet assessed the relations of all strength-related
dimensions to all four defining features in these ways. However, those relations
that have been assessed are remarkably consistent: Each dimension has been
shown to be positively associated with one or more of the four defining features
(for reviews, see Krosnick & Abelson, 1992; Krosnick, Boninger, Chuang,
Berent, & Carnot, 1993; Raden, 1985). Furthermore, only in very few instances
has one of the dimensions been found to be unrelated to one of these features,
and in no case has a dimension been found to be negatively related to one of
the features. Thus, at the very least, all of these dimensions seem related to
strength.

RELATIONS AMONG THE DIMENSIONS

Why might there be such strong similarity among these dimensions in terms of
their correlations with the defining features of attitude strength? One possibility
is that all these dimensions reflect a single underlying construct. That is, although
the various dimensions are clearly conceptually and operationally distinct from
one another, they may share a small set of common causes. One might therefore
think of the confluence of these dimensions as constituting emotional and intellectual engagement in an attitude. Such engagement could be sparked initially,
for example, by recognizing the personal relevance of the issue (Petty & Cacioppo, 1979). This might instigate a sense of importance at first, which might
then inspire extensive thinking and information-gathering, which might ultimately
yield extremity, certainty, expanded knowledge, and so forth (e.g., Boninger et

al., ch. 7, this volume; Petty et al., ch. 5, this volume). Ultimately, all of the attitude dimensions might be uniformly shaped by a set of common causes, leading to such high correlations among the dimensions that they might be viewed as reflecting a single underlying construct. More generally, inducing a high level in any one of these dimensions might, over a period of time, reverberate throughout the system, ultimately producing high levels in them all. Consequently, any departures from perfect association among the dimensions for any given attitude might then simply reflect the fact that these sequential processes have not yet completely unfolded. According to this view, virtually all associations between these dimensions and attitude strength features would be redundant.

The great similarity between the dimensions in terms of their relations to the four defining features of strong attitudes justifies empirical examination of the associations among the dimensions. On the one hand, the dimensions may be highly overlapping with one another and may therefore have essentially identical effects on attitude strength features. Alternatively, it is possible that each of the dimensions is uniquely related to the strength features, enhancing an attitude's persistence, resistance, and impact on cognition and behavior through unique processes. Or, there may be at least some overlap among some of the dimensions that reflect a smaller set of higher order constructs.

Support for the notion of reverberation comes from evidence that some of the attitude dimensions cause others. For example, thinking about an attitude object increases its accessibility (Rennier, 1988). Also, thinking about an attitude can increase its extremity (Tesser, 1978). Thus it is conceivable that once one such dimension is elevated (e.g., an individual comes to perceive the personal relevance of the attitude object and begins to think about it; Petty & Cacioppo, 1979), various cognitive and behavioral processes are set in motion to elevate some or even most of the other dimensions (e.g., accessibility, extremity).

If the dimensions are all perfectly overlapping with one another, it would be most parsimonious to think of them all as manifestations of a single latent construct. And if this is true, it would greatly simplify theory building and empirical testing in this arena, because the array of dimensions currently being addressed by separate research programs could be reduced to a single dimension that could then be studied in a much more streamlined fashion. What might appear to be distinct qualities of attitudes could then be thought of as only one single property, with one set of causes and one set of effects. Future research could then identify and measure or manipulate the most effective indicators of this underlying dimension, and future theory building could focus on that one dimension instead of on a multitude of higher order properties.

Given the clear distinctions between the dimensions in terms of definitions and operationalizations, however, such perfect overlap seems unlikely. Nevertheless, some overlap seems quite plausible, and some groups of dimensions might reflect single underlying constructs. Indeed, there are a number of instances in the attitudes literature where higher order constructs have been measured with a wide variety of different specific measures. For example, investigators have presumed that attitudinal *intensity* can be measured via certainty (Brim, 1955; Guttman & Suchman, 1947; Katz, 1944; McDill, 1959; Suchman, 1950) or extremity (McDill, 1959; Tannenbaum, 1956). Attitudinal *salience* has been measured by questions about importance (Hoelter, 1985; Jackson & Marcus, 1975; Lemon, 1968; Powell, 1977; Tedin, 1980) and frequency of thought (Brown, 1974). One of the most studied higher order constructs, *involvement*, has been assessed by measuring importance (Apsler & Sears, 1968; Borgida & Howard-Pitney, 1983; Gorn, 1975; Howard-Pitney, Borgida, & Omoto, 1986), amount of thought (Bishop, 1990), knowledge (Stember & Hyman, 1949–1950), the confluence of thought, information gathering, and self-interest (Flora & Maibach, 1990), or the confluence of importance, thought, commitment, and social support (Miller, 1965).

Another higher order construct about which there has been a great diversity in approaches is attitude *centrality*. Questions about importance have frequently been used to gauge this construct (Converse, 1964; Judd & Krosnick, 1982; Krosnick, 1986; Petersen & Dutton, 1975; Schuman & Presser, 1981), an approach that comes closest to the definitions of it offered by Smith, Bruner, and White (1956, p. 35) and Freedman (1964). However, Converse (1970) defined *centrality* as the "proportion of 'mental time' that is occupied by attention to the attitude object over substantial periods" (p. 182), which seems closer to the notions of attitude salience and accessibility. At the same time, Lewin (1951), Bem (1970), Katz (1960), and others defined "centrality" as the extent of structural linkage among attitudes, thus resembling Scott's (1968) notion of embeddedness. Yet direct measures of such structural linkage have rarely if ever been used in the attitude literature to operationalize this construct. Thus there is a fair amount of disagreement in the literature about the extent to which these dimensions can be used to measure each other and about which higher order constructs, if any, they reflect.

Even if the dimensions all represent independent but moderately overlapping constructs, questions would arise about the extent to which relations between individual dimensions and defining features of attitude strength are spurious. For example, it is conceivable that attitude accessibility is the sole determinant of attitude-behavior consistency, and that importance and evaluative–cognitive consistency are only associated with attitude-behavior consistency by virtue of their correlations with accessibility. This sort of theoretical viewpoint has been offered most clearly by Fazio (1989), who suggested that at least some attitude attributes (e.g., certainty and direct experience) may enhance an attitude's impact on behavior and information processing by strengthening the object-evaluation link in memory (i.e., the attitude's accessibility). Therefore if multivariate analyses were to be conducted predicting attitude-behavior consistency using accessibility, certainty, direct experience, and other attitude attributes, many of these correlates of consistency might turn out not to be causes of it. On the other hand, if the dimensions are completely nonoverlapping, such multivariate analyses would likely leave all bivariate relations unaltered. Each dimension might have reasonably unique origins and effects. Thus, in order to understand which attitude attributes are directly responsible for attitude strength, it is useful to assess the overlap among the dimensions.

Associations Among the Dimensions

In fact, many correlational studies have assessed the relations among a subset of the various strength-related dimensions and have consistently documented only low to moderately positive correlations. On the basis of this sort of evidence, Raden (1985) concluded that these dimensions are not all reflections of a single underlying, superordinate dimension. Raden did not collect original empirical data, but rather reviewed some of the existing published evidence on associations between some strength dimensions. The literature Raden reviewed provided only a small subset of all possible correlations among these dimensions, but most of the associations he observed were relatively weak. Therefore, Raden asserted that the one construct view of attitude strength should be abandoned in favor of a multiconstruct view in which the dimensions are essentially independent of one another.

However, it is difficult to know exactly what to make of the zero order correlations that were the focus of Raden's study, because they are likely to have been distorted by random and systematic measurement error. Random measurement error attenuates correlations between indicators, and correlated measurement error due to shared method can make correlations either more positive or more negative (see, e.g., Alwin & Krosnick, 1985; Boruch & Wolins, 1970; Green, 1988; Krosnick & Alwin, 1988). Consequently, zero order correlations may either overestimate or underestimate correlations between attitude dimensions. Given Cote and Buckley's (1987) evidence that random and systematic measurement error typically account for more than 50% of the variance in psychological measures, it seems quite plausible that zero order correlations among attitude dimensions are misleadingly attenuated and that there is more overlap among them than Raden (1985) believed there to be.

In order to estimate these correlations more precisely, Krosnick et al. (1993) collected multiple measures of each of ten strength-related dimensions. These investigators then applied structural equation modeling techniques to the resulting data in order to correct for the impact of random and systematic measurement error. In all, Krosnick et al. (1993) estimated four correlation matrices, one for each of four attitude objects. Table 1.1 displays the results involving the dimensions addressed in this book from a typical example, regarding attitudes toward defense spending by the U.S. government (all variables were coded so that positive correlations would be expected). These dimensions include measures presumably tapping accessibility (frequency of talking about the object, as well

TABLE 1.1

Krosnick et al. (1993) Estimates of Correlations Between Latent Attitude Dimensions Corrected for Random Error and Method Covariance (Attitudes on U.S. Defense Spending)

	Talking	Thinking	Perceived Knowledge	Knowledge Listing	Response Latency	Importance	Certainty	Extremity
Thinking	.84							
Perceived Knowledge	.79	.76						
Knowledge Listing	.19	.19	.28					
Response Latency	.34	.49	.25	.11				
Importance	.60	.77	.64	.19	.26			
Certainty	.49	.71	.59	.08	.26	.75		
Extremity	.33	.37	.22	.11	.35	.38	.55	
Evaluative-Cognitive Consistency	-.02	-.02	-.17	-.05	.24	-.14	-.05	.38

as response latency), elaboration (frequency of thinking about the object), the amount of knowledge people had about the object (as assessed via self-perceptions as well as listings of everything people knew about the object), importance, certainty, extremity, and evaluative-cognitive consistency.

Although some of the correlations shown here are relatively strong, most of them are moderate to weak. This is particularly so for the amount of knowledge people could list about the object and for evaluative–cognitive consistency. These results are comparable to those in the other three corrected correlation matrices Krosnick et al. (1993) estimated, highlighting some cases of strong overlap, some cases of moderate overlap, and some cases of no overlap at all.

It is interesting that different means of assessing the same construct appear to have yielded distinct results. For example, self-perceptions of knowledgeability were only weakly associated with the amount of knowledge people were actually able to list about an object. Similarly, some measures that would be expected to be correlated were not. For example, if people possess considerable knowledge about an attitude object, one might expect them to be more confident in their attitudes, but they were not.

Krosnick, Jarvis, Strathman, and Petty (1994) reanalyzed data originally collected by Strathman (1991). Multiple measures of some of the dimensions examined by Krosnick et al. (1993), as well as additional ones were examined. Because of the nature of some of the measures, Krosnick et al. (1994) estimated phantom variable structural equation models (Bollen, 1984; Bollen & Lennox, 1991; MacCallum & Browne, 1993) to correct for the impact of random measurement error. The corrected correlations they obtained for one of their attitude objects (George Bush) are shown in Table 1.2.

Consistent with Krosnick et al.'s (1993) findings, some of these correlations are relatively strong; others are moderate; and many are near zero. Some of the stronger correlations involve importance, certainty, amount of thought, and extremity, and consistently weaker correlations involve evaluative-cognitive consistency, evaluative-affective consistency, and cognitive-affective consistency. In fact, for some of these later variables, surprisingly strong negative correlations appeared (again, the variables were coded so that positive associations would be expected). Thus it seems that the general complexion of Krosnick et al.'s (1993) results were replicated.

Also consistent with Krosnick et al.'s (1993) results, Krosnick et al. (1994) found clear distinctions between self-perception and objective measures of the same construct. For example, the correlation between self-perceptions of knowledgeability and the amount of knowledge subjects listed was .14. Given the apparent distinction between subjective and objective measures of what might be considered the same construct, it seems worthwhile to speculate about the meaning of such a distinction. First, self-perceptions might reflect constructs different from those tapped by the direct measures but equally real and useful. Thus self-perceptions of a construct might even have effects different than those

TABLE 1.2

Krosnick et al. (1994) Estimates of Correlations Between Latent Attitude Dimensions Corrected for Random Error and Method Covariance for Attitudes Toward George Bush

	Thinking	Perceived Knowledge	Knowledge Listing	Response Latency	Importance	Certainty	Extremity	Evaluative-Cognitive Consistency	Evaluative-Affective Consistency
Perceived Knowledge	.78								
Knowledge Listing	.15	.14							
Response Latency	.50	.47	.24						
Importance	.60	.57	.05	.33					
Certainty	.70	.62	.10	.67	.45				
Extremity	.54	.45	.00	.61	.36	.62			
Evaluative-Cognitive Consistency	.02	.06	-.14	.28	.20	.15	.15		
Evaluative-Affective Consistency	-.25	.24	.19	-.55	.03	-.28	.21	-.07	
Cognitive-Affective Consistency	.10	.01	.22	-.10	.09	.09	.16	.07	-.09

of direct measures of it. Second, the self-perceptions and objective measures could tap the same construct, but imperfectly. Because random measurement error has been purged from the corrected correlations in Tables 1.1 and 1.2, this imperfection cannot be attributable to it. Conceivably, though, the imperfection could be due to the presence of method-specific systematic error. It is tempting to view the self-perception data as the more flawed, because it is presumably subject to intentional manipulation by respondents, whereas the objective measures are less susceptible. It is interesting to note, however, that medical researchers have found that self-perceptions of health status contain some valid information that predicts later mortality, over and above the information contained in objective measures of health status (Idler & Angel, 1990). It is thus conceivable that both the self-perceptions and the objective measures of attitude dimensions may both contain useful, valid, and independent information.

Do the Dimensions Reflect a Few Higher Order Constructs?

It seems clear from the evidence we reviewed (i.e., Krosnick et al., 1993, 1994) that there is a considerable amount of independence among the individual strength-related dimensions. However, even if these dimensions are in fact distinct from one another, it is nonetheless possible that two or more of them reflect common, higher order constructs. That is, the set of dimensions may be reflections of a smaller set of underlying latent constructs, and those underlying constructs might produce associations with stability, resistance, and impact on cognition and behavior. In fact, it is possible for all of the dimensions that are at least somewhat correlated with one another to reflect only a single latent construct.

Verplanken (1989, 1991) reported one pair of studies consistent with the notion that a group of strength-related dimensions reflects a higher order construct. He examined the structure of measures of interest, thinking, talking, and feeling involved in an issue, frequency of reading about the issue, desire to express one's opinion on the issue, and other such dimensions. Verplanken treated single indicators of each of these dimensions as if they were all indicators of a single underlying construct; Cronbach's alphas for indices derived from sets of them for three issues were .86, .86, and .75. This suggests that a single factor did indeed account for a great deal of the covariation among the dimensions. The remaining, unexplained covariation may simply represent random or systematic measurement error, or it could represent the existence of a more complex underlying factor structure.

Other investigations have uncovered clear evidence of more complex organizations. For example, Abelson's (1988) analysis of a series of attitude dimensions revealed three clusters of items across a set of issues. The first, which he called "emotional commitment," included items assessing certainty and relevance to self-concept. The second cluster, called "ego preoccupation," included items measuring frequency of thought and importance. And the third cluster, "cognitive elaboration," included items measuring knowledge, as well as others not directly linked to the dimensions of interest here.

A similar investigation was conducted by Lastovicka and Gardner (1979). They also factor analyzed a set of relevant indicators and found yet a different three factor structure. Their first factor included items addressing frequency of talking, knowledge, and interest. The second factor included measures of certainty and ego defensiveness. And the third factor included importance and the relevance of one's social identity and values. Thus Lastovicka and Gardner's (1979) findings were quite different from Abelson's (1988), which raises questions about the reliability of these factor structures.

Krosnick et al. (1993) offered a resolution of this confusion by taking a somewhat different approach to assessing the latent structure of these dimensions. Instead of conducting exploratory factor analyses, these investigators conducted confirmatory factor analyses. Specifically, Krosnick et al. (1993) specified and tested the adequacy of a series of models that presumed two or more dimensions reflected a single underlying construct while controlling for the impact of random and systematic measurement error. Some of the models they tested were suggested by previous investigators' presumptions regarding interchangeability, and some were suggested by theoretical considerations. Despite this, every one of the models Krosnick et al. (1993) evaluated did not fit the observed data and was therefore empirically rejected. Because this approach involved explicit model testing and goodness-of-fit assessment, it seems quite informative. Furthermore, Krosnick et al.'s (1993) findings can explain the inconsistency of previous exploratory factor analyses: That method was apparently being used to uncover latent structure that did not exist. Thus the available evidence seems to support the view that many of the various attributes of attitudes that may contribute to strength are best thought of as distinct from one another.

Also consistent with the notion that many of these dimensions are distinct from one another is evidence that they can have nonoverlapping, independent, interactive, and mediated effects. For example, although attitude importance, intensity, and certainty generally do not regulate the magnitude of question wording effects (Bishop, 1990; Krosnick & Schuman, 1988), evaluative-cognitive consistency (Chaiken & Baldwin, 1981) and extremity (Hippler & Schwarz, 1986) do seem to exert such regulatory influences. Furthermore, these dimensions sometimes interact with one another. For example, Tourangeau, Rasinski, Bradburn, and D'Andrade (1989a, 1989b) showed that question order effects are especially likely to occur among people who are high in ambivalence and consider an attitude to be highly personally important. Similarly, Biek (1992) showed that attitude-defensive biased processing of a persuasive message is most likely among respondents high in knowledge and intensity.

Taken together, this evidence suggests that the one factor view of strength-related attributes may not be viable. Indeed, this evidence suggests that it is difficult to reduce the set of dimensions to a smaller set of latent constructs and that doing so may be counterproductive. Consequently, it seems that a full understanding of attitude strength will require in-depth investigations of each of the attitude dimensions. The chapters in this book attempt to provide a state of the art discussion of many of the most researched dimensions of attitudes related to strength.

THIS BOOK

Although individual researchers have not concentrated exclusively upon single dimensions of attitudes related to strength, there has been a strong tendency for scholars to focus on just one dimension at a time. In organizing a 1991 conference on attitude strength that set this book in motion, we sought to bring together researchers exploring attitude strength to share their findings and perspectives. Our hope was that some direct exchange of ideas among ourselves and integration of our perspectives might be productive. Previously, the findings of individual researchers studying individual attributes had been published in relative isolation from one other. There was not a great deal of cross-citation taking place, and there were not central, overarching issues being addressed in a coordinated fashion from multiple perspectives. Yet the fact that these dimensions all appear to be related to the four defining features of strength suggested a common core to these individual research agendas. This book is intended partly to help make this common core more explicit in ways that might have constructive impact on future studies.

A second important goal of this book is to catalogue and systematize the many diverse findings on attitude strength and related attitude dimensions. Relatively few review articles have been written on this topic to date, so it seemed useful for leading researchers to present their perspectives on the accumulated findings and to suggest directions for future studies. In particular, we asked chapter authors to identify the antecedents of the attitude strength dimension(s) examined in their research programs, the strength consequences of these dimensions, the mechanisms by which these consequences are produced, and the conditions under which they are most likely to appear.

The book begins with Abelson's chapter focused on attitude extremity, the one strength-related dimension that is an attribute of the attitude itself. His emphasis is on the social and interpersonal sources of extremity. In the next three chapters, the focus shifts to thought processes and their impact on strength. Judd and Brauer explore how mere thought, encounters, and expressions can influence attitude extremity. Tesser, Martin, and Mendolia explore the impact of mere thought on extremity and attitude-behavior consistency. The next chapter, by Petty, Haugtvedt, and Smith, examines not mere thought but rather the effects of elaboration of persuasive messages on attitude persistence, resistance, and impact on behavior.

The next few chapters address both the origins and consequences of dimensions defined as subjective perceptions of attitude qualities: Crano reviews work on vested interest; Boninger, Krosnick, Berent, and Fabrigar on importance; Thomsen, Borgida, and Lavine on personal involvement; and Gross, Holtz, and Miller on certainty. Following this group, the next chapters address the causes and effects of structure-related dimensions. First is Fazio on accessibility. Next are three chapters on knowledge: Wood, Rhodes, and Biek; Davidson; and Jaccard, Dittus, Radecki, and Wilson. Thompson, Zanna, and Griffin then report on ambivalence; Chaiken, Pomerantz, and Giner-Sorolla consider evaluative-cognitive and evaluative-affective consistency; and Eagly and Chaiken review implications of interattitudinal and intraattitudinal structure. All of these chapters describe the existing bodies of research documenting the relations of these dimensions to the four defining features of strength. Finally, Erber, Hodges, and Wilson report multivariate analyses exploring the relations of numerous strength-related attitude attributes to attitude stability and resistance to change.

The book's final chapter is intended to provide practical help for investigators interested in conducting studies of strength-related attitude dimensions. In it, Wegener, Downing, Krosnick, and Petty provide an overview of the various ways in which strength-related attributes have been measured and manipulated. These techniques can be easily adapted for use in future investigations.

CONCLUSION

Focus on one strength-related dimension at a time has been the predominant approach employed in attitude strength research in the past. In future years, we suspect, some investigators will continue to concentrate on single dimensions, probing their idiosyncratic features and building models of their causes and effects. At the same time, however, valuable new insights can be produced by multivariate studies considering many dimensions simultaneously. Increasing numbers of investigators may well employ this sort of metadimensional approach in the future, attempting to understand the relations among the strength-related attributes and to identify their unique contributions to attitude strength. We hope that this volume helps to facilitate both sorts of work.

REFERENCES

Abelson, R. P. (1988). Conviction. *American Psychologist, 43*, 267–275.

Ajzen, I., & Madden, T. J. (1986). Prediction of goal-directed behavior: Attitudes, intentions, and perceived behavioral control. *Journal of Experimental Social Psychology, 22*, 453–474.

Alwin, D. F., & Krosnick, J. A. (1985). The measurement of values in surveys: A comparison of ratings and rankings. *Public Opinion Quarterly, 49*, 535–552.

Apsler, R., & Sears, D. O. (1968). Warning, personal involvement, and attitude change. *Journal of Personality and Social Psychology, 9,* 162–166.

Arvey, R. D., Bouchard, T. J., Segal, N. L., & Abraham, L. M. (1989). Job satisfaction: Environmental and genetic components. *Journal of Applied Psychology, 74,* 187–192.

Bem, D. J. (1970). *Beliefs, attitudes, and personal affairs.* Monterey, CA: Brooks/Cole.

Biek, M. A. (1992). *Knowledge and affect as determinants of information processing, attitude stability, and behavior.* Unpublished doctoral dissertation, Texas A & M University, College Station, Texas.

Bishop, G. F. (1990). Issue involvement and response effects in public opinion surveys. *Public Opinion Quarterly, 54,* 209–218.

Bollen, K. A. (1984). Multiple indicators: Internal consistency or no necessary relationship? *Quality and Quantity, 18,* 377–385.

Bollen, K., & Lennox, R. (1991). Conventional wisdom on measurement: A structural equation perspective. *Psychological Bulletin, 110,* 305–314.

Boninger, D. S., Krosnick, J. A., & Berent, M. K. (1995). The origins of attitude importance: Self-interest, social identification, and value-relevance. *Journal of Personality and Social Psychology, 68,* 61–80.

Borgida, E., & Howard-Pitney, B. (1983). Personal involvement and the robustness of perceptual salience effects. *Journal of Personality and Social Psychology, 45,* 560–570.

Boruch, R. F., & Wolins, L. (1970). A procedure for estimation of trait, method, and error variances attributable to a measure. *Educational and Psychological Measurement, 30,* 547–574.

Breckler, S. J. (1984). Empirical validation of affect, behavior, and cognition as distinct components of attitude. *Journal of Personality and Social Psychology, 47,* 1191–1205.

Brim, O. G. (1955). Attitude content-intensity and probability expectations. *American Sociological Review, 20,* 68–76.

Brown, D. W. (1974). Adolescent attitudes and lawful behavior. *Public Opinion Quarterly, 38,* 98–106.

Byrne, D. E. (1971). *The attraction paradigm.* San Diego, CA: Academic.

Chaiken, S. (1980) Heuristic versus systematic information processing and the use of source versus message cues in persuasion. *Journal of Personality and Social Psychology, 39,* 752–766.

Chaiken, S., & Baldwin, M. W. (1981). Affective-cognitive consistency and the effect of salient behavioral information on the self-perception of attitudes. *Journal of Personality and Social Psychology, 41,* 1–12.

Converse, P. E. (1964). The nature of belief systems in the mass public. In D. E. Apter (Ed.), *Ideology and discontent* (pp. 206–261). New York: The Free Press.

Converse, P. E. (1970). Attitudes and nonattitudes: Continuation of a dialogue. In E. R. Tufte (Ed.), *The quantitative analysis of social problems* (pp. 168–189). Reading, MA: Addison-Wesley.

Cote, J. A., & Buckley, M. R. (1987). Estimating trait, method, and error variance: Generalizing across 70 construct validation studies. *Journal of Marketing Research, 24,* 315–318.

Crites, S. L., Fabrigar, L. R., & Petty, R. E. (1994). Measuring the affective and cognitive properties of attitudes: Conceptual and methodological issues. *Personality and Social Psychology Bulletin, 20,* 619–634.

Davidson, A. R., & Morrison, D. M. (1983). Predicting contraceptive behavior from attitudes: A comparison of within- versus across-subjects procedures. *Journal of Personality and Social Psychology, 45,* 997–1009.

Eagly, A. H., & Chaiken, S. (1993). *The psychology of attitudes.* Fort Worth, TX: Harcourt, Brace, Jovanovich.

Ewing, T. N. (1942). A study of certain factors involved in changes of opinion. *Journal of Social Psychology, 16,* 63–88.

Eysenck, (1967). *The biological basis of personality.* Springfield, IL: Thomas.

Fazio, R. H. (1986). How do attitudes guide behavior? In R. M. Sorrentino & E. T. Higgins (Eds.), *The handbook of motivation and cognition: Foundation of social behavior* (pp. 204–243). New York: Guilford.

Fazio, R. H. (1989). On the power and functionality of attitudes: The role of attitude accessibility. In A. R. Pratkanis, S. J. Breckler, & A. G. Greenwald (Eds.), *Attitude structure and function* (pp. 153–179). Hillsdale, NJ: Lawrence Erlbaum Associates.

Fazio, R. H., Chen, J., McDonel, E. C., & Sherman, S. J. (1982). Attitude accessibility, attitude-behavior consistency, and the strength of the object-evaluation association. *Journal of Personality and Social Psychology, 18*, 339–357.

Fazio, R. H., & Zanna, M. P. (1981). Direct experience and attitude-behavior consistency. In L. Berkowitz (Ed.), *Advances in experimental social psychology* (Vol. 14, pp. 161–202). New York: Academic.

Feldman, S. (1989). Measuring issue preferences: The problem of response instability. *Political Analysis, 1*, 25–60.

Festinger, L. (1954). A theory of social comparison processes. *Human Relations, 7*, 117–140.

Festinger, L. (1957). *A theory of cognitive dissonance.* Evanston, IL: Row, Peterson.

Flora, J. A., & Maibach, E. W. (1990). Cognitive responses to AIDS information: The effects of issue involvement and message appeal. *Communication Research, 17*, 759–774.

Freedman, J. L. (1964). Involvement, discrepancy, and change. *Journal of Abnormal and Social Psychology, 69*, 290–295.

Gorn, G. J. (1975). The effects of personal involvement, communication discrepancy, and source prestige on reactions to communications on separatism. *Canadian Journal of Behavioral Science, 7*, 369–386.

Green, D. P. (1988). On the dimensionality of public sentiment toward partisan and ideological groups. *American Journal of Political Science, 32*, 758–780.

Guttman, L., & Suchman, E. A. (1947). Intensity and a zero point for attitude analysis. *American Sociological Review, 12*, 57–67.

Haugtvedt, C. P., & Petty, R. E. (1992). Personality and persuasion: Need for cognition moderates the persistence and resistance of attitude changes. *Journal of Personality and Social Psychology, 63*, 308–319.

Heider, F. (1958). *The psychology of interpersonal relations.* New York: Wiley.

Hippler, H., & Schwarz, N. (1986). Not forbidding isn't allowing: The cognitive basis of the forbid-allow asymmetry. *Public Opinion Quarterly, 50*, 87–96.

Hoelter, J. W. (1985). The structure of self-conception: Conceptualization and measurement. *Journal of Personality and Social Psychology, 49*, 1392–1407.

Hovland, C. I. (1959). Reconciling conflicting results derived from experimental and survey studies of attitude change. *American Psychologist, 14*, 8–17.

Hovland, C. I., Campbell, E. H., & Brock, T. C. (1957). The effects of 'commitment' on opinion change following communication. In C. I. Hovland, W. Mandell, E. H. Campbell, T. C. Brock, A. S. Luchins, A. R. Cohen, W. J. McGuire, I. L. Janis, R. L. Feierabend, & N. H. Anderson, *The order of presentation in persuasion* (pp. 23–32). New Haven, CT: Yale University Press.

Howard-Pitney, B., Borgida, E., & Omoto, A. M. (1986). Personal involvement: An examination of processing differences. *Social Cognition, 4*, 39–57.

Hyman, H. H., & Sheatsley, P. B. (1947). Some reasons why information campaigns fail. *Public Opinion Quarterly, 11*, 412–423.

Idler, E. L., & Angel, R. J. (1990). Self-rated health and mortality in the NHANES-I epidemiologic follow-up survey. *American Journal of Public Health, 80*, 446–452.

Jackson, T. H., & Marcus, G. E. (1975). Political competence and ideological constraint. *Social Science Research, 4*, 93–111.

Johnson, B. T., & Eagly, A. H. (1989). Effects of involvement on persuasion: A meta-analysis. *Psychological Bulletin, 106*, 290–314.

Judd, C. M., & Krosnick, J. A. (1982). Attitude centrality, organization, and measurement. *Journal of Personality and Social Psychology, 42*, 436–447.

Kaplan, K. J. (1972). On the ambivalence–indifference problem in attitude theory and measurement: A suggested modification of the semantic differential technique. *Psychological Bulletin, 77,* 361–372.

Katz, D. (1944). The measurement of intensity. In H. Cantril (Ed.), *Gauging public opinion* (pp. 51–65). Princeton, NJ: Princeton University Press.

Katz, D. (1960). The functional approach to the study of attitudes. *Public Opinion Quarterly, 24,* 163–204.

Kiesler, C. A. (1971). *The psychology of commitment: Experiments linking behavior to belief.* San Diego, CA: Academic Press.

Krosnick, J. A. (1986). *Policy voting in American Presidential elections: An application of psychological theory to American politics.* Unpublished doctoral dissertation, University of Michigan, Ann Arbor.

Krosnick, J. A. (1988a). The role of attitude importance in social evaluation: A study of policy preferences, presidential candidate evaluations, and voting behavior. *Journal of Personality and Social Psychology, 55,* 96–210.

Krosnick, J. A. (1988b). Attitude importance and attitude change. *Journal of Experimental Social Psychology, 24,* 240–255.

Krosnick, J. A., & Abelson, R. P. (1992). The case for measuring attitude strength in surveys. In J. Tanur (Ed.), *Questions about survey questions* (pp. 177–203). New York: Russell Sage.

Krosnick, J. A., & Alwin, D. F. (1988). A test of the form-resistant correlation hypothesis: Ratings, rankings, and the measurement of values. *Public Opinion Quarterly, 52,* 526–538.

Krosnick, J. A., Boninger, D. S., Chuang, Y. C., Berent, M. K., & Carnot, C. G. (1993). Attitude strength: One construct or many related constructs? *Journal of Personality and Social Psychology, 65,* 1132–1151.

Krosnick, J. A., Jarvis, B., Strathman, A., & Petty, R. E. (1994). *Relations among dimensions of attitude strength: Insights from induced variable models.* Unpublished manuscript, Ohio State University, Columbus.

Krosnick, J. A., & Schuman, H. (1988). Attitude intensity, importance, and certainty and susceptibility to response effects. *Journal of Personality and Social Psychology, 54,* 940–952.

LaPiere, R. (1934). Attitudes versus actions. *Social Forces, 13,* 230–237.

Lastovicka, J. L., & Gardner, D. M. (1979). Components of involvement. In J. C. Maloney & B. Silverman (Eds.), *Attitude research plays for high stakes* (pp. 53–73). Chicago: American Marketing Association.

Lemon, N. F. (1968). A model of the extremity, confidence and salience of an opinion. *British Journal of Social Clinical Psychology, 7,* 106–114.

Lewin, K. (1951). *Field theory in social science.* New York: Harper & Row.

Lord, C. G., Ross, L., & Lepper, M. R. (1979). Biased assimilation and attitude polarization: The effects of prior theories on subsequently considered evidence. *Journal of Personality and Social Psychology, 37,* 2098–2109.

MacCallum, R. C., & Browne, M. W. (1993). The use of causal indicators in covariance structure models: Some practical issues. *Psychological Bulletin, 114,* 533–541.

McDill, E. L. (1959). A comparison of three measures of attitude intensity. *Social Forces, 38,* 95–99.

McKechnie, J. L. (Ed.). (1976). *Webster's new twentieth century dictionary of the English language* (2nd ed.). New York: Collins-World.

Miller, L. E., & Grush, J. E. (1986). Individual differences in attitudinal versus normative determination of behavior. *Journal of Experimental Social Psychology, 22,* 190–202.

Miller, N. E. (1965). Involvement and dogmatism as inhibitors of attitude change. *Journal of Experimental Social Psychology, 1,* 121–132.

Petersen, K., & Dutton, J. E. (1975). Certainty, extremity, intensity: Neglected variables in research on attitude-behavior consistency. *Social Forces, 54,* 393–414.

Petty, R. E., & Cacioppo, J. T. (1979). Issue involvement can increase or decrease persuasion by enhancing message-relevant cognitive responses. *Journal of Personality and Social Psychology, 37*, 1915–1926.

Petty, R. E., & Cacioppo, J. T. (1981). *Attitudes and persuasion: Classic and contemporary approaches.* Dubuque, IA: Wm. C. Brown.

Petty, R. E., & Cacioppo, J. T. (1986). *Communication and persuasion: Central and peripheral routes to attitude change.* New York: Springer-Verlag.

Petty, R. E., & Cacioppo, J. T. (1990). Involvement and persuasion: Tradition versus integration. *Psychological Bulletin, 107*, 367–374.

Petty, R. E., Cacioppo, J. T., & Haugtvedt, C. P. (1992). Ego-involvement and persuasion: An appreciative look at the Sherifs' contribution to the study of self-relevance and attitude change. In D. Granberg & G. Sarup (Eds.), *Social judgment and intergroup relations: Essays in honor of Muzafer Sherif* (pp. 147–174). New York: Springer-Verlag.

Powell, J. L. (1977). Satirical persuasion and topic salience. *Southern Speech Communication Journal, 42*, 151–162.

Pratkanis, A. R., & Greenwald, A. G. (1989). A sociocognitive model of attitude structure and function. In L. Berkowitz (Ed.), *Advances in Experimental Social Psychology* (Vol. 22, pp. 245–285). San Diego, CA: Academic.

Raden, D. (1985). Strength-related attitude dimensions. *Social Psychological Quarterly, 48*, 312–330.

Rennier, G. A. (1988). *The strength of the object-evaluation association, the attitude-behavior relationship, and the Elaboration Likelihood Model of persuasion.* Unpublished doctoral dissertation, University of Missouri, Columbia, MO.

Roberts, J. V. (1985). The attitude-memory relationship after 40 years: A meta-analysis of the literature. *Basic and Applied Social Psychology, 6*, 221–241.

Rosenberg, M. (1956). Cognitive structure and attitudinal affect. *Journal of Abnormal and Social Psychology. 53*, 367–372.

Schuman, H., & Johnson, M. P. (1976). Attitudes and behavior. *Annual Review of Sociology, 2*, 161–207.

Schuman, H., & Presser, S. (1981). *Questions and answers in attitude surveys: Experiments on question form, wording, and context.* New York: Academic.

Schwartz, S. H. (1978). Temporal instability as a moderator of the attitude-behavior relationship. *Journal of Personality and Social Psychology, 36*, 715–724.

Scott, W. A. (1968). Attitude measurement. In G. Lindzey & E. Aronson (Eds.), *Handbook of social psychology* (Vol. 2, pp. 204–273). Reading, MA: Addison-Wesley.

Sherif, C. W., Sherif, M., & Nebergall, R. E. (1965). *Attitude and attitude change.* Philadelphia: Saunders.

Smith, M. B., Bruner, J. S., & White, R. W. (1956). *Opinions and personality.* New York: Wiley.

Stember, H., & Hyman, H. (1949–1950). How interviewer effects operate through question form. *International Journal of Opinion and Attitude Research, 3*, 493–512.

Strathman, A. J. (1991). *Investigation of the influence of need for cognition on attitude-behavior consistency.* Unpublished doctoral dissertation, Ohio State University, Columbus, OH.

Suchman, E. A. (1950). The intensity component in attitude and opinion research. In S. A. Stouffer, L. Guttman, E. A. Suchman, P. F. Lazarsfeld, S. A. Star, & J. A. Clausen (Eds.), *Measurement and prediction* (pp. 213–276). Princeton, NJ: Princeton University Press.

Swann, W. B., Jr., & Ely, R. J. (1984). A battle of wills: Self-verification versus behavioral confirmation. *Journal of Personality and Social Psychology, 46*, 1287–1302.

Tannenbaum, P. H. (1956). Initial attitude toward source and concept as factors in attitude change through communication. *Public Opinion Quarterly, 20*, 413–425.

Tedin, K. L. (1980). Assessing peer and parental influence on adolescent political attitudes. *American Journal of Political Science, 24*, 136–154.

Tesser, A. (1978). Self-generated attitude change. In L. Berkowitz (Ed.), *Advances in experimental social psychology* (Vol. 11). New York: Academic.

Tesser, A. (1993). The importance of heritability in psychological research: The case of attitudes. *Psychological Review, 100,* 129–142.

Tourangeau, R., Rasinski, K. A., Bradburn, N., & D'Andrade, R. (1989a). Belief accessibility and context effects in attitude measurement. *Journal of Experimental Social Psychology, 25,* 401–421.

Tourangeau, R., Rasinski, K. A., Bradburn, N., & D'Andrade, R. (1989b). Carryover effects in attitude surveys. *Public Opinion Quarterly, 53,* 495–524.

Verplanken, B. (1989). Involvement and need for cognition as moderators of beliefs-attitude-intention consistency. *British Journal of Social Psychology, 28,* 115–122.

Verplanken, B. (1991). Persuasive communication of risk information: A test of cue versus message processing effects in a field experiment. *Personality and Social Psychology Bulletin, 17,* 188–193.

Weigel, R. H., & Newman, L. S. (1976). Increasing attitude-behavior correspondence by broadening the scope of the behavioral measure. *Journal of Personality and Social Psychology, 33,* 793–802.

Wicker, A. W. (1969). Attitudes versus actions: The relationship of verbal and overt behavioral responses to attitude objects. *Journal of Social Issues, 25,* 41–78.

Wilson, T. D., Kraft, D., & Dunn, D. S. (1989). The disruptive effects of explaining attitudes: The moderating effect of knowledge about the attitude object. *Journal of Experimental Social Psychology, 25,* 379–400.

Wood, W. (1982). Retrieval of attitude-relevant information from memory: Effects on susceptibility to persuasion and on intrinsic motivation. *Journal of Personality and Social Psychology, 42,* 798–810.

2

▼▼▼▼▼▼▼

Attitude Extremity

Robert P. Abelson
Yale University

Different meanings of attitude strength attach to different measures of what is almost certainly a multidimensional concept. Some measures of attitude strength command attention because of ease and frequency of empirical use; some because of theoretical and empirical coherence; and some because they are relevant to important social phenomena. In a recent review of a large number of candidate measures of attitude strength, Krosnick and Abelson (1991) recommended three measures: attitude *importance* for its simplicity and sheer frequency of appearance in a variety of relationships; attitude *accessibility* for its theoretical coherence; and attitude *extremity* for its practical importance. This chapter focuses on the last named, attitude extremity. Extremity has been conventionally measured by self-placement of subjects along a numerical scale of attitude position, usually labeled at the ends with the respective designations, *extremely unfavorable* and *extremely favorable*. *Neutral* may also be labeled, but the meaning of placements at less-than-extreme positions is left to the judgment of the subject—an option whose consequences are discussed later in this chapter. One social arena in which extreme attitudes are consequential is that of intergroup conflict, because conflict can breed attitude extremity, which in turn serves to maintain or increase conflict. I analyze later several interesting social psychological processes that may be implicated in this vicious cycle.

BACKGROUND

Throughout my academic career I have been fascinated by the capacity of holders of very strong attitudes to resist persuasive attempts at change. Public figures and ordinary folks alike often cling tenaciously to beliefs and attitudes that we, as know-it-all academics, are convinced are wrong-headed. Whether the attitudes concern life after death, gay rights, a perceived conspiracy to take over New Jersey, or whatever, we can argue until blue-faced without budging our State Representative or our Uncle Walter an inch.

I have tried various ways to capture the bulldog nature of some attitudes. I once programmed a computer simulation of a rigid ideology (Abelson, 1973; Abelson & Carroll, 1965), namely Senator Barry Goldwater's views on international relations. The senator, a quintessential cold warrior of the 1960s, had an answer for everything in terms of communists doing bad things and free nations doing good things. I discovered that this system could be simulated either by "hot cognition" (Abelson, 1963)—the motivation to avoid cognitive imbalance, and the skill to rationalize it away; or by "cold cognition"—the use of ready-made scripts and explanations for all known events, and a total lack of interest in explaining any anomalous ones.

More recently I offered the proposal that beliefs are like possessions (Abelson, 1986). We define ourselves by our most valued beliefs and attitudes much as we do by our most valued possessions. Loss of valued attitudes and possessions can be identity-threatening, and we mobilize resistance against such losses. There is an interesting parallel between the instrumental and expressive functions of attitudes and of possessions (Abelson & Prentice, 1989; Prentice, 1987). Thus this possession metaphor captures something of the self-enhancing nature of cherished attitudes. In certain respects, however, it is flawed. For example, negative attitudes are well defined, but the analogous concept of negative possessions is not. (Think of the difficulties Heider, 1958, had with the idea of negative unit-relations.) For another example: When you sell a possession, you don't have it anymore; but when you "sell" an attitude, you retain it, too.

I later tried to work out the elements of the common sense concept of conviction (Abelson, 1987). I factor analyzed survey responses to a battery of attitude strength measures on several current issues, and roughly identified three factors, which I called *ego preoccupation*, *emotional commitment*, and *cognitive elaboration*. Scores on these three factors tend to have sensible relations to other variables. However, the item loadings on these factors wobble around from issue to issue, and other factors such as social anchorage can sometimes appear. Although there is some promise in this approach, it is rather laborious and messy.

In the last year or two, I have come full circle to an interest in the apparently simpler variable of attitude extremity. In the 1960s I developed a mathematical model (Abelson, 1964) with implications for the analysis of sociopolitical conflict. My model addressed the question of how the distribution of attitude positions on a given issue would change in a social collectivity, under various assumptions about the social network connecting the individuals, and the amount of attitudinal influence of each individual upon every other individual in the group. In the simplest form of the model, each person's attitude moves toward that of the other, at a rate proportional to the attitude difference between them, and to the probability that they are interacting at any given moment. (Nowak, Szamrej, & Latane, 1990, have advanced a seemingly different model, but despite their wild enthusiasm for the use of nonlinearity, their model is in most respects less general than mine. They make no use of any concept of extremity, and their definition of polarization is peculiarly inappropriate for conflicts between ethnic, racial, or other predefined groups.)

My mathematical exercise, albeit highly circumscribed in its assumptions, yielded a provocative conclusion. The simplest form of the model always led to decreasing variance of attitudes with the passage of time, culminating asymptotically in complete homogeneity of attitude at a scale position equal to the average of the initial attitude positions in the group. I referred to this outcome as the "loss of attitude entropy," and raised the question of its plausibility when real social issues are discussed. We know by personal and mediated experience, and by systematic scholarly reviews (e.g., Coleman, 1957) that harmonious universal agreement is often not achieved. Instead, the change one sees over time is frequently toward greater polarization of attitudes, with two subgroups within the collectivity espousing irreconcilably extreme, opposing positions.

What kinds of processes lead to attitude polarization rather than homogeneity? I only dimly realized it when I wrote my initial paper, but the homogeneity result depends very critically on the psychological assumption that social interaction always produces accommodation, with attitude positions moving to some degree toward each other. Mathematically, homogeneity ensues when nothing maintains the extremity of the most extreme individuals; everyone else on the same side of the issue is more moderate than they, and so they are pulled inexorably toward compromise. An interesting three-dimensional, physical example of the same principle is the operation of Newton's law of gravitation on all heavenly bodies. Each tends to be pulled toward every other, and as noted by physicist Stephen Hawking (1988, p. 5), if the universe weren't expanding, it would collapse due to Newton's law. The moral for attitude distributions is that to prevent homogenization, processes are required that enhance or at least maintain extreme attitudes.

PROCESSES LEADING TO EXTREMIFICATION

It is interesting that the psychological literature contains empirical evidence for many phenomena that increase the extremity of attitudes. These phenomena are relevant in many contexts, but my interest is in their occurrence in situations of intergroup conflict. Table 2.1 lists 13 such phenomena. Evidence for Items 1–7 and Item 10 comes from experimental studies. Items 8, 9, and 11–13 are not (yet) based directly on experiment, but on field observation and theoretical argument.

TABLE 2.1
Phenomena Embodying One or More Polarizing Processes

---

1. Group polarization
2. Insults
3. Thought polarization
4. Expression polarization
5. Belief polarization
6. Salience of group conflict
7. Social modeling and normatization of extremity
8. The "group-in-the-door" effect
9. Formation of hard-core subgroups
10. Commitment and suffering
11. Anger as a cue to attributed malevolence
12. Triggered crowd response
13. Perception of a monolithic outgroup

Group Polarization

One of the most robust phenomena in the experimental social psychology literature is the "group polarization effect" (see Myers & Lamm, 1976). Group polarization arises when a controversial issue is discussed by a group of individuals who are like-minded on the issue. Following discussion, the average attitude position of the participants becomes more extreme on the initially preferred side.

Although consensus pressures are undoubtedly at play in group discussion, the result is not just a simple convergence to the average initial position. If everyone starts out in agreement, say, at Position 7 on a 10-point scale, all group members might move to a new consensus at Position 8. Two lines of explanation for this extremification phenomenon have good empirical support. The most straightforward account is that each discussion participant is exposed to potentially new *arguments* bolstering the shared initial position (Burnstein & Vinokur, 1977). Thus if each member starts out knowing two arguments on the preferred side, he or she might come out of the discussion knowing four or five, thereby tending to further polarize the initial preference. Second, a form of *self-enhancement bias* appears to lead group members individually to try to position themselves a bit more extremely on the issue than their peers, as though to be able to think of themselves and present themselves as being more pure on the issue (Myers, 1978). Although there is ample evidence that this dynamic is present in the discussions of like-minded groups, the situational circumstances which maximize or minimize this self-enhancement bias remain largely unexplored.

A third account has recently been advanced by McGarty, Turner, Hogg, David, and Wetherell (1992), who claim that group members are conforming to an ideal position minimizing the ratio of ingroup heterogeneity to separation from the outgroup. Although it is conceptually elegant, this model tends to underpredict the level of extremity reached by actual groups.

Insults

Negative attitude change in response to a persuasive communication is difficult to produce in the laboratory, but has been shown in a field experiment. Back in the days before ethics committees, Abelson and Miller (1967) arranged for a confederate to insult naive subjects during the course of two-person debates conducted on park benches in Washington Square Park in New York City. The confederate adopted an issue position opposed to that of the subject, and then delivered insults in reply to issue comments by the subject. For example, the insulter might say, "That's just the sort of nonsense I'd expect to hear from people in this place." The results showed that in general the insulted party became more extreme in his initial attitude.

A polarization effect from insults had also been noted by Coleman (1957) in his review of accounts of some 200 unfolding local issue controversies. The effect seems intuitively plausible, although its mediating dynamics are not entirely clear. We hypothesize that it is a primitive tit-for-tat or reciprocity (Cialdini, Green, & Rusch, 1992) response, in which the sharpening of issue disagreement is a social payback for the insult. To absorb offensive remarks without some sort of reciprocation might seem to signal tolerance for further insults. In that sense, response to an insult may resemble that to a threat (Na, 1992) or a dare (O'Neill, 1991). Psychologically, all types of overt challenge tend to dichotomize the options of the target, encouraging resistance, lest weakness be signaled.

Thought Polarization

The previous two polarization effects depend, respectively, on exposure to the attitudes of ingroup members and to slurs from strangers or enemies. What if people with attitude preferences are not exposed to new influences, but are merely encouraged to think about the issue? This, too, leads to attitude polarization—the so-called "thought polarization" effect, a process of individual attitude intensification (Tesser, 1978; Tesser, Martin, & Mendolia, ch. 4, this volume).

It has been found that thought produces attitude polarization only when the issue has previously been "schematized" by the individual—in other words, when the issue has been thought about before and has acquired detailed internal structure. For example (Tesser & Leone, 1977), when male students at the University of Georgia thought about the quality of techniques of tackling in football, or when female students thought about the aesthetics of dress designs, a sizeable average polarization effect occurred; but for the males who thought about dress designs, or females about football, very little polarization was evident.

One may perhaps conceptualize thought polarization as involving imagined or anticipated social interaction with like-minded individuals, thus implicating the same mediating mechanisms as in group polarization. Thought may generate previously unconsidered arguments which, as in group polarization, are consistent with initial attitude, and thereby strengthen it. Additionally or alternatively, thought may pose a challenge to self-image that can be alleviated by adopting a purer, less moderate position.

Expression Polarization

Conceivably, group polarization or thought polarization or both may be promoted by an even simpler underlying mechanism than any thus far mentioned. Fazio's (1989) notion of attitude accessibility is implicated. Exposure to evaluations of an attitude object and the *expression* of evaluations of an attitude object have both been found to increase the attitude's accessibility (Powell & Fazio, 1984). One outgrowth of these findings has been the investigation of whether the expression of evaluations would also increase attitude extremity. And indeed, it appears to do so (Downing, Judd, & Brauer, 1992; Judd & Brauer, this volume)—although the extent and generality of the phenomenon are still unclear. Such "expression polarization" could contribute to group polarization in an obvious way: Group discussion encourages the participants to express their attitudes, perhaps several times, and this in itself could extremify the positions of the group members. As far as thought polarization is concerned, one might adopt the behaviorist view of thought as inner expression. This would lead back to the known conclusion that the more one thought about an attitude object, the more extreme one would become.

Belief Polarization

In investigating the question of whether attitude extremity on an issue could be tempered by exposure to a mixed bag of relevant evidence (e.g., contrary outcomes of studies on whether capital punishment deters crime), Lord, Ross and Lepper (1979) and Lord, Lepper and Preston (1985) found the somewhat surprising result that such exposure increases the polarization of issue partisans. Experimental subjects strongly favoring capital punishment were very begrudging in accepting any evidence against its deterrent effects, but extremely responsive to evidence supporting deterrent effects—so much so that the net effect of an even-handed presentation of evidence on both sides was to increase the extremity of their pro capital punishment attitudes. (The mirror image result held for anti capital punishment subjects).

This effect has been dubbed "belief polarization" or "attitude polarization." It is based on the biased scanning of evidence, and would seem to require that the "evidence" be open to some degree of interpretive ambiguity.

Salience of Group Conflict

A psychological factor of potential consequence for attitude change on an issue is the extent to which the issue is linked to group identities. Research dating back to the 1950s (e.g., Kelley, 1955) has shown that reminding an audience of their group membership (e.g., as Catholics) makes them more resistant to communications finding fault with normative group attitudes (e.g., on divorce). Going one step further, if two groups are unfriendly to one another, one could hypothesize that contention between them might become even worse when existing intergroup difference on an issue is made salient (Doise, 1972; Eiser & Strobe, 1972).

Price (1989) has demonstrated this dynamic in the relatively benign situation of college students disagreeing over the issue of course distribution requirements. Humanities majors tend to oppose broader distributions which would force them to take uncongenial science and math courses, whereas science majors are relatively accepting of breadth. When students were shown a (bogus) student newspaper headline, "Humanities and Science Majors Clash over Distribution Requirements," members of these groups became more polarized on this issue than in the control condition in which the headline simply read, "Humanities and Science Majors Discuss Distribution Requirements."

Such a conflict-salience effect might turn out to be mediated by elementary polarizing processes such as those discussed earlier. Group conflict implies threat to group members (especially to those of the weaker group; Na, 1992). Threat in turn leads under many conditions (Janis & Mann, 1977) to heightened and biased information processing, the conditions for thought polarization and belief polarization. A group polarization process might also be a mediator. If intergroup relations are framed in terms of antagonism, then group members vying to appear good and true ingroup members would be especially likely to position themselves toward the extreme away from the outgroup.

Social Modeling and the Normatization of Extremity

Social modeling effects are legion in psychology, ranging all the way from modeling altruistic behavior (e.g., Bryan & Test, 1967) to modeling aggression (Bandura, Ross, & Ross, 1961). Modeling effects are of major importance for actions with typically low base rates (like stopping on a freeway to help someone change a tire). From this point of view, it is interesting to consider the modeling of the expression of extreme attitudes.

Let us again consider the group polarization phenomenon, and a curious theoretical puzzle it embodies: If it is self-enhancing to be more extreme than one's fellow group members on an issue of concern to the group, what restrains people from being as extreme as possible? Thus, if everyone else is at position 7 on a 10-point scale, why move merely to position 8? Why not go the whole hog and move to position 10?

The answer, we think, is that expression of an overly extreme position may seem socially inappropriate. It is not "cool"; it may mark one as a fanatic. (Recently I saw a triplet of bumper stickers laying out such a message: "Vote NO on Proposition 3. I'm mad but I'm not crazy. Proposition 3 goes too far.")

In my analysis of the valued properties of beliefs (Abelson, 1986), I noted that defensible beliefs were clearly of more value than indefensible ones and that, although making a belief more extreme might have the potential of improving its value, in general an increase in extremity entails a decrease in defensibility. This trade-off exerts a constraint on the motive to become more extreme. Moderation is the usual norm in the United States.

Putting the matter in this way leads one to ask whether there are circumstances under which extremity would become socially desirable, or at least permissible. One such circumstance is seeing one or more others risk the expression of extremity. If conditions are right, and the model recruits a sufficient number of others, we might speak of the *normatization of extremity*.

What are the right conditions for extremity to be modeled? We suggest three necessary conditions: identification, justification, and success. The model must be a respected ingroup figure who convincingly argues that moderate approaches have failed to advance the group's goals; further, the model's initial moves in pursuit of extremity must appear to meet with social approval and/or objective reward. Senator Barry Goldwater, at the height of his popularity in the early 1960s, had attracted a loyal conservative following despite his reputation as an extremist for (among other things) advocating going to the nuclear brink to resist Soviet expansion. He consistently argued that negotiations or mild approaches to the USSR were doomed to failure. Just in case anyone still felt timid, however, he delivered this famous line in accepting the Republican Presidential nomination in 1964: "Extremism in defense of freedom is no vice, and moderation in support of liberty is no virtue." The crowd roared its approval.

The Goldwater phenomenon is one among many examples in which *external threat* lends respectability to extremism. Extremists on one or both sides of a conflict are prone to assert that the acceptance of particular compromise positions is unthinkable. Politically and/or socially, advocacy of such positions may become taboo. If a conflict becomes passionate enough, one can readily imagine that group members espousing tabooed compromise positions might be accused of betrayal. Prevention or reversal of the normatization of extremity requires powerful and credible reassertion and modeling of norms of moderation, which would tend to be successful only if moderation could be presented in a way that promised some success for group interests.

The "Group-in-the-Door" Effect

The well known foot-in-the-door effect (Freedman & Fraser, 1966) involves an escalation of the onerousness of favors requested of a target individual. A person who has complied with a small request is more likely to agree to a later, larger request, even if it comes from a somewhat different requester, and involves a somewhat different favor. The mediating mechanism is thought to be self-labeling by the target person as someone who is helpful.

The escalation of the extremity of activities undertaken by members of a group might obey similar dynamics. Consider a group of students seeking to redress what they regard as an injustice on campus. Pleas through normal channels fail, and then a petition is circulated. There is pressure on individual students to sign; the choice is dichotomous, and relatively benign; signing enhances one's self-concept as a loyal group member.

Soon, another step is required of the fledgling loyalist: He or she is urged to attend a rally. What can be the harm in that? And then a march on the Administration Building. And then. . . . Each step offers a dichotomous choice—either you join with the group, or you fink out. Each step is a little more committal and involves more extreme activities, probably justified with more extreme arguments. Unless discouraged or bored, the individuals in the group will become collectivized, in the sense that self-explanations for behavior refer to the needs and values of the group. With an increase in the prominence of group-centered motives comes an increase in the opportunity for the operation of other extremification processes (e.g., group polarization, group salience, social modeling).

Formation of Hard-Core Subgroups

In thinking about evidence for the foot-in-the-door effect, social psychologists are aware of a potential artifact. If some people refuse the small request, and their data are dropped from consideration, then the set of remaining people will be biased in favor of those who are more agreeable to requests from strangers. This *self-selection* artifact would tend to produce an increase in the proportion of (remaining) subjects agreeing to the later, larger request, without any within-person changes in helpfulness.

The same argument could be applied to the group-in-the-door effect. However, in the group situation, the "artifact" corresponds to a real phenomenon, the formation of a militant, hard-core subgroup. Political scientists, as well as social psychologists, are aware of this effect of self-selection, albeit they come at it from a different direction.

Social choice theorists, addressing the question of how a political actor should choose a position maximizing popular support, appeal to the "median voter theorem." This is a famous mathematical result stating that the optimum positioning on an issue is precisely where the median voter lies. The actor's opponent cannot find a majority either to the left or right of this position, because the median splits the voter population in half. And the opponent may do a good deal worse by straying far from the median.

A twist on this theme comes from an analysis by Paul Johnson (1990) of the voting behavior of union members on setting the size of union dues. Johnson argued, with some empirical support, that the median voter theorem fails because the group may "unravel." Say that each member indicates his preferred yearly dues. The union leader, trained no doubt at the Harvard Business School, pushes through a motion that the median preference will in fact be the actual dues figure. To the leader's dismay, however, the members who voted for the lowest dues find the median figure too high, and they quit the union. A new, higher median thereby obtains, but when it in turn is voted through, the stingiest remaining members quit. And so on, until the group partially or totally unravels.

A similar phenomenon is very plausible for a social or political group whose members have widely differing degrees of ideological fervor. As the group undergoes polarizing processes, even the middling position of the group may become too extreme for the most faint-hearted members, who drop out. This makes the updated middling position even more extreme, and more moderates leave. What eventually survives, if anything, is the hardest core of the most militant members. Such a process has been documented for revolutionary cadres by historian Crane Brinton (1938).

On its face, this process is different from the other polarization processes we have considered, in that group composition is what changes, rather than individual attitudes. However, there is probably a secondary effect of militant subgroup formation in which individual attitudes also change. As the core group contracts to its most fanatic members, individuals motivated to remain in the group may be seduced into the adoption of more extreme orientations.

Commitment and Suffering

The psychological forces underlying the group-in-the-door effect warrant further discussion. Kanter (1972), in her detailed scrutiny of the factors leading to the success of cults and utopian movements, emphasizes the central role played by public *commitment* (see also Kiesler, 1971). Kanter found that groups with especially long histories of survival typically required a variety of commitments from members, including instrumental concessions such as giving up wages and possessions; social commitments forswearing ties to parents, lovers, and old friends in favor of loyalty to the collective; and moral commitment to the rituals and symbols of the group. The irreversibility of such commitments, made in public and continually monitored by group leaders, motivates an ever-deepening attachment to the group and its activities.

We recognize here, of course, a paradigmatic case of dissonance reduction, applied to the question of the permanence of extreme attitudes and behaviors. Most of the polarizing mechanisms we have discussed are short-run processes which will fizzle after a while if extremity has not been normatized. Commitment "fixes" extremity by encouraging continued rationalization of one's involvement with an extreme group.

Such a dissonance dynamic can be even further enhanced if the individual experiences pain and suffering when entering the group or engaging in group activities. Fraternity initiations and their experimental analogues (Aronson & Mills, 1959; Gerard & Mathewson, 1966) are the familiar cases in this category.

Less familiar, but no less cogent, is the historical analysis by Silvan Tomkins (1965) of the increasing militancy of pre-Civil War abolitionists, after each new episode of public ridicule by their contemporaries.

Anger as a Cue for Attributed Malevolence

The next mechanism I discuss has not yet, as far as I know, found its way into the psychological literature (though very similar ideas have.) Let me first illustrate it with an anecdote, then explain the concept, and say how it might operate as a polarizing process.

One afternoon as I was waiting for an approaching bus, a woman beside me stepped out into the street to see whether the bus was at hand. At that moment, a car started backing into the spot where she was standing. She took evasive action, and then shook her fist at the driver and shouted, "You knew!" I supposed her to mean, "You knew I was standing there!" and this struck me as odd. If the driver *knew*, then obviously he wouldn't have backed up that way. It must have been unintentional. Then why did she respond as she did? My reconstruction goes like this: When the car suddenly started towards her, she felt an immediate rush of anger. Then, in interpreting what was happening, she took her own anger into account as well as the behavior of the driver. In the prototypic situation in which one is angry at an intrusive behavior, that behavior is intentional. Thus she attributed intentionality to the driver.

Note that this hypothesized mechanism turns Schachter's (1964) theory of emotion around. The emotion shapes the cognition, rather than the cognition shaping the emotion. This is consistent with Zajonc's (1980) idea that the affective signal arrives before the inferential machinery has a chance to get started. It also accords with the spirit of the initial observation that led Festinger to dissonance theory, namely that the Indian villagers who were thrown into a fearful state by an earthquake invented further impending disasters to justify their fear. Finally, I see this mechanism as a more specific version of Schwarz's (1990) proposition that one's emotions have information value. He considered the positive versus negative character of feelings, but not specific emotions such as anger.

I know of no study that directly tests this postulated anger-as-cue process. One can adduce indirectly relevant research, however. For example, some time ago Lewis (1974) conducted a survey in New Haven, Connecticut, of reactions to the nationwide truckers' strike, which was presented to the respondent as motivated by economic aims. Half of the respondents were told that the strike had been quite violent, and for these subjects, their sympathy with the strikers increased! An explanation of this curious result is that the respondent reasons that if the truckers went so far as to be violent, then there must have been justification on their side.

There are leaps between this result, the anger mechanism, and our general discussion of the polarization of attitudes. The connection is that ingroup members, when angered by (reports of) seemingly intrusive actions by the outgroup, are prone to attribute malevolent intent to the perpetrators. Such attributions tend to support more extreme attitudes on issues central to the group conflict. Hostility is its own amplifier, one might say.

Triggered Crowd Response

Another important dynamic is the behavior of partisan crowds, when angered by an incident interpreted as a provocation by an outgroup. As noted in the Kerner Commission report on the urban riots in the summer of 1965 (National Advisory Commission on Civil Disorders, 1968), virtually every instance of rioting began with some triggering event, often a seemingly trivial one such as a White policeman accosting a Black motorist for a traffic violation. Recent nontrivial examples of triggering events are the death of a 7-year-old Black girl, killed accidentally by a Hasidic Jewish driver in Crown Heights, Brooklyn, and the case of the policemen who beat Rodney King in the famous videotaped episode.

The analysis of crowd or mob behavior has long been a popular enterprise in sociology (LeBon, 1895; Turner & Killian, 1972), but not so much in psychology. I think we have been hampered as a discipline by our reluctance to accord emotions as dignified a theoretical position as we give to information processing. Does any academic social psychologist have a theory of hatred?

In the cases of crowd behavior under discussion here, it might be tempting to regard contagion in the crowd as a special case of the group polarization phenomenon, with an accelerated social reinforcement dynamic enhancing partisan extremity. Several differences between partisan crowd behavior and laboratory or back-fence discussions among like-minded individuals should be noted, however. Crowds can influence action choices of large numbers of individuals, rather than merely attitudes of small numbers of people. The milling (Johnson & Feinberg, 1989), excitement, and shouts of exhortation within crowds are more likely to involve emotional antagonism against outgroups. Furthermore, I think the anger-as-a-cue mechanism is especially strong in crowds. The crowd members are not only cued individually by their own spontaneous feelings of anger, but also by the anger they can read in the faces of their peers. The resulting magnified blame of the outgroup, enhanced by deindividuated fury (Zimbardo, 1969), is a compelling psychological chemistry leading to extremes of aggressive behavior.

Perception of a Monolithic Outgroup

Social psychologists have turned increasing attention to the importance of group identity in self-definition, and in so doing, have theorized about the "collective self." This concerns the perception and internalization of one's own group's interests and worldview. Little has been said about the "collective other," that is, perceptions of the outgroup's interests, particularly the outgroup's *action agenda*.

When bigots or zealots discuss the despised "*they*," comments are not confined to trait stereotypes. Reference is often made to present or impending outgroup actions: *They* are taking over the neighborhood; *they* are going to riot; etc. The image is that of a monolithic *group actor*, with individuals coordinated so as to act as one (Abelson, 1994).

Perceptions of unity of action by a hostile outgroup can be intensified by a number of cues: If outgroup members are seen to behave alike, display group symbols, conform to a powerful leader, and collectively justify extreme actions, among other things, the perception of a monolithic actor is a natural one. It explains these miscellaneous phenomena. It also justifies aggressive collective action by one's own group to forestall or avenge the malevolent actions of the outgroup. Two antagonistic groups, each perceiving the other as a monolithic opponent, will tend to fulfill each other's prophecies by becoming more uniformly extreme themselves.

THE JOINT OPERATION OF POLARIZING PROCESSES

I have listed 13 different mechanisms, each of which would encourage subgroup polarization rather than harmonization of attitudes when an issue is actively debated within a population. Fairly commonly, many of these mechanisms might be simultaneously active. Heated intergroup controversies often can be characterized by the trading of hostile actions and insults, and thus the accumulation of grievances, by the polarization of beliefs about whose cause is just, by the fact of group conflict being quite salient, by self-righteous within-group discussion encouraging group polarization, by the normatization of extremity, and so on.

What kinds of factors might dispose the several polarizing mechanisms to work in concert? In the major class of cases in which opposing issue positions are associated with powerful group identities, many political and historical conditions could contribute to a tendency for the issue to be or to become polarized—the power relationship between the groups, their past and present involvement in controversies on other issues, the accumulation of grievances between them, the actions of political opportunists in fomenting conflict, and so on. Conversely, the mitigation of these conditions would tend to damp the operation of clusters of polarizing processes. Analysis by social psychologists of these important underlying factors would be of both theoretical and applied consequence.

What Does "Extremity" Mean, Anyway?

Throughout my discussion, I have made repeated reference to extremity, the crucial concept in any analysis of polarization. But what does extremity mean? The usual definition in terms of distance from the attitude scale neutral point is conceptually empty. If we said of some subjects that they were 9s instead of 8s on a 10-point scale of opposition to abortion, what claim would we think we were making?

It seems to me that there are as many answers as there are construals of the numerical self-placement task by questionnaire respondents. To analyze how respondents approach this ambiguous task, let us adopt a neo-Bemian point of view. Bem's (1967) famous proposal was that in answering questions about their attitudes, subjects examine their overt behaviors for clues, just as observers would do. The subsequent debate in the literature about this proposal tended to focus on very circumscribed "issues" like how interesting it was to twirl spools in the Festinger and Carlsmith (1959) experiment, or how appealing brown bread is, and the complexity of self-examination for clues to attitudes was not well appreciated.

Imagine a respondent who is pro-life, trying to decide whether he should call himself a 9 or an 8. How should he decide? One way is to call to mind the pro-lifers he knows or can imagine, line them up along a hypothetical scale of extremity, and place himself on the line (perhaps exaggerating for self-enhancement purposes). But this begs the question: How does he know where to place others? My claim is that ratings of attitude extremity are based on the *common sense understanding of what it could mean to be more in favor of* (or opposed to) *something*. No doubt there are individual differences in such understandings, but some reasonable possibilities are listed in Table 2.2.

Clues to intensity of feeling can be illustrated with many examples. In judging another person—or oneself—on intensity of feeling, one can note tendencies toward argument or temper loss, enthusiastic engagement in partisan activities, and the like.

Unqualifiedness of position should be fairly obvious. It is a more extreme antiabortion position to say, "*All* abortions should be immediately forbidden" than to say, "Abortion should be generally discouraged, but permitted in cases of rape, incest, and danger to the mother's health."

The third and fourth meanings are the most germane to the escalation of intergroup conflict. The Israeli citizen is more extreme who endorses beatings of Hamas sympathizers than is his fellow citizen who would not go that far. And in a real sense the most extreme position involves eagerness to administer the beatings oneself. My claim here is that behavioral intentions constitute part of the meaning of attitude extremity, because a good way to tell if you are really

TABLE 2.2
Common Sense Meanings of Extremity

1. Intensity of feeling on the issue
2. Unqualifiedness of issue position
3. Lengths to which the group should go to defend its position
4. Lengths to which the individual would go

for or against something is if you know you are "willing to put your money where your mouth is." These meanings of extremity seem to form a conceptual and sequential hierarchy. To reach the extremes of extremity, so to speak, one first has to have an emotional attachment to the issue. Then, in elaborating the issue, one must brush aside qualifications and hedges. Finally, one must make action commitments to an unqualified position—minimally by cheering from the sideline as one's fellow group members do the dirty work, and maximally by taking extreme actions oneself. Note here that unqualifiedness is a psychologically necessary precondition for willingness to undertake extreme actions. It would be odd to volunteer to bomb an abortion clinic in support of the position that abortions are only sometimes justified.

These distinctions in meaning are important to a clarification of the process of the normatization of extremity. Presumably, the first step is "consciousness raising" of the group member, so that he or she is aware of the connection between the issue and important group values. Second, via the occurrence of some or all of the polarizing mechanisms I have discussed, qualifications on the attitude position are stripped away. (Of course, although I have not highlighted them, there are contrary processes that could operate to maintain or increase attitude qualification.) Finally, if extreme action commitments become normatized, then the conflict may have gone beyond the point of no return. Mob actions and cycles of mutual grievance-inflicting behaviors are likely, and all the polarizing processes stand to be activated. It would be interesting in the context of research on intergroup conflict to try out survey measures of these different variants of extremity.

REFERENCES

Abelson, R. P. (1963). Computer simulation of "hot cognition". In S. Tomkins & S. Messick (Eds.), *Computer simulation of personality*. New York: Wiley.

Abelson, R. P. (1964). Mathematical models of the distribution of attitudes under controversy. In N. Frederiksen & H. Gulliksen (Eds.), *Contributions to mathematical psychology* (pp. 142–160). New York: Holt, Rinehart & Winston.

Abelson, R. P. (1973). Structural analysis of belief systems. In R. Schank & K. Colby (Eds.), *Computer models of thought and language* (pp. 287–339). San Francisco: Freeman.

Abelson, R. P. (1986). Beliefs are like possessions. *Journal for the Theory of Social Behavior, 16,* 223–250.

Abelson, R. P. (1987). Conviction. *American Psychologist, 43,* 267–275.

Abelson, R. P. (1994, July). *Have you heard what they did? Perceptions of the collective other.* Invited address presented at the meeting of the American Psychological Society, Washington, DC.

Abelson, R. P., & Carroll, J. D. (1965). Computer simulation of individual belief systems. *American Behavioral Scientist, 8,* 24–30.

Abelson, R. P., & Miller, J. C. (1967). Negative persuasion via personal insult. *Journal of Experimental Social Psychology, 3,* 321–333.

Abelson, R. P., & Prentice, D. A. (1989). Beliefs as possessions—a functional perspective. In A. R. Pratkanis, S. J. Breckler, & A. G. Greenwald (Eds.), *Attitude structure and function* (pp. 361–381). Hillsdale, NJ: Lawrence Erlbaum Associates.

Aronson, E., & Mills, J. (1959). The effect of severity of initiation on liking for a group. *Journal of Abnormal and Social Psychology, 59*, 177–181.

Bandura, A., Ross, D., & Ross, S. A. (1961). Transmission of aggression through imitation of aggressive models. *Journal of Abnormal and Social Psychology, 63*, 575–582.

Bem, D. J. (1967). Self-perception: An alternative interpretation of cognitive dissonance phenomena. *Psychological Review, 74*, 183–200.

Brinton, C. (1938). *The anatomy of revolution*. New York: Vintage.

Bryan, J. H., & Test, M. A. (1967). Models and helping: Naturalistic studies in aiding behavior. *Journal of Personality and Social Psychology, 6*, 400–407.

Burnstein, E., & Vinokur, A. (1977). Persuasive argumentation and social comparison as determinants of attitude polarization. *Journal of Experimental Social Psychology, 13*, 315–332.

Cialdini, R. B., Green, B. L., & Rusch, A. J. (1992). When tactical pronouncements of change become real change. *Journal of Personality and Social Psychology, 63*, 30–40.

Coleman, J. S. (1957). *Community conflict*. New York: The Free Press.

Doise, W. (1972). Rencontres et representations intergroupes. *Archives de Psychologie, 41*, 303–320.

Downing, J. W., Judd, C. M., & Brauer, M. (1992). Effects of repeated expressions on attitude extremity. *Journal of Personality and Social Psychology, 63*, 17–29.

Eiser, J. R., & Strobe, W. (1972). *Categorization and social judgment*. London: Academic.

Fazio, R. H. (1989). On the power and functionality of attitudes: The role of attitude accessibility. In A. R. Pratkanis, S. J. Breckler, & A. G. Greenwald (Eds.), *Attitude structure and function* (pp. 153–179). Hillsdale, NJ: Lawrence Erlbaum Associates.

Festinger, L., & Carlsmith, J. M. (1959). Cognitive consequences of forced compliance. *Journal of Abnormal and Social Psychology, 58*, 203–210.

Freedman, J. L., & Fraser, S. C. (1966). Compliance without pressure: The foot-in-the-door technique. *Journal of Personality and Social Psychology, 4*, 195–202.

Gerard, H. B., & Mathewson, G. C. (1966). The effects of severity of initiation on liking for a group: A replication. *Journal of Experimental Social Psychology, 2*, 278–287.

Hawking, S. W. (1988). *A brief history of time: From the big bang to black holes*. New York: Bantam.

Heider, F. (1958). *The psychology of interpersonal relations*. New York: Wiley.

Janis, I. L., & Mann, L. (1977). *Decision making: A psychological analysis of conflict, choice, and commitment*. New York: The Free Press.

Johnson, N. R., & Feinberg, W. E. (1989). Crowd structure and process: Theoretical framework and computer simulation model. *Advances in Group Process, 6*, 49–86.

Johnson, P. (1990). Unraveling in democratically governed groups. *Rationality and Society, 2*, 380–393.

Kanter, R. M. (1972). *Commitment and community: Communes and utopias in sociological perspective*. Cambridge, MA: Harvard University Press.

Kelley, H. H. (1955). Group membership and resistance to influence. In C. I. Hovland, I. L. Janis, & H. H. Kelley (Eds.), *Communication and persuasion* (pp. 134–165). New Haven, CT: Yale University Press.

Kiesler, C. A. (1971). *The psychology of commitment: Experiments linking behavior to belief*. New York: Academic.

Krosnick, J., & Abelson, R. P. (1991). Measures of attitude strength. In J. Tanur (Ed.), *Questions about survey questions* (pp. 177–203). New York: Russell Sage.

LeBon, G. (1895). *Psychologie des foules*. Paris: Felix Alcan.

Lewis, S. H. (1974). *An attributional analysis of the perceived legitimacy of social protest*. Unpublished manuscript, Yale University, New Haven, CT.

Lord, C. G., Lepper, M. R., & Preston, E. (1985). Considering the opposite: A corrective strategy for social judgment. *Journal of Personality and Social Psychology, 47,* 1231–1243.

Lord, C. G., Ross, L. & Lepper, M. (1979). Biased assimilation and attitude polarization: The effects of prior theories on subsequently considered evidence. *Journal of Personality and Social Psychology, 37,* 2098–2109.

McGarty, C., Turner, J. C., Hogg, M. A., David, B., & Wetherell, M. S. (1992). Group polarization as conformity to the prototypical group member. *British Journal of Social Psychology, 31,* 1–20.

Myers, D. G. (1978). Polarizing effects of social comparison. *Journal of Experimental Social Psychology, 14,* 554–563.

Myers, D. G., & Lamm, H. (1976). The group polarization phenomenon. *Psychological Bulletin, 83,* 602–627.

Na, E.-Y. (1992). Resistance of identity-relevant beliefs under threat from an antagonistic outgroup. Unpublished doctoral dissertation, Yale University, New Haven, CT.

National Advisory Commission on Civil Disorders. (1968). *Report of the National Advisory Commission on Civil Disorders.* New York: Bantam.

Nowak, A., Szamrej, J., & Latane, B. (1990). From private attitude to public opinion: A dynamic theory of social impact. *Psychological Review, 97,* 362–376.

O'Neill, B. (1991). The strategy of challenges: Two beheading games in medieval literature. In R. Selten & F. Weising (Eds.), *Proceedings of the conference on game theory in the behavioral sciences* (pp. 1–35). New York: Springer-Verlag.

Powell, M. C., & Fazio, R. H. (1984). Attitude accessibility as a function of repeated attitude expression. *Personality and Social Psychology Bulletin, 10,* 139–148.

Prentice, D. A. (1987). Psychological correspondence of possessions, attitudes, and values. *Journal of Personality and Social Psychology, 53,* 993–1003.

Price, V. (1989). Social identification and public opinion: Effects of communicating group conflict. *Public Opinion Quarterly, 53,* 197–224.

Schachter, S. (1964). The interaction of cognitive and physiological determinants of emotional state. In L. Berkowitz (Ed.), *Advances in experimental social psychology* (Vol. 1, pp. 49–80). New York: Academic Press.

Schwarz, N. (1990). Feelings as information. In E. T. Higgins & R. M. Sorrentino (Eds.), *Handbook of motivation and cognition: Foundations of social behavior* (Vol. 2, pp. 527–561). New York: Guilford.

Tesser, A. (1978). Self-generated attitude change. In L. Berkowitz (Ed.), *Advances in Experimental Social Psychology* (Vol. 11, pp. 289–338). New York: Academic.

Tesser, A., & Leone, C. (1977). Cognitive schemas and thought as determinants of attitude change. *Journal of Experimental and Social Psychology, 13,* 340–356.

Tomkins, S. S. (1965). The psychology of commitment. In M. Duberman (Ed.), *The antislavery vanguard* (pp. 270–300). Princeton, NJ: Princeton University Press.

Turner, R. H., & Killian, L. A. (1972). *Collective behavior* (2nd ed.). Englewood Cliffs, NJ: Prentice-Hall.

Zajonc, R. (1980). Feeling and thinking: Preferences need no inferences. *American Psychologist, 35,* 151–175.

Zimbardo, P. (1969). The human choice: Individuation, reason, and order versus deindividuation, impulse, and chaos. *Nebraska symposium on motivation 1969* (Vol. 17, pp. 237–307). Lincoln NE: University of Nebraska Press.

3

▼▼▼▼▼▼▼

Repetition and Evaluative Extremity

Charles M. Judd
Markus Brauer
University of Colorado

As the other chapters in this volume make clear, there are many different components of attitude strength, each perhaps being determined in different ways and having different consequences. Thus, for instance, the subjective importance of an attitude for an individual (Boninger, Krosnick, Berent, & Fabrigar, ch. 7, this volume) may be rather different in both its causes and effects from the accessibility of an attitude (Fazio, ch. 10, this volume). Our focus in this chapter is on one aspect of attitude strength, namely the expressed extremity of the attitude. As one component of attitude strength, expressed extremity is likely to be correlated with other components, such that more extreme attitudes tend to be more subjectively important and more accessible. But just like the other components of attitude strength, extremity may result from particular processes and have particular consequences that are only partially shared with the other components of attitude strength.

As a component of attitude strength, extremity moderates the energizing and directive functions of attitudes, similar to the moderating effects of other strength components. For instance, laboratory studies suggest that extreme attitudes are less susceptible to persuasion attempts than are less extreme attitudes (Ewing, 1942; Osgood, Suci, & Tannenbaum, 1957; Osgood & Tannenbaum, 1955; Sarat & Vidmar, 1976; Tannenbaum, 1956). Extreme attitudes have also been shown to be more consistent with behaviors than less extreme ones (Fazio & Zanna, 1978; Petersen & Dutton, 1975). Extreme attitudes also seem to have pronounced judgmental effects. Judd and Johnson (1981), for instance, found that subjects with extreme points of view overestimate the extremity of others—both others they agree with and others with whom they disagree. Similarly, extreme attitudes seem to be associated with judgments that a larger proportion of others take one's own point of view (Allison & Messick, 1988; Crano, Gorenflo, & Shackelford, 1988). Finally, there is some evidence that attitude congruent information is more likely to be remembered by subjects who adopt extreme points of view than by less extreme subjects (Roberts, 1984). In sum, attitude extremity qualifies as one component of attitude strength by being predictably related to the extent to which attitudes direct and energize behavior, judgment, and memory.

Sorting out the diverse consequences and causes of each of the components of attitude strength is the overarching goal of all the chapters in this book. Our own contribution serves this general goal by focusing on the question of the causes of expressed attitude extremity. A great deal of work has been reported in the literature on various social processes that affect expressed extremity or that lead to polarization of evaluative responses (e.g., Myers, 1978; Myers & Lamm, 1976). Abelson nicely summarized much of this work in his chapter in this volume. Our own intention is to focus not on these social processes that lead to polarization but rather on various cognitive or intrapersonal processes that may lead to greater expressed extremity of evaluations. Although these intrapersonal processes may be set in motion by the social factors of information exchange and social comparison, a thorough understanding of attitude extremity must involve a cognitive elaboration of how information exchange leads to greater or less expressed extremity. This is our intention.

Most of the intrapersonal determinants of expressed extremity that we focus on have to do with the effects of repeated exposure to the attitude object, repeated communications about the object and its attributes, repeated thought devoted to the object, and repeated expressions of the attitude. Each of these activities has been shown to lead to greater expressed extremity under appropriate circumstances. Our goal is to build a comprehensive model to account for these effects, and more broadly, to identify within that model intrapersonal processes that affect expressed attitude extremity. We start out with a quick overview of the various effects that we hope to account for. We then develop a general model of attitude representation, computation, and expression and, within the confines of this model, develop a general account of the intrapersonal factors that affect expressed extremity. In particular, we focus on the effects of repeated exposure, repeated communication, repeated thought, and repeated expression, and show how each of their effects on expressed extremity can be accounted for within the confines of our general model.

THE EFFECTS TO BE EXPLAINED

Simple repeated exposure to an attitude object can lead, under some conditions, to more extreme evaluations of that object. Zajonc (1968) was the first to examine the effects of "mere exposure" on object evaluations. He found that neutral stimuli are evaluated more positively after repeated exposure. This effect was obtained with Chinese ideographs (Zajonc, 1968), nonsense words (Zajonc & Rajecki, 1969), and a variety of other novel neutral stimuli. Perlman and Oskamp (1971), however, found attitude polarization after repeated exposure to photos of people in positive, negative, or neutral settings. People in a positive or neutral setting were liked more with exposure, but people in a negative setting were liked somewhat less after repeated exposure. Similarly, Brickman, Redfield, Harrison, and Crandall (1972), using abstract paintings as stimuli, found that repeated exposure led to greater liking of initially liked paintings but to greater disliking of initially disliked paintings (see Fig. 3.1). Grush (1976) reported similar effects of exposure to unusual words having either positively or negatively valenced meanings.

Repeated exposure to an attitude object that carries an evaluative valence is very similar to repeated exposures to communications about the object, assuming that those communications repeatedly portray the valenced attributes of the object. These communications can either be explicit persuasion attempts (as in repeated exposure to advertisements, e.g., Pechmann & Stewart, 1988; Sawyer, 1981) or simple repeated pairings of the attitude object with valenced attributes or contexts (as in research on the classical conditioning of attitudes, e.g., Cacioppo, Marshall-Goodell, Tassinary, & Petty, 1992; Zanna, Kiesler, & Pilkonis, 1970). Again, both sorts of repeated communications about an attitude object can lead to more polarized or extreme evaluations of the object.

The effects just cited involve either repeated presentations of the object to subjects or repeated communications about the object's valence to subjects. Additional studies have shown that simple instructions to subjects to think about the attitude object for some period of time can lead to more extreme evaluations (Tesser, 1978; Tesser, Martin, & Mendolia, ch. 4, this volume).

Finally, a number of studies have explored the effects of repeated expressions of attitudes about an object on both the subsequent latency of attitude responses and the extremity of those responses (Downing, Judd, & Brauer, 1992; Fazio, Chen, McDonel, & Sherman, 1982; Fazio, Sanbonmatsu, Powell, & Kardes,

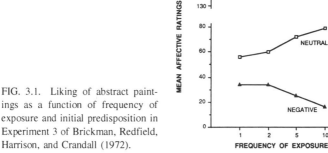

FIG. 3.1. Liking of abstract paintings as a function of frequency of exposure and initial predisposition in Experiment 3 of Brickman, Redfield, Harrison, and Crandall (1972).

1986; Powell & Fazio, 1984). The studies of Fazio and his colleagues have shown shorter latencies as a function of repeated practice at expressing an attitude but no effects on the expressed extremity of the attitude. Downing, Judd, and Brauer (1992) have shown that repeated expressions do lead to more extreme attitude responses so long as the repeated expressions do not occur on traditional likert-type attitude scales. Judd, Drake, Downing, and Krosnick (1991) showed that such practice effects on extremity generalize across related or similar attitude objects.

In sum, there is accumulating evidence that attitude polarization can occur in settings devoid of social interaction. Under appropriate circumstances, repeated exposure to an object, repeated communications about the object, repeated thought about the object, and repeated expressions of evaluation of the object can all lead to greater expressed extremity. To account for these effects in an integrated manner, we present in the next section a very general model of attitude representation and expression. We then examine what processes should lead to more extreme attitudes and what the effects of repetition are within the context of that model. Finally, we return to the effects just enumerated and explore them in more detail from the theoretical perspective of our general model.

A GENERAL MODEL OF ATTITUDE FORMATION, REPRESENTATION, AND OUTPUT

The three panels of Fig. 3.2 present our ideas about attitude representation, attitude computation, and attitude output. The model illustrated in Fig. 3.2 is necessarily a major oversimplification of a very complex set of issues concerning how attitudes are formed, stored, and expressed. Nevertheless, it is a useful heuristic for organizing our thoughts about these issues. We hope that it is sufficiently general and consistent with existing work (Anderson, 1971; Judd & Krosnick, 1989; Zanna & Rempel, 1988) so as to be relatively uncontroversial.

The top panel of Fig. 3.2 presents a very crude representational model, using an associative network analogy. We assume that an attitude object is represented in memory as a node that has associative connections with other object nodes. Stored with the object node are a set of features or attributes of the object and these attributes may be shared with other associated objects. Thus, in the example of Fig. 3.2, the represented object is a particular political candidate and the stored features of that candidate include political stances he or she is believed to adopt, physical and personality attributes, and miscellaneous other characteristics. The representation of this candidate is linked to other candidates, associated events, and other objects also stored in memory and each of these objects has stored features, either the same ones or different ones, as well. Connections between pairs of represented objects and also between objects and their features vary in their associative strength, indicating the probability that one object or feature

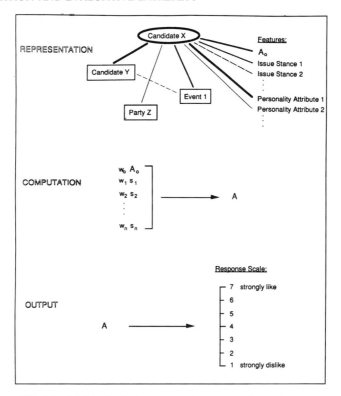

FIG. 3.2. Model of attitude representation, computation, and output.

stored in memory will become activated upon activation of a linked one. Stronger connections are indicated by darker lines in Fig. 3.2. Associative strengths vary not only between the different connections in the model; they also vary over time, with strength of associative links being a function of the recency and frequency of activation. One stored feature is of particular importance for our purposes. We assume that many represented objects have associated evaluations that are stored along with them. This evaluative "feature" is represented as A_o in Fig. 3.2 and the strength of its association with the object may vary, just like the associative strength of any other stored feature.

The middle panel of Fig. 3.2 represents a computational model, based loosely on Anderson's (1971, 1974) information integration theory. This computational model represents the cognitive algebra that is engaged in when a subject is asked to generate a judgment of an object stored in memory. The exact computational form of the model is left unspecified in Fig. 3.2. Our preference is to assume some form of a weighted averaging procedure for combining scale values.

In our case, of course, the primary judgment we are interested in is an evaluative one. To illustrate this component of the model, consider someone who is asked to express her opinion about a political candidate. Several attributes of the candidate may come to mind in deciding about her overall evaluation. Some of these attributes carry positive implications (e.g., the candidate has a lot of experience in office, was born in her hometown, and is pro-choice). Others have more negative connotations (e.g., he has just divorced his second wife and is a strong advocate of nuclear power). These various attributes do not all contribute equally to her overall evaluation: She may weight the candidate's policy stances more heavily than aspects of his personal life, and she may decide that amount of experience in office ought not to influence her overall evaluation much at all.

More formally, the inputs to this computational model, the s_i, consist of the evaluative connotations of each of the attributes or features of the object that are stored in memory and that may be situationally salient. Each of these inputs (scale values in the terminology of information integration theory) contributes to the evaluative judgment A according to its weight, w_i. These weights derive from a variety of factors that include the associative strength of the link between the object and the feature in the representational panel of the model. Features that are brought to mind more easily in evaluating the object will be weighted more heavily in computing that evaluation than features that come to mind less readily. In addition, the magnitude of the weights may vary from context to context and with particular demands imposed by the form of the judgment task. For instance, a question that asks for a candidate evaluation emphasizing the subject's agreement with the candidate's issue stances will obviously result in different weights than an evaluative judgment question asking for an assessment of the candidate's overall leadership ability.

The final note of significance about this computational part of the model is that the stored evaluation, A_o, is included in the computational process as an additional weighted scale value. In some cases, it may be the only scale value with a nonzero value of w_i, resulting in a computed value of A that is simply the stored prior evaluation, A_o. In other cases, prior evaluations may be relatively weak or uninformative and computation with new scale values is intensive. Again, the particular judgmental context and task instructions may influence the size of w_o. Also influencing the magnitude of w_o is the associative strength of the link between the object and A_o in the representational part of the model, as with any feature. Thus well learned or practiced A_o's result in less computation in general than less well learned A_o's.

The bottom panel of Fig. 3.2 represents the translation process whereby a given value of A is output or expressed in some way. In Fig. 3.2 we have assumed that the overt expression of the attitude occurs on a 7-point evaluative scale, with endpoints labeled *strongly like* and *strongly dislike*. But any other form of overt expression of the attitude could have been used instead. The point of this part of Fig. 3.2 is simply to argue that the computed value of A is acted upon in various ways and to varying degrees in fashioning an overt attitude response, be that response a scale response on an attitude questionnaire, a verbal expression, an action that the attitude partially motivates, or whatever.

A host of factors influence this translation process. The scalar aspects of attitude rating scales that influence self-ratings have been relatively well studied. Most obviously, the labeling of the content to be associated with scale values can have a dramatic impact on attitude responses (Ostrom & Upshaw, 1968). More subtle aspects of questionnaire design and the context in which the attitude response is given also influence this process (e.g., Schuman & Presser, 1981). Thus the same A value may result in a more or less favorable response depending on social desirability cues built into the way the question is asked, previous questions which provide cues about appropriate answers for the current question, and so forth. These sorts of cues may also, of course, affect the computation of A and the values of w_i used in that computation. But they can also exert their effects simply by affecting the overt expression of the computed attitude without any effect on the value of A itself. Finally, it seems reasonable to assume that this translation of A into an attitude expression may be more or less effortful depending on prior experience using a particular expression format. Someone who is a perpetual subject in attitude change studies conducted by social psychologists may compute values of A that are essentially "scale values in the head" and that more or less automatically translate into expressed values on self-rating scales. Others, less familiar with such scales, may engage in a much more elaborate process in fashioning the requested attitude expression.

POLARIZATION OF ATTITUDES WITHIN THIS MODEL

Now that the general model has been presented, we turn to processes that may lead to polarization of attitudes within the confines of the model. We consider each component of the model (i.e., representation, computation, and output) in turn. For each, we examine, first, what the general processes are that can lead to greater extremity of evaluation within that component, and second, how various experimental manipulations that involve repetitive exposure, repetitive communication, repetitive thought, and repetitive expression affect the processes leading to polarization. Because the focus in these sections is on manipulations that repeat various cognitive processes, we start off with a general consideration of the known effects of repetition on any cognitive process.

General Effects of Repetition on Cognitive Processes

In general we assume that repetition of any cognitive process strengthens that process, making it more efficient and easier to execute in the future. This assumption is consistent with abundant recent work on the nature of skill and well rehearsed cognitive responses (e.g., Anderson, 1983, 1987; Smith, 1989, 1990; Smith Branscombe, & Bormann, 1988). This general strengthening of processes with repetition should occur in all parts of our general attitude model. Thus, for instance, in the representation component of the model, repeated exposure to a particular feature of an object or repeated retrieval of that feature from memory strengthens the associative link in memory between the object and the feature and thereby facilitates subsequent retrieval of that feature. In the computational component of the model, repeated computation of one's attitude toward a particular object makes that computation more streamlined. Finally, repeated attitude responses using a given response format makes subsequent responses utilizing the same response format easier.

Increasing the strength of a process means both that the process is completed more quickly and that the process becomes simplified over time or "proceduralized" (Anderson, 1983, 1987). The increase in efficiency is due both to an increase in the speed of execution of the individual steps in the process as well as to the simplification or integration of those various steps into fewer and simpler steps. In essence, the process becomes simpler, the inputs to the process become more highly organized, and the process output becomes more predictable. In the following we explore more specifically what exactly this means in the context of each of the components of our general attitude model.

The Representation Component

Processes Affecting Extremity. A given attitude may change in extremity when a new attribute is added to the existing set of features stored in memory or when an old attribute is no longer retained. Adding a new attribute that is evaluatively consistent with the overall evaluation of the attitude object or dropping an old attribute that is evaluatively inconsistent with the overall evaluation should both lead to a more extreme attitude. A second process that can affect attitudinal extremity is a change in the strength of a link between the object and one of its associated features. If the feature is evaluatively consistent with the overall evaluation then an increase in link strength between the attitude object and the feature will generally lead to a more extreme evaluation. Similarly, if the feature is evaluatively inconsistent with the overall evaluation then a decrease in associative strength should result in a more polarized attitude. We return to the example used earlier to illustrate these processes. If we assume that the overall evaluation of the political candidate is positive, then encoding and retaining an additional positive attribute or dropping from memory a previously retained negative attribute should make the attitude even more positive. In the same vein, if one of the positive features stored in memory becomes more closely associated with the candidate, then it should influence the overall evaluation of the candidate more strongly, with the result that the previously positive attitude toward the candidate becomes more extreme. This should also be the result if a negative feature becomes less closely associated with the candidate.

Repetition and the Representation Component. Repetition can influence the efficiency of a number of processes in the representation component of the model, with implications for the processes just outlined that affect extremity. First, and most generally, the representation of the attitude object itself should become simpler and more efficient upon repeated contact with or exposure to the object. Most simply, repeated exposure to the object leads to its representation in memory and more frequent subsequent exposure is associated with easier retrieval of the object. This hypothesis, which seems fairly obvious on its surface, has some interesting implications. Consider a subject who encounters a novel stimulus object. Presumably initial representation of this object in memory requires its classification or categorization along with other related representations that have previously been stored in memory. According to our model and nearly all models of long-term memory organization, storage is not a simple random process; rather each object is linked to other represented objects that share features, attributes, contexts, or other characteristics. As a result, the initial representation of the object in memory entails some selectivity of the features of that object that permit its classification or categorization along with other objects that are represented in memory. Repeated exposure to the object and repeated retrieval of the object from memory means that that selectivity is reinforced. Rather than recognizing and retrieving features of the object that would have led to a different sort of classification of the object in long-term memory, those features that were initially encoded and used for purposes of representation are increasingly brought to mind and the strength of their connections with the object itself increases.

A concrete example may help illustrate the process. Consider an individual exposed to a modern painting for the first time. This object has many, many features that are potentially useful in linking it to categories of other objects that are stored in memory. For instance, one might focus on its colors, its forms, its similarities with the works of known artists, the mood it evokes, and so forth. Initial categorization of the painting depends on selecting some of its myriad features and not others. Subsequent exposure to and recognition of the painting reinforces that selectivity, increasing the strength of the links in memory between those features used for classification and decreasing the strength of links to other features not so used. Certain features become more and more dominant in the subsequent recognition and appraisal of the painting. Others cease to be noticed.

For many of the objects that we encounter, the associated features carry evaluative information and the feature selectivity that happens as a result of categorization and subsequent exposure to and recognition of the object is likely to involve a selectivity of features that share common evaluative implications. This hypothesis presumes that the evaluative implications of an object's features may be used for purposes of classification, storage, and retrieval of the object in memory (Bower, 1981). Again, consider a concrete example in which a subject is exposed to a photo of an unfamiliar person. That person is potentially categorized in many different ways and the choice of features used for categorization is organized in part, we suggest, by the evaluative implications that features share. The subject may initially notice the person's greasy hair, his tender eyes, wild eyebrows, straight nose, and gentle smile. Categorization of the individual may rely in part on a dominant evaluative response to the individual as either generally sympathetic or potentially threatening and dislikeable. Those features with evaluative implications that are consistent with this evaluative categorization are reinforced in the representation of the person in memory. Thus with repeated exposures to the photo and repeated retrieval of the person from memory, the person's tender eyes and gentle smile may be reinforced and the more threatening features disregarded or dismissed, assuming that a generally positive response to the person dominates.

In addition to repeated simple exposure to an object, repeated pairings of an object with a particular feature or context also have implications for the representation of the object. If a particular feature of the object is made salient upon each repetition, then obviously the link between that feature and the object will be strengthened. Similarly, if a context is repeatedly paired with the object, the features of that context may become associated with the object itself and made features of the object. The resulting increase in the strength of links between the object and certain features can presumably happen either as a result of conscious recognition of the features' association with the object (as in repeated messages about the object that underline particular features) or as a result of associative learning processes that may not be consciously mediated (e.g., the association of a conditioned response with the object).

In sum, in the representational component of our model, repeated exposure to an object, repeated pairings of that object with certain features and not others, and repeated retrieval of the object from memory serves to reinforce or strengthen certain features of the object and not others. Repetition increases the selectivity of features in the representation of the object. To the extent that the selectivity is guided by the evaluative implications of an object's features, repeated exposure and retrieval of the object should reinforce the dominant evaluation of the object. Similarly, repeated pairings of the object with evaluative features or contexts should lead to a strengthening of the implied object evaluation.

The Computation Component

Processes Affecting Extremity. In general, attitude polarization can occur in the computation component of the model either through a change in the weights, w_i, or through a change in the scale values, s_i. Giving an attribute a heavier weight during computation of A should generally lead to a more extreme attitude as long as that attribute is evaluatively consistent with the overall evaluation A. When the attribute is evaluatively inconsistent with the overall evaluation, however, then giving it a smaller weight should generally result in attitude polarization. Similarly, changes in scale values in the direction of the overall evaluation may lead to a more extreme attitude.

It should be noted that the processes that lead to attitude polarization in the computation component are not substantially different from those that lead to more extreme attitudes in the representational component. We have earlier argued that the weight of a feature in the computational component depends to a large extent on the strength of the associative link between the feature and the attitude object in representation. In other words, increasing the strength of a link between the object and a feature in the representational component generally results in an increased weight associated with the scale value of that feature in computation. Similarly, adding a new attribute to the list of features stored in long-term memory generally results in assigning the scale value of that feature a nonzero weight during computation.

As indicated earlier, we are assuming some form of weighted averaging computational algebra, following the work of Anderson (1971, 1974). As shown by Judd and Lusk (1984), this has two implications. First, as the evaluative redundancy of the scale values increases, the absolute value of the computed A also increases (assuming that zero values on both s_i and A indicate neutrality). This is just a formal way of saying the obvious: Objects with all good features or all bad ones will have more positive or more negative A values than objects with features that have more varied evaluative connotations. Second, as the number of features increases, the computed value of A will on average be less extreme (i.e., smaller in absolute value) as long as the features are relatively nonredundant (Linville, 1982; Linville & Jones, 1980). With redundant features, however, the inclusion of more features leads to more extreme values of A (given certain assumptions about the value of the initial attitude, A_o, as outlined by Judd & Lusk, 1984).

Repetition and the Computation Component. Repeated computations of an evaluative response to an object make subsequent computations more efficient in two ways. First, and most obviously, the required mental algebra is completed more quickly. Second, the elements of the computational model upon which the mental algebra are performed become fewer and simpler through changes in the weights (the w_i) associated with the stimulus values involved in the computation. This latter effect is due to the reciprocal nature of the relations between the representational and computational components of our model.

The product of the computational component is an implicit global evaluation of the stimulus object. This implicit evaluation (A in the model as portrayed in Fig. 3.2) is subsequently stored in memory, in the representational component of the model, as the stored evaluation (A_o). Upon repetitions of the computation of A, the value of A_o is retrieved from memory and enters into the computational component. Because this stored global evaluation was determined during the previous computational iteration, it is entirely redundant with the stimulus values and the weights used during the computation, unless for some reason these have changed from one computational iteration to the next. As a result, with repetitions of the computational component, the value of A_o that is retrieved acquires a larger and larger weight and the strength of its link with the object in the representational component increases. The stored evaluation of the object comes to mind more readily when one encounters the attitude object and it is weighted more heavily the next time a new evaluative response is generated. Assuming repeated iterations in the same context, involving little change in the relative salience of an object's features, the computational component of the model should become entirely trivial in very short order. Repeated computation comes to mean nothing more than accessing the stored value of A_o, because it has come to have the only nonzero weight in the computation.

The Output Component

Processes Affecting Extremity. When an overt attitude expression or response is required, then the computed value of A must be mapped onto some sort of response scale, i.e., the output component of the model. A polarization of the expressed attitude can be caused by anything that makes the subject choose a more extreme scale value. Obviously the labeling of scale endpoints can have a dramatic effect here (Ostrom & Upshaw, 1968). The more moderate the scale endpoints, the more extreme the rated attitude, given a constant value of the implicit computed A. In the example of Fig. 3.2 the scale points were labeled *strongly like* and *strongly dislike*. Had we defined them simply as *like* or *dislike* the same value of A would presumably result in a more extreme attitude expression. Beyond differences in the extremity of scale endpoints, social desirability cues that are built into the question or into the scale endpoints can also influence expressed extremity. The more the question makes the subject think his or her overall evaluation (A) is toward the socially desirable end of the response scale, the more he or she should shift towards a more extreme self-rating. Previous questions or requests for other evaluations may also induce a response set that leads to more or less extreme responses. Thus if a set of previous questions asked for evaluative responses by allowing subjects only a bipolar choice between relatively extreme responses, then a subsequent response along a continuum may be more extreme than it would be without the previous bipolar responses.

It should be noted that all of these processes are assumed to have a direct effect only on the mapping or output process; that is, they cause the overt expression of the attitude to become more extreme without any necessary effect on the underlying or implicit attitude that is output from the computation component (i.e., A). However, as we argue below, the expressed attitude is likely to be subsequently stored in memory and thus contributes to later computations of the attitude. As a result, the previously mentioned processes may lead indirectly to a polarization of the underlying attitude in addition to a polarization of its expression.

Repetition and the Output Component. What happens when the computed value of A is repeatedly mapped onto some sort of response scale? So long as the response scale remains constant across trials, then this expression component should also become more efficient with practice. In fact, across repeated trials involving the same response scale, it may become so efficient that the overt response becomes essentially indistinguishable from the implicit A value that is the output of the computational component. In other words, the subject learns to generate an implicit evaluative response, A, that is isomorphic with the overt response label given expression on previous response trials. One's attitude essentially becomes a scale response that is stored in memory and retrieved on each trial. In this case, the decrease in latency of response across repeated expression trials is due to increases in efficiency in all three components of the model: The prior value of A_o is retrieved more quickly, the computation is much more efficient since only A_o receives any weight in computation, and the internal or implicit output of the process, A, is the appropriate scalar response that has been learned through previous expressions of the evaluation.

To illustrate, let us consider a woman who is asked to express her opinion about a political candidate. Normally, she is assumed to compute an implicit, abstract attitude (A) which is stored in memory and mapped onto a response scale. When asked to express her attitude several times on different response scales she will retrieve the stored implicit attitude and map it each time onto the particular response scale presented to her. Let us now suppose, however, that she is a habitual respondent to the national election surveys and thus always expresses candidate evaluations on 100-point thermometer scales. Our argument is that as a result of habitually using the same response format, the implicit attitude that she will come to store will be a specific scale value, say the value of 85, rather than a more vague implicit overall evaluation. She will no longer store the conclusion of the computational component as "candidate X is a very capable politician whom I respect a lot" and then go through the mapping process by saying "my attitude can probably be best described by an 85," but she will store in memory "candidate X is an 85."

With changing overt expression formats, increases in efficiency with multiple trials should also be found due to facilitation of the representational and computational components of the model. But the internal output of the computational component may not be in the form of the appropriate scale response. If it is not, then it must be newly translated into an overt expression each time a new response format is encountered. The output of this translation process may be affected by previous response formats that have been used. Assume for instance, that previously used response formats have all been 100-point thermometer scales. Now one encounters a 7-point rating scale anchored with the labels *like* and *dislike*. The translation process should encounter few difficulties in mapping a stored value of A onto this new scale. On the other hand, consider what happens when previous responses have been oral expressions of A, indicating simply an overall summative *like* or *dislike* judgment. In this case, the overt response becomes more strongly associated with the object with more frequent oral expression. When confronted by a 7-point rating scale, anchored with those labels, we suggest that the strong association between the label and the object that has been produced by frequent prior oral expressions should result in relatively confident and extreme self-ratings on the 7-point scale.

Summary of Repetition Effects in the Model

On the one hand, the effects of repetition of a process are quite simple: Repetition increases its efficiency. On the other hand, we have shown that this general principle has numerous implications in the context of our general attitude model. These can be summarized in the following series of propositions.

1. Repeated exposure to an object and repeated retrieval of an object from memory results in feature selectivity. The links of features used for categorization are strengthened and others come to be ignored.

2. When an object has features that have evaluative implications, the selectivity of features across repeated exposure and retrieval trials may involve the selectivity of features based in part of their shared evaluative implications. Thus features that share a dominant evaluative implication come to be linked more strongly to the object across repeated exposure and retrieval trials.

3. Repeated pairings of an object with a particular feature or context strengthens the link between the object and the associated features.

4. Repeated computations of an implicit evaluative response results in a stronger link between the stored evaluation and the object. As a result, the evaluation is more likely to come to mind whenever the object is encountered.

5. Repeated computation of an implicit evaluative response increases computational efficiency. Presuming a constant context, computation quickly comes to mean that the subject simply retrieves the stored implicit evaluation of the object.

6. Repetition of an overt evaluative response leads to greater efficiency of the output component of the model so long as the repeated expression involves the same general response format. In this case the stored implicit evaluation, A_o, may take the form of the overt expression that has been repeatedly given.

7. When a particular response format is repeatedly practiced, the repetition of this overt expression may affect subsequent expressions when confronted by a different response scale. For instance, repeated prior expressions of a global evaluative label will lead to stronger association between the label and the object. When one now encounters an attitude rating scale these stronger associations may lead to a more confident and extreme scale response.

REEXAMINING THE STUDIES OF ATTITUDE POLARIZATION IN LIGHT OF OUR GENERAL ACCOUNT

We now return to the experimental manipulations of repeated exposure, repeated communication, repeated thought, and repeated expression that we briefly discussed at the beginning of the chapter. As we showed there, each of these manipulations has been shown to lead to attitude polarization under appropriate circumstances. Our goal in the present section of the chapter is to discuss these effects in greater detail and show how they can be explained in a relatively parsimonious manner through the general account of the processes that we have just presented.

Repeated Exposure and Communication

Many studies have repeatedly exposed subjects to a stimulus object and then assessed their evaluations of that object. These studies include variations that are of considerable theoretical importance. Some involve the repeated presentation of novel attitude objects having few if any evaluative features or connotations (e.g., exposure to Chinese ideographs; Zajonc, 1968). In other studies, experimenters have manipulated the frequency of exposure to objects that are known to elicit evaluative responses, such as paintings that were known to be generally liked or disliked (e.g., Brickman et al., 1972), or faces (e.g. Hamm, Baum, & Nikels, 1975), or low frequency words (Grush, 1976) having evaluative connotations. Still other studies have involved the presentation of objects accompanied by repeated communications (either explicit or implicit) about certain features of the object known to carry evaluative connotations. Thus for instance Zajonc, Markus, and Wilson (1974) repeatedly showed subjects faces and told them on each trial that the face was that of a criminal or that of a scientist. Similarly, Perlman and Oskamp (1971) showed photographs of individuals to subjects and these individuals were either dressed as priests or prisoners. Other studies have repeatedly exposed subjects to stimulus objects in association with other stimuli known to elicit evaluative responses (e.g., Cacioppo et al., 1992; Zanna et al., 1970). Finally, numerous studies have simply repeated communications about particular evaluative features of objects without actual repeated exposure to the objects themselves (e.g., repeated persuasive communications, Cacioppo & Petty, 1989; Pechmann & Stewart, 1988). Although a general integration of all of this work lies well beyond the scope of this chapter, a consideration of when these different variants on repeated exposure should lead to greater evaluative extremity and when they should not is our present intention.

The best known effect of repeated exposure is the "mere exposure" effect in which repeated exposure to a novel and neutral stimulus object leads to positive evaluations of the object. Although a variety of explanations exist for this effect (see Harrison, 1977; Sawyer, 1981), the one that seems most consistent with the existing literature and that is entirely compatible with our general model of attitude representation and computation has come to be known as the response competition explanation. According to this explanation, a newly encountered stimulus object has many different features that might be used as the basis of classification and representation. In essence, these features compete with each other in terms of how the object is to be categorized with other objects and represented in long-term memory. The response competition hypothesis further assumes that competition among features is associated with negative affect (Berlyne, 1954, 1960; Brown & Farber, 1951). What happens over repeated exposures, as we have outlined in the earlier section of this chapter where we discussed the representation component of our general model, is that certain features are used as the basis of categorization and representation in long-term memory and not others. Thus feature selectivity occurs as a function of repeated exposure, with a concomitant reduction in response competition. This is further accompanied by a decrease in the negative affect associated with response competition, which then generalizes to the represented stimulus object. In other words, the increase in evaluation of a novel neutral stimulus object results from the selection of a subset of the object's features as the basis for categorization and representation. This selection is further reinforced by subsequent exposures to the object, as the features that have been selected as the basis for representation become more and more dominant. Each subsequent exposure in essence reinforces the associative link between the object and those features that were selected for categorization and representation.

Many of the studies in the repeated exposure tradition have used stimuli whose features carry evaluative connotations rather than neutral stimuli. Such stimuli include the abstract paintings of the Brickman et al. (1972) study and the photographs of faces of the Hamm et al. (1975) study. We suggested earlier that the feature selectivity that occurs during initial exposure and representation of such objects is likely to be organized in part by the evaluative connotations of the features. Thus, a few features come to be dominant across repeated exposures and these dominant features are likely to share a dominant evaluative connotation. The extent to which feature selectivity is based on their shared evaluative connotations probably depends, in part, on the strength of the evaluative connotations of the object's features and the extent to which those connotations are consistent with each other.

The selectivity of features across exposures and the reduction in negative affect resulting from the reduction in response competition leads to complex predictions about the effects of repeated exposure to stimuli whose features elicit evaluative responses. On the one hand, the "mere exposure" part of exposure means that the negative affect of response competition is reduced and positive affect is generalized to the stimulus object. On the other hand, as evaluative features that share a dominant evaluative response become more dominant and more redundant across exposure trials, the overall evaluation of the object becomes more and more consistent with the evaluative connotations of those dominant features. In combination, these two effects of exposure mean that repeated exposure to a stimulus object having positive features should increase the extremity of the positive evaluation of the object. Both "mere exposure" and the selectivity of positive features leads to a more positive overall evaluation of the object with more frequent exposure. In the case of an object with features that carry largely negative connotations, the two effects work in opposite directions. "Mere exposure" results in a more positive evaluation of the object. At the same time, if feature selectivity is guided by the evaluative connotations of the object's features, then repeated exposure should lead to more negative evaluations of the object. In combination, these effects predict that a negatively evaluated object can either increase in negativity over multiple exposures or show a weak positivity effect. For objects with strongly negative evaluative features, the selectivity effect ought to dominate the "mere exposure" effect and more negative evaluations should result from more frequent exposure.

Both Brickman et al. (1972) and Hamm et al. (1975) reported that exposure increases liking for initially liked abstract paintings (in the first case) and faces (in the second). For abstract paintings that were initially disliked Brickman et al. (1972) reported that exposure leads to somewhat more extreme negative appraisals. On the other hand, Hamm et al. (1975) reported that negatively evaluated faces are regarded somewhat more positively following repeated exposure. We suggest that the difference in these results is due to the fact that in the case of abstract paintings, features carry strong evaluative connotations and thus feature selectivity is guided by their shared evaluative connotations. In the case of faces, it seems to us that this is less likely to be the case.

When a particular feature of the stimulus object is made salient upon each repeated exposure to the object (e.g., Perlman & Oskamp, 1971; Zajonc et al., 1974), similar predictions about the effects of repetition on evaluations can be made. In this case, the feature that is repeatedly paired with the object should become more strongly associated with the object and the feature's evaluative connotation, if it has one, should be weighted more heavily with increasing repetitions when a final evaluative judgment is asked for. When the evaluative connotation of the associated feature is positive, then repeated presentation of the object and this feature should combine with the positivity effect of "mere exposure" to yield a strong positive effect for repetition. When the associated feature has a negative connotation, then the increased negativity of evaluation that results from a stronger association with the feature across repetitions should work in the opposite direction from the positivity effect of "mere exposure." In both the Zajonc et al. (1974) and Perlman and Oskamp (1971) studies, these conjectures were supported, because repetition of exposure led to a pronounced increase in positivity when the feature that was repeatedly paired with the object was positively valenced. When the paired feature had a negative valence, Perlman and Oskamp found that greater frequency of exposure was associated with more negative evaluations, although the strength of this exposure effect was considerably weaker than exposure effect with a positively valenced feature. Zajonc et al. continued to find a positive exposure effect even for repeated pairings with a negatively valenced feature, although the slope of the exposure effect was considerably weaker than the slope for objects paired with a positively valenced feature.

To explain these apparently discrepant results, we suggest again that the evaluative connotation of the negatively valenced feature in the Zajonc et al. study (i.e., the crime that the person had committed) was less salient or strong than the evaluative connotation of the feature in the Perlman and Oskamp study (the prisoner's outfit that the person wore). Repeated pairings of a negatively valenced feature with the object can overwhelm the "mere exposure" positivity effect if the feature is sufficiently negative. But it may not, if its evaluative connotation is weaker or less apparent.

A number of other studies have paired the repeated presentation of an attitude object with other stimuli that produce affective reactions (e.g., Cacioppo et al., 1992; Staats & Staats, 1958; Zanna et al., 1970). In general, these studies have sought to demonstrate that object evaluations can be classically conditioned (i.e., that the affect associated with the unconditioned stimulus can generalize to the conditioned stimulus). Although such demonstrations have been plagued by alternative explanations arguing that changes in evaluations of the stimulus object are due to experimenter demand characteristics, the accumulating evidence strongly suggests that generalization of positive and negative affect to a stimulus object (particularly a novel one, see Cacioppo et al., 1992) can occur. From the present point of view, these studies are a little different from those just discussed. Rather than underlining a particular feature of the attitude object on each exposure, the object is always paired with another stimulus that has affective properties. What presumably happens is that the affect associated with the paired stimulus is generalized to the attitude object. The more frequent the exposure, the stronger the generalization and the more extreme the resulting attitude toward the object. Consistent with the findings of Cacioppo et al. (1992), it seems reasonable to expect that this generalization across repeated exposures should play a larger role when dealing with relatively novel attitude objects than when dealing with ones that have already been encoded and whose features are already well known. In essence the associated unconditioned stimulus provides a context for the initial representation and storage of the attitude object and this representation exerts an effect on evaluation of the object subsequently.

A final form of repeated exposure involves repeated evaluative communications about an attitude object, often without actual repeated exposure to the object itself. Marketing researchers have been particularly interested in documenting how evaluations of products are affected by the frequency with which subjects are exposed to particular advertising messages about the products (Pechmann & Stewart, 1988). In general, this research shows that repeated exposures to a persuasive communication about an attitude object lead to changes in the object evaluation. The effect of message repetition is initially in the direction advocated by the message. At some point, however, the tedium of being exposed to the same message repeatedly seems to set in and attitudes towards the object may actually move away from the position advocated in the persuasive message. From the point of view of our general model, what repetition of a persuasive message does is to build stronger links in representation and higher weights in computation between the feature of the object that is the focus of the message and the object itself. As a result, the evaluation shifts in the direction of the evaluative connotation of that feature. At some point, however, the subject tires of being told the same thing over and over again and may even come to doubt the credibility or verity of the persuasive communication.

In sum, there seem to be a number of processes that operate when a subject is repeatedly exposed to an attitude object . These processes in combination can explain the diverse effects of repeated exposure to an attitude object on shifts in expressed attitude extremity. On the one hand, with novel objects, simple repeated exposure leads to the development of positive affect toward the object as the object is categorized and represented in long-term memory. The simple process of categorization and representation implies a feature selection process that is accompanied by a decrease in negative affect associated with response competition. Many attitude objects, even though they may not have been encountered before, have highly evaluative features. In this case, feature selectivity may be organized in part by the dominant evaluative response shared by the object's features. Accordingly, across repeated exposure to the object, the dominant evaluative connotation of the selected features is reinforced and evaluations polarize. When the repeated presentation of the object is accompanied by explicit mention of particular evaluative features or is paired with other objects or contexts eliciting strong affective reactions, then the evaluation of the object can be expected to move in the direction of the implied evaluation. This may or may not result in attitude polarization, depending on whether the overall object evaluation is consistent with the evaluative connotation of the paired feature or context. Similar arguments apply to explicit persuasive communications to which subjects are repeatedly exposed.

Repeated Expression

Repeated expression of an evaluation of an object involves not only repeated exposure to that object, but also repeated computation of the value of A and repeated expression of that value with a particular response format. In general, as we have said, repetitive expression increases the strength of the link between A_o and the object in representation. As a result, it increases the weight associated with A_o in the computational part of the model. Finally, repetitive expression with the same response format increases the likelihood that the internal representation of the attitude, i.e., A_o, will assume the form demanded by that format and this will increase the efficiency of expression so long as the response format is unchanged.

Powell and Fazio (1984) were the first to systematically examine the effects of repeated expression. Subjects expressed their attitudes toward various social and political issues with varying frequency. These repeated expressions were always given on 9-point scales, anchored with evaluative labels at the endpoints (e.g., approve–disapprove; advantageous–disadvantageous). The penultimate expression of their attitudes was on a 29-point scale anchored with agree–disagree endpoints. Subsequently, subjects were given a forced choice like–dislike rating task on the computer and the latencies of their responses were recorded. These latencies were strongly affected by the number of prior expressions, as would be predicted by the effects of repetition on both the representation and computation components of our model. Attitudes were expressed more quickly as a result of stronger associative links between stored values of A_o and the attitude object in memory and as a result of prior computational practice and increased weighting of A_o in the computation component. As suggested earlier, with repeated expression, the only object feature with a weight different from zero becomes the stored value of A_o. As a result the computation of a new value of A becomes entirely trivial.

On the penultimate attitude expression, involving a 29-point response scale, Powell and Fazio (1984) report no effects of repetition frequency on the extremity of self ratings. Even though previous responses had all been given on 9-point scales, they all involved scalar self-ratings on scales that spanned a questionnaire page. Repetitive expression of an attitude on one such self-rating scale, it seems to us, should increase the efficiency of subsequent self-ratings on similar scales, even though the actual number of response alternatives may change (from 9 to 29). Through repetition, a particular scalar response is learned and is subsequently produced both efficiently and consistently.

Downing, Judd, and Brauer (1992) replicated these results (see Fig. 3.3) and also ran subjects in an additional condition where the initial repeated attitude

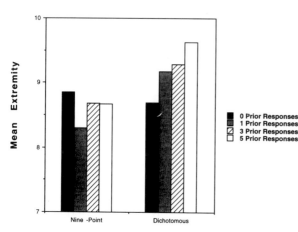

FIG. 3.3. Mean extremity of ratings concerning political issues as a function of frequency of prior responses and expression condition in Experiment 1 of Downing, Judd, and Brauer (1992).

expressions were reported on a forced choice positive–negative format. In this condition, they found that the penultimate ratings on the 29-point scale were more extreme when the attitude had been previously expressed more frequently. Like Powell and Fazio (1984), they found a decrease in the latency of response as a function of the number of prior expressions.

Our general account of repetition effects suggests that practice with a particular response format leads to the internalization of a particular response language. Accordingly, more frequent expressions of an attitude using only verbal labels that will subsequently become response scale endpoints (e.g., like–dislike) leads to more extreme subsequent expressions of attitudes on the rating scales. In essence, the response language that has been practiced becomes a label that is associated with the attitude object and that label is subsequently expressed more quickly and more confidently. Given a subsequent scalar response, greater self-rated extremity ensues.

Downing, Judd, and Brauer (1992) collected data from subjects in an additional condition in which the initial expressions, which varied in frequency across attitude objects, were given orally, unconstrained by any particular response language. In this condition, they found that more frequent expressions were given more quickly and also that self-ratings on the penultimate attitude rating scales varied in extremity as a function of frequency of prior expressions (see Table 3.1). They also found that judges who coded the oral expressions given during the repeated expressions part of the study indicated that those expressions became more extreme the more frequently they had been given. Thus, it seems as if the same sort of associative model may be operative in this oral expression condition as in the condition where repetitive expression was given with a forced-choice response format. Across repetitions, relatively more simple and extreme oral expressions or labels are given in response to the attitude object. These expressions become associated with the object; in essence they become the stored representation of the attitude (i.e., the A_o). Subsequent scalar expressions become therefore more extreme.

TABLE 3.1
Mean Extremity of Ratings Concerning Political Issues as a Function
of Frequency of Prior Responses in Experiment 2
of Downing, Judd, and Brauer (1992)

| | Number of Prior Responses | | | |
	0	1	3	5
29-point Scale Extremity	7.98	7.78	8.20	9.08
	Prior Frequency of Oral Responses			
	0	1	2	3	4
Judged Extremity of Oral Response	2.09	2.09	2.16	2.20	2.28

This simple associative argument should apply to nonevaluative judgments as well as to evaluative ones. That is, if one asks subjects to orally express nonevaluative judgments and if those oral expressions tend to simplify and polarize across trials, then we would predict that more frequent oral expressions should be associated with more extreme expressions, even for nonevaluative judgments. In a third study, Downing, Judd, and Brauer (1992) conducted a nonevaluative replication of the earlier studies to examine this explanation. Subjects were exposed to Chinese ideographs with varying frequencies. Each ideograph was consistently portrayed on a computer terminal in one of nine color shades that varied from a pure red hue to a pure blue (with various shades of purple in between). Thus there were two crossed within subject factors in the design, frequency of exposure (having three levels of three exposures, five exposures, and eight exposures) and color (nine levels). Subjects were told that their job was to learn the color of each ideograph and that they would see some of them more frequently than others. To help them learn the colors, subjects were asked to say out loud the color they judged each ideograph to be, using their own words, each time an ideograph was seen. After all learning trials had been completed, each ideograph was presented in black to the subject who was asked to judge the color in which it had appeared, on a 9-point scale anchored with the verbal labels of "red" and "blue" at the scale endpoints. As expected from the associative analogy to Studies 1 and 2, subjects gave more extreme judgments in the testing phase of the study for ideographs than had been seen more frequently during the learning phase of the study (i.e., for ideographs whose hue had been given expression more frequently). Simply seeing an ideograph more frequently and expressing its color led to more polarized color judgments.

This study suggests that a relatively simple learning explanation may be sufficient to explain the Downing, Judd, and Brauer effects of repeated expression on evaluative extremity. When subjects give expression to their attitudes, they tend to simplify and polarize what they say across repetitions and their internal representation of the attitude assumes the form that has been repeatedly expressed. In essence, they learn the verbal expressions that they have repeated and, as those expressions polarize through repetition, so does the internal representation of their attitude.

Thought Devoted to the Attitude Object

The final manipulation of repetition we have considered is extended thought devoted to the attitude object. As indicated earlier, Tesser and his colleagues (Tesser, 1978; Tesser & Conlee, 1975; Tesser & Cowan, 1975, 1977; Tesser & Leone, 1977) repeatedly showed that instructions to think about an attitude object for some period of time leads to more extreme evaluations of the object. The explanation that Tesser, Martin, and Mendolia (ch. 4, this volume) give for this effect is quite consistent with the general account that we have offered for the varied effects of repetition on expressed extremity. Tesser argued that thought produces greater extremity because it encourages subjects (a) to generate new cognitions that are consistent with one's overall sentiment toward the object, (b) to reinterpret old cognitions about the object so that they manifest greater evaluative consistency with the overall object evaluation, and (c) to suppress old cognitions that are evaluatively inconsistent with the overall object evaluation (see also Tesser, 1978).

Our interpretation of the effects of extended thought is nearly identical to Tesser's explanation. Despite this similarity, we briefly want to identify how each of these three processes fits in our model of attitude representation, computation, and output. The first of these processes, generation of new cognitions that are evaluatively consistent with the dominant evaluation of the object, can be fit within our account by suggesting that thought devoted to an attitude object results in the identification of new features whose evaluative connotations are consistent with the stored overall evaluation. In essence, these additional features acquire nonzero weights in the computation component of the model. More generally, we would suggest that thought increases the weights associated with features whose evaluative connotations are consistent with A_o. Support for this first process comes from Sadler and Tesser (1973) and Tesser and Cowan (1975).

The second process identified by Tesser also fits nicely within our general account. Thought seems to induce polarization by leading to reinterpretations of previously stored object features so that their evaluative connotations are more consistent with the stored overall evaluation. Rather than recomputing the weights that are associated with features, this second process involves the recomputation of the evaluative connotations, or the values of s_i, of those features (Tesser & Cowan, 1977). Other work is also consistent with the argument that ambiguous or neutral information is interpreted to be attitude congruent in cases where subjects are given time to think about their attitudes while examining the ambiguous information. Although Lord, Ross, and Lepper (1979) did not manipulate whether or not subjects spent time thinking about the attitude object, they did find that ambiguous evidence was considered to be attitude congruent when subjects were given extensive time to review that evidence.

Finally the third process suggests that thought leads to the suppression and forgetting of attitude-incongruent information. The hypothesis that attitude incongruent information is less well retained than congruent information has been the subject of extensive research in social psychology over the course of some 50 years (e.g., Levine & Murphy, 1943). Many studies have supported the hypothesis; others have not (e.g., Greenwald & Sakumura, 1967; Waly & Cook, 1966). However, a recent meta-analysis by Roberts (1985) suggests that the effect, although small, is nevertheless robust. What is less clear, from the point of view of Tesser's mediating processes, is whether thought decreases the extent to which incongruent information is kept in memory.

In sum, there is consistent evidence to suggest that thought devoted to an attitude object should increase the number and importance of features whose evaluative connotations are consistent with the overall object evaluation. What is interesting about this conclusion is that the process here seems to closely mirror the process that we have suggested may also be operative upon simple repeated exposure to novel objects whose features are highly evaluative. Simple repeated exposure leads one to focus on those features that are evaluatively consistent with the dominant evaluative response. Extended thought toward the object seems to have a similar effect. The similarity in these processes is all the more remarkable because the effects of simple exposure may occur outside of conscious awareness while the effects of thought would seem to be much more readily accessible and effortful. It is tempting to suggest that a Tesser thought manipulation essentially results in repeated implicit exposure to the attitude object: The subject simply presents the object to him or herself over and over again during thought periods.

A qualification concerning the effects of thought has been demonstrated in research conducted by Chaiken and her colleagues (Chaiken & Yates, 1985; Liberman & Chaiken, 1991). Liberman and Chaiken, for instance, showed that thought does not result in polarization when subjects have highly conflicted or strongly ambivalent attitudes toward the object. In this case, it seems likely to us that there is no single dominant evaluative response that the object elicits. Rather, there are two strongly conflicted evaluative responses, each with its own set of evaluatively consistent features. The subject is simply unable to reconcile the conflicting evaluative implications of the object. One might even suspect that thought in this case would actually increase one's ambivalence toward the object, since thought might lead to greater evaluative consistency of features within each evaluative set.

Our final comment about the effects of thought concerns the demonstrations by Wilson and his colleagues (Erber, Hodges, & Wilson, ch. 17, this volume; Wilson, Kraft, & Dunn, 1989) that thought devoted to the *reasons* underlying one's attitude toward an object results in attitude changes that make them less congruent with behavior. This sort of thought manipulation, rather than increasing the evaluative consistency of the object's features that are stored in memory, seems to cause the subject to concentrate on certain types of features that he or she may not normally emphasize. A subsequently computed overall evaluation may accordingly betray prior evaluations and behaviors toward the object that were based on a different feature weighting scheme.

CONCLUSION

We have attempted to provide a comprehensive model that might account for a large set of diverse experimental findings in the attitude area. Although these findings are themselves relatively complex, it seems to us that they can be integrated with a few general propositions about the effects of repeated exposure to attitude objects and repeated expressions of attitudes toward those objects.

In the most general form, we have suggested that the repetition of a process leads to increased efficiency in the execution of that process. An increase in efficiency means that the process becomes more streamlined and that the dominant response that results from that process is reinforced. Within the confines of the general attitude model that we have outlined, composed of the three components of representation, computation of a response, and expression of that response, this general framework yields a series of more specific propositions that can be used to integrate the diverse findings that we have presented. These more specific propositions include the following:

Repeated exposure to a novel stimulus object leads to the development of positive affect towards that object. This results from a decrease in response competition as repeated exposure leads to a narrowing of focus on a relatively small number of the object's features.

When the features of a novel object are highly evaluative, then a reduction in response competition upon repeated exposure means that features that share the evaluative connotation of the dominant evaluative response are focused on, are more strongly associated with the object in memory, and are weighted more heavily when an overall object evaluation is computed.

Extended thought devoted to an object seems to have effects similar to those found for repeated exposure to an object whose features are highly evaluative. Namely, extended thought seems to produce stronger associations of the object with evaluatively consistent features and increased weighting of those features in attitude computation.

Repeated expressions of an attitude lead to the association of the expressed response with the object. What this means is that the process of expression is made more efficient and the representation of the attitude assumes the form of previous expressions that have been well learned through repetition. Because expressions that are unconstrained by response formats tend to simplify and polarize with repetition, so the associated attitude that is subsequently stored with the object similarly polarizes with repetitive expression.

We believe that these propositions and the model we have developed can be used to integrate a diverse set of experimental findings on factors affecting polarization. In addition, our theoretical approach makes a number of important and somewhat controversial claims which deserve empirical elaboration. For instance, a relatively important implication of our model is that the overt expression of an attitude affects the subsequent representation of that attitude in memory. Our explanation for the polarizing effects of simple repeated expression argues that the attitude becomes more extreme as a result of the response language that the subject employs becoming more simple and more extreme across repetitions. Because this response language is subsequently stored in memory and used in recomputing subsequent evaluations, the polarization of the overt attitude expression potentially leads to the polarization of the stored object evaluation. Thus, according to our model, contextual factors that affect attitude expressions can lead to fundamental changes in the underlying attitude itself.

A second and somewhat novel part of our model is the suggestion that representation of many social objects is based on the selection of features that share evaluative implications. Although we believe that this suggestion is implicit in much earlier research (e.g., Bower, 1981), it seems to us that the organization of social objects in long-term memory is frequently guided by the evaluative implications that those objects have for the perceiver. Thus social perception and representation may be driven by evaluative considerations to a greater degree than is traditionally appreciated. Most models of representation that have been elaborated to deal with the representation of social stimuli that carry strong evaluative connotations have, we believe, failed to sufficiently account for the role that evaluation may play in representation. This may be due largely to the fact that representation models in social psychology have been borrowed largely intact from work in cognitive psychology where stimuli rarely carry affective and evaluative connotations.

In addition to these two points, we conclude by noting that much of the literature on attitude polarization has focused on social interaction processes that lead to polarization. Thus, for instance, highly competitive interactions tend to cause the participants to focus on between-group differences and tend to result in polarized evaluations of attributes that distinguish the groups (Deutsch, 1974; Sherif, Harvey, White, Hood, & Sherif, 1961). Likewise, within-group processes, such as social comparison and information exchange, may reinforce the dominant evaluative responses of the group and polarize individual evaluative judgments (Myers & Lamm, 1976). Although we do not doubt the strength of the effects of social interaction on attitude polarization, it seems to us that the literature has tended to overlook the more basic cognitive processes that may result in polarization in settings where individuals simply focus on particular attitude objects repeatedly, express their attitudes frequently, and spend time deliberating about the objects and their implications. Interestingly, the settings that foster between-group and within-group processes that lead to polarization are also the settings in which object exposure, deliberation, and attitude expression are likely to occur repeatedly. Thus we suspect that the polarizing effects of exposure, reflection, and expression reinforce the polarizing effects of social interaction.

ACKNOWLEDGMENTS

Preparation of this chapter was partially supported by NSF Grant BNS-8806757 to the first author. We gratefully acknowledge the helpful comments of Reid Hastie and Bernadette Park. Markus Brauer is now at the Universität Konstanz, Sozialwissenschaftliche Fakultät, Germany.

REFERENCES

Allison, D. E., & Messick, D. M. (1988). The feature-positive effect, attitude strength, and the degree of perceived consensus. *Personality and Social Psychology Bulletin, 14*, 236–241.

Anderson, J. R. (1983). *The architecture of cognition.* Cambridge, MA: Harvard University Press.

Anderson, J. R. (1987). Skill acquisition: Compilation of weak-method problem solutions. *Psychological Review, 94*, 192–210.

Anderson, N. H. (1971). Integration theory and attitude change. *Psychological Review, 78*, 171–206.

Anderson, N. H. (1974). Cognitive algebra: Integration theory applied to social attribution. In L. Berkowitz (Ed.), *Advances in experimental social psychology* (Vol. 7, pp. 1–101). New York: Academic.

Berlyne, D. E. (1954). A theory of human curiosity. *British Journal of Psychology, 45*, 180–191.

Berlyne, D. E. (1960). *Conflict, arousal, and curiosity.* New York: McGraw-Hill.

Bower, G. H. (1981). Mood and memory. *American Psychologist, 36*, 129–148.

Brickman, P., Redfield, J., Harrison, A. A., & Crandall, R. (1972). Drive and predisposition as factors in the attitudinal effects of mere exposure. *Journal of Experimental Social Psychology, 8*, 31–44.

Brown, J. S., & Farber, I. E. (1951). Emotions conceptualized as intervening variables—with suggestions toward a theory of frustration. *Psychological Bulletin, 48*, 465–495.

Cacioppo, J. T., Marshall-Goodell, B. S., Tassinary, L. G., & Petty, R. E. (1992). Rudimentary determinants of attitudes: Classical conditioning is more effective when prior knowledge about the attitude stimulus is low than high. *Journal of Experimental Social Psychology, 28*, 207–233.

Cacioppo, J. T., & Petty, R. E. (1989). Effects of message repetition on argument processing, recall, and persuasion. *Basic and Applied Social Psychology, 10*, 3–12.

Chaiken, S., & Yates, S. (1985). Affective-cognitive consistency and thought-induced attitude polarization. *Journal of Personality and Social Psychology, 49*, 1470–1481.

Crano, W. D., Gorenflo, D. W., & Shackelford, S. L. (1988). Overjustification, assumed consensus, and attitude change: Further investigation of the incentive-aroused ambivalence hypothesis. *Journal of Personality and Social Psychology, 55*, 12–22.

Deutsch, M. (1974). *The resolution of conflict.* New Haven: Yale University Press.

Downing, J. A., Judd, C. M., & Brauer, M. (1992). Effects of repeated expressions on attitude extremity. *Journal of Personality and Social Psychology, 63*, 17–29.

Ewing, T. N. (1942). A study of certain factors involved in changes of opinion. *Journal of Social Psychology, 16*, 63–88.

Fazio, R. H., Chen, J., McDonel, E. C., & Sherman, S. J. (1982). Attitude accessibility, attitude-behavior consistency, and the strength of the object-evaluation association. *Journal of Experimental Social Psychology, 18*, 339–357.

Fazio, R. H., Sanbonmatsu, D. M., Powell, M. C., & Kardes, F. R. (1986). On the automatic activation of attitudes. *Journal Personality and Social Psychology, 50*, 229–238.

Fazio, R. H., & Zanna, M. P. (1978). Attitudinal qualities relating to the strength of the attitude-behavior relationship. *Journal of Experimental Social Psychology, 14*, 398–408.

Greenwald, A. G., & Sakumura, J. S. (1967). Attitude and selective learning: Where are the phenomena of yesteryear? *Journal of Personality and Social Psychology, 7*, 378–397.

Grush, J. E. (1976). Attitude formation and mere exposure phenomena: A nonartifactual explanation of empirical findings. *Journal of Personality and Social Psychology, 33*, 281–290.

Hamm, N. H., Baum, M. R., & Nikels, K. W. (1975). Effects of race and exposure on judgments of interpersonal favorability. *Journal of Experimental Social Psychology, 11*, 14–24.

Harrison, A. A. (1977). Mere exposure. In L. Berkowitz (Ed.), *Advances in experimental social psychology* (Vol. 10, pp. 39–83). New York: Academic.

Judd, C. M., Drake, R. A., Downing, J. W., & Krosnick, J. A. (1991). Some dynamic properties of attitude structures: Context-induced response facilitation and polarization. *Journal of Personality and Social Psychology, 60*, 193–202.

Judd, C. M., & Johnson, J. T. (1981). Attitudes, polarization, and diagnosticity: Exploring the effects of affect. *Journal of Personality and Social Psychology, 41,* 25–36.

Judd, C. M., & Krosnick, J. A. (1989). The structural bases of consistency among political attitudes: Effects of political expertise and attitude importance. In A. R. Pratkanis, S. J. Breckler, & A. G. Greenwald (Eds.), *Attitude structure and function* (pp. 99–128). Hillsdale, NJ: Lawrence Erlbaum Associates.

Judd, C. M., & Lusk, C. M. (1984). Knowledge structure and evaluative judgments: Effect of structural variables on judgmental extremity. *Journal of Personality and Social Psychology, 46,* 1193–1207.

Levine, J. M., & Murphy, G. (1943). The learning and forgetting of controversial material. *Journal of Abnormal and Social Psychology, 38,* 507–517.

Liberman, A., & Chaiken, S. (1991). Value conflict and thought-induced attitude change. *Journal of Experimental Social Psychology, 27,* 203–216.

Linville, P. W. (1982). The complexity-extremity effect and age-based stereotyping. *Journal of Personality and Social Psychology, 42,* 193–211.

Linville, P. W. & Jones, E. E. (1980). Polarized appraisals of out-group members. *Journal of Personality and Social Psychology, 38,* 689–703.

Lord, E. G., Ross, L., & Lepper, M. (1979). Biased assimilation and attitude polarization: The effects of prior theories on subsequently considered evidence. *Journal of Personality and Social Psychology, 37,* 2098–2109.

Myers, D. G. (1978). Polarizing effects of social comparison. *Journal of Experimental Social Psychology, 14,* 554–563.

Myers, D. G., & Lamm, H. (1976). The group polarization phenomenon. *Psychological Bulletin, 83,* 602–627.

Osgood, C. E., & Tannenbaum, P. H. (1955). The principles of congruity in the prediction of attitude changes. *Psychological Review, 62,* 42–55.

Ostrom, T. M., & Upshaw, H. S. (1968). Psychological perspective and attitude change. In A. C. Greenwald, T. C. Brock, & T. M. Ostrom (Eds.), *Psychological foundations of attitudes* (pp. 217–242). New York: Academic.

Pechmann, C., & Stewart, D. W. (1988). Advertising repetition: A critical review of wearin and wearout. *Current issues and research in advertising, 11,* 285–330.

Perlman, D., & Oskamp, S. (1971). The effects of picture content and exposure frequency on evaluations of negroes and whites. *Journal of Experimental Social Psychology, 7,* 503–512.

Petersen, K., & Dutton, J. E. (1975). Certainty, extremity, intensity: Neglected variables in research on attitude–behavior consistency. *Social Forces, 54,* 393–414.

Powell, M. C., & Fazio, R. H. (1984). Attitude accessibility as a function of repeated attitudinal expression. *Personality and Social Psychology Bulletin, 10,* 139–148.

Roberts, J. V. (1984). Public opinion and capital punishment: The effects of attitudes upon memory. *Canadian Journal of Criminology, 26,* 283–291.

Roberts, J. V. (1985). The attitude–memory relationship after 40 years: A meta-analysis of the literature. *Basic and Applied Social Psychology, 6,* 221–241.

Sadler, O., & Tesser, A. (1973). Some effects of salience and time upon interpersonal hostility and attraction during social isolation. *Sociometry, 36,* 99–112.

Sarat, A., & Vidmar, N. (1976). Public opinion, the death penalty, and the eighth amendment: Testing the Marshall hypothesis. *Wisconsin Law Review, 171,* 171–206.

Sawyer, A. (1981). Repetition, cognitive responses, and persuasion. In R. E. Petty, T. M. Ostrom, & T. C. Brock (Eds.), *Cognitive responses in persuasion.* Hillsdale, NJ: Lawrence Erlbaum Associates.

Schuman, H., & Presser, S. (1981). *Questions and answers in attitude surveys: Experiments on question form, wording, and context.* San Diego, CA: Academic.

Sherif, M., Harvey, O. J., White, B. J., Hood, W. R., & Sherif, C. W. (1961). *Intergroup conflict and cooperation: The robbers cave experiment.* Norman, OK: University Book Exchange.

Smith, E. R. (1989). Procedural efficiency: General and specific components and effects on social judgment. *Journal of Experimental Social Psychology, 25,* 500–523.

Smith, E. R. (1990). Content and process specificity in the effects of prior experiences. In T. K. Srull & R. S. Wyer, Jr. (Eds.), *Advances in social cognition* (pp. 1–59). Hillsdale, NJ: Lawrence Erlbaum Associates.

Smith, E. R., Branscombe, N. R., & Bormann, C. (1988). Generality of the effects of practice on social judgment tasks. *Journal of Personality and Social Psychology, 54,* 385–395.

Staats, A. W., & Staats, C. K. (1958). Attitudes established by classical conditioning. *Journal of Abnormal and Social Psychology, 57,* 37–40.

Tannenbaum, P. H. (1956). Initial attitude toward source and concept as factors in attitude change through communication. *Public Opinion Quarterly, 20,* 413–425.

Tesser, A. (1978). Self-generated attitude change. In L. Berkowitz (Ed.), *Advances in experimental social psychology* (Vol. 11, pp. 289–338). New York: Academic.

Tesser, A., & Conlee, M. C. (1975). Some effects of time and thought on attitude polarization. *Journal of Personality and Social Psychology, 31,* 262–270.

Tesser, A., & Cowan, C. L. (1975). Some effects of thought and number of cognitions on attitude change. *Social Behavior and Personality, 3,* 165–173.

Tesser, A., & Cowan, C. L. (1977). Some attitudinal and cognitive consequences of thought. *Journal of Research in Personality, 11,* 216–226.

Tesser, A., & Leone, C. (1977). Cognitive schemas and thought as determinants of attitude change. *Journal of Experimental Social Psychology, 13,* 340–356.

Waly, P., & Cook, S. W. (1966). Attitude as a determinant of learning and memory: A failure to confirm. *Journal of Personality and Social Psychology, 4,* 280–288.

Wilson, T. D., Kraft, D., & Dunn, D. S. (1989). The disruptive effects of explaining attitudes: The moderating effect of knowledge about the attitude object. *Journal of Experimental Social Psychology, 25,* 379–400.

Zajonc, R. B. (1968). The attitudinal effects of mere exposure. *Journal of Personality and Social Psychology, 9*(pt. 2), 1–27.

Zajonc, R. B., Markus, H., & Wilson, W. R. (1974). Exposure effects and associative learning. *Journal of Experimental Social Psychology, 10,* 248–263.

Zajonc, R. B., & Rajecki, D. W. (1969). Exposure and affect: A field experiment. *Psychonomic Science, 17,* 216–217.

Zanna, M. P., Kiesler, C. A., & Pilkonis, P. A. (1970). Positive and negative attitudinal affect established by classical conditioning. *Journal of Personality and Social Psychology, 14,* 321–328.

Zanna, M. P., & Rempel, J. K. (1988). Attitudes: A new look at an old concept. In D. Bar-Tal & A. Kruglanski (Eds.), *Social psychology of knowledge* (pp. 319–334). New York: Cambridge University Press.

The Impact of Thought on Attitude Extremity and Attitude-Behavior Consistency

Abraham Tesser
Leonard Martin
Marilyn Mendolia
University of Georgia

This volume is concerned with the antecedents and consequences of attitude strength. As noted in some of the earlier chapters attitude strength is multidimensional with a number of related but conceptually distinct facets. In this chapter we examine the role of conscious thought on at least two facets of attitude strength: attitude extremity (polarization) and the attitude-behavior link. In both cases the concern is the mechanisms by which thought has its impact. Finally, because thought about particular attitude objects is consequential, it is important to understand what initiates and directs thought to focus on one object rather than another. We briefly address this question at the end of the chapter.

MERE THOUGHT POLARIZES ATTITUDES

There is an old story about a man who gets a flat tire on a lonely country road only to discover that he does not have a jack handle. The interesting part of the story is in the man's head as he starts down the road to the nearest farmhouse to borrow a jack handle.

> "I'll just find a house and borrow a jack handle."
> "Maybe the person will drive me back to my car and I'll get fixed up in a hurry. Won't that be nice."
> "Maybe he won't lend me a jack handle."
> "Of course he will lend me the handle. Why wouldn't he lend me the handle?"
> "Some people don't like strangers. Maybe he is stingy. I hate people that are stingy and won't help someone out of a jam. A guy like that is awful. He is probably mean to his wife and kids too.

By this time the man is at the farmhouse and ringing the bell. To this day the householder can't figure out why a total stranger would curse and punch him simply for answering the door.

A Demonstration Study

The story, of course, is apocryphal, but the process is quite familiar. Many of us have had the experience of thinking about somebody we dislike (or like). Armed only with our thoughts, even with no new external information, our feelings become polarized. Attitude strength increases. Because the process appears to be ubiquitous (and to involve some interesting, almost autistic psychological dynamics of everyday life), we attempted to capture it for study in the laboratory.

Sadler and Tesser (1973) recruited subjects for a study concerned with "how people form impressions of one another." Each subject and his experimental "partner" (in an adjoining cubicle) were to describe themselves to one another. In actuality, the "partner" was simulated with one of two tape recordings. Subjects were exposed to a recording simulating either a likable "partner" who complimented them or a dislikable "partner" who criticized them. Following this, subjects were instructed to think about their partner or they were distracted from thinking about their partner. Finally, subjects reported their impressions of their partner. As expected, subjects evaluated the likable "partner" positively and the dislikable "partner" negatively. However, this difference was more pronounced for thought-condition subjects than for distraction-condition subjects. In short, mere thought seemed to polarize attitudes.

Thought Affects Other Aspects of Attitude Strength

The ease with which an attitude comes to mind, its accessibility, has been shown to be a good index of attitude strength. More accessible attitudes color our interpretation of situations (Fazio & Williams, 1986; Higgins, King, & Mavin 1982; Houston & Fazio, 1989), are more predictive of behavior (Fazio, Powell, & Williams, 1989; Fazio & Williams, 1986), and are rated as more important (Krosnick, 1989) than less accessible attitudes. Recently, Downing, Judd, and Brauer (1992) found a direct relationship between frequency of expression, that is, thought or attitude accessibility, and extremity of evaluation. (See Judd & Brauer, ch. 3, this volume, for an argument concerning the functional equivalence of thought and repetition.)

Stronger attitudes should persist longer than weaker attitudes. Therefore, thought should be associated with more persistent attitudes. Some of the research connected with the Elaboration Likelihood Model (ELM) is consistent with this expectation (see Petty, Haugtvedt, & Smith, ch. 5, this volume). For example, subjects with greater involvement in a topic might be expected to engage in greater thought about the message than subjects with less involvement. It turns out that the postmessage attitude of high involvement subjects shows greater persistence than that of low involvement subjects (Petty, Haugtvedt, Heesacker, & Cacioppo, cited in Petty, Haugtvedt, & Smith, ch. 5, this volume).

The stronger an attitude the more likely it will drive behavior. There is some indirect evidence concerning this point. Kalgren and Wood (1986) measured subjects' attitudes toward the environment. Subjects were asked to list facts and characteristics they believed to be true about the preservation of the environment and behaviors they had engaged in regarding this topic. We consider these latter measures to be an indirect index of thought. Two weeks later Kalgren and Wood measured recycling and petition signing behavior. The correlation between attitudes and behavior was .19 for subjects at least 1 standard deviation below the mean on the thought index and .84 among subjects 1 standard deviation above the mean on the thought index. In sum, "Attitudes and behavior were strongly related for subjects with relatively high levels of accessibility [thought] and, to a lesser extent, for subjects with moderate levels of accessibility [thought]." (p. 336)

Thought, then, tends to make evaluations more extreme, more accessible, and more enduring. In addition, thought increases the correspondence between evaluations and behavior. Does it also polarize affect? The short answer is yes. Let us assume that people who are made self-conscious by a mirror or other device are thinking more about themselves than people who are not self-focused. Self-focused subjects report more anger as a result of provocation (Scheier, 1976), more favorable responses based on bodily sensations to nudes, more disgust to pictures of mutilated bodies, and more extreme responses to positive and negative mood inductions (Scheier & Carver, 1977).

Nonexperimental data is even more compelling on this score. Nolen-Hoeksema (1987) reviewed evidence that depression is associated with excessive rumination about negative events. Indeed, according to her argument, rumination is an integral component of a causal spiral. Negative events produce ruminative thoughts about the events which drive the affective state to become even more negative resulting in more thought, and so on. Kuhl (1981) suggests that people who respond to failure with thought about the failure are likely to stay depressed because such thought interferes with subsequent performance.

HOW THOUGHT CHANGES ATTITUDES

Thought is not a passive review of one's experiences and knowledge. It is a dynamic and constructive process. Thought changes cognitive content associated with the attitude object and those changes, although predictable, do not follow the canons of objective logic. Often the changes are almost autistic (unless constrained) and follow the dictates of cognitive structures (i.e., schemas). Thought typically strengthens one's attitude because the changes in cognitive content tend to bolster and be in the direction of the initial evaluation. However, thought induced changes are not bound to go in any particular direction. As we see here, thought can decrease attitude strength. Indeed, in the next section we show how the present perspective can explain how thought can uncouple the relationship between attitudes and behavior.

Thought Changes Cognitive Contents: The Effects of Constraints

In our first study (Sadler & Tesser, 1973), described earlier, we asked subjects to write down their beliefs about their partner. Thought subjects recorded more negative cognitions about the dislikable partner and more positive cognitions about the likable partner than their distraction subject counterparts. It is easier to make cognitive changes when one's initial information is ambiguous rather than unambiguous. Consistent with the change hypothesis, Tesser and Cowan (1975) found greater thought generated attitude polarization when subjects thought about others described with ambiguous information than with unambiguous information. Further, thought led to greater reinterpretation of the ambiguous material in the direction of the initial attitude than did distraction.

Reality Constraints

When persons are confronted with "reality" or "logical" constraints while thinking, thought does not have as strong a bolstering effect on attitudes. In one study (Tesser, 1976) women were induced to think about each painting of a series with the painting present; or to think about each with the paintings absent. An additional group was distracted from thinking about the paintings. Thought strengthened attitudes but this effect was reduced in the presence of reality (i.e., the paintings. See Leone, 1984, for a conceptual replication).

Reality constraints need not be dichotomous, either present or absent. Because memory fades, something we were exposed to a minute ago should provide greater constraints than something we were exposed to a week ago. Sanbonmatsu, Kardes, and Sansone (1991) used three time periods to test this hypothesis. They found that people drew stronger inferences in a direction consistent with their overall impression of a product (i.e., a bicycle), after a longer than a shorter period of time without information.

These reality constraint data have implications for the romantic aphorism: Absence makes the heart grow fonder. If one thinks about someone for whom they have positive feelings then the aphorism is likely to be true (e.g., Tesser & Paulhus, 1976). At the same time, if one is thinking about a person who is disliked then the absence of reality constraints can lead to a very negative attitude as in the jack handle story.

Thought can lead to cognitive changes that are inconsistent with sense data. As we have seen, the presence of reality constrains such changes. We do not believe, however, that "reality" results in completely "objective" processing.

Often physical stimuli are ambiguous and subject to multiple interpretations. For example, fans at a sporting event may report exactly the same incident very differently depending on the team they support (Hastorf & Cantril, 1954). Data from the same "scientific study" can cause proponents or both sides of the issue to become more certain of their point of view (Lord, Ross, & Lepper, 1979). However, to the extent that reality is available and its interpretation is relatively clear, we believe that people will be sensitive to the constraints it imposes.

Process Constraints

Thought can also lead to faulty changes in beliefs because the psycho-logical inferencing mechanisms on which those changes are based fall short of formal logic.[1] If that is true, perhaps we can constrain that process by having the individual focus on it. For example, individuals asked to tell us why they feel the way they do are forced to put their thought process into words. Language itself imposes logical constraints. Further, by making their reasoning explicit the logical components become more salient and easier to discount.

This hypothesis was tested with persons who had a particularly strong fear of public speaking (Tesser, Leone, & Clary, 1978). "Process constraint" subjects were induced to make explicit and to focus on the cognitive process by telling why they felt as they did about public speaking. The use of language and explicit reasoning should constrain the process. "Catharsis" subjects were asked to focus on and to experience their feelings about public speaking. Focusing on feelings does not provide cognitive constraints on the thought process. Control subjects were distracted from thinking about public speaking. Each of the subjects then gave a short public speech. Palmar sweat and self-reports of affect indexed fear during the speech. As predicted by the process constraints hypothesis, catharsis subjects experienced the most fear and process constraint subjects showed the least fear. (See Leone, Minor, & Baltimore, 1983, for a study on the combined effects of process and reality constraints.)

In sum, thought appears to change one's cognitions associated with a particular attitude object. Such changes can be inconsistent with reality and do not follow strict logical canons. Therefore, the effects of thought can be reduced with reality and process constraints.[2]

---

[1]According to Liberman and Chaiken (1991) the thought polarization process will also be constrained if thought involves an issue which reflects competing values (e.g., the issue "Should public park lands be opened to mining and exploration in order to promote economic growth and prosperity?" puts valuing nature vs. valuing a prosperous life in competition).

[2]The effects of individual differences on constraint processes are beyond the scope of this chapter. However, Leone and his colleagues have explored the effects of dogmatism (Leone, 1989; Leone, Taylor, & Adams, 1991) and cognitive style (Leone & Ensley, 1985; Leone, Negaran, Aronow, & Groble, 1991) on these processes.

Thought Changes Cognitive Content:
The Necessity for Cognitive Structure

Thought changes cognitive contents and these changes are not random. If they were random some of the changes would be positive and some negative. There would be little net change in attitude and no systematic change over subjects. Because we typically find that attitudes become systematically stronger (particularly in the absence of constraint), there must be some guiding force or principle.

Cognitive Schemas

We believe that cognitive schemas are central to thought driven changes in cognitive content. A schema is ". . . a cognitive structure that represents knowledge about a concept or type of stimulus, including its attributes and the relations among the attributes" (Fiske & Taylor, 1991, p. 98). Any stimulus situation has more information than we can possibly attend to. Schemas direct attention to what is relevant. Often relevant information is missing. Schemas fill in the blanks. "Raw" information is open to multiple interpretations. Schemas reduce that uncertainty. In sum, schemas provide blueprints for cognitive changes. Thought without such a blueprint should produce few changes and those changes should be unsystematic. Thought with such a blueprint should result in systematic changes.

The Role of Schema Complexity: Thesis

The schema hypothesis makes predictions that other explanations do not. If schemas represent a blueprint for change, then the more elaborate and the better developed the schema, the greater the potential is for systematic cognitive change. Schema complexity is difficult to manipulate but one can make educated guesses about differences. For example, most men probably have better developed schemas for thinking about football plays than do most women. Most women probably have better developed schemas for thinking about women's fashions then do most men. Indeed, most men are more familiar with and use more cognitive capacity for thinking about football and most women are more familiar with and use more cognitive capacity for thinking about fashions (Britton & Tesser, 1982). More to the point, compared to distraction, thought tends to strengthen attitudes associated with well-developed schemas (e.g., men's attitudes toward football; women's attitudes toward fashion) more than less well-developed schemas e.g., (men's attitudes toward fashion; women's attitudes toward football; Tesser & Leone, 1977).

The hypothesis that thought with a well-developed schema polarizes attitudes more than thought with a less well-developed schema has been successfully tested several times. For example, persons have better developed schemas for thinking about the personality of individuals than for thinking about the personality of groups (Britton & Tesser, 1982; Millar & Tesser, 1986b). Thought tends to polarize the evaluation of individual personality descriptions more than group personality descriptions (Leone & Ensley, 1985; Millar & Tesser, 1986b; Tesser & Leone, 1977). One measure of schema development is internal consistency. Chaiken and Yates (1985) found that thought induced attitude polarization was positively associated with the affective-cognitive consistency of attitudes toward capital punishment and censorship. Political experts—people who spend a great deal of time thinking about political issues—have better organized representations of candidates and more extreme attitudes than nonexperts (Lusk & Judd, 1988).

The Role of Schema Complexity: Antithesis

Shortly after the early work on schema complexity was published, theoretical ideas and data diametrically opposed to this schema complexity position began to appear. This work, by Patricia Linville, dealt with stereotypes. It suggested that our schemas (stereotypes) for thinking about outgroups are much simpler and not as rich as schemas for thinking about ingroups. Because we have more experience with ingroups, we have more independent dimensions for thinking about ingroups. Therefore, we make less polarized judgments of the ingroup than the outgroup. Why? If a salient stimulus feature is positive and we have few dimensions for judging, then that positivity will be relatively undiluted. On the other hand, if we have many dimensions which are unrelated, that is, some positive and others negative, then that positive feature is likely to be averaged out and the overall judgment should become less extreme.

These arguments are plausible in spite of the fact that the conclusion is 180 degrees from our own. It is not surprising that Linville finds ingroup schemas are, indeed, more complex than outgroup schemas. More important, identical stimulus descriptions evoke less extreme ratings when attributed to an ingroup member than when attributed to an outgroup member, whether ingroup–outgroup status is based on race (Linville & Jones, 1980) or age (Linville, 1982). Even though Linville does not provide her subjects a formal opportunity for thought, these results jar.

The Role of Schema Complexity: Synthesis

Our hypothesis suggests that thought produces more polarization with well-developed schemas. Linville's hypothesis anticipates more polarized evaluations with less well-developed schemas. The data indicate that both expectations are valid! How is that possible?

First, a structural answer exploits subtle, but crucial, differences in the definitions of schema complexity. Our definition had been rather loose and informal. We relied on experience with the domain (Tesser & Leone, 1977), the use of cognitive capacity (Britton & Tesser, 1982), and the "tight" organization of the domain (Chaiken & Yates, 1985). Linville's definition of complexity is relatively formal: It is the number of independent dimensions and her information theoretic metric reflects that definition. Whereas we haphazardly considered both differentiation (e.g., number of dimensions) and integration (e.g., average correlation among dimensions) in thinking about complexity Linville focused exclusively on differentiation. In a brilliant paper, Judd and Lusk (1984) formally proved that these two components of complexity interact in their effects on extremity. When the level of integration (correlation) among dimensions is low, that is, the dimensions are relatively independent, the greater the number of dimensions the less extreme the resulting overall evaluation (the Linville case). When integration is high, the greater the number of dimensions the more extreme the overall evaluation (what we have typically found).

Judd and Lusk (1984) did not manipulate thought but reported results consistent with their hypothesis. Millar and Tesser (1986a, Study 3) manipulated thought and measured the differentiation (number of dimensions) and integration (average correlation among dimensions) of their subjects' schemas for thinking about college courses. The results were precisely in accord with the structural hypothesis. When integration was low we obtained the Linville effect: The greater the number of dimensions associated with the schema the less thought polarized evaluations. When integration was high, the effects we obtained in our early work emerged, again: The greater the number of dimensions associated with the schema the more thought polarized evaluations. In sum, both differentiation and integration[3] must be taken into account if we are to have a more complete understanding of the role of schema complexity in strengthening attitudes.

Second, there is a motivational synthesis. According to Linville, thinking with many independent dimensions results in moderation because good and bad things are more likely to be balanced than with few highly correlated dimensions. This analysis assumes an unbiased thought process. (See Wood, Rhodes, & Biek, ch. 11, this volume, for a similar argument.) However, if the individual were motivated or biased in favor of or against a particular attitude object, a large number of independent dimensions would provide a good selection from which to get support for either side. Few highly correlated dimensions provide little selection. Thus in the presence of bias or motivation we would expect results consistent with our thesis. With little or no bias we would expect the Linville result. Is there a source of bias in our work that is missing in Linville's?

In most of our work, we used a pretest–posttest design; Linville used a posttest-only design. Why is this detail consequential? Giving an initial opinion is a commitment that might provide the necessary motivation to bolster the initial point of view (e.g., Kiesler, 1971). This post hoc reconstruction fits the motivational synthesis nicely, but we (Millar & Tesser, 1986a, Study 2) also designed a study to test it. Subjects were either committed to their pretest evaluation or

---

[3]In a recent paper, Liberman and Chaiken (1991) made the reasonable argument that the structural parameters that facilitate thought induced attitude polarization do so because they induce evaluative consistency among elements of the target stimulus.

they were explicitly told that the pretest was simply practice and would never be looked at again. Schema complexity was manipulated by having subjects evaluate the personality of individuals or groups. (Recall that subjects have less well-developed schemas for thinking about group personality than individual personality.) Finally, subjects were distracted or encouraged to think about the target stimulus. The motivational synthesis held. Uncommitted subjects showed a slight Linville effect: less polarization when thinking with well-developed schemas. Committed subjects showed the effect we originally anticipated: More polarization when thinking with well-developed schemas.

In sum, the notion of schema complexity is, itself, complex. There are at least two important parameters: integration and differentiation. These parameters interact in controlling the effects of thought. Motivational variables add another layer of complexity. In spite of all this complexity, a comprehensible picture of the role of thought in changing attitudes is beginning to emerge.

THOUGHT AND THE DECOUPLING
OF ATTITUDES AND BEHAVIOR

We have argued that mere thought strengthens one's attitude and that such strengthening includes the prediction of behavior. Our argument is not unique. Decision researchers (e.g., Janis & Mann, 1977), psychotherapists (e.g., Rogers, 1951), and others have argued that examined beliefs and feelings are a better guide to action than unexamined ones. In the laboratory, Fazio, Zanna, and Cooper (1978) had people either think or not think about their feelings regarding a series of puzzles. They found that the attitudes of the persons instructed to introspect predicted puzzle-playing behavior better than the attitudes of persons not instructed to introspect.

A glaring contradiction. In spite of the reasonableness and evidence for the expectation that thought makes attitudes better predictors of behaviors there is a systematic body of work that is coherent, well replicated, and carefully designed that contradicts it. Wilson (Wilson, Dunn, Kraft, & Lisle, 1989) and his students have found that thought can disrupt the relationship between attitudes and behaviors.

In a prototypic study, Wilson, Dunn, Bybee, Hyman, and Rotondo (1984) had subjects sample a series of puzzles. (These were the same puzzles used by Fazio et al., 1978.) Some subjects gave their reasons for why they felt the way they did about each of the puzzles. All the subjects recorded their evaluation (attitude) about each. Finally, subjects had an opportunity to play with the puzzles. The amount of time playing with each puzzle was the behavior to be predicted from the evaluations. The results were striking. The average correlation for subjects who were not instructed to analyze their reasons between attitudes and behaviors was .54. The average correlation for subjects who were instructed to analyze their reasons was .17. The difference is large and highly significant. Analyzing reasons for one's feelings led to a decrease in the correlation between attitudes and behaviors.

The work of Wilson is dramatic. It seems inconsistent with a lot of research that has come before and with much of what we believe on a common sense basis. The results are replicable and indisputable. Is it possible to make sense of them?

When Thought Strengthens, When Thought Disrupts: Toward a Mismatch Model of Attitudes and Behavior

The traditional view is that attitudes are relatively lasting predispositions to respond to an object one way or another. Our view is that attitudes are frequently the result of a constructive process reflecting whatever is salient to the individual at the time. (See Wilson & Hodges, 1992, for a lively discussion of this point of view.) Thus by merely thinking about a particular object salient cognitions change and so does the attitude. Tuning in one schema or another schema changes what is salient and thereby changes one's attitude or evaluation. In addition to cognition, feelings may also affect one's evaluation (Zanna & Rempel, 1988). If one's feelings are prepotent at the time the evaluation is made, the evaluation will reflect one's feelings. Why is this important? Knowing that an evaluation may reflect primarily cognition or primarily affect is useful because we (Millar & Tesser, 1992) believe that some behaviors are driven primarily by feelings and emotions, consummatory behaviors, and other behaviors are driven primarily by cognitions, instrumental behaviors. Consummatory behaviors are engaged in for their own sake, enjoyment, or interest value rather than to pursue some distal goal. In contrast, instrumental behaviors are engaged in for distal goals. They enable us to do other things, to get the things we want, or to avoid the things we don't want. If people are focusing on their cognitions or beliefs while constructing their attitudes or evaluations, then those evaluations will be useful in predicting relevant instrumental behaviors but not very useful in predicting consummatory behaviors. If on the other hand, evaluations or attitudes are constructed while feelings are salient, then those attitudes will be useful in predicting consummatory behaviors rather than instrumental behaviors. In short, the aspect of the attitude underlying the evaluation must match the aspect of the attitude driving the behavior if the attitude is to be a useful predictor of behavior. With this in mind, let us go back and examine Wilson's work.

A Reconciliation

Wilson's subjects were asked to give reasons for why they felt the way they did about the attitude objects, whereas our usual thought instructions are unconstrained. Indeed, the instruction to focus on the "why" maps very nicely on to what we think of as process constraints. It makes the attitudes rational, logical, and thereby constrains the polarization process. It also makes salient the cognitive aspect of the attitude. What were the behaviors Wilson examined? The behaviors were the ad lib play with puzzles with no other goal in mind, that is, the behavior was consummatory. Predicting a consummatory behavior with attitudes based on cognition is a mismatch and not likely to be successful, as Wilson found out. Contrast this with the instructions given by Fazio et al. (1978) who used exactly the same task but asked subjects to think about feelings regarding these puzzles. Evaluations taken when feelings are salient should reflect that affect and should effectively predict consummatory behavior, that is, subjects' ad lib play with the puzzles. This, of course, is exactly what Fazio, Zanna, and Cooper found. All of this is post hoc speculation, however. What is needed is a study to test these ideas. Such a study, using the puzzle paradigm, was completed (Millar & Tesser, 1986b). Subjects in the instrumental behavior condition were led to believe that they would be taking an analytic test and that the puzzles would be useful practice for that test. Participants in the consummatory behavior condition were informed that the analytic puzzles would not be useful for the social sensitivity test they were to take. Subjects were given an example of each of five puzzle types and asked to focus on why they felt the way they did about each type of puzzle, that is, to think about what it is about each puzzle that makes it likable and dislikable. The remaining subjects were to analyze how they felt while performing each type of puzzle, that is, to think about feelings they had while performing each type of puzzle. After subjects wrote down their reasons or feelings, they evaluated each of the five puzzle types. Finally, the subjects spent as much time as they wanted with each of the puzzles.

The results conformed to our expectations. When behavior with the puzzles was instrumental, that is, when the puzzles could be used to do well on the analytic test, cognitive attitudes did a better job of predicting behavior, mean r = .42, than affective attitudes, mean r = .01. On the other hand, when the behavior was consummatory, when subjects anticipated a social sensitivity test for which these puzzles were not relevant, affective attitudes predicted behavior better, mean r = .35, than cognitive attitudes, mean r = .18. In sum, the attitude–behavior relationship was maximized when there was a match between the aspects of the attitude driving the evaluation or attitude measure and the aspect of the attitude driving the behavior.

The mismatch model is quite different from other attitude–behavior models. It implies that psychologists should become more analytic with respect to behavior. Given its novelty, a single demonstration is not likely to be taken very seriously. Therefore a replication seems to be important. Even more important, there is a hidden assumption that makes the mismatch model testable. The assumption is that there is a discrepancy between cognitive and affective aspects of the attitude in their implications for behavior. If there were no discrepancy, evaluations based on either aspect would lead to exactly the same prediction and differential effects would not be detectable.

There is some indirect evidence that the operation of the mismatch model is more likely to be observed with attitudes for which the affective and cognitive components are not consistent. For example, Wilson finds that people who are experts or who have thought about the issue for a long time or have had more experience in a domain are less subject to the disruptive effects of analyzing reasons (Wilson, Kraft, & Dunn, 1989). In order to provide a more formal test of the hypothesis, however, we (Millar & Tesser, 1989) designed a study that was identical to the first study in terms of the attitude targets (puzzles), the instrumental versus consummatory behavior manipulation (analytic test vs. sensitivity test), and the thought manipulation (affective vs. cognitive). In this study, however, all subjects listed both their feelings and their cognitions about each puzzle type. A cognitive consistency index was computed by correlating each subject's cognitions (number positive cognitions minus number negative) with his or her feelings (number positive feelings minus number negative) over the puzzle types.

Two theoretically interesting effects emerged. Cognitive attitudes predicted instrumental behaviors better than affective attitudes and affective attitudes predicted consummatory behaviors better than cognitive attitudes. More importantly, the central hypothesis was sustained. The behavior type by focus of thought interaction was moderated by affective-cognitive consistency. For subjects with low consistency, attitudes following a cognitive focus predicted instrumental behavior better than attitudes following an affective focus. In addition, attitudes following an affective focus predicted consummatory behavior better than attitudes following a cognitive focus. This interaction washed out completely for subjects whose beliefs and feelings were highly consistent.

The mismatch hypothesis points to the productivity of taking a more complex view of behavior. The causal aspects of attitudes tend to be correlated in many instances. However, they are theoretically separable and they function quite differently in predicting behavior. A current problem for the model is its inability to identify behavior as clearly consummatory or instrumental. Smoking and drinking appear to be consummatory, whereas the purchase of dishwasher cleanser sounds more instrumental. But what about the purchase of a car? This behavior clearly has both consummatory and instrumental aspects. Behaviors can be primarily consummatory, primarily instrumental, or a mixture. The theory has not been developed to the point of knowing exactly how to identify or classify behaviors.

Generalizing the Mismatch Model

The mismatch model appears to go beyond the relationship between attitudes and behavior (Millar & Tesser, 1992). Some years ago researchers distinguished between classical conditioning and instrumental learning. Classical conditioning was associated with autonomic responses and emotional learning. Instrumental learning concerned responses designed to get rewards. Whereas classical conditioning was simply associative there appeared to be more cognitive mediation in instrumental responses. Theorists now see fewer differences between these forms of learning but they still have different research protocols associated with them.

Interpersonal relationship researchers distinguish communal from exchange relationships (e.g., Clark, Mills, & Powell, 1986). Exchange relationships are based on the exchange of goods and services. People keep track of specific amounts given and received to enable the relationship to function. Communal relationships appear where there is an emotional or potential emotional bond between participants and behavior is based on need. The former looks like what we call instrumental behaviors whereas the latter more like consummatory behaviors.

Aggression researchers make a distinction between hostile aggression and instrumental aggression (Feshbach, 1964). Instrumental aggression is intended to produce some favorable outcome other than the aggressive response itself and is maintained by the perception that the aggressive response will result in reward. Expressive aggression, on the other hand, seems to do no more than allow the individual to express anger or pain. Its antecedents appear to be mostly emotional, that is, anger. Although the fit is not perfect, there appears to be some resonance with the consummatory-instrumental distinction.

A similar distinction has emerged in the helping literature. Empathy precedes altruistic helping (Batson, 1987). Other models, like the reward–cost model (Piliavin, Dovidio, Gartner, & Clark, 1981), see helping as relatively instrumental because it may be used to reduce costs such as feelings of guilt or to gain favor or rewards. Altruistic responding seems to map on to consummatory behavior, whereas reward–cost helping seems to be instrumental. Again, the mapping is crude and imperfect but there appears to be enough resonance to warrant further exploration.

In this section we saw that thought can uncouple attitudes and behaviors (see also Shavitt & Fazio, 1991). We argued that attitudes are a construction based on what's salient at the moment: One's attitude might reflect affect more than cognition or cognition more than affect. If affect drives consummatory behaviors and cognition drives instrumental behaviors then a shift in focus of thought prior to attitude measurement can either strengthen or weaken the relationship between attitudes and behaviors.

WHAT MAKES PEOPLE THINK ABOUT THEIR ATTITUDES?

Thought plays an important role in attitude dynamics. Here is an account of what brings things into consciousness or thought, what keeps it there, and what makes it go away. In many of the previous experiments, subjects were explicitly instructed to think about aspects of their attitudes. It may be rare in the real world that people receive such direct requests. So, if we are to gain a full understanding of the effects of thought on attitudes, then we will have to understand the factors that cause people spontaneously to think.

Our own work on the causes of "self-motivated" thinking have centered primarily on the role of unattained goals (see Martin & Tesser, 1989; Martin, Tesser, & McIntosh, 1993; McIntosh & Martin, 1992). Put simply, we have hypothesized that people tend to think about things they want but do not have (Klinger, 1975; Kuhl, 1981; cf. Lewin, 1951; Miller, Galanter, & Pribram, 1960; Pervin, 1990). A person who has not eaten in days, for example, will repeatedly think about food (Atkinson & McClelland, 1948). The hypothesis that thoughts are initiated and maintained by unattained goals has received considerable empirical support (e.g., Marrow, 1938; Zeigarnik, 1938). In terms of attitude strength this means that attitudes associated with unattained goals are likely to receive more thought than are attitudes not associated with unattained goals. Thus, the former are more likely to polarize than are the latter.

Additional determinants of thought have been explored by Vallacher and Wegner (1987). They focused on people's identification of their own behavior. People tend to move their identifications to higher and higher levels as their skill in performing the behavior increases. A guitar player, for example, may describe his actions as "putting my fingers on the fret board" at first; with greater skill as "playing a song" or as "expressing myself." If a guitarist has difficulty with his playing (e.g., a string breaks), he or she will begin to identify his or her actions at a lower level ("finding the note on another string"). So, the content of a person's thoughts may be determined by the degree to which he or she is making progress in his or her behaviors.

Wicklund (1986) proposed a related model: When there is a breakdown in skilled behavior, people become self-aware. They begin to think about the skills they need to return to a smooth performance. Wicklund (1986) predicted that disruption of behavior causes people to think about themselves, whereas Vallacher and Wegner (1987) suggested that disruption of behavior causes people to think about lower level behaviors. For present purposes, we need only keep in mind that failure to make progress toward a goal may cause people to have thoughts relevant to that goal (self or task) and that these thoughts persist until the person either attains the goal or reconciles him- or herself to not attaining the goal. Thus any attitudes associated with an unattained goal can be strengthened by the repetitive thinking that comes with nonattainment.

Related to the notion of goals is the concept of ego-involvement. Attitude topics are ego-involving to the extent that they are self-definitional (Sherif & Cantril, 1947), they link one to important groups (Sherif, Sherif, & Nebergall, 1965), or they have important consequences for one's well-being (Petty & Cacioppo, 1986). Messages related to ego-involving issues are more likely to be processed thoughtfully than less ego-involving issues (Petty & Cacioppo, 1986). It is tempting to hypothesize that people are also more likely to think about ego-involving topics spontaneously. Issue-involvement and attitude importance are discussed in a number of other chapters (see Boninger, Krosnick, Berent, Fabrigar, ch. 7, this volume, Crano, ch. 6, this volume; Petty, Haugtvedt, & Smith, ch. 5, this volume, Thomsen, Borgida, & Lavine, ch. 8, this volume); so we do not pursue it further here.

Another factor that causes people to think is the desire to come to terms with a negative life event (Horowitz, 1986; Janis, 1971; Parkes, 1972; Silver, Boon, & Stones, 1983). According to Tait and Silver (1989), negative life events possess three features that motivate persistent thinking. First, they often entail an alteration in a person's social roles and/or relationships, or they produce changes in related considerations, such as finances. People engage in thinking until they figure out how to adapt to these changes. Second, they may also instigate a desire to find meaning in the event. Why did my baby die? Is there some lesson I am supposed to learn from this? Finally, negative life events may instigate a desire to discuss the event with others. People may seek out others for advice, comfort, or social comparison. When people talk about their problems, their thoughts about the negative event often dissipate (Pennebaker, 1989). When the need to talk goes unmet, however, people may continue to think about the event. In this case, attitudes related to the event may polarize.

Interestingly, another cause of thinking may be the motivation to stop thinking. Wegner, Schneider, Carter, and White (1987) demonstrated that people's attempts to stop a thought are often unsuccessful and may even lead to greater occurrences of the thought than if they had not attempted to suppress the thought in the first place. According to Wegner et al. (1987), when people attempt to suppress a thought, they are often not 100% successful. The problem is that in order to ascertain if one is not thinking about some object, one has to think about the object. "Am I thinking about a white bear? No, I am not. Well, I guess I just did. How about now? No, I am not thinking about a white bear now. Actually, I am." In this way, the to-be-suppressed thought pops repeatedly into consciousness. Associations are formed between the unwanted thought and whatever else the person happens to be thinking about. These associations can bring the unwanted thought to mind. In this way, attempting not to think about an object or event may make the person more likely to think about that object or event.

Some external factors cause people to think. For example, the mere presentation of an attitude object can make the attitude accessible (Fazio, Powell, & Herr, 1983). And, Berlyne (1957) demonstrated that stimuli that contain some sort of incongruity, surprise, uncertainty, complexity and/or novelty are particularly effective in capturing and holding our attention. For example, people tend to look more at a picture of a giraffe with a lion's head than at a picture of an ordinary giraffe (Berlyne, 1958).

Similarly, we may possess thoughts that are sufficiently complex or novel to hold our attention. For example, we may be more likely to think about attitudes that we have recently developed or that we are unsure of than about attitudes that we have held confidently for a long time. Similarly, if we find ourselves holding attitudes that are incongruent with one another, we may exert considerable cognitive effort in thinking about these beliefs (cf. Clary & Tesser, 1983). In fact, several theories of attitude change are based on this assumption (e.g., balance, congruity, dissonance, value incongruity).

In sum, people in "the real world" may be induced to think about their attitudes if: (a) these attitudes are associated with a highly desired, but unattained goal; (b) the attitudes are associated with issues with which people are trying to come to terms; (c) people attempt to suppress thoughts related to the attitudes; (d) the attitudes are associated with particularly complex or novel stimuli or are themselves novel or complex; and (e) the attitudes are incongruent with other attitudes these people hold. All of these are real-world factors that increase the likelihood that people will maintain thoughts about a given attitude object.

SUMMARY

Thought is a ubiquitous part of one's psychological life. We have attempted to specify what the effects of this activity are for attitude dynamics. The picture we developed is coherent, if not simple. Thought, under the direction of a schema, selects what is to be salient and changes beliefs. If we think of attitudes as an evaluation based on what is salient at the moment of the evaluation then we can see how thought has nontrivial effects on attitudes. The usual effect is for thought to strengthen attitudes. However, this is not always the case. It depends on several variables including the presence or absence of reality or process constraints, the structure of the schema and the motivation of the individual vis-à-vis a particular attitudinal position.

There is evidence that thought both strengthens and weakens the attitude behavior relationship. We suggested that some behaviors are driven by feelings and others are driven by beliefs. Thought can make either feelings or beliefs salient. If attitudes are a construction based on what is salient at the moment then even contradictory effects of thought on the attitude behavior link are understandable.

The genesis of much of the work we have reviewed here was reviewed in 1978 (Tesser, 1978). Although the general model of the effects of thought on attitudes remains, our thinking about schema complexity and the attitude behavior relationship have become more sophisticated. Moreover, we have begun to explore the antecedents of thought. It appears that goal structures, the search for existential meaning, and the desire to avoid particular thoughts play a demonstrable role in initiating, stopping, and determining the focus of thought.

ACKNOWLEDGMENTS

Work on this chapter was facilitated by grants from NSF (BNS 9016578) and NIMH (ROI MH 49487; K05 MH01233-01). We are grateful for this support.

REFERENCES

Atkinson, J. W., & McClelland, D. C. (1948). The effect of different intensities of the hunger drive on thematic apperception. *Journal of Experimental Psychology, 38*, 643–658.

Batson, C. D. (1987). Prosocial motivation: Is it ever truly altruistic? In L. Berkowitz (Ed.), *Advances in experimental social psychology* (Vol. 20, pp. 65–122). New York: Academic.

Berlyne, D. E. (1957). Conflict and information-theory variables as determinants of human perceptual curiosity. *Journal of Experimental Psychology, 53*, 399–404.

Berlyne, D. E. (1958). The influence of complexity and novelty in visual figures on orienting responses. *Journal of Experimental Psychology, 55*, 289–296.

Britton, B. K., & Tesser, A. (1982). Effects of prior knowledge on use of cognitive capacity in three complex cognitive tasks. *Journal of Verbal Learning and Verbal Behavior, 21*, 421–436.

Chaiken, S., & Yates, S. (1985). Affective-cognitive consistency and thought induced attitude polarization. *Journal of Personality and Social Psychology, 49*, 1470–1481.

Clark, M. S., Mills, J., & Powell, M. C. (1986). Keeping track of needs in communal and exchange relationships. *Journal of Personality and Social Psychology, 51*, 333–338.

Clary, G., & Tesser, A. (1983). Reactions to unexpected events: The naive scientist and interpretive activity. *Personality and Social Psychology Bulletin, Q*, 609–620.

Downing, J. W., Judd, C. M., & Brauer, M. (1992). Effects of repeated attitude expressions on response latency and extremity. *Journal of Personality and Social Psychology, 63*, 17–29.

Fazio, R. H., Powell, M. C., & Herr, P. M. (1983). Toward a process model of the attitude-behavior relation: Accessing one's attitude upon mere observation of the attitude object. *Journal of Personality and Social Psychology, 44*, 723–735.

Fazio, R. H., Powell, M. C., & Williams, C. J. (1989). The role of attitude accessibility in the attitude to behavior process. *Journal of Consumer Research, 16*, 280–288.

Fazio, R. H., & Williams, C. J. (1986). Attitude accessibility as a moderator of the attitude perception and attitude-behavior relations: An investigation of the 1984 presidential election. *Journal of Personality and Social Psychology, 51*, 505–514.

Fazio, R. H., Zanna, M. P., & Cooper, J. (1978). Direct experience and attitude-behavior consistency: An information processing analysis. *Personality and Social Psychology Bulletin, 4*, 48–52.

Feshbach, S. (1964). The function of aggression and the regulation of aggressive drive. *Psychological Review, 71*, 257–272.

Fiske, S. T., & Taylor, S. (1991). *Social cognition* (2nd ed.). New York: McGraw-Hill.

Hastorf, A., & Cantril, H. (1954). They saw a game: A case study. *Journal of Abnormal and Social Psychology, 49*, 129–134.

Higgins, E. T., King, G. A., & Mavin, G. H. (1982). Individual construct accessibility and subjective impressions and recall. *Journal of Personality and Social Psychology, 43*, 35–47.

Horowitz, M. J. (1986). *Stress response syndromes* (2nd ed.). New York: Jason Aronson.

Houston, D. A., & Fazio, R. (1989). Biased processing as a function of attitude accessibility: Making objective judgments subjectively. *Social Cognition, 7*, 51–56.

Janis, I. L. (1971). *Stress and frustration.* New York: Harcourt Brace Jovanovich.

Janis, I. L., & Mann, L. (1977). *Decision making: A psychological analysis of conflict, choice, and commitment.* New York: The Free Press.

Judd, C. M., & Lusk, C. M. (1984). Knowledge structures and evaluative judgments: Effects of structural variables on judgment extremity. *Journal of Personality and Social Psychology, 46*, 1193–1207.

Kalgren, C. A., & Wood, W. (1986). Access to attitude-relevant information in memory as a determinant of attitude behavior consistency. *Journal of Experimental Social Psychology, 22*, 328–338.

Kiesler, C. A. (1971). *The psychology of commitment: Experiments linking behavior to belief.* New York: Academic Press.

Klinger, E. (1975). Consequences of commitment to and disengagement from incentives. *Psychological Review, 82,* 223–231.

Krosnick, J. A. (1989). Attitude importance and attitude accessibility. *Personality and Social Psychology Bulletin, 15,* 297–308.

Kuhl, J. (1981). Motivational and functional helplessness: The moderating effect of state vs. action orientation. *Journal of Personality and Social Psychology, 40,* 155–170.

Leone, C. (1984). Thought-induced changes in phobic beliefs: Sometimes it helps, sometimes it hurts. *Journal of Clinical Psychology, 1,* 272–283.

Leone, C. (1989). Self-generated attitude change: Some effects of thought and dogmatism on attitude polarization. *Personality and Individual Differences, 10,* 1243–1252.

Leone, C., & Ensley, E. (1985). Self-generated attitude change: Another look at the effects of thought and cognitive schemata. *Representative Research in Social Psychology, 15,* 2–9.

Leone, C., Minor, S. W., & Baltimore, M. L. (1983). A comparison of cognitive and performance based treatment analogues: Constrained thought versus performance accomplishments. *Cognitive Therapy and Research, 7,* 445–454.

Leone, C., Negaran, C. R., Aronow, R. E., & Groble, M. L. (1991). *Thought, belief constraints, and cognitive style: A client by treatment approach to self-generated reduction of fear.* Unpublished paper, University of North Florida, Jacksonville.

Leone, C., Taylor, L. W., & Adams, K. C. (1991). Self-generated attitude change: Some effects of thought, dogmatism, and reality constraints. *Personality and Individual Differences, 12,* 233–240.

Lewin, K. (1951). *Field theory in social science: Selected theoretical papers.* New York: Harper & Row.

Liberman, A., & Chaiken, S. (1991). Value conflict and thought-induced attitude change. *Journal of Experimental Social Psychology, 27,* 203–216.

Linville, P. W. (1982). The complexity extremity effect and age based stereotyping. *Journal of Personality and Social Psychology, 42,* 193–210.

Linville, P. W., & Jones, E. E. (1980). Polarized appraisals of outgroup members. *Journal of Personality and Social Psychology, 38,* 689–703.

Lord, C. G., Ross, L., & Lepper, M. (1979). Biased assimilation and attitude polarization: The effects of prior theories on subsequently considered evidence. *Journal of Personality and Social Psychology, 37,* 2098–2109.

Lusk, C. M., & Judd, C. M. (1988). Political expertise and the structural mediators of candidate evaluations. *Journal of Experimental Social Psychology, 24,* 105–126.

Marrow, A. J. (1938). Goal tension and recall. *Journal of General Psychology, 19,* 3–64.

Martin, L. L., & Tesser, A. (1989). Toward a motivational and structural theory of ruminative thought. In J. S. Uleman, & J. A. Bargh (Eds.), *Unintended thought* (pp. 306–326). New York: Guilford.

Martin, L. L., Tesser, A., & McIntosh, W. D. (1993). Wanting but not having: The effects of unattained goals on thoughts and feelings. In D. M. Wegner & J. W. Pennebaker (Eds.), *The handbook of mental control* (pp. 552–572). Englewood Cliffs, NJ: Prentice-Hall.

McIntosh, W. D., & Martin, L. L. (1992). The cybernetics of satisfaction: The relation between goal attainment, rumination, and affect. In M. S. Clark (Ed.), *Review of personality and social psychology* (Vol. 14, pp. 222–246). New York: Academic.

Millar, M., & Tesser, A. (1986a). Thought induced attitude change: The effects of schema structure and commitment. *Journal of Personality and Social Psychology, 51,* 259–269.

Millar, M., & Tesser, A. (1986b). Effects of affective and cognitive focus on the attitude-behavior relationship. *Journal of Personality and Social Psychology, 51,* 270–276.

Millar, M., & Tesser, A. (1989). The effects of affective-cognitive consistency and thought on attitude behavior relations. *Journal of Experimental Social Psychology, 25,* 189–202.

Millar, M. G., & Tesser, A. (1992). The role of beliefs and feelings in guiding behavior: The mismatch model. In L. Martin & A. Tesser (Eds.), *The construction of social judgments* (pp. 277–300). Hillsdale, NJ: Lawrence Erlbaum Associates.

Miller, G. A., Galanter, E., & Pribram, K. H. (1960). *Plans and the structure of behavior.* New York: Holt, Rinehart & Winston.

Nolen-Hoeksema, S. (1987). Sex differences in unipolar depression: Evidence and theory. *Psychological Bulletin, 101,* 259–282.

Parkes, C. M. (1972). Components of the reaction to loss of a limb, spouse or home. *Journal of Psychosomatic Research, 16,* 343–349.

Pennebaker, J. W. (1989). Confession, inhibition and disease. *Advances in Experimental Social Psychology, 22,* New York: Academic.

Pervin, L. A. (1990). *Goal concepts in personality and social psychology.* Hillsdale, NJ: Lawrence Erlbaum Associates.

Petty, R. E., & Cacioppo, J. T. (1986). The elaboration likelihood model of persuasion. In L. Berkowitz (Ed.), *Advances in Experimental Social Psychology, 19,* pp. 123–181. New York: Academic.

Piliavin, J. M., Dovidio, J. F., Gartner, S. L., & Clark, R. D. (1981). *Emergency intervention.* New York: Academic.

Rogers, C. R. (1951). *Client-centered therapy: Its current practice, implication, and theory.* Boston: Houghton Mifflin.

Sadler, O., & Tesser, A. (1973). Some effects of salience and time upon interpersonal hostility and attraction. *Sociometry, 36,* 99–112.

Sanbonmatsu, D. M., Kardes, F. R., Sansone, C. (1991). Remembering less and knowing more: The effects of time of judgment on inferences about unknown attributes. *Journal of Personality and Social Psychology, 61,* 546–554.

Scheier, M. F. (1976). Self-awareness, self-consciousness, and angry aggression. *Journal of Personality, 44,* 627–644.

Scheier, M. F., & Carver, C. S. (1977). Self-focused attention and the experience of emotion: Attraction, repulsion, elation and depression. *Journal of Personality and Social Psychology, 35,* 625–636.

Shavitt, S., & Fazio, R. H. (1991). Effects of attribute salience on the consistency between attitudes and behavior predictions. *Personality and Social Psychology Bulletin, 17,* 507–516.

Sherif, C. W., Sherif, M., & Nebergall, R. E. (1965). *Attitude and attitude change.* Philadelphia: W. B. Saunders.

Sherif, M., & Cantril, H. (1947). *The psychology of ego involvements.* New York: Wiley.

Silver, R. L., Boon, C., & Stones, M. H. (1983). Searching for meaning in misfortune: Making sense of incest. *Journal of Social Issues, 39,* 81–102.

Tait, R., & Silver, R. C. (1989). Coming to terms with major negative life events. In J. S. Uleman & J. A. Bargh (Eds.), *Unintended thought* (pp. 351–382). New York: Guilford.

Tesser, A. (1976). Thought and reality constraints as determinants of attitude polarization. *Journal of Research in Personality, 10,* 183–194.

Tesser, A. (1978). Self-generated attitude change. In L. Berkowitz (Ed.), *Advances in Experimental Social Psychology* (Vol. 11, pp. 290–338). New York: Academic.

Tesser, A., & Cowan, C. (1975). Some effects of thought and number of cognitions on attitude change. *Social Behavior and Personality, 3,* 165–173.

Tesser, A., & Leone, C. (1977). Cognitive schemas and thought as determinants of attitude change. *Journal of Experimental Social Psychology, 13,* 340–356.

Tesser, A., Leone, C., & Clary, G. (1978). Affect control: Process constraints vs. catharsis. *Cognitive Therapy and Research, 2,* 265–274.

Tesser, A., & Paulhus, D. (1976). Toward a causal model of love. *Journal of Personality and Social Psychology, 34,* 1095–1105.

Vallacher, R. R., & Wegner, D. M. (1987). What do people think they're doing? Action identification and human behavior. *Psychological Review, 94,* 3–15.

Wegner, D. M., Schneider, D. J., Carter, S. R., & White, T. L. (1987). Paradoxical effects of thought suppression. *Journal of Personality and Social Psychology, 47,* 237–252.

Wicklund, R. A. (1986). Orientations to the environment versus preoccupation with human potential. In R. M. Sorrentino & E. T. Higgins (Eds.), *Handbook of motivation and cognition: Foundations of social behavior* (pp. 64–95). New York: Guilford.

Wilson, T. D., Dunn, D. S., Bybee, J. A., Hyman, D. B., & Rotondo, J. A. (1984). Effects of analyzing reasons on attitude-behavior consistency. *Journal of Personality and Social Psychology, 47,* 5–16.

Wilson, T. D., Dunn, D. S., Kraft, D., & Lisle, D. J. (1989). Introspection, attitude change and attitude-behavior consistency: The disruptive effects of explaining why we feel the way we do. In L. Berkowitz (Ed.), *Advances in experimental social psychology* (Vol. 19, pp. 123–205). Orlando, FL: Academic.

Wilson, T. D., & Hodges, S. D. (1992). Attitudes as temporary constructions. In L. Martin & A. Tesser (Eds.), *The construction of social judgments* (pp. 37–66). Hillsdale, NJ: Lawrence Erlbaum Associates.

Wilson, T. D., Kraft, D., & Dunn, D. S. (1989). The disruptive effects of explaining attitudes: The moderating effect of knowledge about the attitude object. *Journal of Experimental Social Psychology, 25,* 379–400.

Zanna, M., & Rempel, J. K. (1988). Attitudes: A new look at an old concept. In D. Bar-Tal & A. Kruglanski (Eds.), *The social psychology of knowledge* (pp. 315–334). New York: Cambridge University Press.

Zeigarnik, B. (1938). On finished and unfinished tasks. In W. D. Ellis (Ed. & Trans.), *A source book of gestalt psychology* (pp. 300–414). New York: Harcourt, Brace & World. (Original work published 1927)

5

▼▼▼▼▼▼▼

Elaboration as a Determinant of Attitude Strength: Creating Attitudes That Are Persistent, Resistant, and Predictive of Behavior

Richard E. Petty
Curtis P. Haugtvedt
Ohio State University

Stephen M. Smith
North Georgia College

This volume is devoted to understanding the antecedents and consequences of attitude strength. That is, what makes some attitudes persist over time, resist countervailing pressures to change, and impact on other judgments and behaviors?[1] A common strategy in much of the work on attitude strength is to measure

---

[1]The Elaboration Likelihood Model of persuasion (ELM; Petty & Cacioppo, 1986b) identified three consequences of strong attitudes—greater persistence, resistance, and prediction of behavior with strong (central route) rather than weak (peripheral route) attitudes. To these consequences, Krosnick and Petty (ch. 1, this volume) suggested a fourth criterion: Strong attitudes should have a greater impact on other judgments than weak ones. It is important to note, however, that according to the ELM, attitudes can have an impact on other judgments in a number of ways (Petty, Cacioppo, & Haugtvedt, 1992). For example, attitudes could serve as a peripheral cue leading to favorable evaluations of positions that are close to one's own and unfavorable evaluations of deviant ones with little scrutiny of the merits of the positions. The stronger an attitude is, the more likely it is to serve as a cue when the elaboration likelihood is low. In addition, when the elaboration likelihood is high, strong attitudes can bias the ongoing cognitive activity by encouraging counterarguing of messages that take counterattitudinal positions but favorable thinking to proattitudinal appeals. Finally, strong attitudes can influence the extent of message processing (e.g., leading people to scrutinize counterattitudinal messages more closely than proattitudinal ones). Because little research has examined explicitly whether attitudes newly changed as a result of extensive elaboration play a greater biasing role in subsequent judgments than do attitudes changed with little elaboration, we will not discuss this consequence further.

some property of an existing attitude and then examine the strength consequences of attitudes having this property to varying degrees. For example, researchers have measured the extent of knowledge associated with an attitude object (see Davidson, ch. 12, this volume; Wood, Rhodes, & Biek, ch. 11, this volume), or how personally important the attitude object is (see Boninger, Krosnick, Berent, & Fabrigar, ch. 7, this volume), and have determined that the more knowledge associated with an attitude object and the more important the attitude object is perceived to be, the more persistent the attitude toward that object is, the more it is resistant to change, and the more predictive the attitude is of behavior. In contrast to this approach, this chapter is concerned with *creating* new attitudes that are strong rather than weak. That is, this chapter focuses on understanding the processes leading newly changed attitudes to vary in strength—whether this change is from no attitude to some attitude (e.g., no opinion to somewhat favorable), or from one attitudinal position to another (e.g., somewhat favorable to very favorable). We explain that some attitude change processes are likely to produce new attitudes that are relatively strong, but other change processes are more likely to produce weak attitudes.

Some of the earliest research on persuasion suggested that although it was often easy to change people's attitudes (e.g., Knower, 1935, 1936), many of these attitude changes were rather ephemeral and unrelated to people's behaviors (e.g., see Festinger, 1964). That is, the changed attitudes in these studies appeared to be rather weak. However, other studies produced attitude changes that were quite enduring and directive of action (e.g., see Cook & Flay, 1978).

The Elaboration Likelihood Model (ELM) of persuasion was proposed as a means of accounting for the fact that the attitude changes produced in some studies were rather strong, but the changes induced in others were quite weak (Petty, 1977; Petty & Cacioppo, 1981, 1986a). A key postulate of the ELM is that the strength of an attitude is based on the amount of issue-relevant thinking (elaboration) the person has done about the attitude object. That is, when an attitude changes as a result of careful thinking about the merits of the attitude object (*central route* to attitude change), the resulting attitude will be stronger than if the attitude changes because of a relatively simple *cue* in the persuasion setting that induces change by a direct association (e.g., Staats & Staats, 1958), on-line inference (e.g., Bem, 1972), or memory-based heuristic (e.g., Chaiken, 1987) process (*peripheral route* to attitude change). So, in order to understand the strength of attitudes, the ELM indicates that we need to understand the factors that determine whether the attitude is based on careful and effortful thinking rather than on simpler cue processes. According to the ELM, if a variable increases the likelihood that an attitude is based on careful thinking rather than simple cue processes, this variable would also increase the likelihood that the resulting attitude is strong rather than weak.

Understanding how to bring about changed attitudes that are strong rather than weak is of considerable practical as well as conceptual interest. For example, creating unfavorable attitudes toward drugs does little good if these attitudes do not persist over time, resist peer pressure and lead to avoidance of drugs. Similarly, changing attitudes toward political candidates or consumer products does little good if these attitudes do not determine voting or purchases.

We address three issues in this chapter. First, we provide a brief review of the determinants of effortful thinking in persuasion situations. Second, we provide a critical examination of the empirical evidence for the proposition that variables that increase message elaboration encourage stronger attitudes. Finally, we address the issue of *why* increased elaboration would be expected to result in stronger attitudes.[2]

ELABORATION IN ATTITUDE CHANGE SETTINGS

People are confronted with a large number of persuasive communications each day. Because of this, it is impossible to give much thought to all of them—there just is not enough time in the day! Even if there were enough time to think about every message we received, we would not be able to think about them all because some messages are incomprehensible (e.g., presented in very technical language), or are presented too rapidly. Furthermore, even if these ability factors were not an issue, it is likely that some messages would be attended to more than others for motivational reasons. For example, some messages would be more important or interesting than others and thus receive greater scrutiny. In recognition of these factors, a key postulate of the ELM is that for reasons of both limited ability and varying motivation, the extent of careful scrutiny that a persuasive message receives varies with both situational and individual factors (Petty & Cacioppo, 1981, 1986b).

Assessing the Extent of Elaboration

Over the last three decades, considerable research attention has been devoted to uncovering the variables that influence the extent of thinking about a persuasive message. Two procedures have been used most frequently. In one procedure, the quality of the arguments in the message is manipulated along with the variable being tested (e.g., Petty, Wells, & Brock, 1976). The message quality manipulation is developed in pretesting. Two messages on the same topic are prepared such that one communication contains a set of compelling arguments that elicit mostly favorable thoughts and considerable attitude change when people are instructed to evaluate and think about them, and another communication contains a set of specious arguments that elicit mostly unfavorable thoughts and little

---

[2]Although our focus here is on newly changed attitudes, the ELM also predicts that the strength of an existing attitude is tied to the extent to which the attitude is based on considerable issue-relevant cognitive activity rather than low effort cue processes.

attitude change or even boomerang when people are instructed to evaluate and think about them (see Petty & Cacioppo, 1986a; Petty, Wegener, Fabrigar, Priester, & Cacioppo, 1993). For example, if a researcher wanted to know if people thought more about a message of high rather than low personal relevance, the relevance of the message would be varied along with message quality. In order to do this, some college students might be told that a new university regulation was proposed for next year (and thus would have an impact on them) or was proposed for 10 years in the future (and thus would have no personal impact; Apsler & Sears, 1968). The high and low relevance messages would contain either the compelling or specious arguments in favor of the new regulation. If people are not thinking very much about the persuasive message under the low relevance conditions, their attitudes should be affected little, if at all, by the argument quality manipulation. However, if they are thinking carefully about the message under the high relevance conditions, argument quality should have a large effect on attitudes.

A second strategy to assess the extent of thinking in persuasion settings is to have people list their thoughts about the message either during or after exposure to it (e.g., Brock, 1967; Greenwald, 1968). If a variable such as personal relevance increases the extent of thinking about the message, increasing relevance might increase the total number of issue and/or message relevant thoughts generated (e.g., Burnkrant & Howard, 1984). Alternatively, enhanced thinking could increase thoughts that are consistent with the quality of the message, but decrease thoughts that are inconsistent with its quality. For example, if the message is strong, favorable thoughts would increase but unfavorable thoughts would decrease as effortful message evaluation increased, and the total number of issue-relevant thoughts could remain the same (Petty & Cacioppo, 1979). Finally, increased thinking about the message should produce attitudes that are more highly correlated with the valence of the message-relevant thoughts generated (e.g., Chaiken, 1980).[3]

Determinants of Ability to Think About a Message

Using the procedures just described to assess message processing, a number of studies have identified variables that influence a person's ability to think about a persuasive communication. For example, it is perhaps not surprising that people are less able to think about a message if they are distracted by external stimulation during the message presentation than if they are not (e.g., Festinger & Maccoby, 1964). It may be more surprising to realize that this means that including distraction with a message can increase persuasion when the message arguments are specious. This is because when they are distracted from thinking, people will be less able to realize the flaws in the arguments, and thus they are more persuaded

---

[3]Other procedures to assess the extent of elaboration have included simply asking people how much effort they devoted to thinking about a message or issue, and physiological techniques (see Petty & Cacioppo, 1986a).

than when they are able to detect and think about the flaws. However, increasing distraction reduces persuasion when the arguments are compelling, because people are less able to appreciate the merits of the arguments (Petty et al., 1976).

Similar effects have been shown for other variables affecting ability to think about a persuasive message. For example, people are less able to think about a message when they have just completed some vigorous exercise (e.g., Sanbonmatsu & Kardes, 1988). On the other hand, if people are reclining comfortably, they are better able to think than if they are in a more distracting posture such as standing (e.g., Petty, Wells, Heesacker, Brock, & Cacioppo, 1983). People are not able to process some messages because they are incomprehensible (e.g., Eagly, 1974; Ratneshwar & Chaiken, 1991) or are presented too rapidly (e.g., Moore, Hausknecht, & Thamodaran, 1986; Smith & Shaffer, 1991; in press), or the audience has insufficient knowledge to appreciate either the strengths or flaws in the arguments (e.g., Wood, Kallgren, & Priesler, 1985).[4] When a message is sufficiently complex, thinking can be increased by repeating the message a few times (e.g., Cacioppo & Petty, 1989).

Determinants of Motivation to Think About a Message

Motivational factors are also important in influencing the extent of thinking. Perhaps the most studied motivational factor is the personal relevance or importance of the message topic (Johnson & Eagly, 1989). Petty and Cacioppo (1979, 1990) hypothesized that when people think that a message is on a topic of high personal relevance or importance (i.e., the message is relevant to a person's important outcomes, goals, values, groups, possessions, and so forth), they engage in greater message scrutiny than when the message is perceived to be of little relevance or importance.[5] The available evidence is quite consistent with this view (see Boninger et al., ch. 7, this volume; Crano, ch. 6, this volume; Petty, Cacioppo, & Haugtvedt, 1992; Thomsen et al., ch. 8, this volume). The extent to which a message is seen as personally relevant or important has been manipulated in a number of ways including varying the date or location of some policy recommendation so that it would affect the message recipient or not (e.g., Chaiken, 1980; Petty & Cacioppo, 1979), varying the self-relevance of the pro-

---

[4]Knowledge might also have an impact on a person's motivation to think about a message. For example, providing people with a little information about an unfamiliar topic might whet their curiosity if it normally would have been low (e.g., a low involvement issue), but satisfy their curiosity if it is already high and thus diminish interest in processing yet additional information on the topic (see Johnson, 1994, for relevant data).

[5]There are, of course, various degrees of personal relevance, and the amount of thought about a message is expected to be tied to factors such as the perceived magnitude, immediacy, and duration of self-relevant consequences (see Petty & Cacioppo, 1986a). For example a message devoted to an important aspect of the self would elicit greater thought than a message devoted to a trivial aspect of the self, but a message devoted to a trivial aspect of oneself would elicit greater thought than a message devoted to a trivial aspect of someone else.

nouns used in the communication (e.g., Burnkrant & Unnava, 1989), and placing message recipients in front of a mirror so that they would see their self-reflection (Hutton & Baumeister, 1992).

Although inducing a perception of self-relevance is a powerful way to influence thinking, there are, of course, other ways to increase peoples' motivation to think about a communication. For instance, messages that violate peoples' expectancies and induce surprise are thought about more than messages that are consistent with what is expected. Thus, because people generally expect an expert source to provide strong arguments, when an expert presents weak arguments, thinking about the arguments is increased (Maheswaran & Chaiken, 1991). Also, when people find that they disagree with the majority of their peers or agree with the minority, they are surprised and thinking is enhanced over the more expected cases where people learn they agree with the majority or disagree with the minority (Baker & Petty, 1994). In addition, when people expect a message to present the benefits of taking some action but the message instead presents the costs of not taking the action, thinking is increased over cases where the message presents the type of arguments that were expected (Smith & Petty, in press).

Aspects of the message source also influence the extent of thinking about a persuasive communication. For example, when each argument in a message is presented by a different source, the arguments receive greater scrutiny than when all arguments are presented by the same source (e.g., Harkins & Petty, 1981; Moore & Reardon, 1987). This *multiple source effect* is especially likely when the additional sources appear to be providing independent assessments of the issue (e.g., the sources are dissimilar and have not conspired to generate the message; Harkins & Petty, 1987).

Chronic characteristics of the audience also influence their tendency to think about a message. Perhaps the most directly relevant personality variable in this regard is the *need for cognition* (Cacioppo & Petty, 1982). People high in need for cognition enjoy thinking and problem solving, but people low in need for cognition do not. Not surprisingly then, the attitudes of individuals high in need for cognition are based more on their scrutiny of the content of persuasive messages than are the attitudes of individuals low in need for cognition (e.g., Cacioppo, Petty, & Morris, 1983; Haugtvedt, Petty, & Cacioppo, 1992).

Temporary states of the audience can also motivate thinking. For example, being in a good mood can either enhance or reduce thinking about a communication. Positive mood reduces thinking about a message when the message topic is or is expected to be counterattitudinal or depressing (e.g., Bless, Bohner, Schwarz, & Strack, 1990; Worth & Mackie, 1987), but positive mood enhances thinking when the message is or is expected to be proattitudinal or pleasant (Howard & Barry, 1994; Wegener, Petty, & Smith, in press). This suggests that people in a positive mood are protective of their pleasant state and will process a message if it is mood maintaining but will not think about it if it is mood threatening (Petty, Gleicher, & Baker, 1991; Wegener & Petty, 1994). It is interesting to note that simply increasing the momentary accessibility of the audience's attitudes on a topic can increase thinking (Priester, Fabrigar, Wegener, & Petty, 1994). Increasing accessibility might increase processing because when the accessibility of an attitude on a topic is increased, people infer that the topic is more important or relevant (Roese & Olson, 1994).

Various aspects of the persuasion situation itself can also influence motivation to think about the message. For example, thinking can be increased by making people feel personally responsible or accountable for message evaluation such as when they believe that they are the sole message evaluator rather than part of an evaluation team (e.g., Petty, Harkins, & Williams, 1980). In addition, thinking is increased when people are led to believe that they will have to discuss the message with an interviewer (e.g., Chaiken, 1980; see also Tetlock, 1990). A dramatic way to increase thinking about an advocacy is to get the target of influence to generate the message him or herself and then present it to another person (e.g., Greenwald & Albert, 1968; Janis & King, 1957).

Interactions Among Variables

So far, we have considered factors associated with the message, the source, the persuasion context, and the individual message recipient in isolation. However, numerous studies have indicated that various interactions among these variables are important to consider. For example, audience factors can interact with source factors in determining the extent of thinking about a persuasive message. Consider individual differences in self-monitoring (Snyder, 1979). High self-monitors are people who are especially concerned about projecting a desirable self-image. Thus, these individuals are more interested in thinking about what an attractive than an unattractive source says. However, source expertise has little impact on influencing the thinking of these individuals. Low self-monitors, on the other hand, are people who are especially concerned about validity and in projecting their true inner selves to others. Thus, low self-monitors are more likely to think about what an expert than a nonexpert says, but source attractiveness has no impact on the extent of thinking (Snyder & DeBono, 1987).

Other individual differences also interact with source factors. For example, people low in need for cognition (who like to conserve their cognitive resources) are less likely to think about what a clearly honest than a potentially dishonest source says (Priester & Petty, in press). An honest source can be trusted, and thus little scrutiny is needed. A potentially untrustworthy source, however, requires even cognitive misers to exert cognitive effort if they are not to be fooled. The tendency for people to think more about what a potentially untrustworthy rather than a trustworthy source says might account in part for the finding that Caucasian audiences tend to engage in greater thinking about a persuasive message when it is presented by a disliked minority or ethnic group than a liked one (White & Harkins, 1994).

Other interactions among variables have been observed as well. For example, summarizing the main points of a message as rhetorical questions rather than as statements has led to enhanced message processing when a message was low in personal relevance, but using rhetorical questions has disrupted processing when the message was of high relevance (Petty, Cacioppo, & Heesacker, 1981). That is, inserting questions in a message seems to encourage thinking when it normally would be low, but the questions appear to disrupt a person's chain of thought when motivation to think is already high. The potential for such interactions suggests that it is important to consider *all* of the variables present in an attitude change situation that could have an impact on thinking rather than considering variables in isolation.

Summary

The most important point from our discussion so far is that some attitude change situations are characterized by high amounts of thinking, but other situations are characterized by low amounts of thinking. According to the ELM, attitude changes can occur in both types of situations. In high thinking situations, attitude change is based on a careful assessment of the merits of the advocated position. If effortful scrutiny of the message leads to predominately favorable thoughts, then persuasion is likely. But if effortful scrutiny of the message leads to predominately unfavorable thoughts, resistance and even boomerang can occur. In low thinking situations, attitude change stems mostly from various peripheral processes such as identification with the source (Kelman, 1961), and reliance on decision heuristics (Chaiken, 1987; see Eagly & Chaiken, 1993; Petty, Priester, & Wegener, 1994, for reviews).

If the variables we have discussed such as personal relevance, need for cognition, and others, influence the extent to which attitude changes are based on issue-relevant cognitive activity, then these variables should also be associated with variations in the strength of newly changed attitudes. For example, attitudes changed under conditions of high personal relevance should be stronger than attitudes changed the same amount under conditions of low personal relevance. Similarly, the attitude changes produced in people who enjoy thinking should be stronger than the changes produced in people who do not. With this in mind, we next examine the evidence for the proposition that attitude changes that result from thinking about the merits of the advocated position are stronger than attitude changes that result from peripheral processes. We review evidence relevant to each of three strength consequences. Following this, we turn to the question of why issue-relevant thinking is likely to result in strong attitudes.

CREATING PERSISTENT ATTITUDES

The first strength characteristic we consider is the temporal persistence of newly changed attitudes. In our usage, *persistence* refers to the extent to which a newly changed attitude endures over time even if it is never attacked directly. In contrast, *resistance* refers to the ability of an attitude to hold up to an explicit attack. Of course, the overall durability of newly changed attitudes is dependent in part on both persistence processes such as memory decay and resistance processes such as active counterarguing of attacking messages.

In this section, we review studies in which the durability of newly changed attitudes was assessed when no attacks were explicitly provided as part of the study. In a comprehensive review of the literature on attitude change persistence, Cook and Flay (1978) concluded that "overall, persuasion approaches have not often led to absolute persistence, and where they have it is not clear what the mediating variables might have been" (p. 45). In their summary of the research available at the time, Cook and Flay did not identify mediating variables responsible for persistence but instead concluded with a list of moderating variables that they believed discriminated studies that tended to find persistence from those that did not. For example, Cook and Flay noted that studies finding persistence "seem to have had a high degree of personal relevance for subjects" (p. 47).

Petty (1977) also reviewed the existing literature on attitude change persistence and concluded that the variables moderating persistence were those that influenced the likelihood that a person would be motivated or able to think about the message or issue under consideration. For example, research through the late 1970s showed that (a) the self-generation of arguments (e.g., Elms, 1966; Watts, 1967), (b) the use of interesting or involving communication topics (e.g., Ronis, Baumgardner, Leippe, Cacioppo, & Greenwald, 1977), (c) providing increased time to think about a message (e.g., Mitnick & McGinnies, 1958), (d) increasing message repetition (e.g., Johnson & Watkins, 1971), and (e) reducing distraction (e.g., Watts & Holt, 1979) were all associated with increased persistence. That is, the available literature was generally consistent with the notion that both attitude change and its persistence were facilitated when people were encouraged to generate considerable issue and message-relevant "cognitive responses" (Greenwald, 1968). Petty (1977) noted, however, that one problem with the general cognitive response model of persuasion was that attitude changes also could be produced in the absence of diligent cognitive activity (e.g., agreeing with a conclusion simply because the source was touted as an expert), and these cue-based (peripheral) attitude changes appeared to be more transitory. However, no study before 1977 had explicitly varied motivation or ability to think about a persuasive message in order to investigate the *elaboration-persistence hypothesis*—that attitude changes based on issue-relevant elaboration are more persistent than comparable changes based on peripheral cues.

In order to test this hypothesis, one would want to compare at least two groups of people—one group that showed attitude change as a result of engaging in effortful message elaboration, and one group that showed the same amount of change but without such effort. The group that changed following effortful cognitive activity should show greater attitude change persistence than a group that changed to the same extent but changed mostly due to lower effort peripheral processes. Here we review the studies since 1977 that have attempted to provide a test of the elaboration-persistence hypothesis.[6]

Assessing Individual Differences in Elaboration to Examine Persistence

Haugtvedt and Petty (1992) examined the elaboration-persistence hypothesis by studying individual differences in the need for cognition. Recall that research has shown that individuals who are high in their need for cognition (Cacioppo & Petty, 1982) are more influenced by the arguments in a persuasive message and are less influenced by peripheral cues than those who are low in their need for cognition (e.g., Axsom, Yates, & Chaiken, 1987; Haugtvedt et al., 1992).

To test the elaboration-persistence hypothesis, individuals high and low in their need for cognition were exposed to a television advertisement for an answering machine in the context of a television program that contained several ads. The critical ad was designed to contain compelling arguments and sufficient peripheral cues to lead to comparable initial attitude change in both the high and low need for cognition groups. Following exposure to the program and advertisements, individuals completed an attitude questionnaire and responded to other questions. Two days later they returned to the lab and completed a second set of attitude questions about the product and listed their thoughts about it. Although both high and low need for cognition groups formed equally favorable attitudes toward the product immediately following message exposure, only high need for cognition subjects persisted in these attitudes over the 2-day period. The favorable attitudes of low need for cognition subjects showed significant decay over the time period (i.e., they became less favorable).

Although this study is suggestive, because individuals cannot be randomly assigned to high versus low need for cognition status, there might be unmeasured confounds with need for cognition that were responsible for the differential persistence observed. To avoid this potential problem, several studies attempted

---

[6]Some studies have examined the temporal persistence of attitude changes in high and low message elaboration groups in which the two groups did not show equivalent initial attitude change. For example, in two studies Mackie (1987) examined the persistence of attitude change induced by exposure to majority and minority sources. Subjects who found themselves in disagreement with a majority showed change toward that position that persisted one week later. Subjects who found themselves in disagreement with a minority showed little change either initially or one week later. Although Mackie (1987) provided evidence that the initial change in response to the majority was mediated by message elaboration, this research does not provide a strong test of the elaboration-persistence hypothesis because the initial changes induced by the majority (high elaboration) and minority (low elaboration) sources were not comparable. Other studies have also found differences in the magnitude of attitude change due to some variable at Time 1 that persisted at Time 2 (e.g., Sorrentino, Bobocel, Gitta, Olson, & Hewitt, 1988). These studies do not allow a strong test of the elaboration-persistence hypothesis because they do not compare the persistence of thoughtful and nonthoughtful attitude changes. Thus, these studies will not be discussed further.

a procedure that would allow random assignment to high and low elaboration conditions. We discuss these next.

Manipulating Message Discussion/Transmission to Examine Persistence

A few studies have varied the likely extent of cognitive activity during message exposure by comparing message recipients who anticipated discussing the message with another person (cf. Cialdini, Levy, Herman, Kozlowski, & Petty, 1976) or transmitting the substance of the message to another individual (cf. Zajonc, 1960) to people who did not have these expectations when they were exposed to the message. In the first persistence study to use this procedure, Chaiken (1980, Experiment 1) told some undergraduates that they would be interviewed about their opinions on a particular topic and then would discuss their opinions in a group setting. Following this, the subjects read a sample interview on the topic that served as the persuasive message. Participants in the control group were led to believe that they would be interviewed on a topic different from that presented in the sample interview. The persuasive message began with the interviewee giving responses that made him appear either likable or unlikable. Following this, the interviewee presented two or six arguments in favor of the advocated position. Subjects' attitudes toward this position were assessed both immediately following receipt of the message and about 2 weeks later.

Chaiken (1980) hypothesized that subjects expecting to be interviewed on the message topic would be more careful in thinking about the substance of the message than control subjects and thus would be more influenced by the content of the interview (i.e., the manipulation of number of arguments). Control subjects were expected to be more influenced by the likability of the source (i.e., low effort "heuristic" attitude change) than were the interview subjects. Furthermore, if expecting to be interviewed focuses people more on thinking about the message substance, then the attitude changes of interview subjects should show greater persistence than the attitude changes of control subjects.

The results of this study were generally consistent with these hypotheses. For example, simple main effects comparisons indicated that the interview subjects were influenced by the number of message arguments but control subjects were not. Also, control subjects were influenced by the likability of the source, but interview subjects were not. Of particular interest, the attitude changes of subjects scheduled to be interviewed persisted over the time period. However, for control subjects, their initial attitude changes decayed, at least when the source was likable. No decay was present when the source was dislikable, but because this group showed relatively little initial change, a floor effect could have attenuated decay. In sum, the results of this study provide partial support for the elaboration-persistence hypothesis.

In a conceptually similar series of studies, Boninger, Brock, Cook, Gruder, and Romer (1990) examined the persistence of attitude change for individuals exposed to a persuasive message after being placed in a "transmission" versus a "reception" set (Zajonc, 1960). The transmission set subjects were told that their task was to transmit the information in the message to another person. Subjects in the receiver set were informed that they would be receiving additional information on the issue. Following these inductions, subjects read a short persuasive message and reported their attitudes. From 8 to 20 weeks later (depending on the specific study), subjects' attitudes were assessed again in a phone interview. Control subjects received no induction, read an irrelevant message, and responded to the same attitude questions. In each of their studies, both transmission and reception subjects showed initial attitude change toward the advocated position. Of greatest interest, however, transmission subjects showed greater attitudinal persistence than reception subjects. Boninger et al. (1990) speculated that transmitters engaged in greater cognitive effort in processing the message than receivers and that this effort resulted in a more organized cognitive structure that was more likely to endure.[7]

In sum, both Chaiken (1980) and Boninger et al. (1990) found that expecting to transmit or discuss the message with another person at the time of message reception led to greater attitude change persistence than expecting to receive information on the topic or expecting to discuss a different topic. In both cases, the authors hypothesized that differential cognitive activity at the time of message presentation was responsible for the differential attitude change persistence. However, Lassiter, Pezzo, and Apple (1993) argued that the specific procedures used in studies such as these allow for an alternative explanation. In particular, Lassiter et al. (1993) argued that because the subjects never had the discussion (Chaiken, 1980) or never transmitted the information (Boninger et al., 1990), they might continue thinking about the uncompleted task following the message presentation. If so, then it might be the *subsequent* cognitive activity rather than differential thought *during* the message presentation that was responsible for the differential persistence observed.

To provide an initial test of this notion, Lassiter et al. (1993) replicated the Boninger et al. (1990) research but included a condition in which transmitter subjects actually transmitted their message summaries into a tape recorder. Lassiter et al.'s results provided a replication of the Boninger et al. findings when the transmitters left the experimental session with their assigned task incomplete. However, in the group where transmitters were allowed to complete their task at the first session, decay comparable to that of nontransmitters was observed. Thus

---

[7]The persistence results from this research stand in contrast to the findings of Hennigan, Cook, and Gruder (1982), who found that receivers' attitudes persisted to a greater extent than those of transmitters. Boninger et al. suggested that in their research, transmitters tended to assume that the audience had been exposed to the transmission message whereas in the Hennigan et al. research subjects assumed that this was not the case. They speculate that when subjects think that the audience has not been exposed to the message already, more effort goes into memorizing the message rather than elaborating and organizing their impressions of it.

it is possible that a transmission or an interview set does not induce increased elaboration during exposure to the message, but instead increases elaboration following the message as a person continues to think about the message that they were not allowed to transmit or discuss. If people continue to think about the issue periodically until the time of the delayed attitude measure, this considerable post-message cognitive activity could be responsible for the attitude change persistence.

In a recent study, Downing (1994) attempted to replicate the Lassister et al. (1993) research and also investigate the time course of the postmessage cognitive activity. In this study, control subjects who received an irrelevant message were compared with both uninterrupted transmitters (as in Lassister et al., 1993) and groups that were interrupted from transmitting (as in Boninger et al., 1990). The interrupted transmitter groups were delayed from transmitting their messages for periods ranging from just 15 minutes to 8 weeks. After reading a set of instructions that explained that their task was to read an essay and then pass on the information in the essay to someone else, subjects read the appropriate essay, and then completed attitude and thought listing measures. Following this, the uninterrupted transmitters gave a 2-minute talk on the issues raised in the essay they had read. The interrupted transmitters were told that there was not enough time in the session to engage in the transmission task, but they could engage in a separate study. In one interruption condition, subjects were informed that the next study started in 15 minutes. Prior to the initiation of this study, however, subjects were informed that had to transmit the information from the previous study in order to be eligible to participate. Thus in this group, the subjects initially believed that they would not have to transmit the information, but actually transmitted it about 15 minutes later. In the other interrupted conditions, subjects were contacted to participate in a second study either 3 days, 2 weeks, or 8 weeks after their initial participation. As in the 15-minute group, each subject was asked to transmit the information from the earlier study prior to participation in the new experiment. Ten weeks following their participation in the initial session, subjects were contacted by phone and asked about their opinions regarding the critical issue.

The results of the study were very straightforward. First, all groups that read the relevant essay initially displayed attitudes that were similar and more favorable toward the topic than control subjects who read an irrelevant essay. That is, the relevant message produced initial attitude change. When examined 10 weeks later, however, only the interrupted groups showed persistence of this change. The completed transmission group failed to persist. This finding is in accord with Lassiter et al.'s (1993) argument that whether the transmission task is completed or not is critical for the transmitter-persistence effect. Interestingly, however, it did not matter whether the delay in transmission was just 15 minutes or 8 weeks! All interrupted groups showed the same attitude persistence effect. This suggests that it is not the case that transmitter-persistence is due to the fact that people are thinking about the issue over the entire delay period. However, the study also suggests that the transmission set induction does not have its effect on thought processes that take place during receipt of the persuasive communication. Rather, it appears that interrupting the transmission may lead people to engage in some additional thought following message exposure. For example, after learning that the transmission is cancelled, people might think about what they might have transmitted, and this extra period of postmessage elaboration is sufficient to enhance persistence.[8]

Manipulating the Personal Relevance of the Message to Examine Persistence

Given that the persistence results of the Chaiken (1980) and Boninger et al. (1990) studies might be explained by the fact that transmission and discussion sets increase thinking about a message following exposure (Downing, 1994; Lassiter et al., 1993) because people persevere in thinking, at least briefly, when a task is incomplete, it would be desirable to examine a manipulation of message elaboration that is not confounded with task completion. One such manipulation is the personal relevance of the communication. That is, high versus low personal relevance has been shown to increase processing of message arguments *during* message exposure and decrease reliance on peripheral cues (Petty et al., 1992).[9]

In one study examining the elaboration-persistence hypothesis by varying personal relevance, Haugtvedt and Strathman (1990) presented people with an advertisement for a bicycle and informed them just prior to the message presentation that the bike would soon be available in their local area (high relevance) or only in a distant market (low relevance; Petty, Cacioppo, & Schumann, 1983). The ad contained strong arguments and positive cues and was presented on a computer screen for a short time period in the context of six other advertisements. Subjects reported their attitudes toward the advertised brand just after exposure to the series of ads and again 2 days later. Both high and low relevance subjects had equivalent initial attitudes, but only high relevance subjects persisted in their favorability 2 days later.

---

[8]Downing conducted a second study in which both completed and interrupted transmitters had an equivalent 15-minute delay before transmission. The results were the same in that interrupted transmitters showed attitude change persistence but completed transmitters did not.

[9]At least one other study has examined the persistence of attitude changes without confounding the elaboration manipulation with task completion. Chaiken and Eagly (1983) hypothesized that a written communication would elicit greater message elaboration than one presented on video or audiotape and as a result, attitude change in response to a written message should show greater temporal persistence than change produced in the other modalities. Differential persistence in the different modalities was not reliable in this research, however. Perhaps the persistence predictions were not supported because the modality manipulation did not produce clear differences in the extent of initial message content elaboration. Because there is no clear evidence that the modality of message presentation influences the extent of substantive message thinking from this or other studies, we focus on research varying the personal relevance of the message because this manipulation has been associated with differences in elaboration and message-based persuasion in several investigations.

In another study, Petty, Haugtvedt, Heesacker, and Cacioppo (1995, Experiment 1) varied the personal relevance of a message on the topic of instituting comprehensive exams for college seniors by telling some subjects just prior to the message presentation that the exam policy was being proposed for their own university (high relevance) or for a distant university (low relevance). One of two messages was presented. The "positive" message was attributed to a prestigious and credible source and presented six strong arguments in favor of the proposal. A second "negative" message was attributed to a low prestige, nonexpert source and contained six weak arguments in favor of the exams. This message was designed to produce a boomerang effect—attitude change away from the position advocated. Subjects reported their attitudes toward the exam proposal right after exposure to the message and again about 2 weeks later. A control group simply reported their attitudes on the topic at each time interval. The results for this study are presented in Fig. 5.1.

As shown in the figure, high relevance subjects showed only a main effect for message type. That is, the positive message led to more persuasion at both the initial and the delayed testing than did the negative message. This was expected because the high relevance subjects should have processed the substantive message arguments and persisted in the favorable and unfavorable attitudes that resulted from their message processing. However, for low relevance subjects, the effectiveness of the communications decayed over time. That is, although low relevance subjects were more favorable toward the positive than the negative message initially—just like the high relevance subjects—this difference was absent after 2 weeks. This was expected because the low relevance subjects should have been influenced mostly by the favorable or unfavorable cues in the message and these peripheral route attitudes should decay over time.

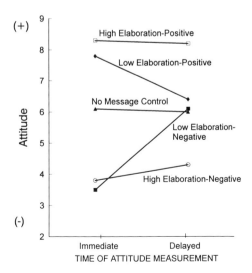

FIG. 5.1. Persistence of attitude change as a function of valence of message and extent of elaboration (as induced by varying issue-relevance). The positive message contained strong arguments and favorable source cues and the negative message contained weak arguments and unfavorable source cues (data from Petty, Haugtvedt, Heesacker, & Cacioppo, 1995, Experiment 1).

Summary

The studies attempting to test explicitly the hypothesis that attitude change persistence is enhanced in conditions where persuasion is associated with effortful message elaboration have provided reasonably good support for it. When attitude change was produced under high elaboration conditions, these changes persisted to a greater extent than the same attitude changes produced under low elaboration conditions. This differential persistence was observed whether the initial change was in the direction advocated by the speaker or in a direction opposite to that advocated.

One issue that warrants further investigation, however, is whether thinking about the message during message presentation is sufficient for persistence, or whether thinking about the message following exposure is necessary. The notion that postmessage thinking might be necessary for persistence is most plausible for studies in which subjects had a specific reason to continue thinking about the topic (e.g., they would be interviewed later on the topic; Chaiken, 1980; or felt tension over an uncompleted task; Boninger et al., 1990). However, even though research clearly demonstrates that being high in need for cognition or exposure to messages on topics of high personal relevance induces greater thinking *during* message exposure than being low in need for cognition or receiving a message on a topic of low personal relevance, it is possible that these situations also induce greater postmessage thought as well.

Because of this, the accumulated studies on the persistence of attitude changes, though suggestive, do not provide unequivocal support for the notion that elaboration during message presentation is responsible for creating strong attitudes. One solution to this problem is to investigate a strength consequence that does not require a delay period so that there would be little time for additional thinking following the message. The resistance paradigm allows for this. That is, in testing a newly changed attitude for its resistance to change, one can subject the new attitude to attack shortly after it is created. A similar case can be made for examining the ability of attitudes to predict behavior. Thus, we turn to these strength consequences next.[10]

CREATING RESISTANT ATTITUDES

In addition to temporal persistence, a second characteristic of strong attitudes is their tendency to be resistant to attacks. Strong attitudes would be expected to change less in the direction of an attacking message than weak attitudes, and strong

---

[10]Another possible solution to the problem would be to measure thoughts at the time of message exposure for high versus low elaboration subjects and conduct mediational analyses. However, it seems likely that requiring low elaboration subjects to generate thoughts at the time of message exposure could modify the natural levels of elaboration that would occur. This induced elaboration could produce the very strength consequences that are under study.

attitudes would require a more vigorous attack than would weak attitudes in order to produce a given amount of change. Although persistence and resistance would commonly co-occur, the resistance and persistence consequences of attitude strength can be separated conceptually and empirically. That is, some attitudes are highly persistent only if they are not challenged. For example, cultural truisms such as "you should get 8 hours of sleep per night," tend to be persistent but not resistant (McGuire, 1964). Also, it is possible for some attitudes to be very resistant to change, but only in the short term. For example, as a result of reactance pressures, an attitude might be momentarily resistant even though it is not very persistent (Brehm, 1966).

As was the case with research on persistence, much of the previous literature has examined existing qualities of attitudes that render them resistant to influence. For example, as documented in other chapters in this volume, attitudes that are important (Boninger et al., ch. 7, this volume), based on extensive knowledge (e.g., Wood et al., ch. 11, this volume), accessible (Fazio, ch. 10, this volume), or structurally consistent (Eagly & Chaiken, ch. 16, this volume), are more resistant to attempts to change them.

A second category of studies has examined how to make existing attitudes more resistant to change. Perhaps the most well-known studies on attitude bolstering are McGuire's (1964) experiments on inoculation theory. McGuire exposed people to weak versions of messages attacking their views to encourage them to develop defenses against future attacks on their attitudes. McGuire's work focused on convincing individuals that their attitudes might be vulnerable to attack and examining different "pretreatments" that would decrease the susceptibility of the attitude. Results of studies inspired by McGuire's perspective have been generally supportive of his view that getting people to think about the strengths and weaknesses of their attitudes prior to an attack makes them more resistant (Adams & Beatty, 1977; Burgoon, Cohen, Miller, & Montgomery, 1978; Pfau & Burgoon, 1988; Suedfeld & Borrie, 1978; Szybillo & Heslin, 1973).

Still other investigators have shown that getting people to think about the underlying basis of their attitudes prior to an attack can increase resistance. Among the manipulations that have been shown to be effective in increasing thought prior to an attacking message and thereby increasing resistance are: (a) providing a forewarning of the topic and position of an impending counterattitudinal advocacy on an involving topic (e.g., Freedman & Sears, 1965, Hass & Grady, 1975; McGuire & Papageorgis, 1962; Petty & Cacioppo, 1977), (b) encouraging people to think about their past behaviors relevant to the attitude (e.g., Ross, McFarland, Conway, & Zanna, 1983), and (c) having subjects think about how their attitudes are related to important values they possess (e.g., Ostrom & Brock, 1968). Each of these manipulations uses thinking to strengthen the link between the attitude and the underlying supportive beliefs, values, and behaviors, and thereby makes it more resistant to change.

Our goal in this chapter, however, is to examine the question of whether attitudes that are newly changed as a result of issue-relevant elaboration are more resistant to subsequent attacks than are comparable attitudes that are newly changed as a result of peripheral route processes. Below, we review studies that have provided evidence pertinent to this *elaboration-resistance hypothesis.*[11]

Examination of the Elaboration-Resistance Hypothesis in the Belief Perseverance Paradigm

One line of research relevant to the elaboration-resistance hypothesis concerns the phenomenon of belief perseverance. Belief perseverance refers to the tendency of individuals to maintain newly created beliefs in the face of subsequent contrary information. The general paradigm used in the belief perseverance work involves creating an initial belief about oneself (Ross, Lepper, & Hubbard, 1975, Experiment 1), another person (Ross et al., 1975, Experiment 2), or about the relationship between two variables such as "preferring risk" and "being a good firefighter" (Anderson, Lepper, & Ross, 1980). In a typical study, following the initial belief creation phase, individuals are then told that the information on which their new belief is based is fictitious. Yet, despite this "debriefing," individuals tend to maintain the initial belief.

According to the elaboration-resistance hypothesis, people whose initial beliefs are based on considerable thought should be especially resistant to the debriefing message. In a study relevant to this idea, Anderson et al. (1980, Experiment 2) first exposed subjects to information suggesting a positive link between risky behavior and firefighting success or a negative relationship between these two variables. Prior to the debriefing message (which indicated that the data they had processed were false), subjects in the high elaboration condition were asked to write an explanation of the relationships they observed. Writing such an expla- nation would require that people think carefully about the informational basis of their new belief. Subjects in the low elaboration condition received the debriefing without being asked to explain the relationship. Following the debriefing, sub- jects' own beliefs about the relationship between riskiness and firefighting success were assessed. These judgments were compared to a control group in which subjects provided their beliefs prior to the debriefing. The control subjects were not asked to write an explanation of the relationship observed and thus provide a good low elaboration control group for the low elaboration debriefing group.

The control subjects showed that in the absence of debriefing, the relevant beliefs were formed. That is, subjects exposed to the positive relationship data

---

[11]We do not consider studies where there is no evidence that resistance is related to a variable known to influence elaboration processes. Nevertheless, some of this research is suggestive. For example, consider the consequences of attitudes formed as a result of personal experience with an object versus attitudes formed via passive exposure to third-party information. To the extent that information gleaned from personal experience is likely to be thought about more than information from third parties, attitudes changed as a result of personal experience should be more resistant to change than attitudes changed as a result of passive information exposure. This is in fact the case (see Wu & Shaffer, 1987).

believed that risky responses were indicative of firefighting success, whereas those exposed to the negative relationship data believed the opposite. Of greater interest is what happened in the two debriefing conditions where the informational basis of subjects' initial beliefs were challenged. Subjects in the low elaboration debriefing condition were still significantly influenced by the data they had processed even after they were told that it was false (i.e., the belief perseverance effect was obtained), though their beliefs were not as strong as those in the no-debriefing control condition. Subjects in the high elaboration debriefing condition, however, maintained their initial beliefs to a greater extent than did subjects in the low elaboration debriefing condition. That is, subjects who were instructed to write an explanation for (i.e., think about) the initial data appeared to be more resistant to the debriefing message—consistent with the elaboration-resistance hypothesis. Another explanation is possible, however, because this study failed to include a high elaboration no-debriefing control group. Because of this, it is possible that the elaboration induction caused high elaboration subjects to form more extreme *initial* beliefs than low elaboration subjects. If so, the difference in beliefs observed after debriefing could have been due not to differential resistance, but to extremity differences that were present prior to debriefing. So, although this study is consistent with the elaboration-resistance hypothesis, more confidence would come from research in which it was clear that the high and low elaboration groups had equivalent beliefs prior to presentation of the undermining communication.[12]

Examination of the Elaboration-Resistance Hypothesis in Persuasion Paradigms

Research using a more traditional attitude change paradigm has solved the problem of differential initial beliefs. In one relevant study, Haugtvedt and Petty (1992) provided subjects who were high or low in need for cognition with an initial message about the safety of a well-known food additive. This initial message contained strong arguments from an expert source and was followed by an opposing message containing weaker arguments from a different expert source. Although both high and low need for cognition individuals were persuaded equally by the initial message, the attitudes of the high need for cognition participants were more resistant to the attacking message (see top panel of Fig. 5.2).

In another study, Petty, Haugtvedt, Heesacker, and Cacioppo (1995, Experiment 2) presented two groups of university students with a message containing

---

[12]In some research on belief perseverance attempting to examine the mediation of the resistance effect, peoples' thoughts about the critical issue have been assessed *after* the discrediting information is presented (e.g., Anderson, New, & Speer, 1985; Davies, 1993). This research has shown that the more a person's thoughts favor their initial beliefs, the more they resist the discrediting information. Because subjects' thoughts are assessed following the attacking message, however, this research does not allow one to determine the extent to which the initial beliefs are based on thought, and whether thoughtful initial beliefs are more resistant to change than nonthoughtful ones.

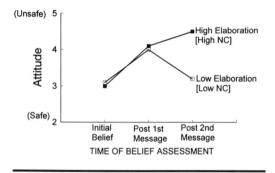

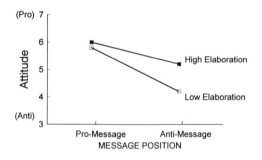

FIG. 5.2.   Resistance of attitudes to attack as a function of extent of elaboration of the initial attitude. In the top panel, elaboration is assessed with the need for cognition scale (data from Haugtvedt & Petty, 1992). In the bottom panel, elaboration is manipulated by varying issue-relevance and distraction (data from Petty et al., 1995, Experiment 2).

seven strong arguments in favor of requiring comprehensive exams as a requirement for graduation. Importantly, the message was also attributed to three college professors from Cornell, Purdue, and UCLA. Half of the subjects were relatively unmotivated to think about the message carefully because they were told that the exam policy was being proposed for a distant university. The experiment also made it somewhat difficult for these subjects to process the message because they were required to engage in a distracting secondary task while being exposed to the communication. The other half of the subjects were considerably more motivated and able to think about the communication because they were told that the proposal was being considered for their own university and the distraction task was made much easier to perform.

Following the initial pro-exam message, subjects reported their attitudes on the topic of senior comprehensive exams. After an irrelevant communication and an attitude assessment on this issue, subjects heard an anti-exam communication. This communication was attributed to a professor at Harvard University and contained somewhat weaker arguments than in the initial exam message. Following this message, subjects once again reported their attitudes on the exam topic. A no-message control condition was included in this study to ensure that subjects showed equivalent changes to the initial pro-exam message.

The attitude results (see bottom panel of Fig. 5.2) revealed a main effect for message direction—people were more favorable toward the exams immediately following the pro- than the anti-exam message. More importantly, an Elaboration X Message interaction revealed that even though high and low elaboration subjects showed similar positive attitudes following the initial pro-exam message, high elaboration subjects were more resistant to the counterpropaganda message than were the low elaboration subjects. High elaboration subjects presumably resisted the second message because their careful analysis of the first message motivated or enabled them to counterargue the second one. Low elaboration subjects presumably succumbed to the second message because they were less motivated or able to defend their new attitudes.

The elaboration-resistance hypothesis suggests that given two equally strong (e.g., compelling arguments and positive cues) but opposite messages, people who think carefully about the first message will be more resistant to the second than people who think relatively little about the first message. Having thought about the initial position carefully not only enables people to bolster their initial attitudes and counterargue an opposing message, but likely gives them the motivational confidence to do so. However, in the tests of the elaboration-resistance hypothesis so far, researchers have used weaker arguments in the second message than in the first. A more stringent test of the hypothesis would come from research in which both the initial and the counter messages were equated in strength. A study by Haugtvedt and Wegener (1994) provided such a test.

Specifically, Haugtvedt and Wegener (1994) developed two messages of equal strength—one in favor of a position, and one opposed to it. The pro and anti messages were developed to contain strong arguments that when considered in isolation elicited the same preponderance of favorable to unfavorable thoughts. Some subjects received the pro–con order of messages, whereas others received the con–pro order. Attitudes were assessed following both messages in order to determine whether attitudes were more favorable toward the initial message (a *primacy effect* indicating relative resistance to the second message), or whether attitudes were more favorable toward the second communication (a *recency effect* indicating lack of resistance). Two separate experiments were conducted. In addition to varying the order of message presentation in each study, they also varied the personal relevance of the communication. In the first study, the relevance of a proposal to institute comprehensive exams for college seniors was manipulated by varying whether the students' own school or a distant university was considering implementation. In the second study, the relevance of a message on nuclear power plants was varied by indicating that the federal government had recommended that new plants be built in the students' own state and surrounding states (high relevance) or in distant states (low relevance). The relevance manipulation, of course, varies the recipients' motivation to think about the messages (Petty & Cacioppo, 1979).

In both studies, participants who encountered the messages under the high elaboration (high relevance) conditions were more influenced by the first than the second message (i.e., a primacy effect). Participants exposed to the messages under low elaboration (low relevance) conditions, however, were more influenced by the second than the first message. These results held regardless of whether the first message was the pro or anti communication. That is, consistent with the elaboration-resistance hypothesis, participants who processed the first message under high relevance conditions showed greater resistance to the second communication than individuals who processed the first message under low relevance conditions.[13]

Summary

The studies explicitly examining the hypothesis that attitude change resistance is enhanced in conditions where initial persuasion is associated with effortful message elaboration have provided consistent support for it. It is important to note that the studies on the resistance of attitude changes address an issue that remained open at the end of our review of studies on the persistence of persuasion. This issue concerned whether effortfully thinking about and elaborating a message during its presentation is sufficient to produce a strong attitude, or whether some thinking about the message following initial exposure is necessary. In studies on attitude resistance, the strength of a newly formed or changed attitude is tested immediately, not days or weeks later as in the persistence paradigm. Yet, the results of the persistence and resistance studies are conceptually identical. For example, just as attitudes formed by people high in need for cognition or in situations of high personal relevance persist over time, attitudes formed by people high in need for cognition or in situations of high personal relevance show resistance to an immediately attacking communication. The research on resistance therefore bolsters the notion that the extent of message elaboration during exposure to the communication is an important determinant of the strength of newly changed attitudes.

CREATING ATTITUDES THAT PREDICT BEHAVIOR

So far, we have argued that understanding the extent of elaboration at the time of attitude change is important for understanding whether a newly changed attitude

---

[13]The elaboration-resistance prediction for message order (i.e., more primacy with greater elaboration of the first message) assumes that the two messages are generally equivalent and processed under similar elaboration conditions. However, if the second message contained much less favorable cues than the first message, then low elaboration subjects would be less likely to show recency because they would be negatively influenced by the unfavorable cues in the second message (Haugtvedt, Wegener, & Warren, 1994). Also, if the arguments in the second message are made much weaker than those in the first message, recency effects would become less likely especially if the elaboration conditions were enhanced between the first and second messages.

will persist over time and be resistant to countervailing messages. Is elaboration also important for understanding whether a new attitude will predict behavior?

In 1964, Festinger provided an early review of research examining the relationship between attitude change and behavior change. At that time he only was able to cite three studies, none of which was designed deliberately to assess this relationship, but also none of which indicated that attitude change translated into behavior change. Unfortunately, little has changed since Festinger's early review. Although a very large body of research has accumulated on the extent to which existing attitudes predict behavior, there is still minimal research in which investigators examine the ability of newly changed attitudes to predict behavior, and even less research where attitudes changed by different processes are compared in their abilities to predict behavior.[14]

Prediction of Behavior From Existing Attitudes

As just noted, most studies of attitude-behavior consistency look at the ability of pre-existing attitudes to predict behavior (see Ajzen, 1988). In a typical study, attitudes, behaviors, and some moderator variable are measured. Studies examining characteristics of the attitudes themselves as well as the people holding the attitudes have been explored and have provided support for the *elaboration-consistency hypothesis* that attitudes formed as a result of issue-relevant thinking are more predictive of behavior than attitudes formed as a result of more peripheral processes. For example, studies have shown that attitudes on policy issues that people consider important predict their voting behavior better than attitudes on unimportant policy issues (e.g., Krosnick, 1988; Schuman & Presser, 1981). To the extent that people have thought about important issues more than unimportant ones (Petty & Cacioppo, 1979; see also Boninger et al., ch. 7, this volume; Crano, ch. 6, this volume; Thomsen et al., ch. 8, this volume), these findings are consistent with the elaboration-consistency hypothesis. Other qualities of attitudes such as accessibility (e.g., Fazio, Powell & Herr, 1983; see Fazio, ch. 10, this volume), knowledge (e.g., Kallgren & Wood, 1986; see Wood et al., ch. 11, this

---

[14]One notable exception is Wilson's program of research on the effects of analyzing reasons on attitude-behavior consistency (see Wilson, Dunn, Kraft, & Lisle, 1989, see Erber, Hodges, & Wilson, ch. 17, this volume). In this research, no persuasive message is presented but participants are simply told to analyze *why* they feel the way they do about some attitude object. The primary conclusion of this research is that if thinking about one's attitude causes a momentary change in attitude because a different set of factors is salient than is normally the case (e.g., the attitude is normally determined by emotional factors but due to the analyzing reasons manipulation the attitude expressed reflects mostly cognitive factors), the new attitude will be less predictive of subsequent behavior than the old one. Presumably if attitude changes that were produced by comprehensive thinking (i.e., considering both the cognitive and emotional factors relevant to the topic) versus focused thinking (i.e., considering only the negative or emotional factors relevant to any issue) were compared, the former attitudes would be more predictive of behavior than the latter ones, but this has not been examined.

volume), affective-cognitive consistency (e.g., Norman, 1975; see Chaiken et al., ch. 15, this volume), and extremity (e.g., Petersen & Dutton, 1975; see Abelson, ch. 2, this volume, Judd & Brauer, ch. 3, this volume) also moderate attitude-behavior consistency and provide support for the elaboration-consistency hypothesis to the extent that all of these variables are plausibly associated with issue-relevant elaboration.

More directly relevant to the elaboration-consistency hypothesis are studies that have examined differences in attitude-behavior consistency for individuals who have thought much versus relatively little about their attitudes. For example, Brown (1974) assessed the attitudes of high school students toward breaking various laws such as using drugs, obeying traffic laws, and so forth. He also measured self-reported compliance with these laws and found greater attitude-behavior consistency for students who reported much, rather than little, thinking about the law. Research on need for cognition (Cacioppo & Petty, 1982) has also supported this proposition. For example, Cacioppo, Petty, Kao, and Rodriguez (1986) found that the attitudes toward the presidential candidates of individuals high in need for cognition were more predictive of their votes than the attitudes of individuals low in need for cognition.

Other individual differences might also be relevant. For example, the attitudes of low self-monitors (Snyder, 1974) are more predictive of behavior than the attitudes of high self-monitors (e.g., Snyder & Swann, 1976; Zanna, Olson, & Fazio, 1980). Given that low self-monitors also tend to be more attentive to the quality of the arguments supporting an advocacy whereas high self-monitors are more concerned about image (e.g., Snyder & DeBono, 1987), differences in the extent of information processing activity may be responsible for this difference. Also, Rholes and Bailey (1983) found that people using higher levels of moral reasoning (Kohlberg, 1958) showed higher attitude-behavior consistency. To the extent that higher levels of moral reasoning correspond to higher levels of attitudinal elaboration, this supports the elaboration-consistency hypothesis. It has also been shown that individuals who assume greater responsibility for their acts are more likely to engage in attitude-consistent behavior (e.g., Ferrari & Leippe, 1992; Schwartz, 1973). Because personal responsibility is associated with elaboration (e.g., Petty et al., 1980), this result is also consistent with the elaboration-consistency hypothesis.

Prediction of Behavior From Newly Changed Attitudes

Although the studies on existing attitudes are suggestive, more confident conclusions could be drawn from research in which new attitudes are created by thoughtful or nonthoughtful means and attitude-behavior consistency assessed. As noted previously, increasing the personal relevance of a persuasive message has been shown to enhance message elaboration. Several studies have manipulated or measured the personal relevance of a communication, measured postcommunication attitudes, and examined attitude-behavior consistency.[15]

In one pertinent study (Sivacek and Crano, 1982; Experiment 2), undergraduate subjects were informed that their university was exploring the possibility of implementing senior comprehensive exams and they then read a message describing these exams. Following message exposure, subjects were given the opportunity to sign petitions opposing the exams and to volunteer their services to a group that opposed the exams. Sivacek and Crano divided their sample into high, moderate, and low relevance groups on the basis of subjects' self-reports of whether the issue was of high or low personal relevance (i.e., would affect them or not). Correlations between subjects' attitudes toward senior comprehensive exams and the relevant petition-signing/volunteering behaviors were largest in the high relevance group. Thus, subjects for whom the message was more personally relevant demonstrated higher attitude-behavior consistency than subjects who considered the message less relevant. If subjects in the high relevance group engaged in greater issue-relevant thought during exposure to the persuasive communication than subjects in the other groups (as would be expected based on numerous studies), this research supports the elaboration-consistency hypothesis (see also, Crano, ch. 6, this volume).

In another study, Petty, Cacioppo, and Schumann (1983) exposed subjects to an advertisement for a consumer product under high or low relevance conditions. The product was endorsed either by a relatively likable or a neutral endorser and contained either strong or weak arguments in support of the product. In the high relevance conditions, subjects read the advertisement after being led to believe that the product would soon be available in their local area and that they would soon have to make a decision about the product category. In the low relevance conditions, subjects read the same ad after being led to believe that the product would not be available in their local area and that they would soon have to make a decision about a different product category. Importantly, the attitudes of the high relevance subjects were more predictive of their intentions to purchase the product ($r = .59$) than were the attitudes of low relevance subjects ($r = .36$; $p < .07$). Although the data would be more convincing if actual product purchases were examined, considerable research shows that behavioral intentions are very highly correlated with actual behavior (see Ajzen & Fishbein, 1980).

In another study using an advertising message, Shavitt and Brock (1986) either instructed subjects to relate a detergent ad to their own experiences (high self-

---

[15]Research on direct experience might also be relevant to the elaboration-consistency hypothesis. Considerable research shows that attitudes newly changed as a result of direct experience are more predictive of behavior than attitudes that are changed as a result of exposure to third-party information (see Fazio & Zanna, 1981). This could be because direct experience increases personal involvement with an issue over indirect experience thereby increasing elaboration of the issue-relevant material presented.

relevance), to try to remember as much of the ad as possible, or they were given no processing instructions. When the subjects returned a week later and were asked to choose a free detergent sample, the attitudes of individuals in the self-relevance condition were more predictive of their product choices than were the attitudes of other subjects. That is, when attitudes toward the products were formed under high elaboration conditions, these attitudes were more predictive of behavior than attitudes formed under the low elaboration conditions.

Leippe and Elkin (1987) also studied the effects of self-relevance on attitude-behavior consistency. In their study, subjects listened to messages on the issue of either senior comprehensive exams or a campus parking fee. To vary the extent of thinking about the message they received, subjects were led to believe that the issue was either highly relevant or irrelevant to their personal lives (Petty & Cacioppo, 1979). As a measure of behavior, Leippe and Elkin had subjects privately write essays on whichever side of the issue they wanted. The attitudes of subjects in the high relevance conditions were more predictive of the content of the essays they wrote than were the attitudes of subjects in the low relevance conditions. That is, the essays subjects wrote more closely mirrored their post-message attitudes when their attitudes toward the topic were formed as a result of high amounts of thinking about the persuasive communication.[16]

Summary

The few studies relevant to the elaboration-consistency hypothesis have provided support for it. That is, when existing attitudes were likely to have been formed as a result of high rather than low amounts of issue-relevant thinking, the attitudes have been better predictors of behavior. This result has occurred when thinking was likely because the individuals under study liked to think (Cacioppo et al., 1986), or the attitudes were on important topics (Krosnick, 1988), or people directly reported having thought about the issues (Brown, 1974). In studies where the ability of newly changed attitudes to predict behavior were examined, the results were the same. The more the newly changed attitudes were likely to be based on issue-relevant thinking, the more they predicted behavior. That is, when subjects were made more inclined to elaborate messages, either because they were instructed to make self-relevant connections (Shavitt & Brock, 1986), or because situational factors such as increased personal relevance (Leippe & Elkin, 1987; Petty et al., 1983; Sivacek & Crano, 1982) compelled them to think about the messages, the resulting attitudes were more highly associated with subsequent behavior toward the attitude object. As was the case with the studies on resistance, these effects were often observable immediately after message exposure. This

---

[16]Leippe and Elkin also manipulated whether subjects expected to discuss the message later ("response involvement"). High response involvement did not enhance message elaboration as assessed by subjects' receptivity to message quality. Thus, not surprisingly, this manipulation did not enhance attitude-behavior consistency.

reinforces the view that variations in thinking during message exposure are sufficient to induce variations in attitude strength.

WHY DOES ELABORATION INCREASE ATTITUDE STRENGTH?

We have argued that when a new attitude is created as a result of considerable issue-relevant thinking, this attitude is stronger than when a new attitude is created by processes requiring little issue-relevant thought. But why is this the case? In explicating the ELM, Petty and Cacioppo (1986a) argued that:

> the process of elaborating issue-relevant arguments involves accessing the schema for the attitude object in order to evaluate each new argument. . . . Under the peripheral route, however, the schema may be accessed only once to incorporate the affect or inference elicited by a salient cue. . . . Under the central route then, the issue-relevant attitude schema may be accessed, rehearsed, and manipulated more times, strengthening the interconnections among the components and rendering the schema more internally consistent, accessible, enduring, and resistant than under the peripheral route. . . . The greater the organization and accessibility of attitudes and attitude-relevant information for persuasion occurring via the central than the peripheral route render people more able to report the same attitude over time, to defend their beliefs, and to act on them. . . . Changes induced under the central route may be accompanied by the subjective perception that considerable thought accompanied opinion formation. This perception may induce more confidence in the attitude, and attitudes held with more confidence may be more likely to be reported over time, to be slower to be abandoned in the face of counter-propaganda, and to be more likely to be acted upon. (p. 22)

These ideas are depicted in Fig. 5.3. That is, according to the ELM, various *antecedent variables* such as need for cognition, personal relevance, issue importance, distraction, and others, influence the extent to which a person is motivated and able to engage in thinking about the issue and the persuasive communication (i.e., *elaboration*). The more attitude change is the result of careful thinking about the merits of the advocacy, the more persistent, resistant, and predictive of behavior the resulting attitude will be. Thus the ELM provides an integrative framework for understanding the *strength consequences* of a wide variety of variables examined in work on attitudes and persuasion. In this chapter we have reviewed various studies that have provided evidence for one or another of the links in the *antecedent variable → elaboration → strength consequence* causal chain.

However, hardly any research has addressed what it is about elaboration that conveys strength properties to newly changed attitudes, or how elaboration conveys strength. For example, is strength produced by elaboration because the greater the issue-relevant thinking, the greater the likelihood that the attitude, beliefs, and knowledge relevant to the attitude become accessible, and the more accessible the attitude, the more it persists, resists and predicts behavior? Or, does elaboration facilitate construction of an attitude schema that is coherent, organized, consistent, and linked to other relevant attitudes, beliefs, and values? Or, does elaboration enhance a person's sense of confidence in the attitude, or its importance, and these constructs are responsible for strength?

Independence of the Strength Consequences

The model in Fig. 5.3 might appear to suggest that the various strength consequences will invariably co-occur since each results from elaboration. However, we have already noted that the strength consequences can be independent. One reason for this is that it is presumably possible to produce the strength consequences and the potential mediating processes such as accessibility in ways other than by varying the extent of thinking. For example, Petty and Cacioppo (1986a) noted that repeatedly pairing peripheral cues with an attitude object could produce an accessible attitude that is relatively persistent. However, individuals with these peripherally based persistent attitudes would still likely be susceptible to counterpersuasion because they would presumably have difficulty mounting a defense of their attitudes if they were attacked with strong arguments.

In a demonstration of the potential independence of attitude persistence and resistance, Haugtvedt, Schumann, Schneier, and Warren (1994) presented one group of participants with an advertising campaign for a consumer product in which the substantive message arguments for the campaign were varied across multiple exposures of the ads. Another group of participants was presented with a campaign in which the ads were varied cosmetically (e.g., different endorsers in each ad), but not in the substantive arguments they presented. That is, the substantive variation strategy involved keeping the peripheral source cues constant across exposures, but presenting different arguments in each ad. The cosmetic variation strategy involved keeping the arguments the same across ad

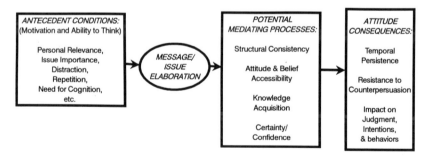

FIG. 5.3. The Elaboration Likelihood Model of attitude strength with potential mediating processes.

exposures, but varying the positive cues contained in the advertisements (see Schumann, Petty, & Clemons, 1990). Substantive variation strategies would be expected to encourage attitude formation via the central route whereas cosmetic variations would encourage attitude formation via the peripheral route.

Previous research comparing central and peripheral routes to persuasion has typically involved a single exposure to a message containing multiple arguments but just one salient cue. Haugtvedt et al. (1994) noted that such research may have provided central route participants with memorial advantages (e.g., multiple retrieval cues) over peripheral route participants. However, if subjects were presented with multiple peripheral cues (cosmetic variation strategy), or if a single cue was repeated multiple times, attitude persistence might be comparable and greater than that obtained in a control condition in which there was just one exposure to an ad. Consistent with this hypothesis, Haugtvedt et al. (1994) found that subjects receiving three exposures of the substantively varied ads, the cosmetically varied ads, or three exposures to a single ad showed greater persistence in attitude change over a 1-week period than subjects who received just one exposure. That is, by the persistence criterion, each of the repetition conditions produced equivalently more favorable attitudes than the single exposure control 1 week after message presentation.

What about resistance? To assess this, after completing the delayed attitude measure, subjects were presented with a message that attacked the product presented in the critical advertisements. On the attitude measure taken after the attacking message, subjects who had received the substantively varied ads showed greater resistance than subjects in any of the other groups. Thus even though the repetition strategies were equally effective in enhancing persistence over one week compared to the single exposure control condition, the different repetition strategies were not equally effective in inducing resistance. Specifically, the attitudes based on exposure to substantively varied ads were more resistant in the face of attack than were the attitudes resulting from the other repetition strategies. That is, repetition and variation of peripheral cues was useful for increasing persistence, but was ineffective in increasing resistance.[17]

Elaboration, Mediation, and Strength

In our review of the elaboration-strength hypothesis, we focused on research showing that when attitudes were changed under conditions that were documented to foster issue-relevant elaboration (e.g., high personal relevance), the attitudes

---

[17]It is also important to note that Fig. 5.3 implies that even if elaboration occurs, the strength consequences will not necessarily follow if one or more of the mediating processes are not induced. For example, it is possible that a person thinking extensively about a message could change in the direction of the advocacy, but become more confused and unconfident than a person relying on an expert source. To the extent that this is true, the model holds that the postulated strength consequences would not hold since the postulated mediating processes are not evident. As noted in the text however, it is not yet clear which of these potential mediating processes are crucial for the strength effects.

were more likely to possess one of the strength consequences than when attitudes were changed under conditions that did not encourage elaboration (i.e., peripheral route change). We devoted little attention to the various processes that might mediate the effects of elaboration on a strength consequence because we were unable to locate a single study that examined all of the steps in the causal chain outlined in Fig. 5.3. Nevertheless, the research we have reviewed above has examined various portions of the causal chain.

One critical link in this chain that we have ignored to this point is whether attitudes changed via elaboration are more likely to be associated with the postulated mediating processes than attitudes changed via peripheral processes. Research on this question is just beginning. For example, in one study Petty, Haugtvedt, and Rennier (1995) examined whether attitudes changed as a result of message elaboration are more accessible than attitudes changed as a result of less effortful peripheral cue processes. To study this, subjects listened to four different messages. Prior to message exposure, the participants were told that their university president had formed two planning committees. One committee was planning for the present and would recommend changes to take effect soon (high relevance), and the other committee was planning for the distant future and was recommending changes that would have no impact on current students (low relevance). The subjects were further told that each committee had solicited ideas from other individuals and groups and that they would hear two suggestions that were made to each of the committees. One of the two suggestions for each committee was presented by a credible source and contained strong arguments in support of the proposal (positive message). The other suggestion for each committee was presented by a low status source and contained weak arguments in support of the proposal (negative message). Based on past research using the personal relevance manipulation, it was expected that high relevance subjects would form their attitudes based on the arguments that were presented, but low relevance subjects would form their attitudes based mostly on the source cues (e.g., Petty, Cacioppo, & Goldman, 1981). Following the message presentation, subjects expressed their attitudes toward each suggestion, and reaction time was assessed. Although high and low relevance subjects formed the same attitudes toward the issues, these new attitudes were expressed more quickly for the high than the low relevance issues. Thus, this study suggests that attitudes formed as a result of issue-relevant cognitive activity are more accessible than attitudes formed in response to peripheral cues.[18]

---

[18]Additional and less direct evidence for the view that elaboration is associated with accessible attitudes comes from work showing that high need for cognition individuals express attitudes more quickly than low need for cognition individuals (Ahlering & Parker, 1989), and from work showing that attitudes toward important issues are expressed more quickly than attitudes toward unimportant issues (Krosnick, 1989). This research is less direct because measured need for cognition and measured importance can tap factors (e.g., knowledge) other than the extent of elaboration.

In addition to suggesting that elaboration should influence one or more of the potential mediating processes, Fig. 5.3 also suggests that manipulating the mediating processes directly should produce strong attitudes. For example, Fazio, Zanna, Ross, and Powell (1992, cited in Zanna, Fazio, & Ross, 1994) investigated whether a manipulation of attitude accessibility could produce more persistent attitudes. In their study, following exposure to a persuasive message, subjects in the high attitude accessibility condition were asked to report their attitudes toward the topic on five different attitude scales. Subjects in the low attitude accessibility condition reported their attitude on only one scale. Subjects in the control condition reported their attitude on one scale after listening to an irrelevant message. After 2 or 3 months, all subjects' attitudes were reassessed in a telephone poll. The high accessibility group showed less decay than the low accessibility group. In fact, even though both high and low accessibility groups were equivalently more favorable toward the issue than controls at the initial testing, only the high accessibility group was more favorable than controls at the delayed testing.

In another study, Petty (1977) examined whether belief rather than attitude accessibility could produce more persistent attitudes. In the relevant conditions of this experiment, subjects were exposed to five strong arguments in favor of raising the driving age and were asked to list five thoughts about these arguments. Then, subjects were asked to continually rehearse either the arguments (argument accessibility) or their thoughts (belief accessibility) to themselves until they memorized them. Attitudes were assessed immediately after the accessibility task and again 1 week later. Although both the argument and belief accessibility groups had more favorable attitudes toward raising the driving age than no-message controls, only the group whose own beliefs were made accessible showed persistence of this attitude the following week.

Thus, both attitude and belief accessibility enhance the persistence of attitude change. However, it is unclear whether these studies have produced a strength consequence in the absence of differential elaboration, or whether the manipulations of attitude and belief accessibility might have induced differential issue-relevant thinking. For example, as students completed each new attitude scale in the research by Fazio et al. (1992), they might have engaged in additional issue-relevant thinking as might have subjects as they rehearsed each of their own beliefs in the research by Petty (1977).

Directions for Future Research

The ELM states that the extent of elaboration mediates the impact of various antecedent variables (e.g., personal relevance) on various strength consequences (e.g., attitude persistence). Figure 5.3 further suggests that other variables (e.g., attitude accessibility) might provide a more proximal mediation of the impact of elaboration on the strength consequences. Because research to date has examined only a few of the links in the full causal chain outlined in Fig. 5.3, it is not yet clear which of the proximal mediating processes (if any) are necessary for the postulated strength consequences of elaboration, which are sufficient, which are neither necessary nor sufficient, and which are both necessary and sufficient.

Thus several interesting issues await additional research. First, will some of the proximal mediating processes be more important than others in accounting for all strength effects for all antecedent variables? For example, might attitude accessibility generally account for more variance in strength than belief organization or any of the other potential mediators? Or, will it turn out that some proximal mediators are more important in accounting for the strength consequences of some antecedent variables than others? For example, will need for cognition effects be mediated by the effects of elaboration on belief accessibility whereas self-relevance effects are mediated by the effects of elaboration on attitude accessibility? Or, more likely, will some proximal mediators be more important in producing some strength consequences than others regardless of the antecedent variables? For example, it seems possible that attitude accessibility alone could produce persistence, but it seems unlikely to induce resistance unless the accessible attitude was also connected to supporting information that would allow counterarguing of an attacking message. Yet, belief accessibility seems capable of providing resistance in the absence of an accessible attitude. Perhaps future research will support the least appealing scenario in which each of the proximal mediators accounts for some strength effects of some antecedent variables in some circumstances. At the moment, it appears that although it may be possible to produce some of the strength consequences without inducing issue-relevant elaboration, inducing issue-relevant elaboration may be the most reliable means of inducing *all* of the consequences associated with strong attitudes.

REFERENCES

Adams, W. C., & Beatty, M. J. (1977). Dogmatism, need for social approval, and the resistance to persuasion. *Communication Monographs, 44*, 321–325.

Ahlering, R. F., & Parker, L. D. (1989, August). *Attitude accessibility and need for cognition.* Paper presented at the annual meeting of the American Psychological Association, New Orleans, LA.

Ajzen, I. (1988). *Attitudes, personality, and behavior.* Chicago: Dorsey.

Ajzen, I., & Fishbein, M. (1980). *Understanding attitudes and predicting social behavior.* Englewood Cliffs, NJ: Prentice-Hall.

Anderson, C. A., Lepper, M. R., & Ross, M. (1980). Perseverance of social theories: The role of explanation in the persistence of discredited information. *Journal of Personality and Social Psychology, 39*, 1037–1049.

Anderson, C. A., New, B. L., & Speer, J. R. (1985). Argument availability as a mediator of social theory perseverance. *Social Cognition, 3*(3), 235–249.

Apsler, R., & Sears, D. O. (1968). Warning, personal involvement, and attitude change. *Journal of Personality and Social Psychology, 9*, 162–166.

Axsom, D. Yates, S., & Chaiken, S. (1987). Audience response as a heuristic cue in persuasion. *Journal of Personality and Social Psychology, 53*, 30–40.

Baker, S. M., & Petty, R. E. (1994). Majority and minority influence: Source-position imbalance as a determinant of message scrutiny. *Journal of Personality and Social Psychology, 67*, 5–19.

Bem, D. J. (1972). Self-perception theory. In L. Berkowitz (Ed.), *Advances in experimental social psychology* (Vol. 6, pp. 1–62). New York: Academic.

Bless, H., Bohner, G., Schwarz, N., & Strack, F. (1990). Mood and persuasion: A cognitive response analysis. *Personality and Social Psychology Bulletin, 16,* 331–345.

Boninger, D. S., Brock, T. C., Cook, T. D., Gruder, C. L., & Romer, D. (1990). Discovery of a reliable attitude change persistence resulting from a transmitter tuning set. *Psychological Science, 1,* 268–271.

Brehm, J. W. (1966). *A theory of psychological reactance.* San Diego, CA: Academic.

Brock, T. C. (1967). Communication discrepancy and intent to persuade as determinants of counterargument production. *Journal of Experimental Social Psychology, 3,* 296–309.

Brown, D. (1974). Adolescent attitudes and lawful behavior. *Public Opinion Quarterly, 38,* 98–106.

Burgoon, M., Cohen, M., Miller, M. D., & Montgomery, C. L. (1978). An empirical test of a model of resistance to persuasion. *Human Communication Research, 5,* 27–39.

Burnkrant, R. E., & Howard, D. J. (1984). Effects of the use of introductory rhetorical questions versus statements on information processing. *Journal of Personality and Social Psychology, 47,* 1218–1230.

Burnkrant, R. E., & Unnava, R. (1989). Self-referencing: A strategy for increasing processing of message content. *Personality and Social Psychology Bulletin, 15,* 628–638.

Cacioppo, J. T., & Petty, R. E. (1982). The need for cognition. *Journal of Personality and Social Psychology, 42,* 116–131.

Cacioppo, J. T., & Petty, R. E. (1989). Effects of message repetition on argument processing, recall, and persuasion. *Basic and Applied Social Psychology, 10,* 3–12.

Cacioppo, J. T., Petty, R. E., Kao, C. F., & Rodriguez, R. (1986). Central and peripheral routes to persuasion: An individual difference perspective. *Journal of Personality and Social Psychology, 51,* 1032–1043.

Cacioppo, J. T. Petty, R. E., & Morris, K. J. (1983). Effects of need for cognition on message evaluation, recall, and persuasion. *Journal of Personality and Social Psychology, 45,* 805–818.

Chaiken, S. (1980). Heuristic versus systematic information processing in the use of source versus message cues in persuasion. *Journal of Personality and Social Psychology, 39,* 752–766.

Chaiken, S. (1987). The heuristic model of persuasion. In M. P. Zanna, J. M. Olson, & C. P. Herman (Eds.), *Social influence: The Ontario Symposium* (Vol. 5, pp. 3–39). Hillsdale, NJ: Lawrence Erlbaum Associates.

Chaiken, S., & Eagly, A. H. (1983). Communication modality as a determinant of persuasion: The role of communicator salience. *Journal of Personality and Social Psychology, 45,* 241–256.

Cialdini, R. B. Levy, A., Herman, C. P., Kozlowski, L. T., & Petty, R. E. (1976). Elastic shifts of opinion: Determinants of direction and durability. *Journal of Personality and Social Psychology, 25,* 100–108.

Cook, T. D., & Flay, B. R. (1978). The persistence of experimentally induced attitude change. In L. Berkowitz (Ed.), *Advances in experimental social psychology* (Vol. 11, pp. 1–57). New York: Academic.

Davies, M. F. (1993). Dogmatism and the persistence of discredited beliefs. *Personality and Social Psychology Bulletin, 19,* 692–699.

Downing, J. (1994). *The role of self-generated cognitive responses in the transmitter-persistence effect.* Unpublished master's thesis, Ohio State University, Columbus.

Eagly, A. H. (1974). Comprehensibility of persuasive arguments as a determinant of opinion change. *Journal of Personality and Social Psychology, 29,* 758–773.

Eagly, A. H., & Chaiken, S. (1993). *Psychology of attitudes.* Fort Worth, TX: Harcourt, Brace, Jovanovich.

Elms, A. C. (1966). Influence of fantasy ability on attitude change through role-playing. *Journal of Personality and Social Psychology, 4,* 36–43.

Fazio, R. H., Powell, M. C., & Herr, P. M. (1983). Toward a process model of the attitude-behavior relation: Accessing one's attitude upon mere observation of the attitude object. *Journal of Personality and Social Psychology, 44,* 723–735.

Fazio, R. H., & Zanna, M. P. (1981). Direct experience and attitude behavior consistency. In L. Berkowitz (Ed.), *Advances in experimental social psychology* (Vol. 14, pp. 161–202). New York: Academic.

Ferrari, J. R., & Leippe, M. R. (1992). Noncompliance with persuasive appeals for a prosocial, altruistic act: Blood donating. *Journal of Applied Social Psychology, 22,* 83–101.

Festinger, L. (1964). Behavioral support for opinion change. *Public Opinion Quarterly, 28,* 404–417.

Festinger, L., & Maccoby, N. (1964). On resistance to persuasive communications. *Journal of Abnormal and Social Psychology, 68,* 359–366.

Freedman, J. L., & Sears, D. O. (1965). Warning, distraction and resistance to influence. *Journal of Personality and Social Psychology, 1,* 262–266.

Greenwald, A. G. (1968). Cognitive learning, cognitive response to persuasion, and attitude change. In A. G. Greenwald, T. C. Brock, & T. M. Ostrom (Eds.), *Psychological foundations of attitudes* (pp. 147–170). New York: Academic.

Greenwald, A. G., & Albert, R. D. (1968). Acceptance and recall of improvised arguments. *Journal of Personality and Social Psychology, 8,* 31–34.

Harkins, S. G., & Petty, R. E. (1981). Effects of source magnification of cognitive effort on attitudes: An information processing view. *Journal of Personality and Social Psychology, 40,* 401–413.

Harkins, S. G., & Petty, R. E. (1987). Information utility and the multiple source effect. *Journal of Personality and Social Psychology, 52,* 260–268.

Hass, R. G., & Grady, K. (1975). Temporal delay, type of forewarning, and resistance to influence. *Journal of Experimental Social Psychology, 11,* 459–469.

Haugtvedt, C. P., & Petty, R. E. (1992). Personality and persuasion: Need for cognition moderates the persistence and resistance of attitude changes. *Journal of Personality and Social Psychology, 63,* 308–319.

Haugtvedt, C. P., Petty, R. E., & Cacioppo, J. T. (1992). Need for cognition and advertising: Understanding the role of personality variables in consumer behavior. *Journal of Consumer Psychology, 1,* 239–260.

Haugtvedt, C. P., Schumann, D. W., Schneier, W. L., & Warren, W. L. (1994). Advertising repetition and variation strategies: Implications for understanding attitude strength. *Journal of Consumer Research, 21,* 176–189.

Haugtvedt, C. P., & Strathman, A. (1990). Situational personal relevance and attitude persistence. *Advances in Consumer Research, 17,* 766–769.

Haugtvedt, C. P., & Wegener, D. T. (1994). Message order effects in persuasion: An attitude strength perspective. *Journal of Consumer Research, 21,* 205–218.

Haugtvedt, C. P., Wegener, D. T., & Warren, W. (1994, May). *Personal relevance, attack source expertise, and resistance of newly changed attitudes.* Paper presented at the annual meeting of the Midwestern Psychological Association, Chicago, IL.

Hennigan, K. M., Cook, T. D., & Gruder, C. L. (1982). Cognitive tuning set, source credibility, and the temporal persistence of attitude change. *Journal of Personality and Social Psychology, 42*(3), 412–425.

Howard, D. J., & Barry, T. E. (1994). The role of thematic congruence between a mood-inducing event and an advertised product in determining the effects of mood on brand attitudes. *Journal of Consumer Psychology, 3,* 1–27.

Hutton, G. G., & Baumeister, R. F. (1992). Self-awareness and attitude change: Seeing oneself on the central route to persuasion. *Personality and Social Psychology Bulletin, 18,* 68–75.

Janis, I. L., & King, B. T. (1957). The influence of role playing on opinion change. *Journal of Abnormal and Social Psychology, 49,* 211–218.

Johnson, B. T. (1994). Effects of outcome-relevant involvement and prior information on persuasion. *Journal of Experimental Social Psychology, 30,* 556–579.

Johnson, B. T., & Eagly, A. H. (1989). Effects of involvement on persuasion: A meta-analysis. *Psychological Bulletin, 106*, 290–314.

Johnson, H. H., & Watkins, T. A. (1971). The effects of message repetition on immediate and delayed attitude change. *Psychonomic Science, 22*, 101–103.

Kallgren, C. A., & Wood, W. (1986). Access to attitude-relevant information in memory as a determinant of attitude-behavior consistency. *Journal of Experimental Social Psychology, 22,* 328–338.

Keating, J. P., & Brock, T. C. (1974). Acceptance of persuasion and the inhibition of counterargumentation under various distraction tasks. *Journal of Experimental Social Psychology, 10*(4), 301–309.

Kelman, H. C. (1961). Processes of opinion change. *Public Opinion Quarterly, 25,* 57–78.

Kohlberg, L. (1958). *The development of modes of moral thinking and choice in the years 10–16.* Unpublished doctoral dissertation, University of Chicago, Chicago, IL.

Knower, F. H. (1935). Experimental studies of changes in attitudes: I. A study of the effect of oral argument on changes of attitude. *Journal of Social Psychology, 6*, 315–347.

Knower, F. H. (1936). Experimental studies of change in attitudes: II. A study of the effect of printed argument on changes in attitude. *Journal of Abnormal and Social Psychology, 30*, 522–532.

Krosnick, J. A. (1988). The role of attitude importance in social evaluation: A study of policy preferences, presidential candidate evaluations, and voting behavior. *Journal of Personality and Social Psychology, 55*(2), 196–210.

Krosnick, J. A. (1989). Attitude importance and attitude accessibility. *Personality and Social Psychology Bulletin, 15*, 297–308.

Lassiter, G. D., Pezzo, M. V., & Apple, K. J. (1993). The transmitter-persistence effect: A confounded discovery? *Psychological Science, 4*, 208–210.

Leippe, M. R., & Elkin, R. A. (1987). When motives clash: Issue involvement and response involvement as determinants of persuasion. *Journal of Personality and Social Psychology, 52*(2), 269–278.

Mackie, D. M. (1987). Systematic and nonsystematic processing of majority and minority persuasive communications. *Journal of Personality and Social Psychology, 53*, 41–52.

Maheswaran, D., & Chaiken, S. (1991). Promoting systematic processing in low-motivation settings: Effect of incongruent information on processing and judgment. *Journal of Personality and Social Psychology, 61*, 13–33.

McGuire, W. J. (1964). Inducing resistance to persuasion: Some contemporary approaches. In L. Berkowitz (Ed.), *Advances in experimental social psychology* (Vol. 1, pp. 191–229). New York: Academic.

McGuire, W. J., & Papageorgis, D. (1962). Effectiveness of forewarning in developing resistance to persuasion. *Public Opinion Quarterly, 26*, 24–34.

Mitnick, L., & McGinnies, E. (1958). Influencing ethnocentrism in small discussion groups through a film communication. *Journal of Abnormal and Social Psychology, 56*, 82–92.

Moore, D., Hausknecht, D., & Thamodaran, K. (1986). Time compression, response opportunity, and persuasion. *Journal of Consumer Research, 13*, 85–99.

Moore, D. L., & Reardon, R. (1987). Source magnification: The role of multiple sources in the processing of advertising appeals. *Journal of Marketing Research, 24*, 412–417.

Norman, R. (1975). Affective-cognitive consistency, attitudes, conformity, and behavior. *Journal of Personality and Social Psychology, 32*, 83–91.

Ostrom, T. M, & Brock, T. C. (1968). A cognitive model of attitudinal involvement. In R. P. Abelson, E. Aronson, W. J. McGuire, T. M. Newcomb, M. J. Rosenberg, & P. H. Tannenbaum (Eds.), *Theories of cognitive consistency: A sourcebook* (pp. 373–383). Chicago: Rand McNally.

Petersen, K. K., & Dutton, J. E. (1975). Certainty, extremity, intensity: Neglected variables in research on attitude-behavior consistency. *Social Forces, 54,* 393–414.

Petty, R. E. (1977). *A cognitive response analysis of the temporal persistence of attitude changes induced by persuasive communications.* Unpublished doctoral dissertation, Ohio State University, Columbus.

Petty, R. E., & Cacioppo, J. T. (1977). Forewarning, cognitive responding, and resistance to persuasion. *Journal of Personality and Social Psychology, 35,* 645–655.

Petty, R. E., & Cacioppo, J. T. (1979). Issue-involvement can increase or decrease persuasion by enhancing message-relevant cognitive responses. *Journal of Personality and Social Psychology, 37,* 1915–1926.

Petty, R. E., & Cacioppo, J. T. (1981). *Attitudes and persuasion: Classic and contemporary approaches.* Dubuque, IA: William C. Brown.

Petty, R. E., & Cacioppo, J. T. (1986a). *Communication and Persuasion: Central and Peripheral Routes to Attitude Change.* New York: Springer-Verlag.

Petty, R. E., & Cacioppo, J. T., (1986b). The Elaboration Likelihood Model of persuasion. In L. Berkowitz (Ed.), *Advances in experimental social psychology* (Vol. 19, pp. 123–205). New York: Academic.

Petty, R. E., & Cacioppo, J. T. (1990). Involvement and persuasion: Tradition versus integration. *Psychological Bulletin, 107,* 367–374.

Petty, R. E., Cacioppo, J. T., & Goldman, R. (1981). Personal involvement as a determinant of argument-based persuasion. *Journal of Personality and Social Psychology, 41,* 847–855.

Petty, R. E., Cacioppo, J. T., & Haugtvedt, C. P. (1992). Involvement and persuasion: An appreciative look at the Sherifs' contribution to the study of self-relevance and attitude change. In D. Granberg & G. Sarup (Eds.), *Social judgment and intergroup relations: Essays in honor of Muzifer Sherif* (pp. 147–175). New York: Springer-Verlag.

Petty, R. E., Cacioppo, J. T., & Heesacker, M. (1981). The use of rhetorical questions in persuasion: A cognitive response analysis. *Journal of Personality and Social Psychology, 40,* 432–440.

Petty, R. E., Cacioppo, J. T., & Schumann, D. W. (1983). Central and peripheral routes to advertising effectiveness: The moderating role of involvement. *Journal of Consumer Research, 10,* 135–146.

Petty, R. E., Gleicher, F., & Baker, S. M. (1991). Multiple roles for affect in persuasion. In J. Forgas (Ed.), *Emotion and social judgments* (pp. 181–200). Oxford: Pergamon.

Petty, R. E., Harkins, S. G., & Williams, K. W. (1980). The effects of group diffusion of cognitive effort on attitudes: An information processing view. *Journal of Personality and Social Psychology, 38,* 81–92.

Petty, R. E., Haugtvedt, C. P., Heesacker, M., & Cacioppo, J. T. (1995). *Message elaboration as a determinant of attitude strength: Persistence and resistance of persuasion.* Unpublished manuscript, Ohio State University, Columbus.

Petty, R. E., Haugtvedt, C. P., & Rennier, G. A. (1995). *Elaboration as a determinant of attitude accessibility.* Unpublished manuscript, Ohio State University, Columbus.

Petty, R. E., Priester, J. R., & Wegener, D. T. (1994). Cognitive processes in attitude change. In R. S. Wyer & T. K. Srull (Eds.), *Handbook of social cognition* (Vol. 2, pp. 69–142). Hillsdale, NJ: Lawrence Erlbaum Associates.

Petty, R. E., Wegener, D. T., Fabrigar, L. R., Priester, J. R., & Cacioppo, J. T. (1993). Conceptual and methodological issues in the Elaboration Likelihood Model of persuasion: A reply to the Michigan State critics. *Communication Theory, 3,* 336–362.

Petty, R. E., Wells, G. L., & Brock, T. C. (1976). Distraction can enhance or reduce yielding to propaganda: Thought disruption versus effort justification. *Journal of Personality and Social Psychology, 34,* 874–884.

Petty, R. E., Wells, G. L., Heesacker, M., Brock, T. C., & Cacioppo, J. T. (1983). The effects of recipient posture on persuasion: A cognitive response analysis. *Personality and Social Psychology Bulletin, 9,* 209–222.

Pfau, M., & Burgoon, M. (1988). Inoculation in political campaign communication. *Human Communication Research, 15,* 91–111.

Priester, J. R., Fabrigar, L. R., Wegener, D. T., & Petty, R. E. (1994, May). *Message elaboration as a function of manipulated attitude accessibility.* Paper presented at the annual meeting of the Midwestern Psychological Association, Chicago, IL.

Priester, J. R., & Petty, R. E. (in press). Source attributions and persuasion: Perceived honesty as a determinant of message scrutiny. *Personality and Social Psychology Bulletin.*

Ratneshwar, S., & Chaiken, S. (1991). Comprehension's role in persuasion: The case of its moderating effect on the persuasive impact of source cues. *Journal of Consumer Psychology, 18,* 52–62.

Rholes, W. S., & Bailey, S. (1983). The effects of level of moral reasoning on consistency between moral attitudes and related behaviors. *Social Cognition, 2,* 32–48.

Roese, N. J., & Olson, J. M. (1994). Attitude importance as a function of repeated attitude expression. *Journal of Experimental Social Psychology, 30,* 39–51.

Ronis, D. L., Baumgardner, M. H., Leippe, M. R., Cacioppo, J. T., & Greenwald, A. G. (1977). In search of reliable persuasion effects: I. A computer-controlled procedure for studying persuasion. *Journal of Personality and Social Psychology, 35,* 548–569.

Ross, L., Lepper, M. R., & Hubbard, M. (1975). Perseverance in self-perception and social perception: Biased attributional processes in the debriefing paradigm. *Journal of Personality and Social Psychology, 32,* 880–892.

Ross, M., McFarland, C., Conway, M., & Zanna, M. P. (1983). Reciprocal relation between attitudes and behavior recall: Committing people to newly formed attitudes. *Journal of Personality and Social Psychology, 45,* 257–267.

Sanbonmatsu, D. M., & Kardes, F. R. (1988). The effects of physiological arousal on information processing and persuasion. *Journal of Consumer Research, 15,* 379–385.

Schumann, D. W., Petty, R. E., & Clemons, D. S. (1990). Predicting the effectiveness of different strategies of advertising variation: A test of the repetition-variation hypotheses. *Journal of Consumer Research, 17,* 192–202.

Schuman, H., & Presser, S. (1981). *Questions and answers: Experiments on question form, wording, and context in attitude surveys.* New York: Academic.

Schwartz, S. (1973). Normative explanations of helping behavior: A critique, proposal and empirical test. *Journal of Experimental Social Psychology, 9,* 349–364.

Shavitt, S., & Brock, T. C. (1986). Self-relevant responses in commercial persuasion: Field and experimental tests. In J. Olson & K. Sentis (Eds.), *Advertising and consumer psychology* (pp. 149–171). New York: Praeger.

Sivacek, J., & Crano, W. D. (1982). Vested interest as a moderator of attitude-behavior consistency. *Journal of Personality and Social Psychology, 43*(2), 210–221.

Smith, S. M., & Petty, R. E. (in press). Message framing and persuasion: A message processing analysis. *Personality and Social Psychology Bulletin.*

Smith, S. M., & Shaffer, D. R. (1991). Celerity and cajolery: Rapid speech may promote or inhibit persuasion through its impact on message elaboration. *Personality and Social Psychology Bulletin, 17,* 663–669.

Smith, S. M., & Shaffer, D. R. (in press). Speed of speech and persuasion: Evidence for multiple effects. *Personality and Social Psychology Bulletin.*

Snyder, M. (1974). Self-monitoring of expressive behavior. *Journal of Personality and Social Psychology , 30,* 526–537.

Snyder, M. (1979). Self-monitoring processes. In L. Berkowitz (Ed.), *Advances in experimental social psychology* (Vol. 12, pp. 86–128). New York: Academic.

Snyder, M., & DeBono, K. G. (1987). A functional approach to attitudes and persuasion. In M. P. Zanna, J. M. Olson, & C. P. Herman (Eds.), *Social influence: The Ontario Symposium* (Vol. 5, pp. 107–125). Hillsdale, NJ: Lawrence Erlbaum Associates.

Snyder, M., & Swann, W. (1976). When actions reflect attitudes: The politics of impression management. *Journal of Personality and Social Psychology, 34,* 1034–1042.

Sorrentino, R. M., Bobocel, D. R., Gitta, M. Z., Olson, J. M., & Hewitt, E. C. (1988). Uncertainty orientation and persuasion: Individual differences in the effects of personal relevance on social judgments. *Journal of Personality and Social Psychology, 55,* 357–371.

Staats, A. W., & Staats, C. K. (1958). Attitudes established by classical conditioning. *Journal of Abnormal and Social Psychology, 57,* 37–40.

Suedfeld, P., & Borrie, R. A. (1978). Sensory deprivation, attitude change, and defense against persuasion. *Canadian Journal of Behavioral Science, 10,* 16–27.

Szybillo, G. J., & Heslin, R. (1973). Resistance to persuasion: Inoculation theory in a marketing context. *Journal of Marketing Research, 10,* 396–403.

Tetlock, P. E. (1990). The impact of accountability on judgment and choice: Toward a social contingency model. In M. P. Zanna (Ed.), *Advances in experimental social psychology* (Vol. 25, pp. 331–376). San Diego, CA: Academic Press.

Watts, W. A. (1967). Relative persistence of opinion change induced by active compared to passive participation. *Journal of Personality and Social Psychology, 5,* 4–15.

Watts, W. A., & Holt, L. E. (1979). Persistence of opinion change induced under conditions of forewarning and distraction. *Journal of Personality and Social Psychology, 37,* 778–789.

Wegener, D. T., & Petty, R. E. (1994). Mood management across affective states: The hedonic contingency hypothesis. *Journal of Personality and Social Psychology, 66,* 1034–1048.

Wegener, D. T., Petty, R. E., & Smith, S. M. (in press). Positive mood can increase or decrease message scrutiny: The hedonic contingency view of mood and message processing. *Journal of Personality and Social Psychology.*

White, P., & Harkins, S. G. (1994). Race of source effects in the Elaboration Likelihood Model. *Journal of Personality and Social Psychology, 67,* 790–807.

Wilson, T. D., Dunn, D. S., Kraft, D., & Lisle, D. J. (1989). Introspection, attitude change, and attitude-behavior consistency: The disruptive effects of explaining why we feel the way we do. In L. Berkowitz (Ed.), *Advances in experimental social psychology* (Vol. 22, pp. 123–205). San Diego, CA: Academic Press.

Wood, W., Kallgren, C. A., & Priesler, R. M. (1985). Access to attitude-relevant information in memory as a determinant of persuasion: The role of message attributes. *Journal of Experimental Social Psychology, 21,* 73–85.

Worth, L. T., & Mackie, D. M. (1987). Cognitive mediation of positive affect in persuasion. *Social Cognition, 5,* 76–94.

Wu, C., & Shaffer, D. R. (1987). Susceptibility to persuasive appeals as a function of source credibility and prior experience with the attitude object. *Journal of Personality and Social Psychology, 52*(4), 677–688.

Zajonc, R. B., (1960). The process of cognitive tuning in communication. *Journal of Abnormal and Social Psychology, 61,* 159–167.

Zanna, M. P., Fazio, R. H., & Ross, M. (1994). The persistence of persuasion. In R. C. Schank & E. Langer (Eds.), *Beliefs, reasoning, and decision making: Psychologic in honor of Bob Abelson* (pp. 347–362). Hillsdale, NJ: Lawrence Erlbaum Associates.

Zanna, M. P., Olson, J. M., & Fazio, R. H. (1980). Attitude-behavior consistency: An individual difference perspective. *Journal of Personality and Social Psychology, 38,* 432–440.

6
▼▼▼▼▼▼▼

Attitude Strength and Vested Interest

William D. Crano
University of Arizona

The study of social attitudes is a defining feature and a fundamental preoccupation of social psychology. For many, what was true in Allport's time is true today—attitudes remain the "most distinctive and indispensable concept in contemporary American social psychology" (Allport, 1935, p. 798). Over the years, some of the central features of this "indispensable concept" have been identified. One of the most important of these is attitude strength, the focus of this volume. Attitude strength usually is described in terms of three qualities: Strong attitudes are *persistent, resistant to change,* and more likely than weak attitudes to be *manifest behaviorally.* Of these three standards, the assumption of attitude-behavior consistency is fundamental, for if attitudes are not associated with behavior, the pertinence of their persistence and resistance is moot. We all recognize the necessity for the functional influence of attitudes on actions. If it did not matter that attitudes have implications for behavior, LaPiere would not be a household name in social psychology.

Considerable evidence indicates that attitudes stand in a functional relationship with attitude-relevant actions (Brewer & Crano, 1994; Zanna, Higgins, & Herman, 1982), but the relationship is neither absolute nor unconditional. Many factors may influence attitude-behavior consistency, and much research has been devoted to their discovery. My purpose is to discuss one such factor: vested interest. In this review, the fundamental conceptualization of vested interest is considered, as are approaches that have approximated the concept. Ego-involvement and attitude importance are reviewed, as is the symbolic politics position, which suggests that vested (or self-) interest does not affect behavior. Finally, some possible components of vested interest are considered. These components provide the theoretical foundation for a more refined vision of the ways this factor prompts attitude-consistent behavior.

VESTED INTEREST: DEFINITION
AND DIFFERENTIATION

Vested interest refers to the extent to which an attitude object is hedonically relevant for the attitude holder. If the attitude object has important perceived personal consequences, the attitude for terminological convenience is labeled of high vested interest. Highly vested attitudes are functionally related to behavior. The more hedonically relevant the attitude object, the more likely is the attitude to be expressed behaviorally, because attitude-congruent behavior promises to prove reinforcing. The significant personal consequences associated with the attitude object need not be objectively important, but must be perceived as such. This emphasis on hedonic consequence distinguishes vested interest from some of the other conceptions of self-interest that are discussed later in this chapter.

Vested Interest and Involvement

Consideration of the personal consequence of attitude objects is a common activity in social psychology. Attention to this issue has been focused recently by a research series concerned with the conceptualization of involvement (Johnson & Eagly, 1989, 1990; Petty & Cacioppo, 1990). This issue is relevant in the present context because vested interest and involvement have similar effects on processes of attitude formation and change, and attitude-behavior consistency. Johnson and Eagly (1989) proposed that involvement be separated into three components: outcome-relevant involvement, value-relevant involvement, and impression-relevant involvement. Although Petty and Cacioppo (1990) maintain that the three-part distinction is premature, the issue has important implications for current models of attitude change. Petty and Cacioppo (1986a, 1986b), for example, maintain that high levels of personal relevance lead to more intensive processing of attitude-relevant communications and, ultimately, to attitudes of greater strength. Such attitudes are more persistent, resistant to persuasion, etc. Personal relevance can subsume all forms of involvement. Although consistent with the general thrust of Petty and Cacioppo's position—highly vested attitudes, too, are likely to lead to greater elaboration of attitude-relevant messages (Agans & Crano, 1992), stronger attitudes, and so on—we adopt a more restricted definition of the involvement-elaboration-attitude strength dynamic. For present purposes, vested interest is defined strictly in terms of the hedonic relevance of an attitude object. The personal consequences associated with an object determine vested interest. Though far from isomorphic, this conceptualization of vested interest corresponds most closely to

Johnson and Eagly's (1989) version of outcome-relevant involvement. This emphasis on consequential outcomes, at the expense of value or impression maintenance, renders the conceptualization of vested interest more narrow than Petty and Cacioppo's (1990) notion of personal relevance (see also Petty, Haugtvedt, & Smith, ch. 5, and Thomsen, Borgida, & Levine, ch. 8, this volume), but this more focused definition is serviceable because it restricts the range of possible factors to be considered when vested interest is at issue. Not all variables that enhance attitude-behavior consistency involve attitude objects of great personal consequence. But attitude objects that *are* personally consequential will be vested, and vested interest, in turn, will foster attitude-consistent action.

Antecedents

The central implication of the vested interest position (that behavior is rational and is undertaken to promote positive personal outcomes) can be traced to the writings of Thomas Hobbes and Adam Smith, and has been carried into the present by rational choice theorists (cf. Mansbridge, 1990; Simon, 1986; Tversky & Kahneman, 1986). The rational choice model assumes that people are motivated to maximize personal outcomes. Indeed, the view of people as rational, self-interested outcome-maximizers is basic to most economic models (cf. Frohlich, 1974; Mueller, 1979). An assumption of this type, which has proved so dominant in the history of ideas, is bound to have stimulated considerable attention and controversy. In social psychology, variations on the vested interest theme have been of concern from the earliest days. The terminology and measurement operations employed to capture the idea have varied, but the basic assumption that consequential attitudes behave differently from inconsequential ones is commonplace. This is not to say that this assumption always has been supported. At times, empirical evidence appears to suggest that personal consequence does not matter much. However, in most such contexts, the critical assumptions of the vested interest orientation have been badly approximated, and such approximations result in a less than perfect realization of the construct. Some past attempts that employed the general notions of personal consequence are considered in the pages that follow. In this discussion, it is important to ponder the lack of isomorphism between the measurement operations used and the conception of vested interest presented to this point.

APPROXIMATIONS TO VESTED INTEREST

Ego-Involvement

Sherif and Hovland (1961) developed the concept of ego-involvement to predict variations in susceptibility to attitude change. What are ego-involved attitudes? According to Sherif and Cantril (1947, p. 93), they are attitudes that "have the characteristic of belonging to *me*, as being part of *me*, as psychologically experienced." The theory posits that attitudes of low ego-involvement will be easier to change than highly ego-involved beliefs. In addition, attempting to change ego-involved attitudes may result in movement contrary to that advocated if the persuasive message is extremely inimical to the established belief (Eiser, 1990; Sherif, Sherif, & Nebergall, 1965). These predictions are derived from classical psychophysical judgment research. Social judgment theory assumes that a persuasive communication that advocates a position relatively close to the target's preferred view will be perceived as more congruent with the established attitude than it really is. As such, a target will be less likely to mount strong defenses against it. Change is facilitated by a perceptual distortion, an *assimilation effect*. If the message is distant from the target's preferred position, it will be viewed as more antagonistic to the established attitude than it is, and strong defenses will be mounted against it. Such biased perceptions are termed *contrast effects*.

Ego-involvement affects perceivers' judgments of the fit between established and advocated positions. With attitudes of low ego-involvement, greater distance is condoned before the advocated position is judged contrary to the established one. With highly charged, ego-involved attitudes, even minor discrepancies are seen as intolerably large. Reviews of research on social judgment disclose that the theory accounts reasonably well for patterns of attitude resistance and change (Eagly & Teelak, 1972; Johnson & Eagly, 1989, 1990; Petty & Cacioppo, 1981; Sherif, Kelley, Rodgers, Sarup, & Tittler, 1973). However, assimilation and contrast, the mediating processes hypothesized as responsible for the change patterns, have not fared well (Petty, Cacioppo, & Haugtvedt, 1992). What, then, is responsible for the sometimes potent effects of ego-involvement on attitude? Arguably, ego-involvement affects attitude change not through the mechanisms of assimilation and contrast, but rather because it is a stand-in, albeit an imperfect one, of vested interest. Ego-involvement is associated with attitude persistence and change to the extent that it reflects people's perceptions of the consequence of an attitude object. When the overlap between these factors is great, ego-involvement *appears* to moderate attitude-behavior consistency. When it is not, ego-involvement has little effect on behavior. By this argument, effects of ego-involvement are apparent, not real; they depend on the incidental relationship between ego-involvement and vested interest.

But are not all ego-involved attitudes vested? Not necessarily. Highly vested attitudes *must* be ego-involving, by definition. An attitude of great hedonic relevance will be assessed as being ego-involving if the usual measures of ego-involvement, based on estimates of latitudes of acceptance and rejection, are employed (e.g., Hovland, Harvey, & Sherif, 1957; Peterson & Koulack, 1969). However, although highly vested attitudes will be experienced as ego-involving, ego-involved attitudes will not necessarily be perceived as vested. One may be ego-involved in an attitude of no hedonic consequence. In such contexts, which entail a lack of overlap between ego-involvement and vested interest, the change predictions of social judgment theory will *not* be supported. In a test of this assertion, Sivacek and Crano (1982) contrasted the utility of the two constructs and confirmed the primacy of vested interest over ego-involvement in predicting attitude-consistent action. When social judgment theory works, it works for reasons other than those theorized. Its power derives from an inadvertent conceptual overlap with vested interest.

Importance

Krosnick and his colleagues have suggested the value of issue importance in predicting attitude-consistent action (cf. Berent, 1990; Boninger, Krosnick, & Berent, in press; Judd & Krosnick, 1989; Krosnick, 1988a, 1988b, 1989, 1990; Krosnick & Schuman, 1988). This research, drawn largely from the social survey tradition of political science, is well-conceived and persuasive. It establishes that people are more likely to vote in accord with their attitudes as perceived issue importance increases. Moreover, some of the underlying causes of this relationship have been identified: They include the greater accessibility of attitudes deemed important, and the positive association between importance and the tendency for voters to assume greater differences between candidates or issues. Boninger et al. (in press) confirmed the impact of self-interest on perceptions of issue importance. Krosnick's issue importance findings are in accord with expectations that may be derived from considerations of vested interest. Nevertheless, for reasons cataloged in the earlier discussion of ego-involvement, it may prove useful to distinguish vested interest from attitude importance.

One factor that differentiates the approaches is scope. As noted, vested interest is concerned with hedonically relevant attitude objects. Importance *can* refer to such matters of personal consequence, but it also can refer to the national, or international moment of an issue, a consideration that may be quite remote from judgments of vested interest. To illustrate this point, let us engage in the following thought experiment. Consider and evaluate the concept of mass starvation in Ethiopia. Is it kind or cruel? Beautiful or ugly? Unpleasant or pleasant? Bad or good? Important or unimportant? My research indicates that almost everyone evaluates starvation in Ethiopia negatively. Who could approve of mass starvation? Who could rate this catastrophe good or beautiful or kind? Most people, too, consider this issue important. Of course, starvation in Ethiopia *is* important—but it is of little hedonic consequence for most North Americans. The attitude is of low vested interest, and thus, it is not likely to incite behavior. If we were to administer our measures to affected Ethiopians, their responses probably would reveal attitude and importance ratings *identical* to those of our North American sample. However, strong attitude-behavior consistency would characterize the Ethiopian sample, given their enormous vested interest in the issue. Subjective vested interest, not the objective importance of the issue, drives attitude-consistent action.

Importance works because it often is a very good proxy for vested interest—it works when importance means "personally consequential." When an importance rating merely reflects acknowledgment of the general gravity of an issue (divorced from personal consequence), it is not vested, and the associated attitude probably will not be reflected in action. The distinction between types of importance (personal importance, national importance, etc.) is not idle. Measures of importance often are largely conjectural. They require people to indicate not whether an issue has a direct bearing on their lives, but rather if it is generally consequential. These measures differ from the approach suggested to assess vested interest because they do not tap the extent to which an issue impinges on respondents' lives. It might be important, but if it does not affect respondents, an issue is not of high vested interest.

Aside from differences used to infer importance and vested interest, there exists a logical distinction between these constructs that merits consideration. Let us review the observations raised in our discussion of ego-involvement, since the thrust of both arguments is similar. By definition, people consider vested attitudes important. As noted, however, important attitudes, as importance often is defined (but see Boninger et al., in press) may not have hedonic implications. Important but nonvested attitudes will not predict behavior. Importance may moderate consistency only to the extent that it is a valid proxy of vested interest.

Cialdini and Petty (1981) made a similar point when they recommended that *issue importance* be differentiated from *personal importance*. While differences exist between the constructs, it is obvious that vested interest is more akin to personal than issue importance. Much of the social survey work on importance involves issues that by any standard are objectively important (e.g., world peace, nuclear disarmament, homelessness, unemployment and poverty), but these issues may or may not be felt as personally consequential. When they are not, behavior consistent with the (objectively important but nonvested) attitude is unlikely.

Self-Interest and Symbolic Politics

Discovery of strong, positive relations between attitudes and behaviors in contexts involving issues of personal importance or high vested interest satisfies both logic and common sense. However, review of the literature on self-interest and political behavior suggests that people often appear to act in ways that, if not inconsistent with rational self-interest, are certainly independent of it. Green and Gerken (1989, pp. 1–2) cited a "burgeoning literature [which] suggests that self-interest has little influence on policy preferences. . . . One study after another has shown that 'self-interest' has little apparent influence on political attitudes." Much of this "burgeoning literature," is based on secondary analyses of political surveys conducted by Sears and his colleagues (cf. Sears & Funk, 1991). Sears theorized that voter behavior is more a function of symbols than self-interest:

> According to this theory, people acquire in early life standing predispositions which influence their adult perceptions and attitudes. In adulthood . . . they respond in a

highly affective way to symbols which resemble the attitude objects to which similar emotional responses were conditioned or associated in earlier life. Whether or not the issue has some tangible consequence for the adult voter's personal life is irrelevant. (Sears, Hensler, & Speer, 1979, pp. 370–371)

The theory of symbolic politics thus refers to people's tendency to be swayed by conditioned affective responses to symbols (e.g., Blacks or rednecks) acquired early in life, which transfer to, or become associated with, other related issues (e.g., busing, integration, Willie Horton).

This conditioning explanation of political behavior seems to demand more of associationism than is warranted. The classical conditioning of complex attitudes remains controversial (cf. Brewer & Crano, 1994; Insko, 1967), and even if such conditioning does occur, an exceptional degree of generalization would be required to move from the classically conditioned 'symbol' to the complex issues that materially affect voters' lives. Consideration of current knowledge regarding the classical conditioning and generalization of complex attitudes (Cacioppo, Marshall-Goodell, Tassinary, & Petty, 1992) raises strong questions about the theoretical underpinnings of symbolic politics. On the other hand, many studies have produced results that fit comfortably within the symbolic politics framework, and appear to provide little if any comfort to proponents of the self-interest school (cf. Green & Gerken, 1989; Kinder, 1986). If classical conditioning cannot provide a plausible basis for the results that appear to favor the symbolic politics camp, then what is responsible for the reported results? It is not possible in the space permitted to address all of the studies undertaken, but a representative example might help to pinpoint some of the sources responsible for the disagreement between proponents of symbolic politics and vested interest.

This illustration is based on a secondary analysis conducted by Sears et al. (1979) of the 1972 Center for Political Studies (CPS) election study. The issue under study is the relationship between self-interest, symbolic (racial) attitudes, and opposition to busing school children to achieve racial balance. To study the contested positions, Sears et al. (1979) defined self-interest with three items (has busing occurred here, do you have children in public school, etc.). Racial intolerance (the symbolic attitude) was measured through the use of an eight-item scale developed via factor analysis. The critical dependent measure was a single 7-point item asking whether busing should be undertaken "to achieve integration," or if it would be wiser to "keep children in neighborhood schools." Owing to scale length alone, it is not surprising that symbolic attitude correlated more strongly with the dependent measure than did the self-interest items.

Although this study is afflicted by many difficult methodological questions (the use of single-item indicators, questionable validity of the critical measures, etc.), the principal problem is the unwarranted assumption of a link between self-interest and attitude. As noted, the White respondents of Sears et al. (1979) were asked whether busing had occurred in their neighborhood, if they had children in public school, and the racial composition of their neighborhood school. Positive answers to the first two questions, and existence of an all-White neighborhood school, were taken as indicative of high self-interest. Sears et al. assumed that highly self-interested people were antagonistic to busing; thus, the correlation between these indicators was taken as indicative of the effect of self-interest on behavior.

This assumption forces acceptance of the proposition in this study that self-interest *inevitably* incites opposition to busing. Even if we were to grant that the self-interest measures are valid, an enormous concession, the assumption of a unidirectional self-interest effect and the correspondent statistical methods used to test it guarantee the predictive failure of self-interest. The assumption of a unidirectional relationship between self-interest and opposition to busing requires that all vested or self-interested respondents be negatively predisposed to busing, and all nonvested respondents be in favor of it. Correlations involving self-interest and opposition to busing will be artificially attenuated to the extent that *either* assumption is false. It is unreasonable to assume that all participants whose sociodemographic status identifies them as self-interested will perceive themselves as vested. It is even less reasonable to assume that all those identified as self-interested will evaluate busing as inimical to their best interests. Vested interest has no necessary implications for attitude direction. A white male applicant to medical school may feel that programs guaranteeing equal opportunity to all, regardless of gender or race, are of great personal consequence. However, we cannot assume on the basis of this perception of vested interest that his attitude toward equal opportunity programs is negative—or positive. The highly vested nature of this issue may impel attitude-consistent actions, but the thrust of the actions will be guided by the content and direction of the attitude. The symbolic attitudes camp appears to have missed this critical point.

Were all the vested respondents of Sears et al. antagonistic to busing? According to their own data, 14% of the sample of ($N = 2,491$) White respondents held neutral-to-positive attitudes toward busing. If any of this group was vested, their data were miscoded, because for these respondents, a *negative* relationship between self-interest (as defined in the study) and opposition to busing supports a self-interest interpretation. A *positive* relationship is consistent with the self-interest hypothesis only for vested respondents having anti-busing attitudes, yet *all data* were coded in this manner. In Sears et al. (1979), and many other studies modeled on its general methodology, these opposing tendencies counteract one another, negating any evidence of self-interest. This process will seriously underestimate the impact of self- or vested interest, and it is inevitable unless all respondents share identical attitudes or, at a minimum, have attitudes that fall on the same side of the scalar neutral point.

The problem works the other way as well. Imagine a subset of respondents who hate Blacks, oppose busing, *but* score low on all the self-interest indicators—that is, they possess no information that busing will be enacted, have no school-age children, and so forth. In the standard correlational approach, these respondents appear to support the symbolic politics position. Their negative attitudes toward blacks correlate with negative attitudes toward busing, even though they are not vested in the issue. In addition, such results are taken as evidence against the case for self-interest. Is this interpretation reasonable? Not unless the self-interest position holds that the *only* determinant of attitude-behavior consistency is self-interest, a form of the hypothesis never proposed by anyone. Logically, even positive symbolic attitude results do not detract from the self-interest position. Sears et al. (1979) failed to find support for the self-interest position not only because their measures were weak, but because the method by which their data were agglomerated in the correlational analysis canceled any self-interest effects that might have occurred.

What Do the Data Really Show?

A reasonable method of investigating the effects of self-interest on attitudes and behavior involves categorizing respondents on the basis of self-interest, and then determining whether attitude-behavior relationships differ systematically as a function of the categorization (as done by Sivacek & Crano, 1982). Rather than ask, "Is there a relationship between self-interest and action," we ask, "Does the relationship between attitude and action differ as a consequence of variation in self-interest?" Symbolic attitudes researchers have answered this question by asserting that self-interest is largely irrelevant. In statistical terms, this means that in Sears et al. (1979), the correlation between attitude and opposition to busing should serve as a valid parameter estimate over all respondents. To determine the validity of this critical assumption, let us construct a confidence interval around the correlation between symbolic attitudes and opposition to busing. As noted, this correlation is reasonably strong ($r = .37$, $N = 1,233$, $p < .001$). The confidence interval (at $p < .00005$) given this value and N would subsume correlations between the values of .25 and .46. Does the attitude/opposition-to-busing correlation for highly vested respondents fall within these intervals?

To answer this question, respondents were divided into vested and nonvested subgroups on the basis of Sears et al.'s own self-interest criteria. Within the vested and nonvested subgroups, correlations involving the eight-item (symbolic) attitude measure and the critical dependent measure were calculated. For vested respondents, the attitude/opposition-to-busing correlation ($r = .51$, $p < .001$, $N = 68$) falls well outside the very liberal confidence interval that was set. This analysis suggests the symbolic politics correlation value is not a reasonable parameter estimate for the vested respondents. The assumption of the irrelevance of self-interest is not supported in this analysis. Does vested interest matter? Based on the same data set used by Sears et al. (1979), there can be no doubt that it does.

The evidence supporting the symbolic politics position is flawed on both conceptual and methodological grounds (Crano & Brewer, 1986). The manner in which the theory has been investigated forces the assumption that certain actions, programs, or positions will be viewed identically by all those similarly affected by them. In Sears et al. (1979), this means that all vested white respondents of necessity were predefined as racists. This is not merely insulting, it is implausible. The methodological approach of the symbolic attitudes school assumes univalent attitudes as a function of membership in a particular sociodemographic category. This assumption is necessary methodologically, but it cannot be supported logically. Campbell (1986) underscored this point when he observed that " 'altruistically' hoarding wealth to pass on to children at the expense of one's own skin-surface hedonism becomes rational self-interest in the biological model" (p. S357). In other words, it is risky to presume what others perceive to be in their self-interest. Not all parents whose children are affected by busing think that busing is detrimental to their children's education. Not all the unemployed believe that a guaranteed job program will work to their advantage. Not all males think that equal employment opportunity for women compromises their own job prospects. Not all Whites feel threatened by Blacks, or Hispanics, or other ethnic minorities. Owing to the methodological approach through which symbolic attitudes have been investigated, such insupportable assumptions are commonplace *and necessary*. Because of the assumption of univalence, the standard approach agglomerates data in ways that *inevitably* bias results against confirmation of a self-interest interpretation.

Although based on an associationist model that appears inadequate to carry the burden asked of it, and tested in a manner that renders its outcomes confounded, the general notion of symbolic politics is not unpersuasive. Of course people's central, self-definitional attitudes are associated with their more peripheral opinions. A hatred of Blacks *should* be associated with a distaste for busing, and this relationship should hold whether or not the attitude holder's own ox is being gored. Whether the observation that "related attitudes correlate" is important is a matter of opinion.

VESTED INTEREST AND ATTITUDE-BEHAVIOR CONSISTENCY: REPRESENTATIVE RESEARCH

How should such research have been conducted? Let us consider the approach taken in the study of vested interest, which has produced results consistent with the hypothesis that beliefs strongly predict behaviors when the issues are of great perceived personal consequence.

The Drinking Age Referendum

In one such study, Sivacek and Crano (1982) took advantage of an opportunity afforded by the state of Michigan, which had instituted a referendum on the legal age at which people might drink alcoholic beverages. At the time of the study, the legal drinking age in Michigan was 18 years. The referendum proposed an increase to 21 years of age. Whatever its merits, the referendum provided an opportunity to study the effects of hedonic relevance, or vested interest, on attitude-behavior consistency. To capitalize on this opportunity, Sivacek and Crano (1982) assessed the referendum-relevant attitudes of a large sample of undergraduate students, 80% of whom were antagonistic to the referendum. These anti-referendum respondents were categorized into three vested-interest subgroups on the basis of age. In this way we hoped to create groups of individuals for whom the perceived personal consequences of the anti-referendum attitude varied. Because some of the students would be of legal age by the time the law's change was enacted, the success or failure of the referendum held little consequence for them. These (anti-referendum) subjects were defined as having attitudes of low vested interest. For other students, the law's change would deprive them from drinking alcoholic beverages legally for at least 2 years. We defined these (anti-referendum) students as having attitudes of high vested interest. Anti-referendum students falling between these extremes were deemed to hold attitudes of moderate vested interest. This approach differs from the symbolic attitudes strategy. We did not infer that everyone affected by the referendum would be antagonistic to it. Had we done so, we would have misidentified 20% of the sample. In this study, unlike the standard symbolic attitudes approach, inaccuracies in defining vested interest would weaken, rather than foster, our hypothesis.

The three groups thus defined did not differ in attitude direction or extremity. They practically could not, since only those having negative attitudes were included in the study. This selection procedure was enacted to rule out differences that might have occurred as a function of attitude (polarity or valence) variations. However, vested interest did differ between groups, and had a major impact on the likelihood that subjects would act on their attitude by joining a group constituted to oppose the referendum and making telephone calls to persuade citizens to vote against it. Nearly half (47%) the participants in the highly vested group agreed to join the anti-referendum campaign; the comparable figures were considerably less for respondents of moderate (26%), or of low, vested interest (12%). The number of telephone calls participants pledged to make in opposition to the referendum also varied significantly as a function of vested interest. On average, high vested interest respondents pledged to call nine voters, whereas those of moderate and low vested attitudes pledged four and two calls respectively.

The Senior Comprehensives Experiment

A second study augmented these results. In this experiment, undergraduate students were approached on the Michigan State University campus and informed that a system of senior comprehensive examinations was being contemplated by a high-level university committee. Students' attitudes toward this possibility were assessed on a highly reliable scale, as were their estimates of the extent to which the imposition of comprehensive examination plan would affect them personally. On the basis of their responses to this scale, students were categorized as having attitudes of high, moderate, or low vested interest. Regardless of attitude—some respondents were in favor of the examination plan—all were given the opportunity to work against implementation of comprehensive examinations. They could (a) sign a petition opposing the examinations, (b) join a group fighting their establishment, and (c) volunteer any number of hours to the group's activities. These anti-referendum behaviors, and a behavioral index that combined all three into a highly reliable measure, were correlated with respondents' attitudes within each of the three vested interest conditions.

The major results of the study are summarized in Table 6.1. As shown, the attitude-behavior correlations within the high vested interest condition were statistically and practically significant. When error was minimized through the use of the index, which combined the three behaviors into a single measure, the resulting correlation accounted for more than 67% of the variance in the attitude-behavior relationship. Consistent with hypotheses, attitude-behavior associations were not nearly as strong among participants of moderate and low vested interest. Indeed, in these groups, two of the three critical behaviors were not significantly related to attitude. However, even among respondents of moderate and low vested interest, the correlations of attitude with the behavior index were statistically significant (although significantly smaller than those found in the highly vested group). In addition to emphasizing the importance of developing behavioral measures as reliable as our attitude scales, these results confirm the value of the concept of vested interest, and suggest that even under conditions of low personal consequence, a reasonable association between attitude and behavior may emerge if solid and sensitive measures are used to measure them.

The results of the comprehensive examination experiment are all the more impressive when it is recognized that the self-interested behaviors of the pro-comprehensive respondents were severely circumscribed. Their only logical option was to refuse to engage in any anti-comprehensive action. If they had been

TABLE 6.1
Correlations Between Attitude and Behavior Measures in
Differentiated Vested-Interest Subgroups (from Sivacek & Crano, 1982)

Vested Interest Condition	Behavior			
	Sign Petition	Volunteer (Yes/No)	No. of Hours Pledged	Behavior Index
High ($n = 27$)	.74**	.60**	.64**	.82**
Moderate ($n = 39$)	.42*	.23	.17	.42*
Low ($n = 30$)	.25	.42*	.24	.53*
Total ($n = 96$)	.38*	.43*	.34	.60**

$*p < .05.$ $**p < .001.$

given the opportunity to work on behalf of the examinations (thereby unrestricting the range of their possible responses), the obtained attitude-behavior correlations could only have increased.

OTHER MANIFESTATIONS OF VESTED INTEREST

Vested Interest and Assumed Consensus

A catalyst that impinges so strongly on attitude-behavior consistency might be expected to have implications for other psychological states as well, and vested interest indeed has been shown to influence corollary aspects of attitude and judgment (cf. Campbell, 1986; Kahneman, Knetsch, & Thaler, 1986; Simon, 1986). For example, vested interest appears to affect people's tendency to overestimate the consensual validity of their attitudes, a bias known variously as the false-consensus or assumed-consensus effect (Crano, 1983; Marks & Miller, 1987; Ross, Greene, & House, 1977). Marks and Miller (1987) have speculated that the false consensus bias might serve as a mechanism to bolster beliefs. If this is so, the tendency should be exacerbated in situations involving personally consequential, or highly vested, attitudes. Because such overestimates would sustain beliefs, it is logical that the more central the attitude, the more important it would be to support it.

To test this possibility, an experiment was conducted under the guise of a survey of public opinion (Crano, 1983). Undergraduate respondents read the following message:

As you might know, the state government has frozen more than $26 million in state support to education. In attempting to deal with this, the university has proposed a number of different plans to cope with the problems that will arise from this loss of revenue. One plan is to collect a ONE TIME ONLY tuition surcharge from . . .

[Manipulation]

underclassmen (that is, freshmen and sophomores). The reasoning behind this plan is that underclassmen will have longer to take advantage of the positive features that the revenue increase will generate and thus should bear this added expense.

[Or]

upperclassmen (that is, juniors and seniors). The reasoning behind this plan is that upperclassmen have had the advantage of the university for a longer period of time, and thus should bear this added expense. (from Crano, 1983, p. 600)

These instructional manipulations were used to create perceptions of either high or low vested interest. In the high vested treatment, respondents learned that the student class *of which they were members* had been singled out to pay a tuition surcharge. This was not in their best (financial) interests, especially since a significant proportion of the student body was not required to share the burden. Students who were informed that others, not they, would bear the financial burden were defined as being of low vested interest.

Manipulation checks disclosed that the participants understood the implications of the surcharge plan. Underclassmen who thought that they had been singled out felt significantly more affected than underclassmen who thought that upperclassmen would be forced to pay. Attitudes of the upperclassmen mirrored those of the underclassmen. Over all participants, attitudes toward the plan were congruent with the vested interest treatment. Those who were to be affected were significantly less favorably disposed toward the plan than those who were not to be taxed. Although this finding is contrary to the general thrust of symbolic attitudes theory, it is consistent with other research that involves direct financial outlays (Green, 1988; Sears & Citrin, 1985). Such research probably entails a closer than usual approximation between operationalized vested interest and self-interest as it actually is perceived (Sniderman & Tetlock, 1986a, 1986b).

Crano's (1983) research was focussed principally on the effect of vested interest on assumed consensus—participants' estimates of the extent to which other students, upperclassmen, and underclassmen alike, agreed with their evaluation of the surcharge plan. This information was obtained by assessing subjects' estimates of the percentage of *all undergraduates attending the university* whom they thought would evaluate the plan as they did. The results of this analysis are presented in Fig. 6.1.

As shown, vested interest had a substantial impact on assumed consensus. Underclassmen who thought they would be affected by the surcharge assumed that nearly 75% of the entire student body would evaluate the plan as they did.

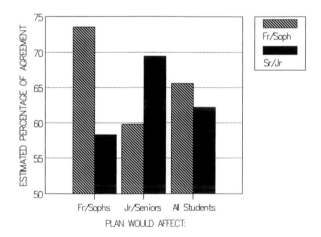

FIG. 6.1.   Effects of vested interest on assumed consensus of attitude.

If the underclassmen were not to be affected, they assumed that less than 60% of the student body would agree with their (low vested) attitude. The same pattern was evident in the consensus estimates of the upperclassmen: those who were to pay the tax assumed that nearly 70% of the student body would share their negative attitude. Those not affected assumed that only about 58% of the student body would agree with their assessment. As in the comparison involving the underclassmen, this difference in consensus proportions was statistically significant. The results represent a remarkable bias in judgment, because everyone *knew* that half the students in the university would *not* be affected by the surcharge. Yet, if they themselves were to be affected, the participants assumed that the overwhelming majority of all students would evaluate the issue as they did.

As was noted, vested interest was correlated significantly with (unfavorable) attitudes toward the surcharge plan. As such, we might wonder whether the assumed consensus bias is merely a result of differences in initial attitude. Auxilliary analysis disclosed that the vested interest-assumed consensus relation persisted even when initial attitude was held constant through partial correlation. This finding indicates that vested interest and assumed consensus share significant variance beyond that attributable to respondents' own attitudes. People for whom an attitude is hedonically relevant appear susceptible to the false consensus bias which, in turn, has important implications for attitudes. As Marks and Miller (1987) showed, high consensus attitudes are more persistent, more resistant to change, and more likely to provoke action.

Vested Interest and Social Comparison

Social comparison, an enduring principle in social psychology (Goethals, 1986), is a related process that might be influenced by vested interest. Recent research implicates vested interest in the social comparison process. Before considering this relationship, let us briefly review the theory. Festinger (1954) assumed that we are motivated to know how we compare with others in terms of beliefs and abilities and, further, that in the absence of objective standards, we will determine our relative position by comparing ourselves with others. Not anyone can serve as a comparison partner, however. If the process is to proceed, we must find someone who is similar to us on the critical dimension. Research findings have not always cooperated with this aspect of the theory. Indeed, in a number of instances, the preferred comparison choice is the most dissimilar person possible (cf. Goethals & Darley, 1987; Kruglanski & Mayseless, 1987; Olson, Herman, & Zanna, 1986). Studies undertaken over the years suggest that the nature of the judgment on which the comparison is sought has important ramifications for the preference of similar or dissimilar comparison partners (Gorenflo & Crano, 1989; Olson, Ellis, & Zanna, 1983). The summary implication of all of this research is that in contexts involving subjective judgments, people prefer to compare with others who are similar to themselves. When objective judgments are at issue, people prefer dissimilar comparison partners. We need not explore in detail the reasons for these variations in preference (cf. Crano & Hannula-Bral, in press), it is sufficient here to note that they exist. People assume that similar and dissimilar comparison sources provide distinct information whose utility varies as a function of the nature of the judgment.

In light of research on the effects of vested interest on assumed consensus, it is reasonable to question whether such assumptions of differential utility will arise when the stakes involved in the comparison are consequential. If vested interest intensifies the presumption of consensus, it might obliterate a preference for similar or dissimilar comparison partners. Why? Because in circumstances of high vested interest, we might assume that most others believe as we do. As such, people holding highly vested attitudes would not be expected to exhibit differential preference for comparison partners, no matter the subjective or objective nature of the judgment task. If everyone believes as I do, it is inconsequential if my comparison partner is like, or unlike, me.

Research by Gorenflo and Crano (1989, Study 2) was undertaken to investigate this possibility. Research participants playing the role of jurors considered a complex court case and made a series of judgments regarding the guilt or innocence of the defendant. Before beginning the case, some were exhorted to stick to the evidence when forming their judgments. They were assured that the information provided was sufficient to make an objective judgment, and they were urged to do so. The remaining participants were informed that jurors in criminal trials almost never have sufficient objective evidence on which to base a judgment of guilt or innocence. Thus, they were to rely upon their own subjective beliefs and values in coming to their decision. In fact, all participants received identical information. After making their decision, they were given the opportunity to compare their judgments with similar or dissimilar comparison partners.

Results were consistent with expectations: Overall, participants who believed that their judgments were subjective chose to compare with partners similar to themselves; those who believed their judgments were objective sought dissimilar comparison partners. This pattern faded in the high vested interest treatment condition. In this condition, participants were informed that they would earn $50 if their postcomparison judgment was most similar to that of an actual jury. In this circumstance, their desire for comparison was significantly amplified but they exhibited no differential partner preference.

This attenuation of preference for one or another type of comparison partner is understandable in light of the assumed consensus findings discussed earlier. People's assumptions that others believe as they do under conditions of high vested interest would attenuate differential preference for similar or dissimilar comparison partners, and this is precisely the result that was obtained. These findings suggest that vested interest can influence the fundamental cause–effect linkages that operate in processes of social comparison (cf. Crano, 1991) and, furthermore, that vested interest may have implications for a broad range of phenomena and psychological processes (Campbell, 1986). Yet, it is clear that as currently constituted, the conceptualization of vested interest is incomplete. A cursory examination of any newspaper discloses numerous examples of attitude-behavior inconsistency in situations that involve highly vested attitudes. For example, studies disclose that most adolescents possess a good understanding of the means by which HIV is transmitted, yet many report having made little or no adjustment in their sexual practices (Basen-Engquist & Parcel, 1992; Jemmott & Jemmott, 1990; Moore & Rosenthal, 1991). Is not the possibility of death from an AIDS-related disease hedonically relevant? If it is, then the basic conceptualization of vested interest as a factor that induces attitude-behavior consistency must be reconsidered.

The AIDS example provides a potential key to unraveling the varying effects of vested interest. Clearly it is no one's self-interest to become HIV positive, yet actions contrary to that attitude are common. Research suggests that adolescents possess a false sense of invulnerability with respect to this disease (Cornell, 1992). Thus it is not objective vulnerability that matters, but its subjective estimate. Are there factors that affect such estimates, short-circuiting attitude-behavior consistency? Examples of the AIDS variety suggest that there is more to vested interest than has been discussed, or discovered, to this point. Many factors appear to influence or moderate the effects of hedonic relevance. If these factors can be specified, greater precision in the manner in which vested attitudes influence behaviors might be purchased. The pages that follow describe an attempt to specify some of the theoretical contours of vested interest—the components of this general feature of attitude strength that intensify or attenuate its impact.

COMPONENTS OF VESTED INTEREST

The attitude literature reveals many factors that might have such an effect, and some of them may be conceptualized as component parts of the global variable identified as vested interest. The component factors most strongly related to vested interest are the focus of the remainder of this chapter. After describing these components, a study designed to assess their interdependence is described. The factors hypothesized to be component parts of the global concept of vested interest are: (a) the actor's *stake* in a given attitude object, (b) the *salience* of the object, (c) the *certainty* that specific consequences will ensue from an attitude-relevant action, (d) the *immediacy* of these consequences, and (e) the actor's *self-efficacy* to enact the requisite (or attitude-implicated) behaviors. Theoretically, the greater the magnitude of these factors, the greater the vested interest, and the more likely are the effects discussed earlier (e.g., attitude-behavior consistency, assumed consensus biases, etc.).

Stake

Stake, also termed *personal consequence*, refers to the subjective perception of the gain–loss consequences attached to an attitude object. Perceived stake is the element most analogous to global vested interest. Petty and Cacioppo (1986a) have suggested that self-interest can vary in terms of the number, magnitude, and duration of consequences associated with an issue or attitude object. All of these features, and probably others besides, affect the subjective perception of stake. We are not concerned with the particular components of stake at this point. It is sufficient that a person, for whatever reason—magnitude of consequences, their number, duration—perceive an attitude object to be of great personal consequence. If this perception holds, the attitude is of high stake. The greater the stake—the more one has to gain or lose—the stronger the attitude. And the stronger the attitude, the more likely are attitude-consistent actions.

Data consistent with this expectation are readily available. In an ingenious field study, Regan and Fazio (1977) assessed the attitudes of Cornell University students toward a housing shortage on campus, which resulted in some undergraduates being forced to live in the hallways of dormitories. As might be expected, most deplored this practice, even though only *some* students had a major stake in the issue— namely, those for whom a dormitory hallway served as their bedroom. Regan and Fazio found the hallway dwellers significantly more willing than other students to work to rectify the problem. Although almost all students' attitudes toward the housing debacle were strong and negative, those who had a stake in the issue were substantially more willing than others to work to effect a change. Stake determined the likelihood of attitudinally implicated action.

Many studies in the elaboration likelihood model (ELM) tradition provide grist for speculation on the manner in which stake operates (cf. Petty & Cacioppo, 1990). This body of research suggests that when stake is high (when the issue is of great personal consequence), people process information systematically (via the "central route"). Argument quality determines persuasive impact. Communications on high-stakes attitudes are more finely elaborated (Petty & Cacioppo, 1984; Petty, Cacioppo, & Goldman, 1981), and this enhanced elaboration may allow a more profound insight into the relevance of an action for a specific attitude. It may be that stake moderates attitude-behavior consistency because the behavioral implications of such attitudes simply are more accessible.

Salience

Research suggests that vivid cues are more likely than nonvivid cues to be noticed, and having been noticed, more likely to affect attributions (McArthur & Post, 1977; Taylor, Fiske, Etcoff, & Ruderman, 1978). Analogous to the effects of vividness is the *salience* of an attitude object. If the object is salient, vested interest will be enhanced, as will the likelihood of attitude-behavior consistency (Sears & Citrin, 1985). Showers and Cantor (1985), Wyer and Srull (1986), and others have shown that the relevance of a construct to a person's goals or needs enhances accessibility, which in turn is linked to attitude strength. Greater accessibility enhances the likelihood of self-interested voting (Young, Borgida, Sullivan, & Aldrich, 1987), and priming the vested interest implications of a political position enhances the likelihood of voters adopting attitudes consistent with these implications (Young, Borgida, Sullivan, & Aldrich, 1991). Apparently, making an attitude object more salient enhances the salience of attitude-relevant outcomes as well.

Vividness, priming, and similar operations may all enhance the salience of the self-interest implications of a position. If an attitude issue is of high salience, its vested implications may be more accessible (cf. Higgins, 1989; Higgins & Bargh, 1987). Research on the effects of *direct experience* is congruent with this speculation (Fazio, Chen, McDonel, & Sherman, 1982). Direct experience with an attitude object enhances attitude strength, and consequent attitude-behavior consistency. It may be that attitudes acquired through direct experience are more salient than those acquired vicariously.

Certainty

The certainty an individual attaches to the gain–loss consequences of an attitude object has important ramifications for vested interest. If the consequences are uncertain, the attitude is not likely to be of high vested interest. For example, a person may have a negative attitude toward AIDS. But vested interest will be attenuated if the individual perceives the relationship between "safe sex" and contracting AIDS to be negligible. Health-promoting sexual behaviors consistent with the high stake AIDS attitude are unlikely. In short, when the gain–loss consequences of an attitude object are uncertain, the attitude will prove hedonically irrelevant.

Evidence for the effects of certainty is available in Tyler and McGraw's (1983) research on antinuclear activists. In a survey of citizens' participation in antinuclear activities, the researchers found activists substantially more certain than nonactivists that a nuclear war would occur. Let us assume that no one has a positive attitude toward thermonuclear war. As such, the attitudes of activists and nonactivists alike toward this occurrence would not be distinguishable on any standard attitude measure. However, participants differed in their degree of certainty that such a cataclysm would come to pass. In our terms, the certainty of the gain/loss consequences of the attitude object, nuclear war, differed between activists and nonactivists. These certainty differences were responsible for variations in attitude strength, and attitude-behavior consistency.

Immediacy

Immediacy refers to the perceived temporal lag interposed between an attitude-implicated act and its presumed consequences. The hedonic relevance of an object whose consequences are removed in time is not as great as one whose consequences are expected to be felt immediately. Thus, a heavy smoker who assumes that the piper, if he is to be paid at all (see earlier section on certainty) will be paid in the distant future, can behave in an attitudinally inconsistent manner because the lack of immediacy attenuates the perception of vested interest. Immediacy thus helps to explain self-destructive behaviors. Research that indirectly supports this position was reported by Schuman, Ludwig, and Krosnick (1986; see also Kramer, Kalick, & Milburn, 1983), who tapped people's attitudes regarding the most important problem facing the United States. Only 6% cited war, or nuclear war. Clearly, people's attitudes toward nuclear war (and its consequences) must be extreme and negative. However, if most assume that such an outcome is "too far in the future to worry about" (Sears & Funk, 1991, p. 72), the attitude will not be strong or vested, and will not induce attitude-consistent action.

Self-Efficacy

The final vested interest component to be tendered is concerned with people's perceptions of their ability to perform actions consistent with the gain–loss implications of the attitude object. This component is termed *self-efficacy*, consistent with Bandura's usage (1977, 1982). Obviously, a number of actions logically spring from almost any attitude, but if these actions are beyond the capability of the actor (for reasons internal or external to the individual), efficacy will be perceived as low. Lack of self-efficacy will attenuate vested interest and attitude-behavior consistency. Returning to the smoker example, consider an individual who has a very negative attitude toward this practice, but simply cannot break the smoking habit. In this case, the vested interest of the (negative) attitude will be attenuated, and attitude-consistent action unlikely.

Self-efficacy appears to affect many aspects of behavior, from political participation (Abramson & Aldrich, 1982; Milbrath, 1981) to positive health practices (Miaman & Becker, 1974). In the laboratory, Ajzen and his colleagues (e.g., Ajzen, 1985; Ajzen & Madden, 1986) showed that self-efficacy (or perceived behavioral control, to use the terminology of the theory of planned behavior) is functionally related to attitude-behavior consistency. In a study of the functional network linking the components of the theory of planned behavior, Ajzen and Madden (1986) reported that self-efficacy not only has a direct effect on behavior, but also an indirect effect through its impact on intentions, which also impinge on behavior.

AN EXPERIMENTAL INVESTIGATION
INTO THE COMPONENTS OF VESTED INTEREST

Crano and Prislin (in press) investigated the utility of this five-component vested interest structure through the use of an experimental technique that expands on the general paradigm used in the study of social distance (cf. Bogardus, 1925; Triandis, 1964). In this approach, different factors (e.g., race, religion, etc.) are combined factorially in a description of a hypothetical stimulus person, and participants evaluate the resulting "gestalt." In Crano and Prislin's (in press) research, a basic scenario was developed involving an issue of relevance to students—the imposition of a system of comprehensive examinations (Johnson & Eagly, 1989). The single-spaced one-page script that participants read describes a day in the life of a student, Jim Johnson, who learns that senior comprehensive exams are being considered by the faculty senate. Jim is strongly opposed to the exams. Features of the scenario are altered systematically so as to manipulate the components of vested interest.

Stake is manipulated by altering the script in such a way that suggests that the actor has or does not "have an enormous stake" in the comprehensive exams. The issue is either salient to the actor, intruding into his thoughts, and appearing on the front page of the student newspaper, or it is deemphasized. Certainty is treated by describing passage of the comprehensive examination plan by the senate as a near certainty, or as highly unlikely. Immediacy is manipulated by altering Jim's class standing as senior or freshman. If passed, he will either take the exams in three months or in three years, depending on class standing. Efficacy is manipulated by the faculty senate's soliciting student opinion, "since many professors have yet to decide on their position" or, alternatively, by suggesting that most professors have already made up their minds on the issue (and hence, self-efficacy is very low).

Factorial combination of the high and low values of these five components results in a (2^5) 32-cell design. A minimum of 30 subjects was assigned randomly to each condition of the study. After subjects read the scenario, manipulation check measures were collected, as were estimates of Jim's attitude toward comprehensive examinations, and the likelihood that he would undertake various specified behaviors to defeat the proposal.

Manipulation Check Analyses

Were the manipulations powerful enough to affect perceptions of the experimental treatments? Previous research (cf. Crano, 1991; Crano & Messé, 1985) suggests that this is not an idle question, for if participants' comprehension of complex social manipulations is not satisfactory, interpretation of results is impossible. In the present research, results disclosed that the manipulations were successful. Five-way analyses of variance were computed on each manipulation check. In every instance, the manipulation of a specific vested-interest component resulted in a highly significant effect on the appropriate measure. In addition, stake was found to have a significant impact on participants' judgments of salience, immediacy, and self-efficacy. The greater the perceived stake in the issue, the greater were estimates of the salience of the issue, its immediacy, and the actor's (i.e., Jim's) ability to affect the issue's outcome.

As noted, Jim Johnson was depicted as being negatively predisposed toward senior comprehensive examinations. This attitude was reflected in participants' estimates of his attitude. Subjects in the high stakes condition assumed more negative attitudes than those in the low stakes treatment.

Expected Action

Did the manipulation of the five hypothesized components of vested interest influence participants' estimates of Jim Johnson's likely behavior? This issue was addressed by eight questions which required participants to estimate the likelihood that Jim would undertake various actions aimed at defeating the proposal. These actions included Jim's calling known professors, calling professors he did not know, signing petitions, volunteering his time to work against the plan, etc. The intercorrelations among the items were strong (coefficient alpha = .82), and the items were combined into a single index of action. Analysis of variance on the action index revealed three significant main effects. Stake profoundly influenced action estimates. Respondents in the high stakes condition assumed that the actor would engage much more intensively in activities directed against the proposal. Salience, too, exerted an influence. Participants in the high salience treatment assumed a higher level of activity against the disliked proposal than did low salience subjects. Self-efficacy was the final significant main effect disclosed in the analysis. When the scenario suggested that the actor had a good chance of affecting the outcome of the vote, participants assumed a higher level of action than when the actor was presented as being relatively powerless to affect it.

IMPLICATIONS AND CONCLUSIONS

How are these results to be interpreted? First, it is necessary to recognize that this research did not manipulate factors that influenced participants' actions, but rather their perceptions of a hypothetical actor whose attitudes and actions they were asked to divine. The relationship between these abstract predictions and the behavior of real people caught in a situation of great personal consequence can only be estimated from this study (cf. Campbell & Stanley, 1963). But the obtained estimates are logical and reasonable, and they are congruent with earlier studies in which actual behavior was observed. Generalization from observation and estimation to motivated action is always treacherous, but at a minimum the results provide encouragement and direction for further explorations into vested interest. The most powerful impression to emerge from all of the analyses is the overpowering impact of stake, or personal consequence, on attitude-consistent action. This might be expected in light of earlier experimental research, but the reach of this factor is impressive, for it influenced not just perceptions of attitude and action, but of other action-relevant components as well. Stake affected participants' perceptions of the perceived salience of the issue to the actor. When stake was high, they assumed that the critical issue would be highly salient. This effect was additive—stake did not interact with, but enhanced the perception of, issue salience. This is important because salience impacted on action. A similar observation can be made with respect to self-efficacy. Analysis disclosed that variations in self-efficacy produced differences in perceptions of the likelihood of the actor's working against the plan. Higher levels of manipulated self-efficacy resulted in higher levels of predicted action. Variations in stake influenced perceptions of self-efficacy. When the stakes were high, participants assumed that the actor would sense a higher level of self-efficacy. Finally, stake affected perceptions of immediacy. The greater the personal consequence of the issue, the more pressing it was perceived to be. Immediacy did not impact strongly on action (its effect was significant at $p < .07$), but it would be a mistake to disregard this factor on the basis of this result alone.

The impact of stake, or personal consequence, provides an explanation for the effects of conceptually related variables shown to affect attitude strength and subsequent attitude-behavior consistency. These variables—ego-involvement, attitude importance, self-interest—may be viewed as indicators, albeit imperfect ones, of vested interest. When these imperfect indicators overlap with personal consequence as, for example, when an important attitude is also highly vested, the indirect indicator works well in predicting subsequent attitude-congruent action. When the indirect measure misses the mark—it is easy to conceive of ego-involving or objectively important issues that have no personal consequence—the lack of overlap of the proxy with the operative variable, vested interest, is ruinous. Failures of this type, attributable to stand-ins that provide an impoverished indication of the operative variable, afford a false reading of its effects, promote misunderstanding, and result ultimately in an underestimation of vested interest's impact on attitudes and attitude-behavior consistency.

ACKNOWLEDGMENT

Preparation of this chapter was facilitated by NSF grant SBR 9396057, for which I am most grateful.

REFERENCES

Abramson, P. R., & Aldrich, J. H. (1982). The decline of electoral participation in America. *American Political Science Review, 76,* 502–521.
Agans, R. P., & Crano, W. D. (1992). *Self-interest and the perception of imminent risk in persuasion.* Unpublished manuscript, University of Arizona, Dept. of Communication, Tucson.
Ajzen, I. (1985). From intentions to actions: A theory of planned behavior. In J. Kuhl & J. Beckmann (Eds.), *Action-control: From cognition to behavior.* Berlin: Springer.
Ajzen, I., & Madden, T. J. (1986). Prediction of goal-directed behavior: The role of intention, perceived control, and prior behavior. *Journal of Experimental Social Psychology, 22,* 453–474.

Allport, G. W. (1935). Attitudes. In C. Murchison (Ed.), *Handbook of social psychology* (pp. 798–884). Worcester, MA: Clark University Press.

Bandura, A. (1977). Self-efficacy: Toward a unifying theory of behavioral change. *Psychological Review, 84*, 191–215.

Bandura, A. (1982). Self-efficacy mechanism in human agency. *American Psychologist, 37*, 122–147.

Basen-Engquist, K., & Parcel, G. S. (1992). Attitudes, norms and self-efficacy: A model of adolescents' HIV-related sexual risk behavior. *Health Education Quarterly, 19*, 263–277.

Berent, M. K. (1990). *Attitude importance and the recall of attitude relevant information.* Unpublished master's thesis, Ohio State University, Department of Psychology, Columbus.

Bogardus, E. S. (1925). Measuring social distance. *Journal of Applied Psychology, 9*, 299–308.

Boninger, D. S., Krosnick, J. A., & Berent, M. K. (in press). The causes of attitude importance: Self-interest, social identification, and values. *Journal of Personality and Social Psychology.*

Brewer, M. B., & Crano, W. D. (1994). *Social psychology.* Minneapolis/St. Paul: West.

Cacioppo, J. T., Marshallgoodell, B. S., Tassinary, L. G., & Petty, R. E. (1992). Rudimentary determinants of attitude—classical conditioning is more effective when prior knowledge about the attitude stimulus is low than high. *Journal of Experimental Social Psychology, 28*, 207–223.

Campbell, D. T. (1986). Rationality and utility from the standpoint of evolutionary biology. *Journal of Business, 59*, S355–S364.

Campbell, D. T., & Stanley, J. C. (1963). Experimental and quasi-experimental designs for research in teaching. In N. L. Gage (Ed.), *Handbook of research on teaching* (pp. 171–246). Chicago: Rand-McNally.

CBS-*New York Times* poll. (1982, May 30). *New York Times*, p. 1.

Cialdini, R. B., & Petty, R. E. (1981). Anticipatory opinion effects. In R. E. Petty, T. M. Ostrom, & T. C. Brock (Eds.), *Cognitive responses in persuasion.* Hillsdale, NJ: Lawrence Erlbaum Associates.

Cornell University Medical College Conference on Health Policy (1992). *Adolescents at risk: Medical-social perspectives.* Boulder: Westview.

Crano, W. D. (1983). Assumed consensus of attitudes: The effect of vested interest. *Personality and Social Psychology Bulletin, 9*, 597–608.

Crano, W. D. (1991). Pitfalls associated with the use of financial incentives (and other complex manipulations) in social research. *Basic and Applied Social Psychology, 12*, 369–390.

Crano, W. D., & Brewer, M. B. (1986). *Principles and methods of social research.* Boston: Allyn & Bacon.

Crano, W. D., & Hannula-Bral, K. (in press). Majority/minority and in-group/out-group social influence in subjective and objective task contexts. *Journal of Experimental Social Psychology.*

Crano, W. D., & Messe, L. A. (1985). Assessing and redressing comprehension artifacts in social intervention research. *Evaluation Review, 9*, 144–172.

Crano, W. D., & Prislin, R. (in press). Components of vested interest and attitude-behavior consistency. *Basic and Applied Social Psychology.*

Eagly, A. H., & Teelak, K. (1972). Width of latitude of acceptance as a determinant of attitude change. *Journal of Personality and Social Psychology, 23*, 388–397.

Eiser, J. R. (1990). *Social judgment.* Pacific Grove, CA: Brooks/Cole.

Fazio, R. H., Chen, J., McDonel, E. C., & Sherman, S. J. (1982). Attitude accessibility, attitude-behavior consistency, and the strength of the object-evaluation association. *Journal of Experimental Social Psychology, 18*, 339–357.

Festinger, L. (1954). A theory of social comparison processes. *Human Relations, 7*, 117–140.

Frohlich, N. (1974). Self-interest or altruism, what difference? *Journal of Conflict Resolution, 18*, 55–73.

Goethals, G. R. (1986). Social comparison theory: Social psychology from the lost and found. *Personality and Social Psychology Bulletin, 12*, 261–278.

Goethals, G. R., & Darley, J. M. (1987). Social comparison theory: Self-evaluation and group life. In B. Mullen & G. R. Goethals (Eds.), *Theories of group behavior* (pp. 21–47). New York: Springer-Verlag.

Gorenflo, D. W., & Crano, W. D. (1989). Judgmental subjectivity/objectivity and locus of choice in social comparison. *Journal of Personality and Social Psychology, 57*, 605–614.

Green, D. P. (1988). *Self-interest, public opinion, and mass political behavior.* Unpublished doctoral dissertation, University of California, Department of Political Science, Berkeley.

Green, D. P., & Gerken, A. E. (1989). Self-interest and public opinion toward smoking restriction and cigarette taxes. *Public Opinion Quarterly, 53*, 1–16.

Higgins, E. T. (1989). Knowledge accessibility and activation: A general model and its application to self-knowledge, automaticity, and vulnerability. In J. S. Uleman & J. A. Bargh (Eds.), *Unintended thought: The limits of awareness, intention, and control.* New York: Guilford.

Higgins, E. T., & Bargh, J. A. (1987). Social cognition and social perception. *Annual Review of Psychology, 38*, 369–425.

Hovland, C. I., Harvey, O. J., & Sherif, M. (1957). Assimilation and contrast effects in communication and attitude change. *Journal of Abnormal and Social Psychology, 55*, 242–252.

Insko, C. A. (1967). *Theories of attitude change.* New York: Appleton-Century-Crofts.

Jemmott, L. S., & Jemmott, J. B. (1990). Sexual knowledge, attitudes, and risky sexual behavior among inner-city Black male adolescents. *Journal of Adolescent Research, 5*, 346–369.

Johnson, B., & Eagly, A. H. (1989). Effects of involvement on persuasion: A meta-analysis. *Psychological Bulletin, 106*, 290–314.

Johnson, B., & Eagly, A. H. (1990). Involvement and persuasion: Types, tradition and the evidence. *Psychological Bulletin, 107*, 375–384.

Judd, C. M., & Krosnick, J. A. (1989). The structural bases of consistency among political attitudes: The effects of political expertise and attitude importance. In A. R. Pratkanis, S. J. Breckler, & A. G. Greenwald (Eds.), *Attitude structure and function* (pp. 99–128). Hillsdale, NJ: Lawrence Erlbaum Associates.

Kahneman, D., Knetsch, J., & Thaler, R. (1986). Fairness and the assumptions of economics. *Journal of Business, 59*, S285–S300, S329–S354.

Kinder, D. R. (1986). The continuing American dilemma: White resistance to racial change 40 years after Myrdal. *Journal of Social Issues, 42*, 151–171.

Kramer, B. M., Kalick, S. M., & Milburn, M. A. (1983). Attitudes toward nuclear weapons and nuclear war. *Journal of Social Issues, 39*, 7–24.

Krosnick, J. A. (1988a). Attitude importance and attitude change. *Journal of Experimental Social Psychology, 24*, 240–255.

Krosnick, J. A. (1988b). The role of attitude importance in social evaluation: A study of policy preferences, presidential candidate evaluations, and voting behavior. *Journal of Personality and Social Psychology, 55*, 196–210.

Krosnick, J. A. (1989). Attitude importance and attitude accessibility. *Personality and Social Psychology Bulletin, 15*, 297–308.

Krosnick, J. A. (1990). Government policy and citizen passion: A study of issue publics in contemporary America. *Political Behavior, 12*, 59–92.

Krosnick, J. A., & Schuman, H. (1988). Attitude intensity, importance, and certainty and susceptibility to response effects. *Journal of Personality and Social Psychology, 54*, 940–952.

Kruglanski, A. W., & Mayseless, O. (1987). Motivational effects in the social comparison of opinions. *Journal of Personality and Social Psychology, 53*, 834–842.

Mansbridge, J. J. (1990). *Beyond self-interest.* Chicago: University of Chicago Press.

Marks, G., & Miller, N. (1987). Ten years of research on the false-consensus effect: An empirical and theoretical overview. *Psychological Bulletin, 102*, 72–90.

McArthur, L. Z., & Post, D. L. (1977). Figural emphasis and person perception. *Journal of Experimental Social Psychology, 13*, 520–536.

Miaman, L., & Becker, M. (1974). The health belief model: Origins and correlates in psychological theory. *Health Education Monographs, 2*, 336–362.

Milbrath, L. W. (1981). Political participation. In S. L. Long (Ed.), *The handbook of political behavior* (Vol. 4). New York: Plenum.

Moore, S., & Rosenthal, D. (1991). Adolescent invulnerability and perceptions of AIDS risk. *Journal of Adolescent Research, 6*, 164–180.

Mueller, D. C. (1979). *Public choice.* New York: Cambridge University Press.

Olson, J. M., Ellis, R. J., & Zanna, M. P. (1983). Validating objective versus subjective judgments: Interest in social comparison and consistency information. *Personality and Social Psychology Bulletin, 9*, 427–436.

Olson, J. M., Herman, C. P., & Zanna, M. P. (Eds.). (1986). *Relative deprivation and social comparison: The Ontario Symposium* (Vol. 4). Hillsdale, NJ: Lawrence Erlbaum Associates.

Peterson, P. D., & Koulack, D. (1969). Attitude change as a function of latitudes of acceptance and rejection. *Journal of Personality and Social Psychology, 11*, 309–311.

Petty, R. E., & Cacioppo, J. T. (1981). *Attitudes and persuasion: Classic and contemporary approaches.* Dubuque, IA: William C. Brown.

Petty, R. E., & Cacioppo, J. T. (1984). The effects of involvement on responses to argument quantity and quality: Central and peripheral routes to persuasion. *Journal of Personality and Social Psychology, 46*, 69–81.

Petty, R. E., & Cacioppo, J. T. (1986a). *Communication and persuasion: Central and peripheral routes to persuasion.* New York: Springer-Verlag.

Petty, R. E., & Cacioppo, J. T. (1986b). The elaboration likelihood model of persuasion. In L. Berkowitz (Ed.), *Advances in experimental social psychology* (Vol. 19, pp. 123–205). New York: Academic.

Petty, R. E., & Cacioppo, J. T. (1990). Involvement and persuasion: Tradition versus integration. *Psychological Bulletin, 107*, 367–374.

Petty, R. E., Cacioppo, J. T., & Goldman, R. (1981). Personal involvement as a determinant of argument-based persuasion. *Journal of Personality and Social Psychology, 41*, 847–855.

Petty, R. E., Cacioppo, J. T., & Haugtvedt, C. P. (1992). Ego-involvement and persuasion: An appreciative look at the Sherifs' contribution to the study of self-relevance and attitude change. In D. Granberg & G. Sarup (Eds.), *Social judgment and intergroup relations: Essays in honor of Muzafer Sherif* (pp. 147–175). New York: Springer-Verlag.

Regan, D. T., & Fazio, R. (1977). On the consistency between attitudes and behavior: Look to the method of attitude formation. *Journal of Experimental Social Psychology, 13*, 28–45.

Ross, L., Greene, D., & House, P. (1977). The false-consensus effect: An egocentric bias in social perception and attribution processes. *Journal of Experimental Social Psychology, 13*, 279–301.

Schuman, H., Ludwig, J., & Krosnick, J. A. (1986). The perceived threat of nuclear war, salience, and open questions. *Public Opinion Quarterly, 50*, 519–536.

Sears, D. O., & Citrin, J. (1985). *Tax revolt: Something for nothing in California* (enlarged ed.). Cambridge, MA: Harvard University Press.

Sears, D. O., & Funk, C. L. (1991). The role of self-interest in social and political attitudes. In M. P. Zanna (Ed.), *Advances in experimental social psychology* (Vol. 24, pp. 1–91). New York: Academic.

Sears, D. O., Hensler, C. P., & Speer, L. K. (1979). Whites' opposition to "busing": Self-interest or symbolic politics? *American Political Science Review, 73*, 369–384.

Sherif, C., Kelley, M., Rodgers, H., Sarup, G., & Tittler, B. (1973). Personal involvement, social judgment and action. *Journal of Personality and Social Psychology, 27*, 311–328.

Sherif, M., & Cantril, H. (1947). *The psychology of ego-involvement.* New York: Wiley.

Sherif, M., & Hovland, C. I. (1961). *Social judgment: Assimilation and contrast effects in communication and attitude change.* New Haven: Yale University Press.

Sherif, M., Sherif, C., & Nebergall, R. (1965). *Attitude and attitude change: The social judgment approach.* Philadelphia: W. B. Saunders.

Showers, C., & Cantor, N. (1985). Social cognition: A look at motivated strategies. *Annual Review of Psychology, 36*, 275–305.

Simon, H. A. (1986). Rationality in psychology and economics. *Journal of Business, 59*, S209–250, S279.

Sivacek, J., & Crano, W. D. (1982). Vested interest as a moderator of attitude-behavior consistency. *Journal of Personality and Social Psychology, 43*, 210–221.

Sniderman, P. M., & Tetlock, P. E. (1986a). Reflections on American racism. *Journal of Social Issues, 42*, 173–187.

Sniderman, P. M., & Tetlock, P. E. (1986b). Symbolic racism: Problems of motive attribution in political analysis. *Journal of Social Issues, 42*, 129–150.

Taylor, S. E., Fiske, S. E., Etcoff, N. L., & Ruderman, A. J. (1978). The categorical and contextual bases of person memory and stereotyping. *Journal of Personality and Social Psychology, 36*, 778–793.

Triandis, H. C. (1964). A note on Rokeach's theory of prejudice. *Journal of Abnormal and Social Psychology, 62*, 184–186.

Tversky, A., & Kahneman, D. (1986). Rational choice and the framing of decisions. *Journal of Business, 59*, S251–S284.

Tyler, T. R., & McGraw, K. M. (1983). The threat of nuclear war: Risk interpretation and behavioral response. *Journal of Social Issues, 39*, 25–40.

Wyer, R. S., & Srull, T. K. (1986) The role of chronic and temporary goals in social information processing. In R. M. Sorrentino & E. T. Higgins (Eds.), *Handbook of motivation and cognition: Foundations of social behavior* (pp. 503–549). New York: Guilford.

Young, J., Borgida, E., Sullivan, J., & Aldrich, J. (1987). Personal agendas and the relationship between self-interest and voting behavior. *Social Psychology Quarterly, 50*, 64–71.

Young, J., Thomsen, C. J., Borgida, E., Sullivan, J., & Aldrich, J. (1991). When self-interest makes a difference: The role of construct accessibility in political reasoning. *Journal of Experimental Social Psychology, 27*, 271–296.

Zanna, M. P., Higgins, E. T., & Herman, C. P. (1982). *Consistency in social behavior: The Ontario symposium* (Vol. 2). Hillsdale, NJ: Lawrence Erlbaum Associates.

7

▼▼▼▼▼▼▼

The Causes and Consequences
of Attitude Importance

David S. Boninger
University of California, Los Angeles

Jon A. Krosnick
Matthew K. Berent
Leandre R. Fabrigar
Ohio State University

In Herzog's (1993) in-depth interviews with animal rights activists, respondents were strikingly consistent in describing their involvement in the movement as the central focus of their lives. Said one respondent, "For my wife and me, [the movement] is the most important aspect of our lives" (p. 115). Another respondent, when asked how important the animal rights movement was in her life, replied, "It *is* my life" (p. 116). Clearly, these individuals' negative attitudes toward what they consider to be abuse of animals are tremendously psychologically significant and motivating. Herzog's interviews revealed that movement participants were constantly thinking and talking about animal rights, trying to convince others to adopt their own attitudes, and even losing close friends and divorcing spouses as the result of their personal investments in those attitudes.

Animal rights does not seem to be a unique issue in this regard. Activists on many other issues routinely exhibit dramatic behaviors expressing attitudes that they apparently consider extremely important personally. Antiabortionists bomb abortion clinics and, in one recent case, went so far as to murder a physician who performed abortions. Environmentalists chain themselves to trees in the face of oncoming heavy machinery to prevent deforestation. Civil rights activists risk personal safety in violent confrontations with Ku Klux Klan members at their rallies. And, of course, the Vietnam War inspired many to protest in ways that risked and sometimes sacrificed their own lives.

Thus people can sometimes care very deeply about one particular attitude to the exclusion of concern about all others. More often, it seems, individuals care a great deal about a few of their attitudes, whereas they attach little or no

159

significance to others. This sort of variation seems as likely to describe attitudes in the political domain as attitudes in other domains, regarding consumer products, social groups, individual people, aspects of the self, places, and many more classes of objects.

What are the cognitive, motivational, and behavioral consequences of attaching personal importance to a particular attitude? What causes individuals to consider some attitudes to be very important while attaching little or no importance to others? In this chapter, we review research that has explored these questions. We begin by defining attitude importance, differentiating it from some closely related constructs, and explaining how it has been operationalized. Next, we review evidence addressing the extent to which important attitudes are strong attitudes, and we outline a series of consequences of importance. Finally, we examine the origins of attitude importance and discuss the implications of all this work for future research.

CONCEPTUAL AND OPERATIONAL DEFINITIONS

Conceptual Definition

Attributes that differentiate strong attitudes from weak ones fall into at least three general categories (see Krosnick & Petty, ch. 1, this volume). Some of these attributes are features of the evaluation itself, such as its extremity (e.g., Judd & Brauer, ch. 3, this volume). Others are features of the cognitive structure in which the attitude is stored in memory, such as the strength of the link between the object and the evaluation (e.g., Fazio, ch. 10, this volume) or the amount of information linked to the attitude (e.g., Wood, Rhodes, & Biek, ch. 11, this volume). Other attitude attributes are subjective judgments or perceptions of the attitude, such as how confident people are in its validity (e.g., Gross, Holtz, & Miller, ch. 9, this volume).

Attitude importance falls into this latter category and is defined as an individual's subjective sense of the concern, caring, and significance he or she attaches to an attitude (e.g., Krosnick, 1988a). To attach great personal importance to an attitude is to care tremendously about it and to be deeply concerned about it. There is nothing subtle about attitude importance, particularly at its highest levels: People know very well when they are deeply concerned about an attitude, and they know just as well when they have no special concern about one. In short, attitude importance is a belief (see Fishbein & Ajzen, 1975), linking an attitude to an attribute (i.e., high, moderate, or low psychological significance).

In our view, attitude importance is consequential precisely because of its status as a belief: Perceiving an attitude to be personally important leads people to use it in processing information, making decisions, and taking action. To understand when this subjective perception is most likely to have impact, it is useful to consider Fazio's (1990a) distinction between spontaneous and deliberative processing. He suggested that people sometimes perform behaviors without actively and effortfully considering relevant attitudes (via spontaneous processing); an extreme example might be a spur-of-the-moment purchase of a candy bar at a supermarket checkout counter. On the other hand, some decisions are made only after very careful thinking about all relevant considerations, including attitudes (via deliberative processing); an extreme example would be deciding whether to marry a particular person.

We expect attitude importance to have its most pronounced effects under these latter conditions, when people can consciously make reference to their beliefs about attitude importance. Importance may also have automatic effects on spontaneous processing as well, as we suggest here. But we suspect that these effects are likely to evolve over time as the result of deliberate choices that people make based upon how much personal importance they attach to particular attitudes. Thus, whereas Fazio (1990a) expected greater effects of attitude accessibility during spontaneous processing, we expect greater effects of attitude importance during deliberative processing.

To attach personal importance to an attitude is to commit oneself to think about the object, to gather information about it, to use that information as well as one's attitude in making relevant decisions, and to design one's actions in accord with that attitude. In this sense, attaching personal importance to an attitude represents a substantial commitment, in some ways analogous to taking a job or making a long-term commitment to an interpersonal relationship. Consequently, we suspect, people are not likely to attach personal importance to an attitude lightly, in response to relatively trivial events. Just as people are "misers" with regard to cognitive processing (e.g., Fiske & Taylor, 1991), they are probably also miserly with their attachments of psychological significance and value to attitudes: Only clear and compelling reasons seem likely to motivate such a psychological investment. So high levels of importance are unlikely to emerge unnoticed over time. Rather, deep and lasting concern is likely to be instigated by significant events of which people are well-aware.

This definition suggests that attitude importance is related to, yet distinct from, other attitudinal constructs, including centrality (Converse, 1964; Krech & Crutchfield, 1948), involvement (Apsler & Sears, 1968; Miller, 1965), ego-involvement (Sherif, 1980; Sherif & Hovland, 1961), ego-preoccupation (Abelson, 1988), salience (Hoelter, 1985; Lemon, 1968), and personal relevance (Petty & Cacioppo, 1986, 1990). These constructs are all conceptually similar to attitude importance, in that they emphasize the significance of an attitude for an individual's psychological system. And, in fact, some discussions of these constructs have explicitly linked them to personal concern, caring, or investment. For instance, Petty, Cacioppo, and Haugtvedt (1992, p. 153) treated personal relevance as synonymous with the "importance" of an attitude object. Krech and Crutchfield (1948) discussed central attitudes in terms of their "importance to the person"

(p. 251). And Sherif and Hovland (1961) described ego-involving attitudes as those that have "intrinsic importance" (p. 197). Thus, all these constructs seem to share a common core of meaning.

However, our conceptual definition of attitude importance is critically different from the most common definitions of these other constructs in one significant respect. Whereas attitude importance is the subjective state of attaching personal importance to an attitude, these other constructs have almost always been defined in terms of links between the attitude object and the self. For example, Katz (1960) and Converse (1964) defined centrality in terms of the number and strength of the links between an attitude and the self-concept. Sherif and his colleagues defined ego-involvement as the extent to which an attitude is related to various aspects of the self (Sherif & Cantril, 1947). To Johnson and Eagly (1989), involvement is the links of an issue to an individual's "important goals and outcomes" (p. 292) or "important values" (p. 290).

In contrast, attitude importance is not *defined* in terms of links to the self. What distinguishes attitude importance from these other constructs is that it is defined as a subjective sense of significance and caring that is attached to an attitude. As we suggest later, links between an attitude and an individual's goals, values, or other aspects of the self may well be causes of attitude importance. Objective conditions presumably influence perceptions of the relevance of an attitude to one's self, and these perceptions of self-relevance may in turn shape decisions about whether or not to attach personal importance to the attitude. But it is conceivable that even in the face of information linking an attitude to oneself, a person may decide not to attach importance to it because of the future cognitive and emotional burdens such a decision would entail. Thus, links to aspects of the self are conceptually distinct from subjective perceptions of importance, although these two constructs seem likely to be bound to one another in a causal chain.

Operational Definition

This concept, a subjective sense of psychological significance, seems best measured via people's self-reports. Certainly, self-reports may be subject to intentional distortion due to self-presentation concerns or unintentional errors due to vague internal cues. Nonetheless, the most direct way to get at the critical self-perception component of the construct seems to be by asking people.

In our own research, for example, we have relied on three principal sorts of questions: asking people how important an attitude object is to them personally, how deeply they care about it, and how concerned they are about it. Thus, our operationalization has stuck close to the conceptual definition of the construct of interest. Our research has focussed on political attitudes, and we have asked people about the personal importance they attached to attitude objects rather than the attitudes themselves. Thus we have asked people, "How important is the issue of abortion to you personally?" rather than addressing the construct of interest more directly by asking "How important is your attitude toward abortion to you personally?"

We have shied away from this latter approach because the word "attitude" is a psychologists' technical term that most people use differently than we do. We feared that there was a significant danger of misunderstanding or confusion (see Abelson, 1988, for a similar argument). In asking about objects, we have presumed that the importance people report attaching to them is an interchangeable proxy for the importance they attach to their attitudes toward those objects. And, indeed, recent studies have shown that these two sorts of judgments are indeed essentially identical for the sorts of political attitudes we examine (median $r = .94$, Fabrigar & Krosnick, 1994a). Furthermore, the reliabilities of items asking about the importance of objects are significantly greater than the reliabilities of items asking about the importance of attitudes (Fabrigar & Krosnick, 1994a). Consequently, it seems advisable to use the former rather than the latter.

Like all other self-report rating measurement approaches employed in questionnaires, our approach to assessing attitude importance is subject to both random and systematic measurement error (see Krosnick, 1986; Krosnick, Boninger, Chuang, Berent, & Carnot, 1993; Marsh, 1986).[1] To minimize the impact of random measurement error, it is necessary to measure importance with multiple items that can be mathematically combined. And to minimize the impact of systematic measurement error due, for example, to response biases (see, e.g., Green & Citrin, 1994), it is helpful to employ different response scales for the different items (e.g., "extremely, very, . . ." vs. "a great deal, a lot, . . .") and average them together. Better yet, one can implement a multitrait-multimethod approach across a range of constructs, thus allowing for statistical isolation of method effects (e.g., Krosnick et al., 1993). Differences across people in their use of rating scales can also be eliminated by measuring the importance of a wide range of attitudes and statistically controlling for shared variance among them in a repeated-measures analysis that focuses on within-person variance in attitude importance (see, e.g., Berent & Krosnick, 1993b).[2] In this sense, measurement and analysis of attitude importance should be carried out just as carefully as, for instance, the measurement and analysis of reaction time (see Fazio, 1990b) in order to obtain precise data. When this is done, attitude importance appears to be a highly crystallized construct, with stability coefficients over 3- to 4-month periods averaging .83 (Krosnick, 1986).

---

[1] In fact, the reliability of single items measuring importance is often in the range of .50 to .60 (Krosnick, 1986). Random errors appear partly because the meanings of response options such as "extremely important" or "very important" are somewhat vague (e.g., Wallsten, Budescu, Rapoport, Zwick, & Forsyth, 1986), so the translation of one's subjective judgments onto such verbal expressions is only approximately accurate. This problem is even greater when a rating scale involves some points labeled only numerically rather with words (see Krosnick & Berent, 1993).

[2] When long rating scales are used (e.g., 0–100 points), we have also found it useful to subject responses to a logarithmic transformation, which focuses analytic attention on variability at the high end of the importance continuum (Krosnick, 1988a).

Because our conceptual definition of attitude importance is distinct from the conceptual definitions of related constructs (in terms of our emphasis on subjective perception), it is not surprising that our operationalization of importance (via self-reports) is quite different from approaches that have often been used to gauge these other constructs. For example, involvement has been gauged through interest in attitude-relevant information (Bishop, 1990; Watts, 1967), amount of attitude-relevant knowledge (Stember & Hyman, 1949–1950), frequency of thought about an attitude object (Bishop, 1990), frequency of talking or reading about it (Watts, 1967), or the confluence of importance, frequency of thought, commitment, and social support (Miller, 1965). Similarly, ego-involvement has been measured via the sizes of latitudes of rejection and noncommitment (Sherif, Sherif, & Nebergall, 1965), via the number of categories used in sorting attitude statements (Sherif & Hovland, 1953), and via membership in social groups known to be behaviorally involved in an issue (Hovland & Sherif, 1952). After correcting for distortion due to random and systematic measurement error, these operations and others used to gauge related aspects of strength are only weakly or moderately associated with subjective self-reports of attitude importance and do not seem to reflect a single higher order construct (Krosnick, Boninger, Chuang, Berent, & Carnot, 1993). Consequently, our operational definition of attitude importance appears to be appropriately intertwined with, but nonetheless distinct from, these other related constructs. The studies reviewed in this chapter included measures of importance conforming to our operational definition, even in cases where the investigators did not discuss their findings in terms of attitude importance.[3]

Personal Versus Collective Importance

One could envision measuring a person's perceptions of the importance of an attitude object at a variety of social levels in addition to the personal level. For example, people could be asked how important an object is for a particular social group, for a country as a whole, or for the entire world. Indeed, a number of studies have explored beliefs about *national* importance by asking respondents what are the country's most important issues or how important is a particular issue for the country as a whole (e.g., Aldrich, Sullivan, & Borgida, 1989; Neuman, 1986, p. 72; Repass, 1971).

---

[3]The correlational approach we and others have taken to studying attitude importance is quite different from experimental manipulations of related constructs (e.g., personal relevance or involvement) conducted in laboratory settings (see Petty, Haugtvedt, & Smith, ch. 5, this volume; Thomsen, Borgida, & Lavine, ch. 8, this volume). Studies employing such manipulations have rarely included measures of attitude importance as manipulation checks and have even more rarely examined whether importance mediated the effects of the manipulations. And of those that did measure importance, some failed to find effects on it (as we discuss later). Therefore, we will not presume that an experimental manipulation of personal relevance or outcome-relevant involvement (Johnson & Eagly, 1989) is informative about attitude importance per se unless importance was measured and examined directly.

Although our measures of personal importance and these measures of national importance may seem similar, they reflect distinguishable constructs. After correcting for random measurement error and correlated error due to measurement method, Fabrigar and Krosnick (1994a) found that personal and national importance clearly reflected distinct, though related, constructs (median $r = .66$). These judgments were also distinguishable in terms of their causes: Whereas personal importance was driven uniquely by self-interest (as we discuss more fully later), national importance was uniquely a function of exposure to news media coverage of the issue (Fabrigar & Krosnick, 1994a; see also Iyengar & Kinder, 1987). Fabrigar and Krosnick also found that personal importance was a significant predictor of five indicators of psychological engagement in a political issue (attitude expression via votes in an election and via telephone calls or letters to politicians, newspapers, or magazines, attitude extremity and accessibility, and memory for attitude-relevant information), whereas national importance had essentially no measurable impact on any of the indicators. These findings are consonant with Cialdini and Petty's (1981, pp. 221–222) view of the persuasion literature as showing that forewarning's effect on an individual is regulated by his or her perception of personal importance, not the importance of an object for people generally. Because very little research has examined national importance judgments and because national importance seems markedly less consequential than personal importance, we focus here on personal importance.

ARE IMPORTANT ATTITUDES STRONG?

According to Krosnick and Petty (ch. 1, this volume), strong attitudes possess four key features: They are resistant to change, are stable over time, have significant impact on cognitive processes (such as attitude formation), and are powerful determinants of social behavior. We now turn to research that has explored whether important attitudes possess these four features.

Resistance to Change and Stability

As one would expect, several studies have shown that important attitudes are unusually resistant to change. For example, Fine (1957) demonstrated that subjects concerned about biological warfare changed their attitudes less in response to a persuasive message than did subjects who were less concerned. And Gorn (1975) replicated this same finding using the issue of Canadian separatism.[4]

---

[4]Consistent with these studies, Rhine and Severance (1970) found that subjects exhibited less attitude change in response to a persuasive message on a topic they considered important (increasing tuition) than in response to a persuasive message on a topic they considered unimportant (increasing acreage in a local park). However, confounds of topic and message with importance make it difficult to know exactly what accounted for the observed differences in persuasion.

Additional research has revealed bolstering of important attitudes even before a persuasive message is encountered. For example, Allyn and Festinger (1961) exposed teenagers to a message advocating a raise in the minimum driving age. Half of the teenagers were forewarned about the message's content and half were not. Forewarning reduced the impact of the persuasive message, but only among teenagers for whom it was important to have a driver's license. Along similar lines, Cialdini, Levy, Herman, Kozlowski, and Petty (1976) found that in response to the news that an individual would be discussing an issue with someone with whom they disagreed, important attitudes became more polarized, whereas unimportant attitudes became more moderate. Thus, people appear to take steps to resist change in important attitudes even before they encounter forces encouraging such change.

There is also evidence suggesting that important attitudes are unusually stable. Correlations between reports of political attitudes made by the same individuals on two or more occasions separated by months or years are stronger when the attitudes involved were more important (Converse, 1964; Feldman, 1989; Hahn, 1970; Kendall, 1954; Krosnick, 1988b; Schuman & Presser, 1981). Recently, Pelham (1991) found the same result with regard to self-views regarding the traits or features people believe they possess: The importance people attached to such self-views was positively associated with their correlational consistency over time.

However, as Krosnick (1988b) pointed out, there is a plausible alternative explanation for this greater consistency. Perhaps people are able to report their important attitudes more *precisely* than they can report their unimportant attitudes, because people presumably think more about the former and therefore have a more refined sense of how they feel about the objects involved. This precision, in and of itself, should reduce the amount of random measurement error in attitude reports and would thereby increase their over-time consistency. In fact, Kendall (1954), Converse (1964), Schuman and Presser (1981), and Feldman (1989) interpreted the relation they observed between importance and over-time consistency as reflecting a difference in this sort of reporting precision, not a difference in the stability of the underlying attitudes involved.

To test this interpretation more precisely, Krosnick (1988b) and Judd and Krosnick (1982) estimated the amount of random measurement error in attitude reports directly (via multiple-indicator structural equation models) and found a nonsignificant, weak *positive* relation between it and attitude importance.[5] Furthermore, after controlling for random measurement error, Krosnick (1988b) found that political attitudes people considered personally important were indeed more stable over several months than were unimportant attitudes.

---

[5]It is also useful to note that reports of unimportant attitudes are apparently not more susceptible to systematic measurement error due to measurement method (Bishop, 1990; Krosnick & Schuman, 1988).

Krosnick and Cornet (1993) found that the relations of importance to stability and reliability varied across the 1976 U.S. presidential election campaign. During the last 4 months of the campaign, higher attitude importance was associated with greater attitude stability and slightly more random measurement error, replicating Krosnick's (1988b) findings. But during the first 5 months of the campaign, important and unimportant attitudes were equally stable, but there was strikingly more measurement error in reports of unimportant attitudes. Krosnick and Cornet (1993) concluded that the stability gap between important and unimportant attitudes is most likely to appear when people are experiencing lots of potentially change-inducing events (i.e., aggressive campaigning), rather than during the relatively quiescent times early in a campaign. Furthermore, these investigators viewed the early-campaign measurement error differences as reflecting the fact that people were not being provoked to think about their unimportant attitudes and therefore had less precise senses of them.

Another source of variation in the importance-stability relation is the positivity or desirability of the attitude one holds. Pelham (1991) proposed that people are motivated to hold positive views of all aspects of themselves. At times, however, people see an aspect of themselves as negative, and they are motivated to make that self-appraisal more positive. This is especially true, said Pelham (1991) for aspects of the self that people consider very important personally. Consider, for example, a man who considers his social skills to be lacking. If he is newly divorced and feels that his social skills are an important self-aspect, then he will be especially motivated to improve his sense of self in this domain and will therefore show greater instability than a person for whom the negative self-appraisal is less important (Pelham, 1991). But once an initially negative appraisal reaches an acceptably positive level, it is unlikely to change thereafter.

Impact on Other Attitudes and Behavior

Also indicating that important attitudes are strong, a great deal of evidence suggests that these attitudes are especially likely to shape other attitudes and behavior.

Attitudes

Theories of cognitive consistency argue that people should be attracted to others who share their attitudes and repelled by others whose attitudes conflict with their own (e.g., Festinger, 1957; Heider, 1958), a prediction confirmed by many studies (e.g., Byrne, 1961, 1971; Newcomb, 1961). This phenomena is one instance of situations described by Fishbein and Ajzen's (1975) theory of reasoned action. This theory asserts that people's attitudes toward an object (e.g., another person) are derived from their beliefs about the attributes of the object (e.g., his or her attitudes) and their attitudes toward those attributes (i.e., agreement or disagreement with them). In any such situation, attributes toward which an individual has more important attitudes should presumably have greater impact on the overall attitude toward the object.

A great deal of evidence on interpersonal attraction is consistent with this idea. For example, attitude similarity is a more powerful determinant of attraction to strangers (Byrne, London, & Griffitt, 1968; Clore & Baldridge, 1968) and to political candidates (Aldrich & McKelvey, 1977; Granberg & Holmberg, 1986; Krosnick, 1988a, 1990a; McGraw, Lodge, & Stroh, 1990; Rabinowitz, Prothro, & Jacoby, 1982; Schuman & Presser, 1981; Shapiro, 1969) when the attitude involved is personally important to the individual. Also, correspondence between an individual's attitudes and his or her friends' attitudes is greater when those attitudes are more important to the person (Tedin, 1974, 1980).

Comparable results have been obtained regarding part-whole attitude effects. Budd (1986) showed that the attributes of cigarette smoking that individuals considered more important were also more strongly correlated with overall evaluations of smoking. Watkins and Park (1972) and Rosen and Ross (1968) reported that attitudes toward one's body parts were more strongly correlated with overall attitudes toward one's body when attitudes toward the body parts were especially important. Individuals' self-esteem is more influenced by satisfaction with dimensions of self-evaluation that are more personally important (Hoelter, 1985; Kaplan, 1980; Marsh, 1986; Pelham & Swann, 1989; Rosenberg, 1965; Showers, 1992). And considerations of economic self-interest have more impact on presidential candidate preferences among people whose attitudes on economic issues are especially important (Young, Borgida, Sullivan, & Aldrich, 1987).[6]

Holtz and Miller (1985) found related evidence in their exploration of social groups, specifically college fraternities and commuting students. On issues about which people had personally important attitudes, they tended to agree with ingroups and disagree with outgroups. But on issues about which people had unimportant attitudes, attitudinal agreement was equivalent for ingroups and outgroups. These findings are consistent with the claim that important attitudes shape people's liking of social groups, whereas unimportant attitudes do not.

Behavior

Some of the most important goals of attitude research are to predict and explain individuals' behavior. Although the attitude-behavior relation is typically not very strong, it would seem likely that the relation would be strong in the case of important attitudes. And as expected, a number of studies have found greater attitude-behavior consistency among people for whom the attitude was more personally important (e.g., Parker, Perry, & Gillespie, 1974; Rokeach & Kliejunas, 1972). For example, Budd (1986) showed that cigarette smoking

---

[6]Some investigators who studied this issue (e.g., Hinckley, Hofstetter, & Kessel, 1974; Marsh, 1986; Niemi & Bartels, 1985) reported some evidence that they viewed as indicating that importance did not regulate part-whole attitude effects. However, Krosnick (1988a) reviewed a variety of methodological features of these investigations that were likely to have masked importance effects.

behavior is better predicted by attitudes toward such behavior when these attitudes are important to individuals. Jaccard and Becker (1985) demonstrated that people's use of birth control methods is best predicted by attitudes that are more important to the individual. And Krosnick (1988a) and Schuman and Presser (1981) showed that attitudes on specific policy issues were more likely to shape voting behavior in elections when the attitudes involved were more important.

Conclusion

Taken together, the evidence presented here indicates that personally important attitudes have the four features of strong attitudes: They are generally resistant and persistent, and they guide attitude formation and behavior. What are the mechanisms and processes whereby important attitudes acquire these characteristics? To address this question, we now turn to research that has examined the influence of attitude importance on exposure to and elaboration of attitude-relevant information, as well as the organization of attitude-relevant knowledge.

MOTIVATION TO PROCESS INFORMATION

In order to understand the sources of the strength of important attitudes, it is useful to consider the effects of attitude importance on the processing of information about attitude objects. Although some psychological theories have described effortful and elaborative information processing strategies in which people may engage (Craik & Tulving, 1975; Wyer & Srull, 1986), many researchers presume that people are cognitive misers and rarely engage in such intensive strategies during the course of daily life (see, e.g., Fiske & Taylor, 1991; Tversky & Kahneman, 1974). More recently, a third perspective has emerged emphasizing the notion that individuals do expend the energy required for elaborative processing when they have unusual motivation to do so (e.g., Fiske & Neuberg, 1990; Petty & Cacioppo, 1986).

When do people decide to engage in effortful processing? One possible answer is that people will do so when information is relevant to an attitude they consider personally important. According to this view, attitude importance may help us to determine when it is adaptive and rational to take a cognitive miser's approach or a more effortful, systematic approach when considering attitude-relevant information. Two areas of research support this notion. First, several studies have demonstrated the influence of attitude importance on exposure to attitude-relevant information. Second, a number of studies have found effects of attitude importance on the degree to which people elaborate upon attitude-relevant information.

Information Exposure

Given the vast array of information that is available to people in their environments every moment of every day, people must selectively expose themselves to only some of that information. If exposure decisions are driven by motivation to process certain types of information, then we would expect attitude importance to instigate strategic exposure. In a test of this hypothesis, Berent and Krosnick (1993a) asked subjects to evaluate political candidates based on statements they made on six policy issues. Subjects were told they could only read statements on three of the six issues for each candidate and were asked to select the three issues about which they wanted to hear. As expected, subjects selected information relevant to important attitudes at the expense of information relevant to unimportant attitudes. Consistent with this finding, Krosnick et al. (1993) found that people who considered an attitude more important reported being more interested in obtaining relevant information.

One way for people to maximize the value of information they gather is to expose themselves to information that they could *not* anticipate. Expending the effort to gather information that could have been guessed anyway hardly seems worthwhile. Therefore, Berent and Krosnick (1993a) hypothesized that making their subjects aware of a candidate's party affiliation would allow them to infer his or her position on issues about which subjects had important attitudes, so subjects' interest in exposure to this information might be reduced. As expected, subjects were able to infer issue positions quite well from candidates' party identifications. However, subjects preferred exposure to information relevant to their important attitudes just as much when given this information as when party affiliations were unknown. This suggests that exposure selections were not influenced by a deliberate, strategic strategy for maximizing information value. Instead, the preference for information relevant to important attitudes seems to have reflected a routinized, habitual behavioral tendency.

Also suggesting that attitude importance inspires selective exposure to information is research on memory by Berent and Krosnick (1993b). These investigators exposed subjects to political statements and administered free recall and recognition memory measures 1 day later. Subjects exhibited better memory for information relevant to more important attitudes when they could selectively expose themselves to such information. When selective exposure was not possible, attitude importance was unrelated to memory. Therefore it appears that attitude importance inspires selective exposure, which yields better memory for information.

Several studies of consumer attitudes documented effects of attitude importance on interest in and exposure to information. For instance, people for whom a product class was more important were more interested in reading information on how the product was made and about its relative quality (McQuarrie & Munson, 1992; Zaichkowsky, 1985).[7] Also, people higher in product importance reported having acquired more information about the product class (Richins, Bloch, & McQuarrie, 1992).

---

[7]Importance in these studies was measured using the Personal Involvement Inventory (for a complete description, see Zaichkowsky, 1985) and the Revised Product Involvement Inventory (for a complete description, see McQuarrie & Munson, 1992). Both of these inventories include ratings of importance, concern, and caring.

Information Elaboration

Once exposed to information, people may be particularly motivated to process it if it pertains to an important attitude (see Petty, Haugvedt, & Smith, ch. 5, this volume). As such, attitude importance may help us determine the amount of effort to invest in processing information. Consistent with this hypothesis, people who care deeply about an attitude are more likely to report thinking about it on a regular basis (Herzog, 1993; Krosnick et al., 1993; Richins et al., 1992).

In a more formal test of this notion, Celsi and Olson (1988) examined the processing of advertisements. They found that when the topic of an ad was relevant to a personally important attitude, subjects spent more time viewing the ad, generated more thoughts about the ad, and generated higher proportions of product-related thoughts and product-related inferences. In another study, Howard-Pitney, Borgida, and Omoto (1986) had subjects watch a debate on drinking-age legislation and complete a thought-listing task. Subjects whose attitudes on this issue were more important generated more message-oriented thoughts and fewer unrelated thoughts.

Further evidence that attitude importance influences selective elaboration was reported by Berent and Krosnick (1993b). In their studies of memory for political information, free recall and recognition memory accuracy were positively related to attitude importance when subjects were given time to elaborate on the information they read or heard (see also Smith & Jamieson, 1972). But when elaboration time was not provided, the memorial advantage of information relevant to important attitudes disappeared. Therefore, it appears that attitude importance inspired selective elaboration of information relevant to personally important attitudes, thereby yielding better memory for it.

CONSEQUENCES OF EXPOSURE AND ELABORATION

If people do indeed selectively expose themselves to and elaborate upon information relevant to important attitudes, then a number of consequences should follow. These include effects upon the attitudes themselves and the knowledge bases accompanying them in memory. We review evidence on these effects next.

Extremity and Accessibility

Tesser (1978) argued that thought about an attitude increases its extremity when the attitude is accompanied by schematically organized knowledge. Therefore, as important attitudes are frequent foci of thinking, it is not surprising that more important attitudes tend to be more extreme (Borgida & Howard-Pitney, 1983;

Brent & Granberg, 1982; Cialdini et al., 1976; Converse & Schuman, 1970; Feldman, 1989; Granberg & Burlison, 1983; Howard-Pitney, Borgida, & Omoto, 1986; Knower, 1936; Krosnick, 1986, 1988a; Krosnick et al., 1993; Lemon, 1968; Rholes & Bailey, 1983; Riland, 1959; Smith, 1982). Because extremity enhances an attitude's strength (see Judd & Brauer, ch. 3, this volume), the extremity of important attitudes is likely to be one source of their strength.

Frequent thought about important attitudes should also presumably strengthen the object-evaluation association in memory and thereby enhance the attitude's accessibility (Fazio, 1989). And indeed, Krosnick (1989) and Tourangeau, Rasinski, and D'Andrade (1991) found that people reported their attitudes on political issues more quickly when those attitudes were more personally important. Also, people whose attitudes on an issue are more important are more likely to mention it as a reason for liking or disliking political candidates during election campaigns (Krosnick, 1988a). Because accessibility strengthens attitudes (see Fazio, ch. 10, this volume), the accessibility of important attitudes is also likely to be one source of their strength.

Consistency of Attitudes with Core Values

Important attitudes are presumed to be more central within attitude systems, in the sense that they are more extensively linked to other attitudes and core elements such as values (e.g., Judd & Krosnick, 1982, 1989; Newcomb, Turner, & Converse, 1965). Therefore, more extensive thinking about such attitudes should enhance their consistency with a person's basic values (Festinger, 1957; Judd & Downing, 1990; Judd & Krosnick, 1989). Indeed, several studies have demonstrated that pairs of political attitudes are more ideologically consistent when one or both of the attitudes involved are personally important (Jackman, 1977; Judd & Krosnick, 1989; Schuman & Presser, 1981; Smith, 1982). Also, more important attitudes have been found to be more consistent with ideological orientations (i.e., liberal and conservative) and with values for equality and individualism (Krosnick, 1990b).

Judd and Krosnick (1982) pointed out that simply examining zero order associations between attitudes and other attitudes or values in this way is potentially problematic. This is because variation in these correlations according to importance could reflect differences in measurement error or polarization instead of in consistency. Judd and Krosnick (1982) therefore conducted structural equation analyses to overcome these problems, and, surprisingly, they found that the factor loadings of concrete policy attitudes on a latent ideology factor did not vary with attitude importance, which questioned the importance-consistency relation. However, later work revealed that comparisons of factor loadings in this way across groups of people cannot be interpreted in the way Judd and Krosnick (1982) thought (Bielby, 1986; Williams & Thomson, 1986). Fabrigar and Krosnick (1994b) developed an analytic approach to overcome this problem and estimate between-attitude consistency while controlling for random measurement error, systematic measurement error, and polarization. As expected, they found that important attitudes were indeed more ideologically consistent with other attitudes than were unimportant attitudes. This evaluative consistency and the structural links in memory that presumably produce it are likely to contribute to the strength of important attitudes (see Chaiken, Pomerantz, & Sorolla, ch. 15, this volume; Eagly & Chaiken, ch. 16, this volume).

Quantity and Accuracy of Attitude-Relevant Knowledge

If people selectively expose themselves to and elaborate upon information relevant to important attitudes, and if the latter yields better memory for that information, then one would expect attitudes that people consider important to be accompanied by more relevant knowledge in memory than unimportant attitudes. A number of studies have documented just such a correlation (e.g., Berent & Krosnick, 1992; Krosnick et al., 1993; Wood, 1982).

Furthermore, Krosnick (1990a) found that the knowledge accompanying more important attitudes is especially likely to be accurate. In his study, voters who attached more importance to their attitudes on a political issue were more likely to accurately perceive the positions taken on the issue by presidential candidates. Because competing candidates tend to take opposing stands on issues, a person higher in attitude importance will tend to perceive a greater discrepancy between the candidates, thus allowing him or her to make a vote choice on the basis of that one issue relatively easily (Krosnick, 1986, 1988a). Along similar lines, Campbell (1986) found that attaching importance to an attitude increased the accuracy of college students' perceptions of the distributions of opinions toward the object among others.

Another set of studies in this area examined systematic bias in perceptions of the distributions of attitudes toward an object in particular groups of people. Campbell (1986) and Krosnick (1992) found that perceptions of groups' attitudes were less susceptible to the false consensus effect (Ross, Greene, & House, 1977) when the attitude involved was more important to the perceiver, and Fabrigar and Krosnick (in press) found that the magnitude of the false consensus effect to be unrelated to attitude importance. Thus, these studies are consistent with the claim that important attitudes do not bias perceptions more than unimportant ones. This is presumably so because people possess more accurate information on which to base their perceptions relevant to important attitudes.

In situations where people lack information on which to base perceptions, however, they are *more* likely to use their own important attitudes to infer the attitudes of others. In a study by Marks and Miller (1982), subjects were shown photographs of attractive or unattractive people and were asked to guess their attitudes on various issues. When subjects' attitudes on an issue were important, they inferred that attractive people held attitudes relatively similar to their own and that unattractive people held relatively dissimilar attitudes. But on issues about which subjects had unimportant attitudes, these attitudes were not used in conjunction with attractiveness to infer the other people's attitudes. Thus, in the absence of any other information, importance inspires people to use available cues (e.g., their own attitudes and the other person's attractiveness) to infer others' attitudes.[8]

Berent and Krosnick (1992) demonstrated that people are very adept at using knowledge associated with important attitudes. Their study assessed the speed and consistency with which subjects made inferences relevant to political attitudes. For example, subjects were asked whether it was likely that people with particular social characteristics (e.g., old or wealthy) would take certain stands on particular political issues (e.g., favor legalized abortion or oppose gun control laws). As expected, inferences relevant to more important attitudes were made more quickly, and these inferences were made more consistently across two occasions.

Taken together, then, this literature indicates that large bodies of accurate knowledge typically accompany important attitudes. And this knowledge presumably enhances their strength (see Wood, Rhodes, & Biek, ch. 11, this volume), at least partly by enhancing people's ability to counterargue. Along these lines, Howard-Pitney, Borgida, and Omoto (1986) demonstrated that people for whom an attitude is personally important are especially likely to generate challenging cognitive responses to counter-attitudinal arguments. Thus, a tendency toward biased cognitive elaboration presumably enhances resistance to attitude change. However, although importance apparently inspires biased elaboration, it does not instigate bias in *perceptions*.

Organization of Attitude-Relevant Knowledge

The extensive exposure and elaboration apparently induced by attitude importance also appears to affect the organization of attitude-relevant knowledge in memory. The process of elaboration involves evaluating and relating newly acquired information to the knowledge already stored in a person's memory. The more one

---

[8]Granberg and colleagues (Brent & Granberg, 1982; Granberg & Brent, 1974; Granberg & Seidel, 1976) examined the association between people's own attitudes on political issues and their perceptions of a presidential candidate's stand on those issues. This association was positive among people who liked the candidate, and it became increasingly strong as people attached more importance to their attitudes on the issue. Granberg and colleagues viewed this evidence as indicating that high importance was associated with greater bias due to projection of one's own attitudes onto liked others. However, Krosnick (1990a) failed to replicate Granberg et al.'s findings with other national survey data. Furthermore, Granberg et al.'s finding is likely to be at least partly if not completely due to similarity-driven evaluation of the candidates and persuasion of voters by candidates (see Krosnick, in press), both of which would constitute manifestations of attitude strength. Therefore, Granberg et al.'s evidence does not provide a strong basis for inferring that importance is associated with greater bias in social perception.

thinks about a new piece of information, the more likely he or she is to recognize what it has in common with previously stored knowledge. As a result, he or she is likely to incorporate the new information into an existing knowledge structure by linking the information either to existing nodes or newly formed nodes (Anderson, 1983; Collins & Loftus, 1975). Therefore, if attitude importance does indeed inspire deeper processing of relevant incoming information, it should also yield a more elaborate organization of relevant knowledge in memory.

Berent and Krosnick (1992) explored this idea in a recent series of experiments. In one study, these investigators measured knowledge organization by examining the order in which pieces of information are retrieved from memory during an open-ended knowledge listing task (see Ostrom, Pryor, & Simpson, 1981). Specifically, items linked to a common node in a cognitive structure should be generated close to each other during such tasks. Berent and Krosnick (1992) had subjects list their knowledge about a political issue and identify pairs of pieces of knowledge they felt were similar. Knowledge organization was gauged by the average number of pieces of information listed between the two items in each pair. As anticipated, subjects whose attitudes on an issue were more important listed psychologically related pieces of knowledge closer to each other.

In another study, Berent and Krosnick (1992) examined the number of dimensions subjects used when organizing their knowledge. Subjects listed all their knowledge about a political issue, grouped together pieces of knowledge they felt were related to one another in some respect, and described why they were related. Next, subjects rated each piece of knowledge written during the listing task according to how well it fit each group descriptor. A measure of multidimensional organization was computed from the knowledge grouping and rating tasks data using a modification of the dimensionality measure proposed by Scott, Osgood, and Peterson (1979). As expected, greater attitude importance was associated with more organizing dimensions, thereby suggesting yet another source of the strength in important attitudes (see Eagly & Chaiken, ch. 16, this volume).

Conclusion

Thus attitudes people consider personally important apparently have a number of structural characteristics that distinguish them from unimportant attitudes. These features may all be the result of selective exposure to and elaboration of relevant information, and they all seem likely to enhance the strength of important attitudes.

THE ORIGINS OF ATTITUDE IMPORTANCE

Finally, we turn to the causes of attitude importance. What makes people care deeply about some attitudes they hold whereas they care little about others?

Hypotheses

At the outset of this chapter, we suggested that links between an attitude object and an individual's goals, values, or social identifications are likely to be causes of attitude importance. Although there has been little empirical work testing these relations until recently, social scientists' speculations for more than 30 years suggest that an attitude may become important to an individual for one of three reasons: self-interest, social identification, and value-relevance (e.g., Key, 1961; Modigliani & Gamson, 1979). Although these causes are not exhaustive of all the potential links to the self, they may represent three particularly potent sets and have been the exclusive focus of recent research.

Self-interest develops when one perceives an attitude to be instrumental to the attainment of one's goals, or to one's tangible rights, privileges, or lifestyle (Sears, Lau, Tyler, & Allen, 1980). Perceived self-interest is likely to be high among people who feel their own personal well-being may be directly affected by an issue in some immediate and concrete manner (Modigliani & Gamson, 1979; Popkin, Gorman, Phillips, & Smith, 1976). And an attitude seems likely to become important to individuals who perceive the attitude object to be linked to their material self-interests (e.g., Apsler & Sears, 1968).

Strong identification with a social group may lead an attitude to become important to a person if the group's rights or privileges are perceived to be at stake (Key, 1961; Modigliani & Gamson, 1979). Also, strong identification with a group that consensually considers an attitude to be important can serve as an impetus for importance, independent of whether rewards for the group are in question (Sherif & Hovland, 1961). Similarly, attitude importance may develop as a result of identification with reference individuals whose interests are perceived to be at stake or who are perceived to care deeply about a particular attitude.

Rokeach (1968) defined a value as an abstract belief (not specific to any attitude object) about proper modes of behavior, about how the world should be, or about the worthiness of various long-term goals. Rokeach (1973) suggested that values are "standards employed . . . to tell us which beliefs, attitudes, values, and actions of others are worth challenging, protesting, and arguing about, or worth trying to influence or change" (p. 13). In this sense, values may tell people which attitudes to consider personally important. The closer the perceived linkage between an attitude object and an individual's values, and the more important the values, the more important the attitude is likely to be to him or her (Campbell, Converse, Miller, & Stokes, 1960; Katz, 1960; Rosenberg, 1956).

Evidence

Tests of these hypotheses come from three different sorts of studies. One study involved introspective accounts of the sources of attitude importance. Other studies were correlational, relating attitude importance to the three classes of predictors. Finally, other studies were experimental, manipulating the antecedents and examining their effects on importance. We review this work in the following section.

An Introspection Study. Boninger, Krosnick, and Berent (1995) asked people to explain why they considered various political attitudes to be personally important or unimportant. Content analyses of explanatory responses revealed that self-interest accounted for a larger proportion (59%) of the statements than social identification (18%) and values (17%). Also, 8% of explanatory statements mentioned the amount of knowledge subjects had on the issue or the amount of information acquisition or thinking they had done on the issue. No other causes of attitude importance were mentioned frequently enough to be recognized by judges.

Correlational Studies. One early correlational study uncovered the expected positive association between self-interest and attitude importance (Lau, Brown, & Sears, 1978). In that study, people who had friends or relatives serving in Vietnam in 1968 reported being more personally concerned about the war than did those who didn't, but only slightly so. But in five correlational studies conducted by Boninger et al. (1995), perceived self-interest was found to be a powerful and consistent predictor of attitude importance (mean $\beta = .33$). Social identification was also a significant predictor (mean $\beta = .33$), as was value-relevance (mean $\beta = .20$).

Boninger et al. (1995) also examined the impact on attitude importance of measures of presumed antecedents of self-interest and social identification. The issue addressed was gun control, and the antecedents were past experiences and likely future experiences of oneself or one's reference group with guns and crime. As expected, these antecedents were significant predictors of attitude importance, though weaker than their subjective counterparts. Furthermore, path analyses suggested that the presumed antecedents were determinants of their subjective counterparts, which in turn shaped attitude importance. These results attest both to the validity of the subjective measures and to their role in mediating the impact of life events on attitude importance. Thus, these studies provide further support for the role of self-interest, social identification, and values in determining attitude importance.

Experimental Studies. Experimental studies have generally provided evidence that self-interest affects importance, although their results have been somewhat mixed. For example, Apsler and Sears (1968) told undergraduates that a change in their university's policy would or would not affect them directly. This self-interest induction succeeded in increasing reports of concern, but failed to significantly alter judgments of personal importance. Similar manipulations of self-interest have succeeded in increasing attitude importance ratings in studies by Madsen (1978) and Brickner, Harkins, and Ostrom (1986) and in one study reported by Sorrentino, Bobocel, Gitta, Olson, and Hewitt (1988), but failed in their other study and in a study by Price (1989). Unfortunately, in cases where a manipulation of self-interest succeeded in increasing attitude importance, there was no explicit assessment of whether perceptions of self-interest mediated the effects on importance.

Boninger et al. (1995) conducted an experiment designed to overcome this limitation and to provide more conclusive causal evidence. Their study manipulated self-interest by inducing some subjects to imagine a self-relevant scenario involving traffic safety. Prior research had demonstrated that imagining an event occurring to oneself increases people's estimates of the likelihood that the event will actually occur to them in the future (Anderson, 1983; Sherman, Cialdini, Schartzman, & Reynolds, 1985). Therefore, Boninger et al. (1995) expected that people who imagined being injured in a traffic accident would come to believe that they were more likely to experience that event. They further anticipated that these subjects would then perceive their self-interests to be more closely tied to the issue of traffic safety. This should, in turn, increase the personal importance these individuals attached to their attitudes on that issue. These expectations were consistently confirmed by Boninger et al. (1995).

DISCUSSION

Summary

In this chapter, we have reviewed evidence showing that important attitudes are strong, and we have explored why they are strong. In short, it seems that important attitudes embody the features of strong attitudes because attitude importance instigates exposure to and elaboration of attitude-relevant information. This heightened motivation to acquire and process information seems to enhance attitude extremity, accessibility, and consistency, as well as the quantity, accuracy, and organization of relevant knowledge in memory.

Thus, the centerpiece of our findings is the notion that important attitudes become strong via their impact on motivation to process relevant information. When faced with the whirlwind of information with which people are often confronted, each individual must decide what to attend to, what to think about, and what to act on in the future. The research we have reviewed suggests that people make these decisions partly by assessing whether incoming information is relevant to a personally important attitude. This may occur either as a result of deliberate, conscious decisions to focus on these attitudes or simply because these attitudes are especially accessible in memory and come to mind automatically as new information is encountered. In any case, the evidence presented here indicates that when information is not relevant to important attitudes, people are more likely to behave like cognitive misers. However, when information is relevant to important attitudes, people are likely to attend to and carefully process that information.

In Fig. 7.1, we have sketched out a causal model that embodies the findings we have reviewed, as well as some additional speculations about the sources of the strength in important attitudes. Self-interest, social identification, and values are causes of attitude importance, which in turn induces selective exposure to and elaboration of relevant information. This more frequent and extensive information processing increases attitude extremity, accessibility, and consistency, as well as knowledge quantity, accuracy, and organization. Each of these latter factors presumably enhance the likelihood that one's behavior will be consistent with the relevant attitude, as well as that attitude's resistance to change and its stability. Finally, we note the likely possibility that performing attitude-consistent behaviors bolsters an attitude and thereby increase its resistance to change and its stability. Although we have omitted from this diagram reciprocal causal influence as well as some direct, unmediated causal effects, we do not mean to suggest that they may not exist. The figure simply documents what we suspect are the primary directions of causal relations and mediational patterns.

In thinking about productive directions for future research, it is useful to note that some relations illustrated in Fig. 7.1 have been supported empirically and some have not yet been tested. First, as we have reviewed in this chapter, attitude importance has been shown to be correlated with all the other variables in the model. Also, experimental manipulations of self-interest have been shown to enhance attitude importance (Boninger et al., 1995) as well as elaboration of relevant information, resistance to attitude change, attitude stability, and impact of attitudes on behavior (Petty & Cacioppo, 1986; Petty et al., ch. 5, this volume; Thomsen et al., ch. 8, this volume).

It will be useful to see whether attitude importance mediates these latter relations, as well as the effects of self-interest, social identification, and values on selective exposure and elaboration and all variables to the right in Fig. 7.1.

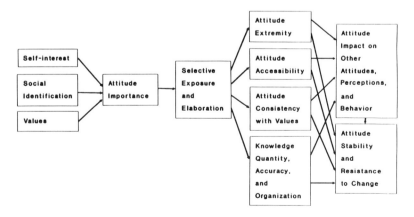

FIG. 7.1. A model of the causes and consequences of attitude importance.

However, conducting such studies is not likely to be possible in single, short laboratory sessions using conventional paradigms. The processes by which attitude importance evolves its consequences are likely to stretch over much longer periods of time. As a result, innovative techniques for these studies will need to be developed.

Importance and Involvement

Another useful direction for future research is exploring the relation of attitude importance to involvement. Involvement has typically been studied by manipulating self-interest in a newly formed attitude in a laboratory setting, whereas attitude importance has usually been studied by measuring it in correlational laboratory and field studies addressing preexisting attitudes. The fact that many findings from these two lines of research are concordant suggests that involvement and attitude importance may be the same construct (see, e.g., Petty & Cacioppo, 1990).

There are, however, two provocative disjunctions between the correlates of importance and involvement. Although attitude importance is positively related to memory for relevant information (Berent & Krosnick, 1993b; Krosnick, 1990a; Krosnick et al., 1993; Wood, 1982), experimentally induced involvement is apparently unrelated to memory for relevant information (Cacioppo, Petty, & Morris, 1983; Petty & Cacioppo, 1979; Petty, Cacioppo, & Goldman, 1981; Petty, Cacioppo, & Heesacker, 1981; Petty, Cacioppo, & Schumann, 1983). Similarly, although attitude importance is positively related to knowledge organization complexity (Berent & Krosnick, 1992), Boninger (1991) failed to find a reliable relation between induced involvement and knowledge organization. There are many possible explanations for these discrepancies (see Berent & Krosnick, 1993b), and we look forward to future research that clarifies their meaning. In the meantime, it may make sense to preserve the possibility that involvement as created in the laboratory and importance as studied in real-world settings may function differently in some regards.

The evidence we have reviewed regarding attitude importance addresses an unresolved issue in the involvement literature. Although some have speculated that attitude involvement mediates the effects of manipulated self-interest on the observed outcomes (e.g., Petty & Cacioppo, 1990), this literature has rarely generated empirical evidence to directly support this presumption. Instead, because the goal of these studies has been to illustrate the impact of self-interest on information processing, measures of importance usually served only as manipulation checks rather than as analytic handles for mediational analysis. The findings we reviewed explicitly link attitude importance both to self-interest and to various strength-related consequences, thus bolstering confidence in the speculation that importance does indeed mediate self-interest's effect.

A debate in the involvement literature also raises some interesting questions for the importance literature. Although Johnson and Eagly (1989, 1990) and Petty and Cacioppo (1990; Petty, Cacioppo, & Haugtvedt, 1992) agreed that involvement is a function of self-interest (or outcome-relevance) and value-relevance, these authors disagreed about whether involvement induced by self-interest affects attitude change via the same processes as involvement induced by value-relevance. Along similar lines, attitude importance induced by self-interest may or may not have the same consequences as importance induced by social identification or values. Research has not yet addressed this question, and it is therefore a worthy focus of future studies.

However, the findings described previously regarding the origins of attitude importance raise questions about tactics that have been used in the past to study this distinction. In their meta-analysis, Johnson and Eagly (1989) treated studies inducing involvement by experimental manipulations of self-interest as exploring outcome-relevant involvement (e.g., Apsler & Sears, 1968). However, Boninger et al.'s (1995) studies found that heightening objective self-interest can also inadvertently enhance social identification and value-relevance. Also, Johnson and Eagly (1989) treated nonexperimental studies that differentiated high and low involvement subjects based on self-reports of issue importance as exploring value-relevant involvement (e.g., Gorn, 1975). Yet the evidence we reviewed previously indicates that issue importance ratings reflect both value-relevance and outcome-relevance. Consequently, the presumed separation of these two sorts of involvement in Johnson and Eagly's (1989) meta-analysis may not in fact have been effective. Thus investigators must be cautious in presuming that they have operationalized one sort of importance or involvement distinctly from the other, and in making assumptions about which source of importance or involvement was manipulated or measured in any particular study.

Other Possible Origins

Self-Perception.   Roese and Olson (1994) proposed a new hypothesis regarding the origins of attitude importance ratings: self-perception processes (e.g., Bem, 1972). These investigators proposed that when asked to report how personally important an attitude is, people may "look to their past behavior for clues, at least to the extent that the attitude is not initially regarded as highly important" (p. 41). Roese and Olson proposed that a person may infer that an attitude is important to him or her if the attitude has been expressed frequently in the past. They also proposed that people may use the "ease with which attitudinal information comes to mind as a heuristic cue for inferring perceived attitude importance" (p. 47). Thus, people might believe that if an attitude comes to mind quickly and easily, it must be important to them.

Roese and Olson (1994) reported an experimental study testing the notions that attitude importance might be caused by people's perceptions of prior attitude expression frequency and attitude accessibility. They had some subjects report their attitudes on an issue five times, whereas others did not express their attitudes at all. This expression manipulation increased later reports of attitude importance and also increased the accessibility of subjects' attitudes (as gauged by response latencies). Furthermore, the effect of the manipulation on importance was mediated by accessibility. Thus, subjects apparently did not infer importance directly from frequency of expression; only accessibility directly shaped importance. This is quite sensible, because the previous expressions were "manded" (to use Bem's term), so there was no reason for subjects to believe that their frequency was informative per se.

The finding that accessibility shapes importance is surprising to us in light of our presumption that importance evolves in noticeable ways as the result of significant events. Consistent with this view, attitude accessibility can explain only a very small proportion of the variance in importance, 10% at most according to Krosnick et al.'s evidence (1993). Also, in Boninger et al.'s (1995) introspection study, less then 10% of the explanations for importance ratings made reference to self-perception indicators such as knowledge levels. Consequently, we suspect that accessibility is not a major source of importance as it exists in everyday life.

Nonetheless, Roese and Olson's (1994) results suggest some interesting possible reinterpretations of previous studies on repeated expression. A number of such studies have documented effects of repeated attitude expression (e.g., stronger attitudinal effects on information processing) that have been attributed to attitude accessibility (see Fazio, ch. 10, this volume). However, Roese and Olson's (1994) finding suggests that these effects may instead have been mediated by attitude importance. That is, attitude importance may have been the *proximal* cause of the effects, whereas repeated expression (and perhaps accessibility) may have been more distal causes, farther back in the causal chain. We look forward to future research exploring these possibilities.

Dissonance Reduction.   Another possible cause of attitude importance is suggested by Festinger's (1957) cognitive dissonance theory. He argued that dissonance is likely to be most powerful when two inconsistent cognitions are highly important to an individual. And one way to reduce this dissonance, Festinger proposed, is to reduce the importance attached to one or both of them. Thus, some of the over-time dynamics in attitude importance may be attributable to the emergence of situations in which cognitive dissonance is created and then resolved. Remarkably, this notion has yet to be tested directly.

However, a related hypothesis suggested by Pelham (1991) has received some empirical attention. He speculated that the importance people attach to their self-views may be determined partly by self-enhancement and self-protection motives. The notion here is that people attach importance to positive self-views and consider negative self-views to be unimportant in order to feel good about themselves. This notion may apply more generally to all types of attitudes: People may attach importance to attitudes they are proud of and may avoid attaching importance to attitudes about which they might be embarrassed. In line with Pelham's (1991) hypothesis, people report attaching more personal importance to positive/complimentary self-views on which they fare favorably than to negative/threatening self-views (Pelham, 1991; Showers, 1992). This notion certainly deserves empirical scrutiny in terms of its applicability to attitudes generally.

Coda

In closing, it seems sensible to address the normative question of whether attitude importance is good or bad, adaptive or harmful, helpful or damaging. And our sense from the literature described previously is that attitude importance serves a positive function for people, in that it makes their lives easier and more manageable by telling them where to focus their time, effort, and energy. That is, importance guides the selection of adaptive strategies in coping with the enormous amount of information in the world around us. We ignore or pay only cursory attention to information relevant to unimportant attitudes so that we have the time and energy to carefully attend to information relevant to important ones. Thus, attitude importance allows us to minimize the cognitive costs of social perception, evaluation, and decision making yet maximize subjective expected utility. In this sense, important attitudes may indeed be indispensable.

REFERENCES

Abelson, R. P. (1988). Conviction. *American Psychologist, 43*, 267–275.

Aldrich, J. H., & McKelvey, R. D. (1977). A method of scaling with applications to the 1968 and 1972 presidential elections. *American Political Science Review, 71*, 111–130.

Aldrich, J. H., Sullivan, J. L., & Borgida, E. (1989). Foreign affairs and issue voting: Do presidential candidates "waltz before a blind audience"? *American Political Science Review, 83*, 123–142.

Allyn, J., & Festinger, L. (1961). The effectiveness of unanticipated persuasive communications. *Journal of Abnormal and Social Psychology, 62*, 35–40.

Anderson, C. A. (1983). Imagination and expectation: The effect of imagining behavioral scripts on personal intentions. *Journal of Personality and Social Psychology, 45*, 293–305.

Apsler, R., & Sears, D. O. (1968). Warning, personal involvement, and attitude change. *Journal of Personality and Social Psychology, 9*, 162–166.

Bem, D. J. 1972). Self-perception theory. In L. Berkowitz (Ed.), *Advances in experimental social psychology* (Vol. 6, pp. 1–62). San Diego, CA: Academic.

Berent, M. K., & Krosnick, J. A. (1992). *Attitude importance and the organization of attitude-relevant knowledge in memory.* Unpublished manuscript, Ohio State University, Columbus.

Berent, M. K., & Krosnick, J. A. (1993a). *Attitude importance and selective exposure to attitude-relevant information.* Unpublished manuscript, Ohio State University, Columbus.

Berent, M. K., & Krosnick, J. A. (1993b). *Attitude importance and memory for attitude-relevant information.* Unpublished manuscript, Ohio State University, Columbus.

Bielby, W. T. (1986). Arbitrary metrics in multiple-indicator models of latent variables. *Sociological Methods and Research, 15*, 3–23.

Bishop, G. F. (1990). Issue involvement and response effects in public opinion surveys. *Public Opinion Quarterly, 54*, 209–218.

Boninger, D. S. (1991). *The effects of cognitive tuning and personal relevance on cognitive organization in persuasion.* Unpublished doctoral dissertation, Ohio State University, Columbus.

Boninger, D. S., Krosnick, J. A., & Berent, M. K. (1995). The causes of attitude importance: Self-interest, social identification, and values. *Journal of Personality and Social Psychology, 68,* 61–80.

Borgida, E., & Howard-Pitney, B. (1983). Personal involvement and the robustness of perceptual salience effects. *Journal of Personality and Social Psychology, 45,* 560–570.

Brent, E., & Granberg, D. (1982). Subjective agreement and the presidential candidates of 1976 and 1980. *Journal of Personality and Social Psychology, 42,* 393–403.

Brickner, M. A., Harkins, S. G., & Ostrom, T. M. (1986). Effects of personal involvement: Thought-provoking implications for social loafing. *Journal of Personality and Social Psychology, 51,* 763–769.

Budd, R. J. (1986). Predicting cigarette use: The need to incorporate measures of salience in the theory of reasoned action. *Journal of Applied Social Psychology, 16,* 663–685.

Byrne, D. (1961). Interpersonal attraction and attitude similarity. *Journal of Abnormal and Social Psychology, 62,* 713–715.

Byrne, D. (1971). *The attraction paradigm.* New York: Academic Press.

Byrne, D., London, O., & Griffitt, W. (1968). The effect of topic importance and attitude similarity–dissimilarity on attraction in an intrastranger design. *Psychonomic Science, 11,* 303–304.

Cacioppo, J. T., Petty, R. E., & Morris, K. J. (1983). Effects of need for cognition on message evaluation, recall, and persuasion. *Journal of Personality and Social Psychology, 45,* 805–818.

Campbell, J. D. (1986). Similarity and uniqueness: The effects of attribute type, relevance, and individual differences in self esteem and depression. *Journal of Personality and Social Psychology, 50,* 281–294.

Campbell, A., Converse, P. E., Miller, W. A., & Stokes, D. E. (1960). *The American voter.* Chicago: University of Chicago Press.

Celsi, R. L., & Olson, J. C. (1988). The role of involvement in attention and comprehension processes. *Journal of Consumer Research, 15,* 210–224.

Cialdini, R. B., Levy, A., Herman, C. P., Kozlowski, L., & Petty, R. E. (1976). Elastic shifts of opinion: Determinants of direction and durability. *Journal of Personality and Social Psychology, 34,* 663–672.

Cialdini, R. B., & Petty, R. E. (1981). Anticipatory opinion effects. In R. E. Petty, T. M. Ostrom, & T. C. Brock (Eds.), *Cognitive responses in persuasion* (pp. 217–236). Hillsdale, NJ: Lawrence Erlbaum Associates.

Clore, G. L., & Baldridge, B. (1968). Interpersonal attraction: The role of agreement and topic interest. *Journal of Personality and Social Psychology, 9,* 340–346.

Collins, A. M., & Loftus, E. F. (1975). A spreading activation theory of semantic processing. *Psychological Review, 82,* 407–428.

Converse, P. E. (1964). The nature of belief systems in mass publics. In D. E. Apter (Ed.), *Ideology and discontent* (pp. 206–261). New York: The Free Press.

Converse, P. E., & Schuman, H. (1970). Silent majorities and the Vietnam war. *Scientific American, 25,* 17–25.

Craik, F. I. M., & Tulving, E. (1975). Depth of processing and the retention of words in episodic memory. *Journal of Experimental Psychology, 104,* 268–294.

Fabrigar, L. R., & Krosnick, J. A. (1994a). *What motivates issue public membership?: Distinguishing between personal importance and national importance.* Unpublished manuscript, Ohio State University, Columbus.

Fabrigar, L. R., & Krosnick, J. A. (1994b). *Attitude importance and inter-attitudinal consistency.* Unpublished manuscript, Ohio State University, Columbus.

Fabrigar, L. R., & Krosnick, J. A. (in press). Attitude importance and the false consensus effect. *Personality and Social Psychology Bulletin.*

Fazio, R. H. (1989). On the power and functionality of attitudes: The role of attitude accessibility. In A. R. Pratkanis, S. J. Breckler, & A. G. Greenwald (Eds.), *Attitude structure and function* (pp. 153–180). Hillsdale, NJ: Lawrence Erlbaum Associates.

Fazio, R. H. (1990a). Multiple processes by which attitudes guide behavior: The MODE model as an integrative framework. *Advances in Experimental Social Psychology, 23,* 75–109.

Fazio, R. H. (1990b). A practical guide to the use of response latency in social psychological research. In C. Hendrick & M. Clark (Eds.), *Research methods in personality and social psychology* (pp. 74–97). Newbury Park, CA: Sage.

Feldman, S. (1989). Measuring issue preferences: The problem of response instability. *Political Analysis, 1,* 25–60.

Festinger, L. (1957). *A theory of cognitive dissonance.* Stanford, CA: Stanford University Press.

Fine, B. J. (1957). Conclusion-drawing, communicator credibility, and anxiety as factors in opinion change. *Journal of Abnormal and Social Psychology, 54,* 369–374.

Fishbein, M., & Ajzen, I. (1975). *Belief, attitude, intention, and behavior: An introduction to theory and research.* Reading, MA: Addison-Wesley.

Fiske, S. T., & Neuberg, S. L. (1990). A continuum of impression formation, from category-based to individuating processes: Influences of information and motivation on attention and interpretation. In M. P. Zanna (Ed.), *Advances in experimental social psychology* (Vol. 23, pp. 1–74). New York: Academic.

Fiske, S. T., & Taylor, S. E. (1991). *Social cognition.* New York: McGraw-Hill.

Gorn, G. J. (1975). The effects of personal involvement, communication discrepancy, and source prestige on reactions to communications on separatism. *Canadian Journal of Behavioral Science, 7,* 369–386.

Granberg, D., & Brent, E. E. (1974). Dove-hawk placements in the 1968 election: Application of social judgment and balance theories. *Journal of Personality and Social Psychology, 29,* 687–695.

Granberg, D., & Burlison, J. (1983). The abortion issue in the 1980 elections. *Family Planning Perspectives, 15,* 231–238.

Granberg, D., & Holmberg, S. (1986). Political perception among voters in Sweden and the US: Analyses of issues with explicit alternatives. *Western Political Quarterly, 39,* 7–28.

Granberg, D., & Seidel, J. (1976). Social judgments of the urban and Vietnam issues in 1968 and 1972. *Social Forces, 55,* 1–15.

Hahn, H. (1970). The political impact of shifting attitudes. *Social Science Quarterly, 51,* 730–742.

Heider, F. (1958). *The psychology of interpersonal relations.* New York: Wiley.

Herzog, H. A. (1993). "The movement is my life": The psychology of animal rights activism. *Journal of Social Issues, 49,* 103–119.

Hinckley, B., Hofstetter, R., & Kessel, J. (1974). Information and the vote: A comparative election study. *American Politics Quarterly, 2,* 131–158.

Hoelter, J. W. (1985). The structure of self-conception: Conceptualization and measurement. *Journal of Personality and Social Psychology, 49,* 1392–1407.

Holtz, R., & Miller, N. (1985). Assumed similarity and opinion certainty. *Journal of Personality and Social Psychology, 48,* 890–898.

Hovland C. I., & Sherif M. (1952). Judgmental phenomena and scales of attitude measurement: Item displacement in Thurstone scales. *Journal of Abnormal and Social Psychology, 47,* 822–832.

Howard-Pitney, B., Borgida, E., & Omoto, A. M. (1986). Personal involvement: An examination of processing differences. *Social Cognition, 4,* 39–57.

Iyengar, S., & Kinder, D. R. (1987). *News that matters.* Chicago: University of Chicago Press.

Jaccard, J., & Becker, M. A. (1985). Attitudes and behavior: An information integration perspective. *Journal of Experimental Social Psychology, 21,* 440–465.

Jackman, M. R. (1977). Prejudice, tolerance, and attitudes toward ethnic groups. *Social Science Research, 6,* 145–169.

Johnson, B. T., & Eagly, A. H. (1989). Effects of involvement on persuasion: A meta-analysis. *Psychological Bulletin, 106,* 290–314.

Johnson, B. T., & Eagly, A. H. (1990). Involvement and persuasion: Types, traditions, and the evidence. *Psychological Bulletin, 107,* 375–384.

Judd, C. M., & Downing, J. W. (1990). Political expertise and development of attitude consistency. *Social Cognition*, *8*, 104–124.

Judd, C. M., & Krosnick, J. A. (1982). Attitude centrality, organization, and measurement. *Journal of Personality and Social Psychology*, *42*, 436–447.

Judd, C. M., & Krosnick. J. A. (1989). The structural bases of consistency among political attitudes: The effects of political expertise and attitude importance. In A. R. Pratkanis, S. J. Breckler, & A. G. Greenwald (Eds.), *Attitude structure and function* (pp. 99–128). Hillsdale, NJ: Lawrence Erlbaum Associates.

Kaplan, H. B. (1980). *Deviant behavior in defense of self.* New York: Academic.

Katz, D. (1960). The functional approach to the study of attitudes. *Public Opinion Quarterly*, *24*, 163–204.

Kendall, P. (1954). *Conflict and mood: Factors affecting stability of response.* Glencoe, IL: The Free Press.

Key, V. O. (1961). *Public opinion and American democracy.* New York: Knopf.

Knower, F. H. (1936). Experimental studies of changes in attitude—III: Some incidence of attitude changes. *Journal of Applied Psychology*, *20*, 114–127.

Krech, D., & Crutchfield, R. S. (1948). *Theory and problems of social psychology.* New York: McGraw-Hill.

Krosnick, J. A. (1986). *Policy voting in American presidential elections: An application on psychological theory to American politics.* Unpublished doctoral dissertation, University of Michigan, Ann Arbor.

Krosnick, J. A. (1988a). The role of attitude importance in social evaluation: A study of policy preferences, presidential candidate evaluations, and voting behavior. *Journal of Personality and Social Psychology*, *55*, 196–210.

Krosnick, J. A. (1988b). Attitude importance and attitude change. *Journal of Experimental Social Psychology*, *24*, 240–255.

Krosnick, J. A. (1989). Attitude importance and attitude accessibility. *Personality and Social Psychology Bulletin*, *15*, 297–308.

Krosnick, J. A. (1990a). American's perceptions of presidential candidates: A test of the projection hypothesis. *Journal of Social Issues*, *46*, 159–182.

Krosnick, J. A. (1990b). Government policy and citizen passion: A study of issue publics in contemporary America. *Political Behavior*, *12*, 59–92.

Krosnick, J. A. (1992). The impact of cognitive sophistication and attitude importance on response order effects and question order effects. In N. Schwarz & S. Sudman (Eds.), *Order effects in social and psychological research* (pp. 203–218). New York: Springer-Verlag.

Krosnick, J. A., & Berent, M. K. (1993). Comparisons of party identification and policy preferences: The impact of survey question format. *American Journal of Political Science*, *37*, 941–964.

Krosnick, J. A., Boninger, D. S., Chuang, Y. C., Berent, M. K., & Carnot, C. G. (1993). Attitude strength: One construct or many related constructs? *Journal of Personality and Social Psychology*, *65*, 1132–1151.

Krosnick, J. A., & Cornet, P. J. (1993). *Attitude importance and attitude change revisited: Shifts in attitude stability and measurement reliability across a presidential election campaign.* Unpublished manuscript, Ohio State University, Columbus.

Krosnick, J. A., & Schuman, H. (1988). Attitude intensity, importance, and certainty and susceptibility to response effects. *Journal of Personality and Social Psychology*, *54*, 940–952.

Lau, R. R., Brown, T. A., & Sears, D. O. (1978). Self-interest and civilians attitudes toward the war in Vietnam. *Public Opinion Quarterly*, *42*, 464–483.

Lemon, N. F. (1968). A model of the extremity, confidence, and salience of an opinion. *British Journal of Social Clinical Psychology*, *7*, 106–114.

Madsen, D. B. (1978). Issue importance and group choice shifts: A persuasive arguments approach. *Journal of Personality and Social Psychology*, *36*, 1118–1127.

Marks, G., & Miller, N. (1982). The effect of certainty on consensus judgments. *Personality and Social Psychology Bulletin, 11*, 165–177.

Marsh, H. W. (1986). Global self-esteem: Its relation to specific facets of self-concept and their importance. *Journal of Personality and Social Psychology, 51*, 1224–1236.

McGraw, K. M., Lodge, M., & Stroh, P. (1990). On-line processing in candidate evaluation: The effects of issue order, issue importance, and sophistication. *Political Behavior, 12*, 41–58.

McQuarrie, E. F., & Munson, J. M. (1992). A revised product involvement inventory: Improved usability and validity. *Advances in Consumer Research, 19*, 108–115.

Miller, N. E. (1965). Involvement and dogmatism as inhibitors of attitude change. *Journal of Experimental Social Psychology, 1*, 121–132.

Modigliani, A., & Gamson, W. A. (1979). Thinking about politics. *Political Behavior, 1*, 5–30.

Neuman, W. R. (1986). *The paradox of mass politics.* Cambridge, MA: Harvard University Press.

Newcomb, T. M. (1961). *The acquaintance process.* New York: Holt, Rinehart & Winston.

Newcomb, T. M., Turner, R. H., & Converse, P. E. (1965). *Social psychology.* New York: Holt, Rinehart & Winston.

Niemi, R. G., & Bartels, L. M. (1985). New measures of issue salience: An evaluation. *Journal of Politics, 47*, 1212–1220.

Ostrom, T. M., Pryor, J. B., & Simpson, D. S. (1981). The organization of social information. In E. T. Higgins, C. P. Herman, & M. P. Zanna (Eds.), *Social cognition: The Ontario symposium on personality and social psychology.* Hillsdale, NJ: Lawrence Erlbaum Associates.

Parker, H. A., Perry, R. W., & Gillespie, D. F. (1974). Prolegomenon to a theory of attitude-behavior relationships. *Pakistan Journal of Psychology, 7*, 21–39.

Pelham, B. W. (1991). On confidence and consequence: The certainty and importance of self-knowledge. *Journal of Personality and Social Psychology, 60*, 518–530.

Pelham, B. W., & Swann, W. B., Jr. (1989). From self-conceptions to self-worth: On the sources and structure of global self-esteem. *Journal of Personality and Social Psychology, 57*, 672–680.

Petty, R. E., & Cacioppo, J. T. (1979). Issue involvement can increase or decrease persuasion by enhancing message-relevant cognitive responses. *Journal of Personality and Social Psychology, 37*, 1915–1926.

Petty, R. E., & Cacioppo, J. T. (1986). The elaboration likelihood model of persuasion. In L. Berkowitz (Ed.), *Advances in experimental social psychology* (Vol. 19, pp. 81–136). New York: Academic.

Petty, R. E., & Cacioppo, J. T. (1990). Involvement and persuasion: Tradition versus integration. *Psychological Bulletin, 107*, 367–374.

Petty, R. E., Cacioppo, J. T., & Goldman, R. (1981). Personal involvement as a determinant of argument-based persuasion. *Journal of Personality and Social Psychology, 41*, 847–855.

Petty, R. E., Cacioppo, J. T., & Haugtvedt, C. (1992). Ego-involvement and persuasion: An appreciative look at the Sherifs' contribution to the study of self-relevance and attitude change. In D. Granberg & G. Sarup (Eds.), *Social judgment and intergroup relations: A festschrift for Muzifer Sherif* (pp. 147–174). New York: Springer-Verlag.

Petty, R. E., Cacioppo, J. T., & Heesacker, M. (1981). The use of rhetorical questions in persuasion: A cognitive response analysis. *Journal of Personality and Social Psychology, 40*, 432–440.

Petty, R. E., Cacioppo, J. T., & Schumann, D. (1983). Central and peripheral routes to advertising effectiveness: The moderating role of involvement. *Journal of Consumer Research, 10*, 134–148.

Popkin, S., Gorman, J. W., Phillips, C., & Smith, J. A. (1976). Comment: What have you done for me lately? Toward an investment theory of voting American. *Political Science Review,* , 779–805.

Price, V. (1989). Social identification and public opinion: Effects of communicating group conflict. *Public Opinion Quarterly, 53*, 197–224.

Rabinowitz, G., Prothro, J. W., & Jacoby, W. (1982). Salience as a factor in the impact of issues on candidate evaluation. *Journal of Politics, 42*, 41–63.

Repass, D. E. (1971). Issue salience and party choice. *American Political Science Review, 65*, 389–400.

Rhine, R. J., & Severance, L. J. (1970). Ego-involvement, discrepancy, source credibility, and attitude change. *Journal of Personality and Social Psychology, 16*, 175–190.

Rholes, W. S., & Bailey, S. (1983). The effects of level of moral reasoning on consistency between moral attitudes and related behaviors. *Social Cognition, 2*, 32–48.

Richins, M. L., Bloch, P. H., & McQuarrie, E. F. (1992). How enduring and situational involvement combine to create involvement responses. *Journal of Consumer Psychology, 1*, 143–153.

Riland, L. H. (1959). Relationship of the Guttman components of attitude intensity and personal involvement. *Journal of Applied Psychology, 43*, 279–284.

Roese, N. J., & Olson, J. M. (1994). Attitude importance as a function of repeated attitude expression. *Journal of Experimental Social Psychology, 30*, 39–51.

Rokeach, M. (1968). *Beliefs, attitudes, and values.* San Francisco: Jossey-Bass.

Rokeach, M. (1973). *The nature of human values.* New York: The Free Press.

Rokeach, M., & Kliejunas, P. (1972). Behavior as a function of attitude-toward-object and attitude-toward-situation. *Journal of Personality and Social Psychology, 22*, 194–201.

Rosen, G. M., & Ross, A. O. (1968). Relationship of body image to self-concept. *Journal of Consulting and Clinical Psychology, 32*, 100.

Rosenberg, M. (1965). *Society and the adolescent self-image.* Princeton, NJ: Princeton University Press.

Rosenberg, M. J. (1956). Cognitive structure and attitudinal affect. *Journal of Abnormal and Social Psychology, 53*, 367–372.

Ross, L., Greene, D., & House, P. (1977). The "false consensus effect": An egocentric bias in social perception and attribution processes. *Journal of Experimental Social Psychology, 13*, 279–301.

Schuman, H., & Presser, S. (1981). *Questions and answers: Experiments on question form, wording, and context in attitude surveys.* New York: Academic.

Scott, W. A., Osgood, D. W., & Peterson, C. (1979). *Cognitive structure: Theory and measurement of individual differences.* New York: Wiley.

Sears, D. O., Lau, R. R., Tyler, T. R., & Allen, H. M., Jr. (1980). Self-interest vs. symbolic politics in policy attitudes and presidential voting. *American Political Science Review, 74*, 670–684.

Shapiro, M. J. (1969). Rational political man: A synthesis of economic and social-psychological perspectives. *American Political Science Review, 63*, 1106–1119.

Sherif, C. W. (1980). Social values, attitudes, and the involvement of the self. In M. M. Page (Ed.), *Nebraska symposium on motivation 1979: Beliefs, attitudes, and values* (pp. 1–64). Lincoln: University of Nebraska Press.

Sherif, C. W., Sherif, M., & Nebergall, R. E. (1965). *Attitude and attitude change.* Philadelphia: W. B. Saunders.

Sherif, M., & Cantril, H. (1947). *The psychology of ego-involvements.* New York: Wiley.

Sherif, M., & Hovland, C. I. (1953). Judgmental phenomena and scales of attitude measurement: Placement of items with individual choice of number of categories. *The Journal of Abnormal and Social Psychology, 48*, 135–141.

Sherif, M., & Hovland, C. W. (1961). *Social judgment: Assimilation and contrast effects in communication and attitude change.* New Haven, CT: Yale University Press.

Sherman, S. J., Cialdini, R. B., Schartzman, D. F., & Reynolds, K. D. (1985). Imagining can heighten or lower the perceived likelihood of contracting a disease: The mediating effect of ease of imagery. *Personality and Social Psychology Bulletin, 11*, 118–127.

Showers, C. (1992). Compartmentalization of positive and negative self-knowledge: Keeping bad apples out of the bunch. *Journal of Personality and Social Psychology, 62*, 1036–1049.

Smith, S. S., & Jamieson, B. D. (1972). Effects of attitude and ego involvement on the learning and retention of controversial material. *Journal of Personality and Social Psychology, 22*, 303–310.

Smith, T. W. (1982). *Attitude constraint as a function of nonaffective dimensions* (General Social Survey Tech. Rep. No. 39). Chicago, IL: National Opinion Research Center.

Sorrentino, R. M., Bobocel, D. R., Gitta, M. Z., Olson, J. M., & Hewitt, E. C. (1988). Uncertainty orientation and persuasion: Individual differences in the effects of personal relevance of social judgments. *Journal of Personality and Social Psychology, 55*, 357–371.

Stember, H., & Hyman, H. (1949–1950). How interviewer effects operate through question form. *International Journal of Opinion and Attitude Research, 3,* 493–512.

Tedin, K. L. (1974). The influence of parents on the political attitudes of adolescents. *American Political Science Review, 68,* 1579–1592.

Tedin, K. L. (1980). Assessing peer and parental influence on adolescent political attitudes. *American Journal of Political Science, 24,* 136–154.

Tesser, A. (1978). Self-generated attitude change. In L. Berkowitz (Ed.), *Advances in experimental social psychology* (Vol. 11, pp. 289–328). New York: Academic.

Tourangeau, R., Rasinski, K. A., & D'Andrade, R. (1991). Attitude structure and belief accessibility. *Journal of Experimental Social Psychology, 27,* 48–75.

Tversky, A., & Kahneman, D. (1974). Judgments under uncertainty: Heuristics and biases. *Science, 185,* 1124–1131.

Wallsten, T. S., Budescu, D. V., Rapoport, A., Zwick, R., & Forsyth, B. (1986). Measuring vague meanings of probability terms. *Journal of Experimental Psychology: General, 115,* 348–365.

Watkins, D., & Park, J. (1972). The role of subjective importance in self-evaluation. *Australian Journal of Psychology, 24,* 209–210.

Watts, W. A. (1967). Relative persistence of opinion change induced by active compared to passive participation. *Journal of Personality and Social Psychology, 5,* 4–15.

Williams, R., & Thomson, E. (1986). Normalization issues in latent variable modeling. *Sociological Methods and Research, 15,* 24–43.

Wood, W. (1982). The retrieval of attitude-relevant information from memory: Effects on susceptibility to persuasion and on intrinsic motivation. *Journal of Personality and Social Psychology, 42,* 798–810.

Wyer, R. S., & Srull, T. K. (1986). Human cognition in its social context. *Psychological Review, 93,* 322–359.

Young, J., Borgida, E., Sullivan, J. L., & Aldrich, J. H. (1987). Personal agendas and the relationship between self-interest and voting behavior. *Social Psychology Quarterly, 50,* 64–71.

Zaichkowsky, J. L. (1985). Measuring the involvement construct. *Journal of Consumer Research, 12,* 341–352.

8
▼▼▼▼▼▼▼

The Causes and Consequences
of Personal Involvement

Cynthia J. Thomsen
Tufts University

Eugene Borgida
University of Minnesota

Howard Lavine
Northern Illinois University

> *Ego-involvement, or its absence, makes a critical difference in human be-*
> *havior. When a person reacts in a neutral, impersonal routine atmosphere,*
> *his [her] behavior is one thing. But when he [she] is behaving personally,*
> *perhaps excitedly, seriously committed to a task, he [she] behaves quite*
> *differently.*
>
> —Allport (1943, p. 459)

Allport suggested 50 years ago that one's level of involvement with a task profoundly influences individual performance. Researchers have followed up on Allport's insight by examining the effects of involvement in a variety of domains. Indeed, personal involvement has figured prominently in theories of persuasion such as social judgment theory (C. W. Sherif, Sherif, & Nebergall, 1965; M. Sherif & Cantril, 1947; M. Sherif & Hovland, 1961), the Elaboration Likelihood Model (ELM; Petty & Cacioppo, 1986), and the Heuristic-Systematic Model (HSM; Chaiken, Liberman & Eagly, 1989); it has been investigated as a moderator of social cognitive heuristics and biases (Harkness, DeBono, & Borgida, 1985) and of attitude-behavior relations (Krosnick, 1988; C. W. Sherif, Kelly, Rodgers, Sarrap, & Tittler, 1973); and has been examined as an influence on impression formation (Berscheid, Graziano, Monson, & Dermer, 1976). Individuals are said to be personally involved with an issue, event, object, or person to the extent that they care about that entity and perceive it as important.

As such, personal involvement is closely related to a variety of other constructs (e.g., *ego-involvement*, M. Sherif & Cantril, 1947; *attitudinal involvement*, Ostrom

& Brock, 1968; *personal or self-relevance*, Petty & Cacioppo, 1986; *attitude importance*, Krosnick, 1988; *attitude centrality*, Judd & Krosnick, 1982). Although these constructs overlap substantially, we use the term *personal involvement* (see Apsler & Sears, 1968; Borgida & Howard-Pitney, 1983; C. W. Sherif, 1980), or simply *involvement*, to highlight the generality of this motivational quality (e.g., it is applicable to domains other than attitudes). Nonetheless, because these various terms have often been used to describe the same (or very similar) phenomena, our review includes studies that are couched in each of these terms. Just as personal involvement has been referred to under a variety of different concept labels, it has also been manipulated and measured in diverse ways, as shall become evident in this chapter. Some of these measures and manipulations are quite face valid, and some have documented construct validity. Others, however, are less straightforward, and results using these measures must be interpreted with caution.

This chapter reviews the conclusions of research on personal involvement, highlighting similarities and differences in findings across the different literatures in which it has been investigated. After presenting a broad theoretical framework that specifies the *sources* of involvement, we discuss research relevant to each source. Next, we consider the *effects* of involvement in the domains of persuasion, impression formation, and social judgment and behavior; the results of this research suggest that attitudes with which individuals are personally involved meet the criteria generally considered to define "strong" attitudes. Finally, we present the results of some recent research that examines the cognitive *structures* and *processes* that seem to mediate the observed effects of personal involvement. Our ultimate goal, then, is to advance toward an integrative social psychological perspective on personal involvement (see Allport, 1943; Greenwald, 1982) that considers its causes or antecedents, its consequences or effects, and the structures and processes that provide a more complete understanding of the linkages between antecedents and consequences.

SOURCES OF PERSONAL INVOLVEMENT: THEORY

Theoretically, individuals should be personally involved with an entity to the extent that it affects, impinges on, reflects, or is otherwise associated with the self (e.g., C. W. Sherif, 1980). There are several aspects of the self with which an entity might be associated. In possibly the earliest and most comprehensive enumeration of the aspects of the self, William James (1890) suggested that the self includes material (e.g., one's body, material possessions), social (e.g., one's lover, offspring), and spiritual (e.g., one's values, politics) aspects. Entities relevant to any of these self-aspects may thus occasion personal involvement. In fact, more recent attempts to explicate the sources of involvement have resulted in taxonomies that in most cases can be mapped onto James' three self-aspects.

TABLE 8.1
Sources of Personal Involvement

Theorist	James (1890)	Katz (1960)	Smith, Bruner, & White (1956)	Fiske & Neuberg (1990)
Domain of Application	The Self	Attitude Functions	Attitude Functions	Impression Formation
Source of Involvement				
Self-Interest	Material	Utilitarian	Object Appraisal	Outcome Dependency
Group Interest	Social/Material	—	—	—
Self-Presentation	Social	—	Social Adjustment	Self-Presentation
Social Identification	Social	—	—	—
Values	Spiritual	Value Expressive	—	Values
Self-Esteem	—	Ego Defensive	Externalization	—
Maintenance		Knowledge	Object Appraisal	

Theorist	Johnson & Eagly (1989)	Boninger et al. (in press)	Greenwald & Breckler (1985)
Domain of Application	Persuasion	Attitudes	The Self
Source of Involvement			
Self-Interest	Outcome-relevant	Self-Interest	The Diffuse Self
Group Interest	—	Social Identification	The Collective Self
Self-Presentation	Impression-relevant	—	The Public Self
Social Identification	—	Social Identification	The Public Self
Values	Value-relevant	Values	—
Self-Esteem Maintenance	—	—	The Private Self

Note. For a discussion of other relevant motivational taxonomies, see Snyder (1992).

The parallels between various accounts of the sources of involvement and James' early description of the aspects of the self are illustrated in Table 8.1.

The idea that relations between an entity and material aspects of the self result in heightened personal involvement is reflected in the concept of outcome dependency within the impression formation literature, and the concept of outcome-relevant involvement in the persuasion domain. It is also similar to Sivacek and Crano's (1982; see also Crano, ch. 6, this volume) concept of "vested interest," to the concept of self-interest in the symbolic politics literature (see Sears & Funk, 1991), and to the utilitarian or adjustive function of attitudes. These theories differ, however, in one important respect: Some of them consider material self-interest as a basis for personal involvement with an entity, whereas others consider self-interest as a source of the attitude per se. The former approaches specify that an entity will be important if it influences one's outcomes, while the latter approaches specify that the valence or direction of one's attitude may be determined by the way in which the entity impacts on one's outcomes. Thus, we may distinguish *self-interest-based involvement* from *self-interest-based attitudes.*[1] Because this chapter is primarily concerned with involvement, theories

[1]Similar distinctions could be made with respect to other bases of involvement discussed later.

of the bases of involvement are most relevant here. Nonetheless, we include in Table 8.1 theories of the motivational bases of attitudes, as well as theories of the sources of involvement, to highlight the substantial similarities that exist across these taxonomies.

Associations between entities and the spiritual aspect of the self may also result in heightened personal involvement. Most classification schemes have incorporated this notion by focusing on a particular aspect of the spiritual self: personal values. For example, functional attitude theories have specified that attitudes may be adopted because they aid the individual in expressing important values (the value-expressive function). Taxonomies of the motives underlying both impression formation and persuasion have also identified values as a potential source of involvement. The most clearly articulated theoretical statement about this type of involvement is provided by Ostrom and Brock (1968), who specified that levels of *value-based involvement* with an entity depend on three factors: (a) the number of values to which the entity is related, (b) the strength of these relations, and (c) the centrality or importance of the relevant values.

The notion that involvement may result from associations between an entity and social aspects of the self has also been incorporated in several classification schemes, although in somewhat different ways. First, an entity can be associated with social aspects of the self because it assists one in securing the positive regard of others. *Self-presentation-based involvement*, as we refer to this type of social motive, is based on the fact that one's association with or orientation toward an entity could influence how others view one (Chaiken, 1980; Leippe & Elkin, 1987; Tetlock, 1983). This type of relationship is specified by the social-adjustive attitude function, the self-presentation motive for impression formation, and the notion of impression-relevant involvement in the persuasion domain. Self-presentation-based involvement has been elicited by leading individuals to expect that they will have to justify their attitude to others (Tetlock, 1983), or by inducing them to make a public commitment to a particular stand before being exposed to a persuasive message on that topic (see Kiesler, 1971).

In a related vein, the social aspect of the self is also implicated when individuals are involved with an entity because of its relevance to groups or individuals with whom they identify (see Kelman, 1958). According to M. Sherif and Cantril (1947), "one important reason why attitudes are affectively charged is the fact that many attitudes prescribe the individual's relationship, status, or role with respect to other individuals or groups" (p. 134). The *social identification basis of involvement* (Boninger, Krosnick, & Berent, 1995) differs from the self-presentation basis in that the former necessarily involves reference groups or that are important to the individual; the latter, in contrast, can be invoked by any individual(s) by whom a person may be evaluated or to whom she or he may be accountable. A third respect in which an entity may be associated with the social aspect of the self may be termed *group interest-based involvement*. This represents involvement with an entity based on its perceived implications for the outcomes of groups that are important to the individual. As such, this motivation can be viewed as a broader form of self-interest (Sears & Funk, 1991).[2]

Finally, sources of involvement have been identified that are not easily assimilated to James' classification of self-aspects. Greenwald (1982) distinguished between involvement based on self-presentation motives, or "concern about evaluation by others," and involvement based on "concern about self-evaluation."[3] *ws*
The latter motive, which we refer to as the *self-esteem maintenance* source of involvement, is invoked by the individual's desire to maintain, protect, or enhance her or his self-esteem (see Koestner, Zuckerman, & Koestner, 1987; Tesser, 1988), and is related to the ego-defensive function of attitudes.[4] Of the six sources of personal involvement that we have identified, four—self-interest, values, group interest, and social identification—represent motives for involvement with a particular entity, including issues, people, and objects. The other two motives— self-presentation and self-esteem maintenance—constitute motives for involvement with a particular task or response (cf. Zimbardo, 1960). Because our primary focus in the present chapter is on attitudinal involvement, we limit our discussion to the self-interest, group-interest, social identification, and value bases of personal involvement.

SOURCES OF PERSONAL INVOLVEMENT: EVIDENCE

Surprisingly little research has explicitly focused on the sources of involvement, and the research that does exist has almost exclusively examined self-interest and value bases, rather than the more social (group-interest and social identification) bases of involvement. Most studies in which involvement has been manipulated have employed self-interest-based manipulations (e.g., Berscheid et al., 1976; Borgida & Howard-Pitney, 1983, Exp. 1; Petty, Cacioppo, & Goldman, 1981). Manipulation checks in several of these studies have provided evidence that self-interest can indeed increase personal involvement (Boninger et al., 1993, Exp. 6; Borgida & Howard-Pitney, 1983, Exp. 1; Brickner, Harkins, & Ostrom, 1986; Leippe & Elkin, 1987; Petty & Cacioppo, 1979, Exp. 1; but see Apsler & Sears, 1968). Unlike self-interest, very few studies have manipulated involvement through values, social identification, or group-interest. One study, to our knowledge, has manipulated involvement by forging associations between attitudes and

---

[2]Boninger and his colleagues' (1993) social identification motive actually subsumes both social identification and group interest sources of involvement in our taxonomy.

[3]Greenwald (1982) also identified a third form of involvement, which he termed "personal importance," although he did not explicitly identify its motivational source.

[4]A fifth function, the knowledge function, has also been included in some functional taxonomies. Attitudes serve the knowledge function when they are held to render the world more comprehensible and predictable. Given that this motivation seems rather more cognitive than motivational, however, it would appear to be an unlikely candidate for arousing intense forms of personal involvement. Thus, it may not be relevant in the present context.

important values (Ostrom & Brock, 1969). Unfortunately, this study (like most experimental studies of self-interest-based involvement) did not include manipulation checks to verify that involvement was successfully aroused. Similarly, we know of only one study that has attempted to manipulate involvement via group-interest or social identification (Boninger et al., 1995, Exp. 6), and this manipulation was unsuccessful. Experimental evidence thus supports the efficacy of self-interest in arousing involvement, but does not address other possible bases of involvement.

A few correlational studies have also examined the relation of personal involvement to its hypothesized sources. In studies using indirect measures of involvement such as the width of respondents' latitudes of rejection, the evidence for these relations is mixed. One such study (Sivacek & Crano, 1982) found no relation between self-interest with respect to the instituting of comprehensive exams and involvement in the issue. However, in a study examining the relations between social identification and personal involvement (C. W. Sherif et al., 1973, Exp. 2), membership in cliques that varied in their characteristic activities and concerns predicted levels of personal involvement with these concerns. Studies employing measures with greater face validity have produced more consistent evidence that the motivational sources described above do indeed produce involvement. Using an "objective" measure of self-interest, Lau, Brown, and Sears (1978) found a significant (although weak) association between self-reported personal concern about the Vietnam War and self-interest (i.e., knowing people serving in Vietnam). Using subjective (self-rated) measures of involvement yields even stronger evidence. Two recent papers have reported research that has explicitly examined the antecedents of involvement by assessing subjects' levels of various motivations with respect to a particular issue and correlating each of these motivations with personal involvement. In one series of studies, Boninger et al. (1995) found that self-interest, social identification/group interest, and value-relevance independently predicted personal involvement across six political issues, with self-interest consistently showing the strongest relations to involvement (mean rs = .61, .40, and .39, respectively). Similarly, Thomsen, Lavine, Borgida, and Sullivan (1993) conducted two studies in which levels of self-interest, value-relevance, and personal involvement were assessed for 14 political issues and three campus issues. In addition to replicating the Boninger et al. finding that self-interest correlates more highly with involvement than does value-relevance (mean rs = .55 and .20, respectively, for political issues, and .53 and .28 for campus issues), Thomsen et al. also used a within-person correlational strategy to more directly examine the relations among self-interest, value-relevance and personal involvement within the cognitive system of the individual. Consistent with the results of the between-subjects analyses, self-interest was revealed to be the stronger predictor of involvement (mean rs = .69 and .26).

In sum, although empirical evidence regarding the antecedents of involvement is not plentiful, it supports the idea that involvement can be aroused by self-interest, values and social identification/group interest. Experimental studies have demonstrated that self-interest can arouse involvement, although comparable evidence is lacking with regard to the other possible sources of involvement. Correlational evidence, in contrast, reveals some support for all of the motivational sources, though it suggests that self-interest is a stronger determinant of involvement than values, social identification, or group interest.

CONSEQUENCES OF PERSONAL INVOLVEMENT

In contrast to the relative paucity of research examining the motivational underpinnings of involvement, a great deal of research has explored the effects of involvement in domains such as persuasion, impression formation, attitude-behavior relations, and social judgment. The remainder of this chapter examines the specific ways in which involved individuals differ from less involved individuals in both cognition and behavior. We conclude by presenting preliminary evidence regarding the structural and processing mechanisms through which involvement may exert its cognitive and behavioral effects.

Persuasion

Perhaps the largest single body of research concerning the effects of personal involvement has been amassed in the persuasion context. There have been two primary approaches to studying the role of involvement in persuasion (for a review, see Johnson & Eagly, 1989; see also Petty, Cacioppo, & Haugtvedt, 1992). From the perspective of social judgment theory (C. W. Sherif et al., 1965; M. Sherif & Hovland, 1961), attitude change should be more difficult to effect to the degree that personal involvement is high. In contrast, dual process theories such as the ELM (Petty & Cacioppo, 1986) and the HSM (Chaiken et al., 1989) suggest that the primary effect of involvement is to increase the amount of effort that the individual is willing to expend in processing a persuasive message. Theoretically, this increased processing may be either biased or objective, depending on such factors as the individual's degree of prior knowledge or forewarning about the impending persuasion attempt (Petty & Cacioppo, 1986).

Although these two theoretical perspectives make somewhat different predictions, each has garnered empirical support from research conducted under its own auspices. For example, in their meta-analysis, Johnson and Eagly (1989) found that studies conducted in the social judgment theory tradition generally show that attitudes are more resistant to change to the extent that they are personally involving; in contrast, studies in the cognitive response tradition show that involvement increases motivation to process persuasive messages, thereby increasing message-relevant thought. As a result, "high involvement subjects [are] more persuaded by strong arguments and less persuaded by weak arguments than [are] low involvement subjects" (p. 302), consistent with both the ELM and the HSM. Cognitive response theorists have also examined the effects of involvement on a number of variables besides persuasion. They have found that relative to uninvolved subjects, those in whom self-interest-based involvement has been heightened also generate more message-oriented thoughts (Howard-Pitney, Borgida, & Omoto, 1986; Leippe & Elkin, 1987) and demonstrate better recall for message arguments in some studies (Leippe & Elkin, 1987) but not in others (Howard-Pitney et al., 1986). The increased processing that results from involvement is also reflected by findings that highly involved subjects are more likely than less involved subjects to infer omitted conclusions from a persuasive message (Kardes, 1988), and that they tend to respond more positively to open-ended than to closed-ended messages (Sawyer & Howard, 1991). Finally, manipulations of self-interest-based involvement lessen the extent to which individuals are influenced by message-irrelevant cues such as the likability (Chaiken, 1980), expertise (Petty et al., 1981), or perceptual salience (Borgida & Howard-Pitney, 1983) of the communicator.

Johnson and Eagly (1989) interpreted the different results obtained by social judgment and cognitive response researchers as reflecting differential effects of value- and outcome-relevant involvement. This conclusion, however, has precipitated some debate (see Johnson & Eagly, 1990; Petty & Cacioppo, 1990). The dispute centers primarily on the question of whether the observed differences between the results of research conducted in these two traditions truly reflect differential effects of value- and outcome-based involvement or whether they instead reflect paradigmatic differences between the two lines of research. Indeed, as Johnson and Eagly acknowledge, these two types of research differ in a number of other respects. Social judgment theorists have typically employed correlational or quasi-experimental approaches, assessing preexisting levels of involvement, whereas cognitive response researchers have almost always experimentally manipulated this variable. Social judgment theorists have also used a wide variety of methods and assessment procedures, many of them quite indirect;[5] in contrast, the involvement manipulations employed by cognitive response theorists have been quite homogeneous, typically varying self-interest in issues such as increased tuition or the institution of comprehensive exams for college seniors by informing

---

[5]Measures typically used by social judgment theorists include the width of individuals' latitudes of noncommitment or rejection (Eagly & Telaak, 1972; Gantt, 1970; C. W. Sherif et al., 1973, Exp. 1; C. W. Sherif et al., 1965) and the number of categories into which they sort attitude statements (C. W. Sherif et al., 1973, Exp. 1; C. W. Sherif et al., 1965, pp. 92–126; M. Sherif & Hovland, 1961). In other cases, social judgment researchers have compared groups of subjects expected to differ in their levels of involvement with respect to a particular issue (e.g., Gorn, 1975; M. Sherif & Hovland, 1961), or compared issues known to differ in their importance to subjects (e.g., Miller, 1965; Rhine & Severance, 1970; C. W. Sherif et al., 1973, Exps. 4–5). Although there is little direct evidence that these methods of assessing or varying involvement actually do so, there is some evidence that these fairly diverse measures are tapping some common construct (e.g., C. W. Sherif et al., 1973, Exp. 2; M. Sherif & Hovland, 1953).

some subjects, but not others, that the policy will affect them personally. A related difference is that the issues used in social judgment research are often much more familiar to subjects than those used in cognitive response research; attitudes toward more familiar issues, in turn, are likely to be characterized by greater prior knowledge, more extremity, and higher levels of personal involvement, among other variables (see Petty & Cacioppo, 1990).

Differences in the conclusions of these two lines of research may thus reflect paradigmatic differences rather than differential effects of value-based and outcome-based involvement. It may be, for example, that low levels of involvement (as induced in experimental studies) lead to enhanced objective thought, whereas higher levels of involvement (as typically measured in correlational studies) lead to greater partisanship, regardless of the source of the involvement. Consistent with this possibility, the handful of correlational studies in which the effects of preexisting differences in self-interest-based involvement have been examined have all shown that self-interest-based involvement can produce partisan biases in the processing of counterattitudinal messages. For example, Borgida and his colleagues (Borgida & Howard-Pitney, 1983, Exp. 2; Howard-Pitney et al., 1986) selected high and low involvement groups based on self-reports of the extent to which an issue was important and the extent to which it affected them personally. They found that high involvement subjects listed more thoughts than low involvement subjects about the position in a debate that was congruent with their own attitude, and counterargued the opposing position more (Howard-Pitney et al., 1986). Others have found evidence that self-interest-based involvement increases resistance to counterattitudinal messages, by comparing either groups (Gorn, 1975) or issues (e.g., Rhine & Severance, 1970) that differ in their levels of self-interest-based involvement.

It should also be noted that there is not a strong theoretical or empirical basis for labelling social judgment studies as investigations of "value-based involvement." Although social judgment theorists have accorded values a prominent role in their view of personal involvement, values are not considered isolated entities, but mechanisms of socialization: "Many ego-involved attitudes are derived from the values or norm system of the person's reference groups" (C. W. Sherif et al., 1965, p. vi); "these values, goals, standards, or norms which become our attitudes are represented by, set by, or created by group activities and social situations that form the constellation of social relationships with which we come in contact" (M. Sherif & Cantril, 1947, p. 114). Social judgment theory therefore seems to have focussed more centrally on social identification motives than on values as a basis of personal involvement. Others have also interpreted social judgment theory in this way (e.g., Greenwald, 1982; Leippe & Elkin, 1987). Similarly, there is little empirical basis for concluding that social judgment research has considered value-based involvement. In fact, there is not a great deal of direct empirical evidence that the measures social judgment theorists have typically employed to assess involvement measure it at all (although involvement as assessed by these measures generally does predict resistance to attitude change, as the theory would suggest). A full assessment of whether different types of involvement have different consequences awaits further research in which source of involvement is unconfounded with research paradigm.

The research reviewed thus far suggests that involvement can have two distinct effects on persuasion. First, personal involvement can increase the amount of thought an individual is willing to devote to a relevant persuasive communication, consistent with the predictions of dual process theories such as the ELM and HSM. Second, personal involvement with an entity can also increase the individual's partisanship with respect to that entity, heightening her or his resistance to attitude change attempts. This is consistent with the predictions of both social judgment theory and cognitive response theories.

A final line of persuasion research is also relevant to the question of whether involvement has different consequences depending on the underlying motivation on which it is based. Although not directly examining the motivational bases of involvement, some evidence suggests that attitudes with different functional bases are most effectively changed via messages that appeal to the corresponding motivation (e.g., DeBono, 1987; Katz, McClintock, & Sarnoff, 1956). Most previous research supporting this idea has taken an individual differences approach. We recently conducted an experimental study to assess whether persuasive communications are more effective when the message appeals to the motivation underlying subject's original involvement with the issue (Lavine, Robertson, & Borgida, 1993). First, in the involvement phase, we manipulated involvement in the issue of University of Minnesota energy policy on the basis of either self-interest or values. In the *self-interest-based involvement condition*, we told subjects that the university's decision to provide for its energy needs with either natural gas or coal would substantially affect future tuition increases, as well as the availability of student services such as campus parking and academic advising. Subjects in the *value-based involvement condition* were informed that the issue would have a substantial impact on the environment (activating the values of natural beauty and protection of the environment). Subjects in a *control condition* simply rated the personal importance of the issue. Next, in the persuasion phase, we presented subjects with a persuasive message that appealed to either their self-interest or their values. In the self-interest condition, the message emphasized the impact of the energy policy on tuition and student services and advocated the less expensive (but less environmentally sound) "coal policy"; in the value-based condition, the message emphasized the impact of the policy on the environment and advocated the "natural gas policy." Three results are of interest here. First, subjects in the involvement conditions rated the issue as higher in importance ($Ms = 4.9$ and 5.5 for self-interest and value-based conditions, respectively) than those in the control condition ($M = 4.3$; $p < .05$). Second, within the two experimental conditions, involvement was based on the intended source; coding of subjects' free-responses regarding the reasons for which the issue was important to them revealed more mentions of self-interest by those in the self-interest condition (55%) than by those in the value condition (24%; $p < .05$), and more mentions of values by those in the value condition (88%) than by those in the self-interest condition (62%; $p < .05$). Finally, as can be seen in Table 8.2, self-interest-based persuasion was more effective among subjects who were involved based on self-interest than among those whose involvement stemmed from value-relevance. Similarly, value-based persuasion was most effective among those whose involvement was based on their values rather than their self-interests ($ps < .05$). Thus, it does appear that the source of involvement plays a role in determining the strategies that will best effect attitude change.

Impression Formation

Researchers have also considered the influence of personal involvement on impression formation. Theorists have suggested that outcome dependency (in our terms, *self-interest*), values, and self-presentation may all motivate involvement in this domain (Fiske & Neuberg, 1990). However, even more than was the case in the persuasion literature, research in the impression formation domain has focused almost exclusively on self-interest-based involvement, and has employed experimental rather than correlational paradigms. In fact, although Fiske and Neuberg (1990) cited values as one of three major sources of involvement, their review does not cite a single published study that has examined value-based involvement.

Outcome dependency has typically been created by leading perceivers to believe that they will later be interacting with a target person in some capacity. The specific form of the anticipated interaction has varied from playing a game (Monson, Keel, Stephens, & Genung, 1982; Omoto & Borgida, 1988), to cooperating (Erber & Fiske, 1984; Neuberg & Fiske, 1987) or competing on a task for which a prize might be won (Ruscher & Fiske 1990), to dating the target person (Berscheid et al., 1976; Harkness et al., 1985; Omoto & Borgida, 1988). Although little comparative research has explored the possibility that these manipulations may elicit different

TABLE 8.2
Attitudes Toward Energy Policy as a Function of
Type of Involvement and Type of Persuasion

	Type of Persuasion	
Type of Involvement	Self-Interest	Values
Self-Interest	4.4	5.1
Values	3.1	6.8
Control	3.9	5.6

Note. $N = 54$. Attitude scores could range 1 to 7; higher scores indicate greater agreement with the persuasive message.

types or amounts of involvement (but see Omoto & Borgida, 1988), it is plausible that they do. Factors such as the structure of the task (e.g., cooperative vs. competitive), the nature of the task (e.g., dating vs. playing a game), attributes of the target (e.g., her or his level of competence), and other aspects of the situation (e.g., manipulated level of "stakes" in the outcome of the task) may all impact the magnitude and/or the type of effects that the target can have on the perceiver.

Like research in the persuasion domain, research on impression formation has shown that increasing self-interest-based involvement can increase the effort subjects are willing to expend in processing information about another person. Thus, compared to subjects who are relatively uninvolved with the target person, outcome-dependent subjects have been found to pay more attention to the target (Berscheid et al., 1976), especially to expectancy-inconsistent information about her or him (presumably because this type of information is most informative; Erber & Fiske, 1984; Ruscher & Fiske, 1990); to take longer to make judgments about the target (Monson et al., 1982); and to better remember information about the target in some studies (Berscheid et al., 1976) but not in others (Erber & Fiske, 1984). Those whose outcomes depend on their partners also make more extreme dispositional attributions about the partners (Berscheid et al., 1976; Erber & Fiske, 1984; Monson et al., 1982). As a result of their greater consideration of individuating information about the target, the impressions of outcome dependent subjects are often less influenced by social group categories and stereotypes, and more strongly related to the actual information provided, than are the impressions of less involved subjects (e.g., Erber & Fiske, 1984; Monson et al., 1982; Neuberg & Fiske, 1987). Similarly, relative to noninvolved subjects, outcome dependent subjects use more complex reasoning strategies when thinking about the target person (Harkness et al., 1985), and their impressions of the target are more predictive of their intended behavior toward the target (Monson et al., 1982).

Fiske and Neuberg (1990) suggest that these effects occur because outcome dependent subjects have enhanced motivation to form accurate impressions. However, they also note that involvement need not always result in objective processing of information about the target. Sometimes, rather than being motivated to form accurate impressions, individuals are motivated to form a particular impression, or to form an impression quickly, regardless of its accuracy (Kruglanski, 1990). Omoto and Borgida (1988) suggested that moderate levels of involvement (e.g., expecting to play a game with the target) may undercut stereotyping and lead to more positive impressions compared to higher levels of involvement (e.g., anticipating a date with the target). This may be analogous to the finding, within the persuasion literature, that involvement sometimes (perhaps at moderate levels) leads to objective processing of the persuasive message, whereas at other times (perhaps at higher levels) it leads to partisan processing and resistance to persuasion. Such biased processing may also be revealed by the finding that, compared to their relatively uninvolved counterparts, outcome-dependent individuals have sometimes been found to form more positive impressions of their partners (Berscheid et al., 1976), although other studies have failed to find this effect (e.g., Erber & Fiske, 1984).

The similarity of the observed effects of involvement for persuasion and impression formation is quite striking, particularly given the differences in how involvement has been operationalized in the two domains. Whereas persuasion researchers have induced involvement by spelling out concrete effects of particular policies for the subject, in the impression formation domain the specific effects that targets will have on subjects remain unspecified. Rather, the perceiver is simply made aware that the target person will have the capability of influencing her outcomes; she often has little basis for predicting the specific consequences the target will have for her. In light of these strong operational differences, the convergence of these literatures constitutes impressive evidence for the generality of involvement effects.

Attitudes, Judgments, and Behavior

A smattering of research has also examined the effects of involvement on other aspects of attitudes. Two studies have demonstrated that involving attitudes, compared to less involving attitudes, are more stable over time (Krosnick, 1988; Petty et al., 1990, cited in Petty et al., 1992). Somewhat more research has examined the possibility that personal involvement moderates the attitude-behavior relation. Several studies have reported significant associations between one's level of personal involvement in an issue and one's likelihood of acting in an attitude-consistent fashion, primarily by correlating various measures of personal involvement with either self-reported behavior (see, e.g., Brown, 1974; Krosnick, 1988; Schuman & Presser, 1981) or actual behavior (Rokeach & Kliejunas, 1972; C. W. Sherif et al., 1973, Exp. 5). Although these studies did not consider the motivational sources of the involvement, a few studies have provided evidence that self-interest-based involvement can increase attitude-behavior relations. Leippe and Elkin (1987) found that attitude was an extremely strong predictor of behavior among subjects who had been told that an issue would affect them personally ($r = .83$), but was much weaker among those in whom self-interest-based involvement had not been induced ($r = .38$; see also Petty, Cacioppo, & Schumann, 1983). Other studies have taken a correlational approach, with similar results (see Regan & Fazio, 1977; Sivacek & Crano, 1982; for parallel findings in the impression formation domain, see Monson et al., 1982).

Attitudes toward issues and objects with which individuals are highly involved may also disproportionately influence their other attitudes and judgments. This hypothesis has been confirmed in research in the disparate domains of interpersonal attraction and political cognition. In the attraction domain, the well-documented finding that similarity breeds attraction has been found to be more pronounced when the individuals are similar in terms of attitudes that are important to the person than when they are similar in less important respects (Byrne, London, & Griffitt,

1968; Clore & Baldridge, 1968). Research has also demonstrated that important political attitudes play a greater role in candidate evaluation than do less important attitudes (e.g., Aldrich & McKelvey, 1977; Krosnick, 1988). Thus, to the extent that individuals are highly involved with a particular attitude, that attitude tends to be used in evaluating others. This may occur because people view attitudes as more informative about others' personality traits to the extent that those attitudes are personally important (Judd & Johnson, 1981). Although research has focused on how important attitudes can influence people's opinions of others, it seems likely that important attitudes may also influence the formation of other kinds of attitudes. It remains for future research to examine this possibility.

STRUCTURAL CONSEQUENCES
OF PERSONAL INVOLVEMENT

Our review thus far suggests that attitudes toward an entity will be stronger to the extent that the individual is personally involved with that entity. Strong attitudes have been characterized as those that are highly predictive of behavior, persistent over time, and resistant to change (Petty et al., 1992; Raden, 1985); as we have seen, there is at least some evidence that personally involving attitudes meet all of these criteria. Further research is clearly needed to address the generalizability of these relations across domains, and to examine possible differences as a function of type of involvement. Beyond establishing the boundary conditions of involvement effects, however, it is important to examine the mediation of these effects. That is, it is important to ask how—through what structural or processing mechanisms—involvement produces its cognitive and behavioral effects. This question implies that beyond its consequences for cognitive and behavioral outcomes, personal involvement may also influence the structural attributes of attitudes that are formed, the processes that are engaged, and the way(s) in which attitudes are stored in memory.

Although most research has focused on the evaluative dimension of attitudes (Ostrom, 1989), attitudes may vary in terms of a variety of structural properties. By structural properties we refer to any attribute with implications for the manner in which attitudes are structured in memory; thus, structural properties include such aspects as attitude extremity (Judd & Brauer, ch. 3, this volume; Judd & Johnson, 1981; Tesser, 1978; Tesser, Martin, & Mendolia, ch. 4, this volume), amount of attitude-relevant information (Wood, 1982; Wood, Rhodes, & Biek, ch. 11, this volume), accessibility (Fazio, ch. 10, this volume; Fazio & Williams, 1986), evaluative-cognitive consistency (Chaiken, Pomerantz, & Giner-Sorolla, ch. 15, this volume; Lavine, Thomsen, & Gonzales, 1993; Rosenberg, 1956), polarization (Bargh, Chaiken, Govender, & Pratto, 1992; Kaplan, 1972; Lavine, Sullivan, Borgida, & Thomsen, 1994), and ambivalence (Kaplan, 1972; Thompson, Zanna, & Griffin, ch. 14, this volume). Most research on these attributes, which Raden (1985) referred to as "strength-related attitude dimensions," has explored relations between specific attitudinal properties and other outcomes, such as behavior. For example, researchers have studied dimensions such as accessibility (Fazio & Williams, 1986) and involvement (C. W. Sherif et al., 1973, Exp. 5) as moderators of the attitude-behavior relation. However, there has been very little integrative research directly examining interrelations among the dimensions (for a review, see Raden, 1985). Neither have theorists devoted much attention to explicating the relations theoretically expected to exist among these properties (although see Krosnick, 1989; Krosnick et al., 1991; Tesser, 1978).

However, some research has directly examined relations between involvement and other structural variables. Most relevant in the present context is research showing that attitudes characterized by high levels of involvement are more extreme (Leippe & Elkin, 1987; Krosnick, 1988; Thomsen et al., 1993), more accessible (Krosnick, 1988, 1989; Lavine, Sullivan, et al., 1994), and thought about more frequently (Howard-Pitney et al., 1986; Omoto & Borgida, 1988) than less involving attitudes. Some of this research has been experimental, manipulating involvement (almost exclusively via self-interest-based manipulations) and observing its effects on extremity (Leippe & Elkin, 1987) or frequency of thought (Omoto & Borgida, 1988; Petty & Cacioppo, 1979). Even in correlational research, however, personal involvement has been ascribed a causal role; that is, involvement has been regarded as an independent variable, whereas other structural variables have typically been treated as dependent variables.

Other research has focused on the interrelationships among attitude extremity, attitude accessibility, and frequency of issue-relevant thought. In a program of research addressing these issues, Tesser and his colleagues (for a review, see Tesser, 1978) demonstrated that mere thought about an attitude object or issue makes the associated attitude more extreme. Theoretically, this occurs because thinking about an issue increases the salience of attitude-consistent beliefs and feelings within the attitudinal knowledge structure. In addition to its relation to amount of issue-relevant thought, attitude extremity is also related to attitude accessibility. Fazio and his colleagues (e.g., Fazio & Williams, 1986) demonstrated that individuals are able to report on their attitude toward an issue more quickly to the extent that their attitude is extreme.

Although the existing research on relations among these attitude dimensions is rather fragmentary, taken together these studies provide several clues regarding their likely causal interrelations. Based on these clues, we, along with our colleague John L. Sullivan, recently conducted two studies to examine a model of the relations between personal involvement and the dimensions of extremity, polarization, issue-relevant thought, and accessibility.[6] We took as our starting

---

[6]Attitude extremity is operationalized in terms of deviation from the midpoint of an attitude scale. Polarization refers to the degree to which the attitude is univalent or unambivalent; operationally, it is defined as the absolute difference between the individual's rating of his or her positive feelings toward the object and comparable ratings of negative feelings toward the object (see Kaplan, 1972). Accessibility refers to the ease or speed with which the attitude is brought to mind, and is typically indexed by the length of time it takes the individual to respond "good" or "bad" to an attitudinal inquiry (Fazio, 1986).

point the finding that involving or important attitudes exert a stronger influence on social perception and behavior than less important attitudes (e.g., Monson et al., 1982; C. W. Sherif et al., 1973). One likely explanation for this effect implicates the greater cognitive accessibility of involving, relative to uninvolving attitudes (Krosnick, 1988, 1989). It has, in turn, been suggested that the greater cognitive accessibility of involving attitudes is due to the fact that they are the target of more frequent conscious thought (Krosnick, 1989).

In our first study (Lavine, Sullivan, et al., 1994), we sought to explore the mediating roles of issue-relevant thought and attitude polarization in the relationship between involvement and accessibility. On the basis of previous research (e.g., Chaiken, 1980; Petty et al., 1981), we expected that increased involvement in an issue would lead to more frequent thought about that issue. Increased issue-relevant thought, in turn, was hypothesized to produce greater internal consistency of the attitudinal knowledge structure, resulting in attitude polarization (Tesser, 1978).[7] Finally, polarized attitudes should provide clearer behavioral cues than weaker or ambivalent attitudes, and thus should be more accessible in memory (Bargh et al., 1992). Conversely, because attitudes based on mixed or weak feelings should be relatively unlikely to play a determining role in an individual's cognition and behavior, their accessibility should decrease over time.

In sum, the hypothesized model suggests the following causal ordering:

$$\text{Involvement} \rightarrow \text{Thought} \rightarrow \text{Polarization} \rightarrow \text{Accessibility}.$$

To evaluate the plausibility of this model, we measured involvement, frequency of thought, attitude polarization and accessibility with respect to each of 14 political issues.[8] Our initial results indicated that important (involving) attitudes are thought about more frequently and are more polarized and accessible than less involving attitudes. To test our model more directly, we assessed whether the heightened accessibility of involving attitudes is due to more frequent thought and more polarized attitudes on these issues, by separately covarying frequency of thought and attitude polarization out of the involvement-accessibility relationship. Our results confirmed the hypothesis that both issue-relevant thought and

---

[7]Although Tesser's theory describes the consequences of mere thought as "attitude polarization," operationally his measure is equivalent to what we refer to as "extremity" (see footnote 5). Although these two measures are correlated (Bargh et al., 1992), we chose to focus on polarization rather than extremity, because the results of preliminary research suggested that polarization is more strongly related to attitude accessibility.

[8]We assessed subjects' involvement in the issues by their rankings of the relative importance of the issues (C. W. Sherif et al., 1973). Issue-relevant thinking was assessed by self-reports of the frequency with which subjects thought about each issue. Attitudes were measured by an independent assessment of the extent of subjects' positive and negative feelings toward the issues. Attitude polarization scores were created by taking the absolute value of the difference between subjects' positive and negative feelings about each issue (see Kaplan, 1972). Finally, the accessibility of subjects' attitudes was assessed by recording response latencies to direct attitudinal inquiries about each issue (Fazio, 1986).

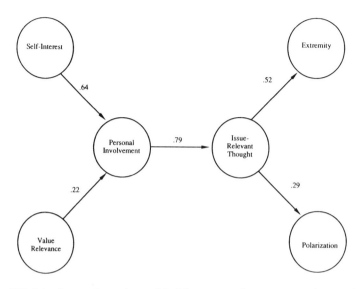

FIG. 8.1. Structural equation model of the causes and consequences of personal involvement.

attitude polarization serve as mediators; when either of these variables was controlled, the previously significant relationship between involvement and accessibility was eliminated (see Lavine, Sullivan, et al., 1994). In addition, controlling for frequency of issue-relevant thought eliminated the significant effect of involvement on polarization, supporting the contention that important attitudes are more polarized because they are thought about more than less important attitudes. This is consistent with Tesser's (1978) model of thought-induced attitude change. Finally, a significant relationship between frequency of issue-relevant thought and attitude accessibility was eliminated by controlling for the influence of polarization. The model was thus strongly supported.[9]

To further investigate the effects of involvement and, in addition, to examine its sources, we conducted an additional study in which we employed covariance structure modeling to test the model depicted in Fig. 8.1 with respect to three issues (sexual harassment, tuition increases, and discrimination against gays and lesbians; Thomsen et al., 1993). The model specifies that self-interest and value-relevance cause involvement, and that involvement causes increased issue-relevant thought, which, in turn, leads to more extreme and polarized attitudes. In this study, we used multiple indicators and multiple methods to assess each of

---

[9]We also tested several alternative models. In the first, attitude polarization mediates the effect of involvement on frequency of issue-relevant thought. In the second, involvement is directly associated with both polarization and accessibility, with the latter two only spuriously related. In the third, accessibility mediates the effects of involvement on frequency of thought and polarization. Each of these models proved inconsistent with some features of the data, and was consequently rejected.

the variables in the model. We then estimated latent constructs for each of the variables (via LISREL 7). Figure 8.1 presents the results for the sexual harassment issue; results for the other issues were similar. All paths specified in the model were statistically significant ($p < .05$), and the model proved an adequate fit to the data (GFI = .88).[10] Consistent with previous research (e.g., Boninger et al., 1995), self-interest and value-relevance were both significantly associated with involvement in an issue, with self-interest having a considerably stronger effect. Moreover, replicating our previous study, we found that involvement directly affects the frequency of issue-relevant thought, which then leads to more extreme and polarized attitudes.

CONCLUSION

What have we learned about the nature of personal involvement? We would argue that researchers have learned quite a bit about its effects, but surprisingly little about its causes. We regard this relative lack of attention to the antecedents of involvement as the single most important deficit in this literature. Although the evidence that exists consistently shows that self-interest is the most potent instigator of involvement among those investigated, it may well be that future research will illuminate other sources of involvement beyond those that have been examined thus far. Not only is the question of what motivates involvement interesting in its own right, it also impinges on our ability to understand the effects of involvement. If different forms or different levels of involvement lead to different consequences, homogeneously referring to the wide variety of assessment and manipulation techniques that have been used in this domain as "involvement" may mask real and important differences among these various sources. Thus, beyond simply specifying the motivational antecedents of involvement, it is necessary to determine whether different forms and levels of involvement have different effects.

Comparisons of the effects of different types or amounts of involvement have been extremely rare (but see Lavine, Robertson, et al., 1993; Leippe & Elkin, 1987; Omoto & Borgida, 1988), and in much of the existing correlational research, the origins of involvement have not been directly examined at all. The one type of involvement that has been studied fairly extensively is self-interest-based involvement, although even here, our ability to generalize about the effects of self-interest-based involvement is hampered by the homogeneity of the manipulations that

---

[10]We tested several alternative models, none of which fit the data as well as our preferred model. In one model, involvement and thought loaded on one factor, with self-interest and value-relevance as causes and extremity and polarization as effects (GFI = .82). In other models, involvement was specified as the single causal factor, with all remaining variables as its effects (GFI = .83). In a third alternative model, the model specified in Fig. 8.1 was re-estimated without method factors (GFI = .83).

have been used, and by researchers' near-total reliance on experimental paradigms. The paucity of research examining the other (value, social identification, group interest) bases of involvement may reflect the greater difficulty of manipulating or assessing these more abstract forms of involvement. However, it can be done (see Ostrom & Brock, 1969),[11] and it is necessary if we are to arrive at a more complete understanding of the consequences of involvement.

At the present, then, our conclusions about the effects of involvement must be tentative, subject to revision pending the results of future research in which different types and/or levels of personal involvement are compared. Nonetheless, some clear and interesting consistencies do emerge across literatures. Those who are highly involved devote more effort to the task at hand, and this occurs with both cognitive (e.g., Petty et al., 1981) and behavioral (e.g., Brickner, Harkins, & Ostrom, 1986) tasks. However, although involvement sometimes results in more sophisticated reasoning strategies and higher quality solutions (e.g., Harkness et al., 1985), it may also lead to strongly biased and partisan processing (Howard-Pitney et al., 1986). Whether processing is objective or biased may be a function of whether the individual's primary motivation is to obtain accurate information or to validate and confirm her or his beliefs and opinions (cf. Fazio, 1979). It seems likely that type and/or level of involvement influence which of these motivations will predominate, and a delineation of the circumstances under which each can be expected is an important task for future research. Future research may also reveal that while involvement has certain common general effects, specific effects may also emerge depending on the individual's specific goals within the situation (see Omoto & Borgida, 1988).

Although the largest accumulation of research on personal involvement is within the persuasion domain, a variety of other effects of involvement have been observed in other domains. These include a positive relation between involvement and the strength of attitude-behavior relations (e.g., C. W. Sherif et al., 1973, Exp. 5); a stronger impact of involving than of noninvolving attitudes on evaluations of others (e.g., Clore & Baldridge, 1968); an association between involvement and attitudinal persistence and stability over time (e.g., Krosnick, 1988); a decreased reliance upon judgmental heuristics among those who are highly involved (Borgida & Howard-Pitney, 1983; Chaiken, 1980; Petty et al., 1981; but see Taylor, Crocker, Fiske, Sprinzen, & Winkler, 1979); increased complexity of thought (e.g., more sophisticated strategies for assessing covariation) among those who are involved (Harkness et al., 1985; Sanbonmatsu, Shavitt,

---

[11]Ostrom and Brock (1969) experimentally manipulated value-based involvement by creating associations between attitudes and values, and found that those for whom central (i.e., important) values had been associated with their attitudes were more resistant to subsequent attitude change attempts than subjects whose peripheral values had been linked to their attitudes. Although they did not include a manipulation check to ascertain that involvement was indeed aroused by the value-bonding procedure, this study provides the clearest evidence to date of effects of value-based involvement on persuasion.

& Sherman, 1991); and heightened perceptions of the extent to which others agree with one for involving, relative to noninvolving issues (Crano, 1983). Additional effects will most likely emerge in future research as well.

We hope that researchers will devote increasing attention to illuminating the structural consequences of involvement, and to specifying the cognitive processes by which involvement exerts its effects on various cognitive and behavioral outcomes. Our own research, along with that of others, suggests that many of the effects of involvement may occur because people devote increased thought to involving entities. This increased thought, in turn, leads to more univalent or polarized attitudes (Tesser, 1978) and to heightened cognitive accessibility of the attitude (Krosnick, 1989). Because accessibility has been demonstrated to have a number of consequences (see, e.g., Higgins & King, 1981), involvement may, in this way, have far-reaching effects. Finally, on a methodological note, we believe that a multimethod approach to the elucidation of the causes and consequences of involvement, involving both correlational and experimental methods and converging operationalizations of involvement, will be most likely to advance our understanding of this construct. To be sure, such an approach drives our current research agenda. Although the accumulation of research on involvement across diverse research domains is impressive and suggestive, work remains to be done before a more complex and comprehensive model of personal involvement can be articulated.

REFERENCES

Aldrich, J. H., & McKelvey, R. D. (1977). A method of scaling with application to the 1968 and 1972 presidential elections. *American Political Science Review, 71,* 111–130.

Allport, G. W. (1943). The ego in contemporary psychology. *Psychological Review, 50,* 451–478.

Apsler, R., & Sears, D. O. (1968). Warning, personal involvement, and attitude change. *Journal of Personality and Social Psychology, 9,* 162–166.

Bargh, J. A., Chaiken, S., Govender, R., & Pratto, F. (1992). The generality of the automatic attitude activation effect. *Journal of Personality and Social Psychology, 62,* 893–912.

Berscheid, E., Graziano, W., Monson, T., & Dermer, M. (1976). Outcome dependency: Attention, attribution, and attraction. *Journal of Personality and Social Psychology, 34,* 978–989.

Boninger, D. S., Krosnick, J. A., & Berent, M. K. (1995). The causes and consequences of attitude importance: Self-interest, social identification and values. *Journal of Personality and Social Psychology, 68,* 61–80.

Borgida, E., & Howard-Pitney, B. (1983). Personal involvement and the robustness of perceptual salience effects. *Journal of Personality and Social Psychology, 45,* 560–570.

Brickner, M. A., Harkins, S. G., & Ostrom. T. M. (1986). Effects of personal involvement: Thought-provoking implications for social loafing. *Journal of Personality and Social Psychology, 51,* 763–769.

Brown, D. W. (1974). Adolescent attitudes and lawful behavior. *Public Opinion Quarterly, 38,* 98–106.

Byrne, D., London, O., & Griffitt, W. (1968). The effect of topic importance and attitude similarity-dissimilarity on attraction in an intrastranger design. *Psychonomic Science, 11,* 303–304.

Chaiken, S. (1980). Heuristic versus systematic information processing and the use of source versus message cues in persuasion. *Journal of Personality and Social Psychology, 39*, 752–766.

Chaiken, S., Liberman, A., & Eagly, A. H. (1989). Heuristic and systematic information processing within and beyond the persuasion context. In J. S. Uleman & J. A. Bargh (Eds.), *Unintended thought* (pp. 212–252). New York: Guilford.

Clore, G. L., & Baldridge, B. (1968). Interpersonal attraction: The role of agreement and topic interest. *Journal of Personality and Social Psychology, 9*, 340–346.

Crano, W. D. (1983). Assumed consensus of attitudes: The effect of vested interest. *Personality and Social Psychology Bulletin, 9*, 597–608.

DeBono, K. G. (1987). Investigating the social-adjustive and value-expressive functions of attitudes: Implications for persuasion processes. *Journal of Personality and Social Psychology, 52*, 279–287.

Eagly, A. H., & Telaak, K. (1972). Width of the latitude of acceptance as a determinant of attitude change. *Journal of Personality and Social Psychology, 23*, 388–397.

Erber, R., & Fiske, S. T. (1984). Outcome dependency and attention to inconsistent information. *Journal of Personality and Social Psychology, 47*, 709–726.

Fazio, R. H. (1979). Motives for social comparison: The construction-validation distinction. *Journal of Personality and Social Psychology, 37*, 1683–1698.

Fazio, R. H. (1986). How do attitudes guide behavior? In R. M. Sorrentino & E. T. Higgins (Eds.), *Handbook of motivation and cognition: Foundations of social behavior* (pp. 204–243). New York: Guilford.

Fazio, R. H., & Williams, C. J. (1986). Attitude accessibility as a moderator of the attitude-perception and attitude-behavior relations: An investigation of the 1984 presidential election. *Journal of Personality and Social Psychology, 51*, 505–514.

Fiske, S. T., & Neuberg, S. L. (1990). A continuum of impression formation, from category-based to individuating processes: Influences of information and motivation on attention and interpretation. In M. P. Zanna (Ed.), *Advances in experimental social psychology* (Vol. 23, pp. 1–74). New York: Academic.

Gantt, V. W. (1970). Attitude change as a function of source credibility and levels of involvement. *Dissertation Abstracts International, 31*, 3074A.

Gorn, G. J. (1975). The effects of personal involvement, communication discrepancy, and source prestige on reactions to communications on separatism. *Canadian Journal of Behavioral Science, 7*, 369–386.

Greenwald, A. G. (1982). Ego task analysis: An integration of research on ego-involvement and self-awareness. In A. Hastorf & A. M. Isen (Eds.), *Cognitive social psychology* (pp. 109–147). New York: Elsevier/North-Holland.

Greenwald, A. G., & Breckler, S. J. (1985). To whom is the self presented? In B. R. Schlenker (Ed.), *The self and social life* (pp. 126–145). New York: McGraw-Hill.

Harkness, A. R., DeBono, K. G., & Borgida, E. (1985). Personal involvement and strategies for making contingency judgments: A stake in the dating game makes a difference. *Journal of Personality and Social Psychology, 49*, 22–32.

Higgins, E. T., & King, G. (1981). Accessibility of social constructs: Information-processing consequences of individual and contextual variability. In N. Cantor & J. F. Kihlstrom (Eds.), *Personality and social interaction* (pp. 69–121). Hillsdale, NJ: Lawrence Erlbaum Associates.

Howard-Pitney, B., Borgida, E., & Omoto, A. M. (1986). Personal involvement: An examination of processing differences. *Social Cognition, 4*, 39–57.

James, W. (1890). *The principles of psychology.* New York: Holt, Rinehart, & Winston.

Johnson, B. T., & Eagly, A. H. (1989). Effects of involvement on persuasion: A meta-analysis. *Psychological Bulletin, 106*, 290–314.

Johnson, B. T., & Eagly, A. H. (1990). Involvement and persuasion: Types, traditions and the evidence. *Psychological Bulletin, 107*, 375–384.

Judd, C. M., & Johnson, J. T. (1981). Attitude polarization, and diagnosticity: Exploring the effect of affect. *Journal of Personality and Social Psychology, 41*, 26–36.

Judd, C. M., & Krosnick, J. A. (1982). Attitude centrality, organization, and measurement. *Journal of Personality and Social Psychology, 42,* 436–447.

Kaplan, K. J. (1972). On the ambivalence-indifference problem in attitude theory and measurement: A suggested modification of the semantic differential technique. *Psychological Bulletin, 77,* 361–372.

Kardes, F. R. (1988). Spontaneous inference processes in advertising: The effects of conclusion omission and involvement on persuasion. *Journal of Consumer Research, 15,* 210–224.

Katz, D. (1960). The functional approach to the study of attitudes. *Public Opinion Quarterly, 24,* 163–204.

Katz, D., McClintock, C., & Sarnoff, D. (1956). The measurement of ego defense as related to attitude change. *Journal of Personality, 25,* 465–474.

Kelman, H. C. (1958). Compliance, identification, and internalization: Three processes of attitude change. *Journal of Conflict Resolution, 2,* 51–60.

Kiesler, C. A. (1971). *The psychology of commitment.* New York: Academic.

Koestner, R., Zuckerman, M., & Koestner, J. (1987). Praise, involvement, and intrinsic motivation. *Journal of Personality and Social Psychology, 53,* 383–390.

Krosnick, J. A. (1988). The role of attitude importance in social evaluation: A study of policy preferences, presidential candidate evaluations, and voting behavior. *Journal of Personality and Social Psychology, 55,* 196–210.

Krosnick, J. A. (1989). Attitude importance and attitude accessibility. *Personality and Social Psychology Bulletin, 15,* 297–308.

Krosnick, J. A., Boninger, D. S., Chuang, Y. C., & Carnot, C. G. (1991). *Attitude strength: One construct or many constructs?* Unpublished manuscript, Ohio State University, Columbus.

Kruglanski, A. W. (1990). Motivations for judging and knowing: Implications for causal attribution. In E. T. Higgins & R. M. Sorrentino (Eds.), *Handbook of motivation and cognition: Foundations of social behavior* (Vol. 2, pp. 333–368). New York: Guilford.

Lau, R. R., Brown, T. A., & Sears, D. O. (1978). Self-interest and civilians' attitudes toward the war in Vietnam. *Public Opinion Quarterly, 42,* 464–483.

Lavine, H., Robertson, B., & Borgida, E. (1993). *Self-interest- and value-based involvement: Implications for persuasion processes.* Unpublished manuscript, University of Minnesota, Minneapolis.

Lavine, H., Sullivan, J. L., Borgida, E., & Thomsen, C. J. (1994). *The relationship of national and personal issue salience to attitude accessibility on foreign and domestic policy issues.* Unpublished manuscript, Northern Illinois University, DeKalb.

Lavine, H., Thomsen, C. J., & Gonzales, M. H. (1993). *Political expertise and value-attitude relations: The value-based mediation of political attitude consistency.* Unpublished manuscript, University of Minnesota, Minneapolis.

Leippe, M. R., & Elkin, R. A. (1987). When motives clash: Issue involvement and response involvement as determinants of persuasion. *Journal of Personality and Social Psychology, 52,* 269–278.

Miller, N. (1965). Involvement and dogmatism as inhibitors of attitude change. *Journal of Experimental Social Psychology, 1,* 121–132.

Monson, T. C., Keel, R., Stephens, D., & Genung, V. (1982). Trait attributions: Relative validity, covariation with behavior, and prospect of future interaction. *Journal of Personality and Social Psychology, 42,* 1014–1024.

Neuberg, S. L., & Fiske, S. T. (1987). Motivational influences on impression formation: Outcome dependency, accuracy-driven attention, and individuating processes. *Journal of Personality and Social Psychology, 53,* 431–444.

Omoto, A. M., & Borgida, E. (1988). Guess who might be coming to dinner: Personal involvement and racial stereotyping. *Journal of Experimental Social Psychology, 24,* 571–593.

Ostrom, T. M. (1989). Interdependence of attitude theory and measurement. In A. R. Pratkanis, S. J. Breckler, & A. G. Greenwald (Eds.), *Attitude structure and function* (pp. 11–36). Hillsdale, NJ: Lawrence Erlbaum Associates.

Ostrom, T. M., & Brock, T. C. (1968). A cognitive model of attitudinal involvement. In R. P. Abelson, E. Aronson, W. J. McGuire, T. M. Newcomb, M. J. Rosenberg, & P. H. Tannenbaum (Eds.), *Theories of cognitive consistency: A sourcebook* (pp. 373–383). Chicago: Rand-McNally.

Ostrom, T. M., & Brock, T. C. (1969). Cognitive bonding to central values and resistance to a communication advocating change in policy orientation. *Journal of Experimental Research in Personality, 4,* 42–50.

Petty, R. E., & Cacioppo, J. T. (1979). Issue-involvement can increase or decrease persuasion by enhancing message-relevant cognitive responses. *Journal of Personality and Social Psychology, 37,* 1915–1926.

Petty, R. E., & Cacioppo, J. T. (1986). The elaboration likelihood model of persuasion. In L. Berkowitz (Ed.), *Advances in experimental social psychology* (Vol. 19, pp. 123–205). Orlando, FL: Academic.

Petty, R. E., & Cacioppo. J. T. (1990). Involvement and Persuasion: Tradition and integration. *Psychological Bulletin, 107,* 367–374.

Petty, R. E., Cacioppo, J. T., & Goldman (1981). Personal involvement as a determinant of argument-based persuasion. *Journal of Personality and Social Psychology, 41,* 847–855.

Petty, R. E., Cacioppo, J. T., & Haugtvedt, C. P. (1992). Ego-involvement and persuasion: An appreciative look at the Sherifs' contribution to the study of self-relevance and attitude change. In D. Granberg & G. Sarup (Eds.), *Social judgment and intergroup relations: Essays in honor of Muzafer Sherif* (pp. 147–175). New York: Springer-Verlag.

Petty, R. E., Cacioppo, J. T., & Schumann, D. (1983). Central and peripheral routes to advertising effectiveness: The moderating role of involvement. *Journal of Consumer Research, 10,* 135–146.

Raden, D. (1985). Strength-related attitude dimensions. *Social Psychology Quarterly, 48,* 312–330.

Regan D. T., & Fazio, R. H. (1977). On the consistency between attitude and behavior: Look to the method of attitude formation. *Journal of Experimental Social Psychology, 13,* 28–45.

Rhine, R. J., & Severance, L. J. (1970). Ego-involvement, discrepancy, source credibility and attitude change. *Journal of Personality and Social Psychology, 16,* 175–190.

Rokeach, M., & Kliejunas, P. (1972). Behavior as a function of attitude-toward-object and attitude-toward-situation. *Journal of Personality and Social Psychology, 22,* 194–201.

Ruscher, J. B., & Fiske, S. T. (1990). Interpersonal competition can cause individuating processes. *Journal of Personality and Social Psychology, 58,* 832–843.

Sanbonmatsu, D. M., Shavitt, S., & Sherman, S. J. (1991). The role of personal relevance in the formation of distinctiveness-based illusory correlations. *Personality and Social Psychology Bulletin, 17,* 124–132.

Sawyer, A. G., & Howard, D. J. (1991). Effects of omitting conclusions in advertisements to involved and uninvolved audiences. *Journal of Marketing Research, 28,* 467–474.

Sears, D. O., & Funk, C. L. (1991). The role of self-interest in social and political attitudes. In M. P. Zanna (Ed.), *Advances in experimental social psychology* (Vol. 24, pp. 1–91). New York: Academic.

Sherif, C. W. (1980). Social values, attitudes, and involvement of the self. In M. M. Page (Ed.), *Nebraska symposium on motivation: Beliefs, attitudes, and values* (pp. 1–64). Lincoln: University of Nebraska Press.

Sherif, C. W., Kelly, M., Rodgers, L., Sarrap, G., & Tittler, B. I. (1973). Personal involvement, social judgment, and action. *Journal of Personality and Social Psychology, 27,* 311–328.

Sherif, C. W., Sherif, M., & Nebergall, R. E. (1965). *Attitude and attitude change: The social judgment-involvement approach.* Philadelphia: Saunders.

Sherif, M., & Cantril, H. (1947). *The psychology of ego-involvements.* New York: Wiley.

Sherif, M., & Hovland, C. I. (1953). Judgmental phenomena and scales of attitude measurement: Placement of items with individual choice of number of categories. *Journal of Abnormal and Social Psychology, 48,* 135–141.

Sherif, M., & Hovland, C. I. (1961). *Social judgment: Assimilation and contrast effects in communication and attitude change.* New Haven, CT: Yale University Press.

Sivacek, J., & Crano, W. D. (1982). Vested interest as a moderator of attitude-behavior consistency. *Journal of Personality and Social Psychology, 43*, 210–221.

Smith, M. B., Bruner, J. S., & White, R. W. (1956). *Opinions and personality*. New York: Wiley.

Snyder, M. (1992). The motivational foundations of behavioral confirmation. In M. P. Zanna (Ed.), *Advances in experimental social psychology* (Vol. 25, pp. 67–122). New York: Academic.

Taylor, S. E,. Crocker, J., Fiske, S. T., Sprinzen, M., & Winkler, J. D. (1979). The generalizability of salience effects. *Journal of Personality and Social Psychology, 37*, 357–368.

Tesser, A. (1978). Self-generated attitude change. In L. Berkowitz (Ed.), *Advances in experimental social psychology* (Vol. 11, pp. 289–338). New York: Academic.

Tesser, A. (1988). Toward a self-evaluation maintenance model of social behavior. In L. Berkowitz (Ed.), *Advances in experimental social psychology* (Vol. 21, pp. 181–227). New York: Academic.

Tetlock, P. E. (1983). Accountability and complexity of thought. *Journal of Personality and Social Psychology, 45*, 74–83.

Thomsen, C. J., Lavine, H., Borgida E., & Sullivan, J. L. (1993). *A covariance structure model of the causes and consequences of personal involvement*. Unpublished manuscript, Tufts University, Medford, MA.

Wood, W. (1982). Retrieval of attitude-relevant information from memory: Effects on susceptibility to persuasion and on intrinsic motivation. *Journal of Personality and Social Psychology, 42*, 798–810.

Zimbardo, P. G. (1960). Involvement and communication discrepancy as determinants of opinion conformity. *Journal of Abnormal and Social Psychology, 60*, 86–94.

9

▼▼▼▼▼▼▼

Attitude Certainty

Sharon Ruth Gross
University of Southern California

Rolf Holtz
Lamar University

Norman Miller
University of Southern California

To date, a coherent picture of the nomological net in which the concept of certainty is located and its convergent or discriminant validity with respect to other measures of attitude strength is lacking. Instead, only disjointed theorizing and findings exist from which, it is hoped, future work will weave a cohesive whole. Early researchers focused on relations among measures of attitude intensity and on the consequences of certainty. Recent work attends more to its antecedents. Like many measures of attitude strength, certainty has both cognitive and affective components. A state of uncertainty not only connotes insufficient information to act, but also is assumed to be aversive (e.g., Gerard & Greenbaum, 1962), or at least to arouse an affective state that differs from certainty (Roseman, 1984).

We begin by defining *certainty*, explicitly distinguishing subjective conceptualizations (on which we focus) from objective ones. We then position subjective certainty in relation to other measures of attitude strength, considering in particular the conceptual relation between attitude extremity and certainty. Then, in separate sections, we discuss antecedents of certainty and its consequences. In a final section, we present suggestions for new research.

CONCEPTUAL DEFINITION OF CERTAINTY

Conceptually, we define certainty as a subjective sense of conviction or validity about one's attitude or opinion (Festinger, 1950, 1954). Whereas objective certainty is associated with accuracy or objective correctness, and requires compari-

215

son with a measure of external reality, subjective certainty does not.[1] Appropriate synonyms of subjective certainty are a sense of attitude or opinion confidence, conviction, certitude, commitment, correctness, surety, or firmness.

Across three studies of telephone and in-person interviews, Abelson (1988) factor analyzed 15 measures of opinion conviction about five relatively salient and important attitude issues: belief in God, desirability of nuclear power, divestment from companies doing business in South Africa, legalization of abortion, and mandatory AIDS testing. Three five-item clusters emerged: *subjective certitude*[2] *(certainty/correctness, crystallization/involvement, steadfastness/stability, moral values, action/intention to behave), ego preoccupation* (thought, strength, importance, concern, affect), and *cognitive elaboration* (longevity, centrality, instrumentality, knowledge, ease of explaining/attitude accessibility).[3] Subjective certitude corresponds most closely to our conceptualization of attitude certainty. In contrast to this evidence for a convergence among subsets of conviction or strength measures, others have concluded, on the basis of literature review (Raden, 1985) or their own empirical comparison of strength measures concerning important social issues (Krosnick, Boninger, Chuang, Berent, & Carnot, 1993), that there is no common underlying construct of attitude strength. We next present some discussion and findings relevant to this debate.

Relation Between Extremity and Certainty

More often than not, attitude extremity and certainty have been conceptually and empirically confounded. For example, Abelson (1990) ascribes three meanings to extremity: "The attitude object might attach to a number of strong values held by the individual; the attitude might be sweeping in its lack of qualification . . . ;

---

[1]Confidence (e.g., Peterson & Pitz, 1988) and correctness (e.g., Hanley & Collins, 1989) are often conceptualized as likelihood or probability measures about events that are based in reality (see Smithson, 1989 for the difference between probability and possibility). Subjects who are aware that an objectively correct answer exists are asked to report their confidence about the correctness of their attitude. This use differs from our conceptualization of certainty. Of note is that conformity is greater (both publicly and privately) when an objectively correct response can be known (Insko, Drenan, Solomon, Smith, & Wade, 1983). This suggests that pluralistic ignorance (e.g., D. T. Miller & McFarland, 1987), that is, believing that others' correctness is greater than one's own, is more likely when there is an objectively correct response than a subjective one. Laughlin and Ellis (1986) argued that tasks with demonstrably correct answers engender greater use of logic whereas judgmental tasks engage normative processes.

[2]We consider Abelson's (1988) alternate label (subjective certitude) a better descriptor of this factor than *emotional commitment*. Whereas he views this factor as "noncognitive," we believe that it contains cognitive components.

[3]The word or phrase before the slash is Abelson's (1988) label. Any word(s) after the slash is a term we judge to be a synonym. Most are self-evident but one needs explanation. Generally, attitude crystallization refers to resistance to change (cf. Krosnick & Abelson, 1992), or stability. Within this study, however, Abelson defines it as responses to statements in the form: My beliefs about 'X' express the real me. As such, they may represent personal involvement. Steadfastness was measured from statements in the form: I can't imagine ever changing my mind.

or the attitude might be extreme because one deems it legitimate to go to great lengths to defend it . . ." (p. 179). Although these may be properties of extreme attitudes, we do not believe they are exclusive properties. It seems likely that they can characterize attitudes that have other strength-related attributes such as importance, centrality, certainty, and a broad latitude of rejection. However, whereas earlier researchers emphasized an equivalence between extremity and certainty (e.g., Cantril, 1946; Mehling, 1959; Osgood, Suci, & Tannenbaum, 1957; Suchman, 1950), later researchers do not (e.g., Krosnick & Abelson, 1992; Krosnick et al., 1993).

Some procedures used to assess attitude strength confound extremity and certainty. Commonly, measures of attitude extremity or polarization employ a bipolar scale with a neutral midpoint. Deviance from the midpoint reflects increasing degrees of attitudinal extremity (e.g., slightly, moderately, strongly agree/disagree).[4] It also reflects attitudinal certainty. Extremity and certainty can, however, be measured independently.

Attitudes are specific reactions to an attitude object that are based on affective and belief components. A measure designed to emphasize the opinion or belief component of attitude extremity might use a continuum of statements that varies the inclusiveness of the attitude object, the intensity of its attribute, or both. Note that although intended as a measure of belief strength, if positively or negatively valenced attributes of the attitude object are included in the set, then affective response is also measured. Alternatively, one might solicit attributes associated with an attitude object and weight them by the value of the attribute. In either case, the extremity of response would reflect certainty. Instead, to measure attitude certainty directly, one might ask "How certain are you that you like/dislike (depending on the outcome on the attitude measure) the attitude object?" Again, such a measure should correlate positively with measures of the extremity of beliefs, as well as direct measures of attitude, and attitude extremity as defined by a combination of relevant attributes and their valence. However, although we view both extremity and certainty as conceptually linked to attitude strength, certainty captures components that are independent of extremity. Especially important is that certainty measures are responsive to felt differences in attitudinal intensity held by those with middling (nonextreme) attitudes.

In comparison with those whose attitudes are more extreme, people with middling attitudes vary more in their certainty (e.g., McCroskey, Prichard, & Arnold, 1967–1968). Sherif and Hovland (1961) noted that some people may hold "extreme neutral" attitudes, and many have noted that neutral responses to attitude scales may have different meanings for different people (e.g., Converse & Traugott, 1986; Diab, 1965). This diversity among those who hold middling attitudinal positions attenuates correlations between certainty and extremity.

---

[4]In addition to the typical operationalization of extremity as deviation from a scale midpoint, an equally appropriate one is deviation from the modal or median response. The latter is used by Johnson (1940) and is discussed in a subsequent section (Social Influence and Social Support).

The self as an attitude object might have unique consequences for the relation between extremity and certainty. As a manifestation of the importance of the role played by consistency motivation in self-definition, one might expect high certainty about self-traits regardless of their extremity. In consonance with our previous analysis, however, for issues related to self-knowledge too, Pelham (1991) found that certainty was associated with extremity of self-view, whereas importance was associated with the positivity of their valence. Supporting the link between extremity and certainty, subjects were more certain about how they ranked their worst and best attributes relative to their peers (e.g., very certain about being among the bottom 5%—or top 95%—of college students in musical talent), than their average ones. In contrast, they rated their best attributes as most important and their worst attributes as least important. Further, over a 10-week period, certainty was more stable than importance.

In sum, we suggest that extremity and certainty share conceptual and empirical meaning, but whereas extremity connotes certainty, certainty does not necessarily imply extremity.

Relation Between Ambiguity and Certainty

One might ordinarily expect a negative correlation between attitude certainty and both *ambiguity* and *ambivalence*, but there is little relevant research. Whereas ambiguity generally describes the degree of stimulus clarity, ambivalence describes a conflicted internal state and/or behavior. Ambiguous or unclear input should cause less certainty (e.g., size of fictitious animals, homophones) than clear stimuli (e.g., size of real animals, spoken words with a pronunciation that has a unique meaning). Situational cues (e.g., framing), however, can change the perception of a stimulus that ordinarily has multiple meanings into one that has a clear single interpretation (e.g., Newman & Uleman, 1990).

Although ambivalence is an internal state of conflict, one might feel as certain about being ambivalent as about being unambivalent. For example, many teachers will be certain of their ambivalence about an impending strike, feeling favorable because they consider the board of education offer unfair, but against it because they do not want to lose income. Generally, awareness of internal conflict leads to uncertainty in the behavioral sense of approach/avoidance (e.g., Abelson & Levi, 1985). Consequently, although certain about one's ambivalence, one feels uncertain when asked a general question such as "Do you support the strike?" Without awareness of internal conflict, greater certainty is felt about the dominant tendency toward the attitude object. For example, in reports of self-awareness of their feelings, repressives were less aware of their ambivalence and more certain about their feelings than nonrepressives (Sincoff, 1992). Liberman and Chaiken (1991) examined the effects of thought (vs. distraction) on attitude certainty[5]

---

[5]Although they considered their attitude response measure (-7 = definitely not, $+7$ = definitely yes) to be a measure of attitude extremity, it conceptually corresponds to our definition of certainty.

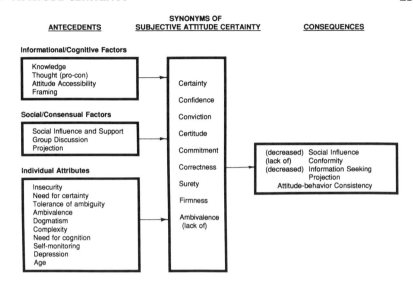

FIG. 9.1.   Antecedents and consequences of subjective attitude certainty.

using an attitude issue (e.g., should the CIA have the authority to open the mail of citizens as part of its efforts against foreign spies?) that raised potentially conflicting values (freedom vs. national security). They compared subjects for whom the two values were in conflict with those for whom they were not. Thought about the issue only increased certainty among those for whom one value was more dominant, thus supporting the view that ambivalence reduces attitude certainty.

In general, people are less certain (have greater ambivalence) about the desirability of an object when the number of its good and bad attributes is similar (Lemon, 1968). Stimuli that are of low ambiguity tend to be judged with high confidence (reviews: Tajfel, 1969; Vickers, Smith, Burt, & Brown, 1985).

ANTECEDENTS OF ATTITUDE CERTAINTY[6]

Many factors affect attitude certainty (see Fig. 9.1). We first discuss two major classes of external factors that enter into theorizing about uncertainty reduction, informational/cognitive and social/consensual, and then consider personal attributes.

---

[6]We omit discussion of studies that examine self-confidence because they typically concern abilities rather than attitudes (e.g., Altmaier, Leary, Halpern, & Sellers, 1985; Zuckerman, 1985). Some studies on over- or underconfidence are excluded because they concern the objective accuracy of the attitude (e.g., Sanbonmatsu, Kardes, & Sansone, 1991; von Winterfeldt & Edwards, 1986).

Informational/Cognitive Factors

In information theory (Shannon & Weaver, 1949), the degree to which an outcome is informative depends on the amount of uncertainty it reduces. Accordingly, there can be no information without prior uncertainty. That is, complete certainty inhibits information seeking and encoding. Uncertainty is defined as increasing when there are more alternatives and when the likelihood that each might occur approaches equivalence. The greater the number of possible outcomes (events or choices), the more informative is the occurrence of a particular outcome because it eliminates more alternatives. Because the weather is more variable in Denver than in Santa Monica, learning that the sun is shining in Denver is more informative than learning that it is shining in Santa Monica. Berlyne (1965), in his three-factor theory of motivation to seek information, adds importance (defined by its relevance for action decisions) and subjective probability that the information received is reliable and informative to the information theory definition of uncertainty. Aside from information or knowledge per se, other related cognitive factors such as thought, accessibility, and framing, are relevant aspects of individual psychology.

Knowledge. Experience can provide knowledge. Direct experience with an attitude object increases both latitude of rejection and opinion certainty (cf. Sample & Warland, 1973; Sherif, Kelly, Rodgers, Sarup, & Titler, 1973). In a nationwide survey of 1,359 business investors, those with less investing experience had less confidence in their investment decisions (Estes & Hosseini, 1988). The amount of prior experience women had with children predicted their maternal confidence during their current child's toddler years (Gross, Rocissano, & Roncoli, 1989). Although a greater amount of relevant information generally increases certainty (e.g., Sidanius, 1988), sometimes it does not. For example, individuals who examined less information about alternatives were more certain about their decision than those who engaged in a more exhaustive search (Zakay, 1985). Experienced clinicians displayed less overconfidence in their diagnoses than inexperienced clinicians (Garb, 1986).

That confidence increases as the balance of evidence favors a response (Vickers et al., 1985) seems obvious. If a search provides preponderant evidence for one's attitude, or experience reveals a consistent effect, certainty will be high. When instead, information, knowledge, or experience presents inconsistencies, it is reduced.

Thought. Knowledge requires thought, but thought does not necessarily confer knowledge. Yet, thought sometimes augments attitude strength. Cognitive elaboration is associated with attitude extremity (e.g., Brock & Brannon, 1992) and certainty (Abelson, 1988). Based on Tesser's (1978) hypothesis that mere thought is sufficient to polarize attitudes, we expected and found attitude certainty to covary with amount of thought (Miller, Gross, & Holtz, 1991, pp. 187–195). To manipulate amount of thought, subjects were assigned different numbers (0–2) of rating tasks about issues on which they had initially expressed their attitude. Each task required that they think again about the attitude topic. Their certainty monotonically increased as a function of the number of tasks. *Hindsight bias* (Hawkins & Hastie, 1990) may in part reflect this effect of thought. Once given an outcome, people feel they could have predicted it—that it is obvious (e.g., "I knew Sally and John would be the ones to stay married," ". . . to get divorced," etc.). They deny that the outcome made them retrospectively feel subjectively certain about what is now (either actually or ostensibly) objectively certain. Because hindsight bias concerns beliefs, it can apply to attitudes as well (cf. Gage, 1991). Journal editors, too, can fall prey to it. Even when submitted research is novel, it is likely to be deemed obvious after reading it, and thus unpublishable (N. Miller & Pollock, 1994).

Amount of thought, however, need not necessarily increase certainty. In a study described previously in our discussion of ambiguity, among persons for whom an attitude topic aroused conflicting values, thought decreased their attitude certainty (Liberman & Chaiken, 1991). Further, situational factors can instigate either supportive or nonsupportive thought. For example, forewarning of exposure to a counterattitudinal message elicits rehearsal of belief-supporting thoughts which buffer the effect of the message (McGuire, 1961). Without such warning, attitudes are more susceptible to change. In contrast, Wilson, Dunn, Kraft, and Lisle (1989) hypothesized that thinking about reasons for feeling as one did about an attitude object might lower attitudinal confidence by stimulating consideration of alternative points of view. Although generating reasons did not reduce certainty in any of their five studies,[7] other research is more supportive of their general hypothesis. Certainty of success did decrease as a decision deadline was approached (e.g., Gilovich, Kerr, & Medvec, 1993; Kruglanski & Webster, 1991), presumably due to thoughts about accountability and potential causes of failure. Also, as the number of choice alternatives (e.g., Kruglanski, Peri, & Zakai, 1991), or the cost of being wrong (e.g., Cohen, Jaffray, & Said, 1985) increased, certainty decreased; probably as a result of positive thoughts about the alternatives. Whereas Wilson et al. (1989) suggested that thinking about reasons leads to biased recall based on suboptimal sampling, Millar and Tesser (1986) argued that it increases the salience of the cognitive component of attitude at the expense of its affective component and thereby decreases attitude-behavior consistency.

Attitude Accessibility. Attitude confidence has long been thought to be associated with greater accessibility (e.g., Johnson, 1939; Kellogg, 1931; Volkmann, 1934). A frequently used measure of attitude accessibility is the speed

---

[7]They also found no effect on measures of latitude of acceptance/rejection, or response time to the attitude questionnaire.

with which an attitude is expressed (Fazio, 1990). Eyewitnesses who were certain about their choice of a suspect from a lineup made faster identifications than those less certain (Smith, Kassin, & Ellsworth, 1989). Similarly, those more certain about their answers to trivia questions spoke louder and faster than less confident persons (Kimble & Seidel, 1991). The foregoing could be interpreted as implying that certainty antecedes accessibility. A self-perception perspective, however, suggests the opposite (Bem, 1972). When asked, "Do you want your bedroom painted purple?," the alacrity and vehemence with which you respond "No!" may add to your felt certainty about your attitude. Faster recall is associated with an inference of increased validity of one's thoughts (e.g., reviews: Bargh, 1989; Jacoby & Kelley, 1990). Three contributors to attitude accessibility or availability have been considered determinants of confidence: familiarity, internal consistency, and salience (e.g., Tversky & Kahneman, 1982). The first is related to degree of exposure to an attitude object, the second to the relative support for alternative attitudes toward the object, and the third to the distinctiveness of the attitude object or the amount of concentrated attention paid to it at the time of encoding. Biased retrieval of instances occurs as a function of these factors and, in turn, leads to overconfidence (Tversky & Kahneman, 1973). This bias reflects certainty.

Framing. Framing (or cognitive priming) affects attitude certainty. Women who read a pamphlet describing the benefits lost by not performing breast self-examinations (negative frame) were more confident that the procedure would enable them to detect a lump than those who read either one that was neutral, one that described the benefits gained by performing it (positive frame), or nothing (Meyerowitz & Chaiken, 1987). Nonvalenced frames, such as category-based expectancies, can also affect certainty. After learning that they would be reading about an extravert, subjects were more certain that they had seen nonincluded descriptors of extroverts than those who expected to learn about introverts (Cantor & Mischel, 1977). Biased recall did not occur when no personality category information was provided.

The type of decision problem can frame the decision process that one selects. If one wants an economy car and must choose between a Toyota and a Cadillac, only the disliked attributes of the excluded choice need be examined. The closer the chosen alternative is to one's ideal, the greater the post-decision confidence (e.g., Zakay & Dil, 1984). Comparison of similar makes and models, such as Toyota *Camry* and Nissan *Maxima*, requires consideration of more discrete pieces of information (e.g., preference for appearance, mileage, maintenance history) and a weighing of trade-offs, making lost benefits salient, and reducing certainty about one's final decision. People who are uncertain about social issues are more susceptible to priming effects when the issue is important to them, or if, regardless of its importance, they know that their attitude leans in one direction or the other (Tourangeau, Rasinski, Bradburn, & D'Andrade, 1989).

Social/Consensual Factors

Other theorizing emphasizes the role of social consensus in uncertainty reduction: discovering that our attitudes are normative (conformity: e.g., Sherif, 1935, 1936), shared by people with whom we identify (self-categorization: Turner, Hogg, Oakes, Reicher, & Wetherell, 1987; social identity: Tajfel & Turner, 1986), shared by others in informal conversation (social communication: Festinger, 1950), or shared by those we seek for comparison (social comparison: Festinger, 1954). Alternatively, rather than direct comparison, we often assume that others share our attitude by projecting our own opinions onto those others (projection: Allport, 1924; Gerard & Orive, 1987). Actual comparison between self and others is at times either undesirable or unobtainable. Social projection[8] can function as a stand-in for social comparison in that it is the psychological or internal manufacture of an external consensus which, in turn, theoretically functions to decrease attitude uncertainty. Few phenomena have been as well studied and multiply confirmed as has social projection, suggesting it has broad pervasiveness and hence, potential importance (e.g., reviews: Marks & Miller, 1987; Mullen, Atkins, Champion, Edwards, Hardy, Story, & Vanderklok, 1985; Sherwood, 1981). In addition, it is linked to other theorizing that rests on the premise that attitude uncertainty is reduced by observing consensus among others' positions. A more elaborated consideration of theorizing about projection will raise issues that apply to other theories (e.g., social comparison, self-categorization) which assume that a reduction of uncertainty is mediated by a consensual process (induced by an antecedent condition, such as exposure to an influence attempt).

In Allport's (1924) theorizing about the mediating role of projection in augmenting attitude certainty, he started with the assumption that it will be elicited by exposure to a persuasive message in the presence of a group. He argued that it has three features: It is attributive, reciprocative, and enhancive. First, one assumes that the other listeners share one's own reactions, an attributive process. Second, this attribution is reflected. One experiences the attitude that one is forming (as a consequence of the speaker's statements) as not merely emanating from the speaker, but also, from others present, thereby making the projection reciprocative. One sees those others as believing or intending to act in a manner consonant with one's own developing beliefs and intentions. This reciprocal feature is, in turn, enhancive. It has a normative effect which increases the strength

---

[8]The literature concerning similarity projection employs a host of terms (cf. N. Miller & Pollock, 1994, for a comprehensive list). Our use of the term refers to distorted similarity/dissimilarity between self and other and implies no additional psychodynamic processes. It operationally corresponds to assimilative projection, assumed similarity, attributive projection, autistic projection, comparison projection, direct similarity, false consensus effect, reference projection, social comparison, social judgment, and social projection. It does not correspond to cassandrian/panglossian projection, causal attribution, causal projection, classical (Freudian) projection, complementary projection, complimentary/supplementary projection, defensive projection, rationalized projection, or thematic projection.

of whatever new attitude one is developing in response to the speaker's persuasive appeal.

Gerard and Orive (1987), building on Allport, hypothesized that either knowing or assuming (projecting) attitude similarity to others creates the social support necessary to augment certainty to a level sufficient for action. In seeming accord with Allport, they stated that the projection process requires the physical presence of others. In addition, they emphasized that the perception of similarity between self and others must occur on attributes relevant to the attitude object. Finally, three ingredients were seen as increasing the likelihood of projection: insufficient certainty to act, imminent need for action, and action importance.

A limiting feature of these theories is their explicit focus on intragroup phenomena. Because differences in social settings can prime different aspects of one's social identity and thereby affect motivational focus, a more comprehensive model must include interpersonal and intergroup settings as well. Furthermore, in studies of assumed similarity (review: Marks & Miller, 1987) and the false consensus effect (meta-analysis: Mullen et al., 1985), in which measurements typically are taken when subjects are alone, consensual bias (i.e., projected attitudinal similarity) is found despite the absence of other persons to serve as eliciting stimuli for the perception of reciprocal projection. Thus, although a projection (or social comparison, or self-categorization) process may more readily be elicited when others are physically, rather than merely symbolically present (Wilder & Shapiro, 1991), at least with respect to projection, these extensive literatures clearly cast doubt on the assumption that the physical presence of others is necessary.

As previously described, theory positions projection as mediating the effect that exposure to an influence attempt has on subsequent certainty about the new attitude produced by that attempt. Tests of any mediational model must provide evidence confirming the process that allegedly links antecedent, mediating, and dependent variables. This requires conceptualizing the mediating variable as both a dependent and an independent variable, and examining it experimentally from both perspectives. A variety of antecedents can increase one's uncertainty and need for social support—which is the motivational state that presumably instigates a projective process, but also can motivate social comparison, self-categorization, bias, prejudice, and so forth. For instance, threatening circumstances, which suggest that the attitude of one's ingroup is inferior, as for example, when one belongs to a minority group (e.g., Griffin, Dunning, & Ross, 1990; Mullen, 1991), or low-status group (e.g., Brewer, 1979; Mackie, 1984), augment one's need for social support. Consequently, stronger projection of similarity between self and ingroup is expected and found in minority (e.g., Mullen & Hu, 1989) and low-status groups (e.g., Mullen, Brown, & Smith, 1992). Other factors may moderate the mediating process. Whereas competition constrains group members from projecting similarity to the outgroup (e.g., Mackie & Cooper, 1984), cooperation might extend it to them. Similarly, the opportunity for social mobility (e.g., Ellemers, Van Knippenberg, De Vries, & Wilke, 1988) should increase projected similarity to the outgroup. The substantive content of the attitude topic raised in an influence attempt should also moderate the degree to which social support is sought. It will affect the aspect of identity that is made salient: individual, group-based, or neither. For instance, whereas uncertainty about group-relevant issues may elicit projection, there is less reason to project on issues solely relevant to one's individual identity (e.g., Marks, 1984) because this component of self is not based on external consensus. Moreover, projected similarity on such issues would only undermine self-enhancing perceptions of uniqueness (e.g., Brewer, 1991). Finally, theoretically expected effects of projection on conviction must be examined directly (e.g., Holtz & Miller, 1985). For instance, because projection is the assumption of consensual validation, its effects on certainty are, as expected, stronger for attitudes initially founded on a normative basis than for those based on informational material (e.g., Wagner & Gerard, 1983).

In subsequent sections, however, we present evidence that certainty, not uncertainty, elicits projection and we describe within-study instances of failures to obtain the expected covariation between projected similarity and attitude certainty. The hazards of making an inference from the absence of an effect notwithstanding, accumulated instances of such lack of covariation, along with evidence that uncertainty fails to elicit the projective process, constrain the scope of, if not cast doubt on, the validity of any theory of projection-mediated attitude certainty. Other theoretical models, in which specific process events such as felt social support (e.g., Festinger, 1954; Tajfel & Turner, 1956; Turner et al., 1987) are postulated to mediate increased attitude certainty, will likewise need to be decomposed experimentally to enable examination of the consistency with which expected covariations are confirmed (cf. Harrington & Miller, 1993).

Social Influence and Social Support. As stated, most theories of uncertainty reduction include aspects of social influence. Generally, discovery that comparable others agree with our attitude causes us to feel more certain about it, whereas discovery that they disagree shakes our confidence. There is more empirical evidence for the former than the latter. This may be due partially to the fact that the uncertainty caused by discovery that similar others disagree is often short-lived. Consider the finding that people who are influenced by others (i.e., change their attitude) do not show a decrease, but rather, an increase in confidence (Krech, Crutchfield, & Ballachey, 1962, p. 519). What happened to their uncertainty on discovering that others disagreed with them? The methodologies typically used in studies of social influence do not assess this uncertainty. When measures are positioned before and after an exposure to social influence, although an attitude change score is meaningful, a certainty change score usually is not. The certainty assessed at Time 2 typically concerns the new attitude, not the change in certainty about the original attitude prior to abandoning it. McGarty, Turner, Oakes, and Haslam (1993) reasoned that if subjects were situationally constrained so that they could not change their attitude, then one could meaningfully assess the effect of social influence (i.e., feedback about agreement or disagreement with own opinion by others) on certainty. After estimating the number of dots they saw on a screen, subjects expressed their confidence in their judgment. Feedback then indicated that the mean response of others was either close to (agreement) or far from (disagreement) their own. Subjects then reestimated their confidence in their original judgment. In the absence of any possibility to change their opinion, certainty increased when others agreed with them and decreased when they disagreed. The effects of these procedures on perceptions of one's own and one's group's ability showed that disagreement decreased confidence in both one's own and the group's ability and caused subjects to reject the group as a relevant reference group.

Typically, within experimental paradigms, subjects are asked to indicate their own attitude along an agree-disagree continuum and to rate their certainty only about their own attitude. Johnson's (1940) study is an exception that offers insights into the effect of social influence on certainty. He used some of Thurstone's (Thurstone & Chave, 1929) scaled statements to determine respondents' attitudes toward war and toward censorship; the scaled values of these statements ranged from 0 (*extremely anti*) to 11 (*extremely pro*). For each issue, respondents dichotomously indicated which of 20 attitude statements (with a mean scale value of 5.5 across the 20 statements for each issue) they accepted. They also expressed their confidence in accepting or rejecting each statement on a scale anchored by 0% (*guess*) and 100% (*complete certainty*), thereby indicating their degree of certainty about whether or not a statement represented their attitude. To examine the effect of social influence, Johnson determined the degree of consensus about each attitude statement (viz., absolute difference between the numbers of respondents who accepted and rejected each statement). Within each attitude domain, the correlation between consensus for each of the 20 statements and mean attitude certainty across subjects for each statement was .68 for war and .54 for censorship. Johnson concluded that "It is clear that *group confidence is directly related to group agreement* [italics his]" (p. 219). That is, there is greater certainty about attitudes that the majority either accepts or rejects and less certainty about those on which people are divided.

Group Discussion. Group polarization, a discussion-induced increase in attitude extremity, is one of the most well established findings in social psychology (review: Isenberg, 1986). Although a group decision can be predicted by the prediscussion mean (e.g., Gigone & Hastie, 1993), group discussion commonly reinforces the pre-discussion attitude (e.g., Burnstein & Vinokur, 1977; Tanford & Penrod, 1986) and increases attitude confidence (e.g., Myers & Kaplan, 1976; Ng, 1984; Sniezek & Henry, 1990; Stasser, Taylor, & Hanna, 1989), whereas an interpersonal discussion may not (e.g., Turner, Wetherell, & Hogg, 1989). Group discussion affects certainty by not only providing information about both where one's attitude lies on a continuum (range of attitudes) and its normativeness (degree of social support), but also by the substantive information that arises in the discussion. Different types of group discussion, however, do not increase attitude certainty equivalently. For instance, groups are more satisfied with and confident about a unanimous decision than either their own prediscussion attitude or a majority decision (e.g., Hastie, Penrod, & Pennington, 1983). One reason for the relation between unanimity and attitude certainty is that a unanimity rule promotes greater discussion of the majority viewpoint than does a majority rule (Hoffman, 1979). As a result, it provides more consistent substantive information in support of a position, as well as stronger normative pressure to agree (Kameda & Sugimori, 1993). Thus, unanimity and majority rules differ in their informational as well as their normative consequences. On the other hand, when a group is made to feel that there is a correct answer for their task, they are less likely to ignore unshared information (Stasser & Stewart, 1992). In turn, to the degree that contradiction does indeed exist in individually held information that otherwise would not be discussed, this increases the perception of heterogeneity and conflict. And, until a consensus emerges, it will reduce attitudinal certainty.

Projection. To operationalize attitude projection as an independent variable, the most direct procedure is to instruct or require subjects to engage in attitude estimation. We know of no studies other than our own (e.g., Holtz & Miller, 1985, 1989 [cited in Miller, Gross, & Holtz, 1991], 1992) that have examined the effect of projection on attitudinal certainty from this perspective. Nor do we know of published studies that assess directly the key underlying variable theoretically postulated to account for its contribution to increased certainty—felt social support or consensus.

Lower status should not only threaten one's social identity, but also increase the need for social support. Theory argues that this need can be fulfilled by assuming greater attitudinal similarity to the ingroup (projection), which, in turn, will increase opinion certainty. Holtz (1992) asked new and veteran fraternity members to estimate the attitudes of either other active members (ingroup), or pledges (potential ingroup members) before they indicated their certainty about their own attitudes. The veteran members projected greater attitude similarity to their ingroup (active members) than to the more peripheral target (pledges), and also reported greater certainty about their attitudes than those in a no-projection condition. Although new members, too, assumed their attitudes were more similar to other actives than to pledges, this opportunity to project failed to increase their attitude certainty beyond that of those in the no-projection control condition. Thus, contrary to a model of projection-mediated attitude certainty (in which projected similarity to the target of projection predicts whether or not certainty will be augmented), although the relatively lower status of the new members apparently increased their tendency to project themselves as more similar to the high-status members, it left them relatively uncertain about those beliefs. By contrast, when new members estimated the attitudes of pledges, they projected dissimilarity to them and subsequently reported increased attitude certainty. Apparently, distancing themselves from others whose status was even lower than their own bolstered their certainty. Yet veteran members, whose status was secure, projected even greater dissimilarity to pledges than did new members. But for them, distancing themselves from this lowest status group did not increase their certainty.

Intergroup competition is another circumstance that can threaten social identity, increase group members' need for social support, and consequently, by augmenting projections of similarity within the ingroup, might increase attitude certainty. In a laboratory study on the effect of a cooperative versus a competitive goal structure on projected attitude similarity and attitude certainty (cf. N. Miller, Gross, & Holtz, 1991, pp. 186–187), subjects were assigned to one of two 3-person groups on the alleged basis of their relative preference for the paintings of Klee or Kandinsky. In separate rooms, each group evaluated a painting by each artist on several dimensions. To manipulate goal structure, eligibility for a prize purportedly would depend on either the combined responses of the groups to a series of art-related issues (cooperation) or the better of the two groups' responses (competition). Projection was manipulated by instructing subjects to estimate the attitudes of either ingroup members, outgroup members, or neither, on art-relevant issues. Assumed attitude similarity to the projection target on the art issues and certainty about own art-related attitudes were the key measures. Although the ingroup projection conditions produced equivalently high levels of assumed similarity under cooperation and competition as well as equivalent levels of attitude certainty, these levels of certainty did not exceed those in the no-projection conditions. The outgroup projection condition yielded both greater distancing of the outgroup and greater attitude certainty under competition as compared to cooperation. However, the difference in certainty under competition versus cooperation was as great in the no-projection conditions as in the outgroup projection conditions—effects contrary to the view that projected outgroup dissimilarity mediates differences in attitude certainty found under competition and cooperation. That is, if uncertainty is reduced (or certainty is increased) by the perception of dissimilarity from the outgroup (projection), then it should not be reduced without projection. But in this study, it was.

A more direct manipulation of threat to social identity also failed to produce the expected covariation between projection and attitude certainty. In a series of three field studies (Gross, Holtz, & Miller, 1991, as cited in N. Miller et al., 1991), threat was manipulated by telling (or not telling) male commuter students or university apartment dwellers about opposition to their own attitudes by a higher-status outgroup (fraternity members). Then, subjects were either required or not required to estimate ingroup positions (project) on an array of attitude issues. Threatened identity led subjects to display ingroup solidarity by projecting greater attitude similarity between self and ingroup, but concomitantly failed to increase their attitude certainty. Further questioning whether projection augments certainty, it did not increase certainty any more than did other conditions that equivalently manipulated subjects' thought about the attitude issues (e.g., a recognition recall task, a rating of the ease or difficulty of assessing own attitude). Although there is overlap between the concepts *projection* and *induced thought*, the two are not isomorphic. In all instances of projection one must necessarily think about the issue. Obviously, however, all instances of induced thought about an attitude do not require that subjects think about or estimate the attitudes of others (projection). Support for projection as an antecedent of certainty requires evidence of greater certainty than that elicited by thought per se.

An alternative approach to assessing whether induced attitude projection increases certainty is to examine the consequences of statistically removing its effect. In a laboratory study which crossed projection target (ingroup, outgroup, no-projection) with the social climate of groups that were in competition with each other, subjects were assigned to one of two homogeneous 6-member groups on the basis of alleged dot over-/underestimation and sent to different rooms to work on a group task (Holtz & Miller, 1992). In the warm climate condition, the leader (an experimental assistant) sat with the group in a circle and employed a democratic leadership style. In the cold climate condition, group members sat single-file facing the front of the room. The leader, who sat slightly to the side, employed an autocratic style. Standardized feedback led each group to think that its task performance had been demeaned by the other group, thereby establishing group differentiation and bias. Those in the warm climate conditions projected similarity to the ingroup and dissimilarity to the outgroup and in both projection conditions exhibited more attitude certainty than those in the no-projection condition. In contrast, within the cold climate conditions, projection onto the ingroup failed to increase assumed similarity to ingroup (compared to the outgroup) or attitude certainty (compared to the no-projection control). Mediation analyses (Judd & Kenny, 1981) showed that the effects of the social climate manipulation on attitude certainty were not mediated by projected attitude similarity/dissimilarity, but instead, by felt emotional support.

In sum, rather than mediating (causing) conviction in response to an influence attempt, as argued by theory (Allport, 1924; Gerard & Orive, 1987), projection may be one among a number of variables that, along with attitude strength, are outcome variables that covary as a function of some combinations of antecedent situational variables, but with other combinations, do not.

Individual Attributes

Individual attributes, as well as situational factors, have received attention as antecedents of attitude certainty.

Certainty as a Personality Trait. A long history of research on the authoritarian personality (e.g., Adorno, Frenkel-Brunswik, Levinson, & Sanford, 1950), though manifestly focused on measuring "right" or conservative political ideology, also has been concerned with assessment of certainty or rigidity as a personality trait (review: Christie, 1991). In its original conceptualization, it incorporates a causal interpretation similar to that adopted by Allport and Hartman (1925) concerning the relation between extremism and insecurity, namely, one based on psychoanalytic conceptualizations concerning ego strength. Briefly, Allport and Hartman (1925) had subjects report their attitude, intensity of interest or feeling, and certainty on an array of social and political issues. For each issue, intensity and certainty were highly correlated ($rs \geq .90$) and those whose opinions reflected an extremely radical or reactionary view were generally more confident than those who were less extreme. Extremists shared many personal characteristics that differentiated them from the centrists leading the authors to view extremism as a personality trait. They also interpreted the expressed certainty of extremists as a motivational consequence of their stand, as compensating for a sense of insecurity inherent in taking extreme (generally minority) positions. Altemeyer (1988), who provides the best current measure of authoritarianism, abandons the psychoanalytic underpinnings of many earlier instruments.

Next, we briefly discuss recent additions to a comprehensive list of scales for assessing certainty as an individual difference. The Certainty Orientation Scale (Sorrentino & Short, 1986) concerns one's need for certainty. Under conditions of low justification (e.g., ambiguous stimulus, less knowledge), persons with a greater need for certainty are more certain about their attitudes (cf. Sorrentino, Raynor, Zubeck, & Short, 1990). Similarly, those with less ambivalence (Budner, 1962; Raulin, 1984), more dogmatism (Palmer & Kalin, 1991; Rokeach, 1960), or preference for complexity (Eisenman & Boss, 1970) exhibit greater attitude extremity and certainty. Another recent measure is the Need for Cognitive Closure Scale (cf. Kruglanski, Webster, & Klem, 1993). When information is sparse, persons with a higher need for closure should be more certain (Kruglanski, Peri, & Zakai, 1991).

The Need for Cognition Scale (Cacioppo & Petty, 1982) assesses the tendency to engage in and enjoy thinking. It includes subscales that measure cognitive confidence, persistence, and complexity (Tanaka, Panter, & Winborne, 1988). One might expect persons with a higher need for cognition to be more certain about their attitudes. That is, those with a higher need give more thought to their conclusions thereby creating not only greater certainty, but also greater accuracy. Further, the belief that eyewitness confidence reliably predicts identification accuracy has a common sense appeal. However, neither need for cognition, nor self-monitoring (Snyder & Gangestad, 1986) moderated the accuracy-confidence correlation in eyewitness accounts (e.g., Kassin, Rigby, & Castillo, 1991). Furthermore, in a study of the 1984 presidential election, individuals who differed in their need for cognition also differed in their preelection knowledge but not in their attitude confidence (Cacioppo, Petty, Kao, & Rodriguez, 1986). Perhaps those with a higher need for cognition not only become more knowledgeable, but also require more information in order to be as certain as those with a lower need.

Depression may be associated with a disjunction between accuracy and certainty. Whereas depressives have been described as more accurate in assessing others' traits (e.g., Coyne, 1976a, 1976b), they profess less certainty about their estimates (e.g., Campbell & Fehr, 1990; Pietromonaco, Rook, & Lewis, 1992). For instance, compared to normals and dysthymics, depressives reported that they *thought* they saw a flicker at the same level of intensity as did the other two groups, but a greater level of intensity was required in order for them to report that they *knew* they saw it (Herskovic, Kietzman, & Sutton, 1986).

In sum, although attitude certainty may be an aspect of personality, direct links between potentially relevant personality measures, general extremity/certainty of response style, and attitudinal certainty on specific content domains have not been well-studied. Nor is there evidence on the convergent or discriminant validity of seemingly relevant personality measures.

Age. It is interesting to note that we develop an understanding of the meaning of certainty by about the age of 4. Three-year-olds do not distinguish among the clue words *know*, *think*, or *guess* (as given by puppets concerning the whereabouts of a hidden object), but 4-year-olds do (Moore, Bryant, & Furrow, 1989). Similarly, among French children aged 4 to 5, 40% correctly differentiated the modifiers *savoir* (to know) and *croire* (to think) when used in sentences describing the location of a hidden object (Bassano, 1985). Both tolerance of ambiguity and confidence seem to increase with age. Compared to their undergraduate self-ratings, middle-aged alumnae (early 40s–50s) exhibited increased confidence, decisiveness, and tolerance of ambiguity (Helson & Wink, 1992).

CONSEQUENCES OF ATTITUDE CERTAINTY

Examination of some consequences of induced certainty provides findings that border on being vacuous, if not tautological. For instance, when the probability of experiencing an aversive event later in the experiment was absolutely certain (100% likelihood), as opposed to less certain (0%, 25%, 50%, or 75%), subjects reported feeling more negative affect (Andersen & Lyon, 1987). Perhaps somewhat less vacuous, and providing another example in which absolute certainty is the threshold for a change in response, is research on the devaluation of an expected reward that is not received. Allen (1964) had subjects choose and rank the 2 records they most preferred among 15. He manipulated their certainty of receiving the two as gifts (due to an oversupply) by telling subjects what percentage of them (e.g., either 100%, 95%, or 5%) would get both instead of only one. Then, after actually receiving only one, they were asked to revalue them. The record not received was only devalued by those led to anticipate that they were absolutely certain to receive it.

In this section we describe empirical evidence regarding the effects of subjective attitudinal certainty on: social influence, seeking information, projection, and the strength of the bond between attitudes and behavior (or the intention to behave).

Social Influence

It is generally accepted that subjective uncertainty creates a predisposition to be influenced (e.g., Krech, Crutchfield, & Ballachey, 1962; Moscovici, 1976). Factors likely to augment uncertainty, and thereby increase susceptibility to social influence are: (a) a difficult task, (b) ambiguous stimuli, (c) others perceived as more competent than self, (d) lack of social support for one's views, or (e) focus on an unimportant issue (reviews: Allen, 1965; Allen & Wilder, 1977; Jones & Gerard, 1967; Kiesler & Kiesler, 1969). People often conform to the expectations as well as the behavior and admonitions of others (e.g., Harris, 1991), but those who are certain can resist this pressure. Swann and Ely (1984) divided subjects to be interviewed (targets) into those who were more or less certain about their own classification as an introvert or extrovert. Interviewer subjects received bogus information which described the target as possessing the trait opposite to the target's self-depiction. The interviewer's certainty about this false depiction was manipulated by varying the alleged consensus among observers about this characterization of the target. Targets' certainty about their own trait interacted with the certainty induced in interviewers about the targets' possession of this opposing trait. Targets who were certain of their own trait always behaved in a manner consistent with their self-conception; they were not influenced by the interviewer. By contrast, targets who were less certain about their possession of this trait only behaved in a self-consistent manner when the interviewer was uncertain (i.e., was open to either alternative). When, for instance, interviewers were certain that an extrovert was an introvert, they consequently confronted the uncertain target mainly with questions about her introversion, leading the target to conform increasingly to the interviewers' expectancy across three consecutive interviews. Thus, the social influence of a single other may only affect the behavior of those who are uncertain. However, social impact theory (Latané, 1981; Latané & Wolf, 1981), the Asch (1956) studies, and much conformity research suggest stronger effects when multiple sources attempt a single direction influence.

Information Seeking

Certainty about an attitudinal belief perpetuates its confirmation, often creating a self-fulfilling prophecy that further augments one's certainty (e.g., Snyder & Swann, 1978, Study 3; Swann & Giuliano, as cited in Swann & Ely, 1984). In addition to the previously described conformity effects among those who are uncertain, Swann and Ely (1984) showed that the firmness of one's expectation guides information seeking. Recall that interviewers were led to have high or low certainty that the extrovert confronting them was an introvert. Those led to be certain tended to affirm their expectations by asking expectancy-confirming questions, whereas those uncertain, were not so single-minded.

Projection

In opposition to models linking projection to attitude certainty, certainty rather than uncertainty increased projection (Marks & Miller, 1985). This questions the assumption that uncertainty is the motivational antecedent that elicits the projective process. After reading about an ambivalent court case and indicating their verdict, subjects were made to feel certain or uncertain about their choice. They received either bogus GSR feedback (Study 2) or information that knowledgeable others agreed or disagreed with their verdict (Study 3), or they received no information. They then estimated the degree to which other specific individuals and their peers would share their view. In comparison to the no-projection conditions, experimentally induced certainty consistently increased projected attitude similarity whereas uncertainty did not. Persons induced to be certain not only behave in a manner consistent with their certainty (e.g., Swann & Ely, 1984), but also are more likely to assume that others view the world similarly.

From this standpoint, projection is merely one among an array of measures generally symptomatic of confidence. Consequently, in group settings, it typically will covary with variables associated with confidence, such as, for example, group cohesiveness. In research on minority-majority influence, influential minorities generally display stronger cohesion and stronger attitude conviction than majorities (Kruglanski & Mackie, 1990). Thus, various covariates of group cohesion, such as perceived ingroup homogeneity, perceived outgroup homogeneity, perceived intergroup distinctiveness, outgroup derogation, and ingroup favoritism, ordinarily will be accompanied by attitude certainty. However, these measures will not covary in all circumstances. Consider the effects of outgroup attack on an ingroup position that had not been previously questioned. In a symbolic ingroup setting, in which other ingroup members are not present, outgroup attack is more likely to direct energy toward affirming group membership and support, as displayed on measures assessing perceived similarity between other group members and self (projection) on group-relevant attributes. Yet, confidence about the specific attitude that was attacked may remain shaken. When instead ingroup members are present, and the outgroup only symbolically represented, knowledge of their attack is less likely to shake confidence, resulting in covariation between attitude conviction and projected similarity to the ingroup, not only on group-relevant attributes, but the specific attitude dimension as well. The affective state of the actor also may be critical. When negative affect is turned inward, to be expressed as depression, guilt, or self-doubt, adjustive mechanisms may lead to the seeking of social support (projection of similarity to ingroup) but at the same time, lessen attitude confidence.

Attitude-Behavior Consistency

Attitude strength is considered to be the bond that links attitude and behavior. Researchers have assessed it with various measures, including certainty, and have examined its role as a potential moderator of attitude-behavior consistency (e.g.,

Raden, 1985). As an index of attitude strength, certainty has implications for the stability,[9] range, and reliability of an attitude. An attitude held with certainty will be difficult to change; it will be stable (e.g., Babad, Ariav, Rosen, & Salomon, 1987; Swann, Pelham, & Chidester, 1988) and behaviors associated with that attitude similarly should be stable (e.g., Fishbein & Ajzen, 1975).

As previously discussed, knowledge affects certainty and can be obtained from direct experience with the attitude object. Fazio and Zanna (1978) expected attitudinal certainty (about volunteering to act as a subject in future experiments) and clarity (the width of the latitude of rejection) to be stronger as a consequence of the amount of prior direct experience with the attitude object (past participation in experiments) and to increase attitude-behavior consistency. After trichotomizing subjects with respect to each strength measure, they found that those in the highest and middle thirds showed high attitude-behavior consistency, whereas those low on each did not. They interpreted their outcome as showing that "The qualities do not appear to influence consistency independently," and that "direct experience may influence consistency only indirectly through its effect upon certainty and latitude of rejection" (p. 405). Supportive information, apart from direct experience, may be important. Certainty about voting for a candidate predicted intention-behavior consistency (i.e., future vote) only when there was a positive correlation between certainty and both information about the candidate and prior voting experience (i.e., number of times voted; Davidson, Yantis, Norwood, & Montano, 1985).[10]

Studies of smokers and drinkers suggest instrumental distortion of certainty in the service of retaining a preferred behavior. People may know that important others disapprove of a behavior they do not wish to change. However, whereas concern for the opinions of those others may not easily be relinquished, certainty about their degree of disapproval may more easily be distorted. Although both smokers and nonsmokers thought that important others (parents, friends, boy/girl-friend) would disapprove of smoking, smokers were more certain about their own beliefs about smoking and less certain about their opinions of how their smoking would be viewed by others than were nonsmokers. After controlling for the intention to behave, among those with high certainty about how such important others would view their behavior (viz., mostly nonsmokers), the attitude they attributed to those others predicted their behavior. For those with low certainty (viz., mostly smokers), it did not (Budd, 1986; see Budd & Spencer, 1984, for replication with drinkers and nondrinkers).

Despite the appeal of the view that the attitude-behavior relationship is stronger when one is more certain about one's attitude, it may be premature to accept it. Correlational studies that examine the moderating effect of certainty on attitude-

---

[9]Raden's (1985) report that certainty and stability are independent rests on a single study (Schwartz, 1978) which operationalized uncertainty as lack of an attitude about a topic. This conceptualization differs from our own.

[10]Complicating the issue, however, the association between certainty and amount of information differed for the winning ($r = .37$) and losing ($r = .08$) candidate.

behavior consistency must not only consider the interpretive problems that Dawes and Smith (1985) raise about such correlations, but also the consequences of statistical regression to the mean. The effect of statistical regression is intuitively obvious for scores on three 1-hour tests given during course "X." Students scoring high on Tests A and B are more likely to score high on C than are those who score high on A, but low on B. Given that the tests are imperfectly correlated (e.g., $r = .5$), among two sets of students who score equally high on A, those who score high on B will regress less on C than will those who scored low on B. This tautology is equally true if one examines the moderating effect of scores on C when predicting scores on A from scores on B (or any other such pairings of the three). Now consider a researcher who obtains three measures in a correlational study (e.g., Acock & DeFleur, 1972): (a) self-reports of attitude about marijuana in high school, (b) self-reports of friends' attitudes about marijuana in college (perhaps using social support as a "stand-in" index of attitude certainty), and (c) voting behavior in graduate school regarding the legalization of marijuana. It is of course quite possible that social support does indeed truly increase attitude-behavior consistency. However, if (a), (b), and (c) are positively, but imperfectly correlated, regression inevitably produces an outcome that seemingly confirms this plausible hypothesis. Those high on (a), if also high on (b), are more likely to be high on (c). Just as the three 1-hour tests all (imperfectly) measured a common underlying construct (knowledge of the content of course "X"), one's self-reported attitude about marijuana, one's selection of friends, and one's vote about its legalization may all reflect a common underlying attitude about drugs rather than the dynamic causal interpretation that social support (attitude certainty) increases attitude-behavior consistency. This latter view would be strongly challenged by analyses that examined the moderating effect of social support on the prediction of high school attitude from graduate school voting behavior. Regression requires (will produce) an identical outcome to that obtained with the reverse temporal sequence, but in this second case, the causal interpretation is precluded by the backward temporal sequence of events. If such a "backward analysis"—predicting (a) from (c) as moderated by (b)—yields the same outcome as the forward analysis—which predicts (c) from (a), as moderated by (b)—the regression interpretation is the more parsimonious one (Campbell & Clayton, 1961).[11]

FUTURE RESEARCH

We have glossed over a fundamental contradiction in the preceding sections. On the one hand, we noted that social support contributes strongly to certainty. At the same time, although we have argued that attitude extremity indexes certainty,

---

[11]The effect of statistical regression to the mean has been well discussed (e.g, McNemar, 1940; Thorndike, 1942) with respect to matching designs involving two variables, and by Campbell and Erlebacher (1970) with respect to matching designs involving three variables. The three variable situation, however, is most clearly explained in Campbell and Clayton (1961).

extremists often hold positions for which there is little consensus, as in Allport and Hartman (1925). As previously described, knowledge, thought, direct experience, and so on, can sometimes account for certainty in the absence of social support. However, anecdotal experience suggests that persons who take an extreme position with strong conviction are sometimes no more knowledgeable than less certain centrists. Sometimes such persons take their extreme view in the absence of a known supportive ingroup. This leads us to speculate that there are two sources of effect on direct measures of attitude certainty: true confidence and compensatory confidence. With true confidence, there is no felt need to self-justify. The attitude is grounded in the presence of social support and consensus for the position, and/or rests on knowledge, and/or has become strongly integrated into individual (vs. social) identity and hence, like a preference for an ice cream flavor, requires neither social support nor evidence for subjective conviction. Compensatory confidence reflects, instead, a lack of confidence and is exhibited in the absence of consensus or knowledge and prior to integration of the attitude into self-identity.

Meta-analysis of the false consensus effect provides indirect support for this distinction. Those who hold a majority position *underestimate* the true consensus that exists for their position! That is, the actual percentage of people who endorse the majority position exceeds the estimate of this percentage made by those holding the majority view. Moreover, the stronger the actual consensus for their attitude, the more they underestimate consensus. It is only those holding nonconsensual (minority) positions who produce the commonly cited false consensus main effect of consensual overestimation. They do so by overestimating consensus by a magnitude larger than the underestimation of those who hold a majority position (Mullen & Hu, 1989). This suggests that the greater the social support for a position in external reality, the less need to exaggerate its presence. At the same time, reflecting reality, both a person holding a majority and a person holding a minority position will (correctly) estimate greater consensus for the majority position. For example, 20% of a subject population may be smokers and 80% nonsmokers. The nonsmoking majority may estimate its prevalence to be 70% while the smoking minority estimates the prevalence of nonsmokers to be 65%. Note that although both groups correctly identify nonsmoking as the behavior of the majority, the minority (smokers) underestimates the prevalence of nonsmokers (−15%) more than the majority (nonsmokers) underestimates its own prevalence (−10%). The false consensus effect itself does not refer to reality. Instead, it is the relative comparison between the estimates made by members of the two populations about the prevalence of a single attitude or behavior (e.g., smokers estimate the prevalence of smokers to be 35%, whereas nonsmokers estimate that 30% are smokers). Taken in conjunction with the previously reported findings of Johnson (1940) linking consensual support to attitude certainty, these results emphasize the important contribution that consensus makes to conviction. Note also, however, that despite our opening theoretical arguments linking extremity to certainty, the two types of extremists, majority and minority, behave very differently in the false consensus research. This difference is reflected more broadly in the intergroup relations literature, as seen in the more general confidence of those in power, in the numerical majority, or of higher status (Ng & Cram, 1988). When unthreatened, groups exhibit less bias (meta-analysis: Mullen, Brown, & Smith, 1992). It is such considerations that lead us to propose that there are two types of certainty associated with extreme positions—true and compensatory.

It makes no sense to propose such a distinction unless the two types of certainty can be distinguished. The *biopsychosocial arousal regulation model* (Blascovich, 1992) provides a promising possibility. This model differentiates cardiovascular responding to challenges and threats. When engaged in an active task and personally challenged, but not threatened (i.e., success is likely and self-confidence is high), myocardial reactivity increases and vascular reactivity decreases. In contrast, when personally threatened (i.e., failure is likely and self-confidence is low), the cardiovascular pattern is reversed. Applied to certainty, true certainty should produce increased myocardial and decreased vascular reactivity, whereas compensatory certainty should elicit the opposite pattern. Among those at each extreme of an attitude dimension (and previously assessed as being equivalently certain about the correctness of their view) asked to think about or explain their attitude, we would expect the two extremes to differ in their cardiovascular responding when there is: (a) normative consensus about the good and bad ends of an attitudinal continuum, and/or (b) clear numerical (majority) support for one extreme, and/or (c) an absence of strong arguments in support of one extreme, and (d) the attitude is not a strong component of individual identity. We would not expect to find differences between those with opposing extreme views when: (a) both extremes are numerical minorities, and/or (b) the attitude dimension is a personal preference (e.g., favorite color, for which it is generally accepted that there is no right or wrong attitude), and/or (c) there is no prevalence information, as when the issue is novel, and/or (d) the attitudes are based on strong informational foundations, and (e) the attitudes have been integrated into their respective self-identities. The motivational consequences of compensatory certainty may, of course, lead to true certainty, as when supporting information is sought and obtained and/or when a social support group of other similar extremists is found, or the attitude is incorporated into the self-concept.

Many other issues have not received sufficient attention by researchers. These include: the conceptual distinctiveness and overlap of certainty with extremity, ambiguity, and ambivalence; the implications for attitude change when individuals differ in their certainty about holding a neutral attitude, or are equally certain about their opinions, but vary in opinion extremity; the relative contribution of social support versus supporting information to an increase in certainty about attitudes based on affect versus reasons (cognitions); and, the contribution of social support versus information to certainty about attitudes that differ in the degree to which they are related to one's group identity versus individual identity.

CONCLUSION

The certainty with which attitudes are held has been examined as a measure of attitude strength for more than 70 years. We argue that studies of attitudinal extremity also speak on certainty. However, whereas extremity implies certainty, certainty is, to a degree, independent of attitudinal extremity due to the fact that people with neutral (nonextreme) attitudes vary in their certainty about being neutral.

Generally, research on the causes of change in attitudinal certainty has been more interesting than that on its consequences. We subclassified the antecedents into those that are cognitive, social, and individual in nature. At the informational/cognitive level, attitude certainty is a function of the degree of supportive thought, knowledge, and/or information about the attitude object. At the social/consensual level, it is a function of the degree of social support people have for their attitude. In examining causes of a change in attitude certainty, however, one is struck by the lack of consistency. Almost every finding has exceptions. Attention to the distinction between attitudes that reflect individual versus social identity may be useful for ordering the relative contribution of these two types of factors. Finally, the idea that certainty might be a stable, characterological attribute, despite its long history, continues to prompt new individual difference measures such as authoritarianism, need for certainty, tolerance of ambiguity, ambivalence, dogmatism, cognitive complexity, and need for cognition. More empirical evidence on the convergent and discriminant validity of existing measures is needed rather than efforts to develop new ones.

Integration of findings about the effect of consensual support on certainty led us to postulate two types of certainty: true and compensatory. Although, in response to direct measures of certainty, those who enjoy a majority attitude and those who suffer minority support may describe themselves as possessing equal conviction about their attitudes, we suggest that different motivations drive this outcome. Minorities often misperceive their degree of social support and engage in defensive projection as a means of compensating for their lack of certainty about the correctness of a position not shared by many others. In contrast, majorities, having confirmation about the correctness of their position, may more strongly be driven to capture individual distinctiveness.

Clearly, 70 years have proved insufficient to provide a satisfying account of the dynamics of opinion certainty. Perhaps, however, less additional time will be needed to weave a cohesive whole out of the fragments we have discussed.

REFERENCES

Abelson, R. P. (1988). Conviction. *American Psychologist, 43,* 267–275.

Abelson, R. P. (1990). *Psychological processes that make intergroup controversies worse.* Paper presented at the annual meeting of the International Society for Political Psychology, Washington, DC.

Abelson, R. P., & Levi, A. (1985). Decision making and decision theory. In G. Lindzey & E. Aronson (Eds.), *Handbook of social psychology* (3rd ed., Vol. 1, pp. 231–309). New York: Random House.

Acock, A. C., & DeFleur, M. L. (1972). A configural approach to contingent consistency in the attitude-behavior relationship. *American Sociological Review, 37,* 714–726.

Adorno, T. W., Frenkel-Brunswik, E., Levinson, D. J., & Sanford, R. N. (1950). *The authoritarian personality.* New York: Harper & Row.

Allen, V. L. (1964). Uncertainty of outcome and post-decision dissonance reduction. In L. Festinger (Ed.), *Conflict, decision, and dissonance* (pp. 34–42). Palo Alto, CA: Stanford University Press.

Allen, V. L. (1965). Situational factors in conformity. In L. Berkowitz (Ed.), *Advances in experimental social psychology* (Vol. 2, pp. 133–175). New York: Academic.

Allen, V. L., & Wilder, D. A. (1977). Social comparison, self evaluation, and conformity to the group. In J. M. Suls & R. L. Miller (Eds.), *Social comparison processes* (pp. 187–208). Washington, DC: Hemisphere.

Allport, F. H. (1924). *Social psychology.* Boston, MA: Houghton Mifflin.

Allport, F. H., & Hartman, D. A. (1925). The measurement and motivation of atypical opinion in a certain group. *American Political Science Review, 19,* 735–760.

Altemeyer, B. (1988). *Enemies of freedom.* San Francisco: Jossey-Bass.

Altmaier, E. M., Leary, M. R., Halpern, S., & Sellers, J. E. (1985). Effects of stress inoculation and participant modeling on confidence and anxiety: Testing predictions on self-efficacy theory. *Journal of Social and Clinical Psychology, 3,* 500–505.

Andersen, S. M., & Lyon, J. E. (1987). Anticipating undesired outcomes: The role of outcome certainty in the onset of depressive affect. *Journal of Experimental Social Psychology, 23,* 428–443.

Asch, S. E. (1956). Studies of independence and conformity: A minority of one against a unanimous majority. *Psychological Monographs: General and Applied, 70,* 1–70.

Babad, E. Y., Ariav, A., Rosen, I., & Salomon, G. (1987). Perseverance of bias as a function of debriefing conditions and subjects' confidence. *Social Behaviour, 2,* 185–193.

Bargh, J. A. (1989). Conditional automaticity: Varieties of automatic influence in social perception and cognition. In J. S. Uleman & J. A. Bargh (Eds.), *Unintended thought* (pp. 3–51). New York: Guilford.

Bassano, D. (1985). Five-year-olds' understanding of "savoir" and "croire." *Journal of Child Language, 12,* 417–432.

Bem, D. J. (1972). Self-perception theory. In L. Berkowitz (Ed.), *Advances in experimental social psychology* (Vol. 6, pp. 1–62). New York: Academic.

Berlyne, D. E. (1965). *Structure and direction in thinking.* New York: Wiley.

Blascovich, J. (1992). A biopsychosocial approach to arousal regulation. *Journal of Social and Clinical Psychology, 11,* 213–237.

Brewer, M. B. (1979). Ingroup bias in the minimal intergroup situation: A cognitive-motivational analysis. *Psychological Bulletin, 86,* 307–324.

Brewer, M. B. (1991). The social self: On being the same and different at the same time. *Personality and Social Psychology Bulletin, 17,* 475–482.

Brock, T. C., & Brannon, L. A. (1992). Liberalization of commodity theory. *Basic and Applied Social Psychology, 13,* 135–144.

Budd, R. J. (1986). Predicting cigarette use: The need to incorporate measures of salience in the theory of reasoned action. *Journal of Applied Social Psychology, 16,* 663–685.

Budd, R. J., & Spencer, C. (1984). Latitude of rejection, centrality, and certainty: Variables affecting the relationship between attitudes, norms, and behavioral intention. *British Journal of Social Psychology, 23,* 1–8.

Budner, S. (1962). Intolerance of ambiguity as a personality variable. *Journal of Personality, 30,* 29–50.

Burnstein, E., & Vinokur, A. (1977). Persuasive argumentation and social comparison as determinants of attitude polarization. *Journal of Experimental Social Psychology, 13,* 315–332.

Cacioppo, J. T., & Petty, R. E. (1982). The need for cognition. *Journal of Personality and Social Psychology, 42,* 116–131.

Cacioppo, J. T., Petty, R. E., Kao, C. F., & Rodriguez, R. (1986). Central and peripheral routes to persuasion: An individual difference perspective. *Journal of Personality and Social Psychology, 51,* 1032–1043.

Campbell, D. T., & Clayton, K. N. (1961). Avoiding regression effects in panel studies of communication impact. *Studies in Public Communication, 3,* 99–118.

Campbell, D. T., & Erlebacher, A. (1970). How regression artifacts in quasi-experimental evaluations can mistakenly make compensatory education look harmful. In J. Hellmuth (Ed.), *Compensatory education: A national debate* (Vol. 3, pp. 185–210). New York: Browner/Mazel.

Campbell, J. D., & Fehr, B. (1990). Self-esteem and perceptions of conveyed impression: Is negative affectivity associated with greater realism? *Journal of Personality and Social Psychology, 58,* 122–133.

Cantor, N., & Mischel, W. (1977). Traits as prototypes: Effects on recognition memory. *Journal of Personality and Social Psychology, 35,* 38–48.

Cantril, H. (1946). The intensity of an attitude. *Journal of Abnormal and Social Psychology, 41,* 129–135.

Christie, R. (1991). Authoritarianism and related constructs. In J. P. Robinson, P. R. Shaver, & L. S. Wrightsman (Eds.), *Measurements of personality and social psychological attitudes* (pp. 501–571). New York: Academic.

Cohen, M., Jaffray, J. Y., & Said, T. (1985). Individual behavior under risk and under uncertainty: An experimental study. *Theory and Decision, 18,* 203–225.

Converse, P. E., & Traugott, M. W. (1986). Assessing the accuracy of polls and surveys. *Science, 234,* 1094–1098.

Coyne, J. C. (1976a). Toward an interactional description of depression. *Psychiatry, 39,* 28–40.

Coyne, J. C. (1976b). Depression and the response of others. *Journal of Abnormal Psychology, 85,* 186–193.

Davidson, A. R., Yantis, S., Norwood, M., & Montano, D. E. (1985). Amount of information about the attitude object and attitude-behavior consistency. *Journal of Personality and Social Psychology, 49,* 1184–1198.

Dawes, R. M., & Smith, T. L. (1985). Attitude and opinion measurement. In G. Lindzey & E. Aronson (Eds.), *The handbook of social psychology* (3rd ed., Vol. 1, pp. 509–566). Hillsdale, NJ: Lawrence Erlbaum Associates.

Diab, L. N. (1965). Some limitations of existing scales in the measurement of social attitudes. *Psychological Reports, 17,* 427–430.

Eisenman, R., & Boss, E. (1970). Complexity-simplicity and persuasibility. *Perceptual and Motor Skills, 31,* 651–656.

Ellemers, N., Van Knippenberg, A., De Vries, N., & Wilke, H. (1988). Social identification and permeability of group boundaries. *European Journal of Social Psychology, 18,* 497–513.

Estes, R., & Hosseini, J. (1988). The gender gap on Wall Street: An empirical analysis of confidence in investment decision making. *Journal of Psychology, 122,* 577–590.

Fazio, R. H. (1990). A practical guide to the use of response latency in social psychological research. In C. Hendrick & M. S. Clark (Eds.), *Research methods in personality and social psychology* (pp. 74–97). Newbury Park, CA: Sage.

Fazio, R. H., & Zanna, M. P. (1978). Attitudinal qualities relating to the strength of the attitude-behaviour [sic] relationship. *Journal of Experimental Social Psychology, 14,* 398–408.

Festinger, L. (1950). Informal social communication. *Psychological Review, 57,* 271–282.

Festinger, L. A. (1954). A theory of social comparison processes. *Human Relations, 7,* 117–140.

Fishbein, M., & Ajzen, I. (1975). *Belief, attitude, intention, and behavior: An introduction to theory and research* (ch. 3). Menlo Park, CA: Addison-Wesley.

Gage, N. L. (1991). The obviousness of social and educational research results. *Educational Researcher, 20,* 10–16.

Garb, H. N. (1986). The appropriateness of confidence ratings in clinical judgment. *Journal of Clinical Psychology, 42*, 190–197.

Gerard, H. B., & Greenbaum, C. W. (1962). Attitudes toward an agent of uncertainty reduction. *Journal of Personality, 30*, 485–495.

Gerard, H. B., & Orive, R. (1987). The dynamics of opinion formation. In L. Berkowitz (Ed.), *Advances in experimental social psychology* (Vol. 20, pp. 171–202). San Diego, CA: Academic.

Gigone, D., & Hastie, R. (1993). The common knowledge effect: Information sharing and group judgment. *Journal of Personality and Social Psychology, 65*, 959–974.

Gilovich, T., Kerr, M., & Medvec, V. H. (1993). Effect of temporal perspective on subjective confidence. *Journal of Personality and Social Psychology, 64*, 552–560.

Griffin, D. W., Dunning, D., & Ross, L. (1990). The role of construal process in overconfident predictions about the self and others. *Journal of Personality and Social Psychology, 59*, 1128–1139.

Gross, D., Rocissano, L., & Roncoli, M. (1989). Maternal confidence during toddlerhood: Comparing preterm and full term groups. *Research in Nursing and Health, 12*, 1–9.

Hanley, G. L., & Collins, V. L. (1989). Metamemory judgments of the origin and content of course information: Comparing text and lecture materials. *Journal of Educational Psychology, 81*, 3–8.

Harrington, H., & Miller, N. (1993). Do group motives differ from individual motives? Considerations regarding process distinctiveness. In M. A. Hogg & D. Abrams (Eds.), *Group motivation: Social psychological perspectives* (pp. 149–172). New York: Harvester Wheatsheaf.

Harris, M. J. (1991). Controversy and cumulation: Meta-analysis and research on interpersonal expectancy effects. *Personality and Social Psychology Bulletin, 17*, 316–322.

Hastie, R., Penrod, S., & Pennington, N. (1983). *Inside the jury.* Cambridge, MA: Harvard University Press.

Hawkins, S. A., & Hastie, R. (1990). Hindsight: Biased judgments of past events after the outcomes are known. *Psychological Bulletin, 107*, 311–327.

Helson, R., & Wink, P. (1992). Personality change in women from the early 40s to the early 50s. *Psychology of Aging, 7*, 46–55.

Herskovic, J. E., Kietzman, M. L., & Sutton, S. (1986). Visual flicker in depression: Response criteria, confidence ratings and response times. *Psychological Medicine, 16*, 187–197.

Hoffman, R. L. (Ed.). (1979). *The group problem solving process: Studies of a valence model.* New York: Praeger.

Holtz, R. (1992). *Length of group membership, assumed similarity, and opinion certainty: The dividend for veteran members.* Unpublished manuscript.

Holtz, R., & Miller, N. (1985). Assumed similarity and opinion certainty. *Journal of Personality and Social Psychology, 48*, 890–898.

Holtz, R., & Miller, N. (1992). *Group climate, thoughts, and opinion certainty.* Unpublished manuscript.

Insko, C. A., Drenan, S., Solomon, M. R., Smith, R., & Wade, T. J. (1983). Conformity as a function of the consistency of positive self-evaluation with being liked and being right. *Journal of Experimental Social Psychology, 19*, 341–358.

Isenberg, D. J. (1986). Group polarization: A critical review and meta-analysis. *Journal of Personality and Social Psychology, 50*, 1141–1151.

Jacoby, L. L., & Kelley, C. M. (1990). An episodic view of motivation: Unconscious influences of memory. In E. T. Higgins & R. M. Sorrentino (Eds.), *Handbook of motivation and cognition* (Vol. 2, pp. 451–481). New York: Guilford.

Johnson, D. M. (1939). Confidence and speed in the two-category judgment. *Archives of Psychology, 34*, 1–53.

Johnson, D. M. (1940). Confidence and the expression of opinion. *The Journal of Social Psychology, Society for the Psychological Study of Social Issues Bulletin, 12*, 221–242.

Jones, E. E., & Gerard, H. B. (1967). *Foundations of social psychology.* New York: Wiley.

Judd, C. M., & Kenny, D. A. (1981). *Estimating the effects of social interventions* (ch. 10). New York: Cambridge University Press.

Kameda, T., & Sugimori, S. (1993). Psychological entrapment in group decision-making: An assigned decision rule and a groupthink phenomenon. *Journal of Personality and Social Psychology, 65,* 282–292.

Kassin, S. M., Rigby, S., & Castillo, S. R. (1991). The accuracy-confidence correlation in eyewitness testimony: Limits and extensions of the retrospective self-awareness effect. *Journal of Personality and Social Psychology, 61,* 698–707.

Kellogg, W. N. (1931). Time of judgment in psychometric measures. *American Journal of Psychology, 43,* 65–86.

Kiesler, C. A., & Kiesler, S. B. (1969). *Conformity.* Reading, MA: Addison-Wesley.

Kimble, C. E., & Seidel, S. D. (1991). Vocal signs of confidence. *Journal of Nonverbal Behavior, 15,* 99–105.

Krech, D., Crutchfield, R. S., & Ballachey, E. L. (1962). *Individual in society: A textbook of social psychology.* Cambridge, UK: Cambridge University Press.

Krosnick, J. A., & Abelson, R. P. (1992). The case for measuring attitude strength in surveys. In J. M. Tanur (Ed.), *Questions about questions: Inquiries into the cognitive bases of surveys* (pp. 177–203). New York: Russell Sage Foundation.

Krosnick, J. A., Boninger, D. S., Chuang, Y. C., Berent, M. K., & Carnot, C. G. (1993). Attitude strength: One construct or many related constructs? *Journal of Personality and Social Psychology, 65,* 1132–1151.

Kruglanski, A. W., & Mackie, D. M. (1990). Majority and minority influence: A judgmental process analysis. In W. Stroebe & M. Hewstone (Eds.), *European review of social psychology* (Vol. 1, pp. 229–261). Chichester, England: Wiley.

Kruglanski, A. W., Peri, N., & Zakai, D. (1991). Interactive effects of need for closure and initial confidence on social information seeking. *Social Cognition, 9,* 127–148.

Kruglanski, A. W., & Webster, D. M. (1991). Group members' reactions to opinion deviates and conformists at varying degrees of proximity to decision deadline and of environmental noise. *Journal of Personality and Social Psychology, 61,* 212–225.

Kruglanski, A. W., Webster, D. M., & Klem, A. (1993). Motivated resistance and openness to persuasion in the presence or absence of prior information. *Journal of Personality and Social Psychology, 65,* 861–876.

Latané, B. (1981). The psychology of social impact. *American Psychologist, 36,* 343–356.

Latané, B., & Wolf, S. (1981). The social impact of majorities and minorities. *Psychological Review, 88,* 438–453.

Laughlin, P. R., & Ellis, A. L. (1986). Demonstrability and social combination processes on mathematical intellective tasks. *Journal of Experimental Social Psychology, 22,* 177–189.

Lemon, N. F. (1968). A model of the extremity, confidence and salience of an opinion. *British Journal of Social and Clinical Psychology, 7,* 106–114.

Liberman, A., & Chaiken, S. (1991). Value conflict and thought-induced attitude change. *Journal of Experimental Social Psychology, 27,* 203–216.

Mackie, D. (1984). Social comparison in high-and low-status groups. *Journal of Cross-Cultural Psychology, 15,* 379–398.

Mackie, D., & Cooper, J. (1984). Attitude polarization: Effects of group membership. *Journal of Personality and Social Psychology, 46,* 575–585.

Marks, G. (1984). Thinking one's abilities are unique and one's opinions are common. *Personality and Social Psychology Bulletin, 10,* 203–208.

Marks, G., & Miller, N. (1985). The effect of certainty on consensus judgments. *Personality and Social Psychology Bulletin, 11,* 165–177.

Marks, G., & Miller, N. (1987). Ten years of research on the false-consensus effect: An empirical and theoretical review. *Psychological Bulletin, 102,* 72–90.

McCroskey, J. C., Prichard, S. V. O., & Arnold, W. E. (1967–1968). Attitude intensity and the neutral point on semantic differential scales. *Public Opinion Quarterly, 31*, 642–645.

McGarty, C., Turner, J. C., Oakes, P. J., & Haslam, S. A. (1993). The creation of uncertainty in the influence process: The roles of stimulus information and disagreement with similar others. *Journal of Experimental Social Psychology, 23*, 17–38.

McGuire, W. J. (1961). Resistance to persuasion conferred by active and passive prior refutation of the same and alternative counterarguments. *Journal of Abnormal and Social Psychology, 63*, 326–332.

McNemar, Q. A. (1940). A critical examination of the University of Iowa studies of environmental influences upon the I.Q. *Psychological Bulletin, 37*, 63–92.

Mehling, R. (1959). A simple test for measuring intensity of attitudes. *Public Opinion Quarterly, 23*, 576–578.

Meyerowitz, B. E., & Chaiken, S. (1987). The effect of message framing on breast self-examination attitudes, intentions, and behavior. *Journal of Personality and Social Psychology, 52*, 500–510.

Millar, M. G., & Tesser, A. (1986). Effects of affective and cognitive focus on the attitude-behavior relationship. *Journal of Personality and Social Psychology, 51*, 270–276.

Miller, D. T., & McFarland, C. (1987). Pluralistic ignorance: When similarity is interpreted as dissimilarity. *Journal of Personality and Social Psychology, 53*, 298–305.

Miller, N., Gross, S., & Holtz, R. (1991). Social projection and attitudinal certainty. In J. Suls & T. A. Wills (Eds.), *Social comparison: Contemporary theory and research* (pp. 177–209). Hillsdale, NJ: Lawrence Erlbaum Associates.

Miller, N., & Pollock, V. E. (1994). Meta-analysis and some science-compromising problems of social psychology. In W. R. Shadish & S. Fuller (Eds.), *The social psychology of science* (pp. 230–261). New York: Guilford.

Moore, C., Bryant, D., & Furrow, D (1989). Mental terms and the development of certainty. *Child Development, 60*, 167–171.

Moscovici, S. (1976). *Social influence and social change.* London: Academic.

Mullen, B. (1991). Group composition, salience, and cognitive representations: The phenomenology of being in a group. *Journal of Experimental Social Psychology, 27*, 297–323.

Mullen, B., Atkins, J. L., Champion, D. S., Edwards, C., Hardy, D., Story, J. E., & Vanderklok, M. (1985). The false consensus effect: A meta-analysis of 115 hypothesis tests. *Journal of Experimental Social Psychology, 21*, 262–283.

Mullen, B., Brown, R., & Smith, C. (1992). Ingroup bias as a function of salience, relevance, and status: An integration. *European Journal of Social Psychology, 22*, 103–122.

Mullen, B., & Hu, L. (1989). Perceptions of ingroup and outgroup variability: A meta-analytic integration. *Basic and Applied Social Psychology, 18*, 233–252.

Myers, D. G., & Kaplan, M. F. (1976). Group-induced polarization in simulated juries. *Personality and Social Psychology Bulletin, 2*, 63–66.

Newman, L. S., & Uleman, J. S. (1990). Assimilation and contrast effects in spontaneous trait inference. *Personality and Social Psychology Bulletin, 16*, 224–240.

Ng, S. H. (1984). Intergroup allocation bias before and after group discussion. *Journal of Social Psychology, 124*, 95–103.

Ng, S. H., & Cram, F. (1988). Intergroup bias by defensive and offensive groups in majority and minority conditions. *Journal of Personality and Social Psychology, 55*, 749–757.

Osgood, C. E., Suci, G. J., & Tannenbaum, P. H. (1957). *The measurement of meaning* (pp. 155–159). Urbana: University of Illinois Press.

Palmer, D. L., & Kalin, R. (1991). Predictive validity of the dogmatic rejection scale. *Personality and Social Psychology Bulletin, 17*, 212–218.

Pelham, B. W. (1991). On confidence and consequence: The certainty and importance of self-knowledge. *Journal of Personality and Social Psychology, 60*, 518–530.

Peterson, D. K., & Pitz, G. F. (1988). Confidence, uncertainty, and the use of information. *Journal of Experimental Psychology: Learning, Memory, and Cognition, 14*, 85–92.

Pietromonaco, P. R., Rook, K. S., & Lewis, M A. (1992). Accuracy in perceptions of interpersonal interactions: Effects of dysphoria, friendship, and similarity. *Journal of Personality and Social Psychology, 63*, 247–259.

Raden, D. (1985). Strength-related attitude dimensions. *Social Psychology Quarterly, 48*, 312–330.

Raulin, M. L. (1984). Development of a scale to measure intense ambivalence. *Journal of Consulting and Clinical Psychology, 52*, 63–72.

Rokeach, M. (1960). *The open and closed mind.* New York: Basic Books.

Roseman, I. J. (1984). Cognitive determinants of emotion: A structural theory. *Review of Personality and Social Psychology, 5*, 11–36.

Sample, J., & Warland, R. (1973). Attitude and prediction of behavior. *Social Forces, 51*, 292–304.

Sanbonmatsu, D. M., Kardes, F. R., & Sansone, C. (1991). Remembering less and inferring more: Effects of time of judgment on inferences about unknown attributes. *Journal of Personality and Social Psychology, 61*, 546–554.

Schwartz, S. H. (1978). Temporal instability as a moderator of the attitude-behavior relationship. *Journal of Personality and Social Psychology, 36*, 715–724.

Shannon, C. E., & Weaver, W. (1949). *Mathematical theory of communication.* Urbana: University of Illinois Press.

Sherif, C. W., Kelly, M., Rodgers, H. L., Sarup, G., & Titler, B. L. (1973). Personal involvement, social judgment, and action. *Journal of Personality and Social Psychology, 27*, 311–328.

Sherif, M. (1935). A study of some social factors in perception. *Archives of Psychology, 27*, No.187.

Sherif, M. (1936). *The psychology of social norms.* New York: Harper & Row.

Sherif, M., & Hovland, C. I. (1961). *Social judgment: Assimilation and contrast effects in communication and attitude change.* New Haven, CT: Yale University Press.

Sherwood, G. G. (1981). Self-serving biases in person perception: A reexamination of projection as a mechanism of defense. *Psychological Bulletin, 90*, 445–459.

Sidanius, J. (1988). Political sophistication and political deviance: A structural equation examination of context theory. *Journal of Personality and Social Psychology, 55*, 37–51.

Sincoff, J. B. (1992). Ambivalence and defense: Effects of a repressive style on normal adolescents' and young adults' mixed feelings. *Journal of Abnormal Psychology, 101*, 251–256.

Smith, V. L., Kassin, S. M., & Ellsworth, P. C. (1989). Eyewitness accuracy and confidence: Within- versus between-subjects correlations. *Journal of Applied Psychology, 74*, 356–359.

Smithson, M. (1989). *Ignorance and uncertainty: Emerging paradigms.* New York: Springer-Verlag.

Sniezek, J. A., & Henry, R. A. (1990). Revision, weighting, and commitment in consensus group judgment. *Organizational Behavior and Human Decision Processes, 45*, 66–84.

Snyder, M., & Gangestad, S. (1986). On the nature of self-monitoring: Matters of assessment, matters of validity. *Journal of Personality and Social Psychology, 51*, 125–131.

Snyder, M., & Swann, Jr., W. B. (1978). Hypothesis testing processes in social interaction. *Journal of Personality and Social Psychology, 36*, 1202–1212.

Sorrentino, R. M., Raynor, J. O., Zubeck, J. M., & Short, J. C. (1990). Personality functioning and change: Informational and affective influences on cognitive, moral, and social development. In E. T. Higgins & R. M. Sorrentino (Eds.), *Handbook of motivation and cognition* (Vol. 2, pp. 193–228). New York: Guilford.

Sorrentino, R. M., & Short, J. C. (1986). Uncertainty, motivation, and cognition. In R. M. Sorrentino & E. T. Higgins (Eds.), *Handbook of motivation and cognition* (Vol. 1, pp. 379–403). New York: Guilford.

Stasser, G., & Stewart, D. (1992). Discovery of hidden profiles by decision-making groups: Solving a problem versus making a judgment. *Journal of Personality and Social Psychology, 63*, 426–434.

Stasser, G., Taylor, L. A., & Hanna, C. (1989). Information sampling in structured and unstructured discussion of three- and six-person groups. *Journal of Personality and Social Psychology, 57*, 67–78.

Suchman, E. A. (1950). The intensity component in attitude and opinion research. In S. A. Stouffer, L. Guttman, E. A. Suchman, P. F. Lazarsfeld, S. A. Star, & J. A. Clausen (Eds.), *Measurement and prediction* (pp. 213–276). Princeton, NJ: Princeton University Press.

Swann, W. B., Jr., & Ely, R. J. (1984). A battle of wills: Self-verification versus behavioral information. *Journal of Personality and Social Psychology, 46,* 1287–1302.

Swann, W. B., Pelham, B. W., & Chidester, T. R. (1988). Change through paradox: Using self-verification to alter beliefs. *Journal of Personality and Social Psychology, 54,* 268–273.

Tajfel, H. (1969). Social and cultural factors in perception. In G. Lindzey & E. Aronson (Eds.), *Handbook of social psychology* (2nd ed., Vol. 3., pp. 315–394). Reading, MA: Addison-Wesley.

Tajfel, H., & Turner, J. C. (1986). The social identity theory of intergroup behaviour. In S. Worchel & W. G. Austin (Eds.), *Psychology of intergroup relations* (2nd ed., pp. 7–24). Chicago: Nelson-Hall.

Tanaka, J. S., Panter, A. T., & Winborne, W. C. (1988). Dimensions of the need for cognition: Subscales and gender differences. *Multivariate Behavioral Research, 23,* 35–50.

Tanford, S., & Penrod, S. (1986). Jury deliberations: Discussion content and influence processes in jury decision making. *Journal of Applied Social Psychology, 16,* 322–347.

Tesser, A. (1978). Self-generated attitude change. In L. Berkowitz (Ed.), *Advances in experimental social psychology* (Vol. 11, pp. 290–338). New York: Academic.

Thorndike, R. L. (1942). Regression fallacies in the matched groups experiment. *Psychometrika, 7,* 85–102.

Thurstone, L. L., & Chave, E. J. (1929). *The measurement of attitude.* Chicago: University of Chicago Press.

Tourangeau, R., Rasinski, K. A., Bradburn, N., & D'Andrade, R. (1989). Carryover effects in attitude surveys. *Public Opinion Quarterly, 53,* 495–524.

Turner, J. C., Hogg, M. A., Oakes, P. J., Reicher, S. D., & Wetherell, M. S. (1987). *Rediscovering the social group: A self-categorization theory.* Oxford, UK: Blackwell.

Turner, J. C., Wetherell, M. S., & Hogg, M. A. (1989). Referent informational influence and group polarization. *British Journal of Social Psychology, 28,* 135–147.

Tversky, A., & Kahneman, D. (1973). Availability: A heuristic for judging frequency and probability. *Cognitive Psychology, 5,* 207–232.

Tversky, A., & Kahneman, D. (1982). Judgment under uncertainty: Heuristics and biases. In D. Kahneman, P. Slovic, & A. Tversky (Eds.), *Judgment under uncertainty: Heuristics and biases* (pp. 3–20). New York: Cambridge University Press.

Vickers, D., Smith, P., Burt, J., & Brown, M. (1985). Experimental paradigms emphasising [sic] state or process limitation: II. Effects on confidence. *Acta Psychologica, 59,* 163–193.

Volkmann, J. (1934). The relation of the time of judgment to the certainty of judgment. *Psychological Bulletin, 31,* 672–673.

von Winterfeldt, D., & Edwards, W. (1986). *Decision analysis and behavioral research.* Cambridge, UK: Cambridge University Press.

Wagner, W., & Gerard, H. B. (1983). Similarity of comparison group, opinions about facts and values and social projection. *Archiv fur Psychologie, 135,* 313–324.

Wilder, D. A., & Shapiro, P. (1991). Facilitation of outgroup stereotypes by enhanced group identity. *Journal of Experimental Social Psychology, 27,* 431–452.

Wilson, T. D., Dunn, D. S., Kraft, D., & Lisle, D. J. (1989). Introspection, attitude change, and attitude-behavior consistency: The disruptive effect of explaining why we feel the way we do. In L. Berkowitz (Ed.), *Advances in experimental social psychology* (Vol. 22, pp. 287–343). New York: Academic.

Zakay, D. (1985). Post-decisional confidence and conflict experienced in a choice process. *Acta Psychologica, 58,* 75–80.

Zakay, D., & Dil, D. (1984). Degree of post-decisional confidence as a function of the distances of the offered alternatives from an "ideal" alternative. *Archiv fur Psychologie, 136,* 293–300.

Zuckerman, D. M. (1985). Confidence and aspirations: Self-esteem and self-concepts as predictors of students' life goals. *Journal of Personality, 53,* 543–560.

10

▼▼▼▼▼▼▼

Attitudes as Object-Evaluation Associations: Determinants, Consequences, and Correlates of Attitude Accessibility

Russell H. Fazio
Indiana University

It now has been over 10 years since my colleagues and I first suggested that attitudes can be viewed as associations in memory between an attitude object and one's evaluation of the object, and that the strength of this association determines the accessibility of the attitude from memory (Fazio, Chen, McDonel, & Sherman, 1982). This view, and its assorted implications, have proven very fruitful—much more so than I had envisioned at the time. What was initiated as a program of research aimed at illuminating a process by which attitudes might guide behavior mushroomed into a fairly general perspective with broad implications for a number of phenomena beyond our original concerns with attitude-behavior consistency. Issues revolving around this theoretical perspective have absorbed my laboratory for over a decade. The goal of this chapter is to provide an overview of what we have learned over the years regarding the determinants, consequences, and correlates of attitude accessibility. Along the way, I point to some of the many interesting questions that remain to be addressed.

ATTITUDES AS OBJECT-EVALUATION ASSOCIATIONS

Within our model, an attitude is viewed as an association in memory between a given object and a given summary evaluation of the object. As is common in the attitude literature, the term *object* is used in a very broad sense. Individuals may hold evaluations of a wide variety of potential attitude objects, including social issues, categories of situations, categories of people, and specific individuals, as well as physical objects. The term *evaluation* is meant broadly also. It may range in nature from a very "hot" affect to a "colder" more analytical judgment of one's favorability or unfavorability toward the object. Furthermore, this evaluative summary may itself be based upon various sources of information, such as emotions that the attitude object produces for the individual (as in the case of a conditioned emotional response, e.g., Cacioppo, Marshall-Goodell, Tassinary, & Petty, 1992; Krosnick, Betz, Jussim, & Lynn, 1992; Zanna, Kiesler, & Pilkonis, 1970), beliefs that the individual holds about the attitude object's instrumentality (e.g., Fishbein, 1963), and/or previous behavioral experiences with the object (e.g., Bem, 1972; Fazio, 1987; Fazio & Zanna, 1981). Regardless of the precise hot versus cold nature of the evaluation and regardless of the basis for the evaluation, the attitude itself is viewed as an association between the object and the evaluation.

Attitude Accessibility

This conceptualization of attitudes has important implications for attitude accessibility, that is, for the likelihood that the attitude will be activated from memory automatically when the object is encountered. The term *automatic* refers to the attitude being activated effortlessly and inescapably. In the words of Shiffrin and Dumais (1981), a process can be characterized as automatic if it leads to the activation of some concept or response "whenever a given set of external initiating stimuli are presented [in the present case, the attitude object], regardless of a subject's attempt to ignore or bypass the distraction" (p. 117).

The strength of any construct based on associative learning can vary. The mere mention of "bacon" probably activates "eggs" from your memory. Similarly, the date "April 15" probably activates thoughts regarding taxes. These are well-learned associations. In contrast, although we are well aware that the European continent includes the country of Belgium, it is unlikely that Belgium is spontaneously activated from memory upon mention of Europe for very many people.

We argue that attitudes can be considered in the same way. That is, the strength of the object-evaluation association can vary. This associative strength is postulated to be the major determinant of the likelihood that the attitude will be activated from memory upon the individual's encountering the attitude object. Some attitudes involve sufficiently strong associations that the mere presentation or mention of the object (e.g., "snake" to a snake phobic) is likely to activate the evaluative associate. Other attitudes (e.g., one's evaluation of Belgium) may involve weaker associations that are not readily activated.

The Attitude–Nonattitude Continuum. In an effort to build upon the distinction that Converse (1970) proposed between attitude and nonattitudes, we refer to such variations in associative strength and to their impact upon attitude activation as the attitude–nonattitude continuum. For Converse, the distinction centered on the possibility that a person may respond to an item on a survey even though he or she has never given any consideration to the attitude object prior to being asked the survey question. We have suggested that Converse's dichotomy might be more fruitfully viewed as a continuum (Fazio, Sanbonmatsu, Powell, & Kardes, 1986). At the nonattitude end of the continuum is the case of an individual not having any a priori evaluation of the object stored in memory. It is not available. When faced with an attitudinal inquiry, the individual is forced to construct an evaluation on the spot on the basis of whatever relevant attributes of the object might be available in memory or in the current context. As we move along the continuum, an evaluation is available in memory and the strength of the association between the object and the evaluation increases, as does the attitude's capability for automatic activation. Thus, toward the upper end of the continuum is the case of a well-learned association—sufficiently so that the evaluation is capable of being activated automatically from memory upon observation of the attitude object. In such a case, the individual faced with an attitudinal inquiry has to do very little cognitive work to respond; his or her summary evaluation of the object is automatically activated from memory.

Latency of Response to a Direct Attitudinal Inquiry. Over the years, we have conducted a number of empirical tests of the central premise that associative strength determines attitude accessibility. Initial tests involved the latency with which individuals could respond to a direct inquiry about their attitudes. The reasoning was that the more accessible any associated evaluation might be from memory, the less cognitive work the individual would have to do to respond to the query and, hence, the less time the individual would require. In these experiments, associative strength has been manipulated by inducing individuals to note and rehearse the association by virtue of their being required to express their attitudes repeatedly. In one such study (Fazio et al., 1982, Experiment 3), an appropriate ruse was employed to have subjects copy their attitudinal ratings of the attitude objects on to multiple forms. In other studies (e.g., Powell & Fazio, 1984), subjects have completed a questionnaire containing semantic differential items and the number of times that a given attitude object or issue appeared on the questionnaire (each time followed by a different semantic differential scale) was varied experimentally. In yet another variation of this manipulation (e.g., Fazio et al., 1986, Experiment 3; Roskos-Ewoldsen & Fazio, 1992a, Experiment 2), we have presented each attitude object an equivalent number of times, but varied how often a given attitude object was paired with an evaluative question (e.g., "good or bad?," "like or dislike?") versus some control question (e.g., "one syllable word?," "animate or inanimate?"). The thrust of these manipulations is to induce the subject to rehearse the association between a *given* object and a *given* evaluation (see the cognitive literature on consistent mapping, e.g., Schneider & Fisk, 1982; Schneider & Shiffrin, 1977).

Each of these forms of the attitude rehearsal manipulation has affected response latencies in a subsequent task in which subjects were asked to indicate their attitudes as quickly and accurately as possible. Subjects responded more quickly to those objects concerning which they earlier had expressed their attitudes repeatedly. A recent experiment observed this same effect when a full week separated the attitude rehearsal phase of the experiment and the latency task (Fazio, Zanna, Ross, & Powell, 1994).

These latency findings are consistent with the assumption that attitudes involving relatively strong associations are capable of automatic activation. However, these data do not establish the automaticity of any such process. After all, the subjects' very goal during the latency task was to express a judgment of the object. Responding quickly does not necessarily mean that the evaluation was activated automatically. Instead, the evaluation may have been retrieved or constructed via an effortful process, but one that was performed with relative efficiency (see Smith, 1989).

Automatic Attitude Activation. Subsequent research addressed this issue by employing priming paradigms that have the potential to provide indications that an attitude has been activated from memory despite the subject's involvement in a task for which their attitudes are completely irrelevant (e.g., Fazio, Powell, & Herr, 1983; Fazio et al., 1986). One such paradigm (Fazio et al., 1986) focuses on the extent to which a given prime facilitates responding on any given trial of the task in which the subject is involved. In our research, critical trials began with the presentation of the name of an attitude object as a prime. From the subject's perspective this prime was a *memory word* that was to be recited aloud at the end of the trial. However, the subject's primary task concerned an evaluative adjective that was presented very shortly after the prime; the subject was to indicate the connotation of the adjective as quickly as possible. The datum of interest was the latency with which the subject did so and, more specifically, the extent to which the subject's responding was facilitated by the prime. For example, does presentation of "cockroach" to a subject with a negative attitude toward cockroaches facilitate the subject's responding that an evaluatively congruent adjective such as "disgusting" has a negative connotation?

We observed more such facilitation on trials involving congruency between the subject's evaluation of the primed object and the evaluative adjective than on trials characterized by incongruency. However, consistent with the notion of an attitude–nonattitude continuum, this effect varied as function of the associative strength that characterized the individual's attitude. The pattern of facilitation was more pronounced in the case of strong object-evaluation associations than in the case of weaker ones. In the first two experiments reported in Fazio et al. (1986), preexisting associative strength was assessed on the basis of the latency with which the subject responded to a direct query about his or her attitude—the very measure that our earlier research had found to be sensitive to associative strength. Objects that the subject had responded to relatively quickly or slowly during an initial task had been selected as primes idiosyncratically for each subject. Thus, operationally, these experiments established a relation between latency of response to a direct query and the pattern of facilitation. The faster subjects could respond when faced with a direct query about their attitudes, the more facilitation the attitude object produced on evaluatively congruent trials of the adjective connotation task relative to incongruent trials. Conceptually, the results suggest a relation between associative strength and the automatic attitude activation.

In recognition of the correlational nature of these two studies, the Fazio et al. (1986) work included a third experiment in which associative strength was manipulated experimentally via repeated attitudinal expression. Once again, we found evidence of automatic attitude activation—greater facilitation on evaluatively congruent trials than on evaluatively incongruent ones. However, this effect was enhanced significantly for those attitude objects toward which the subject had rehearsed the object-evaluation association, thus providing experimental corroboration for the earlier correlational findings.

These findings regarding the moderating role of associative strength have been replicated numerous times, both within my laboratory (Sanbonmatsu & Fazio, 1986; Sanbonmatsu, Osborne, & Fazio, 1986) and independent laboratories (Bargh, Chaiken, Govender, & Pratto, 1992). A recent meta-analysis of nine experiments examining the effect of associative strength on automatic activation has attested to its reliability, $p < .0000005$ (Fazio, 1993). Furthermore, the research by Bargh et al. (1992) and that by Sanbonmatsu et al. (1986) replicated the original findings in experimental contexts that differ in some potentially important ways from the original procedures. Bargh et al. established that the attitude activation effect is observable even when an interval of two days separates the initial attitude assessment phase (which involves the subjects indicating their attitudes toward each attitude object as quickly as possible and serves as the basis for selecting the objects that are to serve as primes) and the priming phase of the experiment. Their research also indicated that the effect does not vary as a function of whether experimental instructions do or do not call special attention to the prime as a memory word that the subject is required to announce aloud at the end of the trial. Finally, Sanbonmatsu et al. (1986) obtained the effect with a word identification task instead of the adjective connotation task. In this experiment, the target adjective initially was masked by a block of dots which gradually disappeared until the word became legible. The subject's task was to press a key as soon as he or she was able to identify the word and then recite it aloud. The extent to which evaluatively congruent primes facilitated identification was examined. The effects replicated those observed with the adjective connotation task.

DETERMINANTS OF ATTITUDE ACCESSIBILITY

The obvious question that arises concerns the determinants of attitude accessibility. Actually, given our conceptualization, the question should be phrased as: What determines the strength of the object-evaluation association in memory?

To be frank, this is not a question to which we have yet devoted nearly the attention that it merits. At this point in time, I only can offer two general principles (and some relevant evidence) regarding the determinants of associative strength.

Attitude Rehearsal

The first principle is based on associative learning and stems directly from the view of attitudes as object-evaluation associations. **The more often individuals note and rehearse the object-evaluation association, the stronger it becomes.** It is, of course, this principle of which we have taken advantage in experiments that have manipulated associative strength via repeated attitudinal expression. When people are induced to copy their attitude ratings over and over again, when they are induced to evaluate an attitude object over and over again on multiple semantic differential scales, or when through the course of a task they simply indicate "like" or "dislike" in response to an object each of the multiple times that it appears, the association is strengthened. More generally, I would suggest that anything that calls one's attention to the associated evaluation will serve as an additional trial of associative learning and strengthen the association. The effects of repeated attitudinal expression that have been observed on the speed with which individuals can respond to an attitudinal inquiry and on the likelihood of automatic attitude activation provide direct support for this principle.

Perceived Diagnosticity

The second principle that I can offer concerns the basis for the individual's evaluation. Like Zanna and Rempel (1988), and as mentioned earlier, I endorse the view that attitudinal evaluations may be based on a variety of sources of information (see Shavitt & Fazio, 1991, for one such illustration), including the emotions that an attitude object creates, beliefs about the value of attributes that the object possesses, and prior behavior toward the object. I also would argue that people are sensitive to the diagnosticity of the evidentiary base upon which they are relying. Through their previous learning, individuals may come to trust some classes of information as more indicative of their attitudes than are other classes of information. More attitudinally diagnostic grounds for an evaluation may have more impact in that the evaluation implied by such classes of information may be noted (consciously or nonconsciously) more readily. As a result, the object and the evaluation may be associated more strongly. Thus, I would propose that: **The greater the perceived diagnosticity of the informational basis for an attitude, the more strongly individuals associate the object and the evaluation.**

Sensory Information. What sort of informational bases might people learn to view as especially trustworthy and diagnostic? Some evidence suggests that sensory reactions might be so viewed. Wu and Shaffer (1987) found that individuals, whose preference for a given peanut butter was formed following a taste test, held their attitudes more confidently and were more resistant to counterpersuasion than individuals whose preference was based upon information that they had read. Wu and Shaffer suggested that attitudes based on such sensory experience may be more accessible from memory.

Emotional Reactions. Similarly, emotional reactions to an attitude object may be perceived as diagnostic. Experiments that have instructed participants to focus on the feelings that attitude objects (various intellectual puzzles) generate have found the resulting attitudes to be relatively more predictive of later free-play behavior than attitudes among control subjects for whom focusing on feelings was not emphasized (Fazio, Zanna, & Cooper, 1978) or among subjects who were instructed to focus on the reasons for their feelings (Millar & Tesser, 1986; Wilson, Dunn, Bybee, Hyman, & Rotondo, 1984). Neither of these investigations directly assessed attitude accessibility. Nonetheless, it may be that emotional reactions to an object form what is viewed as a very trustworthy basis for evaluation. The resulting attitude may involve a sufficiently strong object-evaluation association that the evaluation is activated automatically upon observation of that object during the free-play period and, hence, influences behavior.

A recent investigation by Fazio and Powell (1992) did obtain evidence consistent with the proposition that attitudes based on emotional reactions to an object are characterized by relatively greater attitude accessibility. This particular investigation is part of a larger project concerned with the hot versus cold nature of the evaluation that comes to be associated with an attitude object. In examining this distinction, we conducted some multidimensional scaling research regarding over 80 evaluative adjectives—work which led us to the conclusion that the "language of evaluation" can be characterized as a two-dimensional space involving valence and emotionality. The adjectives ranged from positive to neutral to negative and from relatively cold (e.g., objectionable, valuable) to relatively hot (e.g., disgusting, terrific). Most relevant for the present purposes are the normative data that we collected from judges to guide the interpretation of the multidimensional space. Some judges rated the extent to which each adjective implied a positive versus negative evaluation. Additional judges rated the extent to which each adjective implied an evaluation that was arrived at on the basis of an emotional reaction.

These normative data regarding the valence and emotionality of each adjective were employed in a subsequent investigation as a means of assessing the nature of individuals' attitudes. The 20 objects involved in this study were selected from the game Personal Preference™, which includes cards that show a color photograph of a wide number of objects and activities, along with a label printed under the photograph. Some examples of the stimuli we employed as attitudes objects are: roller coasters, snakes, anchovies, listening to an opera, and donating blood. As their initial task, subjects were shown slides of these 20 cards, as well as a number of fillers, and instructed to indicate whether they liked or disliked the object or activity as quickly as possible. Obviously, the latency of these responses provides data relevant to the accessibility of subjects' attitudes. In a subsequent task, subjects were presented with a list of 24 evaluative adjectives that had been chosen as representative of the multidimensional space. The subjects were instructed to circle two to four adjectives that described their evaluations of each attitude object.

Using the normative data from the judges, we calculated the mean valence implied by the endorsed adjectives, as well as the mean emotionality, for each of the 20 attitude objects for any given individual. In this way, we could compute within-subject correlations between the emotionality of a given individual's evaluation and the accessibility of the individual's attitude. Averaged across subjects, this correlation was highly significant (mean $r = .27$, $p < .001$), and remained so even after controlling for the extremity of the valence associated with the endorsed adjectives (mean $r = .17$, $p < .001$). The hotter the adjectives that the subject found descriptive of a given object (irrespective of the extremity of valence implied by those adjectives), the faster the subject's latency of response to that object. Thus, attitudes with a more emotional basis appear to be characterized by stronger object-evaluation associations. Individuals appear to trust their emotional reactions as very diagnostic of their evaluations of an object.

Behavioral Information. Similarly diagnostic is our freely chosen behavior. Indeed, this is the central postulate of self-perception theory (Bem, 1972; Fazio, 1987). Just as observers heavily weigh another's behavior in considering the dispositions that the target person might possess (Amabile & Kabat, 1982), people view their own behavior to be a highly reliable and relevant indication of their attitudes. This reasoning implies that those classes of behavior that are viewed as dispositionally informative according to self-perception theory—namely, freely performed unmanded behavior—should promote the formation of relatively strong object-evaluation associations in memory. Fazio, Herr, and Olney (1984) found support for this hypothesis in each of two experiments in which attitude accessibility was measured via latency of response. In one experiment, subjects first completed a lengthy inventory that listed behaviors relevant to religion by checking those that they had performed. Some subjects did so with respect to a time frame of the past year. Because the subjects were college students, it was assumed that the behaviors would have been performed freely. Other subjects completed the inventory with respect to their childhood on the assumption that the behaviors would have been required by parents. These less recent and presumably more manded behavior form a less appropriate basis for self-inference than is true of the other condition. This manipulation had no effect on attitudes or on the extremity of attitudes on a measure of attitudes toward religion that subjects then completed. The two conditions did not differ from each other, nor from a control condition that did not review past religious behaviors. However, the manipulation did affect the accessibility of attitudes toward religion. As their final task, subjects participated in a response time task involving attitudinal inquiries concerning both religion and a variety of filler issues. Latencies on the religion trials were significantly faster for those subjects who had reviewed their recent behaviors than for the subjects from either of the other two conditions. Thus, the opportunity to review unmanded behaviors strengthened the object-evaluation association in memory. A second experiment, which tested the hypothesis by inducing subjects to perform a new behavior under manded or unmanded conditions, obtained a similar effect.

Also relevant to the general principle regarding attitudinally diagnostic classes of information is research concerning the effect of attitude formation via direct versus indirect experience with an attitude object. Attitudes based on direct experience exert a greater impact upon subsequent behavior than those based on indirect experience (Fazio & Zanna, 1981). In pursuing the mechanisms that might underlie this effect, we have found that attitude accessibility is affected by the manner of attitude formation (e.g., Fazio et al., 1982, Experiments 1 and 2). Subjects are able to express their attitudes more quickly when asked to do so following direct experience than following indirect experience (see Doll & Ajzen, 1992, for a replication). Furthermore, attitudes based upon direct experience also are more likely to be activated automatically upon observation of the object (Fazio et al., 1983). Depending on the nature of the attitude object and one's direct experience with it, the diagnostic value of sensory, emotional, and/or behavioral information may contribute to this effect. During direct experience, sensory and emotional reactions to the object may occur, as well as behavior from which an attitude can be inferred. Such information appears to provide particularly diagnostic bases for an attitude—more so than the consideration of knowledge acquired through indirect experience with the attitude object.

This is not to say that analytic evaluations of the attributes that characterize an attitude object necessarily involve weak associations. Indeed, research by Petty and his colleagues (see Petty, Haugtvedt, & Smith, ch. 5, this volume) indicates that attitudes stemming from the central processing of a persuasive message are more accessible from memory than those resulting from peripheral processing. Under some circumstances, individuals may undertake such a careful analysis of the available data that they view the evidence as very diagnostic and consciously associate the object and the analytic evaluation strongly. The very factors that motivated the deliberation may induce individuals to note the outcome of the analysis repeatedly—in effect, rehearsing the summary evaluation. Furthermore, the act of careful analysis and elaboration may itself involve attitude rehearsal as the examination of different pieces of evidence leads to the same evaluation repeatedly.

CONSEQUENCES OF ATTITUDE ACCESSIBILITY

Let me now turn to the consequences of attitude accessibility. This is indeed what the brunt of the research program has concerned over the years. The essence of what we have found is that all the power and functionality that was ascribed to attitudes by such theorists as Allport (1935) is much more true of relatively accessible attitudes than of less accessible attitudes. In other words, position along the attitude–nonattitude continuum determines the power and functionality of the attitude for the individual.

Some of our research on the consequences of attitude accessibility has involved our measuring the strength of the preexisting object-evaluation association via the response latency technique that already has been described. In other work, we have manipulated the strength of the association. The general strategy that has been followed whenever possible in testing any given hypothesis is to conduct pairs or series of experiments—at least one of which involves the measurement of associative strength and at least one of which involves the experimental manipulation of associative strength. In this way, we typically have been able to collect both correlational and experimental evidence regarding the hypothesis.

On the Power of Accessible Attitudes

Behavior.   As noted earlier, the initial focus of the research program was the issue of attitude-behavior consistency and the process(es) by which attitudes might guide behavior. As a result, a number of studies have examined attitude-behavior consistency as a function of the accessibility of the attitude from memory. For example, enhancing the strength of object-evaluation associations via repeated attitudinal expression has been found to increase attitude-behavior consistency (Fazio et al., 1982, Experiment 4). Subjects who formed attitudes toward various intellectual puzzles on the basis of indirect experience displayed greater consistency between these attitudes and their subsequent free-play behavior if they had been induced to rehearse their attitudes toward the various puzzle types. The attitudes of these individuals were more likely to be activated from memory upon their observation of any given puzzle type during the free-play period. In terms of our model of the attitude-to-behavior process, these activated attitudes—as opposed to on-the-spot constructions that may have been unduly influenced by some momentarily salient feature—guided appraisals of a given puzzle type during the free-play period.

Converging evidence is provided by studies which measured preexisting attitude accessibility, rather than manipulating it. In an investigation concerning the 1984 presidential election, Fazio and Williams (1986) measured attitudes toward then President Reagan, as well as the accessibility of those attitudes. Accessibility was measured via latency of response to a direct query and the sample was divided into high and low accessibility groups by performing a median split distinguishing those who responded relatively quickly from those who responded relatively slowly at *each and every* level of the response scale. This classification procedure ensured that the attitude distributions in the high and low accessibility groups were perfectly equivalent. Despite having been assessed nearly four months prior to the election, attitudes among the high accessibility respondents were much more predictive of voting behavior than were attitudes among the low accessibility respondents.

Similar findings regarding a moderating role of attitude accessibility in the domain of voting behavior have been obtained by Bassili (in press), who measured response latencies in the context of a computer-assisted telephone interview. The critical question concerned the party for whom the respondent intended to vote in the 1990 Ontario Provincial election. High and low accessibility groups, which were created in the same manner as in the Fazio and Williams study, differed markedly with respect to the relation between voting intention and eventual voting behavior. The relation was much stronger for the high accessibility sample, thus replicating the Fazio and Williams findings in the context of a phone survey. Bassili's findings also illustrate that his intriguing adaptation of latency measures may prove generally useful (and feasible) for survey researchers (see Dovidio & Fazio, 1992).

Evidence of the moderating role of attitude accessibility also has been obtained when actual behavior, as opposed to the self-report of voting behavior, has been assessed. Fazio, Powell, and Williams (1989) examined the relation between attitude accessibility and attitude-behavior consistency in a study whose behavioral measure involved participants' actual selection of consumer products. After collecting attitude and response latency data regarding a large set of products, these investigators allowed subjects to select 5 of 10 products to take home as partial reimbursement for their having participated. Both within-subject and between-subject analyses that centered upon the impact of accessibility, while considering equivalent attitude scores, proved supportive of the hypothesis. (The between-subject analyses also controlled for differences in subjects' baseline speed of responding to attitudinal inquiries by considering latencies for the target products in relation to the latencies for the filler products; see Fazio, 1990b, for a discussion of this methodological issue.) The more accessible subjects' attitudes, the more product selection was consistent with those attitudes.

In sum, a variety of investigations have demonstrated the impact of attitude accessibility on attitude-behavior consistency. Because accessible attitudes are more likely to be activated automatically from memory, the individual's appraisal of the object in the immediate situation is more likely to reflect his or her attitude. The appraisal does not have to be constructed on the spot and, hence, is not unduly influenced by some momentarily salient and potentially idiosyncratic feature of the object. This sort of attitude-to-behavior process, which I have referred to as a spontaneous mode, can be contrasted to a more deliberative process in which the individual reflects upon attributes of the attitude object more extensively. The recently proposed MODE model hypothesizes that *m*otivation and *o*pportunity act as *de*terminants of spontaneous versus deliberative attitude-to-behavior processes (Fazio, 1990a). Research by Sanbonmatsu and Fazio (1990) and Schuette and Fazio (in press) indicated that deliberative processing is more likely when individuals have sufficient motivation and opportunity to engage in the effort of retrieving and considering attribute knowledge.

In the context of the present concerns, it is important to note that the role of attitude accessibility is postulated to differ as a function of processing mode. The impact of attitude accessibility is much more direct in the case of a spontaneous process. The central issue concerns the extent to which the appraisal of the object in the immediate situation embodies the automatically activated attitude or is constructed on the spot. Given sufficient motivation and opportunity, individuals are hypothesized to deliberate about the attributes of the attitude object (i.e., to be more data-driven than theory-driven), regardless of the attitude's accessibility from memory. Any influence of attitude accessibility is relatively indirect in nature. An automatically activated attitude may influence the "data" that are considered by, for example, biasing the sample of relevant information that is retrieved from memory and/or directing attention to information that tends to be attitudinally congruent. In theory, a purely deliberative process could be free of even such indirect influences of attitude accessibility (see Schuette & Fazio, in press, for evidence regarding motivated individuals overcoming the biasing influences of a relatively accessible attitude).

Information Processing. Historically, attitudes have been presumed to influence not only an individual's overt behavior but also judgments of information relevant to the attitude object. Our model of the attitude–nonattitude continuum clearly predicts that such information processing will be biased to the extent that the individual's attitude is highly accessible from memory and, hence, capable of automatic activation from memory upon mention of the attitude object. This role of attitude accessibility has been examined empirically. Indeed, the Fazio and Williams (1986) election study included judgments of the performances of the presidential and vice presidential candidates during the nationally televised debates. As expected, Reagan supporters judged the Republican candidates' performances more positively than did individuals with a more negative attitude toward Reagan. However, attitude accessibility moderated this relation; it was stronger among those individuals with relatively accessible attitudes toward Reagan than among those with less accessible attitudes.

Similar evidence regarding biased processing was obtained in two studies that concerned attitudes toward the death penalty (Houston & Fazio, 1989). As in research conducted by Lord, Ross, and Lepper (1979), the subjects read detailed summaries of two purported studies concerning the deterrent efficacy of capital punishment. One of the studies came to a favorable conclusion concerning the deterrent effect of capital punishment while the other came to an unfavorable conclusion. The subjects' task was to evaluate how well conducted and convincing each study was. In the first of the two experiments that we conducted using this methodology, attitude accessibility was measured via latency of response to a direct query. In the second, attitude accessibility was manipulated via repeated attitudinal expression. In both cases, the data indicated that the extent of biased processing of the supposed research evidence concerning capital punishment depended on attitude accessibility. When attitudes were highly accessible, the relation between attitudes toward the death penalty and judgments of the quality of the research was substantial. Individuals who were pro-death penalty regarded the study that reached a favorable conclusion about capital punishment as better conducted and more convincing than the other study; individuals who were opposed to the death penalty viewed the study that reached an unfavorable conclusion to be of higher quality. Such biased processing was less apparent among individuals with relatively inaccessible attitudes. Thus, the findings clearly indicate that highly accessible attitudes serve as a filter through which attitude-relevant information is processed and judged.

Some recent research in the domain of persuasion also is relevant to the hypothesis that attitude accessibility moderates the extent to which judgments are consistent with attitudes. Obviously, recipients of a persuasive message may possess attitudes toward the source of the message—attitudes that may vary in their accessibility from memory. Just as suggested by our model, the impact of source likability upon persuasion is moderated by the accessibility of the attitude toward the source (Roskos-Ewoldsen & Fazio, 1992a). If one's liking for the source is capable of automatic activation from memory upon mention of the source, then persuasion is enhanced.

Attitude Stability and Persistence Over Time. The findings regarding attitude accessibility and information processing strongly imply that accessible attitudes are likely to be resistant to counterinformation and, hence, relatively more stable over time than are less accessible attitudes. The Houston and Fazio work involved presentation of what can be characterized as a persuasive countermessage. However, accessible attitudes affected judgments of the credibility of this information. Similarly, the nationally televised debates investigated in the Fazio and Williams study provided a wealth of information that could have served as the basis for a change in one's attitudes toward the candidates. Yet attitudes, especially accessible ones, influenced judgments of the candidate's performances.

In effect, the Fazio and Williams study provided an opportunity to examine attitude stability over a 4-month period, while the public was exposed to an extensive political campaign. The attitudinally congruent processing that was apparent with respect to the debate performance presumably would have occurred throughout the campaign. Because they would have engaged in less biased processing, those individuals with less accessible attitudes would have been more receptive to counterinformation and, hence, been more likely to modify their attitudes during the 4-month interval between attitude measurement and the election. The voting data revealed that attitude ratings expressed in the summer were less predictive of eventual voting behavior among those individuals with relatively less accessible attitudes. Thus individuals with relatively inaccessible attitudes during the summer preceding the election were more likely to experience a change of heart during the course of the campaign.

Bassili and Fletcher (1991) also found more accessible attitudes to be more resistant to counterargument. Like the research by Bassili (in press) that was summarized earlier, this study involved the use of latency measures in the context of a telephone survey. After responding to a question that concerned their attitudes toward job quotas for women, the respondents were confronted with a counterargument. Respondents who supported quotas were asked if they would feel the same even if having quotas meant not hiring the best person for the job. Those who opposed quotas were asked if they would feel the same even if it meant that women remained economically unequal. This procedure allowed Bassili and Fletcher to see how pliant the respondents' attitudes toward quotas might be. Some individuals changed their mind when confronted with the counterargument (referred to as *movers*), whereas others did not (*nonmovers*). Analyses of the latencies of response to the initial question regarding quotas revealed that the nonmovers had responded significantly faster than the movers. Thus those individuals for whom attitudes were sufficiently accessible that they were able to respond relatively quickly were relatively less influenced by the counterargument.

Also relevant to the influence of attitude accessibility on attitude stability is recent research by Hodges and Wilson (1994), which concerned the impact of self-generated information made salient by individuals' considering the reasons for their attitudes. Several weeks after having assessed attitudes toward then President Reagan, as well as the accessibility of subjects' attitudes, these investigators contacted subjects for participation in a phone survey. The subjects were asked to explain why they felt the way they did about various issues, including Reagan. As has been commonly observed in such research (e.g., Wilson et al., 1984), the reasons that subjects listed were not in perfect accordance with their previously measured attitudes. Subjects with attitudes of high or low accessibility described reasons that were equivalently discordant in this regard; the correspondence between judges' rating of the attitude implied by the listed reasons and the prior attitude score did not vary as a function of attitude accessibility. Nonetheless, the impact of these now salient reasons upon subsequent attitude expressions did vary with attitude accessibility. Immediately after having generated their reasons, the subjects once again provided an evaluation of Reagan. Subjects whose attitudes were relatively low in accessibility (as assessed weeks earlier) more strongly based their evaluation on the momentarily salient reasons than did subjects with more accessible attitudes. Apparently, the latter individuals could easily retrieve their previously stored, and strongly associated, evaluation of Reagan from memory. Not needing to construct an attitude on the spot, they were relatively less influenced by the salient "reasons" information.

The observation that accessible attitudes are relatively stable is relevant to a long-standing issue regarding the persistence of attitude change. Attitude change in response to a persuasive message typically does not persist over time (Cook & Flay, 1978). Yet, research by Ross, Zanna, and their colleagues has revealed that such persistence can be enhanced. Inducing the individual with the newly modified attitude to consider past behaviors relevant to the attitude issue—what the investigators refer to as *autobiographical recall*—bolsters the attitude. Such reconstruction of the past is influenced by the new attitude; people recall their past behaviors as having been consistent with their current attitudes (Ross, McFarland, & Fletcher, 1981). The consequence of grounding the newly modified attitude in past behaviors is that the attitude is more resistant to counterpersuasion (Ross, McFarland, Conway, & Zanna, 1983) and more persistent over time (Lydon, Zanna, & Ross, 1988).

In considering why autobiographical recall might bolster newly modified attitudes, Zanna, Fazio, and Ross (1994) noted the similarity between the recall induction that was employed in this research and the study by Fazio et al. (1984) that was described earlier (see p. 254). Reviewing recent religious behaviors enhanced the accessibility of attitudes toward religion. In the same manner, recalling and reviewing past behaviors relevant to a newly modified attitude (albeit in a biased manner emphasizing past behaviors that are congruent with the new attitude) may enhance the accessibility of the attitude. By viewing the current attitude as having followed from highly diagnostic past behavior, the individual may more strongly associate the attitude object and the evaluation than he or she otherwise would have. The resulting accessibility of the attitude may then promote its relative persistence over time.

This reasoning was tested in two experimental replications. Subjects' attitudes toward vigorous physical exercise were modified by exposure to a persuasive communication. In the experimental condition, the accessibility of these new attitudes was enhanced by our standard means of repeated attitudinal expression. When subjects were retested at a later point in time (14 weeks later in Experiment 1 and 9 weeks later in Experiment 2), these experimental subjects displayed greater persistence than did the control subjects who had not been induced to expressed their newly modified attitudes repeatedly. Averaged across the two replications, the attitudes of the control subjects had dissipated to their original position, whereas the experimental subjects continued to show evidence of attitude change. Thus, enhancing the accessibility of the newly modified attitude enhanced its persistence over time. These findings provide additional confirmation regarding the impact of attitude accessibility on attitude stability.

In sum, the power and influence that attitudes exert vary as a function of the attitude's position along the attitude–nonattitude continuum. Relative to attitudes toward the nonattitude end of the continuum, attitudes that are highly accessible from memory more strongly influence both behavior toward the object and judgments of information relevant to the object. They also are more stable over time.

On the Functionality of Accessible Attitudes

In addition to influencing the individual's judgments and behavior, accessible attitudes are of functional value for the individual. Historically, theorists have considered attitudes to be constructs that accomplish a great deal for the individual (Allport, 1935; Katz, 1960; Smith, Bruner, & White, 1956). The social world consists of an amazingly complex and chaotic universe of objects, which individuals must somehow structure in order to function smoothly. Attitudes allow us to structure objects, issues, and people on an evaluative dimension, which then has potential consequences for our perceptions of these objects in any given situation and our approach or avoidance tendencies. As noted by Smith et al. (1956), by providing "a ready aid in 'sizing up' objects and events in the environment," an attitude toward an object saves the person from "the energy-consuming and sometimes painful process of figuring out *de novo* how he shall relate himself to it" (p. 41). Presumably, having categorized the elements in one's social world into good and bad enables the individual to progress easily through daily life. What to approach and what to avoid is clear. In this way, the individual is in a position to maximize the likelihood of having positive day-to-day life experiences and to minimize the occurrence of aversive experiences.

The implications of my model for this notion of functionality are obvious. The degree to which an attitude provides the individual with the ready aid mentioned earlier would appear to depend on the extent to which the attitude is capable of being activated automatically from memory when the individual observes the attitude object. The likelihood of such automatic activation depends on the strength of the object-evaluation association. It is attitudes that involve a strong association that are truly functional. By virtue of their accessibility from memory, such attitudes free the individual from the processing required for reflective thought about his or her evaluation of the object. Simply put, the individual does not have to *work* as hard. Motivated by such reasoning, my colleagues and I have conducted a number of experiments concerning the functionality of attitudes in the last few years.

The Ease of Decision-Making. One hypothesis that follows directly from this reasoning is that decision making should require less effort when it involves attitudes that are relatively accessible from memory than when it does not. A recent series of experiments employed measures of physiological reactivity as an indicant of the extent of effort expenditure during decision making (Fazio, Blascovich, & Driscoll, 1992; Blascovich et al., 1993). The experiments all involved a common paradigm in which the critical task required subjects to express a preference between pairs of abstract paintings. The difficulty of the task was enhanced by having the trials of this pairwise preference task proceed at a fairly rapid rate. We were interested in the extent to which subjects displayed reactivity (elevated blood pressure in the Fazio et al. studies, and skin conductance as well as a variety of cardiovascular measures in the Blascovich et al. studies) while performing this task and, in particular, sought to determine whether individuals who had developed attitudes toward each painting in an earlier phase of the experiment would display less reactivity than those who had not.

An attitude rehearsal manipulation occurred before the pairwise preference task. Some subjects judged their liking for each painting repeatedly. Other subjects performed a *color-naming* task; for each painting, they announced the predominant color, the percentage of the painting that consisted of that color, and any other colors appearing in the painting. Thus the manipulation permitted a comparison of subjects whose attitudes were at different positions along the attitude–nonattitude continuum. As expected, subjects in the attitude rehearsal condition displayed less reactivity when they later performed the pairwise preference task than did subjects in the color-naming condition (Blascovich et al., 1993, Experiment 1; Fazio et al., 1992, Experiments 2 and 3).

Importantly, similar effects were obtained by Blascovich et al. (Experiment 2) in an experiment in which the attitude rehearsal manipulation was conducted within subjects instead of between subjects. The importance of the within-subjects design is that it ensured that all subjects were equivalently familiar with the task of evaluating paintings and had received equivalent practice at the procedure of doing so. Despite our having equated for task novelty and procedural efficiency in this way, subjects displayed greater reactivity when the pairwise preference task involved paintings that had been in the color-naming set than when it involved paintings that had been in the attitude-rehearsal set. Analogous findings were obtained in a within-subjects experiment in which the latency with which subjects could make their pairwise preference decisions served as the dependent measure (Fazio et al., 1992, Experiment 4). Subjects were able to make these decisions more quickly when they were deciding between two alternatives from the attitude-rehearsal set than when deciding between two alternatives from the color-naming set.

These findings indicate that accessible attitudes can ease decision making. The attitude-rehearsal task led subjects to develop associations in memory between each painting and their evaluation of the painting. Activation of these evaluations during the pairwise preference task made that task less demanding. In contrast, when lacking an accessible attitude, subjects had to construct an evaluation of each alternative painting during each trial of the pairwise preference task, which required more effort. Thus an accessible attitude does provide the individual with a ready aid in sizing up the object.

The Quality of Decision Making.   A second benefit of possessing attitudes was apparent in the research previously summarized. The experiments also provided evidence that the subjects who had undergone attitude rehearsal made decisions that were of better quality than the control subjects did. At the end of each experiment, the subjects were given unlimited time to rank photos of each painting in terms of their liking for them. We counted the number of times that each subject's expressed pairwise preferences concurred with these rank-order-ings. In each experiment, the scores in both conditions were well above chance, indicating that subjects did take the pairwise preference task seriously. But, on the average, concurrences were significantly more numerous in the attitude rehearsal condition than in the control condition. This finding suggests that accessible attitudes can guide decision making in a relatively satisfying direction that one is less likely to modify when an opportunity for reappraisal later arises.

Naturally, our interpretation of this finding relates to the work that we have done on the attitude-to-behavior process. An attitude that is highly accessible from memory is likely to be activated upon one's observation of the attitude object. As a result, an individual who possesses such a preexisting attitude is likely to arrive at immediate perceptions of the object that concur with his or her affect. When a person lacks an accessible attitude and is forced to rely upon a quick, on-the-spot appraisal of an object, the person is more likely to be unduly influenced by momentarily salient characteristics of the object. As a result, the individual may make a decision that is not reflective of his or her attitude. In effect, the individual makes a mistake. Through such a mechanism, accessible attitudes may result in decisions that ultimately are relatively more satisfying (see Erber, Hodges, & Wilson, ch. 17, this volume, for a related discussion).

The Orienting Value of Attitudes.   Experiments concerning yet another sense in which accessible attitudes are functional—what we refer to as their *orienting value*—also have been conducted (Roskos-Ewoldsen & Fazio, 1992b). Obviously, we cannot attend to all the stimuli that enter our visual field. A truly functional system would in one way or another direct its attention to those stimuli that have the potential for some hedonic consequences—to those that we like or dislike. Thus attitudes, or at least accessible ones, may serve an orienting value in the sense that they direct our attention to certain kinds of objects. The hypothesis that we have forwarded is that objects toward which one has a strongly associated evaluation in memory (which we termed *attitude-activating* objects) automatically attract attention.

Four experiments tested this hypothesis. The basic procedure involved a brief presentation (1,500 ms) of slides, each of which consisted of line drawings of six objects arranged in a circle. Immediately after each slide, the subjects were asked to list as many of the objects as possible. If attitude-activating objects do attract attention, then subjects should be more likely to notice such objects. In Experiment 1, we measured the extent to which an object was attitude activating for a given subject. That is, we measured attitude accessibility via our standard means of latency of response to an attitudinal inquiry. Experiment 2 involved a manipulation of attitude accessibility via our standard means of attitude rehearsal. The findings from the two experiments paralleled one another. Regardless of whether attitude accessibility was measured or manipulated, objects toward which subjects had accessible attitudes were more likely to have been noticed. In

Experiment 3, evidence of incidental attention was observed; subjects were more likely to notice those objects towards which they had rehearsed attitudes, despite their being involved in a task in which attending to these items was neither required nor optimal. In addition, this experiment indicated that the greater attention-drawing properties of objects toward which the individual possessed accessible attitudes held true regardless of the extremity of the attitude.

The fourth and most crucial experiment demonstrated that the locus of these observed effects did reside, at least partly, in an attentional component. Performance in a visual search task that involved subjects' indicating whether a display included a target item was examined. In this way, attention could be assessed independent of any processes involving memory for the objects. Through instruction and training, our subjects knew that a target item would not appear in certain positions of the visual display. However, when these to-be-ignored distractor positions depicted objects toward which the subjects possessed accessible attitudes, their presence interfered with subjects' ability to search for a target item.

Collectively, these findings demonstrate that the extent to which objects attract attention as they enter our visual field depends, at least in part, on the accessibility of our attitudes toward the objects. If a strongly associated evaluation of the object exists in memory, then that object attracts attention. Hence, we are likely to notice those objects that we have personally defined as likable—those that can provide some reward or satisfaction—those that we wish to approach. Likewise, we are likely to notice those objects toward which we have a strongly associated negative evaluation—those that can hurt us—those that we wish to avoid. What we "see" appears to be influenced by accessible attitudes. By orienting our attention to objects that have the potential for hedonic consequences, accessible attitudes ready us to respond appropriately. In this way, such attitudes can promote an individual's maximizing positive outcomes and minimizing negative ones.

Adjustment to College Life. The laboratory research summarized above indicates that accessible attitudes serve to ease decision making, enhance the quality of decisions, and to orient visual attention in a fruitful manner. A large-scale, correlational investigation relevant to the functional value of attitudes also has been conducted (Fazio, 1992). The purpose of this study was to complement the picture that has emerged from our laboratory experiments with a direct assessment of the relation between possessing accessible attitudes and mental health. The underlying premise was that individuals who enter a new life setting already possessing attitudes toward some of the issues and objects about which they will have to make decisions may find adjustment to this new setting easier than will individuals who lack strong, preexisting attitudes. Entrance to college constitutes such a major transition.

More than 200 freshmen participated in two sessions. The first occurred during their first 2 weeks on campus and involved (a) an assessment of the accessibility of their attitudes toward a variety of academic concerns, including specific courses, possible majors, and academic activities, (b) a self-report assessment of the amount of stress that they had experienced in recent weeks, namely the College Student Life Events Scale (see Levine & Perkins, 1980; Linville, 1987), and (c) standard mental health inventories such as the Hopkins Symptoms Checklist and the Beck Depression Inventory, as well as self-assessments of physical health (e.g., the Cohen-Hoberman Inventory of Physical Symptoms, Cohen & Hoberman, 1983). Two months later, the subjects once again completed the health inventories.

The findings have proved both complex and exciting. Attitude accessibility (average latency of response to attitudinal inquiries concerning the academically relevant target issues adjusted for baseline speed of responding on trials involving filler issues) was not directly predictive of later mental or physical health. Indeed, there is little reason to expect it to be. If one's life situation is such that he or she is experiencing minimal stress, then the individual has both the opportunity and resources to reflect upon academically oriented decisions. Having accessible attitudes toward such issues will make little difference. However, if other life events are imposing additional stressors, then having accessible attitudes in the academic domain can free resources for coping with such stressors. Thus attitude accessibility may serve as a *buffering* variable. Hierarchical multiple regression analyses predicting mental health at Time 2 revealed significant three-way interactions involving mental health at Time 1, stress, and attitude accessibility. Attitude accessibility and initial mental health jointly moderated the extent and nature of the relation between stress at Time 1 and mental health at Time 2. Overall, stress was predictive of poorer mental health at Time 2—just as is typically observed in such studies (e.g., Linville, 1987; Rholes, Michas, & Shroff, 1989). Among individuals whose initial mental health was relatively good, greater stress at Time 1 was associated with a decrement in adjustment at Time 2. However, the possession of accessible attitudes appeared to insulate individuals from the negative conse-quences of stress in that this relation was attenuated among such individuals. Apparently, knowing their likes and dislikes with respect to academic life and, thus not having to deliberate extensively in order to make academically relevant decisions, permitted these individuals to focus their cognitive and emotional resources on coping effectively with the stressors that they were experiencing. It also was the case that attitude accessibility related to recovery from dysphoria. Among those individuals whose initial mental health was relatively poor, lower stress at Time 1 was predictive of greater improvement in mental health by Time 2. However, this recovery was more pronounced for individuals with relatively accessible attitudes.

The rather complex pattern summarized here held true for scores on both the Hopkins Symptom Checklist and the Beck Depression Inventory, as well as for the self-assessments of physical health. Thus, it appears that freshmen who enter college knowing their likes and dislikes regarding academically relevant issues have an easier time coping with any life stressors that they may experience. Apparently, it does pay to know one's likes and dislikes.

Attitudes, then, are very functional constructs for an individual to possess. To the extent that they are accessible from memory, attitudes ease decision making, enhance the quality of those decisions, automatically orient attention productively, and free resources for coping with other stressors. It is important to note, however, that these benefits are not achieved without some costs. In particular, there is a sense in which accessible attitudes can leave the individual fairly closed minded. By virtue of their automatic activation from memory and by their influence on subsequent information processing, such attitudes can inhibit the individual from according sufficient merit to qualities of the object that are attitudinally incongruent. Thus opportunities for experiencing a "change of heart" are diminished. In a case in which both the object, and one's likely outcomes upon interacting with the object, remain stable over time, this poses no difficulty. Indeed, it is this presumed constancy that makes accessible attitudes generally functional; the individual is attentive to, and approaches (or avoids), objects that are likely to yield positive (or negative) outcomes, as personally defined. The accessible attitudes guide the individual through a "safe" route in day-to-day life. However, if the object actually has changed over time, an individual with a relatively accessible attitude may be less inclined to judge the object in terms of the new qualities that it exhibits than will an individual with a less accessible attitude. In this sense, the former individual is less open to a new experience with the attitude object—an experience that could, as in the case of prejudice, for example, prove quite rewarding despite a negative attitude toward the target as originally conceived. Future research will need to examine such costs of accessible attitudes.

A CONCEPTUAL FRAMEWORK FOR VIEWING INDICES OF ATTITUDE STRENGTH

Correlates of Attitude Accessibility

Over the years, our research has identified a number of correlates of attitude accessibility. Some of these were mentioned while discussing the determinants and consequences of attitude accessibility. Attitude accessibility relates to the informational basis for the attitude (e.g., direct vs. indirect experience), to the emotionality of the attitude, and to the frequency of attitudinal expression. Attitude accessibility also relates to the stability of the attitude over time and to its extremity.

Additional information regarding such correlates is available from the study mentioned earlier that employed Personal Preference™ game cards as stimuli. In addition to assessments of attitude accessibility and emotionality, this study included Kaplan's (1972) measures of ambivalence, polarization, and total affect, as well as an assessment of confidence in one's attitude. Given the nature of the study, it was possible to compute within-subject correlations across the 20 attitude objects and, then, to test whether the average correlation differed from zero. Attitude accessibility, as measured by the latency with which subjects could indicate their attitude toward each object, correlated significantly with each of these measures. The greater the polarization, the total affect, and the attitudinal confidence, the greater the accessibility of the attitude. The greater the ambivalence, the less the accessibility.

Similar findings were observed by Bargh et al. (1992), who pursued a normative approach to a number of these same relations. Various samples of subjects provided data concerning each of 92 attitude objects. For each measure of interest, a mean across subjects was calculated for each object. Correlations were then examined across the objects. Those objects characterized by the greater average attitude accessibility also were characterized by greater attitude polarization and less ambivalence, as indexed by Kaplan's techniques, and by greater consensus of opinion across subjects. They also were characterized by a greater likelihood that the subjects would judge the object consistently across two experimental sessions. In other words, attitude consistency or stability was related to attitude accessibility.

Finally, a number of researchers have found evidence that the extent to which the individual is involved in the issue, has some self-interest with respect to the issue, or regards the issue as important is related to attitude accessibility (Boninger, Krosnick, Berent, & Fabrigar, ch. 7, this volume; Krosnick, 1989; Thomsen, Borgida, & Lavine, ch. 8, this volume).

Some Conceptual Distinctions

This brief overview of some of the empirical literature regarding correlates of attitude accessibility raises important conceptual questions. In my view, it is imperative that research efforts move beyond attempts to examine a host of such variables simultaneously in the hope that some meaningful structure might emerge from a factor-analytic hopper. Given the measurement error involved, the unknown influences that measuring one variable might have upon the subsequent measure of another variable, and the likely dependence of any observed relations on the particular attitude issues that are investigated, I find it doubtful that replicable factors will emerge. Instead, I believe that it is important to draw some critical conceptual distinctions and to consider the impact that any given variable might have in the context of predictions generated from a conceptual framework.

In previous discussions of the attitude-behavior relation, distinctions have been drawn between qualities of the person, of the situation, and of the attitude as a means of conceptualizing the growing literature on moderating variables (e.g., Fazio & Zanna, 1981). The first two classes are sufficiently clear. However, in no small part due to my own usage of the term, the notion of *qualities of the attitude* has become blurred over the years. It is important to distinguish between qualities of the attitude as represented in memory and antecedents or consequences of such qualities. Thus some variables that have been referred to as attitudinal qualities (e.g., the manner of attitude formation) may be more properly considered antecedents of the representation of the attitude in memory; others may be more appropriately considered consequences (e.g., attitude stability).

In the present framework, qualities of the attitude (and, hence, the concept of attitude strength) refers solely to variables that focus on the representation of the attitude in memory. Included as attitudinal qualities are: (a) attitude accessibility, that is, the strength of the object-evaluation association in memory and the resulting capability for automatic activation, (b) attitude ambivalence, that is, the likelihood that the object will activate both positive and negative evaluations simultaneously (Thompson, Zanna, & Griffin, ch. 14), and (c) affective-cognitive discrepancy, that is, the extent to which any affectively based and cognitively based evaluations that might be activated in response to the attitude object are consistent with one another (Chaiken, Pomerantz, & Giner-Sorolla, ch. 15, this volume; Norman, 1975). The extremity of the attitude is not considered a quality of the attitude (nor is Kaplan's closely related construct of polarization). Instead of restricting attitudes to a valence dichotomy and employing extremity as a measure of strength, I prefer to view attitudes as evaluations of an object that can range from very positive to very negative. Thus extremity reflects not a quality of the attitudinal representation, but the attitude per se. A more extreme attitude is a different attitude (see Thompson, Zanna, & Griffin, ch. 14, for a similar view). Someone who views comedian George Carlin as "moderately amusing" has a different attitude than someone who views him as "very amusing." Even among individuals with the very same evaluation of Carlin, there may be considerable variability regarding the strength of the attitude—variability that can be appreciated by reference to qualities of the attitude.

Also not considered qualities of the attitude are such variables as attitude (or issue) importance (Boninger, Krosnick, Berent, & Fabrigar, ch. 7, this volume), self-interest (Thomsen, Borgida, & Lavine, ch. 8, this volume), vested interest (Crano, ch. 6, this volume), conviction (Abelson, 1988), involvement (Sherif, Kelly, Rodgers, Sarup, & Tittler, 1973), and commitment (Kiesler, 1971). Instead, these are properties describing the *relationship* between the individual and the issue. The nature of this relationship certainly has implications for the strength of the attitude. However, these variables are more appropriately considered antecedents of attitude strength than indicants of attitude strength.

The same is true of a variety of variables relating to the knowledge base from which the attitude has been formed. The sheer amount of knowledge regarding the attitude object that is available to the person (Davidson, ch. 12) or easily retrievable (Wood, Rhodes, & Biek, ch. 11), the extent to which the information has been processed elaborately (Petty, Haugtvedt, & Smith, ch. 5, this volume), and whether the knowledge base stems from direct or indirect experience with the attitude object (Fazio & Zanna, 1981) reflect not qualities of the attitude but properties of the *representation* of the attitude object or issue itself. They too can be considered antecedent variables that may influence attitude strength.

Conversely, a variable that has been labeled both attitude stability (e.g., Doll & Ajzen, 1992; Schwartz, 1978) and attitude consistency (Bargh et al., 1992)—essentially, the extent to which an individual's attitude persists over time—can itself be considered a consequence of attitude strength. Persistence is not so much a quality of the attitude as it is as consequence of a strong attitude. The person is resistant to counterinfluence, be it overt persuasive pressure or subtle contextual cues that vary from one expression of attitude to another. Such resistance is the outcome of the biased information processing fostered by a strong attitude and, thus, is conceptually parallel to other indicants of the power and functionality of the attitude.

Crosscutting these distinctions between qualities of the attitude and antecedents or consequences of such qualities is an important distinction regarding the methods by which such variables are measured. Bassili (1993a, 1993b) distinguished measures that essentially involve impressions of one's attitude, which he refers to as meta-attitudinal measures, from those that do not require a subjective judgment regarding the state of one's attitude. For example, confidence in one's attitude is necessarily meta-attitudinal, and such variables as attitude importance and knowledgeability often are measured in a meta-attitudinal fashion. In a telephone survey similar to the Bassili and Fletcher (1991) study described earlier, Bassili (1993a) found that a number of such meta-attitudinal measures were less related to resistance to persuasion than attitude accessibility and ambivalence were. Furthermore, the meta-attitudinal measures did not account for any unique variance in predicting such resistance. Bassili suggested that individuals may derive their meta-attitudinal judgments from qualities of the attitude as represented in memory and/or direct antecedents of such qualities. The extent to which they do so may determine how well the meta-attitudinal measure serves as an indicant of attitude strength. Recent research by Roese and Olson (1994) supports Bassili's argument that meta-attitudinal judgments sometimes may be a consequence of qualities of the attitude. When attitude accessibility was experimentally enhanced, an increase in subjects' judgments of the importance of the attitude issues was observed.

Direct Versus Indirect Effects of Moderating Variables

With these conceptual distinctions in mind, one can ask whether a given class of variables affects any of the indicants of the power and functionality of the attitude. For the sake of simplicity, the ensuing discussion focuses on one such indicant, the extent to which the attitude influences behavior. Qualities of the *person*, of the *situation*, of the *representation* of the attitude object, of the person's *relationship* to the object, and of the *attitude* itself each affect attitude-behavior consistency. As noted earlier, evidence of such moderating effects exists for each of these classes of variables.

One also can ask, as is particularly appropriate in a volume devoted to attitude strength, whether any given person, situation, representation, or relationship variable exerts its impact as a result of the influence it has on qualities of the attitude itself. Obviously, this is a complex question regarding the process(es) by which the variables affect behavior. Sometimes the impact of these variables on attitude-behavior consistency may be a direct one; other times, their impact may be mediated by attitude qualities.

Spontaneous Versus Deliberative Behavior. The MODE model (Fazio, 1990a) is particularly relevant to this issue. As mentioned earlier, the role of such attitude qualities as attitude accessibility depends on whether the attitude-to-behavior process is spontaneous or deliberative in nature. Given sufficient motivation and opportunity, individuals will consider the raw data, that is, the information that is available regarding the attributes of the decision alternatives, instead of relying on preexisting summary constructs. As such, the influence of the preexisting attitude and its strength may be minimal. Any effect of person, situation, representation, or relationship variables is likely to be largely direct in nature—mediated only in part, if at all, by qualities of the attitude. Instead, the moderators directly influence the information that is sampled and how it is evaluated and weighted. For example, some individuals may weigh normative information heavily; some may pay little attention to the expectation of others. Likewise, some individuals may have a rich and extensive representation of the object that allows them to consider more relevant information than other people. In any case, attitude-behavior consistency will be apparent to the extent that the evaluative implications of the data that are considered during this deliberative processing match the evaluation that was expressed at an earlier point in time.

It is in the case of a more spontaneous attitude-behavior process that attitude qualities such as accessibility should play a substantial role. It is when individuals lack either the motivation or the opportunity to deliberate that they are most strongly influenced by preexisting summary constructs available in memory (see Kruglanski, 1989). Thus, the influence of person, situation, representation, and relation moderators occurs as a consequence of their impact upon qualities of the attitude. It is in this sense that a variable such as attitude accessibility provides an understanding of how these other moderators influence attitude-behavior consistency.

Directing Versus Energizing Behavior. Allport (1935) characterized attitudes as having the potential to be both directive and dynamic. Attitudes guide behavior in one direction or another and, according to Allport, may energize or motivate behavior. This distinction is not one that has received attention in modern approaches to the study of attitudes. Although the directive influence of attitude is undoubtedly a central concern, I am reluctant to ascribe any energizing value to attitudes. Like others, I do not see why the "mere fact that one has an attitude would . . . produce behavior in and of itself" (Calder & Ross, 1973, p. 7). Nevertheless, a conceptually parallel distinction (implicit in Allport's theorizing) does not require the ascription of any additional properties to the attitude concept, and yet is relevant to the various classes of moderating variables that have been identified. Behavioral opportunities often present themselves during the course of daily life. A canvasser knocks on our door requesting a donation. We encounter a person whom we like or dislike while walking down the street. An acquaintance invites us to participate in a pro-choice rally. Our attitudes can direct our response to such behavioral opportunities as they present themselves. The presence of an environmental trigger, that is, the individual's naturally encountering an attitudinally relevant behavioral opportunity, permits qualities of the attitude to moderate the attitude's influence upon the behavioral response. In such cases, and particularly when motivation and opportunity for deliberation are lacking, the accessibility of the attitude will play a central role.

Responses to a behavioral opportunity can be contrasted with situations in which the environmental trigger is lacking. These are cases in which individuals actually *seek out* opportunities to behaviorally promote their attitudes (e.g, Festinger, Riecken, & Schachter, 1956). It certainly is appropriate to consider attitudes as guiding the direction of any such self-initiated behavior, but what seems particularly influential with respect to the decision to initiate advocacy is the nature of the relation between the person and attitude issue. Such variables as involvement, importance, vested interest, conviction, and commitment—properties describing the individual's attachment to the issue—are likely to determine the extent to which individuals seek out opportunities to behave pro-attitudinally. Although individuals with such an intense relation to the issue are likely to hold attitudes of remarkable strength—highly accessible attitudes, involving no ambivalence and strong consistency between affect and cognition—these attitudinal qualities would not appear to be exerting influence on the search for behavioral opportunities. Instead, the behavior is energized by the person's intense attachment to the issue.

Much work remains to be done concerning the interplay between the various classes of variables noted by the conceptual framework—both theoretical and empirical work. It seems evident that the processes involved will vary in complex ways. The particular variable that has been the focus of my research program—attitude accessibility—is relevant to spontaneously driven responses to behavioral opportunities. In such cases, the greater the attitude's capability for automatic activation, the greater the directive influence of the attitude.

RECENT CRITIQUES OF THE MODEL

Future research should continue to examine the antecedents and consequences of attitude accessibility, as well as its relation to other indices of attitude strength. Many important questions remain. It is gratifying to see that the theoretical model and research program have spawned related research by other investigators concerning such matters. However, three recently published articles are critical of one aspect or another of the work. On the assumption that readers familiar with this literature might be interested in my perspective, it may be illuminating to discuss each briefly before concluding this chapter. More important, any clarification that I can provide regarding the conceptualization, measurement, and manipulation of attitude accessibility may facilitate our progressing effectively toward the goal of understanding the interplay among factors related to attitude strength.

Bargh, Chaiken, Govender, and Pratto (1992)

Bargh et al. conducted three experiments employing the paradigm developed by Fazio et al. (1986) to study automatic attitude activation. Despite their characterizing the results as calling my model into question, I view the Bargh et al. data as very consistent with my theoretical perspective. Two contentions of Bargh et al. are of major importance. First, on the basis of their having observed evidence of automatic attitude activation, not only for individuals' strongest attitudes ("fast" primes or those for which latencies of response to a direct query were fastest), but also for relatively weak attitudes ("slow" primes or those for which latencies were slowest), Bargh et al. concluded that automatic attitude activation was "a pervasive and relatively unconditional phenomenon" (p. 893). Yet, their very own data indicated that the automatic activation effect depended on the strength of the object-evaluation association in memory. Although the so-called slow primes involved attitudes that were sufficiently strong to produce automatic activation, the magnitude of this effect was reliably smaller than for the fast primes. Bargh et al.'s meta-analysis of their experiments revealed that, far from being unconditional, attitude activation was greater for the stronger than for the weaker attitudes—just as it was in the Fazio et al. experiments.

　　Bargh et al.'s contention that this outcome—attitude activation for weaker attitudes but significantly greater activation for stronger attitudes—is inconsistent with my model appears to be based on a construal of the model as restricting the capability for automatic activation to some necessarily small percentage of attitudes. Our research has never sought to estimate some point on the attitude–nonattitude continuum that demarcates those attitudes with sufficient associative strength to be capable of automatic activation from those not capable. Instead, our concern has been with the extent to which attitude activation varied as a function of measured or manipulated associative strength. Although the relation need not be perfectly linear, the essential notion is that greater associative strength yields a greater likelihood of automatic attitude activation. The model is limited to making predictions in relative terms. Whether a given association is sufficiently strong to be capable of automatic activation cannot be determined in any a priori fashion, nor can the percentage of attitudes that might be characterized by sufficient strength. We can only predict that a given association is more likely to have such capability than a weaker association—exactly what the Bargh et al. data revealed.

The second conclusion that Bargh et al. drew stemmed from an examination of how the attitude activation effect varied as a function of a large number of variables. Although the latency with which individuals could respond to a direct attitudinal inquiry was predictive of attitude activation, Bargh et al.'s normative research, as mentioned earlier, had identified a number of correlates of such latencies. Regression analyses employing each of these potential predictors led Bargh et al. to conclude that attitude activation is "a function not of variations in the accessibility of the individual subjects' attitudes but of features of the object representation or its evaluation that are constant across individuals" (p. 906). In other words, Bargh et al. maintained that attitude activation was determined normatively, not idiosyncratically. A number of characteristics of these regression analyses, which led to a substantial underestimation of the relation between idiosyncratic associative strength and automatic attitude activation, are noted in Fazio (1993). For example, the analysis failed to control adequately for individual differences in baseline speed of responding. Doing so is essential, for the very same latency has very different meaning when considered in the context of the individual distributions of two subjects with varying baseline speeds of responding (see Fazio, 1990b, for a general discussion of this issue). The only degree of control that the Bargh et al. regression included for gross individual differences was that each subject's mean latency during the adjective connotation task served as a covariate. However, general speed at reporting the connotation of an adjective did not adequately control for individual differences in the speed of judging attitude objects. A substantial portion of the individual differences evident in the attitude latency task was independent of the baseline speed of responding that individuals exhibited during the adjective connotation task (see Fazio, 1993, for details). Reanalyses of the data that corrected this problem, as well as others, revealed the superiority of the idiosyncratic measure of associative strength (a given individual's latency of response) in predicting automatic attitude activation over the various normative measures (latency, extremity, ambivalence, polarization, and consensus or consistency) that Bargh et al. examined. Even after partialling out the influence of various correlates, idiosyncratic latency was predictive of attitude activation. Thus, the Bargh et al. data provide additional support for my model's central premise that automatic attitude activation depends on the idiosyncratic strength of the association in memory between an object and an individual's evaluation of the object.

Doll and Ajzen (1992)

Recent research by Doll and Ajzen (1992) is characterized by a similarly inadequate adjustment for baseline speed of responding. In an interesting modernization of the puzzle paradigm, these researchers manipulated whether subjects were introduced to a set of computer video games via direct or indirect experience. This manipulation affected (a) the latency with which individuals responded to attitudinal inquiries regarding the games (thus, replicating the Fazio et al., 1982, experiment), (b) the consistency between expressed attitudes and later free-play behavior (thus, replicating Regan & Fazio, 1977, and Fazio & Zanna, 1978), and (c) the stability of attitudes from pre- to post-free-play (see Watts, 1967). Attitudes based on direct experience were relatively more accessible from memory, more predictive of behavior, and more stable over time. However, mediational analyses failed to reveal any influence of accessibility on the relation between the manner of attitude formation and attitude-behavior consistency. In fact, controlling for attitude latencies, if anything, accentuated the relation. In contrast, controlling for attitude stability reduced the relation, leading Doll and Azjen to conclude that the effects of the manner of attitude formation were mediated solely by the stability of the attitude over time.

However, various characteristics of the attitude latency measure should lead one to question the extent to which Doll and Azjen adequately assessed attitude accessibility. The number of response options to the attitudinal queries, seven, was quite high. On some trials, some subjects may have spent time debating whether to respond with, say a "5" or a "6." Such mapping on to the response scale has nothing to do with accessing an evaluation from memory, yet is represented in the latency that was observed. More important, individual differences in general baseline speed of responding clearly were not handled satisfactorily. Each subject's attitude latencies were adjusted for the mean latency to "read a one-sentence description of the subsequent set of questions" and to then "press one of two keys to continue" (p. 14). Given that individual differences in the latency with which adjective connotation could be reported did not adequately control for individual differences in the latency with which attitude objects could be judged in the Bargh et al. research, it seems unlikely that individual differences in reading a sentence provide an adequate estimate of baseline differences in speed of responding to the attitudinal queries.

Various findings of Doll and Ajzen's also call into question the validity of their measure of attitude accessibility. Faster latencies were not associated with greater attitude-behavior consistency, thus failing to replicate my laboratory's work involving the predictive power of measures of attitude accessibility, as well as that of Bassili (in press). This finding also is inconsistent with experimental results showing that enhancing the accessibility of attitudes via repeated attitudinal expression increases attitude-behavior consistency (Fazio et al., 1982, Experiment 4). Indeed, if anything, faster latencies in the Doll and Ajzen study were predictive of lower consistency, which explains why controlling for latency differences accentuated the effect of direct versus indirect experience on attitude-behavior consistency and suggests that individuals with fast baseline speeds of responding (for some unknown reason) tended to behave inconsistently. Finally, Doll and Ajzen observed no relation between their latency measure and attitude stability, thus failing to replicate the Bargh et al. finding noted earlier.

The only positive suggestion that the data provide concerning the validity of the latency measure is the confirmation of the expected effect of the experimental manipulation. As noted elsewhere (Fazio, 1990b), the various difficulties with the latency measure that I mentioned previously are not critical problems when mean latencies across various experimental conditions are being compared. Given random assignment to condition, these factors simply add to the error variance. Presumably, average baseline speed of responding was equivalent across the conditions. A strong manipulation can produce enough of a signal to be apparent through the noise, which was the case in this experiment. However, when one is attempting to use latency as an individual difference measure, that is, to identify position along a continuum, the difficulties noted earlier pose serious problems. They can lead to an ordering of individuals on the continuum that has little or no validity.

At a conceptual level, I agree with Doll and Ajzen's reasoning regarding the importance of attitude stability. While one interacts with the attitude objects, attitudes are more likely to change if one has not had previous behavioral experience with the attitude objects. However, what Doll and Ajzen neglect to consider is the process by which such attitude stability is promoted. By what mechanism do attitudes based upon direct experience remain relatively stable over time? The attitude accessibility model addresses this question and maintains that it is as a consequence of their greater likelihood of being activated from memory that such attitudes remain relatively impervious to counterinformation.

Downing, Judd, and Brauer (1992)

These investigators conducted an intriguing series of experiments concerning the effects of repeated attitudinal expression on attitude extremity (also see Judd & Brauer, ch. 3). Our work employing the various forms of a repeated expression manipulation that were described earlier has yielded effects on attitude accessibility with no accompanying effects on attitude extremity (e.g., Powell & Fazio, 1984). In contrast, Downing et al. identified a particular form of repeated expression which produced not only an enhancement of attitude accessibility as measured by response latency but also attitude polarization. A forced-choice, dichotomous evaluation, but not repeated judgments on 9-point scales, yielded polarization. Downing et al. argued that individuals' memory for the earlier scalar ratings inhibited any tendency toward polarization on the final scalar rating. An alternative explanation acknowledged by the authors themselves is that the dichotomous form of repeated expression and the scalar form differ with respect to the availability of a neutral response option. The latter permits the respondent to assign a neutral rating out of either indifference or ambivalence. The dichotomous judgment forces the respondent to take a stand and, having done so, he or she may continue to display a more extreme attitude on the final scale. This "neutrality" hypothesis suggests that any polarizing effect of dichotomous attitude rehearsal is limited to issues for which the respondent would have employed a neutral point if one were available.

In consideration of such a possibility, Downing et al. conducted a second study in which the attitudinal expressions were oral responses unconstrained by any particular scale format. With increasing repetitions, these responses became simpler, more concise, and more extreme. Although unconstrained by scale format, these oral expressions are not free of constraints. Social norms frown upon repeating oneself over and over again in front of the very same audience. Thus, it is not clear how this finding relates to rehearsal that is privately expressed or devoid of any implicit pressure to vary one's expressions.

One of the reasons that I question the generality of the research findings is that my laboratory also has employed a forced-choice, dichotomous form of repeated expression and did not obtain any evidence of resulting attitude polarization. Although Downing et al. are certainly correct that one such data set does not permit a statistically powerful test for attitude polarization (Fazio et al., 1986, Experiment 3), the research by Roskos-Ewoldsen and Fazio (1992b) does not suffer from any such limitation. In this experiment, subjects repeatedly expressed their attitudes toward each object assigned to an attitude rehearsal set in a dichotomous fashion. They also made repeated judgments of whether an object was animate or inanimate for each object in a control set. At the end of the experiment, subjects made a scalar evaluation of each object. Given that judgment task was counterbalanced across the two sets of objects, it was possible to compute the mean extremity of final attitudes when an object had been assigned to the attitude rehearsal set and when it had been assigned to the control set. Averaged across the objects, the means were virtually equivalent. Despite the large number of observations involved in this test (59 subjects expressing attitudes toward 54 objects) and the resulting statistical power, no effect of repeated attitudinal expression was apparent on attitude extremity. This finding implies that any polarizing effect of repeated expression may be more limited than suggested by Downing et al.

We recently completed an experiment examining the generality of the polarization effect across levels of initial attitude extremity (Fazio & Powell, 1994). From an initially large pool of subjects who had provided attitude ratings of a number of issues on a -3 to $+3$ scale, we selected subjects who had rated a minimum of six issues at the neutral point, 3 at $+1$, 3 at -1, 3 at $+2$ or $+3$, and 3 at -2 or -3. For these subjects, then, six issues were available at each of three levels of initial extremity—neutral (0), mild (1), and extreme (2 or 3). Tailored questionnaires were constructed for each individual varying the number of times that issues appeared on an initial questionnaire that involved forced-choice, dichotomous attitude expressions. All but two issues from each set appeared on a second questionnaire that involved a scalar rating. All the issues were presented during a subsequent attitude latency task. These latency data replicated the effects observed by Powell and Fazio (1984) and Downing et al. (1992). Regardless of level of initial attitude extremity, latencies were faster with increasing numbers of earlier attitude expressions.

Unlike the latency data, the main effect of prior expressions on attitude extremity was qualified by a significant interaction with level of initial extremity. No polarization was evident for either initially mild or initially extreme attitudes. Only initially neutral attitudes were polarized as a function of earlier dichotomous expressions. Thus the effect observed by Downing et al. was apparent only for initially neutral attitudes, just as suggested by the neutrality hypothesis. Obviously, more research needs to be conducted on the specific conditions that promote polarization. However, the present findings suggest that any such consequence of attitude rehearsal is limited to cases in which the respondent is induced to modify an initially neutral stance.

CONCLUSION

In closing, it is appropriate to quote Allport (1935), who offered a strong assertion regarding the power and functionality of attitudes.

> Without guiding attitudes the individual is confused and baffled. Some kind of preparation is essential before he can make a satisfactory observation, pass suitable judgment, or make any but the most primitive reflex type of response. Attitudes determine for each individual what he will see and hear, what he will think and what he will do. To borrow a phrase from William James, they "engender meaning upon the world"; they draw lines about and segregate an otherwise chaotic environment; they are our methods for finding our way about in an ambiguous universe. (p. 806)

Allport's assertion appears to be true of some kinds of attitudes, but not others. The extent to which an attitude is characterized by such power and functionality varies as a function of the strength of the association in memory between the attitude object and the individual's evaluation of the object. With greater associative strength, and, hence, a greater capability for automatic activation, attitudes exert greater influence. There is very good reason to be skeptical of the power and functionality of attitudes characterized by weak object-evaluation associations in memory. However, as we move up the attitude–nonattitude continuum, Allport's enthusiasm regarding the importance of attitudes is more and more appropriate.

ACKNOWLEDGMENTS

Preparation of this chapter was supported by Research Scientist Development Award MH00452 and Grant MH38832 from the National Institute of Mental Health. I thank John Bassili, Edward Hirt, Jon Krosnick, Richard Petty, and Mark Zanna for their helpful comments on an earlier draft.

REFERENCES

Abelson, R. P. (1988). Conviction. *American Psychologist, 43,* 267–275.

Allport, G. W. (1935). Attitudes. In C. Murchison (Ed.), *Handbook of social psychology* (pp. 798–844). Worcester, MA: Clark University Press.

Amabile, T. M., & Kabat, L. G. (1982). When self-descriptions contradict behavior: Actions do speak louder than words. *Social Cognition, 1,* 311–335.

Bargh, J. A., Chaiken, S., Govender, R., & Pratto, F. (1992). The generality of the automatic attitude activation effect. *Journal of Personality and Social Psychology, 62,* 893–912.

Bassili, J. N. (1993a, January). *Procedural versus meta-attitudinal indices of attitude strength.* Paper presented at the Social Psychology Winter Conference, Park City, UT.

Bassili, J. N. (1993b). Response latency versus certainty as indices of the strength of voting intentions in a CATI survey. *Public Opinion Quarterly, 57,* 54–61.

Bassili, J. N. (in press). Response latency and the accessibility of voting intentions: What contributes to accessibility and how it affects vote choice. *Personality and Social Psychology Bulletin.*

Bassili, J. N., & Fletcher, J. (1991). Response-time measurement in survey research. *Public Opinion Quarterly, 55,* 331–346.

Bem, D. J. (1972). Self-perception theory. In L. Berkowitz (Ed.), *Advances in experimental social psychology* (Vol. 6, pp. 1–62). New York: Academic.

Blascovich, J., Ernst, J. M., Tomaka, J., Kelsey, R. M., Salomon, K. L., & Fazio, R. H. (1993). Attitude accessibility as a moderator of autonomic reactivity during decision making. *Journal of Personality and Social Psychology, 64,* 165–176.

Cacioppo, J. T., Marshall-Goodell, B. S., Tassinary, L. G., & Petty, R. E. (1992). Rudimentary determinants of attitudes: Classical conditioning is more effective when prior knowledge about the attitude stimulus is low than high. *Journal of Experimental Social Psychology, 28,* 207–233.

Calder, B. J., & Ross, M. (1973). *Attitudes and behavior.* Morristown, NJ: General Learning Press.

Cohen, S., & Hoberman, H. M., (1983). Positive events and social support as buffers of life change stress. *Journal of Applied Social Psychology, 13,* 99–125.

Converse, P. E. (1970). Attitudes and non-attitudes: Continuation of a dialogue. In E. R. Tufte (Ed.), *The quantitative analysis of social problems* (pp. 168–189). Reading, MA: Addison-Wesley.

Cook, T. D., & Flay, B. R. (1978). The temporal persistence of experimentally induced attitude change: An evaluative review. In L. Berkowitz (Ed.), *Advances in experimental social psychology* (Vol. 11). New York: Academic.

Doll, J., & Ajzen, I. (1992). Accessibility and stability of predictors in the theory of planned behavior. *Journal of Personality and Social Psychology, 63,* 754–765.

Dovidio, J. F., & Fazio, R. H. (1992). New technologies for the direct and indirect assessment of attitudes. In J. M. Tanur (Ed.), *Questions about questions: Inquiries into the cognitive bases of surveys* (pp. 204–237). New York: Russell Sage Foundation.

Downing, J. W., Judd, C. M., & Brauer, M. (1992). Effects of repeated expressions on attitude extremity. *Journal of Personality and Social Psychology, 63,* 17–29.

Fazio, R. H. (1987). Self-perception theory: A current perspective. In M. P. Zanna, J. M. Olson, & C. P. Herman (Eds.), *Social influence: The Ontario symposium* (Vol. 5, pp. 129–150). Hillsdale, NJ: Lawrence Erlbaum Associates.

Fazio, R. H. (1990a). Multiple processes by which attitudes guide behavior: The MODE model as an integrative framework. In M. P. Zanna (Ed.), *Advances in experimental social psychology* (Vol. 23, pp. 75–109). New York: Academic.

Fazio, R. H. (1990b). A practical guide to the use of response latency in social psychological research. In C. Hendrick & M. S. Clark (Eds.), *Review of personality and social psychology* (Vol. 11, pp. 74–97). Newbury Park, CA: Sage.

Fazio, R. H. (1992, January). *On the value of knowing one's likes and dislikes.* Paper presented at the Social Psychology Winter Conference, Park City, UT.

Fazio, R. H. (1993). Variability in the likelihood of automatic attitude activation: Data re-analysis and commentary on Bargh, Chaiken, Govender, and Pratto (1992). *Journal of Personality and Social Psychology, 64,* 753–758, 764–765.

Fazio, R. H., Blascovich, J., & Driscoll, D. M. (1992). On the functional value of attitudes: The influence of accessible attitudes upon the ease and quality of decision making. *Personality and Social Psychology Bulletin, 18,* 388–401.

Fazio, R. H., Chen, J., McDonel, E. C., & Sherman, S. J. (1982). Attitude accessibility, attitude-behavior consistency, and the strength of the object-evaluation association. *Journal of Experimental Social Psychology, 18,* 339–357.

Fazio, R. H., Herr, P. M., & Olney, T. J. (1984). Attitude accessibility following a self-perception process. *Journal of Personality and Social Psychology, 47,* 277–286.

Fazio, R. H., & Powell, M. C. (1992). [The emotionality of evaluations]. Unpublished raw data. Indiana University.

Fazio, R. H., & Powell, M. C. (1994). *Attitude expression, extremity and accessibility: When does attitude expression promote polarization?* Unpublished manuscript, Indiana University, Bloomington.

Fazio, R. H., Powell, M. C., & Herr, P. M. (1983). Toward a process model of the attitude-behavior relation: Accessing one's attitude upon mere observation of the attitude object. *Journal of Personality and Social Psychology, 44,* 723–735.

Fazio, R. H., Powell, M. C., & Williams, C. J. (1989). The role of attitude accessibility in the attitude-to-behavior process. *Journal of Consumer Research, 16,* 280–288.

Fazio, R. H., Sanbonmatsu, D. M., Powell, M. C., & Kardes, F. R. (1986). On the automatic activation of attitudes. *Journal of Personality and Social Psychology, 50,* 229–238.

Fazio, R. H., & Williams, C. J. (1986). Attitude accessibility as a moderator of the attitude-perception and attitude-behavior relations: An investigation of the 1984 presidential election. *Journal of Personality and Social Psychology, 51,* 505–514.

Fazio, R. H., & Zanna, M. P. (1978). On the predictive validity of attitudes: The role of direct experience and confidence. *Journal of Personality, 46,* 228–243.

Fazio, R. H., & Zanna, M. P. (1981). Direct experience and attitude-behavior consistency. In L. Berkowitz (Ed.), *Advances in experimental social psychology* (Vol. 14, pp. 162–202). New York: Academic.

Fazio, R. H., Zanna, M. P., & Cooper, J. (1978). Direct experience and attitude-behavior consistency: An information processing analysis. *Personality and Social Psychology Bulletin, 4,* 48–51.

Fazio, R. H., Zanna, M. P., Ross, M., & Powell, M. C. (1994). *Attitude accessibility and attitudinal persistence.* Unpublished manuscript, Indiana University, Bloomington.

Festinger, L., Riecken, H. W., & Schachter, S. (1956). *When prophecy fails.* New York: Harper & Row.

Fishbein, M. (1963). An investigation of the relationship between beliefs about an object and attitude toward that object. *Human Relations, 16,* 233–240.

Hodges, S. D., & Wilson, T. D. (1994). Effects of analyzing reasons on attitude change: The moderating role of attitude accessibility. *Social Cognition, 11,* 353–366.

Houston, D. A., & Fazio, R. H. (1989). Biased processing as a function of attitude accessibility: Making objective judgments subjectively. *Social Cognition, 7,* 51–66.

Kaplan, K. J. (1972). On the ambivalence-indifference problem in attitude theory and measurement: A suggested modification of the semantic differential technique. *Psychological Bulletin, 77,* 361–372.

Katz, D. (1960). The functional approach to the study of attitudes. *Public Opinion Quarterly, 24,* 163–204.

Kiesler, C. A. (1971). *The psychology of commitment.* New York: Academic.

Krosnick, J. A. (1989). Attitude importance and attitude accessibility. *Personality and Social Psychology Bulletin, 15,* 297–308.

Krosnick, J. A., Betz, A. L., Jussim, & Lynn, A. R. (1992). Subliminal conditioning of attitudes. *Personality and Social Psychology Bulletin, 18,* 152–162.

Kruglanski, A. W. (1989). *Lay epistemics and human knowledge.* New York: Plenum.

Levine, M., & Perkins, D. V. (1980, August). *Tailor making life events scale.* Paper presented at the meeting of the American Psychological Association, Montreal.

Linville, P. W. (1987). Self-complexity as a buffer against stress-related illness and depression. *Journal of Personality and Social Psychology, 52,* 663–676.

Lord, C. G., Ross, L., & Lepper, M. R. (1979). Biased assimilation and attitude polarization: The effects of prior theories on subsequently considered evidence. *Journal of Personality and Social Psychology, 37,* 2098–2109.

Lydon, J., Zanna, M. P., & Ross, M. (1988). Bolstering attitudes by autobiographical recall: Attitude persistence and selective memory. *Personality and Social Psychology Bulletin, 14,* 78–86.

Millar, M. G., & Tesser, A. (1986). Effects of affective and cognitive focus on the attitude-behavior relation. *Journal of Personality and Social Psychology, 51,* 270–276.

Norman, R. (1975). Affective-cognitive consistency, attitudes, conformity, and behavior. *Journal of Personality and Social Psychology, 32,* 83–91.

Powell, M. C., & Fazio, R. H. (1984). Attitude accessibility as a function of repeated attitudinal expression. *Personality and Social Psychology Bulletin, 10,* 139–148.

Regan, D. T., & Fazio, R. H. (1977). On the consistency between attitudes and behavior: Look to the method of attitude formation. *Journal of Experimental Social Psychology, 13,* 28–45.

Rholes, W. S., Michas, L., & Shroff, J. (1989). Action control as a vulnerability factor in dysphoria. *Cognitive Therapy and Research, 13,* 263–274.

Roese, N. J., & Olson, J. M. (1994). Attitude importance as a function of repeated attitude expression. *Journal of Experimental Social Psychology, 30,* 39–51.

Roskos-Ewoldsen, D. R., & Fazio, R. H. (1992a). The accessibility of source likability as a determinant of persuasion. *Personality and Social Psychology Bulletin, 18,* 19–25.

Roskos-Ewoldsen, D. R., & Fazio, R. H. (1992b). On the orienting value of attitudes: Attitude accessibility as a determinant of an object's attraction of visual attention. *Journal of Personality and Social Psychology, 63,* 198–211.

Ross, M., McFarland, C., & Fletcher, G. J. O. (1981). The effect of attitude on the recall of personal histories. *Journal of Personality and Social Psychology, 40,* 627–634.

Ross, M., McFarland, C., Conway, M., & Zanna, M. P. (1983). Reciprocal relation between attitudes and behavior recall: Committing people to newly formed attitudes. *Journal of Personality and Social Psychology, 45,* 257–267.

Sanbonmatsu, D. M., & Fazio, R. H. (1986, October). *The automatic activation of attitudes toward products.* Paper presented at the meeting of the Association for Consumer Research, Toronto.

Sanbonmatsu, D. M., & Fazio, R. H. (1990). The role of attitudes in memory-based decision making. *Journal of Personality and Social Psychology, 59,* 614–622.

Sanbonmatsu, D. M., Osborne, R. E., & Fazio, R. H. (1986, May). *The measurement of automatic attitude activation.* Paper presented at the meeting of the Midwestern Psychological Association, Chicago.

Schneider, W., & Fisk, A. D. (1982). Degree of consistent training: Improvements in search performance and automatic process development. *Perception & Psychophysics, 31,* 160–168.

Schneider, W., & Shiffrin, R. M. (1977). Controlled and automatic human information processing: I. Detection, search, and attention. *Psychological Review, 84,* 1–66.

Schuette, R. A., & Fazio, R. H. (in press). Attitude accessibility and motivation as determinants of biased processing: A test of the MODE model. *Personality and Social Psychology Bulletin.*

Schwartz, S. H. (1978). Temporal instability as a moderator of the attitude-behavior relationship. *Journal of Personality and Social Psychology, 36,* 715–724.

Shavitt, S., & Fazio, R. H. (1991). Effects of attribute salience on the consistency between attitudes and behavior predictions. *Personality and Social Psychology Bulletin, 17,* 507–516.

Sherif, C. W., Kelly, M., Rodgers, H. L., Sarup, G., & Tittler, B. I. (1973). Personal involvement, social judgment, and action. *Journal of Personality and Social Psychology, 27,* 311–328.

Shiffrin, R. M., & Dumais, S. T. (1981). The development of automatism. In J. R. Anderson (Ed.), *Cognitive skills and their acquisition*. Hillsdale, NJ: Lawrence Erlbaum Associates.

Smith, E. R. (1989). Procedural efficiency: General and specific components and effects on social judgment. *Journal of Experimental Social Psychology, 25*, 500–523.

Smith, M. B., Bruner, J. S., & White, R. W. (1956). *Opinions and personality*. New York: Wiley.

Watts, W. A. (1967). Relative persistence of opinion change induced by active compared to passive participation. *Journal of Personality and Social Psychology, 5*, 4–15.

Wilson, T. D., Dunn, D. S., Bybee, J. A., Hyman, D. B., & Rotondo, J. A. (1984). Effects of analyzing reasons on attitude-behavior consistency. *Journal of Personality and Social Psychology, 47*, 4–16.

Wu, C., & Shaffer, D. R. (1987). Susceptibility to persuasive appeals as a function of source credibility and prior experience with the attitude object. *Journal of Personality and Social Psychology, 52*, 677–688.

Zanna, M. P., Fazio, R. H., & Ross, M. (1994). The persistence of persuasion. In R. C. Schank & E. Langer (Eds.), *Beliefs, reasoning, and decision making: Psycho-logic in honor of Bob Abelson* (pp. 347–362). Hillsdale, NJ: Lawrence Erlbaum Associates.

Zanna, M. P., Kiesler, C. A., & Pilkonis, P. A. (1970). Positive and negative attitudinal affect established by classical conditioning. *Journal of Personality and Social Psychology, 14*, 321–328.

Zanna, M. P., & Rempel, J. K. (1988). In D. Bar-Tal & A. W. Kruglanski (Eds.), *The social psychology of knowledge* (pp. 315–354). New York: Cambridge University Press.

11

▼▼▼▼▼▼▼

Working Knowledge and Attitude Strength: An Information-Processing Analysis

Wendy Wood
Nancy Rhodes
Michael Biek
Texas A&M University

Television news programs often use a debate-type format to present controversial issues, with proponents from each side of the disagreement presenting their views in sequence. Imagine that you are watching a debate concerning an issue that you do not know much about, say a controversy over the best method of allocating funds for medical research. One likely response in such a circumstance is to flip the channel to a more easily understood presentation. But assuming that you decide to watch, you hear the first speaker advocate a broadly based research effort to identify a cure for the target disease. You may have some difficulty understanding the details of her arguments, but in general they seem well thought-out and reasonable—that is, until the opposing arguments are presented. The opposing speaker, arguing for a narrowly focused investigation into a particularly promising cure, also presents highly plausible arguments, and you may think, "Why didn't that occur to me?" Contrast your response to that of the two experts whose livelihood is tied up in their ongoing debate on the topic (and who may have faced off against each other on other news shows earlier in the evening). While the first speaker is outlining her views, the second is probably busy countering each of the arguments. They do not experience the uncomfortable flip-flop in attitudes likely to characterize the responses of the less well-informed viewers.

The different reactions of the viewers and the debate participants derive in part from their different levels of knowledge on the topic. Knowledgeable people are expert reasoners and information processors in the relevant domain. They can use their extensive store of beliefs and prior experiences to interpret and evaluate new information on the topic, including any new material that surfaces during the debate. The uninformed have greater difficulty attending to, comprehending, and evaluating relevant information. They may fail to notice, misinterpret, or incorrectly evaluate many important points. In this chapter we consider how knowledge affects processing of new, topic relevant information as well as the effects of knowledge on attitude judgments. Although knowledge typically facilitates processing, we shall see that its implications for attitude judgments are complex.

Consistent with the theme of this book, one function of knowledge is to help maintain strong attitudes. Attitudes are typically considered strong when they are resistant to change and persistent over time. Knowledgeable people with strong attitudes are careful, expert processors of new information, but their processing is biased to bolster and protect their favored attitude position. This closed-minded orientation generates considerable stability and persistence in attitude judgments. For example, if one of the speakers in our debate had conducted the initial, ground-breaking research into a drug treatment, her resulting strong feelings about this issue might generate a closed-minded, defensive use of knowledge. She might interpret all evidence as supporting a focused research effort into this particular treatment.

Many analyses of attitude strength have recognized that knowledge contributes to especially potent attitudes. Strong attitudes are often thought to be built on an extensive, well-organized knowledge structure that provides an informational basis for reactions to the attitude object. For example, according to Eagly and Chaiken (1993, ch. 16, this volume), strong attitudes are embedded in an extensive knowledge structure composed of an interconnected set of beliefs, feelings, and behaviors. Similarly, strength in terms of conviction in one's views is thought to derive in part from "cognitive elaboration," reflecting an extensive mental network of beliefs and prior experiences (Abelson, 1988; Petty, Haugtvedt, & Smith, ch. 5, this volume). In addition, a strong, important attitude (i.e., linked to a person's needs and goals) is thought to be associated with a highly structured schema organizing large amounts of attitude-relevant knowledge in memory (Berent & Krosnick, in press).

Knowledge not only contributes to the maintenance of strong attitudes, it can also facilitate objective, unbiased processing of information. In this role, knowledge will not always attenuate attitude change. Because knowledgeable people can attend to, understand, and recognize the merits in a wide variety of new information, they may be very likely to change their attitudes to align with a cogent, well reasoned position. For example, our expert researchers are more likely than naive viewers to attend to, understand, and recognize the implications of new research data. When presented with a breakthrough in research, they may change their judgments to a greater extent than less knowledgeable individuals.

In this chapter we discuss how knowledge contributes to the closed-minded maintenance of strong attitudes as well as to an open-minded orientation focused on validity of attitude judgments. By knowledge, we mean *working knowledge*, or the amount of attitude-relevant information one can retrieve from memory (Agans, Wood, & Rhodes, 1992; Biek, Wood, Nations, & Chaiken, 1993; Kallgren & Wood, 1986; Wood, 1982; Wood & Kallgren, 1988; Wood, Kallgren, & Preisler, 1985). People with extensive working knowledge can access a considerable store of attitude-relevant beliefs and prior experiences, whereas people with lesser knowledge possess a relatively impoverished base of information concerning the attitude issue.

The Construct of Working Knowledge

Opinion in good men is but knowledge in the making. (John Milton, 1644)

When you know a thing, to hold that you know it, and when you do not know a thing, to allow that you do not know it—this is knowledge. (Confucius)

Knowledge is learning well retained. (Dante)

As these quotations illustrate, knowledge is a multifaceted construct that can be defined in a variety of ways. Working knowledge was designed to represent the beliefs and prior experiences that spontaneously come to mind when one is confronted with an attitude issue, and not necessarily the full wealth of one's supporting information base (Wood, 1982). Knowledgeable people use this information retrieved from memory to perceive, interpret, and respond to subsequent encounters with the attitude object. The relatively impoverished store of beliefs and experiences of people low in working knowledge hinders their ability to receive and evaluate new, attitude-relevant information.

This definition of knowledge as amount of information relevant to the attitude object has considerable precedent in the attitude literature. For example, Converse (1970) argued that the cognitive component of attitude centrality or strength is represented in the "sheer amount of ancillary information held by the subject with respect to the object" (p. 183). Similarly, Rosenberg and Abelson (1960) proposed that people's "cognitive files" of information relevant to the attitude object have important implications for their willingness to change the attitude.

Our definition of working knowledge has emphasized ability to process new information. Working knowledge can be aligned with other variables that affect facility at information processing; lack of knowledge should limit capacity to process new information, much like time pressure (Kruglanski, 1989), cognitive resources drained by mood states (Mackie & Worth, 1989), and distraction (Petty & Brock, 1981). Working knowledge differs from these other variables, however, in that it is topic bound and affects processing only in a particular attitude domain (Wood, 1982).

To assess working knowledge, research participants are asked to list beliefs and prior experiences relevant to a particular object or social issue. Although this procedure does not constrain participants to support their attitudes, most beliefs and experiences generated through this procedure are evaluatively consistent with subjects' favored attitude positions. For example, content coding of the knowledge protocols generated by subjects in the research by Biek et al. (1993) indicated that 93% of the beliefs and prior experiences listed on the topic of preservation of the environment (by both high and low knowledge persons) were supportive of subjects' pro-preservation attitudes.

Consider the following working knowledge protocol from a subject in a recent experiment who was strongly in favor of preservation of the environment and highly knowledgeable on the topic (from Biek et al., 1993). He listed the following beliefs concerning the environment:

We are responsible for its upkeep and preservation.

Sacrifices are worth saving the environment.

We have not inherited the world from our ancestors: We have borrowed it from our children.

We are destroying our environment at an alarming rate.

He also listed the following behaviors:

I take classes and research.

I carpool.

I wrote articles.

I give money to environmental organizations.

I talk to people.

I eat only albacore tuna (no dolphins killed).

In this experiment, the subject returned to the lab one week later and read a counterattitudinal persuasive message, arguing against preservation. We examined his processing of the message as a function of working knowledge. He proved not to be influenced by the message because he countered the message arguments with the ideas and actions in the knowledge protocol. That is, the arguments in our message that (a) preservation hinders economic and techno-logical development and increases unemployment, and (b) lower air standards would allow for the burning of coal, which would reduce our dependence on foreign oil, were countered by the subject's notion that personal and economic sacrifices are worthwhile. Specifically, when listing his thoughts about the message, the subject indicated that "our personal convenience (economics) is a small price to pay for environmental preservation." The subject also reiterated that we are personally responsible for the environment, arguing that "we have a respon-sibility to preserve the environment because we are the ones destroying it." In this way, beliefs and past experiences on the attitude topic facilitated the evalu-ation of new, relevant information. Subjects with minimal knowledge in this experiment were unable to draw on an extensive information base to help interpret the antipreservation message and were less able to critically evaluate it.

The undirected recall procedure used to assess working knowledge generates a very different information base than that obtained when subjects are specifically asked to justify their opinions (cf. Erber, Hodges, & Wilson, ch. 17, this volume). In the process of explaining to others why they feel the way they do, people may emphasize plausible, easily justifiable reasons and fail to recognize the less rational bases for their attitudes. As Erber et al.'s (ch. 17, this volume) research has demonstrated, the resulting biased sample of reasons can mislead people about the true basis for their attitudes.

When knowledge is assessed through amount of information recalled from memory, the construct is potentially confounded with verbal facility or IQ. If people who can access greater amounts of information from memory are higher in verbal ability, then the information-processing effects we attribute to working knowledge might really reflect the broader construct of verbal skills. This confound has been eliminated through two procedures in our research. First, we typically obtain measures of working knowledge on a variety of issues, in addition to the critical attitude topic. As would be expected if the knowledge measure reflects issue-specific information and not general verbal skills, knowledge on the critical attitude topic, but not on unrelated ones, successfully predicts responses on that topic. Thus, for example, Wood (1982) found that extent of knowledge on the topic of abortion was not related to evaluation of new information on an unrelated topic, preservation of the environment (see also Biek, Wood, & Chaiken, in press). The second procedure we have used to differentiate working knowledge from broader dispositional variables such as verbal skills is to measure these directly, for example by administering the verbal portion of an IQ test. This score is then used as a covariate in analyses predicting evaluation of new information from working knowledge. Including such direct measures of verbal ability has in no case reduced the impact of working knowledge (e.g., Agans et al., 1992). Thus, the effects of working knowledge reflect the extent of one's topic-specific information base and not broad dispositional variables such as verbal skills.

Working knowledge appears to be related to other topic-specific informational qualities of attitudes. For example, Wood (1982) found that people high in working knowledge concerning preservation of the environment reported having more frequent thoughts about the environment in the past than less knowledgeable people. Furthermore, respondents appeared to be aware of their extent of working knowledge: When asked to rate their knowledgeability, people high in working knowledge report they know more than those low in working knowledge (Agans et al., 1992; Wood, 1982). On a correlational basis, however, the association between working knowledge and self-reports of knowledge is not especially large ($r = .29$, $p < .01$, Agans et al., 1992).

Working knowledge does not, however, appear to be consistently related to affective qualities of attitudes, such as extremity of the attitude position or intensity of affect. Although extent of working knowledge has proved not to be correlated with extremity of attitudes or rated intensity of affective reactions on a variety of issues, including preservation, AIDS prevention, and current news events (Biek, 1992; Perse, 1990; Wood et al., 1985; Wood & Kallgren, 1988), one study did find that greater knowledge about abortion was linked to greater affective intensity on this topic (Biek, 1992). Furthermore, for many attitude domains, considerable variability appears across subjects in the relation between knowledge and affect, with some people indicating uniformly high or low levels of both constructs, and others demonstrating little consistency across constructs. Thus, working knowledge may be linked to other informational attitude qualities, but the link between knowledge and affective qualities appears to vary with attitude domain and for individuals within each domain.

Our approach can be contrasted with alternate treatments of knowledge that emphasize the accuracy of information. A standard device for assessing knowledge is to evaluate the factual correctness of people's thoughts and beliefs through objective tests (Fiske, Lau, & Smith, 1990; Krosnick & Milburn, 1990; Lodge & Hamill, 1986). Knowledgeable people are then defined as those with extensive correct information on the issue. Indeed, sometimes accuracy is important. Inaccurate information may be less stable than accurate understanding. If the expectations of people with incorrect (vs. correct) knowledge are more likely to be challenged by subsequent events, then incorrect knowledge may be especially likely to change given experience with the attitude object (Davidson, ch. 12, this volume).

Accuracy tests will often not be useful, however, because they may fail to capture the extent of one's *subjectively* important knowledge on an attitude issue. Even when people possess accurate knowledge they may not rely on it because it is not subjectively meaningful. Instead, they may use objectively inaccurate information because it is subjectively compelling. Furthermore, for many attitude issues the correctness, or validity, of critical components of knowledge is unclear. For example, on the topic of abortion, it is difficult to determine the relative accuracy of the pro-life position that life begins at conception with the pro-choice view that life begins when the fetus is independently viable. Supporting this distinction between objective facts and subjectively important information, in recent research, extent of working knowledge on AIDS prevention was not closely related to scores on standardized tests of accuracy of factual knowledge on this topic (rs ranged from $-.07$ to $.25$, Biek, 1992). Thus, people with a minimal grasp of objective facts may possess a considerable base of working knowledge that represents their subjectively valid understanding of and experiences with the attitude topic.

Knowledgeability may be associated with a variety of organizing structures in memory. In the study of expertise, experts differ from novices not only in amount of content knowledge but also in the extent to which they possess an integrated, well-organized system of relevant information (Fiske, Kinder, & Larter, 1983; Fiske, Lau, & Smith, 1990). Highly organized structures may be characterized by

the number of either independent or correlated dimensions of information underlying one's judgments (Judd & Lusk, 1984; Linville, 1982; Tesser, Martin, &
Mendolia, ch. 4, this volume) as well as by the consistency between the evaluative
implications of one's beliefs and overall evaluation (Chaiken & Yates, 1985;
Rosenberg, 1968) or one's affective responses and overall evaluation (Chaiken,
Pomerantz, & Giner-Sorolla, 1993). Given that a well-organized structure of
information in memory is likely to facilitate access to attitude-relevant beliefs and
experiences, people high (vs. low) in working knowledge may possess a more
efficient, better organized structure of information in memory related to the attitude
issue. However, it is unclear at this point exactly what form such a structure might
take. Recent developments in parallel distributed processing suggest that information is not stored in memory in static patterns, but rather knowledge is represented
in terms of the strength of connections among units of information, allowing
patterns to be recreated during retrieval from memory (McClelland, Rumelhart, &
Hinton, 1986). Instead of a localized store, or structure of knowledge about an issue,
information may be distributed across connections in a large number of processing
units, with retrieval requiring simultaneous (i.e., parallel) consideration of many
pieces of information. Any of these organizational structures in memory might be
associated with extensive working knowledge.

Origins of Working Knowledge

*Knowledge must come through action; you can have no test which is not fanciful,
save by trial.* (Sophocles)

As this quote suggests, direct behavioral experience with an attitude object is an
important source of information (Fazio & Zanna, 1981). Our understanding of
the qualities and features of attitude objects frequently develops through direct
exposure. For example, extensive knowledge may be acquired through repeated
encounters with an object or a person over time, as with developing friendships.
Continued interaction with friends confers a rich store of information, including
both specific past events (e.g., the many times they agreed to babysit your children) and general beliefs about their attributes (e.g., nurturance and supportive-
ness). Extensive knowledge may also be acquired through limited, but highly
meaningful direct experiences. For example, one may have acquired a detailed
picture of a new boss's interaction style and major likes and dislikes after only
a single interaction with him or her (see Fiske & Neuberg's, 1992, discussion
of outcome dependence in impression formation). Our measure of knowledge
explicitly incorporates an experiential component that reflects such past experiences with an attitude object—working knowledge is assessed from retrieval of
past experiences as well as retrieval of beliefs.

Attitude-relevant knowledge is also likely to originate from indirect exposure
to attitude objects, including discussions with others (Robinson & Levy, 1986)

and media presentations (McGuire, 1986; Roberts & Maccoby, 1985). During the span of a given day, people are exposed to numerous pieces of information from these indirect sources, only some of which are retained and retrieved upon subsequent confrontation with the attitude object or issue. When are people likely to acquire knowledge through such experiences? Research on the determinants of political "information holding" (Clarke & Kline, 1974), a construct similar to working knowledge, provides some insight. Information holding represents how informed one is about public affairs, which is measured from the number of political issues one spontaneously identifies as important as well as the number of possible solutions and political figures mentioned relevant to these issues. As would be expected, greater information holding is associated with greater reports of exposure to news media (Clarke & Fredin, 1978; Clarke & Kline, 1974). However, simple exposure is only one contributor to knowledge acquisition. Information holding concerning news events appears to be associated with extensive processing of media presentations: More informed people report greater attention to news programs, greater comprehension of them, and greater thought about and cognitive elaboration of them (Perse, 1990). Thus, exposure to new information, along with careful processing of this material, appears to facilitate knowledge acquisition. In the next sections of the chapter we consider how one's existing levels of knowledge, in conjunction with one's processing goals, determine reactions to new information.

A General Framework for the Effects of Knowledge on Information Processing

People can be knowledgeable on attitude issues they feel intensely about as well as on issues that aren't associated with strong feelings. Our initial research on working knowledge was conducted with a single attitude topic, preservation of the environment (i.e., Kallgren & Wood, 1986; Wood, 1982; Wood & Kallgren, 1988; Wood et al., 1985). This issue provided an ideal context in which to study knowledge when people are relatively dispassionate and objective. Although preservation was considered an important global goal by our college student subjects, it did not appear to generate intense affective reactions for most students. More recently, when investigating other attitude issues, we considered the effects of knowledge for passionately held attitudes associated with intense affect.

In general, affective reactions to an attitude object consist of emotions, feelings, moods, and sympathetic nervous system activity. The intensity of these affective responses can be assessed from the extremity of subjects' ratings, on a series of bipolar semantic differential scales, of how the attitude object makes them feel. The intensity of affective reactions are important to understanding the role of knowledge because affect is one indicator of attitude strength. Attitudes have most often been termed "strong" when a high degree of affect or conviction is associated with the attitude judgment (Raden, 1985).

Potent feelings indicative of strong attitudes are most likely to ensue when the attitude domain concerns defining aspects of one's self-concept, for example: as a liberal or conservative political philosophy might be to "political elites," when the attitude implicates broader religious or social values; as with the highly pitched emotional arguments associated with abortion, or when the domain is associated with important outcomes for the self (cf. Crano, ch. 6, this volume); as the personal involvement in research identifying a cure for a disease affected one of the participants in the hypothetical debate with which we began this chapter. For issues that elicit intense positive or negative affect, people use their knowledge to bolster and protect existing evaluations of the attitude object because change would be threatening to their self-concept, to personal outcomes, or to higher order values. With strong attitudes, then, knowledge contributes to one's defensive armorarium, maintaining attitudes against change.

From a structural perspective, strong attitudes derive their potency from the organization of attitude-relevant material in memory (Eagly & Chaiken, 1993; ch. 16, this volume). Strong attitudes built on considerable knowledge and affect are linked to a tightly connected, emotionally charged network of information and feelings in memory related to the attitude judgment. Change in any one aspect of the network will likely have disruptive effects on related material. To reduce the likelihood of such a "domino effect," people with strong attitudes process information in a biased manner, reacting more favorably to information that supports their favored position than information that challenges it.

When affective reactions are mild, attitudes cannot be described as especially strong, and little motivation exists for biased processing of new information in order to bolster and protect the attitude. Attitudes characterized by considerable knowledge but minimal affect are likely to arise when people are motivated by validity concerns and wish to hold the best, most accurate opinion on an issue. Such an attitude issue might, for example, be judged to be of general importance to society but to have few personal implications for one's own immediate outcomes. Under such circumstances, knowledge enables dispassionate, objective processing of new material; it enhances people's ability to receive and make sense out of new information in an informed, impartial manner. Knowledge in the absence of intense affect can thus confer general information processing expertise, enhancing one's ability to assess the validity of new information, irrespective of whether it challenges or supports existing attitudes and beliefs.[1]

Consider the alternate case of attitudes associated with limited knowledge. Minimal knowledge limits ability to carefully process details of new attitude-relevant information. Attitudes built on intense affect with limited knowledge

---

[1]Our presentation of knowledge and affect as a dichotomy representing high or low values is a convenient heuristic. Indeed, extent of knowledge and intensity of affect can assume a range of values. We present these constructs as assuming only two levels in order to most clearly characterize the information processing and attitude change effects associated with amount of knowledge and amount of affect.

are likely to be subjectively experienced as "gut-level evaluations" accompanied by little justification or explanation. These attitudes may arise from culturally specified normative practices (e.g., the prohibition in many western societies against eating insects) and may be found with attitude objects that appear highly threatening (e.g., some forms of racial prejudice, the phobic object for sufferers of phobias). The intense feelings associated with such attitude objects are likely to provide a strong guide for responding more favorably to supportive information than to challenging information. However, limited knowledge renders people unable to understand in detail the implications of much new, attitude-relevant information or to evaluate its strengths and weaknesses. Such an attitude may be characterized as strong, in the sense that it organizes and directs subsequent responses and yields a closed-minded orientation toward new material. But it is unlikely to provide a sufficient information base for a careful, considered analysis of relevant information.

For other attitude issues, limited knowledge is associated with minimal affect. Attitudes derived from minimal knowledge and feelings are likely to arise when issues appear to have few implications for ones' self-concept or immediate outcomes and to be only vaguely associated with cherished values and goals. Political attitudes may often exemplify this orientation, with the general public having only minimal information and affect concerning much government legislation. With such attitude issues, people are unlikely to be biased processors who evaluate new information by whether it supports or opposes their attitudes. In addition, their meager information base is likely to be insufficient to conduct a careful, informed analysis of the details of incoming information. In such a case, people may be subject to a variety of motivations, including economy in judgments; the limited affective significance of such attitude topics may encourage a relatively quick, low effort analysis of new, attitude-relevant information.

In the remainder of the chapter we consider in some detail the effects of knowledge on information processing. We rely on sequential models of persuasion to represent the effects of knowledge given intense affect and biased processing to maintain strong attitudes and the effects of knowledge given minimal affect and objective processing (Converse, 1962; Janis & Hovland, 1959; McGuire, 1968, 1985; Rhodes & Wood, 1992). With these models, recipient attributes such as knowledge affect reactions to new information in a series of stages. Attitude stability or change is a consequence, or outcome, of the effects of knowledge and feelings on reception of new information (i.e., attention to and comprehension of it) and then on evaluation of what is received.[2] In addition,

---

[2]We do not argue that influence will always proceed according to these sequential steps. Research on preference judgments suggests that simple preferences for people as well as nonhuman stimuli sometimes form in the absence of conscious attention to and recognition of the stimulus object (Bornstein, 1989; Zajonc, 1980). Thus the stages we identify in information processing may occur simultaneously or may, under some conditions, occur in a different sequence than specified in the present chapter.

we will consider how, given minimal knowledge and ability to process message content, new information can be evaluated based on simple, relatively low effort decision rules, or cognitive heuristics (Chaiken, Liberman, & Eagly, 1989).

KNOWLEDGE AND INFORMATION PROCESSING ABILITY

Knowledge Enhances Reception: Objective Processing

The desire of knowledge, like the thirst of riches, increases ever with the acquisition of it. (Stern, 1760)

For topics on which people do not have strong attitudes, knowledge facilitates objective, unbiased reception of new information. Reception processes refer to both attention and comprehension. Thus, the expert medical researchers in the debate at the beginning of this chapter are more likely than the uninformed viewers to seek out and attend to new material on the debate topic and are more likely to understand its significance for the broader issue. The link between knowledge and reception has been noted in many areas of investigation. For example, in the study of mass persuasion, greater political awareness, as indexed by interest in politics and general factual knowledge about the political system, is thought to be associated with greater exposure to and understanding of campaign messages (Converse, 1970; Zaller, 1987, 1989). The effect of knowledge on reception is illustrated in the top left panel of the information processing model presented in Fig. 11.1. We speculate that knowledge not only facilitates overall reception, but also has directive effects. That is, given attitude issues associated with minimal affect and an unbiased orientation to new information, knowledgeable people are likely to selectively attend to and comprehend information that promises to provide especially valid, truthful insight into the issue. Their expertise allows them to distinguish the useful from less useful material.

Knowledge affects message reception for a variety of reasons. In the political realm, high levels of accurate knowledge about the political system are thought to be an aspect of cognitive engagement. According to Converse (1962), "There is a strong correlation between the mass of stored political information and the motivation to monitor communication systems for additional current information" (p. 586). In addition, knowledge is linked to reception because it enhances one's ability to attend to and comprehend new information. The practice and learning associated with the acquisition of knowledge facilitates processing of domain-relevant material (see Kahneman, 1973; Norman, 1976; Posner, 1982). Thus, knowledgeable people need to allocate less mental effort to attend to and encode topic-relevant information than people with minimal knowledge. The effects of knowledge on reception may also stem from motivational factors; to the extent that recipients can assess their own abilities to attend to and comprehend the message, knowledge will affect information acquisition through self-efficacy

Knowledge and objective processing:	Knowledge and biased processing:
Given minimal affect toward attitude object, knowledge enhances validity seeking.	Given intense affect toward attitude object, knowledge enhances ability to defend/bolster existing attitude.

Implications for processing

Greater knowledge enhances **reception**, especially of valid information. Lesser knowledge reduces reception.	Greater knowledge enhances biased **reception**: Greater attention to and comprehension of information supporting than challenging initial attitudes. Lesser knowledge reduces reception of all information.
Greater knowledge enhances objective, **critical evaluation** of new information. Lesser knowledge reduces critical evaluation.	Greater knowledge enhances biased **critical evaluation**: Greater favorability to information supporting than challenging initial attitudes. Lesser knowledge reduces critical evaluation.
Lesser knowledge enhances reliance on **heuristic cues**.	Lesser knowledge enhances selective reliance on **heuristic cues**: Greater use of cues supporting than challenging initial attitudes.

Implications for attitude change

Extensive knowledge typically associated with minimal change because of high critical evaluation, but change greater when processing is dependent on reception rather than evaluation, when message content is evaluated as valid, or when heuristic cues imply validity.	**Extensive knowledge** typically associated with minimal change because of biased reception and evaluation.
Minimal knowledge associated with considerable change with positive heuristic cues and minimal change with negative cues.	**Minimal knowledge** typically associated with minimal change because of selective use of heuristic cues.

FIG. 11.1.   Stages in processing incoming information and attitude change as a function of knowledgeability on topics eliciting intense or moderate affect.

beliefs (Chaiken, Liberman, & Eagly, 1989). That is, less knowledgeable people may not attempt to attend to and interpret a message because they judge they have insufficient basis for doing so, whereas knowledgeable people may not be hindered by such self-doubts. The motivation of those with low knowledge may additionally be sapped by frustration and other negative emotions generated by the lack of success achieved when attempting to attend to and interpret the message (Eagly, 1974; Eagly & Warren, 1976).

Initial, suggestive evidence for the prediction that knowledge drives information acquisition has been provided by research correlating initial knowledge levels on political issues with later reports of media use and news exposure (e.g., Atkin, Galloway, & Nayman, 1976; McCombs & Mullins, 1973). To provide more direct evidence that knowledge promotes attention to and comprehension of new information, we conducted a meta-analytic review of our own past research that measured highly knowledgeable and less knowledgeable subjects' reception of arguments presented in a persuasive message. Meta-analysis is a statistical reviewing technique in which the outcomes of separate studies are combined to yield an estimate of an effect across a whole body of literature (Hedges & Olkin, 1985). In the reviewed research, subjects' working knowledge was assessed in a preliminary experimental session. During the experiment, subjects read a persuasive appeal on the issue of preservation of the environment. Reception was assessed in terms of accuracy at an unannounced free-recall task at the end of the session, in which subjects wrote down all of the message arguments they could remember. The recall findings of the studies were first converted to standardized mean differences (ds), representing the mean number of arguments recalled by knowledgeable subjects minus the mean recalled by less knowledgeable ones, divided by the common standard deviation. The effects were then weighted by the inverse of the variance associated with each estimate (a technique that gives the larger samples, representing the more precisely estimated effects, the greatest weight), and combined (see Table 11.1). As anticipated, for counterattitudinal messages knowledgeable subjects recalled more message arguments than less knowledgeable ones. Furthermore, the nonsignificant homogeneity test ($Q = 2.87$, ns) suggested that the effects were drawn from a common population. Thus, the apparent variability across effect sizes can be attributed to random error and does not require substantive interpretation. Little evidence was available concerning recall of arguments in proattitudinal messages, but the available data suggest a less pronounced recall difference between high and low knowledge recipients for this type of appeal.

TABLE 11.1
Relation Between Knowledge and Recall of Message Arguments

	Effect Size (d) and 95% Confidence Interval			
	Counterattitudinal Messages	N of Subjects	Proattitudinal Messages	N of Subjects
Wood (1982)	0.44 (−0.05/0.94)	65		
Wood, Kallgren, & Preisler (1985)	0.52 (0.08/0.97)	120		
Wood & Kallgren (1988)	0.52 (0.05/1.00)	105		
Biek, Wood, Nations, & Chaiken (1993)				
Experiment 1	1.06 (0.11/2.02)	20	−0.35 (−0.95/0.25)	26
Experiment 2	0.17 (−0.36/0.69)	56	0.09 (−0.40/0.58)	53
Mean overall effect	0.47 (0.23/0.70)			

Note. Positive numbers represent greater recall of arguments by high knowledge than low knowledge recipients. Negative numbers represent greater recall by low than high knowledge recipients.

In general, the facilitative effects of knowledge on reception for counterattitudinal messages support our argument that knowledgeable people have greater ability and higher motivation to attend to and comprehend message arguments than less knowledgeable ones. However, the free recall measure used in this research, like other measures of argument retention (e.g., recognition accuracy), is not an ideal indicator of reception processes. As Eagly and Chaiken (1984, 1993) argue, retention not only involves encoding and interpreting the information in messages, which are the components of reception, but also involves integrating this with the information already in memory and finally retrieving it during the recall or recognition test. Thus it is unclear whether the effects of knowledge on recall stem from reception, integration, or retrieval processes. To assess the effects of knowledge on reception more directly than is possible with retention measures, we recently conducted a study examining the effects of knowledge on selective attention to persuasive messages (Agans et al., 1992).

To measure attention in a context that simulates the multiple processing demands typical of real life settings, we adapted a procedure traditionally used in studies of selective exposure (Cotton, 1985; Frey, 1986). Subjects were told that we were interested in how people read newspaper and magazine articles in everyday contexts. They were seated at a computer terminal and given the option of reading an editorial on the critical attitude topic, preservation of the environment, or reading a "humor column," actually adapted from a newspaper column by Dave Barry. The attitude-relevant message opposed subjects' opinions and was labeled "Editorial Against Preservation of the Environment." The environmental message, like the humor column, was written in an easily comprehended style. Subjects chose to read either the preservation editorial, the humor column, chose to read both, or to read neither, and they read them at their own pace.

Selective attention was measured from the article that subjects chose to read first (or the only article they read), as well as the percentage of time subjects devoted to reading the environmental article given their total reading time (i.e., including the humor column). Because knowledgeable people are cognitively engaged in the issue and motivated to obtain new information about it, they were expected to attend relatively closely to the preservation message. Indeed, knowledgeable people, in comparison to less knowledgeable ones, were marginally more likely to select the environmental article to read first and they devoted a significantly greater percentage of their reading time to this article. Thus, greater knowledge was associated with a stronger tendency to seek out and attend to fresh material relevant to the knowledge base, in comparison to unrelated material.

In this study, reading time and choice of article reflected selective attention to the environmental article over an alternative reading choice. This positive relation between knowledge and selective attention is all the more noteworthy given that knowledgeable people would be expected to be especially efficient at learning and mastering the content of relevant information. Indeed, in contexts emphasizing learning speed, knowledgeable people may be faster, more proficient readers than less knowledgeable ones. In contexts like our experiment, however, in which reading time is an indicator of interest in and willingness to attend to and think about an issue (vs. other, distracting material), knowledge has a positive relation to reading time. In general, the findings of our meta-analysis of earlier research on message retention and our more recent experimental work on selective attention provide convergent evidence that existing levels of working knowledge enhance attention to new information.

Attention to new material is an initial stage by which people maintain or change their attitudes in response to fresh information. For this new information to affect attitudes, recipients should also understand or comprehend the material attended to and then evaluate the material by establishing links with existing knowledge and feelings. Given the extensive research, especially in cognitive and educational psychology, suggesting that new material is useful to the extent that a recipient is sufficiently prepared to receive it, we will not discuss here the processes by which knowledge facilitates comprehension (see also Eagly, 1974; Eagly & Warren, 1976). In the next section of the chapter, we consider the implications of knowledge for evaluation of new material once it is received.

Knowledge and Evaluation of Messages: Objective Processing

Knowledge is apparent not only in the affirmation of what is true, but in the negation of what is false. Charles Caleb Colton (1825)

Evaluation of new information consists of affirming, favorable reactions as well as negating, unfavorable reactions. Evaluation is comparable to what has traditionally been labeled *yielding* or *resisting* processes in influence. No direct measures of yielding were identified in early tests of sequential influence models. Instead, yielding processes were inferred from attitude scores after exposure to the persuasive material, in particular from the discrepancy between obtained and predicted attitude change (predicted on the basis of level of retention and the overall correlation between retention and opinion change, McGuire, 1968).

Evaluation processes can be directly assessed from the favorability of recipients' cognitive responses to new information. According to the heuristic/systematic model (HSM, Chaiken, 1980; Chaiken, Liberman, & Eagly, 1989) and the elaboration likelihood model (ELM, Petty & Cacioppo, 1986a, 1986b; Petty, Unnava, & Strathman, 1991), cognitive responses can reflect critical, careful evaluations of the central content of new information, indicative of systematic or central processing, or can reflect reliance on simple evaluative decision rules, or cognitive heuristics, such as "people agree with those they like." In this section, we consider how extensive knowledge enables detailed evaluation of the content of new information, and in a later section we consider how limited knowledge promotes reliance on heuristic rules.

As indicated in the left panel of Fig. 11.1, knowledge confers the ability and motivation to evaluate the content of persuasive messages and other new information. As the figure suggests, for attitude topics associated with extensive working knowledge but minimal affect, little motivation exists for biased processing to maintain existing views. On such issues, knowledgeable people are experts at assessing the validity, or cogency, of new information. Knowledge affects evaluation for several reasons. The beliefs and experiences knowledgeable people retrieve from memory provide a basis for evaluating new material. Existing knowledge provides a standard from which to detect the strengths and weaknesses of incoming information. In contrast, people with minimal knowledge do not possess the informational background necessary to distinguish strong, valid information from that which is weaker and less valid. In addition to greater ability, knowledge may also be associated with greater motivation to critically evaluate new information. If knowledgeable people believe they have greater capacity to evaluate the message than less knowledgeable ones, they may be more likely to attempt to do so. Furthermore, they may be less likely to experience frustration and other negative emotions that can deter critical analysis. Thus, for ability and motivational reasons, knowledgeable recipients should be more likely to critically evaluate the content of new information than less knowledgeable people.[3]

Several experiments have suggested that recipients' knowledge affects the extent to which they critically evaluate the content of an influence appeal (Biek et al., 1993; Wood, 1982; Wood & Kallgren, 1988; Wood et al., 1985). For example, Wood et al. (1985) measured subjects' working knowledge and opinions on the topic of preservation of the environment in an initial experimental session. One week later, subjects read a persuasive message containing strong, cogent arguments or weak, specious ones advocating a position opposed to preservation. The study also manipulated message length, and the effects of this variable are discussed later in the section of the chapter on heuristic processing. As expected, the cognitive responses or thoughts of subjects while reading the message indicated that knowledge enabled extensive critical evaluation: Knowledgeable subjects reported having a greater number of critical, negative thoughts than less knowledgeable ones and, as illustrated in Table 11.2, they indicated a greater number of thoughts concerning the content of the message than less knowledgeable ones. This pattern of findings provides nice support for the model depicted in Fig. 11.1, in which knowledgeable people possess the ability and motivation

---

[3]As Petty and Cacioppo (1986a) argue, knowledge can fill a variety of additional roles in message evaluation. For example, knowledge may feature as a message argument when a persuasive message contains a reference to knowledge as an argument in the appeal (e.g., claiming that knowledgeable people are more likely to endorse the message position than less knowledgeable ones). Alternately, simple decision rules to accept or reject the message (Chaiken, 1980) might be based on knowledge; people who believe themselves knowledgeable might reject an appeal because they think they already possess substantial support for their own judgment, rendering further consideration of the topic unnecessary.

TABLE 11.2

Evaluations of the Message and Postopinions on Preservation of the Environment (from Wood, Kallgren, & Preisler, 1985)

	Low Knowledge				High Knowledge			
	Strong Message		Weak Message		Strong Message		Weak Message	
	Long Message	Short Message	Long Message	Short Message	Long Message	Short Message	Long Message	Short Message
Global thoughts about message	1.17	1.70	1.99	1.68	1.60	1.33	0.84	1.79
Content-specific thoughts about message	0.81	1.30	0.64	0.93	1.85	1.26	1.73	1.37
Adjusted postopinions	4.92	3.59	5.86	4.21	4.01	3.95	2.93	2.76

Note. Higher numbers represent greater number of thoughts and, for postopinions, greater change toward the anti-preservation message. Postopinions are adjusted on the basis of preopinions on the message topic.

to engage in more extensive critical evaluation of the content of new information, in comparison to less knowledgeable ones.

Objective Processing and Openness or Resistance to Influence

Reception and Attitude Change: Objective Processing.   The extent to which people receive and evaluate incoming information has implications for attitude change (see bottom left panel of Fig. 11.1). When attitude change requires attending to and understanding the content of a message, then knowledge should facilitate change. Because the highly knowledgeable participants in our medical research debate can attend to and comprehend technical details of arguments, they may be persuaded by such material to change their attitudes. We speculate that knowledgeable people will be especially likely to change their views due to heightened reception when attitudes are based directly on the message content received, and little evaluation of this material occurs. For example, if message content is encoded veridically in memory without evaluation (cf. Mackie & Asuncion, 1990), or people are distracted from evaluation, then knowledgeable people, who receive more content, should be more influenced by the message than less knowledgeable ones.

In contrast, when recipients have only limited knowledge about an attitude issue, they should be able to receive only a limited amount of difficult material, and their attitudes may be relatively impervious to change. Indeed, survey research linking political knowledge with the stability of political attitudes has yielded a pattern supporting this idea. People with minimal knowledge tend to be extremely stable in their opinions, presumably because they do not receive the details of most messages and are not exposed to information that might challenge their beliefs (Converse, 1962; Zaller, 1987, 1989, 1990).

Evaluation and Attitude Change: Objective Processing.   In many contexts, however, opinion change is not simply a function of reception, but also varies with evaluation of what has been received. Considering the effects of knowledge on evaluation leads to very different attitude change predictions than outlined in the preceding section on reception. Because knowledgeable people can use their considerable information base to detect weaknesses in all but the strongest, most compelling appeals, they are likely to resist change. Less knowledgeable people are easier to influence because they are less able to identify deficiencies in new information. Evaluation rather than reception is especially likely to be important in the standard psychology influence experiment, given the typically few distractions for subjects' attention and the easily understood text (cf. Eagly & Chaiken, 1993). Thus, when everyone can receive the new information and influence is dependent on evaluation, knowledgeable (vs. less knowledgeable) people tend to have more stable attitudes because they can resist change to all but the most cogently reasoned new material.

The pattern of opinion change findings from the Wood et al. (1985) study presented in Table 11.2 is consistent with the idea that evaluation mediates the link between knowledge and attitude change; knowledgeable recipients proved to be more influenced by the message containing strong rather than weak arguments, whereas recipients with low knowledge tended to be influenced by both weak and strong messages. Furthermore, additional analyses on the processes underlying change revealed that, for knowledgeable but not unknowledgeable people, greater attitude change was associated with greater numbers of positively valenced thoughts concerning details of message content (e.g., thoughts such as, "It's true that preservation is expensive").

However, these findings do not reveal the exact nature of the evaluation process underlying the resistance to change associated with extensive knowledge. Although we have argued that, in the absence of intense affective reactions toward an attitude topic, knowledgeable people are expert *objective* processors of attitude-relevant information, we have no direct evidence of objectivity. It remains possible that the knowledgeable people in our research resisted change because they evaluated new information in a biased manner (Petty & Cacioppo, 1986a). In this research, bias would be represented by a correspondence between the advocated position and recipients' evaluation of the message as compelling or not. Biased resistance, as a tendency to evaluate new information in a directional manner that supports initial attitudes, thus can be detected from more favorable evaluation of congenial messages than challenging ones. Knowledge might facilitate biased, defensive evaluation because knowledgeable (vs. less knowledgeable) people are better able to identify weaknesses in opposing views while generating additional supportive data for congenial perspectives. Because our early research used only counterattitudinal messages (i.e., Wood, 1982; Wood & Kallgren, 1988; Wood et al., 1985), it does not indicate whether the critical evaluation and resistance to change associated with high knowledge is best characterized by a biased or by an objective orientation.

We recently conducted a series of experiments designed to examine directly the objective versus biased nature of message evaluation. Biek et al. (1993) presented knowledgeable and less knowledgeable subjects with a message on the issue of preservation of the environment that either opposed subjects' views, or were generally compatible with them. As we noted at the beginning of the chapter, our college students tended to rate this issue as invoking only moderate affect. The counterattitudinal message argued against preservation whereas the proattitudinal messages supported environmental causes. The proattitudinal messages were constructed so that they advocated positions either slightly less extreme than subjects' own (Biek et al., 1993, Study 1) or slightly more extreme (Study 2). In addition, the messages were of moderate strength so that recipients were not constrained to generate only favorable or unfavorable evaluations. If knowledge is associated with objective criticality, then knowledgeable subjects should unfavorably evaluate and resist the moderately strong messages, whether proattitudinal or counterattitudinal. If knowledge is associated with a biased orientation, then knowledgeable subjects should respond more favorably to the pro- than counterattitudinal message. In both accounts, less knowledgeable subjects should respond favorably to both messages.

The findings strongly confirmed that knowledge on issues like preservation of the environment confers an objectively critical processing orientation indicative of validity seeking. In both experiments, knowledgeable subjects (when their opinions were compared with no-message control groups) proved resistant to both the proattitudinal messages congruent with their views as well as the counterattitudinal message that opposed their views. Low knowledge subjects were more readily influenced by both pro- and counterattitudinal messages and demonstrated significant opinion change when compared with no-message control subjects. Furthermore, analyses on recipients' thoughts while reading the message revealed that knowledgeable recipients generated more counterarguments to proattitudinal and counterattitudinal messages than did less knowledgeable ones. These findings are consistent with the data from Table 11.2 indicating that knowledgeable subjects resist all but the most cogently argued persuasive appeals (Wood et al., 1985). Thus, it appears that subjects knowledgeable about preservation engaged in a dispassionate, objective evaluation of the validity of new information rather than a biased analysis designed to defend their existing attitudes.

In summary, then, knowledgeability can facilitate attitude change to new information through heightened reception of the material or can attenuate attitude change (to all but highly cogent, well-reasoned information) through increased critical evaluation. Knowledge thus has a variety of effects on influence when people are objective processors, depending on the relative importance of the reception and evaluation mediators. In the next section of this chapter we consider how knowledge affects these mediating processes and influence when people are motivated to maintain strong attitudes. Finally, we present a broad model that specifies how reception and evaluation combine in their effects on influence.

WORKING KNOWLEDGE AS A CONTRIBUTOR
TO ATTITUDE STRENGTH

The only fence against the world is a thorough knowledge of it. (Locke, 1693)

People do not always use knowledge in the objective, dispassionate search for truth described in the preceding section. As we have already argued, knowledge can also contribute to the biased resistance processes that maintain strong attitudes. When people feel intensely about an attitude issue, their attitudes have strong, potent effects on reactions to new information. Knowledgeable people holding such strong attitudes are able to process the details of incoming information in a way that bolsters and protects their initial judgment. Less knowledgeable people with strong attitudes are not able to draw on an extensive information base and cannot process details of new material in a way that maintains their views.

The defensive orientation associated with strong attitudes is likely to direct reactions to new information at each stage of information processing. As illustrated in the right panel of Fig. 11.1, a biased orientation has implications for reception of new information, evaluation of it, and eventual attitude change or stability.

Knowledge and Reception: Defensive Processing. At the reception stage, we speculate that knowledgeable people with intense affective reactions to the attitude issue will not attend equally to all information. Consider the highly knowledgeable medical researchers participating in the debate at the beginning of the chapter. If an issue is associated with intense affect for the debate participants and their attitudes are strong, they are likely to attend selectively to the discussion in order to garner evidence for weaknesses in the opposing view and strengths in their own. The relatively less knowledgeable viewers may have strong attitudes but they will be less effective at discriminating when to attend and when not to attend to new material in order to maintain their views.

Although evidence for selective exposure to maintain and bolster a favored opinion or decision has been inconsistent in experimental research in social psychology, directed attention and exposure appears most likely when people are highly committed to a decision or position (Cotton, 1985; Frey, 1986; Kunda, 1990). For example, during the extensively broadcast Senate hearings of the Watergate affair in the 1970s, committed supporters of then President Nixon reported less attention to and interest in media reports than nonaligned, uncommitted voters (Sweeney & Gruber, 1984). In contrast, voters who had supported McGovern rather than Nixon in the previous election reported greater attention to and interest in the hearings than nonaligned voters. Not surprisingly, comprehension and knowledge of the incident were also affected by voters' favored positions. McGovern supporters indicated greater factual knowledge of the affair than the nonaligned group, who in turn knew more than the Nixon supporters. In general, we speculate that when attitudes are strong, knowledgeable people will be especially adept at avoiding challenging information and at seeking out supportive material. People who feel strongly about an issue but are less knowledgeable may be less proficient at selectively receiving new information; their lack of knowledge leaves them without an informed guide to negotiate the various attacking and supportive pieces of information they are exposed to during the course of a typical day.

Knowledge and Elaboration: Defensive Processing. As indicated in the right panel of Fig. 11.1, knowledgeable people with intense feelings may not only be biased receivers of new information but also may evaluate new infor-

mation in a way that is congenial with their initial views. Fortunately, we have
direct empirical evidence for this prediction concerning biased evaluation. Biek
et al. (in press) directly examined the relations among affective intensity, knowledge, and evaluation of new material. In the study, college students' working
knowledge and affective intensity were assessed with regard to personal AIDS
risk. Affective intensity was measured by having subjects rate their feelings about
their personal risk for contracting AIDS on a series of 7-point bipolar scales
(e.g., angry, afraid). One week later, subjects read a series of (actually hypothetical) findings from research studies, some of which suggested that the AIDS risk
of various sexual behaviors for college students is very low, indicating little need
for preventive measures, and others that it is very high, suggesting considerable
need for prevention (a procedure adapted from Lord, Ross, & Lepper, 1979).
Subjects rated their agreement with each finding and then indicated their thoughts
while reading the experimental results.

As expected, only subjects with strong attitudes, as indicated by intense affect,
used their knowledge in detailed, biased processing of the research evidence.
That is, to the extent high affect/high knowledge subjects were favorable toward
AIDS risk prevention, they agreed more with the studies indicating high risk for
AIDS than those indicating low risk. Furthermore, this processing bias was
manifest in subjects' evaluations of the various experimental findings. Subjects
with attitudes derived from intense affect and considerable knowledge generated
greater numbers of favorable thoughts and fewer unfavorable thoughts to studies
congruent with their initial attitudes toward AIDS risk than to studies opposing
their attitudes. Interestingly, when affect was less intense and thus attitudes were
not strong, knowledge did not enable biased processing. Subjects with minimal
or moderate affect and high knowledge did not show any tendency to respond
more favorably to studies congenial with (vs. discrepant from) their initial
attitudes. This finding replicates earlier research with the topic of preservation
of the environment (Biek et al., 1993) and provides direct evidence for a central
argument in this chapter: Knowledge contributes to the biasing, defensive effects
associated with strong attitudes when the attitude issue generates intense affect.
When affect is minimal, knowledge enables objective and not biased processing
of the details of incoming information.

In addition, Biek et al. (in press) found no evidence of biased processing by
subjects low in knowledge and high in affect concerning AIDS prevention or by
those low in both knowledge and affect. Although it may seem surprising that
intense affect alone was not sufficient to instigate biased processing, it is important to keep in mind that high affect/low knowledge subjects were limited in
cognitive support of any kind for their attitude judgments. Their minimal information base would have rendered it difficult to evaluate the studies in a biased
manner; they could not selectively support experimental results congenial with
(vs. opposed to) their views. However, as we discuss in the following section
on heuristic processing, for attitude issues that elicit intense affect but minimal

knowledge, people may engage in forms of biased processing that do not require careful, directed evaluation of message content.

In summary, the overall pattern of findings from Biek et al.'s (in press) research is indicative of an interaction between knowledge and affective intensity. Knowledgeable people motivated to defend their attitudes by the possession of strong affect were biased in their evaluation of new information. They responded more favorably to material supporting their views than to material opposing them. Knowledgeable people with minimal affect surrounding their opinions were not driven to defensive processing of the new information and instead appeared to evaluate it in the relatively objective manner associated with a validity-seeking orientation.

Reception and Attitude Change: Defensive Processing. As illustrated in the bottom right panel in Fig. 11.1, the effects of knowledge on reception and evaluation have implications for attitude stability. That is, the biased processing of new information that characterizes knowledgeable people with intense affect generates stable attitudes resistant to change. The effect of biased reception on subsequent attitudes was suggested in the aforementioned study on reactions to the Watergate incident (Sweeney & Gruber, 1984). The biased reception that apparently accompanied strong attitudes, with supporters of President Nixon avoiding information relevant to the incident and supporters of McGovern seeking out relevant information, resulted in remarkably stable attitudes in these two groups. However, the nonaligned, uncommitted voters, who appeared to be moderately exposed to the information indicting Nixon, changed to be less favorable toward both Republicans and Nixon across the 2-month period of the study. We speculate that the biased reception associated with high levels of knowledge paired with high affect bolsters and protects people's initial attitudes, much like the committed voters in Sweeney and Gruber's (1984) research.

Evaluation and Attitude Change: Defensive Processing. Attitude stability also results from knowledgeable people's biased evaluation of the information received (see bottom right panel of Fig. 11.1). According to Converse (1962, 1964), the highly stable opinions characteristic of political partisans can be attributed to their biased, directional evaluation of new information; despite the considerable exposure to new political ideas that likely accompanies high political involvement and knowledgeability, such individuals appear to maintain their attitudes through favorable evaluation of supportive material and derogation of challenging information. Although survey investigations of political attitudes have provided little direct evidence of the hypothesized reception and evaluation mediators, surveys documenting the stability of attitudes over time are consistent with the idea that biased reception and evaluation of new information generates stability among those highly involved in politics (e.g., Zaller, 1987). We speculate that, when attitudes are strong, the biased reception and evaluation of knowledgeable (vs. less knowledgeable) people will serve to maintain existing attitudes and dispositions.

HEURISTIC EVALUATION OF MESSAGES

Knowledge is of two kinds: we know a subject ourselves, or we know where we can find information upon it. Samuel Johnson (1775)

In addition to directly processing the content of new information themselves, people may seek out and base their attitude judgments on other cues or sources of informed opinion. In past research (Chaiken, 1980; Chaiken et al., 1989), message recipients have been presented with a variety of noncontent cues that potentially provide information about the message, including the attributes of the communicator (e.g., likability, credibility) and structural features of the message itself (use of statistics, lengthy arguments). These noncontent cues are relatively easy to receive. When such easily received cues are linked to acceptance or rejection of new information in people's implicit theories (e.g., the supposed untrustworthiness of communicators with shifty eyes), then evaluation of new material can be based on these simple theories, or cognitive heuristics.

As illustrated in Fig. 11.1, low knowledge recipients should be especially likely to rely on heuristic processing strategies. Their limited attention, comprehension, and evaluation concerning the details of new information makes it difficult for them to base acceptance on the quality of message content, and renders them especially dependent on easily received cues. In addition, to the extent that low knowledge people are aware of their processing limitations, they may self-consciously direct their attention to heuristic cues in order to avoid frustration and likely failure at interpreting the confusing-seeming message content. Furthermore, to the extent that low knowledge people are concerned with cognitive economy in judgments, they are likely to rely on heuristic and other relatively efficient evaluation strategies.[4]

Several studies have provided support for the idea that low knowledge recipients are more likely to rely on heuristic processing strategies than knowledgeable ones (Wood & Kallgren, 1988; Wood et al., 1985). For example, the study by Wood et al. mentioned earlier, which manipulated the strength of the arguments in a message against preservation of the environment, also varied a heuristic cue, the length of the appeal. The long and short versions of the messages were identical except for the amount of detail provided concerning each argument. As can been seen in Table 11.2 presented earlier in this chapter, less knowledgeable

---

[4]Although low knowledge may generally preclude systematic or central analysis of the message, high knowledge does not necessarily preclude heuristic analyses (cf. Chaiken, Liberman, & Eagly, 1989). Heuristic analyses may proceed simultaneously with systematic evaluation of the message, and may at times augment or replace these content evaluations.

recipients showed greater attitude change to long than short messages, consistent with the idea that they were relying on the heuristic "message length implies strength." Message length had little impact on persuasion for knowledgeable subjects. Subjects' cognitive responses further indicated that low knowledge subjects were relying on a heuristic strategy in evaluating the message. That is, they generated a higher number of general, global thoughts about the message and fewer specific thoughts about details of message content than high knowledge subjects. Correlational analyses linking influence to mediators of change further revealed that, for recipients with minimal knowledge, a greater percentage of global, noncontent-oriented message thoughts favorable toward the advocated position (such as, e.g., "I agreed with what he said") tended to be associated with greater influence (although this relation did not achieve significance).

Source attributes can also serve as cues in heuristic processing. In a study by Wood and Kallgren (1988), again using the preservation topic, message recipients with little knowledge followed the rule, "expert sources can be trusted," and proved to be more persuaded by expert than nonexpert communicators. Similarly, following the rule, "people agree with those they like," low knowledge recipients proved to be more persuaded by likable than unlikable communicators. Furthermore, correlational analyses to evaluate mediators of opinion change suggested that for low knowledge recipients, greater numbers of positive than negative communicator-oriented thoughts enhanced attitude change (Wood & Kallgren, 1988).

Although our findings with preservation of the environment, a topic on which most subjects have only minimal or moderate affect, suggest that heuristic processing is used objectively to evaluate the validity of new information, it may also play a role in biased evaluations of the message. When attitudes are strong, people may bolster and protect existing views through heuristic analyses (Chaiken et al., 1989). Heuristic processors highly motivated to hold valid opinions are likely to rely on cues that will maximize this goal by, for example, seeking out and favorably evaluating the opinions of experts or the conclusions of scholarly research articles. Alternately, heuristic processors motivated to maintain existing views may selectively rely on cues likely to yield supportive information. For example, Republicans may evaluate a proposed social policy by basing their support on endorsement by a well-known conservative commentator, such as William F. Buckley, with little understanding of the details of the proposal itself. Democrats with limited understanding of the proposal might base their attitudes on the opinions of another expert, such as Ted Kennedy.

Thus, people with little knowledge will not always be protected from new information by their minimal reception of message content. When heuristic cues are available and recipients' attention is sufficient to reveal the main contours of the appeal, recipients may change their opinions through heuristic processing strategies. Messages accompanied by positive (i.e., influence-enhancing) cues may be highly influential for recipients with little knowledge of the message topic. In addition, given a choice of cues, people may selectively rely on those that meet their processing goals. When concerned with obtaining a valid opinion, people may be especially sensitive to cues that imply high or low validity, and when concerned with maintaining a strong attitude, people may selectively rely on cues that defend and bolster existing views.

MODELING ATTITUDE STABILITY AND CHANGE: DEFENSIVE VERSUS OBJECTIVE PROCESSING

Previous modeling approaches to attitude stability and change have typically relied on the outcome pattern of attitude change findings to provide insight into mediating processes (McGuire, 1968; Rhodes & Wood, 1992; Zaller, 1987, 1989). In particular, an inverted-U-shaped relation between recipient attributes, such as knowledge, and change in attitudes has been taken as evidence for reception and evaluation processes as mediators of attitude change. That is, a finding of minimal attitude change for individuals low in knowledge would be indicative of their limited reception of new information. A finding of minimal attitude change for individuals high in knowledge would be indicative of their extensive critical evaluation of new information. A finding of greater attitude change for people with middle levels of knowledge (vs. low or high) would be indicative of these individuals receiving moderate amounts of new information and having only moderate motivation and ability to critically evaluate and reject it.

Although past research reviews have been notably successful at identifying this inverted-U pattern across diverse recipient attributes and research literatures (e.g., Rhodes & Wood, 1992; Zaller, 1987), we speculate that the exact relation between attributes such as knowledge and attitude change outcomes will vary depending on a variety of factors, including recipients' processing goals and resulting objective versus defensive processing of new material as well as the strength or cogency of the influence appeal. Knowledge can confer objective ability to process information when people are oriented toward validity seeking or can enable biased processing to protect and bolster existing views. For objective processing of weak or moderately strong messages, we would indeed expect the inverted-U-shaped relation between knowledge and attitude change to emerge. However, when objectively processing strong, cogent arguments, even knowledgeable people are likely to react favorably and change their views, thus generating a positive linear relation between knowledge and influence (cf. Wood et al., 1985). Alternately, when an issue elicits intense affect and attitudes are strong, knowledgeable people are likely to demonstrate resistance to opposing views through biased reception and biased evaluation processes. If knowledge enhances effectiveness at defensive processing of message content, an inverse relation between knowledge and attitude change may obtain, with knowledgeable people demonstrating the least change.

The predictions of sequential models of influence become even more complex when we recognize the possibility of attitude change through heuristic analyses.

Heuristic processing provides an avenue for change in attitudes despite limited ability to receive and evaluate the central features of new information. Thus, people with little attitude-relevant information, who may be unable to receive or evaluate much new information, may respond favorably and change their opinions when the novel information is associated with easily received positive heuristic cues (e.g., likable source, endorsement of message by valued others). Thus, low levels of knowledge may be associated with greater opinion change than specified by predictive models that emphasize processing of message content.

SUMMARY AND CONCLUSIONS

In this chapter we considered how knowledge contributes to the closed-minded, defensive orientation to new information characteristic of strong attitudes. Attitudes built on considerable affect and extensive working knowledge direct and organize the processing of new information in a way that maintains the original views. These strong attitudes bias the processing of new, attitude-relevant information, so that supportive information is more likely to be received and to be favorably evaluated than opposing information. The closed-minded orientation associated with strong attitudes shields them against change.

We also considered how knowledge enables objective, dispassionate processing of new information. When an attitude issue is associated with minimal affect and attitudes are not especially strong, knowledge enhances the ability to conduct a critical, objective analysis of new information relevant to the issue. For attitudes built on extensive knowledge and minimal affect, people are expert information processors oriented to attaining accurate views. In this case, knowledge enhances the ability to receive new information and to critically evaluate its strength, with more favorable evaluations accorded to stronger, more cogent arguments regardless of their congruency with people's existing views. An objective processing orientation renders the attitudes of knowledgeable people susceptible to change from valid, cogent appeals.

We also speculated that attitudes built on minimal attitude-relevant knowledge but intense affect can be characterized as strong because they are likely to direct processing to defend existing views. Although minimal knowledge limits the ability to receive and evaluate the details of new information, biased processing may take the form of selective use of heuristic rules, or simple guides to message acceptance or rejection. Strong attitudes derived from high affect but low knowledge may be maintained through reliance on cues, such as communicator attributes or structural features of the message, that suggest support for congenial perspectives and rejection of opposing views. This biased processing and closed-minded orientation again shields attitudes from change.

Finally, for attitude issues associated with minimal knowledge and limited affect, people are not likely to be expert information processors or to be motivated to defend their views. For such issues, people may be concerned primarily with cognitive economy in judgments; they are likely to employ relatively effortless, efficient strategies to evaluate new information, such as relying on easy-to-receive heuristic cues. Influence should be a function of the heuristic cues associated with new information. Messages associated with positive cues are likely to be favorably evaluated and influential whereas those associated with negative cues are likely to be unfavorably evaluated and not successful at generating influence.

From the perspective of attitude strength, we have argued that knowledge affects the form of the resistance processes associated with strong attitudes: with extensive knowledge, resistance is generated through biased processing of the details of the new information (i.e., biased reception and evaluation); and with minimal knowledge resistance occurs through less demanding strategies, such as biased use of heuristic cues. We speculate that, in addition to affect intensity, a variety of affect- and motivation-related qualities, including extremity of attitudes (Judd & Brauer, ch. 3, this volume) and vested interest (Crano, ch. 6, this volume), may confer strength-related biased processing and resistance. Similarly, working knowledge may be but one example of a variety of informational and structural features of attitudes. The form of the resistance effects associated with strong attitudes may depend on these other informational and structural properties in much the same manner as we have outlined with knowledge. For example, greater amounts of direct experience with an attitude object and greater consistency between an attitude and relevant cognitions in memory might provide an informational basis enhancing expertise at reception and evaluation of new information. From this perspective, then, attitude strength is not a unitary construct associated with a single structural property or feature (cf. Krosnick, Boninger, Chuang, Berent, & Carnot, 1993) and strong attitudes can be bolstered and protected through a variety of information-processing mechanisms.

ACKNOWLEDGMENTS

Preparation of this chapter was supported by a grant to Wendy Wood from the National Institute of Mental Health (#MH49895-01) and a research fellowship to Michael Biek from the College of Liberal Arts, Texas A&M University. Michael Biek is now at Jury Analysts, State College, Pennsylvania.

REFERENCES

Abelson, R. P. (1988). Conviction. *American Psychologist, 43*, 267–275.
Agans, R., Wood, W., & Rhodes, N. D. (1992, August). *Selective attention to persuasive messages as a function of working knowledge.* Paper presented at the 100th annual convention of the American Psychological Association, Washington, DC.

Atkin, C. K., Galloway, J., & Nayman, O. B. (1976). News media exposure, political knowledge and campaign interest. *Journalism Quarterly, 53,* 231–237.

Berent, M. K., & Krosnick, J. A. (in press). The relation between attitude importance and knowledge structure. In M. Lodge & K. McGraw (Eds.), *Political information processing.* Ann Arbor: University of Michigan Press.

Biek, M. (1992). *Knowledge and affect as determinants of information processing, attitude stability, and behavior.* Unpublished doctoral dissertation, Texas A&M University, College Station.

Biek, M., Wood, W., & Chaiken, S. (in press). Working knowledge and cognitive processing: On the determinants of bias. *Personality and Social Psychology Bulletin.*

Biek, M., Wood, W., Nations, C., & Chaiken, S. (1993). *Working knowledge and persuasiveness of proattitudinal and counterattitudinal messages.* Unpublished manuscript, Texas A&M University.

Bornstein, R. F. (1989). Exposure and affect: Overview and meta-analysis of research, 1968–1987. *Psychological Bulletin, 106,* 265–289.

Chaiken, S. (1980). Heuristic vs. systematic information processing and the use of source vs. message cues in persuasion. *Journal of Personality and Social Psychology, 39,* 752–766.

Chaiken, S., Liberman, A., & Eagly, A. H. (1989). Heuristic and systematic information processing within and beyond the persuasion context. In J. S. Uleman & J. A. Bargh (Eds.), *Unintended thought* (pp. 212–252). New York: Guilford.

Chaiken, S., & Yates, S. (1985). Affective-cognitive consistency and thought induced attitude polarization. *Journal of Personality and Social Psychology, 49,* 1470–1481.

Clark, P., & Fredin, E. (1978). Newspapers, television and political reasoning. *Public Opinion Quarterly, 42,* 143–160.

Clark, P., & Kline, F. G. (1974). Media effects reconsidered: Some new strategies for communication research. *Communication Research, 1,* 224–240.

Converse, P. E. (1962). Information flow and the stability of partisan attitudes. *Public Opinion Quarterly, 26,* 578–599.

Converse, P. E. (1964). The nature of belief systems in mass publics. In D. Apter (Ed.), *Ideology and discontent* (pp. 201–261). New York: Free Press.

Converse, P. E. (1970). Attitudes and nonattitudes. In E. R. Tufte (Ed.), *The quantitative analysis of social problems* (pp. 168–189). Reading, MA: Addison-Wesley.

Cotton, J. L. (1985). Cognitive dissonance in selective exposure. In D. Zillman & J. Bryant (Eds.), *Selective exposure to communication* (pp. 11–33). Hillsdale, NJ: Lawrence Erlbaum Associates.

Eagly, A. H. (1974). Comprehensibility of persuasive arguments as a determinant of opinion change. *Journal of Personality and Social Psychology, 29,* 758–773.

Eagly, A. H., & Chaiken, S. (1984). Cognitive theories of persuasion. In L. Berkowitz (Ed.), *Advances in experimental social psychology* (Vol. 17, pp. 268–359). Orlando, FL: Academic.

Eagly, A. H., & Chaiken, S. (1993). *The psychology of attitudes.* New York: Harcourt Brace.

Eagly, A. H., & Warren, R. (1976). Intelligence, comprehension, and opinion change. *Journal of Personality, 44,* 226–242.

Fazio, R. H., & Zanna, M. P. (1981). Direct experience and attitude-behavior consistency. In L. Berkowitz (Ed.), *Advances in experimental social psychology* (Vol. 14, pp. 161–202). Orlando, FL: Academic.

Fiske, S. T., Kinder, D. R., & Larter, W. M. (1983). The novice and the expert: Knowledge-based strategies in political cognition. *Journal of Experimental Social Psychology, 19,* 381–400.

Fiske, S. T., Lau, R. R., & Smith, R. A. (1990). On the varieties and utilities of political expertise. *Social Cognition, 8,* 31–48.

Fiske, S. T., & Neuberg, S. (1992). A continuum of impression formation, from category-based to individuating processes: Influences of information and motivation on attention and interpretation. In M. P. Zanna (Ed.), *Advances in experimental social psychology* (Vol. 23, pp. 1–74). Orlando, FL: Academic.

Frey, D. (1986). Recent research on selective exposure to information. In L. Berkowitz (Ed.), *Advances in experimental social psychology* (Vol. 19, pp. 41–80). New Haven: Yale University Press.

Hedges, L. V., & Olkin, I. (1985). *Statistical methods for meta-analysis.* San Diego, CA: Academic.

Janis, I. L., & Hovland, C. I. (1959). Postscript: Theoretical categories for analyzing individual differences. In I. L. Janis, C. I. Hovland, P. B. Field, H. Linton, E. Graham, A. R. Cohen, D. Rife, R. P. Abelson, G. S. Lesser, & B. T. King (Eds.), *Personality and persuasibility* (pp. 255–279). New Haven: Yale University Press.

Judd, C. M., & Lusk, C. M. (1984). Knowledge structures and evaluative judgments: Effects of structural variables on judgment extremity. *Journal of Personality and Social Psychology, 46,* 1193–1207.

Kahneman, D. (1973). *Attention and effort.* Englewood Cliffs, NJ: Prentice-Hall.

Kallgren, C. A., III, & Wood, W. (1986). Access to attitude-relevant information in memory as a determinant of attitude-behavior consistency. *Journal of Experimental Social Psychology, 22,* 328–338.

Krosnick, J. A., Boninger, D. S., Chuang, Y. C., Berent, M. K., & Carnot, C. G. (1993). Attitude strength: One construct or many related constructs? *Journal of Personality and Social Psychology, 65,* 1132–1151.

Krosnick, J. A., & Milburn, M. A. (1990). Psychological determinants of political opinionation. *Social Cognition, 8,* 49–72.

Kruglanski, A. W. (1989). *Lay epistemics and human knowledge: Cognitive and motivational bases.* New York: Plenum Press.

Kunda, Z. (1990). The case for motivated reasoning. *Psychological Bulletin, 108,* 480–498.

Linville, P. W. (1982). The complexity-extremity effect and aged-based stereotyping. *Journal of Personality and Social Psychology, 42,* 193–210.

Lodge, M., & Hamill, R. (1986). A partisan schema for political information processing. *American Political Science Review, 8,* 505–519.

Lord, C. G., Ross, L., & Lepper, M. R. (1979). Biased assimilations and attitude polarization: The effects of prior theories on subsequently considered evidence. *Journal of Personality and Social Psychology, 27,* 2098–2109.

Mackie, D. M., & Asuncion, A. G. (1990). On-line and memory-based modification of attitudes: Determinants of message recall-attitude change correspondence. *Journal of Personality and Social Psychology, 59,* 5–16.

Mackie, D., & Worth, L. T. (1989). Processing deficits and mediation of positive affect in persuasion. *Journal of Personality and Social Psychology, 57,* 27–40.

McClelland, J. L., Rumelhart, D. E., & Hinton, G. E. (1986). The appeal of parallel distributed processing. In D. E. Rumelhart, J. L., McClelland, & the PDP Research Group (Eds.), *Parallel distributed processing: Explorations in the microstructure of cognition* (Vol. 1, pp. 3–44). Cambridge, MA: MIT Press.

McCombs, M., & Mullins, L. E. (1973). Consequences of education: Media exposure, political interest, and information-seeking orientations. *Mass Communication Review, 4,* 37–61.

McGuire, W. J. (1968). Personality and susceptibility to social influence. In E. F. Borgatta & W. W. Lambert (Eds.), *Handbook of personality theory and research* (pp. 1130–1187). Chicago: Rand McNally.

McGuire, W. J. (1985). Attitudes and attitude change. In G. Lindzey & E. Aronson (Eds.), *Handbook of social psychology* (Vol. 2, 3rd ed., pp. 233–346). New York: Random House.

McGuire, W. J. (1986). The myth of massive media impact: Savagings and salvagings. In G. Comstock (Ed.), *Public communication and behavior* (Vol. 1, pp. 173–257). San Diego, CA: Academic.

Norman, D. A. (1976). *Memory and attention: An introduction to human information processing.* New York: Wiley.

Perse, E. M. (1990). Media involvement and local news effects. *Journal of Broadcasting and Electronic Media, 34,* 17–36.

Petty, R. E., & Brock, T. C. (1981). Thought disruption and persuasion: Assessing the validity of attitude change experiments. In R. Petty, T. Ostrom, & T. Brock (Eds.), *Cognitive responses in persuasion* (pp. 55–79). Hillsdale, NJ: Lawrence Erlbaum Associates.

Petty, R. E., & Cacioppo, J. T. (1986a). The elaboration likelihood model of persuasion. In L. Berkowitz (Ed.), *Advances in experimental social psychology* (Vol. 19, pp. 123–205). Orlando, FL: Academic.

Petty, R. E., & Cacioppo, J. T. (1986b). *Communication and persuasion: Central and peripheral routes to attitude change.* New York: Springer-Verlag.

Petty, R. E., Unnava, R., & Strathman, A. J. (1991). Theories of attitude change. In H. Kassalian & T. Robertson (Eds.), *Handbook of consumer behavior* (pp. 161–165). Englewood Cliffs, NJ: Prentice-Hall.

Posner, M. I. (1982). Cumulative development of attentional theory. *American Psychologist, 37,* 168–179.

Raden, D. (1985). Strength-related attitude dimensions. *Social Psychology Quarterly, 48,* 312–330.

Rhodes, N. D., & Wood, W. (1992). Self-esteem and intelligence affect influenceability: The role of message reception. *Psychological Bulletin, 111,* 156–171.

Roberts, D. F., & Maccoby, N. (1985). Effects of mass communication. In G. Lindzey & E. Aronson (Eds.), *Handbook of social psychology* (Vol. 2, pp. 539–598). New York: Random House.

Robinson, J. P., & Levy, M. R. (1986). Interpersonal communication and news comprehension. *Public Opinion Quarterly, 50,* 160–175.

Rosenberg, M. J. (1968). Hedonism, inauthenticity, and other goads toward expansion of a consistency theory. In R. P. Abelson, E. Aronson, W. J. McGuire, T. M. Newcomb, M. J. Rosenberg, & P. H. Tannenbaum (Eds.), *Theories of cognitive consistency: A sourcebook* (pp. 73–111). Chicago: Rand McNally.

Rosenberg, M. J., & Abelson, R. (1960). An analysis of cognitive balancing. In C. I. Hovland & M. Rosenberg (Eds.), *Attitude organization and change: An analysis of consistency among attitude components* (pp. 112–163). New Haven: Yale University Press.

Sweeney, P. D., & Gruber, K. L. (1984). Selective exposure: Voter information preferences and the Watergate affair. *Journal of Personality and Social Psychology, 46,* 1208–1221.

Wood, W. (1982). The retrieval of attitude-relevant information from memory: Effects on susceptibility to persuasion and on intrinsic motivation. *Journal of Personality and Social Psychology, 42,* 798–810.

Wood, W., & Kallgren, C. A., III. (1988). Communicator attributes and persuasion: A function of access to attitude-relevant information. *Personality and Social Psychology Bulletin, 14,* 172–182.

Wood, W., Kallgren, C. A., III, & Preisler, R. M. (1985). Access to attitude-relevant information in memory as a determinant of persuasion: The role of message attributes. *Journal of Experimental Social Psychology, 21,* 73–85.

Zaller, J. (1987). Diffusion of political attitudes. *Journal of Personality and Social Psychology, 53,* 821–833.

Zaller, J. (1989). Bringing Converse back in: Modeling information flow in political campaigns. In J. A. Stimson (Ed.), *Political analysis* (Vol. 1, pp. 181–220). Ann Arbor: University of Michigan Press.

Zaller, J. (1990). Political awareness, elite opinion leadership, and the mass survey response. *Social Cognition, 8,* 125–153.

Zajonc, R. B. (1980). Feeling and thinking: Preferences need no inferences. *American Psychologist, 35,* 151–175.

12
▼▼▼▼▼▼▼

From Attitudes to Actions to Attitude Change: The Effects of Amount and Accuracy of Information

Andrew R. Davidson
Columbia University

In this chapter I examine the dynamic processes linking attitudes and actions and the role that attitude strength plays in moderating these processes. I am particularly interested in two key stages of a continuous sequence: the influence of an initial attitude on the performance of a subsequent behavior and, in turn, the effect of feedback resulting from the performance of that behavior in changing the initial attitude. Attitude strength should moderate both of these stages. First, strong attitudes should be more likely to lead to attitude-consistent actions. Second, strong attitudes should be more resistant to change in the face of feedback following the performance of the behavior—more generally, strong attitudes should evidence greater temporal consistency.

Given the potential consequences of attitude strength for the attitude–action–attitude change sequence, an important question is what determines whether an attitude is strong or weak. This chapter focuses on the role of information about the attitude object as an antecedent of attitude strength, and delineates two dimensions of attitudinal information—amount and accuracy. I develop a framework relating each of these dimensions to the attitude–action–attitude change sequence. Specifically, for the attitude-action link, attitude strength should depend on the amount of information that one has about the attitude object. The more information on which an attitude is based the more likely it is that subsequent behavior will be consistent with the attitude. For the second stage of the sequence (the impact of feedback resulting from the performance of the behavior on the initial attitude), attitude strength will depend on the accuracy of the information that buttressed the initial attitude. The more accurate the information, the less likely it is that the attitude will change following the performance of the behavior.

In this review I use the term *attitude* quite broadly, and have included articles that employ measures of evaluation of the target behavior and measures of behavioral intention. I have adopted the simplifying assumption that my hypotheses about the role of attitude relevant information apply to both evaluative and intention measures. Overall, the range of studies that are reviewed here appear to be consistent with this assumption. It is certainly possible, however, that some differences do exist in the manner in which amount and accuracy of information affect the relation of evaluation and intention to behavior. This would be an interesting topic for future research. For the present, I have attempted to specify the type of attitude measure used in each of the reviewed studies.

FROM ATTITUDES TO ACTIONS: THE ROLE OF AMOUNT OF INFORMATION

Information stored in memory has traditionally been viewed as a primary determinant of evaluative judgments (Allport, 1935; McGuire, 1985). Building on this perspective, theorists (e.g., N. H. Anderson, 1981; Fishbein & Ajzen, 1975) have developed information-processing models that specify how people integrate pieces of information to form attitudes. Although much of this research seeks to determine the validity of different algebraic models of information integration, the research also has identified one variable—amount of information about the attitude object— that has important implications for the study of the attitude-behavior relation.

The role of amount of information first became evident in one of the more conceptually problematic findings to emerge from research on information integration, the *decelerating set-size* effect. *Set-size* refers to the finding that the evaluative judgment of an object becomes more extreme as the number of pieces of information about the object increases, even when the value of each piece of information is held constant. Of greater pertinence to our interest in amount of information, the effect is *decelerating*; each successive piece of information has a smaller and smaller impact on the overall evaluation. That is, the effect of an additional piece of information on an attitude is dependent on the amount of information that is already available about the attitude object.

The decelerating set-size effect has been widely investigated because it is inconsistent with the simplest forms of both the averaging model and its primary competitor, the adding model (Davidson & Morrison, 1982; Yamagishi & Hill, 1981). The simple averaging model predicts no set-size effect; adding information of equal value should not change the average value. Similarly, the simple adding model predicts no deceleration; holding the value of the information constant, each piece of information should have an equal additive effect on the summary evaluation.

The most accepted explanation for the decelerating set-size effect takes into account an initial attitude toward the object (N. H. Anderson, 1965). This initial attitude is hypothesized to be averaged with the value of the items of new information gained. As a result, each additional piece of information increases the extremity of evaluation but at a decelerating rate. Anderson (1971, 1981) has further specified the determinants of whether the initial attitude will be more versus less resistant to change following exposure to a new piece of information. He hypothesized that an initial attitude, based on a substantial amount of information, will demonstrate less change in response to a new piece of information than will an attitude based on lesser amounts of information. According to information integration theory, this effect will occur because the magnitude of the weight parameter, associated with the initial attitude, is a function of the amount of information on which the attitude is based. An existing attitude, that is based on a substantial amount of information, will have a much greater weight parameter than will a new piece of information and, as a result, the initial attitude will show little change.

The decelerating set-size effect highlights the role of amount of information about the attitude object as an important determinant of the impact that new information will have on attitude change. The deceleration of the set-size effect, as predicted by the averaging model, has been demonstrated in a large number of studies (e.g., N. H. Anderson, 1965, 1967, 1968; T. Anderson & Birnbaum, 1976; Sloan & Ostrom, 1974). Due to the averaging process, the effect of a new piece of information would be relatively dramatic when one has very little existing information about the attitude object and would be comparatively minor for a topic about which one has a substantial amount of information.

I have introduced the effect of amount of information by focusing on research findings from the relatively formal information-integration paradigm. It is important to note that the moderating role of amount of information also has been discussed and demonstrated within the context of more traditional studies of attitude change. For example, Rosenberg (1968) was one of the first attitude researchers to speculate about the consequences of amount of information when he argued that old and familiar attitude objects would be harder to change than new and unfamiliar objects. More recently, Wood (1982) and her colleagues (Wood, Kallgren, & Preisler, 1985), in an interesting series of studies, found that subjects' amount of attitude-relevant information determined the impact of counterattitudinal messages on attitude change. Subjects with little information, in comparison to those with greater information, changed their opinions to be more consistent with the message position. For a more detailed description of this research, see Wood, Rhodes, and Biek, ch. 11 (this volume).

In summary, there is substantial support for the hypothesis that the amount of information that one has about an attitude object is a determinant of the extent of attitude change resulting from exposure to new information or to a counterattitudinal communication. It follows that amount of information should also moderate the degree of relation between attitudes and behavior, particularly if there is a time lag between the measurement of attitude and behavior and if the respondent is exposed to new information during that interval. The process would operate in the following manner: Respondents express an attitude at Time 1 and are subsequently exposed to new information about the attitude object. Those with weak attitudes, based on little information, will be susceptible to attitude change and, as a result, will exhibit low consistency between their Time 1 attitudes and their Time 2 behaviors. Those with strong initial attitudes will be less likely to experience attitude change and will, therefore, have higher Time 1 attitude to Time 2 behavior correlations.

A number of studies have provided indirect evidence that is consistent with the hypothesized process. First, it is clear that attitude change often occurs in the interval between the measurement of attitudes and behavior, thereby contributing to the frequently noted lack of attitude-behavior consistency. The longer the time interval, the higher the probability of exposure to new information and, in turn, attitude change (Davidson & Jaccard, 1979; Erber, Hodges, & Wilson, ch. 17, this volume; Fishbein & Coombs, 1974; Fishbein & Jaccard, 1973; Kelley & Mirer, 1974; Norman, 1975; Schuman & Johnson, 1976; Schwartz, 1978). Second, the greater the amount of attitude change, the lower the congruence between initial attitudes and subsequent action (Davidson & Beach, 1981; Davidson & Jaccard, 1979). Not surprisingly, for those respondents who do exhibit attitude change, the new as opposed to the initial attitude is more predictive of behavior (Davidson & Beach, 1981). Because amount of information about the attitude object moderates the effect of new information on attitude change, it should also serve to identify respondents at greater risk of apparent attitude-behavior inconsistency due to attitude change during the interval of the study.

I now turn to a description of two longitudinal studies, that my colleagues and I have conducted, investigating the role of amount of information about the attitude object and attitude-behavior consistency. The studies examined naturally occurring attitude change. We did not manipulate the respondents' receipt of new information about the attitude object. Rather, we timed the waves of our longitudinal surveys so that respondents were likely to receive additional information about the attitude object during the interval between the measurement of their attitudes and behavior.

The Voting Study

Our first study (Davidson, Yantis, Norwood, & Montano, 1985) investigated the amount of information that respondents had about political candidates as a determinant of the consistency between their intentions and voting behaviors. We interviewed undergraduates, who were eligible to vote in an upcoming mayoral election, approximately 10 days prior to the election and assessed their intentions to vote for each of the two candidates and their amounts of information about the candidates. Intention to vote for each candidate was measured on a 7-point scale that ranged from "extremely unlikely" to "extremely likely." The procedure for measuring amount of information required the subjects to list their information and beliefs about each candidate. This could include both positions that the candidate had taken on specific issues and beliefs that they had about the candidate that could cause them to vote for and against the candidate. For each candidate they were asked to write only one idea per line and were given 2.5 minutes to list their beliefs. Virtually all subjects completed the listing task before the time was over. Two judges independently rated the number of pieces of information and their judgments evidenced high interrater reliability (r's = .87 and .88, for the two candidates). Voters were asked, after the election, for whom they had voted.

We hypothesized an interaction between intentions and information in the prediction of behavior, with intentions based on larger amounts of information being more predictive of subsequent behavior. The hypothesis was tested through the use of hierarchical regression analysis. To predict behavior, intention was entered first in the regression equation, followed by amount of information, and finally, by the intention × information interaction term.

Table 12.1 presents the results of the regression analysis. Voting intention had a correlation of moderate strength with voting behavior for both candidates. For neither candidate did amount of information contribute significantly to the prediction of voting behavior. The explicit test of the hypothesis is represented by the intention × information interaction term. In support of the hypothesis, for both candidates, the inclusion of the interaction term significantly and substantially increased the amount of variance accounted for in the criterion, For Candidate A, adding the intention × information interaction term to the main effects of intention and information explained an additional 17% of the variance in behavior. The comparable increase for Candidate B was 12%. The regression coefficient associated with each interaction term was positive, indicating that as information increased so did the correlation between intention and behavior.

TABLE 12.1
Hierarchical Regression of Voting Behavior on Behavioral Intention,
Information, and the Intention × Information Interaction

Variable	R	Change in R^2	F Test, Change in R^2
Candidate A			
Intention	.325**	.106	4.96**
Information	.387**	.044	2.13
Intention × Information	.568***	.173	10.22***
Candidate B			
Intention	.261*	.068	3.07*
Information	.300	.022	0.97
Intention × Information	.460**	.122	6.17**

Note. N = 44.
*p < .10. **p < .05. ***p < .01.

Although the hierarchical regression analysis demonstrated that amount of information moderated attitude-behavior consistency, it does not help us decide if amount of information is a new and independent effect or merely an alternative measure of some other previously established moderator of attitude-behavior consistency. We are particularly interested in determining whether amount of information contributes independent variance to the prediction of attitude-behavior consistency over and above any effects attributable to attitude certainty and prior experience with the attitude object. Focusing first on certainty, Sample and Warland (1973) found that respondents who reported being very certain about their voting attitudes exhibited greater attitude-behavior consistency than did those who expressed their attitudes with less certainty. It might be the case that certainty and amount of information are alternative indicators of attitude strength.

Similarly, it has been shown that attitudes formed on the basis of direct behavioral experience with the attitude object are more predictive of later behavior than are attitudes formed through indirect nonbehavioral experience (see Fazio & Zanna, 1981, for a review). It could be argued that amount of information also is dependent on the manner in which the attitude is formed, with direct experience with the attitude object leading to both attitude-behavior consistency and greater amounts of information about the attitude object. To rule out these plausible alternative hypotheses we conducted a series of partial-correlation analyses to learn whether the effect of amount of information was reduced to nonsignificance when either attitude certainty or direct experience with the attitude object was held constant.

Subjects' certainty about their attitude toward voting for each candidate was measured on a scale that ranged from extremely uncertain about their attitude (1) to extremely certain (7). Three aspects of prior direct behavioral experience with the attitude object were assessed: the number of times the subject had previously voted, whether or not the subject had voted in the primary election, and whether the subject had voted for Candidate A or B in the primary. To provide a straightforward dependent variable for these analyses, voting intention and voting behavior were combined in one variable assessing intention-behavior consistency. For each candidate, respondents were coded consistent (1) if they either (a) scored above the median on the intention measure and voted for the candidate, or (b) scored below the median and did not vote for the candidate. All other response patterns were coded as indicating attitude-behavior inconsistency (0).

The simple correlation of each potential moderator with intention-behavior consistency is shown in the first column of Table 12.2. In agreement with the hierarchical regression analyses, amount of information about the candidate had a significant correlation with intention-behavior consistency and was the strongest single determinant of consistency. The voting experience variables had marginally significant, but consistent, positive correlations with intention-behavior consistency. Attitude certainty moderated attitude-behavior consistency for Candidate A but not for Candidate B.

TABLE 12.2

Simple and Partial Correlations of Information, Prior Experience Variables,
and Certainty with Intention–Behavior Consistency

Variable	Simple Correlation	Correlation with Intention–Behavior Consistency				
		Partialed Variable				
		Information	Voting Frequency	Voted in Primary	Voted for A or B in Primary	Attitude Certainty
Candidate A						
Information	.47***	—	.42***	.42***	.45***	.38***
Voting frequency	.24*	.08	—	.13	.18	.17
Voted in primary	.24*	.08	.13	—	.16	.17
Voted for A or B in primary	.18	.06	.07	−.01	—	.16
Attitude certainty	.38***	.23*	.35**	.35**	.37***	—
Candidate B						
Information	.46***	—	.42***	.42***	.41***	.45***
Voting frequency	.20*	.03	—	.10	.10	.18
Voted in primary	.21*	.04	.12	—	.05	.19
Voted for A or B in primary	.23*	.07	.15	.11	—	.21*
Attitude certainty	.10	−.02	.05	.04	.04	—

Note. N = 44.
*p < .10. **p < .05. ***p < .01.

A series of partial correlations were then computed to determine if the information, experience, and certainty variables each had an independent effect on intention-behavior consistency. As presented in columns 2–6 of Table 12.2, the correlation of each potential moderator with consistency was computed after the effect of any shared variance with each of the other moderators was separately partialed out of the relation. The relation of information to consistency remained relatively strong even when the experience and certainty variables were held constant. In contrast, the experience consistency correlations dropped to a nonsignificant level when information was held constant, and the effect of attitude certainty was inconsistent across the two candidates.

The results of the hierarchical regression and the partial correlation analyses indicate that strong attitudes—those capable of guiding subsequent behaviors—are buttressed by greater amounts of information. Whereas attitudes lacking this informational support are less likely to be related to subsequent behaviors. Moreover, the moderating effect of information is independent of any effects attributable to attitude certainty and prior experience with the attitude object, two more established determinants of attitude-behavior consistency. I now turn to a second study which was designed to extend the boundary conditions of the information effect on attitude-behavior consistency.

The Influenza Vaccination Study

To determine if the moderating effect of amount of information is limited to voting behavior, my colleagues and I (Davidson et al., 1985) investigated the determinants of attitude-action consistency for a health behavior, obtaining an influenza vaccination. The study also extended the prior findings to an elderly sample of respondents of more limited educational attainment.

In addition, this research examined the utility of a self-report measure of amount of information about the attitude object for identifying the likelihood that subjects will demonstrate attitude-behavior consistency. It seems clear that the self-report and thought-listing procedures are vulnerable to different sources of error variance. Thought-listing is more susceptible to the compulsiveness of the subject and self-report is probably more influenced by self-presentation biases. The self-report measure also presents subjects with the difficult tasks of evaluating their amount of information on a topic, contrasting their level of information with that of others, and translating that judgment to a rating scale. These tasks are probably more difficult if all respondents have substantial amounts of information about the attitude object. However, despite these unique sources of variance, we assume that the two measures share some common variance, and that the usefulness of the self-report measure will depend on that degree of overlap. For the present attitude object, influenza vaccinations, a topic about which most respondents are not information saturated, we expect an adequate degree of overlap.

Approximately 400 U.S. veterans, who were identified by a Veterans Administration (VA) outpatient care unit as being at risk for developing influenza complications, served as the respondents in the study. Risk factors included being 65 years of age or older, or having a chronic health condition (heart disease or diabetes mellitus). The average age of the veterans was 65.3, and approximately half the sample had not completed high school.

Respondents were initially interviewed prior to the flu season and the following variables were assessed: (a) a dichotomous measure of whether or not they intended to have a flu shot during the year, (b) how well informed they were about the flu shot on a 7-point scale ranging from "completely uninformed" to "completely informed," and (c) a dichotomous measure of whether or not they had ever had a flu shot in the past. The latter measure was included to continue the investigation of the role of prior experience in determining attitude-behavior consistency. At the start of the flu season all respondents were sent a letter by the VA recommending that they obtain a flu shot at the VA outpatient care unit. When the flu season was over, respondents were recontacted by mail to learn whether or not they had obtained a flu shot. Actual clinic records were used to verify these self-reports and, for 99% of the respondents, the two sources of information yielded identical information.

As in the voting study, it was hypothesized that respondents with greater amounts of information about the attitude object would be more likely to exhibit intention-behavior consistency. Respondents were divided into two groups: intention-behavior consistent and intention-behavior inconsistent. Consistent respondents either intended to have a flu shot and did receive one or did not intend a flu shot and did not have one. In contrast, inconsistent respondents behaved in the way opposite of their initial intentions. Consistent and inconsistent respondents were then compared in terms of both their amount of information about the flu shot and whether they previously had a vaccination. The data are presented in Table 12.3. In support of our hypothesis, consistent respondents were significantly better informed about the flu shot than were inconsistent respondents. Similarly, consistent respondents were more likely to have previously had a flu shot than were inconsistent respondents. Partial correlation analyses indicated that each of the moderators made significant independent contributions to the prediction of attitude-behavior consistency.

Our studies demonstrated clear support for the hypothesis that attitudes based on substantial amounts of information are more predictive of subsequent behavior. Moreover, the influence of amount of information was independent of two other moderators of the attitude-behavior relation—attitude certainty and prior experience with the attitude object. Our confidence in the effect of information on the attitude-behavior relation is increased by the consistent findings reported by other researchers, to which we now turn.

Research by Other Investigators

Kallgren and Wood (1985), used a longitudinal research design similar to that of our voting and influenza vaccination studies, and examined the interrelation of information, attitudes, and behavior concerning preservation of the environment. During an initial interview, subjects responded to an attitude measure and listed their information about the topic. A pro-environment behavioral index was constructed based on the subjects' actions over the next few weeks (e.g., signing and circulating pro-environmental petitions, participating in a recycling project).

TABLE 12.3
Mean Information and Prior Experience Levels and *t* Tests of Differences
Between Intention–Behavior Consistent and Inconsistent Respondents

Variable	Consistent	Inconsistent	t
Information[a]	5.25	4.49	2.29*[c]
Experience[b]	.76	.51	3.27**[d]

[a]Ratings were made on a 7-point scale ranging from 1 (completely uninformed) to 7 (completely informed).
[b]Scored as 0 (no prior flu shot) or 1 (prior flu shot).
[c]N = 329.
[d]N = 331.
*p < .025. **p < .01.

Consistent with the findings already cited, there was a linear relation between amount of information and consistency; for each increment in the amount of attitude–relevant information there was a corresponding increment in attitude–action consistency. In addition to demonstrating the moderating effect of information, this study extended the boundary conditions of the effect in the following way. Ajzen and Fishbein (1977) have distinguished between attitude-behavior studies that measure variables at a global versus a specific level. In our research we assessed highly specific attitudes and behaviors (e.g., voting for a specific candidate), whereas in the Kallgren and Wood study a global attitude (environmental preservation) and behavior (based on an aggregate behavioral index) were measured.

A second series of studies, reported by Wilson, Kraft, and Dunn (1989), also support the concept that attitudes, based on greater amounts of information, are stronger and more likely to guide subsequent behavior. Their support, however, is more subtle than that provided by either our studies or those of Kallgren and Wood. Wilson and his colleagues discovered that asking people to think about the reasons for their attitudes can have a strong disruptive effect on the attitude-behavior relation (see Wilson, Dunn, Kraft, & Lisle, 1989). Those asked to analyze their reasons have lower attitude-action consistency than do control subjects. Recently, their reanalysis of some of their previous work, in conjunction with data from additional studies, has shown that the disruption from analyzing reasons only occurs for those with relatively little knowledge about the attitude object (Wilson et al., 1989). That is, those with greater amounts of information are more likely to be immune to this powerful manipulation and to exhibit greater attitude-behavior consistency.

Discussion

Taken together, these studies provide strong evidence that amount of attitude relevant information moderates attitude-action consistency. Although the studies do demonstrate the replicability of the effect, they have not adequately clarified a number of issues central to this phenomenon. The primary topics requiring further specification are the theoretical meaning that should be assigned to a high score on the information measures and the process linking information to attitude-behavior consistency.

We have broadly defined a piece of information as the perceived relation of an attitude object to an attribute. The greater the number of such cognitions available to the respondent, the better informed the individual was considered to be about the attitude object. Accordingly, in the voting study we used an information-listing task to measure the amount of information available. The studies by Wood and her colleagues used a similar information-listing procedure (Kallgren & Wood, 1985; Wood, 1982; Wood et al., 1985). It is important to note that in contrast to our assumption about what the listing task assessed, they believed that they were measuring ease of access to information stored in memory.

This difference in interpretation has occurred because the number of items listed in this task is mutually determined by the amount of information stored in memory and the ease with which this information can be accessed. To obtain a high score on the listing task, both factors are necessary, but neither is sufficient.

It seems reasonable, however, to assume that the extent to which thought listing is measuring ease of access rather than amount of information available will depend on the attitude topic. For information saturated attitude objects (i.e., those topics for which practically all respondents have a large set of cognitions), it is likely that information listing is primarily assessing ease of access. Whereas when the attitude object is one in which the respondents have less information, it is more likely that amount of information is being assessed. Implicitly, the two research groups have acted in ways that are consistent with this view. Wood's group attempted to measure ease of access via thought listing and, accordingly, selected a broad and popular attitude topic about which their undergraduate subjects had a lot of information: preservation of the environment. We desired to measure the amount of information available to the respondent and, as a result, selected topics that our respondents had less familiarity with—influenza vaccinations, mayoral (as opposed to presidential) elections, and local election initiatives. Clearly, these assumptions need to be tested before we can tighten our theoretical grasp on the constructs being measured by the thought listing and self-report measures of information.

Additional research is also needed on the process by which amount of attitude relevant information moderates attitude-behavior consistency. Although each of the attitude-behavior studies that we have reviewed speculated about process, not one directly tested the hypothesized process. For the present, there are two probable mechanisms—stability and accessibility—by which amount of information could moderate attitude-behavior consistency. The stability mechanism is the process we advanced. Attitudes based on substantial amounts of information are more likely to guide subsequent behavior because they are resistant to change in the face of new information. The accessibility mechanism follows from the research of Fazio and his colleagues (Fazio, ch. 10, this volume; Fazio, Chen, McDonel, & Sherman, 1982; Fazio, Powell, & Herr, 1983). They argue that for attitudes to guide behavior they must be accessed from memory upon contact with the attitude object. If amount of information were related to attitude accessibility, then information could moderate attitude-behavior consistency even in the absence of attitude change.

Certainly both of these processes are plausible, and it would be surprising if only one mechanism was the sole determinant of the information effect; different situations and behaviors should evoke different attitude-to-behavior processes. For example, Sherman and Fazio (1983) argued that the infrequent, deliberate, and consequential behaviors that my colleagues and I have investigated—obtaining an influenza vaccination and voting—are those which are least likely to be driven by an accessibility mechanism. For other behaviors, that are less the result of conscious decision making, automatic attitude-to-behavior processes are more likely.

In summary, this portion of the chapter has focused on the first link of the attitude–action–attitude change sequence. The research literature indicates that amount of information is a reliable determinant of the strength of the attitude-action link. Additional studies are required, however, to clarify the specific processes by which information leads to attitude-action consistency. I now turn to the second link of the sequence and analyze attitude change following the performance of the behavior, as a function of the accuracy of the information that buttressed the initial attitude.

FROM ACTIONS TO ATTITUDE CHANGE: THE ROLE
OF ACCURACY OF INFORMATION

I have defined a piece of information as the perceived relation of an attitude object to an attribute. When the attitude object is a specific behavior (e.g., obtaining an influenza vaccination) these perceived relations tend to link the behavior to expected outcomes (e.g., avoiding the flu, enduring a long wait at the physician's office, having a painful arm). Such information, in the form of expectations about future outcomes, plays a central role in many models of attitude formation, and virtually every model of decision making.

In the attitude literature, the role of expectations in affecting attitudes perhaps can best be seen in Fishbein and Ajzen's (1975) theory of reasoned action. According to their theory, attitudes are a function of one's expectations about the consequences of performing a behavior and the evaluation of those consequences. A person will have a positive or negative attitude toward performing the behavior based on a balancing of the positive expectations against the negative expectation. Expectations about the future outcomes of behavior are also the primary variables in subjective expected utility and expectancy-value models of decision making (Beach, 1982; Lee, 1971; Pagel & Davidson,1984).

One limitation of the research on the Fishbein and Ajzen model, and decision models in general, is that it has provided primarily static tests of the attitude formation and decision making processes. We have learned that information in the form of expectations does guide decisions but we have learned little about how people adjust their attitudes if their expectations are disconfirmed by their actual experiences. That is, how do people respond if their experiences demonstrate that their initial expectations were inaccurate? Given that expectations are predictions about the events that will occur after the behavior is enacted, it is surprising that researchers have not shown a greater interest in investigating expectation–experience discrepancies as a determinant of attitude change. The major decision theories, particularly the utility-based theories, do suggest a dynamic process. For example, in the Fishbein and Ajzen (1975) framework, it is proposed that performance of a behavior may lead to a new or revised set of expectations which may, in turn, change attitudes regarding the performance of the behavior. The problem is that these notions have not been adequately specified or tested in the empirical literature.

The purpose of this section is to describe a model that my colleagues and I have developed (Kalmuss, Davidson, & Cushman, 1992; Davidson, Kalmuss, & Cushman, 1992), which links the accuracy of the information on which an initial attitude is based to attitude change following the performance of the behavior. I then describe some of the research that tests this model.

Consistent with the attitude and decision models cited earlier, we assume that attitudes about performing specific behaviors are guided by expectations concerning the future outcomes of the behavior. Initial experience with the behavior provides a significant opportunity to compare outcomes with expectations. The direction and magnitude of any resulting expectation–experience discrepancies are important determinants of attitude change. When initial information about the outcomes of the behavior is accurate, resulting in a close match between expectations and experiences, attitudes toward the behavior will remain unchanged. However, experiences that are, on balance, markedly more negative or positive than expected will result in attitude change. Although expectation-experience discrepancy is most likely after initial experience with the behavior, subsequent experiences can also lead to a revision of expectations and, in turn, a change of attitudes. To more fully describe the model I refer to the behavior that we and others investigating expectation–experience discrepancies have focused on—parenting. Parenting is a rich area for this type of research because first-time parents often have inaccurate information and expectations about the impacts that parenting will have on their lives.

According to our model, women form expectations regarding how parenting will affect their lives, prior to having their first child, and, based on these expectations, make family size decisions. The expectation information may or may not be correct but it is assumed that attitudes and decisions are determined by what the individual perceives to be true, as opposed to what is actually true. A number of studies have documented the relationship between parenting expectations and fertility attitudes (Adler, 1979; Beach, Campbell, & Townes, 1979; Davidson & Jaccard, 1975, 1979; Fawcett, 1983). The probability of divergence between expectation and experience is perhaps greatest following the birth of the first child. The actual experience of parenting could be more negative, more positive, or similar to what was expected prior to the birth. The larger the overall discrepancy between parenting expectations and experiences, the more likely a woman is to make a change in her intended family size. We hypothesize the following linear relation between expectation–experience discrepancies and change in fertility intentions: Parenting experiences that are, on balance, more negative than expected will lead to a decrease in intended family size; experiences that match expectations will be least likely to yield a change in fertility intentions;

and, experiences that are more positive than expected will cause an upward shift in fertility intentions.

Research from two surprisingly disparate areas—marketing studies of consumer satisfaction and sociological investigations of the transition to parenthood—provides important underpinnings for our model of attitude change. In attempting to understand the determinants of consumer satisfaction, Oliver (1980) also focused on discrepancies between expectations and experiences. His approach is based on Helson's (1964) adaptation level theory, which posits that one perceives stimuli in relation to an adapted standard. Applying this model to marketing, expectations about specific product attributes are assumed to function as that standard adaptation level against which actual experiences with product attributes are evaluated. Satisfaction with the product is thought to be based on the extent to which experiences with the product attributes either exceed or fall short of one's expectations (adaptation level).

Oliver's conceptualization is important because it has identified the potential role of expectancy disconfirmations in determining satisfaction and it has grounded these disconfirmations in a broader theoretical context. However, there has been difficulty in operationalizing the model, and attempts to assess the key construct of expectancy disconfirmation at the attribute level, have not yielded "encouraging results" (Oliver, 1980). As a result, Oliver (1980) and other consumer satisfaction researchers (e.g., Bearden & Teel, 1983; LaBarbera & Mazursky, 1983; Westbrook, 1987) have moved away from attempting to measure expectancy disconfirmation at the individual attribute level and have substituted a simple summary measure of disconfirmed expectancies—"was the product worse or better than expected." This postpurchase summary measure is well correlated with postpurchase satisfaction. Although this correlation is consistent with the hypothesis that expectancy disconfirmation is related to dissatisfaction, a compelling test of an expectation–experience model requires evidence that discrepancies measured at the attribute level are related to dissatisfaction and attitude change.

Greater success in measuring expectation–experience discrepancies can be found in a few investigations of the transition to parenthood. In the initial study, Belsky (1985) investigated the determinants of change in marital satisfaction across the transition to parenthood. Men and women expecting their first children completed a questionnaire assessing their expectations about how the addition of a child to the family would affect a number of dimensions of their lives—primarily relations with the spouse, shared caregiving assistance, and relations with friends and family. At 3 and 9 months postpartum, parents completed the same questionnaires, this time reporting the actual effect on their lives. A measure of expectation–experience discrepancies was created on the basis of the difference between prenatal expectations and postbirth experiences. As predicted, parents whose postnatal experiences turned out less positive and more negative than anticipated reported more negative change in their marriages.

Ruble, Fleming, Hackel, and Stangor (1988) also reported the results of a longitudinal study designed to evaluate the hypothesis that violated expectations with respect to sharing child care and housekeeping responsibilities contributed to increases in women's marital dissatisfaction. They found that the more negative the discrepancy between prebirth expectations and postbirth experiences, the more likely the woman was to report negative feelings about her marital relationship. My colleagues and I (Kalmuss, Davidson, & Cushman, 1992) have extended this research by looking more broadly at the consequences of inaccurate prebirth parenting expectations. Rather than focusing on marital satisfaction, we have examined the impact of violated parenting expectations on the ease of adjustment to motherhood, as indexed by such variables as life satisfaction and life stress. We found that discrepancies between prebirth parenting expectations and postbirth experiences significantly affected the ease of adjustment to parenthood.

The results of these studies support two key aspects of our proposed model of attitude change. First, they demonstrate that the prebirth expectations of many parents are inaccurate and that these inaccuracies influence the respondents' affective reactions to the transition to parenthood. Although in many situations perceivers "see" what they expect to see (Darley & Fazio, 1980; Snyder, 1984), for parenting behaviors it appears that expectations do not completely dominate experiences. As Jussim (1986) has argued, even strong expectations can be disconfirmed when experience is clearly inconsistent with expectations. Second, the studies indicate that it is not the nature of experiences alone that determines the evaluation of these experiences. Rather, the evaluations are shaped by how experiences match expectations (Heider 1958; Kelley & Thibaut, 1978). Difficult parenting experiences that are accurately anticipated lead to less dissatisfaction than unexpected parenting difficulties.

Although research on the transition to parenthood demonstrates the feasibility and value of the expectation–experience paradigm, it does not provide an adequate test of our model linking the accuracy of the information, on which an initial attitude is based, to attitude change following the performance of the behavior. The primary problem is that the transition-to-parenthood studies have focused only on the general outcomes of marital and life satisfaction, and have not considered specific actions that people take when they face disconfirmed parenting expectations. For example, research has not determined if expectation–experience discrepancies lead to changes in either decisions or attitudes toward the specific behavior. Recently my colleagues and I (Davidson, Kalmuss, & Cushman, 1992) completed an investigation designed to provide a more complete test of our proposed model of attitude change.

The Parenting Study

We recruited a sample of approximately 500 pregnant women from private obstetrical practices for this longitudinal study. Women were initially interviewed during the final 4 months of pregnancy and again at 12 months following the birth of the child. None of the women had previously given birth. At each interview we measured intentions about the total number of children women planned to have in their completed family. Change in these intentions represented the primary dependent variable in the study.

At the pregnancy interview we assessed women's parenting expectations for 12 months postbirth, and parallel assessments of actual experiences were made at the 12-month postnatal interview. Prebirth parenting information was considered to be accurate if it was consistent with actual experience. Our selection of expectation and experience items was guided by a review of the fertility and transition to parenthood literature and by our intent to create a measure capturing a wide range of women's expectations about parenting. Women were asked 25 questions concerning their parenting expectations. Items assessed expectations in the following broad areas: relationship with spouse, relationship with extended family and friends, physical well-being, financial well-being, desire to work, maternal satisfaction, maternal competence, and caregiving assistance from spouse.

All expectations and experiences were measured on 7-point scales. For example, for the expectations concerning relationship with spouse (e.g., amount of time together) respondents were asked to contrast the way things usually were to the way they would be when the baby was 12 months old. Responses ranged from "a very large decrease" to "a very large increase." The same questions were repeated at 12 months postpartum and phrased in terms of actual experiences or amounts of change. Each item was coded in the direction of high scores (7) reflecting positive childbearing expectations and experiences. Summary expectation and experience variables were constructed by summing the items within each of the content areas, dividing by the number of items, and then summing the resultant scores. These summary measures of expectations and experiences were used to model change in fertility intentions.

Twenty-eight percent of the women changed their intended family size between the pregnancy and 12-month postbirth interview. Approximately equal numbers of women decreased and increased their plans (15% and 13%, respectively). Identifying the determinants of these changes is our primary interest.

The hypothesis that changes in fertility intentions are determined by discrepancies between expectations and experiences was tested using multiple regression. Following the recommendations of Cronbach and Furby (1970) and Cohen and Cohen (1983), we utilized a regression method, as opposed to a difference score method, for the analysis of change. The dependent variable was the fertility intention at 12-months postpartum, and a key variable in the regression equation was the fertility intention at pregnancy. This partials out of the 12-month intention any variance attributable to the fertility intention at pregnancy, leaving only variance accounted for by change in intention. Similarly, for the expectation–experience discrepancy, we included both the expectations at pregnancy and the experiences at 12-months postpartum as independent variables in the equation. This partials out of the experience measure any effects of initial expectations, leaving only the variance attributable to experiences that deviated from expectations. Based on our expectation–experience model of intention change, we predict a positive and significant coefficient for the experience variable.

In addition to the central theoretical elements, the model also contained two other behavior-specific factors that should lead to a reduction in intended family size: having serious labor or delivery complications, and having a child with a very difficult temperament. Finally, the regression analysis included a set of control variables in order to more adequately specify our model and better estimate the effects of expectation–experience discrepancies on change in intention.

The results of our model of the determinants of change in intended family size are shown in Table 12.4. In support of the central hypothesis of the study, parenting experiences, net of expectations, had a significant and positive effect on change in intended family size ($b = .073$, $t = 3.48$, $p < .001$). When their actual experiences did not match their expectations, women responded by changing their fertility plans. Experiences that were more negative than expected resulted in a decrease in intended family size. This effect was observed even after controlling for the effects of other variables thought to influence change in intended family size.

For comparison purposes, the expectation–experience hypothesis was retested using experience–expectation difference scores. Prebirth expectations were subtracted from postbirth experiences and the difference scores were summed to yield an index of experience–expectation discrepancy. The index was entered into the regression model depicted in Table 12.4 in the place of parenting experiences and expectations. The results from the difference score analysis were the same

TABLE 12.4
Regression Coefficients for Determinants of Change in Intended Family Size:
Pregnancy to 12 Months Post-Birth[a]

Variable	Regression Coefficient	t Statistic
Family size intention at pregnancy	.699***	17.25
Parenting experiences	.073***	3.48
Parenting expectations	−.049*	−2.01
Difficult child temperament	−.121*	−2.20
Pregnancy problems	−.320*	−2.02
Husband's expected family size	.147	1.32
Child not the preferred sex	.372	1.70
Marital duration	−.116**	−3.06
Age	−.033	−1.17
Work status	.140	.88
Income	−.011	−.24
R square	.63***	
F	69.10	
df	(11, 450)	

[a]The dependent variable is intended family size at the end of the interval.
*$p < .05$. **$p < .01$. ***$p < .001$.

as those obtained when experience and expectation were each included in the model. The experience–expectation difference score had a significant positive effect on change in fertility intentions. In summary, the data provide consistent support for the validity of the expectation–experience hypothesis.

Expectations, net of experiences, had a significant negative effect on change in intended family size ($b = -.049$, $t = -2.01$, $p < .05$). Because our model did not make a specific prediction about this variable, we are lacking a sound theoretical basis for interpreting this effect. However, we are not the first to observe a negative and significant expectation effect in this behavioral domain; Ruble et al. (1988) reported such a finding in their study of change in marital satisfaction following the birth of the first child. These findings suggest the interesting conclusion that optimistic expectations, independent of actual experience, can result in a negative transition to parenthood and reduced fertility intentions. Conversely, overly pessimistic expectations can yield an increase in intended family size.

As expected, the variables assessing negative child temperament and unexpected pregnancy problems had significant negative effects on change in intended family size. The set of control variables had no reliable influence on change in intended family size, with the exception of marital duration. The negative impact of this variable indicated that, net of all the other effects, the longer the woman delayed having her first child, the more likely she was to reduce her intended family size.

It is important to note that we have obtained support for our model of expectation–experience discrepancies in a sample of married, White, predominantly middle-class women with no history of infertility or multiple miscarriages. This sample was chosen to provide an initial test of the model on a sample whose fertility plans and parenting experiences were not overly shaped by social, health, or economic factors. The impact of expectancy violations may be different in samples that are less advantaged. A needed step in this line of research is to determine the validity of the model with a more diverse sample of women.

Discussion

I have organized this chapter in terms of two stages of a continuous sequence: the influence of an initial attitude on the performance of a subsequent behavior, and the effect of feedback resulting from the performance of that behavior in changing the initial attitude. I assumed that attitude strength would play a role in each of these stages. At the first stage, strong attitudes should be more predictive of behavior than should weak attitudes. At the second stage of the sequence, strong attitudes should be less likely to change as the result of feedback following the performance of the behavior. Two dimensions of information about the attitude object—amount and accuracy of information—were viewed as antecedents of attitude strength.

The first section of the chapter reviews work on amount of information and attitude-behavior consistency. There is a substantial amount of research demonstrating that subjects' amount of attitude-relevant information determines the impact of new information on attitude change. Similarly, attitudes supported by greater amounts of information are more likely to lead to attitude-behavior consistency. However, attitudes lacking this informational support are less likely to be related to subsequent behaviors. The latter section of the chapter reviews work on the second link of the sequence and analyzes attitude change following the performance of the behavior, as a function of the accuracy of the information that buttressed the initial attitude. Although there is less research on this topic, the existing studies indicate that respondents with accurate expectations about the outcomes of their behaviors are less likely to experience dissatisfaction and attitude change.

It is interesting to speculate whether the two dimensions of information—amount and accuracy—have broader effects on the attitude–action–attitude change sequence than we have discussed. Specifically, does accuracy of information affect the attitude-action stage and does amount of information moderate the action-attitude change stage? In the absence of data, it seems reasonable to expect that attitudes based on accurate information will evidence greater temporal stability and will be better predictors of subsequent behavior than will attitudes based on inaccurate information. Even if the respondent lacks direct behavioral experience with the attitude object, inaccurate information could be susceptible to change from any of a variety of indirect experiences (e.g., observing the outcomes of others' behaviors, the media). However, the magnitude of the effect of accuracy of information on attitude-behavior consistency probably will be constrained because, aside from direct behavioral experience, it is somewhat rare that we receive compelling evidence that our information and expectations are inaccurate.

It is harder to conceive of how amount of information could moderate the impact of action on attitude change. Moreover, any observed effect might be attributable to the relation of amount of information to accuracy of information. The limited available data suggest a relation of weak to moderate strength between these variables. For example, Scott (1969) reported significant correlations between amount of information (measured by thought-listing) and accuracy of information (measured by a factual test) that ranged from .38 to .34. The interrelation of accuracy and amount of information and the potential impact of accuracy of information on attitude-behavior consistency are important topics for future inquiry.

ACKNOWLEDGMENT

Preparation of this chapter was supported by research grant R01-HD23915 from the National Institute of Child Health and Human Development.

REFERENCES

Adler, N. E. (1979). Decision models in population research. *Journal of Population, 2,* 187–202.

Ajzen, I., & Fishbein, M. (1977). Attitude-behavior relations: A theoretical analysis and review of empirical research. *Psychological Bulletin, 84,* 888–918.

Allport, G. W. (1935). Attitudes. In C. Murchison (Ed.), *Handbook of social psychology* (pp. 798–844). Worcester, MA: Clark University Press.

Anderson, N. H. (1965). Averaging versus adding as a stimulus combination rule in impression formation. *Journal of Experimental Psychology, 70,* 394–400.

Anderson, N. H. (1967). Averaging model analysis of the set-size effect in impression formation. *Journal of Experimental Psychology, 75,* 158–165.

Anderson, N. H. (1968). Application of a linear-serial model to a personality-impression task using serial presentation. *Journal of Personality and Social Psychology, 10,* 354–362.

Anderson, N. H. (1971). Integration theory and attitude change. *Psychological Review, 78,* 171–206.

Anderson, N. H. (1981). *Foundations of information integration theory.* New York: Academic.

Anderson, T., & Birnbaum, M. H. (1976). Test of an additive model of social inference. *Journal of Personality and Social Psychology, 33,* 655–662.

Beach, L. R. (1982). Decision making: Diagnosis, action selection and implementation. In L. McAlister (Ed.), *Choice models for buyer behavior* (pp. 185–200). Greenwich CT: JAI.

Beach, L. R., Campbell, F. L., & Townes, B. D. (1979). Subjective expected utility and the prediction of birth planning decisions. *Organizational Behavior and Human Performance, 24,* 18–28.

Bearden, W. O., & Teel, J. E. (1983). Selected determinants of consumer satisfaction and complaint reports. *Journal of Marketing Research, 20,* 21–28.

Belsky, J. (1985). Exploring individual differences in marital change across the transition to parenthood: The role of violated expectations. *Journal of Marriage and the Family, 47,* 1037–1044.

Cohen, J., & Cohen, P. (1983). *Applied multiple regression correlation analysis for the behavioral sciences* (2nd ed.). Hillsdale, NJ: Lawrence Erlbaum Associates.

Cronbach, L. J., & Furby, L. (1970). How should we measure "change" or should we? *Psychological Bulletin, 74,* 68–80.

Darley, J. M., & Fazio, R. H. (1980). Expectancy confirmation processes arising in the social interaction sequence. *American Psychologist, 35,* 867–881.

Davidson, A. R., & Beach, L. R. (1981). Error patterns in the prediction of fertility behavior. *Journal of Applied Social Psychology, 11,* 455–488.

Davidson, A. R., & Jaccard, J. J. (1975). Population psychology: A new look at an old problem. *Journal of Personality and Social Psychology, 31,* 1073–1082.

Davidson, A. R., & Jaccard, J. J. (1979). Variables that moderate the attitude-behavior relation: Results of a longitudinal survey. *Journal of Personality and Social Psychology, 37,* 1364–1376.

Davidson, A. R., Kalmuss, D., & Cushman, L. (1992). *Change in behavioral intentions: The role of expectation-experience discrepancies.* Manuscript submitted for publication.

Davidson, A. R., & Morrison, D. M. (1982). Social psychological models of decision making. In. L. McAlister (Ed.), *Choice models for buyer behavior* (pp. 91–112). Greenwich, CT: JAI.

Davidson, A. R., Yantis, S., Norwood, M., & Montano, D. E. (1985). Amount of information about the attitude object and attitude-behavior consistency. *Journal of Personality and Social Psychology, 49*(5), 1184–1198.

Fawcett, J. T. (1983). Perceptions of the value of children: Satisfaction and costs. In R. A. Bulatao, R. D. Lee, P. E. Hollerbach, & J. Bongaarts (Eds.), *Determinants of fertility in developing countries: Vol. 1. Supply and demand for children.* New York: Academic.

Fazio, R. H., Chen, J., McDonel, E. C., & Sherman, S. J. (1982). Attitude accessibility, attitude-behavior consistency, and the strength of the object-evaluation association. *Journal of Experimental Social Psychology, 18,* 339–357.

Fazio, R. H., Powell, M. C., & Herr, P. (1983). Toward a processing model of the attitude–behavior relation: Assessing one's attitude upon mere observation of the attitude object. *Journal of Personality and Social Psychology, 44*, 723–735.

Fazio, R. H., & Zanna, M. P. (1981). Direct experience and attitude-behavior consistency. In. L. Berkowitz (Ed.), *Advances in experimental social psychology* (Vol. 14, pp. 161–202). New York: Academic.

Fishbein, M., & Ajzen, I. (1975). *Belief, attitude, intention and behavior.* Reading, MA: Addison-Wesley.

Fishbein, M., & Coombs, F. S. (1974). Basis for decision: An attitudinal analysis of voting behavior. *Journal of Applied Social Psychology, 4*, 95–124.

Fishbein, M., & Jaccard, J. J. (1973). Theoretical and methodological considerations in the prediction of family planning intentions and behavior. *Representative Research in Social Psychology, 4*, 37–51.

Heider, F. (1958). *The psychology of interpersonal relations.* New York: Wiley.

Helson, H. (1964). *Adaptation level theory: An experimental and systematic approach to behavior.* New York: Harper & Row.

Jussim, L. (1986). Self-fulfilling prophecies: A theoretical and integrative review. *Psychological Review, 93*(4), 429–445.

Kallgren, C. A., & Wood, W. (1985). Access to attitude-relevant information in memory as a determinant of attitude-behavior consistency. *Journal of Experimental Social Psychology, 22*, 328–338.

Kalmuss, D., Davidson, A. R., & Cushman, L. (1992). Parenting expectations, experiences and adjustment to parenthood: A test of the violated expectations framework. *Journal of Marriage and the Family, 54*, 516–526.

Kelley, H., & Thibaut, J. (1978). *Interpersonal relations: A theory of interdependence.* New York: Wiley-Interscience.

Kelley, S., & Mirer, T. W. (1974). The simple act of voting. *American Political Science Review, 68*, 572–591.

LaBarbera, P. A., & Mazursky, D. (1983). A longitudinal assessment of consumer satisfaction/ dissatisfaction: The dynamic aspect of the cognitive process. *Journal of Marketing Research, 20*, 393–404.

Lee, W. (1971). *Decision theory and human behavior.* New York: Wiley.

McGuire, W. J. (1985). Attitudes and attitude change. In G. Lindzey & E. Aronson (Eds.), *The handbook of social psychology* (3rd ed., Vol. 2, pp. 234–326). New York: Random House.

Norman, R. (1975). Affective-cognitive consistency, attitudes, conformity, and behavior. *Journal of Personality and Social Psychology, 32*, 83–91.

Oliver, R. L. (1980). A cognitive model of the antecedent and consequences of satisfaction decisions. *Journal of Marketing Research, 17*, 460–469.

Pagel, M., & Davidson, A. R. (1984). A comparison of three social-psychological models of attitude and behavioral plan: Prediction of contraceptive behavior. *Journal of Personality and Social Psychology, 47*, 517–533.

Rosenberg, M. J. (1968). Discussion: Impression processing and the evaluation of old and new objects. In R. P. Abelson, E. Aronson, W. J. McGuire, T. M. Newcomb, M. J. Rosenberg, & P. H. Tannenbaum (Eds.), *Theories of cognitive consistency: A sourcebook.* Chicago: Rand McNally.

Ruble, D. N., Fleming, A. S., Hackel, L. S., & Stangor, C. (1988). Changes in the marital relationship during the transition to first time motherhood: Effects of violated expectations concerning division of household labor. *Journal of Personality and Social Psychology, 55*, 78–87.

Sample, J., & Warland, R. (1973). Attitude and the prediction of behavior. *Social Forces, 51*, 292–304.

Schuman, H., & Johnson, M. (1976). Attitudes and behavior. *Annual Review of Sociology, 2*, 161–207.

Schwartz, S. (1978). Temporal instability as a moderator of the attitude-behavior relationship. *Journal of Personality and Social Psychology, 36*, 715–724.

Scott, W. A. (1969). Structure of natural cognitions. *Journal of Personality and Social Psychology*, *12*, 261–278.

Sherman, S. J., & Fazio, R. H. (1983). Parallels between attitudes and traits as predictors of behavior. *Journal of Personality*, *51*, 308–345.

Sloan, L. R., & Ostrom, T. M. (1974). Amount of information and interpersonal judgment. *Journal of Personality and Social Psychology*, *29*, 23–29.

Snyder, M. (1984). When belief creates reality. *Advances in Experimental Social Psychology*, *18*, 62–113.

Westbrook, R. A. (1987). Product/consumption-based affective responses and postpurchase processes. *Journal of Marketing Research*, *24*, 258–270.

Wilson, T. D., Dunn, D. S., Kraft, D., & Lisle, D. J. (1989). Introspection, attitude change, and attitude-behavior consistency: The disruptive effects of explaining why we feel the way we do. In L. Berkowitz (Ed.), *Advances in experimental social psychology* (Vol. 19, pp. 123–205). San Diego, CA: Academic.

Wilson, T. D., Kraft, D., & Dunn, D. S. (1989). The disruptive effects of explaining attitudes: The moderating effect of knowledge about the attitude object. *Journal of Experimental Social Psychology*, *25*, 379–400.

Wood, W. (1982). Retrieval of attitude-relevant information from memory: Effects on susceptibility to persuasion and on intrinsic motivation. *Journal of Personality and Social Psychology*, *42*, 798–810.

Wood, W., Kallgren, C. A., & Preisler, R. M. (1985). Access to attitude-relevant information in memory as a determinant of persuasion: The role of message attributes. *Journal of Experimental Social Psychology*, *21*, 73–85.

Yamagishi, T., & Hill, C. T. (1981). Adding versus averaging models revisited: A test of a path-analytic integration model. *Journal of Personality and Social Psychology*, *41*, 13–25.

13
▼▼▼▼▼▼▼

Methods for Identifying Consequential Beliefs: Implications for Understanding Attitude Strength

James Jaccard
Carmen Radecki
Tracey Wilson
Patricia Dittus
State University of New York, Albany

The concepts of *attitude extremity*, *importance*, and *intensity* are becoming of increasing theoretical import in the attitude literature. Two individuals may hold identical attitudes towards an object, yet their behavior or reactions to persuasive communications about that object may be quite different. Concepts such as attitude extremity, importance, and intensity, as well as affective ambivalence, cognitive ambivalence, belief heterogeneity, involvement, cognitive elaboration, emotional commitment, salience, accessibility, belief polarization, vested interest, value relevance, hot versus cold cognitions, and affective-cognitive consistency are all variables that have been studied under the general rubric of "attitude strength" to explain why individuals with similar evaluations of an attitude object behave differently with respect to that object.

One major thrust of this research has focused on distinctions between evaluative and cognitive foundations of attitudes and the interplay between these components. The evaluative component refers to how positive or negative an individual feels about an attitude object, whereas the cognitive component refers to the specific beliefs that the individual has about the attitude object. Much of the research in the area of attitude strength has explained differences in attitude resistance to change and attitude–behavior consistency in terms of evaluative and cognitive components. For example, Wood and her associates (Wood, 1982; Wood & Kallgren, 1988; Wood, Kallgren, & Presler, 1985) have argued that the number of beliefs that an individual possesses about an attitude object is related to how susceptible the individual will be to persuasive messages because more knowledgeable people can draw upon a broader base of attitude-relevant knowledge to counterargue the arguments within a message. Tesser (Sadler & Tesser, 1973; Tesser & Conlee, 1975) and others (e.g., Linville & Jones, 1980; Judd & Lusk, 1984) have examined how the process of thinking about an attitude object interacts with the number of beliefs about that object in influencing attitude polarization. According to this work, thinking about an attitude object will lead an individual to add new beliefs that are consistent with those in the existing belief system, thereby polarizing the attitude. The amount of polarization decreases with increasing numbers of independent beliefs, but increases with a greater number of correlated beliefs. Davidson, Yantis, Norwood, and Montano (1985) and others (e.g., Kallgren & Wood, 1986) have documented a relationship between the number of beliefs underlying an attitude and attitude-behavior consistency: The greater the number of beliefs, the greater the correspondence between attitudes and behaviors. Finally, attitude-cognitive consistency is related to attitude-behavior consistency as well as polarization (e.g., Chaiken & Yates, 1985; Norman, 1975).

Underlying much of this research, as well as research in related domains, is the need to identify the cognitions that underlie an individual's attitude or behavior and to differentiate between beliefs that are relatively important or consequential in influencing attitudes versus beliefs that are not. For example, according to the research reviewed earlier, attitudes that derive from many beliefs should behave differently in response to certain variables (e.g., persuasive attempts) than attitudes that derive from only a few beliefs. There have been literally hundreds of studies to identify the "important" perceptions that underlie attitudes about such topics as voting behavior, drug use, family planning behavior, blood donation behavior, consumer purchase decisions, career–marriage orientations, absenteeism, smoking behavior, use of city services, AIDS-related risk behavior, and dieting, to name only a few. These studies have used a diverse set of methods for assessing what beliefs underlie an attitude, drawing on a wide range of theoretical and empirical frameworks.

In this chapter, we first briefly review selected research that has compared methods designed to identify beliefs that underlie attitudes. These measurement strategies are crucial to research on attitude strength because they ultimately shape the way in which a researcher characterizes a cognitive structure underlying an attitude. We conclude that there is a relative lack of convergence between methods for identifying cognitions that underlie attitudes and discuss the theoretical and practical implications of this. We then present a theoretical framework that incorporates the construct of importance and permits both idiographic and nomothetic analyses of the relationships between beliefs, attitudes, and behavior. Finally, we develop the implications of the framework for research on attitude strength.

DEFINING BELIEF IMPORTANCE

There are many ways of defining belief importance. Most theorists agree that a belief is a perceived association between an attitude object and some attribute, characteristic, outcome, goal, or value and the strength of the belief is represented by the strength of the association. The strength of this association has been defined in the literature using either a structural or a relational approach. The structural approach defines belief importance in terms of some quality of the belief per se. For example, some theorists define a belief as being an important one if it is strongly linked to an outcome or value that is important to the individual. If gaining weight is highly adverse to a woman considering using birth control pills and she is certain that they would induce weight gain, then this belief is said to be an important one. Relational approaches to defining belief importance focus on the extent to which variations in the belief (either its strength or evaluation) are related (in a causal sense) to variations in attitudes. For example, a belief is said to be important for an attitude if it is a primary cause of that attitude (i.e., changes in the belief produce changes in the attitude). Some beliefs, when changed, will yield little or no change in attitude, and these beliefs can be said to be less important or less consequential than beliefs that, when changed, yield substantial changes in attitude. Thus, the relational approach requires that the investigator determine if a belief has causal implications for an attitude and that he or she quantify the degree of causal implication that the belief has.

MEASURING COGNITIVE STRUCTURES
UNDERLYING AN ATTITUDE

Seven major approaches to measuring belief importance have been used extensively in the attitude literature, all employing a relational perspective. All of the approaches have advocates as well as detractors and numerous controversial issues arise within the context of each. Our purpose here is only to provide a sense of the major strategies that have been used in the attitude literature.

One set of procedures for identifying beliefs that underlie an attitude is based on free elicitation methodology where individuals are asked to spontaneously generate consequences, outcomes, or attributes that they think are associated with the attitude object (e.g., Fishbein, 1972; Fishbein & Ajzen, 1975; Rosenberg & Oltman, 1962). An underlying assumption of this strategy is that those beliefs that are mentioned by an individual are important in influencing his or her attitude toward the behavior and that those beliefs that are not mentioned are of lesser importance, if any at all. Some researchers have further suggested that more readily accessible beliefs are more important than those that are less accessible (e.g., Szalay & Deese, 1978).

A second set of approaches for determining whether a belief underlies an attitude is based on subjective probability models (e.g., Fishbein & Ajzen, 1975; Jaccard & King, 1977; Jaccard, Knox, & Brinberg, 1979; McGuire, 1960, 1981; Wyer, 1970, 1972; Wyer & Hartwick, 1980). As an example, in Wyer's framework, one index of the extent to which a belief underlies a positive attitude toward some object is the absolute difference between two subjective probabilities, $p(A|B)$ and $p(A|B')$. $p(A|B)$ is the subjective rating by an individual that he or she would have a positive attitude given that belief B is true and $p(A|B')$ is the subjective rating by the individual that he or she would have a positive attitude given that belief B is not true. As the difference between the conditional probabilities increases, the belief has greater implications for the attitude.

A third set of approaches to assess belief importance is based on behavioral process methodologies (e.g., Jacoby, 1975, 1978). The method involves providing an individual potential access to an array of information about attitude objects and then permitting the individual to acquire as much or as little information as he/she wishes in order to arrive at an evaluation of the object. The importance of belief dimensions is inferred from what, and in what order, an individual asks for information.

A fourth approach to measuring belief importance is a direct rating method. For example, Johnson and Jaccard (1981) asked respondents to indicate the importance of different factors in influencing their evaluations of various career/marriage options on a 21-point scale ranging from 0 (extremely unimportant) to 20 (extremely important). Such ratings also have been used in research comparing subjective versus objective weighting of cues by individuals and has generally found lack of correspondence between the two (e.g., Wiggins, 1973).

A fifth set of approaches to determining whether a belief underlies an attitude is based on conjoint analysis and functional measurement analysis. Conjoint analysis involves forming descriptions of hypothetical objects based on the factorial manipulation of different attribute dimensions. For example, a set of eight cameras might be described based on the factorial manipulation of three dimensions with two levels each (e.g., cost, type of lens, and size). An individual would rank order the stimuli in terms of preference, and the resulting data are analyzed to infer the relative weights assigned to each attribute. In functional measurement, rather than ranking the stimuli, the individual rates each stimulus on a response dimension (e.g., how favorable the individual feels about it). Functional measurement incorporates an error theory into its analysis by obtaining test-retest ratings of each stimulus and uses a relative range index to reflect the relative importance of the dimensions being manipulated (see Anderson, 1981).

A sixth set of approaches to assessing the cognitions that may underlie an attitude is based on correlational strategies. A set of beliefs are measured and then correlated with a measure of attitude. For example, a correlation might be computed between ratings of agreement with the statement "using birth control pills will make me gain weight" and a measure of the attitude toward using birth control pills. The absolute value of the correlation is an index of the extent to which the belief underlies the attitude. Alternatively, the belief ratings could be entered into a multiple regression equation, and the (standardized) regression coefficients could be interpreted as the importance of each belief in determining the attitude. Note that the correlational approach does not yield a separate importance index for each individual, but rather can only be applied at the group level by calculating a correlational index across individuals.

A final method involves presenting individuals with pairs of attributes and asking them to indicate which of the two is more important to them in making a decision about or forming an evaluation of an object (e.g., Edwards, 1957). All possible pairs of a set of attributes are presented, and then paired comparison analysis using Thurstonian theory is applied to derive scale values of the relative importance of the attributes on an interval level scale. As with correlational analyses, this method only yields importance indices across a group of individuals.

Few studies have directly compared the convergence between two or more of the importance indices (e.g., Cook & Stewart, 1975), and most of the studies have been limited in scope. We have conducted a series of more extensive investigations that has examined the extent to which the different measures converge in their characterizations of the number and type of beliefs that underlie an attitude. For example, Jaccard and Sheng (1985) assessed convergence for an elicitation measure, importance ratings, two subjective probability indices, two indices from a behavioral process methodology, and two correlational indices. Interestingly, the measures generally were uncorrelated or only slightly correlated (in the 0.10 to 0.20 range). The two behavioral process measures showed inter-correlations of approximately 0.50 with each other, which is not surprising given that they were derived from the same methodology. The importance ratings revealed correlations of approximately 0.30 with the subjective probability index. Other than this, the correlations between indices were low and nonsignificant (less than 0.15). We have replicated this general trend of low convergence with other importance indices using a wide range of measures and methodological approaches (e.g., Dittus & Jaccard, 1992; Jaccard, Brinberg, & Ackerman, 1986).

These results have important implications for studies that address the question of how differences in cognitive structures affect the resistance of attitudes to change and how attitudes relate to behavior. According to our results, the way in which a researcher characterizes a cognitive structure will be method dependent. Which measure is the best or the correct one for determining what and how many beliefs underlie an attitude? One way to answer this question would be to address the issue empirically. This would involve the design of change studies in which one approach would predict that a change in a belief will lead to a change in attitude, whereas another approach would predict that this would not be the case. Ultimately, a sufficient number of studies could be conducted so as to yield insights into the change implications of the different indices.

Alternatively, it might be argued that each of the indices measures belief importance to a certain degree, but that importance is a multidimensional construct. The relative lack of correlation between indices results from the different measures tapping into different aspects of importance. For example, the elicitation index appears to measure, albeit imperfectly, factors that people consciously consider in their decisions. The direct rating index and the subjective probability indices may instead indicate whether a given consequence *could* be important in influencing a decision were it to be made salient and manipulated. This multidimensional perspective implies that the theoretical foundations of each index needs to be elaborated in greater detail and integrated into our theorizing about cognitive structures and attitudes, a task that awaits further elaboration in the attitude literature.

A THEORETICAL NETWORK

It became evident to us that a multiple method approach to characterizing cognitive structures underlying attitudes was crucial and that these methods must be embedded within the context of a broader theoretical network of the relationships between beliefs, attitudes, intentions, and behavior. The next section describes such a framework. We begin by highlighting the core constructs of the theory. We describe a method for the assessment of the extent to which beliefs underlie an attitude that is multimethod in its orientation and which has been empirically borne out as being fruitful. We then consider the implications of the theory for a wide range of phenomena in the attitude literature.

Our framework conceptualizes the belief–attitude–behavior relationship from a decision-making perspective. When making a decision in a familiar situation, individuals typically accept the suggestion of impulse, habit, custom, or rule, without serious reflection. Most behavioral decisions in everyday life are of this character. However, when the decision is perceived as being important or when impulse, habit, or custom are questioned, then the individual will reflect on the matter, considering one or more courses of action. Our framework is concerned with thoughtful behavioral decisions.

There are at least eight activities in which an individual can engage during decision making. The first is *problem recognition*, where an individual determines that a problem exists and that a decision must be considered. Second is *goal identification*, where the individual specifies, a priori, the purpose of the decision, that is, the ideal outcome of the decision. Third is *option generation/identification*, in which the individual thinks of potential alternative solutions to the problem at hand. Fourth is *information search*, in which the individual seeks information, either about what additional options might be available or about the properties of one or more of the options under consideration. Fifth is the *assessment of option information*, in which the individual considers the information he or she has about different decision options. In doing so, the individual forms an attitude toward performing each option. Given p decision options, the preference structure is the set of p attitudes. Sixth is the *choice process*, where one of the decision options is chosen for purposes of future behavioral enactment. Seventh is *behavioral translation*, where the individual translates the decision into overt behavior. Eighth is *postdecision evaluation*, in which the individual reflects on the decision after the chosen option has been enacted and evaluates the decision process in light of the outcomes that have resulted. Not all of the activities will necessarily be performed by the individual, nor must they be performed in the sequence described.

Preference Structures

Many behaviors of interest to attitude theorists can be conceptualized as a choice between behavioral alternatives (e.g., choice of a birth control method, choice of a career), and the individual may be said to have an attitude towards each of these alternatives. Consistent with subjective-expected-utility theory, an individual will choose to perform that option towards which the most positive attitude is held (Jaccard, 1981; Jaccard & Becker, 1985).

Perceptual Structures

One of the major determinants of this preference structure is the individual's beliefs about the various decision options. These beliefs are represented in the form of a perceptual structure matrix. For a given topic (e.g., choice of a birth control method), the individual is aware of a set of options from which to choose (e.g., birth control pills, condoms, diaphragm). Each option varies on one or more informational dimensions (e.g., effectiveness in preventing pregnancy, health risks, cost, convenience in using). The perceptual structure matrix characterizes the individual's perceptions of each option on each dimension, as illustrated in Table 13.1. The cell entries refer to the extent to which the individual believes the option is "good" or "bad" (typically measured on a −5 to +5 rating

TABLE 13.1
Perceptual Structure Matrix

	Option 1	Option 2	Option 3	. . . .	Option p
Dimension 1	R_{11}	R_{12}	R_{13}	. . . .	R_{1p}
Dimension 2	R_{21}	R_{22}	R_{23}	. . . .	R_{2p}
Dimension 3	R_{31}	R_{32}	R_{33}	. . . .	R_{3p}
.					
.					
.					
Dimension m	R_{m1}	R_{m2}	R_{m3}	. . . .	R_{mp}

Note. Cell entries represent ratings of each option on a given dimension in terms of how good or bad the option is on the dimension.

scale) on the dimension in question. For example, the pill might be perceived as being "very good" in terms of its effectiveness in preventing pregnancy, but "bad" in terms of the health risks associated with it.

Linking Perceptual Structures and Preference Structures

Perceptual structure and preference structures can be linked using Anderson's information integration theory. According to information integration theory, the way in which individuals integrate information to form attitudes can be characterized in terms of cognitive algebra. In general, two broad classes of integration rules can be distinguished. Compensatory rules are those in which the negative features of an option can be offset by positive features of the option. Noncompensatory rules are those in which positive qualities do not offset negative qualities. The occurrence of a negative feature on a given dimension may lead to a negative attitude, independent of the positive features of that option on other dimensions. Within each of these general classes of integration rules, there are submodels of the integration process. For example, included among the different types of compensatory rules, are the constant weight averaging rule, the differential weight averaging rule, the constant weight summation rule, and the differential weight summation rule. Functional measurement methodology permits the investigator to assess the type of integration rule that is operating, as well as how the individual pieces of information are valued by the individual. A powerful feature of the methodology is that it can be applied on an idiographic basis.

Functional measurement usually involves factorially manipulating different types of information and then obtaining measures of attitude toward each of the resulting hypothetical stimuli. For example, eight hypothetical methods of birth control can be described in a $2 \times 2 \times 2$ factorial design manipulating effectiveness, health risks, and convenience. Attitudes toward each of the eight birth control methods would then be obtained and analyzed via functional measurement methods. Our research has suggested that the number of dimensions that are potentially relevant to a decision topic, such as the choice of a birth control method, frequently ranges between 10 and 15. Obviously, it is not feasible to orthogonally manipulate all dimensions, because the number of hypothetical options would be overwhelming. The number of stimuli can be reduced by assuming, for example, additive integration rules and using a fractional factorial design. However, this approach is unsatisfactory because the nature of the integration rule must be assumed and not empirically tested.

One solution is to manipulate only a small number of informational dimensions. In our framework, we typically manipulate three dimensions with three levels per factor. The dimensions can differ for each individual studied and are selected by identifying the three most important dimensions to the individual. We identify these dimensions using a multimethod strategy. First, based on a literature review and interviews with experts in the topic area of interest, we compile a list of dimensions that are potentially relevant to the decision. We then conduct a pilot study with a representative group of individuals of the target population who participate in an elicitation task in which they spontaneously generate important dimensions and advantages and disadvantages for the decision being studied. The initial list generated by experts is then augmented (if necessary) with frequently mentioned dimensions not initially included. Infrequently mentioned dimensions may be deleted from the list. Thus, we use elicitation data at an aggregate level to assist us in compiling a list of potentially relevant dimensions. Next we present the individual with the list of dimensions and ask him or her to rank order the dimensions in terms of how important each dimension is in influencing whether the individual feels positive or negative about a given option.

Our importance measure is essentially a variant of the direct rating approach described earlier, although it is based on a rank order task. We chose this approach over the other candidates for several reasons. First, of all the importance measures, the direct rating method was one of the few to exhibit some convergent validity (albeit low levels) with one or more other measures (e.g., the conditional probability index). Second, the search measures from behavioral process methods and the probability measures were considered to be impractical, especially if our procedure is to be used in survey research. Third, the correlational and paired comparison approaches were rejected because they could only be applied at the nomothetic level. Fourth, we had little confidence in the elicitation methods over and beyond helping us to generate an overall list of relevant dimensions because our research suggests that such methods are particularly vulnerable to transitory influences. Finally, as will be seen, we also use a functional measurement based index of importance for purposes of assessing importance convergence. Such convergence tends to be high, given the procedures and framework that we use.

Individuals are asked to rank the dimensions on two different occasions (usually 1 week apart), and the three highest ranked dimensions are selected for manipulation in the functional measurement task. We have found that the reliability of rankings across sessions is quite high, at least in terms of the same dimensions occurring within the top three. Given that one has identified the dimensions to be manipulated in a functional measurement task, the selection of values that will be used to manipulate a dimension is of primary importance, because it can influence the outcome of the analysis. When forming an evaluative judgment about a behavioral option, people probably translate specific values of a dimension into three to five general subjective categories on the dimension of interest (Jaccard & Wood, 1988). For example, a birth control method that is 75% effective might be translated into the category "moderately bad" on a dimension of effectiveness and an attitude formed accordingly. Each category will have a range of values associated with it. For example, any birth control method that has an effectiveness rate between 65% and 75% might be classified as "moderately bad." Our methodology manipulates informational dimensions in terms of three general categories, corresponding to "moderately bad," "neutral," and "moderately good" on the dimension. These verbal descriptors are quite general and can be applied to both qualitative and quantitative informational dimensions. They also are directly tied to the ratings made in the perceptual structure matrix, an important aspect of the methodology.

Based on these considerations, descriptions of 27 hypothetical objects are formulated vis-à-vis the factorial manipulation of the three most important dimensions. The individual completes the functional measurement task by rating the 27 stimuli on the same attitude scale used to assess the preference structure (usually a 21 point, −10 to +10, unfavorable–favorable scale). The task is repeated on multiple (e.g., three) occasions, and functional analysis is then undertaken to isolate the relevant integration rule and the subjective values of the response dimensions (see Anderson, 1981, or Jaccard & Becker, 1985). An advantage of this approach is that a formal error theory is applicable, thus permitting the researcher to consider the effects of measurement error.

One potential problem with the use of the previous approach is that it involves hypothetical stimuli. Analyses in such situations may yield conclusions that do not correspond to how beliefs are related to attitudes in real-world applications. In addition, it may be that the dimensions manipulated are irrelevant or improperly chosen and that the method of manipulation is suspect. We have devised a procedure for addressing this issue. Consider a choice situation involving 10 existing methods of birth control. We first obtain measures of the preference structure and the perceptual structure matrix. We next administer the functional measurement task, as already described. Based on the $3 \times 3 \times 3$ ANOVA (analysis of variance) of the attitude ratings, it is possible to develop a mathematical model that describes the relationship between beliefs and attitudes in the context of the hypothetical stimuli. More specifically, the model would predict that an attitude toward a given option is equal to the grand mean of the ratings plus any statistically significant treatment effects from the ANOVA. The data from the perceptual structure matrix (that contains ratings of each existing method on each informational dimension) can be used to identify the cell in the factorial design that an existing method falls within. A predicted attitude score based on the ANOVA model can then be calculated for that cell and compared with the observed attitude in the preference structure. If the functional measurement task is unreasonable (because it has omitted important dimensions or made inappropriate assumptions), then one would expect a poor correspondence between predicted and observed attitudes. Our research has generally found good correspondence between predicted and observed preference structures.

Example data from one of our subjects for an analysis of birth control decisions is presented in Table 13.2. This individual is currently using the pill, which is consistent with the attitudinal pattern in the preference structure. The three highest ranked dimensions for the individual were health risks, effectiveness, and spontaneity. The functional measurement analysis suggests a combination of compensatory and noncompensatory mechanisms. If either effectiveness or health

TABLE 13.2
Functional Measurement Analysis for Subject 5

Cell Means									
		Good Spont			Med Spont			Poor Spont		
	Eff:	Good	Med	Poor	Good	Med	Poor	Good	Med	Poor
	Good	6.00	0.00	−9.67	4.00	0.00	−9.67	−6.00	−9.67	−9.67
HR	Med	2.00	−5.00	−9.67	0.00	−5.00	−9.67	−9.67	−9.67	−9.67
	Poor	−9.67	−9.67	−9.67	−9.67	−9.67	−9.67	−9.67	−9.67	−9.67

Perceptual Structure Ratings								
	Pill	Diaph	Condom	IUD	Rhythm	Sponge	Foam/C	Withdraw
HR	+1	+1	+1	−5	+5	+3	+3	+5
Eff	+5	+3	+1	+4	−5	−3	−5	−5
Spon	+5	−4	−5	+5	−1	−5	−5	−5

Preference Structure								
	Pill	Diaph	Condom	IUD	Rhythm	Sponge	Foam/C	Withdraw
Pred Att	5.7	−8.5	−9.3	−9.7	−9.7	−9.7	−9.7	−9.7
Obser Att	7	−8	−8	−10	−10	−10	−10	−10

Note. Grand Mean = −6.59
Main Effect Means:
   Health Risks: −3.85   −6.26   −9.67
   Effectiveness: −3.63   −6.48   −9.67
   Spontaneity: −5.04   −5.48   −9.26

risks are poor, the attitude toward the method is quite negative, irrespective of
the standing on other dimensions. If spontaneity is poor, the attitude is also quite
negative, although if the method is good in terms of effectiveness and health
risks, this can offset the negative impact of poor spontaneity. Given moderate to
good spontaneity, then the evaluation of methods seems to be a compensatory
function of health risks and effectiveness, given that neither of these dimensions
is unsatisfactorily poor. A set of predicted attitudes based on the ANOVA model
from the functional measurement analysis, and with interpolations from the
perceptual structure ratings, corresponds reasonably well with the observed preference structure. The relative range indices suggest that all of the dimensions
are important and can be ordered in terms of health risks, effectiveness, and
spontaneity. This is consistent with the ranks provided by the individual in the
initial ranking task.

A powerful feature of this framework is that it can be applied in its entirety
to a single individual. It is possible to determine if an individual's attitude is
consistent with his or her behavior (by predicting behavior from the most positive

attitude in the preference structure) and it is possible to examine the relationship between beliefs and attitudes for a given individual. This is not the case for most theories of the relationships between beliefs, attitudes, and behavior. For example, using the traditional expectancy-value framework, it is impossible to assess the relationship between these variables without recourse to nomothetic analysis. In addition, measurement assumptions about response metrics in our framework are minimal, which is not true of across-individual analyses (which must assume individuals use and interpret rating scales in the same way). Our only assumption is that an individual interprets the scales the same way when rating different behavioral alternatives. Finally, the idiographic approach we adopt avoids problems due to heterogeneous weights that typify the dominant correlational approaches in the attitude area.

IMPLICATIONS FOR RESEARCH ON ATTITUDE STRENGTH

We have conducted numerous empirical applications of our framework with considerable success (see, e.g., Jaccard, 1981; Jaccard & Becker 1985; Jaccard & Wood, 1988). We briefly describe some of these studies as we consider the implications of our approach for research on attitude strength.

Defining Attitude-Behavior Consistency

Much of the research on attitude strength uses cognitive and attitudinal variables to predict attitude–behavior consistency. Such consistency frequently is defined in terms of correlations between attitudes and behavior, with high correlations implying strong attitude–behavior correspondence. Our theoretical framework permits the assessment of attitude–behavior correspondence on a per individual basis without recourse to a nomothetic framework.

Consider the six individuals in Table 13.3 who chose between two political candidates in an election. The first column indicates the candidate voted for and the second and third columns indicate the attitude toward each candidate (on a -10 to $+10$ scale). The fourth column presents the predicted choice based on the analysis of the preference structure (i.e., the option with the most positive attitude). For each individual, there is perfect correspondence between attitudes (as reflected in the predicted choice) and behavior. However, an across-subject correlation between the attitude toward Candidate A and whether or not Candidate A was chosen yields a near zero correlation ($r = 0.15$). As well, there is a negligible correlation ($r = 0.30$) between the attitude toward Candidate B and choice of B. The correlational analysis suggests that for this group of individuals, attitudes are unrelated to behavior, whereas this is not true from the perspective of preference structure analysis. Numerous studies have found that the within-

TABLE 13.3
Attitude–Behavior Consistency

Individual	Observed Choice	Candidate A	Candidate B	Predicted Choice
1	A	4	3	A
2	A	2	1	A
3	A	8	7	A
4	B	4	5	B
5	B	2	3	B
6	B	6	7	B

subject, across-alternative approach that we propose outperforms more traditional nomothetic approaches when predicting attitudes from behavior (e.g., Jaccard, 1981; Jaccard & Becker, 1985).

Attitude-Cognitive Consistency

Several studies have examined the impact of attitude-cognitive consistency on other variables, such as the degree of consistency between attitudes and behavior (e.g., Norman, 1975). Most of these studies have operationalized attitude-cognitive consistency using expectancy-value models. These models derive a cognitive index by multiplying certainty and value ratings for each of n beliefs about the attitude object and then summing these products across beliefs. In some research, this cognitive sum (CS) is correlated with a direct measure of attitude, typically a semantic differential scale. A low correlation is taken to imply that the attitude does not derive from cognitive foundations, whereas a high correlation implies that the attitude has a strong cognitive base. Such correlation coefficients must be computed across individuals, hence no index of attitude-cognitive consistency is available on a single subject basis. Most researchers have circumvented this problem by standardizing CS and attitude scores across individuals (thereby placing them on a common metric), and then calculating the absolute difference between the scores for a given individual. This absolute difference is interpreted as an index of attitude-cognitive correspondence.

Our theoretical framework suggests several difficulties with this paradigm. First, the index of attitude-cognitive consistency is based on a combinatorial model that is of limited applicability. The summation of belief products assumes a combinatorial rule among beliefs that is compensatory in character when, in fact, noncompensatory or combinations of compensatory and noncompensatory processes may be operating. A researcher might conclude that an individual's attitudes are independent of cognitions not because this is the case, but because the researcher has applied the wrong (combinatorial) model when evaluating the correspondence between the two. Our research suggests that this may indeed be the case. Most individuals seem to combine beliefs using both noncompensatory and compensatory rules, as illustrated by the example individual in the previous section. Strictly compensatory models seem to be the exception rather than the rule and hence probably should not be used to determine attitude-belief correspondence. By contrast, our theoretical framework permits an explicit evaluation of belief-attitude consistency by means of a formal comparison of the predicted and observed preference structures for a given individual. Because the predicted preference structure is based on an empirically derived integration rule, it is not restricted to the assumption of compensatory mechanisms.

Second, in our theoretical framework, belief-attitude correspondence can be directly assessed on an individual by individual basis by comparing predicted and observed preference structures for a given individual. This circumvents the strong (and dubious) measurement assumptions that the "absolute difference" method makes (i.e., that each individual uses and interprets the rating scales in exactly the same way). It also avoids the problem of defining consistency based on nomothetic considerations. For example, because the standardization of measures is performed across individuals, it follows that the consistency score for a given person is dependent on the response tendencies of other individuals. A more desirable approach is to define attitude-cognitive consistency for a given individual independent of the response patterns or tendencies of other individuals.

The utility of our approach for studying the implications of attitude-cognitive consistency can be illustrated with data we have collected on condom use. Consider the theoretical framework in Fig. 13.1a. According to this model, attitude-belief consistency is influenced by how much direct experience an individual has had with the attitude object. The more experience the individual has had with the attitude object, the greater will be the consistency between attitudes (i.e., evaluations) and beliefs. Direct experience with the attitude object also is assumed to influence attitude-behavior consistency. The more experience the individual has had with the attitude object in the past, the more consistent his or her current attitudes will be with current behavior. The model in Fig. 13.1a predicts that a significant correlation should be observed between attitude-belief consistency and attitude-behavior consistency. However, this correlation can be completely explained by the common influence of direct experience on the two variables and, in this sense, the correlation is spurious. An alternative model is presented in Fig. 13.1b. This model states that direct experience influences both attitude-behavior and attitude-belief consistency, but that attitude-belief consistency is associated with attitude-behavior consistency over and above this common influence. There is an additional psychological mechanism that is contributing to the association between attitude-belief consistency and attitude-behavior consistency, perhaps a need for consistency in general.

These two models make different predictions about the partial correlation between measures of attitude-belief consistency and attitude-behavior consistency holding direct experience constant. Model A predicts the partial correlation will

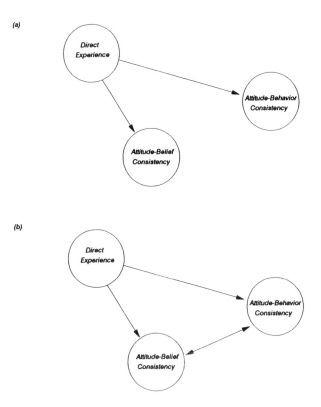

FIG. 13.1.   Two models of the effects of direct experience.

be zero, whereas Model B predicts the partial correlation will be nonzero. We tested the two models (as well as other models) using data collected from 178 sexually active college students in the context of our theoretical framework. Direct experience was measured as a self-report of the number of times that the individuals had used condoms in the past. Belief-attitude correspondence was measured as a difference score between the predicted attitude toward using condoms vis-à-vis our functional measurement approach and the actual attitude toward using condoms, as measured on our traditional attitude scale. Attitude-behavior consistency was defined as a dichotomous measure. If the attitude toward the condom was the most favorable attitude among the set of eight birth control methods assessed in the preference structure, and if the individual indicated that he or she is currently using condoms, then attitudes were scored as being consistent with behavior (i.e., a score of 1 was assigned to the attitude-behavior consistency measure). Similarly, if the attitude toward the condom was not the most favorable among the set of eight birth control methods in the preference structure and if the individual indicated he or she is not currently using condoms, then a score of 1 was also assigned to the consistency measure. All other cases were assigned a score of 0 (e.g., the condom was the most favorably evaluated method but it was reported as not currently being used, or the condom was not rated as the most positively evaluated method but it was reported as currently being used).

Our analyses yielded correlational patterns that were consistent with Model B as opposed to Model A. Direct experience was correlated 0.43 with attitude-belief consistency and 0.41 with attitude-behavior consistency. The partial correlation between the two consistency measures was 0.33, suggesting that the common influence of direct experience is not the sole determinant of the correlation between the two forms of consistency.

Interestingly, traditional analyses of these data yielded no relationships between any of the variables. For example, the traditional approach focused on the correlation between the attitude toward condoms and current use of condoms using typical, across-subject analyses. This correlation was near zero ($r = 0.02$). To test if the relationship between attitudes and behavior differed as a function of direct experience using the traditional approach, we conducted a multiple regression analysis regressing current behavior onto attitude toward the condom, direct experience, and a product term between attitude and experience. Only the direct experience variable yielded a significant regression coefficient, suggesting that attitude-behavior consistency did not differ as a function of direct experience. In short, when attitude-behavior consistency and attitude-belief consistency were defined using traditional, across-subject methodologies, none of the observed relations using our approach were apparent. Clearly the methods used to define consistency make a difference.

Number of Beliefs and Resistance to Change

Several studies make theoretical predictions about the dynamics of attitudes based on the number of beliefs that presumably underlie an attitude (see Wood, ch. 11, and Davidson, ch. 12, this volume). One approach to assessing the number of beliefs is a thought listing task in which individuals list all of their thoughts at any given moment. The thought listing procedure makes no distinctions between the relative importance of beliefs in a more quantitative sense. By contrast, in our functional measurement analyses of belief structures, we can estimate the number of beliefs that underlie an attitude using the results of the ANOVA on attitude ratings. The approach we use is to count the number of belief dimensions in the functional measurement task that yield a statistically significant F and an eta square (or relative range index) that is equal to or greater than some minimal value (e.g., that account for at least 5% of the variance in attitude judgments). Two individuals may have an equal number (e.g., three) of belief dimensions underlying their attitudes, but the patterning of the relative contributions of the three dimensions might be distinct. For example, the eta squares for the three dimensions for one individual might be 0.70, 0.10, and 0.10, whereas for another individual the eta squares might be 0.30, 0.30, and 0.30. The first individual has a cognitive structure in which one belief dimension has a major impact on attitude and the other dimensions, though important, are much less influential: what we would call a *concentrated* structure. The second individual has a more *diffuse* belief structure, in which all three belief dimensions contribute about equally to the attitude. Even though the number of underlying beliefs is the same, the patterning of the relative importance of the beliefs is distinct.

Our research has shown that such differential patterns can be important in terms of understanding attitude change. For example, consider the two individuals noted above who had the same overall attitude toward an over-the-counter headache remedy but whose underlying belief structures were concentrated versus diffuse. A persuasive message aimed at any of the three dimensions would be equally effective in changing attitudes for the second individual but not the first individual. The individual with the concentrated belief structure would exhibit more or less resistance to attitude change relative to the second individual, depending on what belief dimension is addressed in the persuasive message. If perceptions on the second or third belief dimensions are changed as a result of a persuasive message, then the first individual will show more resistance than the second individual to attitude change, everything else being equal. If only the first dimension is addressed in the persuasive message, the reverse will occur. Note also that neither individual may exhibit change in their behavior (and thus both would appear to be resistant to change), if the persuasive message did not change the preference structure in such a way as to alter which option is the most positively evaluated among the option set.

Preliminary research that we have conducted in several content domains has suggested a small correlation between attitude importance (i.e., how important an attitude is perceived as being to an individual) and the diffuseness of the belief structure: more important attitudes tend to be associated with belief structures that are more diffuse (see also Berent & Krosnick, in press). This suggests that more important attitudes can be successfully attacked in persuasive messages from a broader range of perspectives (i.e., with respect to a wider variety of belief dimensions) than less important attitudes, everything else being equal.

Our theoretical framework makes evident that the relationship between the number of beliefs underlying an attitude and behavior change is a complex one that will depend on many additional factors. These include the relative importance of the belief for the attitude (as indexed by an eta square or relative range index), the kind of combinatorial rule that dictates how beliefs are combined to influence attitude (e.g., compensatory versus noncompensatory), the diffuseness of the belief structure, and the nature of the preference structure within which the attitude toward a given option is embedded.

Attitudes Toward Behavioral Alternatives

A unique aspect of our theoretical framework is the emphasis on studying attitudes and beliefs structures for an entire set of behavioral alternatives. In our view, two individuals can have identical attitudes toward a behavioral alternative but exhibit very different behavior with respect to that alternative depending on the attitudes toward other behavioral alternatives. For example, two women may indicate a slightly positive attitude toward using birth control pills (e.g., +1 on a −3 to +3 unfavorable–favorable scale). If one women feels quite negative about all other forms of birth control, she will probably choose the pill as her major method of birth control. If the other women feels negative about most other methods of birth control, but feels more positive toward the diaphragm than the pill, then she probably will not use the pill (and instead will use the diaphragm). It is only when the attitudes toward the other options are examined that the differential behavior of the women makes sense relative to their attitude ratings about the pill.

Although we have not explored it in any depth empirically, we suggest that researchers in the attitude strength area consider the utility of obtaining attitudinal measures across behavioral options and to treat such data in a within-subject as opposed to across-subject perspective. For example, our theoretical framework emphasizes the importance of measuring attitudes for each behavioral option. One could also obtain a measure of attitude extremity, attitude intensity, attitude certainty, and attitude importance for each behavioral alternative in an option set (see Krosnick & Abelson, 1992; Krosnick, ch. 1, this volume for possible ways in which these measures could be obtained). These might be used in a complimentary way to understand attitude change and attitude-behavior dynamics. For example, if a given option is the most positively evaluated *and* it is the most intense, then it may be more likely to be translated into behavior than one that is relatively low in intensity. It is conceivable to think of individuals with identical preference structures but quite different patterns of intensity, certainty, and importance ratings across options, and these differences may be psychologically consequential.

Attitude Extremity

Numerous investigators have studied the construct of attitude extremity. Research has suggested that repeated exposure to an attitude object, under certain conditions, can lead to more extreme attitudes (e.g., Downing, Judd, & Brauer, 1992) and that attitudes become more polarized when individuals are induced to think about their attitudes (e.g., Tesser, 1978). We have conducted research that has examined the effects of attitude extremity on attitude-behavior correspondence. In traditional analyses of attitude extremity, the focus is on defining extremity from a nomothetic perspective: An individual's attitude is said to be extreme if it is more polarized than attitudes of other individuals. Extremity for one individual depends on how extreme the attitudes are for other individuals included in the analysis. Within our framework, the focus is not on such across-individual definitions of extremity, but rather the focus is on within-individual extremity across the behavioral options that are available. An attitude is said to be extreme for an individual if it is highly discrepant from attitudes towards other behavioral options.

Our initial hypothesis was that the more extreme an attitude is (relative to attitudes towards other options), the more likely it is that the attitude would be consistent with behavior. An extreme negative attitude would consistently result in non-choice of the behavioral option, and an extreme positive attitude would consistently result in choice of the behavioral option. In general, the data have borne out this hypothesis. When an attitude is much more positive than other attitudes in the choice set (as indexed by its discrepancy from the second most favorable option), it tends to be the chosen option (which, in turn, leads to behavioral performance). When an option is much more negative than other attitudes in the choice set (as indexed by its discrepancy from the second most negative attitude), it is virtually never chosen.

We have, however, observed some important qualifications of this relationship, at least in the case of extremely positive attitudes. The phenomena is best illustrated with data that we have collected on the choice of a bank by college students. Our research found that a number of students (about 10%) currently had checking accounts at banks that they believed were inferior to other banks (i.e., their attitude toward their own bank was less favorable than their attitude toward another bank in the option set). Further analyses revealed that these individuals were cognizant of the differences in the quality of service between their bank and the "best" bank, but they felt that the disadvantages of switching banks (in terms of the inconvenience of having to travel to a new bank, the wait for new checks, etc.) outweighed the advantages of the superior service offered by another bank (which they were unaware of when they made their initial choice). The students were thus content to continue to use the second most positively evaluated option because of the perceived costs of switching to another alternative. This suggests that behavioral performance will be a function of how extreme an attitude is (in the case of extreme positive attitudes) *and* the perceived costs of switching to another option. Even though an attitude toward an option may be extremely positive (relative to other options in the attitude set), it still may not be translated into behavior if the perceived costs of switching are sufficiently negative.

We have developed a strategy for assessing the interplay of these two variables. First, we obtain a description of the individual's current bank in terms of the perceptual structure matrix. We then focus on a single belief dimension, usually the one rated most important by the individual. We then describe a new bank which is equivalent in all respects to the individual's current bank except one, namely it has a slightly better standing on the targeted belief dimension. For example, the interest rate paid by the individual's current bank might be 3%, and the alternative bank is said to offer an interest rate of 3.5%. We then ask the individual to report if he or she would switch banks given this difference. If the response is no, we then increase the discrepancy (e.g., to 4%) and ask the question again. This process is repeated until the minimum discrepancy on a belief dimension for switching is isolated. This information can be gathered for multiple belief dimensions either univariately (i.e., in isolation, as described earlier), or multivariately (in combination). These "thresholds for switching" can then be used to predict when extremely positive attitudes will be translated into behavior and when they will not be. When analyzing the two most positively evaluated options, if the most extreme attitude is associated with a belief structure that exceeds the switching thresholds, then the attitude will be translated into behavior (i.e., the option will be chosen). By contrast, if the most extreme attitude is associated with a belief structure that does not exceed the values of the switching thresholds, then it is less likely that the attitude will be translated into behavior. This is indeed what our research has found.

In summary, attitude extremity can be defined on either a within-subject or across-subject basis. When defined on a within-subject (across-option) basis, extremely negative attitudes almost always result in nonperformance of a behavioral option. Extremely positive attitudes may or may not result in behavioral performance, depending on the switching thresholds. If the switching thresholds are exceeded, then extremely positive attitudes will translate into behavior. If the switching thresholds are not exceeded, then extremely positive attitudes may or may not be translated into behavior.

Resistance to Change

Our theoretical framework also has implications for research perspectives on resistance to change, some of which have already been mentioned. For example, our analysis suggests that a behavior will be resistant to change to the extent that the discrepancy between the two most positively evaluated options is large, everything else being equal. If for one individual, the attitude toward Options A and B in a two-option choice set are +8 and −8, whereas for another individual the attitudes are +3 and +2, then it is likely that changing behavior away from Option A will be much more difficult for the first individual than for the second individual, everything else being equal. Preference structure analysis thus may account for individual differences in resistance to change when the dependent variable of focus is a behavior or behavioral choice. By the same token, it should be possible to make behaviors more resistant to change by designing messages to increase the difference between the two most positively evaluated options (e.g., by raising the attitude for Option A or lowering the attitude for Option B).

When the focus of analysis is attitudinal resistance to change, our framework suggests that attitudes will display resistance to change based on the number of beliefs that underlie the attitude, the combinatorial rule by which beliefs are integrated to influence attitude, and the particular beliefs that the persuasive message targets. For example, if the combinatorial rule is a compensatory averaging one and the persuasive message has the effect of adding a new belief, then individuals with greater numbers of determinant (i.e., important) beliefs will be more resistant to change than individuals with fewer beliefs. However, if the combinatorial rule is a compensatory summation one, then under the same circumstances, the number of beliefs underlying the attitude will be unrelated to resistance to persuasion. Recognition of such dynamics leads to the possibility that attitudes show differential resistance to persuasive attempts because of differences in combinatorial rules underlying the various attitudes.

CONCLUDING COMMENTS

An increasing amount of research is examining how the dynamic interplay between attitudes and the cognitive structures underlying them influence such constructs as attitude-behavior consistency and resistance to persuasion. We reviewed methods for assessing the relative importance of beliefs that underlie an attitude and found a general lack of convergence between diverse methodologies: The extent to which a given cognition is said to be important is highly method dependent. These findings are important because they suggest that the way cognitive systems underlying attitudes are characterized will be heavily influenced by the strategy used to assess the cognitive structure. The results also highlight the need to incorporate the importance construct and measures into a broader theoretical framework that uses multiple methods of assessment. We presented one such theoretical framework and then developed the implications of the approach for research on attitude strength. The emphasis of the approach is on a within-individual as opposed to an across-individual perspective and emphasizes the need to consider perceived alternative courses of action vis-à-vis behavioral decision theory. Although the framework is still evolving, it shows some promise for conceptualizing and guiding research on attitude strength.

REFERENCES

Anderson, N. H. (1981). *Foundations of information integration theory.* New York: Academic.

Berent, M. K., & Krosnick, J. A. (in press). The relation between attitude importance and knowledge structure. In M. Lodge & K. McGraw (Eds.), *Political information processing.* Ann Arbor: University of Michigan Press.

Chaiken, S., & Yates, S. (1985). Affective-cognitive consistency and thought-induced attitude polarization. *Journal of Personality and Social Psychology, 49,* 1470–1481.

Cook, R. L., & Stewart, T. R. (1975). A comparison of seven methods for obtaining subjective descriptions of judgmental policy. *Organizational Behavior and Human Performance, 13,* 31–45.

Davidson, A. R., Yantis, S., Norwood, M., & Montano, D. E. (1985). Amount of information about the attitude object and attitude-behavior consistency. *Journal of Personality and Social Psychology, 49*, 1184–1198.

Dittus, P., & Jaccard, J. (1992). *Belief salience and importance.* Unpublished manuscript, State University of New York, Department of Psychology, Albany.

Downing, J. A., Judd, C. M., & Brauer, M. (1992). Efffects of repeated expressions on attitude extremity. *Journal of Personality and Social Psychology, 63*, 17–29.

Edwards, A. (1957). *Attitude scaling.* New York: Wiley.

Fishbein, M. (1972). Towards an understanding of family planning behaviors. *Journal of Applied Social Psychology, 2*, 219–227.

Fishbein, M., & Ajzen, I. (1975). *Attitude, intention, and behavior: An introduction to theory and research.* Reading, MA: Addison-Wesley.

Jaccard, J. (1981). Attitudes and behavior: Implications of attitudes towards behavioral alternatives. *Journal of Experimental Social Psychology, 17*, 286–307.

Jaccard, J., & Becker, M. (1985). Attitudes and behavior: An information integration perspective. *Journal of Experimental Social Psychology, 21*, 440–465.

Jaccard, J., Brinberg, D., & Ackerman, L. (1986). Assessing attribute importance: A comparison of six methods. *Journal of Consumer Research, 12*, 463–468.

Jaccard, J., & King, G. W. (1977). A probabilistic model of the relationship between beliefs and behavioral intentions. *Human Communications Research, 3*, 332–342.

Jaccard, J., Knox, R., & Brinberg, D. (1979). Prediction of behavior from beliefs: An extension and test of a subjective probability model. *Journal of Personality and Social Psychology, 37*, 1239–1248.

Jaccard, J., & Sheng, D. (1985) A comparison of six methods for assessing the importance of perceived consequences in behavioral decisions: Applications from attitude research. *Journal of Experimental Social Psychology, 33*, 1–23.

Jaccard, J., & Wood, G. (1988). The effects of incomplete information on the formation of attitudes towards behavioral alternatives. *Journal of Personality and Social Psychology, 54*, 580–591.

Jacoby, J. (1975). Perspectives on a consumer information processing research program. *Communications Research, 2*, 203–215.

Jacoby, J. (1978). The emerging behavioral process technology in consumer decision making research. *Advances in Consumer Research, 6*, 220–232.

Johnson, S., & Jaccard, J. (1981). Life structure decisions: Factors related to career-marriage priorities. *Journal of Applied Developmental Psychology, 2*, 212–228.

Judd, C. M., & Lusk, C. M. (1984). Knowledge structures and evaluative judgments: Effects of structural variables on judgmental extremity. *Journal of Personality and Social Psychology, 46*(6), 1193–1207.

Kallgren, C. A., & Wood, W. (1986). Access to attitude-relevant information in memory as a determinant of attitude-behavior consistency. *Journal of Experimental Social Psychology, 22*, 328–338.

Krosnick, J. A., & Abelson, R. P. (1992). The case for measuring attitude strength in surveys. In Judith M. Tanur (Ed.), *Questions about questions: Inquiries into the cognitive bases of surveys.* New York: Russell Sage Foundation.

Linville, P. W., & Jones, E. E. (1980). Polarized appraisals of out-group members. *Journal of Personality and Social Psychology, 38*, 689–703.

McGuire, W. J. (1960). A syllogistic analysis of cognitive relationships. In M. J. Rosenberg, C. I. Hovland, W. J. McGuire, R. P. Abelson, & J. W. Brehm (Eds.), *Attitude organization and change* (pp. 65–111). New Haven: Yale University Press.

McGuire, W. J. (1981). The probabilogical model of cognitive structure and attitude change. In R. Petty, T. Ostrom, & T. Brook (Eds.), *Cognitive responses in persuasion.* Hillsdale, NJ: Lawrence Erlbaum Associates.

Norman, R. (1975). Affective-cognitive consistency, attitudes, conformity, and behavior. *Journal of Personality and Social Psychology, 32*, 83–91.

Rosenberg, M., & Oltman, P. (1962). Consistency between attitudinal affect and spontaneous cognitions. *Journal of Psychology, 54*, 450–485.

Sadler, O., & Tesser, A. (1973). Some effects of salience and time upon interpersonal hostility and attraction during social isolation. *Sociometry, 36*, 99–112.

Szalay, L. B., & Deese, J. (1978). *Subjective meaning and culture: An assessment through word associations.* Hillsdale, NJ: Lawrence Erlbaum Associates.

Tesser, A. (1978). Self-generated attitude change. In L. Berkowitz (Ed.), *Advances in Experimental Social Psychology* (Vol. 11, pp. 222–248). New York: Academic.

Tesser, A., & Conlee, M. C. (1975). Some effects of time and thought on attitude polarization. *Journal of Personality and Social Psychology, 31*, 262–270.

Wiggins, J. S. (1973). *Personality and prediction.* Reading, MA: Addison-Wesley.

Wood, W. (1982). Retrival of attitude-relevant information from memory: Effects on susceptibility to persuasion and on intrinsic motivation. *Journal of Personality and Social Psychology, 42*(5), 798–810.

Wood, W., & Kallgren, C. A. (1988). Communicator attributes and persuasion: Recipients' access to attitude-relevant information in memory. *Personality and Social Psychology Bulletin, 14*(1), 172–182.

Wood, W., Kallgren, C. A., & Presler, R. M. (1985). Access to attitude-relevant information in memory as a determinant of persuasion: The role of message attributes. *Journal of Experimental Social Psychology, 21*, 73–85.

Wyer, R. S. (1970). The quantitative prediction of belief and opinion change: A further test of subjective probability model. *Journal of Personality and Social Psychology, 12*, 559–571.

Wyer, R. S. (1972). Test of a subjective probability model of social evaluation processes. *Journal of Personality and Social Psychology, 22*, 279–286.

Wyer, R. S., & Hartwick, J. (1980). The role of information retrieval on conditional inference processes in belief formation and change. In L. Berkowitz (Ed.), *Advances in Experimental and Social Psychology* (Vol. 13, pp. 196–222). New York: Academic.

Let's Not Be Indifferent About (Attitudinal) Ambivalence

Megan M. Thompson
Mark P. Zanna
Dale W. Griffin
University of Waterloo

Lay people and psychological theorists alike tend to think in dichotomies, or at least in bipolar terms. For example, we tend to think about good versus evil, liberal versus conservative, masculine versus feminine, and so on. So what would we say about somebody who evaluated an attitude object as both good and evil? At first glance we might be inclined to view these responses as irrational or improbable. After all, how could a person evaluate something as being *both* positive and negative? In the attitude domain, these sorts of inconsistencies between the experiences which underlie an attitude have been traditionally considered to contribute to error variance, and treated as barriers to exact measurement (Ajzen & Fishbein, 1980; Wicker, 1969).

However, who of us have not felt torn and unsure of our attitudes from time to time? Rather than crazy or implausible, we propose that these instances represent *ambivalent* attitudes. This chapter reconceptualizes attitude structure as two dimensional in nature and details the challenges encountered in the course of developing a valid measure of ambivalence. We first provide an historical background of the concept of ambivalence in attitude theory. Next, we present a critical analysis of three measures of ambivalence, two of which have been previously used in the literature to assess attitudes of this nature. We then propose a new method for calculating ambivalence scores that circumvents the problems associated with previous ambivalence measures. Results of two studies are then presented which underscore the validity of the present approach to the measurement of ambivalence, and the particular formula that we suggest interested researchers employ. Finally, the concept of ambivalence is integrated with other attitude strength variables.

THE HISTORY OF AMBIVALENCE
IN ATTITUDE THEORY

Traditionally attitudes have been conceived in dichotomous (or bipolar) terms. For example, we describe people as being pro or con some issue. Nonetheless, even the earliest theorizing regarding attitudes pays homage to the complexity inherent in the construct. Thurstone and Chave (1929) defined an attitude as "the sum-total of a man's inclinations and feelings, prejudice or bias, preconceived notions, ideas, fears, threats and convictions about any specific topic. Thus a man's attitude about pacifism means here all that he feels and thinks about peace and war" (p. 7). This definition underscores the duality that has characterized, and we believe to some extent hampered, attitude theory and research. Although in principle the construct may be multidimensional, in reality attitudes are largely treated as unidimensional summary statements (Fazio, 1986).

As early as 1935, some theorists had begun to take issue with the unidimensional approach to attitudes (Allport, 1935), arguing that much of the richness of the attitude construct was lost with a single component model of attitudes. Such thinking gave rise to the tripartite model of attitudes (Katz & Stotland, 1959; Rosenberg & Hovland, 1960; Smith, 1947; Zanna & Rempel, 1988). According to the Zanna and Rempel model, overall evaluations are those generalized expressions of positivity and negativity regarding an attitude object. The affective component of an attitude refers to emotions and feelings evoked in an individual by a specific attitude object. The cognitive component of an attitude is represented by those beliefs and thoughts that are associated with an attitude target. Because they separate the components of an attitude, these models most readily invite the consideration of the notion of ambivalent attitudes.

Although studies have demonstrated the robustness of the tripartite model (see Breckler, 1984; Breckler & Wiggins, 1989; Kothandapani, 1971; Ostrom, 1969), traditionally there has been little acknowledgment of the existence of inconsistencies among the components of an attitude. Even the advent of cognitive dissonance theory (Festinger, 1957), which explicitly introduced the notion that cognitive elements could be dissonant to one another (Petty & Cacioppo, 1983), has done little to change this state of affairs. Rather, the considerable interest generated by this theory appeared to give dissonance a life of its own, and the idea of ambivalence failed to be integrated into existing attitude theory.

Certainly, some earlier research has suggested that affective experience associated with attitude objects can be two-dimensional. For example, Abelson and his colleagues (Abelson, Kinder, Peters, & Fiske, 1982) demonstrated that subjects associated both positive and negative emotions, relatively independently, with various political candidates. Other studies have shown that positive and negative affect become increasingly independent of each other as the temporal distance from the target event increases (Diener & Emmons, 1984). As well, separate dimensions of liking and disliking have been hypothesized to better reflect the dynamics of interpersonal relationships (Rodin, 1978). Is it possible that even the *evaluative dimension* is better conceived of as two-dimensional? Further, how might this notion of greater dimensionality begin to be translated into traditional attitude measurement strategies?

It seemed reasonable to begin with conflict theory (Brown & Farber, 1951; Miller, 1944; Mowrer, 1960) which provided the first operational definition of ambivalence. Ambivalence was thought to be the result of a particular configuration of response alternatives. Specifically, the response alternatives (a) must have contradictory implications; (b) be of subjectively equal significance or strength; and (c) occur in instances where goal or end states are equally desirable and available, and where compromise/escape is not a salient option.

Although developed independently, Lewin's (1951) field theory contains elements very similar to those proposed by conflict theorists. Lewin hypothesized that a state of tension would exist within a system whenever a psychological need or goal exits. These states are often associated with positive and negative valences, or those forces pointing toward or away from a goal region. These opposing forces produce three major types of conflict. The first is the result of positive forces of equal strength (e.g., Buridan's ass starving between two stacks of hay). The second occurs when two negative forces or outcomes are encountered (e.g., "being stuck between a rock and a hard place"). The third type of conflict occurs when equally strong positive and negative forces are encountered (e.g., "should I stay or should I go now?").

Although Lewin introduced the concept into the sphere of social psychology in general, Scott (1966, 1968) was the first to cite ambivalence as a *property* of an attitude. Despite its innovation, Scott's conceptualization of ambivalent attitudes has been largely neglected by attitude theory. One reason for this neglect was the influence of consistency theories which continued to dominate attitude theory. This perspective, which emphasizes the drive to seek consistency across all aspects of experience, is certainly at odds with the notion of ambivalence. Further, the very structure of semantic differentials did not provide respondents with the opportunity to express ambivalent attitudes. Indeed, semantic differential measures invite us to construe attitudes as falling at some point along an evaluative dimension, assessed by such bipolar scales as: favorable–unfavorable, positive–negative, good–bad, or like–dislike. These conceptual and methodological forces combined to thwart the acknowledgment, or expression, of ambivalence.

KAPLAN: OVERLAP OF WEAKER EVALUATION AND STRONGER EVALUATION

This state of affairs might have continued indefinitely had it not been for the efforts of Kaplan (1972). In trying to solve the problem of what it means to check the midpoint, or "neutral," category of a semantic differential scale, he provided the next step in the assessment of ambivalent attitudes. He noted that by checking the midpoint on traditional semantic differential scales subjects could give a response which was "*neither* positive nor negative" or "*equally* positive and negative." By raising this possibility he made a clear distinction between *indifference* and *ambivalence* and suggested that individuals could, in fact, hold ambivalent attitudes. That is, he proposed that individuals could evaluate something both positively and negatively, and attempted to devise a procedure to measure attitudinal ambivalence.

There are two aspects of Kaplan's procedure that bear further description here: his procedure for collecting positive and negative evaluations and his definition of ambivalence, that is, the way he proposed to combine positive and negative evaluations to determine the degree to which attitudes were ambivalent. To foreshadow, we believe his procedure for collecting positive and negative evaluations makes sense, though his definition of ambivalence is, perhaps, problematic.

In order to collect positive and negative evaluations, Kaplan simply split semantic differential scales at the neutral point and asked subjects to indicate both how positively and how negatively they evaluated the attitude object. For example, to assess the positive component of the attitude he would ask subjects something like the following, "Considering only the positive qualities of X and ignoring its negative ones, evaluate how positive its positive qualities are on the following 4-point scale: (a) not at all positive; (b) slightly positive; (c) quite positive; (d) extremely positive." Then to assess the negative component of the attitude, he would ask, "Considering only X's negative qualities and ignoring its positive ones, evaluate how negative its negative qualities are on the following 4-point scale: (a) not at all negative; (b) slightly negative; (c) quite negative; (d) extremely negative."

Perhaps the first questions to be asked are whether subjects can answer such questions; whether their responses are, at least, somewhat distinct, and how they relate to standard, bipolar semantic differentials. In Kaplan's, as well as in our own experience, subjects do not find this task at all problematic. Further, subjects' responses do show a remarkable degree of independence. In Kaplan's studies the correlations between his positive and negative scales were far from −1.00. In fact, he reports a mean correlation of only −.05. In our data, we find correlations in the −.40 range. Further, in our studies, the more the filler material between the assessment of the positive and negative components, the smaller the correlation. Nevertheless, it seems that asking subjects about their positive and negative evaluations does not generate completely redundant information. For Kaplan's, as well as our purposes, then, this procedure does seem to have the potential to assess ambivalent attitudes. Finally, it is interesting to note that scores obtained from standard, bipolar semantic differentials do correlate quite highly with the algebraic difference of the positive and negative components. In Kaplan's data these correlations ranged from .89 to .97.

We should note that in other areas of research, the apparent independence of semantically opposite constructs has sometimes proven to be illusory. For example, although survey data show Americans' attitudes towards Democrats and Republicans to be uncorrelated, structural equation modeling of the same data has revealed that the latent constructs underlying these attitude measures are actually correlated at −.85 (Green, 1988)! That is, by controlling both random measurement error and systematic response error, the latent variable analysis indicates that these apparently "independent" attitudes are well captured by a single bipolar dimension. Similar analyses of mood reports (Bentler, 1969; Green, Goldman, & Salovey, 1992) have shown that whereas positive and negative mood scales appear to tap separate dimensions (e.g., a correlation of −.27 between happy and sad), the latent constructs underlying these scales are strongly bipolar (e.g., a correlation of −.85 after random and nonrandom error are controlled).

These conclusions could pose a challenge to our formulation. Fortunately, however, we have both indirect and direct evidence that similar measurement artifacts do not underlie our findings. First, unlike the two domains mentioned earlier (attitudes toward political parties and mood reports) where a bias toward "yea-saying" was identified, the demand characteristics present in our studies all pull towards bipolar consistency: An answer of "extremely positive" about a positive component of a given attitude leads to a demand to answer "not at all negative" about the negative component of that same attitude (or vice versa). This consistency demand is reflected in the fact that the magnitude of the negative correlation between positive and negative scales is greatest when they are measured close to each other, that is, when there is relatively little filler material between them. Our direct evidence comes from a LISREL analysis of our own data (Thompson, Zanna, & Griffin, 1992) which revealed that latent variables representing positive and negative components of a given attitude were *not* more highly correlated after random and systematic error were controlled (correlations between positive and negative components of about −.4 increased only to about −.5 to −.6.)[1]

Kaplan's translation of Scott's definition of ambivalence begins with the calculation of total affect, or the sum of the positive and negative components, regardless of valence (in our research each component is scored from 1, "not at all," to 4, "extremely") and subtracting from that number the polarization, or the difference between the positive and negative components, of an attitude. More colloquially, ambivalence is represented by the *overlapping* space between the positive and negative components of an attitude. Thus, upon closer inspection, this formula for ambivalence is simply double the amount of the weaker evalu-

---

[1]Our LISREL analyses revealed another interesting result. When positive and negative components were assessed close together, that is, without much filler material in between, the correlated error terms were *negative* in sign. Note that a yea-saying response bias implies that correlated errors would be positive: Agreement with one scale implies agreement with another scale, even if the two scales have opposite connotations. However, negative correlated errors are exactly what a consistency bias would yield. Agreement with one scale implies disagreement with another. Such a bias works against our finding of relative independence.

TABLE 14.1
Ambivalence (Kaplan): Overlap of Weaker Evaluation with
Stronger Evaluation (or, 2 × Weaker Evaluation)

Negative Component	Positive Component			
	1	*2*	*3*	*4*
1	2	2	2	2
2	2	4	4	4
3	2	4	6	6
4	2	4	6	8

ation. Table 14.1 presents ambivalence scores, calculated according to Kaplan's formula.

As can be seen, there is more ambivalence in the 4/4 case (Positive = 4/Negative = 4) than in the 3/3 case, and so on. Also, there is more ambivalence in the 4/4 case than in the 4/3 case, and so on. These scores fit nicely with the conceptualizations of ambivalence of laypersons and attitude theorists alike. The more extreme and similar the positive and negative scores, the greater the ambivalence. However, there is a serious problem with this formulation. Holding constant the weaker component, subjects who differ in what may be called attitude polarization, which can be thought of as the difference between the stronger and weaker component, have the *same* ambivalence score—and this may offend our intuitions. For example, someone who gives a response of 2 on the negative component will have an ambivalence score of 4, regardless of whether he or she gives a response of 2, 3, or 4 on the positive component. Intuitively the greater polarization in these cases should be associated with less ambivalence, regardless of the fact that the overlap of the negative and the positive components is equal. Specifically, someone who scores 4 on the positive component and 2 on the negative component should have less ambivalence than someone who scores 2 on both components. Thus, Kaplan seems to have introduced a reasonable methodology to collect both positive and negative evaluations of attitude objects, but he may not have provided a good operational definition of ambivalence.

KATZ: POSITIVE × NEGATIVE COMPONENT

Katz, and his colleague Hass, who have done some very interesting and important research concerning racial attitudes, also sought to measure ambivalence (e.g., Hass, Katz, Rizzo, Bailey, & Eisenstadt, 1991; Katz & Hass, 1988). They created a Pro-Black attitude scale from items intended to tap friendly sentiments about Blacks as the minority underdog and an Anti-Black attitude scale from items intended to tap criticism of Blacks as lacking such moral qualities as discipline, self-reliance, and ambition. Interestingly, Katz and Hass (1988) have found the Pro-Black and Anti-Black scales to be largely independent. Of particular interest are the authors' conceptual and operational definition of ambivalence. Their conceptual definition argues that:

> The magnitude of ambivalence a person experiences is conceptually related to both the *similarity* and the *extremity* of his or her positions on the two relevant attitudinal dimensions. A person who has similar Pro-Black and Anti-Black scores should experience more conflict and ambivalence than a person who is high on one scale and low on the other. However, holding similarity constant, ambivalence will be greater for a person who scores high on both scales than for a person who scores low on both. (Hass et al., 1991, p. 87)

This definition has much in common with previous conceptualizations of ambivalence. A person will have an ambivalent attitude if he or she is inclined to give it equivalently strong positive and negative evaluations. Furthermore, the authors propose a different way to measure ambivalence:

> Because ambivalence scores should reflect both the extremity and similarity of responses on the Pro- and Anti-Black scales, we define ambivalence in terms of the product of the two component scale scores rather than the sum of the two scores. The product of the Pro and Anti scores is more influenced than the sum by both the extremity and the similarity of the two scores. Therefore, multiplying the scores is more consistent with the theoretical model. (Hass et al., 1991, p. 87)

The important question is, of course, does this operational definition improve on the problem inherent in Kaplan's definition? A closer inspection of their formula suggests that, unfortunately, this operational definition seems to exacerbate the problem. As seen in Table 14.2, holding constant subjects' responses on the weaker component, increases in evaluation on the stronger component does not decrease ambivalence as one might hope, but instead actually *increases* ambivalence.

To specifically illustrate the problem with this measure, locate the row which corresponds to a score of 1 on the negative component. Theoretically, the combination of a score of 1 on the negative component and 4 on the positive

TABLE 14.2
Ambivalence (Katz): Positive Component × Negative Component

Negative Component	Positive Component			
	1	*2*	*3*	*4*
1	1	2	3	4
2	2	4	6	8
3	3	6	9	12
4	4	8	12	16

component represents the most polarized attitude and, by definition, the least ambivalence. However, according to the Katz formulation this combination of scores produces the *highest* ambivalence score in that row. Therefore, it appears that the Katz and Hass' suggestion for how to calculate ambivalence may not be entirely satisfactory, either. (Incidentally, the sum of the positive and negative component suffers from the same problem.)

JAMIESON: RATIO OF WEAKER COMPONENT
SQUARED TO STRONGER COMPONENT

Given these myriad problems with the measures to date, finding a more conceptually and empirically sensitive measure was necessary. Recently, we discovered that Jamieson, also troubled by the Kaplan and the Katz measures, developed a formula to measure ambivalence. Jamieson's formula involves calculating the ratio of the weaker component to the stronger component. In order to *reward* (or weight) intensity even more (or to *penalize* indifference), he suggests that the weaker component be squared. Thus, ambivalence, according to Jamieson, is the square of the weaker component divided by the stronger component (Jamieson, personal communication, June 23, 1991). Interestingly, this formula is one of a family of equations proposed initially by conflict theorists (Brown & Farber, 1951) and later considered as a measure of ambivalence by Scott (1966). Ambivalence scores, as calculated by this formula, are presented in Table 14.3.

As can be seen, ambivalence scores using this formula don't offend our intuitions. For example, if the subject gives a response of 2 on the negative component, he or she receives increasingly lower ambivalence scores as the positive component increases from 2 to 4. All of this appears to circumvent the problems associated with previous measures of ambivalence devised by Kaplan and Katz. However, it may not be intuitively obvious how important conceptual aspects of ambivalence are captured using this formula. In fact, Jamieson's measure was empirically derived. Specifically, he compared subjects' answers to the separate positive and negative components with their responses to standard

TABLE 14.3
Ambivalence (Jamieson): Ratio of Weaker Component Squared
to Stronger Component

Negative Component	Positive Component			
	1	*2*	*3*	*4*
1	1.00	.50	.33	.25
2	.50	2.00	1.33	1.00
3	.33	1.33	3.00	2.25
4	.25	1.00	2.25	4.00

semantic differentials concerning the same attitude issues. He found that the bipolar responses did not represent a simple summation of the positive and negative components of the attitude. Rather, this summation of the separate components tended to overshoot subjects' responses to the bipolar attitude items. His formula attempted to correct for this. Therefore, although the Jamieson formula certainly overcomes the problems with the measures of Katz and Kaplan, like its historical counterparts it has an arbitrary aspect to its formulation. For instance, it is not clear why the formula takes the square of the weaker component and not, for instance, the cube of the weaker component (or, as suggested by Brown and Farber, the cube of the weaker component divided by the square of the stronger component). And so we continued our search.

GRIFFIN: SIMILARITY (IN MAGNITUDE) AND INTENSITY OF COMPONENTS

Recall that there are two necessary and sufficient conditions of ambivalence. The first condition is that the two attitude components must be similar in magnitude. As the difference in magnitude between the two components increases (i.e., the similarity in magnitude between the two components decreases), the attitude becomes more polarized in the direction of the stronger component. Second, ambivalence involves attitude components which are of at least moderate intensity. With similarity held constant, ambivalence increases directly with intensity. Thus, the optimal formula would be one which is comprised of the two conditions which, when found together, result in ambivalence. Griffin translated these notions *directly* into his formula for the assessment of ambivalence. Specifically, ambivalence equals similarity of components plus intensity of components. Similarity of components is assessed by subtracting the absolute difference of the positive (P) and negative (N) components from 4 (so that similarity ranges from 4, when the positive and negative components are equivalent in magnitude, to 1, when the positive and negative components are maximally different). Intensity (or extremity) of components is assessed by averaging the positive and negative components. So, ambivalence, according to Griffin, is: $4-|P-N|$ plus $(P+N)/2$. In order to allow the "1,1" case to have an ambivalence score of 1, the constant 4 is subtracted from this formula. Thus, to calculate ambivalence, subtract the absolute difference between the two components from the average of the two components, $(P+N)/2 - |P - N|$. (Interestingly, the computional formula for ambivalence suggests that ambivalence can also be thought of as equal to the intensity of the components corrected by the dissimilarity in their magnitude, or, in other words, polarization.) The range of possible ambivalence scores according to this formula are presented in Table 14.4.

As can be seen by comparing Tables 14.3 and 14.4, the Griffin formula produces scores which are extremely similar to those generated by the Jamieson

TABLE 14.4
Ambivalence (Griffin): Similarity + Intensity of Components

Negative Component	Positive Component			
	1	2	3	4
1	1.0	.5	0	−.5
2	.5	2.0	1.5	1.0
3	0	1.5	3.0	2.5
4	−.5	1.0	2.5	4.0

formula. However, there are some differences between the two equations. Some researchers (e.g., Jamieson) have suggested that being "not at all positive (negative)" regarding an attribute should be represented by a score of 0, rather than a 1 as we have used. Although these two scoring systems produce essentially equivalent ambivalence scores for equations that do not involve multiplication of the positive and negative components (such as the Kaplan and Griffin formulae), they do result in slightly different outcomes for equations that do involve multiplication of the two components (such as the Katz and Jamieson formulae). Put simply, when multiplication is involved, the 0 to 3 system produces ambivalence scores of zero whenever one of the components is zero (i.e., is "not at all"), regardless of the value of the other component. Thus, although virtually identical when the 1 to 4 scoring is used, the Jamieson and the Griffin equations do produce small differences when one component is "not at all" and the 0 to 3 scoring system is employed. (If one desires to make even small distinctions among the cases where one component is zero, or "not at all," as we do, then one would not be inclined to use the Jamieson equation with a 0 to 3 scoring system. We will revisit this issue after we present our first study.)

More importantly, only the Griffin formula separately, and independently assesses the similarity and intensity dimensions of ambivalent attitudes. This feature allows one to determine the relative contribution of each dimension. Furthermore, one can also determine whether the multiplicative relation or interaction of the similarity and intensity dimensions relates to some external criterion over and above the simple main effects of similarity and intensity.[2]

To review, Table 14.5 presents the various formulations we have considered so far. Perusing this table, one can see both similarities and differences between the various measures. All agree that the 4/4 case is more ambivalent than the 3/3 case, which in turn is more ambivalent than the 2/2 case, and so on. They also agree that the 4/4 case is more ambivalent than the 4/3 case, which in turn

---

[2]Of course, the Jamieson equation could be decomposed into an intensity dimension (consisting of the score on the weaker component) and a similarity dimension (consisting of the ratio of the score on the weaker component to the score on the stronger component). Such a decomposition would allow one to assess the importance of each dimension of ambivalence.

TABLE 14.5
Comparison of Ambivalence Measures

Positive Score	Negative Score	Kaplan	Katz	Jamieson	Griffin
4	4	8	16	4.00	4.00
4	3	6	12	2.25	2.50
4	2	4	8	1.00	1.00
4	1	2	4	.25	−.50
3	3	6	9	3.00	3.00
3	2	4	6	1.33	1.50
3	1	2	3	.33	0
2	2	4	4	2.00	2.00
2	1	2	2	.50	.50
1	1	2	1	1.00	1.00

is more ambivalent than the 4/2 case, and so on. Where they disagree is in those cases where the weaker component (in this example, the negative component) is held constant and the stronger component (in this example, the positive component) varies, for example, the 2/2, 3/2, versus 4/2 cases. In these cases, Kaplan's measure results in no difference in ambivalence scores, Katz's measure results in more ambivalence with greater discrepancies between the positive and negative components, whereas both the Jamieson and Griffin measures result in less ambivalence with greater discrepancies. Thus, although similar in many respects, it is clear that the Jamieson and Griffin measure differ most from the Katz measure, with the Kaplan measure being in between, that is somewhat different from each. As a final point of comparison, it may be of interest to note that a modified version of the Griffin measure, in which intensity is given twice the weight of similarity, turns out to be equivalent to Kaplan's original measure.

CRITERION VALIDITY: THE RELATION
OF AMBIVALENCE MEASURES
TO AN EXTERNAL STANDARD

With these various formulae in mind, we conducted a preliminary study to determine: (a) the consistency of the various ambivalence measures across various scales and attitude issues; (b) the relation among the various measures of ambivalence; and (c) the relation between the various ambivalence measures and a more direct, self-report measure of ambivalence, which served as sort of an external criterion or gold standard. We assessed subjects' attitudes toward two issues: euthanasia and mandatory AIDS testing.

To assess the *positive* component of subjects' attitude toward euthanasia, for example, we asked the following three questions:

1. Think about your attitude toward or evaluation of euthanasia, that is al-
    lowing patients with terminal illnesses to end their own lives.

    Considering only the favorable qualities of euthanasia and ignoring
    the unfavorable characteristics, *how favorable is your evaluation* of eutha-
    nasia?

Not at all	Slightly	Quite	Extremely
Favorable	Favorable	Favorable	Favorable

2. Think about your *feelings or emotions* when I mention euthanasia.

    Considering only your feelings of satisfaction toward euthanasia and
    ignoring your feelings of dissatisfaction, *how satisfied do you feel* about
    euthanasia?

Not at all	Slightly	Quite	Extremely
Satisfied	Satisfied	Satisfied	Satisfied

3. Think about your *thoughts or beliefs* when I mention euthanasia.

    Considering only the beneficial qualities of euthanasia and ignoring the
    harmful characteristics, *how beneficial do you believe* euthanasia to be?

Not at all	Slightly	Quite	Extremely
Beneficial	Beneficial	Beneficial	Beneficial

To assess the *negative* component of subjects' attitude toward euthanasia we
asked three comparable questions:

1. Think about your attitude toward or evaluation of euthanasia, that is al-
    lowing patients with terminal illnesses to end their own lives.

    Considering only the unfavorable qualities of euthanasia and ignoring
    the favorable characteristics, *how unfavorable is your evaluation* of eutha-
    nasia?

Not at all	Slightly	Quite	Extremely
Unfavorable	Unfavorable	Unfavorable	Unfavorable

2. Think about your *feelings or emotions* when I mention euthanasia.

    Considering only your feelings of dissatisfaction toward euthanasia and
    ignoring your feelings of satisfaction, *how dissatisfied do you feel* about
    euthanasia?

Not at all	Slightly	Quite	Extremely
Dissatisfied	Dissatisfied	Dissatisfied	Dissatisfied

3. Think about your *thoughts or beliefs* when I mention euthanasia.

Considering only the harmful qualities of euthanasia and ignoring the beneficial characteristics, *how harmful do you believe* euthanasia to be?

_____	_____	_____	_____
Not at all	Slightly	Quite	Extremely
Harmful	Harmful	Harmful	Harmful

The positive and the negative questions were separated by a filler questionnaire and although the evaluation question was always asked first, the order of feeling and belief questions was counterbalanced.

Following the theoretical work of Zanna and Rempel (1988) and the empirical work of Batra (Batra & Ahtola, 1991) and Breckler (1984), we tried to assess the positive and negative component of subjects' overall evaluation of the attitude object as well as the positive and negative emotions *and* beliefs they associated with the attitude object. We return to these distinctions later, but for now just think about our questions as two halves of three evaluative semantic differential scales.

Finally, subjects responded to 10 questions, also developed by Jamieson (1988), embedded in a larger questionnaire that directly assessed the degree to which they experienced ambivalence toward the attitude issues. For example, subjects were asked to indicate the extent to which statements such as "I'm confused about (euthanasia) because I have strong thoughts about it and I can't make up my mind one way or another," "I find myself feeling 'torn' between two sides of the issue of (euthanasia)," and "My mind and heart seem to be in disagreement on the issue of (euthanasia)" characterized their feelings about euthanasia on a 9-point scale with endpoints labeled, "extremely uncharacteristic (or extremely characteristic) of my attitude."

Turning to the results, it is important to point out that in this study, as well as in subsequent studies using three and five social issues, we have found individual differences in ambivalence. That is, although we do not find strong relations across issues in attitudes per se (that is, if someone is pro-euthanasia, he or she is equally likely to be pro or con mandatory AIDS testing), we do find that if an individual is ambivalent on one social policy issue, he or she is likely to be relatively ambivalent on another. Therefore, in the research that follows, our ambivalence measures are derived by calculating ambivalence according to a particular formula, initially, at the level of each particular scale within an issue, and, then, averaging across scales and issues.[3]

The first question, then, is how internally consistent are the various ambivalence measures. As can be seen in the diagonal of Table 14.6 the alphas ranged from .58 to .68 in this 6-item (or two-issue) study. (In our 15-item [or five-issue] study, alphas ranged from .72 to .78.) It is also interesting to note the level of ambivalence reported by our subjects. Examining the means, it is clear that

---

[3]The overall pattern of results generally holds for each issue in our studies.

TABLE 14.6
Relation Among Ambivalence Measures

	Kaplan	Katz	Jamieson	Griffin	Direct
Kaplan	(.68)				
Katz	.71	(.66)			
Jamieson	.75	.67	(.61)		
Griffin	.77	.66	.98	(.58)	
Direct	.32	.21	.37	.40	(.88)
Means	3.66	5.71	1.37	1.31	3.78
	[.83]	[1.52]	[.48]	[.58]	[1.54]

Note. $N = 146$. Cronbach alphas in parentheses. Standard deviations in brackets.

subjects reported a moderate, though not great, amount of ambivalence, regardless of how it was calculated.

The next question concerns how these various measures relate to one another. Of course, we expected reasonably high correlations. As seen in Table 14.6, reasonably high correlations were, indeed, what we found.[4] The general pattern among these indices confirmed our earlier predictions. The Griffin and Jamieson formulae were virtually identical ($r = .98$) to each other, and both were less related to the Katz measure (r's = .66, & .67, respectively). Finally, the magnitude of the correlations for the Kaplan measure fell in between these, indicating that it was somewhat distinct from both the Griffin ($r = .77$) and Jamieson ($r = .75$), as well as the Katz ($r = .71$) measures.

More importantly, how do each of the measures relate to the direct, self-report measure of ambivalence (which, incidentally, also appears to be consistent across items and issues, alpha of .88)? As can be seen in Table 14.6, it would appear that both the Griffin ($r = .40$) and the Jamieson ($r = .37$) version of ambivalence are reasonably correlated with the direct, self-report measure; at least, these measures are more highly correlated with this criterion than the Kaplan ($r = .32$) and, especially, the Katz ($r = .21$) measures.[5]

Of course, one could question the criterion variable of direct ambivalence, our so-called gold standard. We would not argue against the notion that more work needs to be done to validate, and especially, discriminably validate, the various ambivalence measures. For example, in future research investigators might ask which formula or formulae best discriminate between issues that are consensually thought to produce more or less ambivalence or between people who are thought to be more or less ambivalent or between situations hypothesized to produce more or less ambivalence, and so on. But for now, because it appears

---

[4]This pattern held for the 5-issue study as well.

[5]Given the rather large *n* and the rather large correlations among the various ambivalence measures, only the comparison between the Jamieson and Kaplan measures fails to be at least marginally significant.

to be conceptually superior and, because in our preliminary study, it also has superior predictive power, we recommend that researchers use the Griffin formulation.

Having settled on this measure, we conducted two additional analyses as further explorations of the Griffin formulation of ambivalence. First, we performed a hierarchical multiple regression analysis in order to determine the relative contribution of similarity, intensity, and the interaction of similarity and intensity to the experience of ambivalence. The dependent variable was the measure of direct, simultaneous ambivalence. The similarity and intensity components were entered simultaneously in a first block, followed by the cross product of similarity and intensity in a second step. Before presenting the results of the regression analysis, we should mention that similarity and intensity were virtually unrelated to each other ($r = -.09$, ns). Results of this regression analysis indicated that similarity was a highly significant predictor of simultaneous ambivalence ($p < .001$), that intensity was a marginally significant predictor ($p = .10$), and that the interaction of similarity and intensity did not relate to the criterion. These findings suggest that in the present research, at least, the similarity in magnitude of the positive and negative components was more important in the phenomenological experience of ambivalence than was the intensity of the components. This is not surprising as the magnitude of the ambivalence experienced in this research was moderate at best. In research which taps issues of greater ambivalence, we might expect intensity to play a greater role in the genesis of ambivalence. In any event, we note that the present formulation easily affords the opportunity for investigators to examine the unique main and interactive effects of the two components of ambivalence, that is, similarity and intensity, on any variable of interest.

Second, we looked at only those cases where subjects' weaker component was "not at all." Recall that even in these cases the Griffin equation implies that increases on the stronger component result in less ambivalence. In contrast, the Jamieson equation, coupled with a 0 to 3 scoring system, explicitly predicts that when the weaker component is "not at all," ambivalence will be zero regardless of the magnitude of the stronger component. Interestingly, the correlation between the magnitude of the stronger component and subjects' scores on the measure of direct, simultaneous ambivalence was significantly negative, supporting the Griffin formulation.

CONSTRUCT VALIDITY: THE ANTECEDENTS OF AMBIVALENT ATTITUDES

We used the Griffin formula in an additional study which was designed to assess possible antecedents of ambivalence (Thompson & Zanna, in press). In the present context, this study explores the construct validity of our general strategy regarding the measurement of ambivalence adopted here and, more specifically, the Griffin formula itself. We picked three individual difference variables to investigate. Two can best be thought of as personality variables. One, Need for Cognition (NFC), was expected to be negatively related to ambivalence. This prediction is based on the notion that individuals high in the tendency "to engage in and enjoy effortful cognitive endeavors" (i.e., high NFC individuals, see Cacioppo & Petty, 1982) would be more likely to work through or reconcile contradictory information about attitude objects. That is, the greater the NFC, the less the ambivalence. The other, Personal Fear of Invalidity (PFI) (Thompson, Naccarato, & Parker, 1989) derived from Kruglanski's theory of lay epistemology (Kruglanski, 1989), was expected to be positively related to ambivalence. Individuals high in the tendency to be concerned with their errors and the consequences of their decisions (i.e., high PFI individuals) would be less likely to effectively work through or reconcile contradictory information about attitude objects. It is the underlying concern with error, characteristic of PFI, which would interfere with the high PFI individuals ability to resolve inconsistencies. Indeed, such individuals abhor closure, as the act of closure increases the likelihood that an error might be made. Therefore, the greater the PFI, the more the ambivalence.

The other individual difference variable we chose to investigate can be thought of not so much as a personality variable, but more as a situational variable designed to distinguish individuals in terms of their experience with or involvement in the attitude issues. Basically, we asked our subjects to indicate the extent to which they had followed the various issues in the media as well as the extent to which they had engaged in a variety of activities related to the issues (such as signing petitions and donating money) and the extent to which they viewed the issues as personally relevant. Here we expected (acknowledging a general tendency toward cognitive consistency) that greater experience or involvement would be negatively related to ambivalence. That is, the greater the involvement, the less the ambivalence. We also expected, however, that involvement might very well moderate the effects of our personality variables such that the predicted effects of NFC and PFI would hold primarily, or only, for those individuals who had relatively high involvement in the issues. To test these notions we assessed subjects' attitudes toward five social policy issues (legalizing euthanasia, AIDS, reinstating capital punishment, free abortion clinics, and making drinking and driving laws more punitive). We also assessed their NFC and PFI as well as their involvement with the issues.

As indicated in Table 14.7, both predictions concerning the personality variables were supported. Compared to those low in the NFC, subjects high in the NFC (i.e., those above the median in NFC) did hold less ambivalent attitudes, $F(1,84) = 4.82$, $p = .03$; in contrast, subjects high in PFI (i.e., those above the median in PFI) compared to those low in PFI held more ambivalent attitudes, $F(1,84) = 4.57$, $p = .03$. Incidentally, NFC and PFI are unrelated ($r = -.03$, ns).

As can be seen in Table 14.8, there was only a slight, and not significant tendency for involvement to be related to less ambivalence overall.[6] More interestingly,

---

[6]Again, involvement was generally consistent across the five social policy issues.

TABLE 14.7
Mean Ambivalence as a Function of Need for Cognition
and Personal Fear of Invalidity

NFC	PFI	
	Low	High
Low	.65	.99
	(25)	(20)
High	.56	.65
	(19)	(24)

Note. Cell *n*'s in parentheses.

involvement did interact with both personality variables in the expected direction. Put simply, the effect for NFC, that is, the greater the NFC, the less the ambivalence, held only for those individuals with relatively high experience with the social policy issues, NFC × Involvement: $F(1,80) = 4.07$, $p = .05$. Similarly, the effect for PFI, that is, the greater the PFI, the more the ambivalence, also held only for those relatively high in involvement, PFI × Involvement: $F(1,80) = 3.27$, $p = .07$. Involvement, then, seems to potentiate the effects of the personality variables. Highly involved individuals high in NFC and low in PFI were the least ambivalent of all the subjects ($M = .22$); involved individuals high in PFI and low in NFC were the most ambivalent ($M = 1.09$).[7]

Thus, there do seem to be individual differences in attitudinal ambivalence and these individual differences do seem to be related to NFC, PFI, and involvement in predictable ways. Although of interest to those concerned with the antecedents of attitudinal ambivalence, these results also underscore the validity of this approach to the measurement of this construct.

AMBIVALENCE CALCULATED WITHIN
AND BETWEEN ATTITUDE COMPONENTS

Although there are many future directions for research, including research on the antecedents of ambivalence—after all the present research is entirely correlational in nature—we would like to suggest one additional type of ambivalence that we find especially intriguing and believe is worthy of future investigation. Recall that we didn't pick just any three semantic differential scales to split. We picked one,

---

[7]The same general pattern of results was obtained when we divided the involvement questionnaire into its component parts of media exposure (e.g., number of news articles read per week), activism (e.g., attending rallies, signing petitions), and personal relevance. As well, the correlations between media exposure and activism ($r = .41$, $p < .001$), and personal relevance ($r = .44$, $p < .001$), as well as activism and personal relevance ($r = .39$, $p < .001$) suggested that these components were reasonably related to each other. For these reasons, we collapsed these components into a more general involvement variable.

TABLE 14.8
Mean Ambivalence as a Function of Involvement, Need for Cognition,
and Personal Fear of Invalidity

	Low Involvement	
	PFI	
NFC	Low	High
Low	.68	.89
	(13)	(10)
High	.80	.68
	(11)	(13)
	High Involvement	
	PFI	
NFC	Low	High
Low	.62	1.09
	(12)	(10)
High	.22	.59
	(8)	(11)

Note. Cell n's in parentheses.

favorable–unfavorable, that with our instructions, was meant to tap overall evaluation. If, following Zanna and Rempel (1988), one conceives of attitudes as overall evaluations based on affect, cognition and past behavior, then one could conceive of this scale as *the* measure of ambivalence. If so, then, one could also ask what is overall ambivalence due to: affective ambivalence (or torn feelings), or cognitive ambivalence (or mixed beliefs) and/or affective/cognitive ambivalence (or when your mind tells you one thing, but your heart something else).

To measure affective ambivalence one could use the satisfied–dissatisfied scale, which, with our instructions, was meant to assess affective ambivalence, or torn emotions. To measure cognitive ambivalence one could use the beneficial–harmful scale, which, again with our instructions, was meant to capture cognitive ambivalence, or mixed beliefs. Of course, to create more reliable measures of overall ambivalence, affective ambivalence, and cognitive ambivalence, one would want to have several scales designed to assess each construct. Following Batra's factor analytic work on evaluative semantic differential scales, we suggest using scales such as positive–negative and good–bad to measure overall ambivalence, pleasant–unpleasant to measure affective ambivalence, and useful–useless to measure cognitive ambivalence. (In addition to, or possibly instead of, using multiple scales, researchers might also consider employing more open-ended positive and negative belief-elicitation procedures as well as positive and negative emotion-elicitation procedures, cf. Esses, Haddock, & Zanna, 1993).

Within this scheme the question still remains, however, of how to measure affective/cognitive ambivalence. These sorts of conflicts arise when one's heart says one thing and one's head another thing. Actually, there are two forms of affective/cognitive ambivalence: (a) positive affective/negative cognitive ambivalence, and (b) negative affective/positive cognitive ambivalence. To be ambivalent within the affective or the cognitive domain, one must, of course, be equivalently high on both the positive and negative component. To be ambivalent across domains, however, one must be polarized in opposite directions in each domain. So, an individual will experience a great deal of affective/cognitive ambivalence on euthanasia, for example, if he or she is strongly pro-euthanasia within the affective domain, but strongly con-euthanasia within the cognitive domain, or vice versa.

When individuals are pro (or neutral) the issue within the affective domain and con (or neutral) the issue within the cognitive domain, we suggest measuring what might be called, *pro-affective/con-cognitive* ambivalence by substituting the term, *positive affective–negative affective* + 1, for the positive component, and the term, *negative cognitive–positive cognitive* + 1, for the negative component, in Griffin's formula. A score of 1 is added to the difference scores to eliminate zeroes and to create a scale which ranges from 1 to 4, where 1, in effect, means not at all polarized on the dimension and 4 means extremely polarized on the dimension. The relevant cases, and the resulting pro-affective/con-cognitive scores, are depicted in Tables 14.9 and 14.10. Thus, someone who is maximally pro-affective ([pos affective–neg affective] + 1 = 4) *and* maximally con-cognitive ([neg cognitive–pos cognitive] + 1 = 4) will achieve the maximum pro-affective/con-cognitive ambivalence score of 4.0.

When individuals are pro (or neutral) the issue within the cognitive domain and con (or neutral) the issue within the affective domain, we suggest measuring, what might be called, *pro cognitive/con affective* ambivalence by substituting the term *positive cognitive–negative cognitive* + 1, for the positive component, and the term, *negative affective–positive affective* + 1, for the negative component, in Griffin's formula. Someone who is maximally pro-cognitive *and* maximally con-affective will achieve the maximum pro-cognitive/con-affective ambivalence score.

Two additional points need to be made about these measures. First, subjects who give equal positive and negative affective ratings *and* equal positive and negative cognitive ratings would appear in the upper left hand cell of *both* a pro-affective/con-cognitive and a pro-cognitive/con-affective ambivalence table. Obviously, we can't differentiate whether these subjects' affective/cognitive ambivalence is due to pro-affective/con-cognitive or pro-cognitive/con-affective ambivalence and, obviously, we can't count them twice! This is not a problem, however, if we are merely interested in obtaining a score on affective/cognitive ambivalence (and not concerned with whether such a score represents pro-affective/con-cognitive or pro-cognitive/con-affective ambivalence); if so, and

TABLE 14.9
Calculation of Pro Affective and Con Cognitive Components

Pos Affective	−	Neg Affective	+ 1 =	Pro Affective
4		4		= 1
4		3		= 2
4		2		= 3
4		1		= 4
3		3		= 1
3		2		= 2
3		1		= 3
2		2		= 1
2		1		= 2
1		1		= 1

Neg Cognitive	−	Pos Cognitive	+ 1 =	Con Cognitive
4		4		= 1
4		3		= 2
4		2		= 3
4		1		= 4
3		3		= 1
3		2		= 2
3		1		= 3
2		2		= 1
2		1		= 2
1		1		= 1

typically this will be the case, these subjects simply get a (single) affective/cognitive ambivalence score of 1. Second, so far we have neglected cases (presumably, the majority of cases) where subjects are polarized in the same direction on *both* the affective and cognitive dimensions. Because, by definition, these subjects do not experience affective/cognitive ambivalence, we simply propose assigning them a score of −1 on this measure.

Although based on only one scale per issue in the present research, we nevertheless did exploratory (descriptive) analyses in our 5-issue study (Thompson & Zanna, in press) to determine the relation among these various measures of ambivalence. Unfortunately (for us), the vast majority of subjects (81%) were polarized in the same direction on both the affective and cognitive dimensions. Thus, there was virtually no affective/cognitive ambivalence for these issues. Correlational analyses of the other three measures did indicate two sets of findings. First, affective and cognitive ambivalence were significantly related ($r = .51, p < .001$) to each other, and each correlated significantly with overall evaluative ambivalence (r's = .60, .61, $p < .001$, respectively). Second, a standard multiple

TABLE 14.10
Pro Affective/Con Cognitive Ambivalence

Con Cognitive (Negative Polarization on Cognition)	Pro Affective (Positive Polarization on Affect)			
	1	2	3	4
1	1.0	.5	0	-.5
2	.5	2.0	1.5	1.0
3	0	1.5	3.0	2.5
4	-.5	1.0	2.5	4.0

regression analysis revealed that each uniquely accounted for variance in evaluative ambivalence (affective ambivalence: $\beta = .47$, $t = 4.51$, $p < .001$); cognitive ambivalence: $\beta = .47$, $t = 4.43$, $p < .001$). Thus, for issues such as euthanasia, AIDS testing, and reinstating capital punishment, evaluative ambivalence seems to be related to both torn feelings (affective ambivalence) and mixed beliefs (cognitive ambivalence), but not to mismatches between heart and mind (affective/cognitive ambivalence). Therefore, in future research it will be important to include issues thought to be high in affective/cognitive ambivalence (such as organ donation or using condoms) in order to put the current formulation to a more adequate test.

Nevertheless, thinking about ambivalence and, especially, the notion that individuals can be polarized in opposite directions on two different dimensions of evaluation may have interesting implications for other attitudinal phenomena. Consider, for example, the domain of interpersonal attraction. We know from past research that evaluations of others are multidimensional. One dimension can be characterized as affection or liking; the other as admiration or respect. Thus, although we often both like and respect or both dislike and disrespect others, we all know people we like, but do not respect (for example, imagine a person who is warm and caring, but also dependent and not very assertive) as well as people we respect, but do not particularly like (for example, imagine a person who is intellectually desirable or agentic, but not very socially desirable or communal). How, then, might we characterize our overall evaluations or attitudes toward such individuals? Well, such attitudes are likely to be ambivalent, and such ambivalence *is* likely to be due, not to mixed evaluations within the dimensions of affection and/or admiration, but to mixed evaluations between these two dimensions.

Thus, for example, if we were to assess liking independently from disliking and respect independently from disrespect on our 4-point scales, a person who holds a positively polarized evaluation on affection (i.e., who rates someone 4 on liking and 1 on disliking) and a negatively polarized evaluation on admiration (i.e., who rates the same person 1 on respect and 4 on disrespect), would exhibit maximum amount of what might be called pro-affection/con-admiration ambivalence. In future research we plan to determine whether the attitudes that men (particularly male chauvinists) hold toward women in general, and toward various subcategories of women, such as housewives, in particular, can be characterized in this fashion.

THE RELATION OF AMBIVALENCE
TO ATTITUDE STRENGTH CONCEPTS

In order to see how ambivalence is related to attitude strength, or, more precisely, variables thought to assess attitude strength, it might be helpful first to indicate how we conceptualize attitudes and, especially, the property of attitude strength. Following Zanna and Rempel (1988), we believe attitudes are overall summary evaluations of attitude objects or topics. In this view attitude extremity is not a property of an attitude. A more extreme attitude is not a stronger attitude, but simply a different attitude. How are such summary evaluations derived? Again following Zanna and Rempel (1988), we believe attitudes are based on knowledge (i.e., cognitive, affective, and behavioral information) concerning the attitude object. Thus, knowledge is also not a property of an attitude, but a determinant of attitude. An attitude based on direct experience with the attitude object, for example, is not by necessity a stronger attitude, but simply an attitude derived from different (and/or more) information than an attitude based on indirect experience (cf. Fazio & Zanna, 1981).

How, then, do we conceptualize attitude strength? Put simply, we believe attitudes can vary with respect to several properties, possibly as a consequence of how they were formed in the first place, including accessibility, importance, ego-involvement or commitment, and ambivalence. These properties may make an attitude strong or weak in the sense that they moderate the consequences of attitudes in terms of persistence, resistance to persuasion, and influences on information processing and behavior. For example, manipulations designed to increase the accessibility of newly formed attitudes seem to increase the persistence of persuasion (cf. Fazio, Zanna, Ross, & Powell, 1992).

Given this model of attitudes and attitude strength, let us return to our original question: How does ambivalence relate to knowledge, extremity, and the various attitude strength concepts? First, concerning knowledge, it would seem on the basis of our second study that ambivalence is not strongly related to the amount of knowledge or experience. Inconsistent knowledge, due to reality constraints and/or competing values or construals (cf. Tetlock's, 1989, work on the relevance of inconsistent values to policy issues), would seem to be necessary for ambivalence, but the amount of knowledge per se does not seem to be related to ambivalence. Second, since Kaplan (1972), all formulations of ambivalence necessarily correlate negatively with extremity (or polarization): the more extreme the attitude, the less the ambivalence. At this point in our research program we (as others) have chosen not to unconfound this relation. In future research, however, it might be interesting to create an unconfounded measure by calculating a preliminary measure of ambivalence according to the Griffin formula and then, *for each point or position along the bipolar, evaluative continuum*, by using a median (or tertile) split determine a final (unconfounded) ambivalence score. For example, those above the median Griffin score (at each point on the bipolar continuum) could be given a final ambivalence score of 1; those below the median, a final score of −1 (or those in the upper, middle, and lower tertiles scores of 1, 0, and −1, respectively).

Turning to those attitudinal properties that do seem to be related to attitude strength, such as accessibility, importance, and commitment, the main point to make is that ambivalence—because it is made up of two contradictory components—is conceptually, at least, independent of most other attitude strength variables. One can hold ambivalent attitudes about important and unimportant issues, about issues to which one is committed or not, and so on. And even though ambivalence may relate negatively with attitude accessibility (that is, the greater the ambivalence, the less accessible the overall summary evaluation or attitude), this may have more to do with the fact that highly ambivalent attitudes contain two highly accessible, contradictory components.

One attitude strength variable, affective-cognitive consistency (see Chaiken, ch. 15, this volume), however, ought to be related to ambivalence. Specifically, traditional measures of affective–cognitive consistency should be related to what we have called affective/cognitive ambivalence. Thus, when overall evaluative ambivalence is based primarily on affective/cognitive ambivalence (which, as the reader will recall, was *not* the case in the present research), ambivalence ought to be negatively related to affective–cognitive consistency. These possibilities should be explored in future research.

If ambivalence is not strongly related to other attitude strength concepts, are ambivalent attitudes stronger or weaker or neither stronger nor weaker than nonambivalent attitudes? For example, is the attitude-behavior relation more or less robust when attitudes decrease in ambivalence? This is an interesting question, and although research by Katz and Hass has addressed this sort of issue, future research needs to specifically investigate this problem. If holding an ambivalent attitude is like having, at least, two somewhat contradictory attitudes towards an object or issue, then we can ask about the differential strength of each attitude or component. If, for example, the positive and negative component are both highly accessible, behavior is not likely to follow from the overall (presumably unstable) summary evaluation. If, on the other hand, one component is chronically more accessible or even temporarily more accessible than the other (due, for example, to a mood induction or a value-salience manipulation which primes one of the components— or, more generally, to situational or contextual factors that influence what characteristics of the attitude object are salient or even how the attitude object is construed in the given instance), then we should be able to make clear predictions about behavior. Past research by Katz and Hass and their colleagues has, indeed, demonstrated that situational manipulations can, in fact, lead individuals with ambivalent attitudes to behave in more polarized ways than individuals with less ambivalent attitudes. Thus, although the overall summary evaluation may appear to be weak when attitudes are ambivalent, the individual components may, in principle at least, have the capacity to be strong. And perhaps in many, if not most, situations one component is likely to be more accessible than the other. Clearly, these possibilities provide additional directions for future research.

CONCLUSION

In conclusion, we believe that it is time to take the concept of attitude ambivalence seriously. At last we have the conceptual and methodological tools to measure ambivalence. So, now it is time to get on with the business of determining the causes and consequences of holding such volatile and, in our view, interesting attitudes.

ACKNOWLEDGMENTS

Preparation of this chapter was facilitated by a Doctoral Fellowship from the Social Sciences and Humanities Research Council of Canada to Megan M. Thompson. The research on which this chapter is based was supported, in part, by a research grant from the Social Sciences and Humanities Research Council of Canada to Mark P. Zanna.

The authors thank two anonymous reviewers of an earlier manuscript for pointing out (in no uncertain terms) the flaw in Kaplan's formulation of ambivalence. Further, we thank colleagues John Holmes and David Jamieson for helping us understand the concept of ambivalence and the importance of studying it; Cynthia Thomsen for helping us conceptualize affective/cognitive ambivalence; and the authors of the other chapters in the volume who, as participants of the Ohio State University Symposium on "Attitude Strength," commented on an earlier version of this chapter (Zanna & Thompson, 1991). Finally, we thank the editors of this volume, Rich Petty and Jon Krosnick, and our colleagues Russ Fazio and Victoria Esses for their constructive suggestions on the present chapter.

REFERENCES

Abelson, R. P., Kinder, D. R., Peters, M. D., & Fiske, S. T. (1982). Affective and semantic components in political person perception. *Journal of Personality and Social Psychology, 42,* 619–630.

Ajzen, I., & Fishbein, M. (1980). *Understanding attitudes and predicting social behavior.* Englewood Cliffs, NJ: Prentice-Hall.

Allport, G. (1935). Attitudes. In C. Murchison (Ed.), *Handbook of social psychology* (pp. 789–844). Worchester, MA: Clark University Press.

Batra, R., & Ahtola, O. T. (1991). Measuring the hedonic and utilitarian sources of consumer attitudes. *Marketing Letters, 2,* 159–170.

Bentler, P. M. (1969). Semantic space is (approximately) bipolar. *The Journal of Psychology, 71,* 33–40.

Breckler, S. J. (1984). Empirical validation of affect, behavior, and cognition as distinct components of attitudes. *Journal of Personality and Social Psychology, 47,* 1191–1205.

Breckler, S. J., & Wiggins, E. C. (1989). Affect versus cognition in the structure of attitudes. *Journal of Experimental Social Psychology, 25,* 253–271.

Brown, J. S., & Farber, I. E. (1951). Emotions conceptualized as intervening variables with suggestions toward a theory of frustration. *Psychological Bulletin, 48,* 465–480.

Cacioppo, J. T., & Petty, R. E. (1982). The need for cognition. *Journal of Personality and Social Psychology, 42,* 116–131.

Diener, E., & Emmons, R. A. (1984). The independence of positive and negative affect. *Journal of Personality and Social Psychology, 47,* 1105–1117.

Esses, V. M., Haddock, G., & Zanna, M. P. (1993). Affect, cognition and attitudes toward social groups. In D. Mackie & D. L. Hamilton (Eds.), *Affect, cognition and stereotyping: Interactive processes in group perception* (pp. 137–166). New York: Academic.

Fazio, R. H. (1986). How do attitudes guide behavior? In R. M. Sorrentino & E. T. Higgins (Eds.), *The handbook of motivation and cognition: Foundations of social behavior* (pp. 204–243). New York: Guilford.

Fazio, R. H., & Zanna, M. P. (1981). Direct experience and attitude-behavior consistency. In L. Berkowitz (Ed.), *Advances in experimental social psychology* (Vol. 14, pp. 161–202). New York: Academic.

Fazio, R. H., Zanna, M. P., Ross, M., & Powell, M. C. (1992). *Attitude accessibility and attitudinal persistence.* Unpublished manuscript, Indiana University.

Festinger, L. (1957). *A theory of cognitive dissonance.* Palo Alto, CA: Stanford University Press.

Green, D. P. (1988). On the dimensionality of public sentiment toward partisan and ideological groups. *American Journal of Political Science, 32,* 758–780.

Green, D. P., Goldman, S. L., & Salovey, P. (1992). Measurement error masks bipolarity in affect ratings. *Journal of Personality and Social Psychology, 64,* 1029–1041.

Hass, R. G., Katz, I., Rizzo, N., Bailey, J., & Eisentstadt, D. (1991). Cross-racial appraisal as related to attitude ambivalence and cognitive complexity. *Personality and Social Psychology Bulletin, 17,* 83–92.

Jamieson, D. W. (1988, June). *The influence of value conflicts on attitudinal ambivalence.* Paper presented at the annual meeting of the Canadian Psychological Association, Montreal.

Kaplan, K. J. (1972). On the ambivalence-indifference problem in attitude theory and measurement: A suggested modification of the semantic differential technique. *Psychological Bulletin, 77,* 361–372.

Katz, D., & Stotland, E. A. (1959). A preliminary statement to a theory of attitude structure and change. In S. Koch (Ed.), *Psychology: A study of science* (Vol. 3, pp. 423–436). New York: McGraw-Hill.

Katz, I., & Hass, R. G. (1988). Racial ambivalence and American value conflict: Correlational and priming studies of dual cognitive structures. *Journal of Personality and Social Psychology, 55,* 893–905.

Kothandapani, V. (1971). Validation of feeling, belief, and intention to act as three components of attitudes and their contribution to the prediction of contraceptive behavior. *Journal of Personality and Social Psychology, 19,* 321–333.

Kruglanski, A. W. (1989). Lay epistemic processes and contents: Another look at attribution theory. *Psychological Review, 87,* 70–87.

Lewin, K. (1951). *Field theory in social science: Selected theoretical papers.* R. Cartwright (Ed.). New York: Harper & Row.

Miller, N. E. (1944). Experimental studies in conflict. In J. V. Hunt (Ed.), *Personality and the behavior disorders* (Vol. 1, pp. 431–465). New York: Ronald Press.

Mowrer, O. H. (1960). *Learning theory and behavior.* New York: Wiley.

Ostrom, T. M. (1969). The relationship between affective, behavioral, and cognitive components of attitude. *Journal of Experimental Social Psychology, 5,* 12–30.

Petty, R. E., & Cacioppo, J. T. (1983). *Attitudes and persuasion: Classic and contemporary approaches.* Dubuque, IA: Wm. C. Brown Publishers.

Rodin, M. J. (1978). Liking and disliking: Sketch of an alternate view. *Personality and Social Psychology Bulletin, 4,* 473–478.

Rosenberg, M. J., & Hovland, C. I. (1960). Cognitive, affective, and behavioral components of attitude. In M. J. Rosenberg, C. I. Hovland, W. J. McGuire, R. P. Abelson, & J. W. Brehm (Eds.), *Attitude organization and change: An analysis of consistency among attitude components* (pp. 1–14). New Haven, CT: Yale University Press.

Scott, W. A. (1966). Measures of cognitive structure. *Multivariate Behavior Research, 1,* 391–395.

Scott, W. A. (1968). Attitude measurement. In G. Lindsey & E. Aronson (Eds.), *The handbook of social psychology* (Vol. 2, pp. 204–273). Reading, MA: Addison-Wesley.

Smith, M. B. (1947). The personal setting of public opinions: A study of attitudes toward Russia. *Public Opinion Quarterly, 11,* 507–523.

Tetlock, P. E. (1989). Structure and function in political belief systems. In A. R. Pratkanis, S. J. Breckler, & A. G. Greenwald (Eds.), *Attitude structure and function* (pp. 129–151). Hillsdale, NJ: Lawrence Erlbaum Associates.

Thompson, M. M., Naccarato, M. E., & Parker, K. (June 1989). *Measuring cognitive needs: The development and validation of the personal need for structure (PNS) and personal fear of invalidity (PFI) measures.* Paper presented at the annual meeting of the Canadian Psychological Association, Halifax.

Thompson, M. M., & Zanna, M. P. (in press). The conflicted individual: Personality-based and domain-specific antecedents of ambivalent social attitudes. *Journal of Personality.*

Thompson, M. M., Zanna, M. P., & Griffin, D. W. (1992). *A latent variable analysis of attitudinal ambivalence.* Unpublished manuscript, University of Waterloo.

Thurstone, L. L., & Chave, E. J. (1929). *The measurement of attitude.* Chicago: University of Chicago Press.

Wicker, A. W. (1969). Attitudes vs. actions: The relationship of verbal and overt behavioral responses to attitude objects. *Journal of Social Issues, 25,* 41–78.

Zanna, M. P., & Rempel, J. K. (1988). Attitudes: A new look at an old concept. In D. Bar-Tal & A. W. Kruglanski (Eds.), *The social psychology of knowledge* (pp. 315–334). Cambridge, UK: Cambidge University Press.

Zanna, M. P., & Thompson, M. M. (1991, September). Let's not be indifferent about (attitudinal) ambivalence. R. E. Petty & J. A. Krosnick (Chairs), *Attitude Strength: Antecedents and Consequences,* Symposium conducted at the Ohio State University conference on attitudes, Nags Head, NC.

15

▼▼▼▼▼▼▼

Structural Consistency and Attitude Strength

Shelly Chaiken
Eva M. Pomerantz
Roger Giner-Sorolla
New York University

Attitudes are people's evaluations of "objects" as diverse as capital punishment, equality, Japanese, essay exams, me, and writing a chapter for Rich and Jon's book on attitude strength. According to our conception of attitudes (Eagly & Chaiken, 1993), they develop on the basis of affective, cognitive, and behavioral responding to attitude objects (or related cues) and represent, or summarize, the evaluative implications of one or a mixture of these three response classes. Thus a person's abstract evaluation, or attitude toward an object, may be based on one or more of these three types of input (see also Zanna & Rempel, 1988). Once an attitude is formed, a mental representation of the abstract evaluation and also of associated affects, beliefs, and behaviors may be stored in memory. Attitudes and these other aspects of attitude structure may thus be activated upon exposure to the attitude object or to related cues (see also Fazio, 1989; Higgins, 1989).

Several interesting structural properties of attitudes follow from this conceptualization (see Eagly & Chaiken, 1993). In this chapter we pay most attention to one of these properties, one that we believe represents an especially important source of an attitude's *strength*. We call this structural property *evaluative-cognitive consistency*, even though it has classically been labeled *affective-cognitive consistency* (e.g., Chaiken & Baldwin, 1981; Norman, 1975; Rosenberg, 1968; but see Scott, 1969). The earlier label reflects the fact that this structural property was introduced into the attitudes literature when many psychologists used the term *affect* as a synonym for evaluation. Like other recent conceptions of attitude (e.g., Millar & Tesser, 1989; Zanna & Rempel, 1988) ours views evaluation and affect as conceptually distinct. Moreover, the way in which evaluative-cognitive consistency has been operationalized (and, for the most part, discussed) in past research is entirely congruent with the label we use here. Evaluative-cognitive consistency refers to attitude-belief consistency. More specifically, it refers to the degree of consistency that exists between a person's overall, abstract evaluation of an attitude object and the evaluative meaning of his or her beliefs about the object.[1]

We summarize research showing that attitudes relatively high in evaluative-cognitive consistency *behave* the way attitude theorists and researchers expect strong attitudes to behave. For example, such attitudes are stable, they predict overt behavior, and they are relatively resistant to social influence attempts. We also discuss evidence suggesting that such attitudes are strong because they are accompanied by a well-organized set of supporting cognitions that mutes the change impact of new counterattitudinal information and that also enables their possessors to actively refute such information. In addition, we summarize data indicating that evaluative-cognitive consistency is not reducible to other common indicators of attitude strength.

This chapter also addresses a second structural property of attitudes, one which is indicated by our empirical findings on evaluative-cognitive consistency and by our conception of attitude. We call this property *evaluative-affective consistency*. It refers to attitude-affect consistency. More specifically, it refers to the degree of consistency that exists between people's overall evaluations of attitude objects and the evaluative meaning of the emotions, feelings, moods, and sympathetic nervous system activity they experience in relation to these objects (Eagly & Chaiken, 1993). We suggest that simultaneous consideration of evaluative-cognitive and evaluative-affective consistency provides a means of diagnosing the cognitive versus affective *basis* of people's attitudes, and that knowledge of an attitude's structural basis is crucial to understanding the concept of attitude strength. This chapter charts the theoretical and empirical road that led to these ideas.

EMERGENCE OF THE ATTITUDE–NONATTITUDE INTERPRETATION OF EVALUATIVE-COGNITIVE CONSISTENCY

Beginning in the late 1950s and continuing during the next decade, evaluative-cognitive consistency was discussed by several theorists in several contexts (e.g., Abelson & Rosenberg, 1958; Festinger, 1957; Fishbein, 1963; Rosenberg, 1956, 1960a, 1960b, 1968; Scott, 1969; Zajonc, 1968). In a broad discussion of cognitive

---

[1]In fact, in our framework the label *affective-cognitive consistency* for this structural property is inappropriate because it implies a different structural property. In our conception, *affective-cognitive* consistency refers to a "heart versus mind" type of ambivalence—the degree to which the evaluative meaning of the affect people experience in relation to attitude objects (e.g., emotions) is consistent with the evaluative meaning of the beliefs they hold about these objects (Eagly & Chaiken, 1993).

structure, Scott (1969) described evaluative-cognitive consistency as existing when liked objects are seen as possessing desirable characteristics and disliked objects are seen as possessing undesirable characteristics. Scott did not emphasize a particular causal interpretation of evaluative-cognitive consistency, but the emerging expectancy-value models of attitude did (e.g., Fishbein, 1963; Fishbein & Ajzen, 1975; Rosenberg, 1956). As is well known, these models and related ones (e.g., Anderson, 1968) emphasize that people form attitudes by learning about the attributes of objects. In other words, the evaluative content of people's beliefs determines their attitudes. Yet theories of cognitive consistency, which also emerged during this period (e.g., Abelson & Rosenberg, 1958; Festinger, 1957; Heider, 1958), suggested that the opposite causal sequence was also possible. In the interest of maintaining cognitive consistency, people might be prone to attribute good characteristics to liked objects and bad characteristics to disliked objects. Both causal perspectives highlight a core assumption of traditional and modern attitude theory: Evaluations of attitude objects tend to be consistent with the evaluative meaning of the attributes that people ascribe to these objects.

Attitudes and beliefs may generally be correlated, but there is no compelling reason to assume high correspondence for all persons for all attitude objects in all situations. The idea that evaluative-cognitive consistency is a *variable* property of attitude structure was emphasized by Milton Rosenberg (1960a, 1968).

Rosenberg's (1956) early research helped demonstrate the viability of an expectancy-value model of attitude. This work showed that attitudes, operationalized as evaluations, were generally consistent with beliefs, operationalized as *instrumentality-value* products. To give a contemporary example, subjects opposed to capital punishment would tend to see this policy as hindering positively evaluated goals or values, and as facilitating negatively evaluated goals. In subsequent work Rosenberg (1960a, 1960b, 1968) turned his attention to studying inconsistency between attitudes and beliefs, and the antecedents and consequences of inconsistency. Exposure to persuasive communications was viewed as a major instigator of attitude-belief inconsistency. Moreover, in line with the cognitive consistency theme that dominated this period, Rosenberg proposed that inconsistency would motivate people to restore consistency by changing their attitudes, their beliefs, or both. Several studies provided support for these ideas (see Rosenberg, 1960a, 1960b, 1968).

Most important for present purposes, Rosenberg's (1968) research documented considerable individual difference variation in evaluative-cognitive consistency. Furthermore, this research program provided preliminary evidence that the attitudes expressed by low consistency persons are more likely than those expressed by high consistency persons to (a) change in response to persuasion attempts, and in the absence of explicit influence inductions, to (b) fluctuate between initial and delayed assessments of attitude.

Rosenberg (1968) considered two main explanations for low evaluative-cognitive consistency. First, inconsistent people may hold beliefs whose evaluative meaning is truly discrepant from their attitudes. Because motivation for consistency-restoring change was presumed to increase when people think "closely" about inconsistency and because completing initial attitude and belief questionnaires could stimulate such thought, the test–retest instability of low evaluative-cognitive consistency subjects and their greater susceptibility to persuasion could, Rosenberg reasoned, reflect consistency-restoring attitudinal reorganization.

Although Rosenberg (1968) did not entirely discount this explanation, he favored a second, _vacuity_ interpretation. In this view people low in evaluative-cognitive consistency lack both genuine beliefs about the attitude object and a genuine attitude toward it. The inconsistency inferred from these persons' responses to attitude and belief questionnaires is thus more apparent than real. People with "vacuous" attitudes comply with implicit research demands to answer such questionnaires, but they are uncertain how to respond and so respond in an unreliable, top-of-the-head manner. In the terminology of public opinion researchers, people low in evaluative–cognitive consistency were viewed by Rosenberg as expressing _nonattitudes_ (Converse, 1970).

By contrast, people high in evaluative-cognitive consistency were presumed to hold genuine beliefs that supported genuine attitudes—well-articulated attitudes that reflect a stable "dispositional orientation" toward the object (Rosenberg, 1968). The proposal that these persons, and not low consistency persons, hold "true" attitudes reflected Rosenberg's (e.g., 1956) expectancy-value perspective, that attitudes are based on beliefs. To the extent that an attitude appeared inconsistent with measured beliefs, its origin was sufficiently unclear to warrant the label "vacuous" or "nonattitude."

This attitude-nonattitude interpretation of evaluative-cognitive consistency prompted most of the research summarized in the next section. It also provides a reasonable account of most studies' main findings. Yet some findings, and detailed aspects of others, argue for a more refined view of this construct, one that regards high evaluative-cognitive consistency as indicating more than "just a genuine attitude" and one that regards low evaluative-cognitive consistency as potentially diagnostic of a genuine attitude based primarily on affective input.

MEASUREMENT, CORRELATES, AND CONSEQUENCES OF EVALUATIVE-COGNITIVE CONSISTENCY

Assessment of Evaluative-Cognitive Consistency

The relatively small research literature on evaluative-cognitive consistency has used common procedures for measuring this structural property of attitudes. We illustrate them with reference to an attitude object featured in some of our research, capital punishment. Subjects indicate the extent to which they favor versus oppose this policy and then rate it on several semantic differential scales (e.g., good vs. bad; foolish vs. wise). The average of these direct, self-report measures of attitude provide a measure of overall *evaluation*.[2] The *cognitive* aspect of subjects' attitudes is assessed by having them complete two scales for each of a set of 10 or so goals or values that have been pretested for their relevance to the focal issue; for capital punishment we have used values such as *concern for human life, protection of society, morality,* and *individual rights*. On the first, *instrumentality* scale, subjects rate the extent to which they believe that capital punishment helps (vs. hinders) the attainment of the stated value (e.g., "protection of society"). On the second, *value* scale subjects indicate how positive (vs. negative) they consider the stated value. The two ratings are multiplied and these (instrumentality × value) products are then summed across value-items to form one index which conveys the evaluative meaning of subjects' endorsed beliefs (Rosenberg, 1956, 1968).

Most studies have followed Rosenberg (e.g., 1968) by determining level of evaluative-cognitive consistency through a ranking procedure: Subjects are rank ordered in terms of the positivity of their evaluation scores and then again on the basis of the positivity implied by their scores on the cognitive index. The absolute value of the discrepancy between each subject's position in these two rankings reflects his or her level of evaluative-cognitive consistency, with smaller difference scores signifying higher consistency (e.g., Chaiken & Baldwin, 1981; Norman, 1975). In a conceptually identical procedure, the evaluation index and the cognitive index are standardized, and the absolute difference of these z-scores is calculated. As in the ranking procedure, smaller difference scores signify higher levels of evaluative-cognitive consistency (e.g., Zimmerman & Chaiken, 1994; Fazio & Zanna, 1978).

Measurement Validity

Rosenberg (1968) assumed that evaluative-cognitive consistency taps a *domain specific* rather than a general, trait-like individual difference. Several findings support this assumption. Chaiken and Baldwin (1981) entertained the possibility that the tendency to endorse beliefs congruent with one's attitudes might merely reflect a more general tendency to be concerned about the social desirability of one's behavior. Arguing against this idea, their subjects' evaluative-cognitive consistency scores (on the topic of environmentalism) were unrelated to their scores on a chronic measure of social desirability concern (Crowne & Marlow, 1964). Norman (1975) provided more direct evidence for the domain specificity conception. He showed that subjects' evaluative-cognitive consistency scores on the issue of volunteering for psychological research were uncorrelated with their evaluative-cognitive consistency scores on two other issues (e.g., prohibition of

---

[2]Evaluation could be assessed using only the single-item favorability measure or only the multi-item semantic differential index (e.g., Norman, 1975), but reliability concerns have led us to favor the composite index.

cigarette smoking in classrooms). Our own research, which has concerned social policy issues, corroborates these null results (Chaiken & Baldwin, 1981; Chaiken et al., 1992; Chaiken & Yates, 1985). For example, structural consistency on the topic of capital punishment does not reliably predict structural consistency on the topics of censorship or abortion-on-demand.

Norman (1975) also ruled out the idea that evaluative-cognitive consistency scores merely tap the general reliability of subjects' responses to attitudinal items. In addition, his research as well as our own studies have confirmed that observed differences between high and low evaluative-cognitive consistency subject groups are not attributable to potential confounds such as valence or extremity differences in these groups' initial attitudes. In fact, across multiple samples and issues the modal finding of relevant research is that subjects' evaluative-cognitive consistency scores are not reliably correlated with their (overall) evaluation scores, their cognitive index scores, or with the extremity of these scores (e.g., Chaiken & Baldwin, 1981; Chaiken & Yates, 1985; Norman, 1975; Scott, 1969; for an exception, see Krosnick, Boninger, Chuang, Berent, & Carnot, 1993).

Because existing research has relied on the instrumentality × value ratings we have described to assess the cognitive aspect of subjects' attitudes, it is arguable that the demonstrated properties of attitudes high in evaluative-cognitive consistency (e.g., resistance to change) follow only from their congruency with beliefs involving terminal and instrumental values such as *freedom* and *responsibility* (Rokeach, 1968), rather than from their congruency with beliefs of all kinds. Despite their empirical focus, Rosenberg (1968) and subsequent investigators have favored the more general interpretation of evaluative-cognitive consistency (e.g., Chaiken & Baldwin, 1981; Fazio & Zanna, 1978; Norman, 1975).

There is also evidence that people identified as high or low in consistency based on instrumentality × value endorsements would be identified similarly based on less restrictive cognitive measures (Chaiken & Baldwin, 1981; Chaiken & Yates, 1985). Most notably, Chaiken and Yates (1985) assessed evaluative-cognitive consistency in the standard manner and, weeks later, had subjects write essays explaining their attitudes. Content analyses of these essays revealed that high consistency subjects expressed a greater proportion of *attitude-congruent* beliefs and a smaller proportion of *attitude-incongruent* and neutral beliefs than low consistency subjects. Moreover, there was no evidence that this difference was confined to subjects' beliefs about the value implications of the attitude objects studied in this research.

Temporal Stability and Attitude-Behavior Correspondence

A traditional assumption of attitude theory is that attitudes, at least strong ones, are relatively stable and predictive of behavior. Replicating Rosenberg's (1968) initial stability findings, Norman (1975) obtained a substantially higher test–retest correlation for attitudes toward volunteering for psychological research among psychology students who manifested relatively high (vs. relatively low) evaluative-cognitive consistency on this topic (rs = .85 vs. .32).[3] We have observed the same difference in temporal stability, on the issue of capital punishment (Chaiken & Pomerantz, 1992).

Attitude stability and attitude-behavior correspondence often go hand in hand, probably because stability mediates the predictability of behavior from attitudes measured at an earlier time (Doll & Ajzen, 1992; Fazio & Zanna, 1981), but possibly because strong attitudes independently produce both outcomes (e.g., Fazio, 1986, 1989). Consistent with either possibility, Norman's (1975) research confirmed a positive relation between degree of evaluative-cognitive consistency and degree of attitude-behavior correspondence. In several replications, high consistency subjects' volunteering attitudes correlated substantially with subsequent measures of their volunteering behavior (e.g., signing up for a study promising no financial or "subject hour" compensation; r = .62, p < .05). By contrast, low consistency subjects' exhibited little attitude-behavior correspondence (e.g., r = −.28, ns). Although Fazio and Zanna (1978) failed to replicate these findings,[4] they did find some evidence that evaluative-cognitive consistency related more strongly to attitude-behavior correspondence as subjects' past behavioral experience with the attitude object (volunteering for experiments) decreased (see also Schlegel & DiTecco, 1982).

Resistance to Social Influence

Another assumption of attitude theory is that strong attitudes are more difficult to influence than weak attitudes or, most certainly, nonattitudes. As noted earlier, Rosenberg (1968) presented preliminary data indicating that persons high in evaluative-cognitive consistency are more difficult to persuade than persons low in such consistency. In a study designed to replicate and extend these findings, we measured the evaluative-cognitive consistency of subjects' attitudes toward censorship and subsequently assessed their agreement with and cognitive responses to a counterattitudinal message on this topic; procensorship subjects read an anticensorship message, and anticensorship subjects read a procensorship message (Chaiken, 1982). Our agreement data were weak but in line with Rosenberg's (1968) results. Although the study's counterattitudinal messages were equally

---

[3]This and other references to high versus low consistency subject groups refer to researchers' comparisons of subjects whose evaluative-cognitive consistency scores are below versus above the median of the distribution or (in some studies) in the bottom versus top tertile or quartile of the distribution.

[4]Although the reasons for the disparity between these data sets are unclear it should be noted that Fazio and Zanna's (1978) behavioral measure was administered during the same session in which attitudes were assessed whereas Norman's (1975) behavioral measures were administered approximately 3 weeks after the assessment of attitudes.

discrepant from high and low consistency subjects' initial attitudes, high consistency subjects were somewhat less persuaded by them ($p = .12$).[5] More interesting, although the two consistency groups did not differ in their *global* cognitive responses to the message (e.g., "poorly argued essay"), high consistency subjects generated a significantly greater number of explicit *counterarguments* ($p < .05$; e.g., "[you] can't just link decrease in sexual crimes to viewing uncensored material").

In a very different test of the resistance hypothesis, Norman (1975, Experiment 3) found that subjects whose attitudes toward volunteering for psychological research showed high consistency were somewhat less likely than low consistency subjects to conform to relevant behavior exhibited by an experimental accomplice ($p < .10$). For example, when asked by an experimenter to attend additional experimental sessions after first hearing the accomplice refuse this request, 52% of the high consistency subjects and 68% of the low consistency subjects also refused.

Chaiken and Baldwin (1981) investigated another social influence phenomenon. One implication of Bem's (e.g., 1972) self-perception theory is that people's attitudes can be influenced by manipulating the salience (or accessibility) of past attitude-relevant behaviors.[6] In a clever demonstration of this influence principle, Salancik and Conway (1975) found that subjects expressed more positive (or more negative) attitudes toward being religious after completing questionnaire items worded so as to increase the salience of their past proreligious behaviors (or their past antireligious behaviors). Chaiken and Baldwin adapted Salancik and Conway's procedures to investigate attitudes toward being an environmentalist. Subjects were asked to place a checkmark next to each of 26 pro- and antiecology behaviors that applied to them. In the proenvironment version, pro-ecology behaviors were phrased to make endorsement likely and antiecology behaviors were phrased to make endorsement unlikely (e.g., "I *occasionally* carpool rather than drive separately," "I *frequently* leave on lights in rooms I'm not using"). The reverse phrasing characterized the antienvironment version of the behavior questionnaire (e.g., "I *frequently* carpool . . . ," "I *occasionally* leave on lights . . .").

Chaiken and Baldwin's (1981) major hypothesis was that this manipulation would exert a greater impact on subjects whose preexperimental environmentalist attitudes were low in evaluative-cognitive consistency. If such persons possess weak attitudes or nonattitudes they should be especially prone to infer their attitudes from salient behavioral information. By contrast, such information should impact less on high consistency persons to the extent that they possess strong "internal cues" regarding their attitudes (Bem, 1972). Internal cues for

---

[5]This and other p-values for unpublished work reported in this chapter are based on two-tailed tests of significance, even when (as in the present instance) one-tailed tests are easily justified and would tell a more compelling story.

[6]For the reverse phenomenon, that attitudes influence people's recall of past behaviors, see Ross (1989).

these persons would entail a set of beliefs that largely support their overall attitudes. In accord with averaging models of attitudes (e.g., Anderson, 1968, 1981) the presence of such cognitions should function to dampen the change impact of small amounts of new information, in this case salient behavioral information. Alternatively, high consistency subjects might be more prone to actively refute the attitudinal implications of this information, in line with Chaiken's (1982) persuasion findings. For either or both reasons, high consistency subjects would be relatively unaffected by the study's self-perception induction.

The results confirmed Chaiken and Baldwin's hypothesis. Completing the proenvironment (vs. antienvironment) version of the behavioral questionnaire led to reliably more positive environmentalist attitudes and stronger environmentalist self-perceptions among low evaluative-cognitive consistency subjects but not among high evaluative-cognitive consistency subjects. Moreover, regression analyses showed that high consistency subjects' postmanipulation attitudes and self-perceptions were best predicted by their preexperimental attitudes and self-perceptions, whereas low consistency subjects' postmanipulation attitudes and self-perceptions were best predicted by the pro- or antiecology behaviors they had been induced to endorse.[7]

This research also presented direct evidence that high consistency persons' beliefs are more highly organized than those of low consistency persons. As part of this study subjects indicated the extent to which they agreed with five ecology-related belief statements (e.g., "More nuclear power stations should be built," "Nonbiodegradable consumer goods such as colored tissue and toilet paper should be outlawed"). Analyses showed that high consistency subjects' responses to these belief statements were more highly intercorrelated than the responses of low consistency subjects.[8] In retrospect, these findings are not surprising because beliefs that are highly correlated with evaluation—the hallmark of evaluative-cognitive consistency—should also be correlated with one another. Nonetheless, they corroborate the idea that differences in cognitive organization underlie differences in evaluative-cognitive consistency. As discussed later in this chapter, however, this conclusion does not preclude the possibility that evaluative-cognitive *inconsistency* may sometimes be a product of other factors (i.e., absence of an attitude or a genuine attitude based on noncognitive input).

---

[7]As implied by our earlier discussion of measurement validity, the valence and extremity of high and low consistency subjects' preexperimental attitudes did not differ reliably in this research. For brevity we ignore such findings in summarizing other studies of ours in this chapter. It suffices to say that valence/extremity differences have been atypical in our research and, when found, have been statistically controlled for.

[8]High (vs. low) consistency subjects' responses to these ecology-items were also more highly correlated with their overall attitudes toward being an environmentalist (average rs = .40 vs. .07), a result consistent with our earlier point that existing findings on evaluative-cognitive consistency may not hinge on using instrumentality × value items to assess the cognitive aspect of subjects' attitudes.

Thought-Induced Attitude Polarization

Understanding how thought affects attitudes is central to understanding resistance, because influence inductions often motivate people to contemplate their attitudes. Tesser and colleagues have shown that having people think about their attitudes often causes these attitudes to become more extreme (see Tesser, Martin, & Mendolia, ch. 4, this volume). Tesser (1978) has also argued and presented evidence for the view that this *polarization* effect is dependent on the presence of a well-developed knowledge structure or "schema" in regard to the attitude object. Such structures lead to polarization because they foster attitude-congruent thinking—for example, generating new attitude-consistent beliefs, and resolving inconsistent beliefs through refutation or reinterpretation. Without a schema, thinking about the attitude object is assumed to produce irrelevant or evaluatively inconsistent beliefs as often as it produces consistent cognitions. Thus with poorly organized knowledge structures, thought causes little or no polarization (see also Liberman & Chaiken, 1991).

Chaiken and Yates (1985) reasoned that if evaluative-cognitive consistency taps well-organized knowledge about attitude objects, the attitudes (i.e., evaluations) of high consistency persons ought to polarize more as a function of thought than the attitudes of low consistency persons. To test this hypothesis, they first identified subjects whose capital punishment attitudes were high or low in evaluative-cognitive consistency and (other) subjects whose censorship attitudes were high or low in evaluative-cognitive consistency. Subsequently these subjects participated in a study in which they were asked to write down their "thoughts and feelings" about both of these topics. To assess polarization, subjects indicated their attitudes toward both topics (and several control topics) before and after writing each essay.

The polarization data provided strong support for Chaiken and Yates' hypothesis (for a replication, see Moreno, Sheposh, & Coverdale, 1987). Thinking about capital punishment led to significant attitude polarization on this topic (and not other topics) only among high consistency capital punishment subjects. Similarly, thinking about censorship led to significant attitude polarization on this topic (and not other topics) *only* among high consistency censorship subjects.[9] Additional results supported Tesser's (1978) assumption that schema-guided evaluatively congruent thinking mediates thought-induced attitude polarization. Polarization scores for high evaluative-cognitive consistency subjects were positively associated with the proportion of attitude-consistent thoughts expressed in their (relevant) essays ($r = .37$, $p < .05$) and negatively associated with the proportion of attitude-inconsistent thoughts expressed ($r = -.31$, $p < .05$). In

---

[9]As discussed earlier in this chapter, structural consistency is largely a domain specific individual difference. Moreover, Chaiken and Yates' (1985) decision to use both the capital punishment and censorship issues was based on two pilot studies showing little relation between subjects' consistency scores on the two issues ($rs = .06$ and .11, both ns).

contrast, the thoughts that low consistency subjects expressed were undiagnostic of the extent to which their attitudes polarized, stayed the same, or moderated after thought.

Content analyses of the essays that subjects wrote yielded several additional findings. Overall, high (vs. low) consistency subjects listed only marginally more attitude-relevant beliefs about the attitude object ($p = .12$).[10] Yet, as noted earlier in this chapter, the beliefs that high consistency subjects expressed were more congruent with their measured attitudes than those expressed by low consistency subjects. The most striking difference obtained in this content-analysis, however, was the greater tendency of high consistency subjects to probe the implications of discrepant information, by generating *refutational thoughts* that discredited or minimized the importance of inconsistent information (e.g., "There are those who argue that capital punishment serves as a deterrent to crime, but until now there seem to be very few statistics that support their claims"; "It may not be too rational to kill someone for killing someone else, but it is necessary to prevent an uprise of criminal acts"). This finding coheres with Chaiken's (1982) persuasion study, which found greater counterarguing of a counterattitudinal message by high consistency subjects.

Attitudinal Selectivity

One of the oldest propositions of attitude theory is that attitudes exert selective effects at virtually all stages of information-processing (see Eagly & Chaiken, 1993; Chaiken, Giner-Sorolla, & Chen, in press). Consistent with the idea that selectivity effects should be more pronounced when attitudes are strong we have investigated the extent to which evaluative-cognitive consistency moderates the impact of attitudes on *judgment* and on *memory*.

Lord, Ross, and Lepper (1979) presented subjects who held extreme attitudes for or against capital punishment with mixed evidence concerning this policy's efficacy as a deterrent to murder. Subjects evaluated two articles, one presenting statistical evidence supportive of deterrence, and one presenting data suggesting that capital punishment actually increases murder rates. The results revealed that subjects judged attitude-congruent articles more positively than attitude-incongruent articles. For example, pro-capital-punishment subjects regarded the prodeterrence article as much more convincing and as reporting a much better conducted study than the antideterrence article. In a replication of this study, Houston and Fazio (1989) obtained a stronger selective judgment effect among subjects whose capital punishment attitudes were highly accessible. In fact, the data for low accessibility subjects showed virtually no impact of attitude on judgment.

---

[10]Because subjects had 7 minutes to write their essays, it is unclear whether this knowledge difference tendency (if at all replicable) should be attributed to differences in the accessibility or availability of attitude-relevant knowledge.

We also conducted a replication of the Lord et al. (1979) study, in order to examine the moderating effect of evaluative-cognitive consistency (Pomerantz, Margolies, & Chaiken, 1993). Unlike Lord and colleagues we did not recruit only subjects with extreme capital punishment attitudes. Nonetheless, the tendency for our subjects to preferentially evaluate the attitude-congruent article was robust ($p < .001$). Our main hypothesis was that this selective judgment effect would be evident especially among subjects whose attitudes were high in evaluative-cognitive consistency. This interaction hypothesis received some support ($p = .10$). Importantly, though, the effect was reliable for low consistency subjects ($p < .05; p < .001$ for highs). Analysis of the favorability of subjects' open-ended comments about the research articles also supported our interaction hypothesis ($p < .01$): The tendency to generate more positive than negative comments about attitude-congruent articles, and more negative than positive comments about attitude-incongruent articles was reliably greater for high consistency subjects. Yet the basic selectivity effect again held for low consistency subjects ($p < .05$; $p < .001$ for highs).[11]

The impact of attitudes on people's memory for incoming attitude-relevant information is another important selectivity phenomenon. Traditionally, researchers have hypothesized a "congeniality" bias, the tendency for attitude-congruent information to be better remembered. Indeed, Robert's (1985) meta-analysis of the attitude-memory literature yielded a small but reliable congeniality effect.

The small congruency effect observed in this meta-analysis and the fact that many studies have found no reliable memory effects, and others superior memory for incongruent information (e.g., Cacioppo & Petty, 1979; Jones & Aneshansel, 1956) suggested to us that taking attitude structure into account might help elucidate the attitude-memory literature. In particular, we reasoned that evaluative-cognitive consistency might moderate both the size and the direction of the attitude-memory relation. If low consistency persons possess weak or vacuous attitudes, memory should favor neither congruent nor incongruent information. In contrast, the attitude-memory relation ought to be sizeable for high consistency persons. Yet, in considering the direction of this relation we doubted that high consistency persons would exhibit a congruency effect. Instead, our earlier findings showing greater counterarguing and refutational thinking by high consistency persons led us to hypothesize that they would better remember attitude-incongruent information. To the extent that these persons process attitude-discrepant information systematically, by actively trying to refute it, better (immediate) memory for such information should ensue (e.g., Chaiken, 1980).

These ideas were tested by exposing high and low consistency subjects to six pro- and six anti-capital-punishment belief statements (Zimmerman & Chaiken,

---

[11]Attitude accessibility and extremity were also measured in this study. Neither variable was correlated with evaluative-cognitive consistency ($rs < .07$), nor did statistically controlling for these variables affect the magnitude of the interaction effects discussed in the text.

1994). These statements (and filler statements) were presented by a slide projector and subjects indicated both their agreement and their familiarity with each statement. After a distractor task, subjects were asked to write down as many capital punishment statements as they could recall.

Analysis of the study's recall data yielded a reliable interaction between evaluative-cognitive consistency and the congruency of attitude-relevant information ($p < .005$). As anticipated, high consistency subjects recalled more incongruent than congruent belief statements ($Ms = 2.43$ vs. 2.00). The surprise in these data were the results for low consistency subjects. Contrary to our expectation that their attitudes would impact little on memory, they showed much better memory for *congruent* (vs. incongruent) belief statements ($Ms = 2.80$ vs. 2.00).[12] We return to this finding shortly.

Other Attitude Strength Variables

The chapters in this book reveal that quite a few variables have been proposed as indicators of *attitude strength*. Indeed, one purpose of the volume is to elucidate these variables' interrelations. The correlations we and others have observed between evaluative-cognitive consistency and other strength variables indicate little overlap.

We have already noted that evaluative-cognitive consistency does not typically correlate with the *extremity* of people's attitudes (e.g., Chaiken & Baldwin, 1981; Chaiken & Yates, 1985; Norman, 1975; cf. Krosnick et al., 1993). It also appears to be unassociated with measures of *attitude accessibility, direct behavioral experience* with attitude objects, and the *latitude of rejection*, or range of attitudinal positions people deem objectionable (e.g., Chaiken & Giner-Sorolla, 1992; Fazio & Zanna, 1978; Krosnick et al., 1993; Pomerantz et al., 1993; see also footnote 11). Nor does evaluative-cognitive consistency show a consistently reliable correlation with various self-report indicators of attitude strength such as how *certain* people feel about their attitudes, how *important* they consider the attitude object, or the extent to which they consider their attitudes to be *central* to their sense of self (e.g., Zimmerman & Chaiken, 1994; Krosnick et al., 1993; Pomerantz et al., 1993). In fact, such correlations are typically close to zero (e.g., Krosnick et al., 1993).

Chaiken and Yates' (1985) finding that high consistency subjects generated marginally more beliefs than low consistency subjects, in an essay-writing task, suggests that evaluative-cognitive consistency may covary with the extensiveness of people's knowledge about attitude objects or their ability to quickly retrieve issue-relevant knowledge from memory (see Wood, Rhodes, & Biek, ch. 11, this volume; see also footnote 10). Yet Krosnick et al. (1993) observed near-zero

---

[12]The value of taking attitude structure into account in examining the attitude-memory relation should be clear from these data: Analyses which ignored evaluative-cognitive consistency yielded a trivially small recall trend favoring congruent over incongruent information ($Ms = 2.41$ vs. 2.21, *ns*).

correlations between evaluative-cognitive consistency and both a self-report measure and a thought-listing measure of extent of issue-relevant knowledge. The implications of these null correlations between evaluative-cognitive consistency and other indicators of attitude strength are discussed in the next section.

REVISING THE ATTITUDE-NONATTITUDE CONCEPTION OF EVALUATIVE-COGNITIVE CONSISTENCY

According to the attitude-nonattitude conception of evaluative-cognitive consistency, high consistency persons hold beliefs about attitude objects and thus genuine attitudes toward those objects whereas low consistency persons lack both beliefs and genuine attitudes. When queried about their attitudes such persons express top-of-the-head judgments that are best labeled "vacuous" or "nonattitudes" (Converse, 1970). This conception, originally proposed by Rosenberg (1968), has been a useful heuristic in guiding research on evaluative-cognitive consistency. It also provides a simple account of demonstrations that high (vs. low) consistency persons' expressed attitudes are more stable, more predictive of behavior, and more resistant to social influence inductions. Nonetheless, other findings argue for a richer conception of evaluative-cognitive consistency than that implied by the attitude-nonattitude distinction. Most notably, certain findings call into question the assumption that low evaluative-cognitive consistency signifies the absence of a genuine attitude.

High Evaluative-Cognitive Consistency

If the difference between high and low consistency attitudes rested mainly on the possession of beliefs about a given attitude object, evaluative-cognitive consistency ought to correlate reliably with knowledge about that attitude object. Yet the data we have reviewed indicates that the association between these constructs is slight at best (Chaiken & Yates, 1985; Krosnick et al., 1993). This lack of significant covariation is important because it helps clarify that the constructs address distinctive aspects of attitude-relevant knowledge. Knowledge measures typically assess either the amount or accessibility of people's knowledge about attitude objects, without regard to its congruency with overall attitude. By contrast, evaluative-cognitive consistency explicitly taps the degree to which the evaluative meaning of people's beliefs is congruent with their attitudes, without regard to how much knowledge they have. Both structural properties are important dimensions of attitude strength (Eagly & Chaiken, ch. 16, this volume; Wood, Rhodes, & Biek, ch. 11, this volume); in combination, they may prove to be particularly important.

It is therefore probably not whether beliefs are held or how many are held that best characterizes the difference between attitudes high and low in evaluative-cognitive consistency. Instead, and in accord with its measurement, it is the degree to which the beliefs one holds about an attitude object are evaluatively congruent with one's overall attitude. Associated with this tendency for beliefs to be more or less correlated with attitude is their tendency to be more or less correlated with one another. Thus high consistency persons' beliefs are more internally consistent in their implied evaluation of the attitude object than those of low consistency persons (Chaiken & Baldwin, 1981; Chaiken & Yates, 1985). We have also seen that high consistency persons are more prone than low consistency persons to counterargue information that challenges their attitudes (Chaiken, 1982; Chaiken & Yates, 1985).

These key differences between attitudes high and low in evaluative-cognitive consistency lead us to regard this construct as a source of attitude strength. Attitudes high in evaluative-cognitive consistency are strong insofar as they are accompanied by a highly organized set of supportive cognitions. Such knowledge represents a valuable *cognitive resource*, enabling people to defend their attitudes through an active, *systematic* analysis of attitude-discrepant information (see Chaiken, Liberman, & Eagly, 1989).

A neglected but important aspect of Rosenberg's (1968) attitude–nonattitude conception is the expectancy-value assumption that high consistency persons' beliefs cohere with their attitudes because such persons have formed their attitudes on the basis of their beliefs. Neither we nor other investigators have explicitly tested this causal explanation of high evaluative-cognitive consistency attitudes. This is a significant omission of research because, as noted earlier in this chapter, attitude-belief congruency could be caused by other mechanisms, such as the tendency to align one's beliefs with one's attitude in the interests of restoring or maintaining cognitive consistency. Nonetheless, our emerging understanding of low evaluative-cognitive consistency, which we turn to in the following paragraph, leads us to favor the idea that high evaluative-cognitive consistency is indeed diagnostic of the extent to which a person's attitude toward some object has been derived from, and thus summarizes, their cognitive experience with that object.

Low Evaluative-Cognitive Consistency

A number of findings in the literature are difficult to reconcile with the idea that low evaluative-cognitive consistency signifies the absence of a genuine attitude. If low consistency persons' attitudes were as ephemeral as implied by the attitude-nonattitude conception, evaluative-cognitive consistency ought to correlate at least modestly with at least some other presumed indicators of attitude strength. Although data of this type are available for most attitude strength variables that theorists have proposed, our review revealed virtually no association between any of them and evaluative-cognitive consistency.

To a certain extent our selective judgment findings also question the vacuity interpretation of low evaluative-cognitive consistency (Pomerantz et al., 1993). Compared to high consistency subjects in that experiment, low consistency subjects showed less partisan processing and judgments of mixed (pro- and counterattitudinal) scientific evidence. Yet, in absolute statistical terms, they did process and judge this information in a reliably partisan manner. The most striking indictment against the vacuity interpretation, however, comes from our attitude-memory study (Zimmerman & Chaiken, 1994). That study revealed a substantial congeniality bias in recall of attitude-relevant information for low consistency subjects. If these subjects truly held nonattitudes, no memory advantage for proattitudinal (or counterattitudinal) information ought to have been observed.

What could account for the null correlations between evaluative-cognitive consistency and other strength variables; the highly reliable selective judgment and selective memory effects we have observed for low consistency subject samples; and the fact that some of the resistance experiments we reviewed yielded differences between high and low consistency subject groups that were statistically marginal (Chaiken, 1982; Norman, 1975)? In harmony with aspects of the attitude-nonattitude conception we believe that low evaluative-cognitive consistency may indicate the absence of a genuine attitude or, at the least, a weak attitude insofar as it lacks a clear, internal cognitive structure. Yet, departing from the attitude-nonattitude conception, we suggest that low evaluative-cognitive consistency may also indicate the presence of a genuine attitude that is grounded more in *affective* than cognitive experience. According to the latter view, low consistency persons might well possess genuine beliefs about an attitude object (although they could as well lack beliefs). Yet their attitudes toward that object primarily derive from, and thus summarize, their affective experience with the object.

The attitudes of at least some persons who exhibit low evaluative-*cognitive* consistency, then, might nonetheless exhibit high evaluative-*affective* consistency. These persons' affect-based attitudes would correlate negligibly with the evaluative implications of endorsed (or generated) beliefs, but they would cohere with the evaluative meaning of the emotions and feelings these persons experience in relation to the object. Of course, other persons who exhibit low evaluative-cognitive consistency might also exhibit low evaluative-affective consistency. Such persons' expressed attitudes would summarize neither relevant cognitive nor affective experience with attitude objects. Attitudes of this sort would be especially weak, possibly earning the label nonattitudes, because they lack a coherent, internal structure of either cognitive or affective associations (see Eagly & Chaiken, ch. 16, this volume).[13] To complete our 2 × 2 taxonomy we speculate

---

[13]It might of course be argued that such persons' attitudes are quite genuine but derive mainly from *behavioral* experience with the attitude object. Although we do not entirely discount this possibility we think it is likely that behavioral experience shapes attitudes primarily by yielding cognitive and affective information about the attitude object and one's responses to it (see Eagly & Chaiken, 1993, ch. 16, this volume).

that (a) attitudes high in evaluative-cognitive consistency but low in evaluative-affective consistency may be diagnostic of attitudes that are primarily derived from and thus summarize people's cognitive experiences with attitude objects,[14] and that (b) attitudes high in both types of structural consistency may be diagnostic of attitudes that reflect both cognitive and affective experience with attitude objects.

The next section of this chapter summarizes our preliminary efforts to explore the utility of distinguishing between evaluative-cognitive and evaluative-affective consistency. These empirical endeavors do not directly test the idea that the two forms of structural consistency distinguish cognitively based attitudes from affectively based attitudes, an ultimate concern of our research program. Instead they examine several preliminary assumptions—that the two types of consistency are empirically distinguishable, and that attitudes low in both forms of consistency are weaker in several senses than attitudes high in either or both forms.

EVALUATIVE-COGNITIVE
AND EVALUATIVE-AFFECTIVE CONSISTENCY
AS INDEPENDENT SOURCES OF ATTITUDE
STRENGTH

Assessment of Evaluative-Affective Consistency

We have measured evaluative-affective consistency using procedures that parallel those developed to assess evaluative-cognitive consistency. Overall evaluation of the attitude object is measured as described earlier in this chapter. The *affective* aspect of subjects' attitudes is assessed by having them rate how "thinking about" the attitude object makes them "feel" (see Breckler, 1984; Breckler & Wiggins, 1989). Subjects respond on several bipolar *adverb* scales chosen for their relevance to the attitude object; for capital punishment we have used scales anchored by emotions such as angry (vs. glad), disgusted (vs. not at all disgusted), displeased (vs. pleased), and uncomfortable (vs. comfortable). Responses to these scales are summed to form one affective index of attitude and, after standardizing this index and the evaluation index, the absolute value of their difference is computed. Thus smaller difference scores signify higher levels of evaluative-affective consistency.

Evaluative-affective consistency appears to be distinct from evaluative-cognitive consistency: In two samples, the correlation between these measures has

---

[14]By hypothesizing that such attitudes are cognitively based we do not mean to imply that their possessors necessarily lack affective experience with the attitude object (although this is an obvious possibility). What we do mean to imply is that, regardless of amount of affective experience, its evaluative implications do not play an appreciable role in shaping the person's attitude toward the object.

been negligible (rs = .07 and .14). Because our research has thus far examined only the issue of capital punishment, these and other findings reported below should be considered preliminary.

Attitude Accessibility

We have noted that evaluative-cognitive consistency does not correlate reliably with attitude accessibility, operationalized as response time to an attitude inquiry. Yet numerous studies support the idea that accessibility is an important indicator of attitude strength (see Fazio, ch. 10, this volume). Based on our speculation that attitudes representing all but the low–low combination of evaluative-cognitive and evaluative-affective consistency are strong in the sense that they have a coherent structural basis we hypothesized that they would all exhibit greater accessibility than the latter, low–low attitudes.

To test this hypothesis we recruited a random sample of students who had completed capital punishment versions of our structural consistency measures at the beginning of the semester. During the laboratory session that subjects subsequently attended they responded to computer-presented scales assessing their favorability toward capital punishment and other issues. Subjects indicated their attitudes by pressing one of nine buttons on the computer's keyboard whose labels ranged from −4 (strongly oppose) to +4 (strongly favor). Response times for the capital punishment issue were subsequently submitted to a two-way analysis of variance whose factors represented subjects above versus below the median on evaluative-cognitive consistency and evaluative-affective consistency, respectively (Chaiken & Giner-Sorolla, 1992). The results of this analysis were encouraging. Neither main effect approached significance. However, a near significant interaction between the two types of consistency emerged (p = .06). Consistent with our expectations, the mean response time for subjects low in both types of consistency (M = 10.19 seconds) was slower than the mean response time for the other three subject groups combined (M = 7.55 seconds). Differences between the latter three subject groups were all nonsignificant.

Attitude Stability

As a second test of the idea that attitudes high in either or both types of structural consistency are stronger than those low in both types, we examined the temporal stability of attitudes toward capital punishment (Chaiken & Pomerantz, 1992). Approximately 6 weeks after completing our structural consistency measures in their classrooms, subjects completed an attitude questionnaire in a laboratory setting. Overall attitude toward capital punishment was assessed on a 7-point scale in the laboratory and a 9-point scale in the classroom pretest; both scales were anchored by "strongly oppose" and "strongly favor." The correlation between these attitude ratings was examined after categorizing subjects (via median splits) as high versus low in evaluative-cognitive consistency and high versus low in evaluative-affective consistency.

Replicating Norman's (1975) stability results, the test–retest correlation was larger among subjects whose attitudes were higher in evaluative-cognitive consistency (rs = .75 vs. .53, p < .05). Of greater interest due to its novelty, we also observed reliably greater temporal stability for attitudes that were higher in evaluative-*affective* consistency (rs = .76 vs. .53, p < .05). Of most interest, however, were the test–retest correlations obtained when the two types of structural consistency were considered jointly. As expected, this index of temporal stability was substantially smaller for subjects whose attitudes were low in both types of consistency (r = .35) than it was for (a) subjects high in both types of consistency (r = .83, p_{diff} < .05), (b) subjects low in evaluative-cognitive consistency but high in evaluative-affective consistency (r = .69, p_{diff} < .05), or (c) subjects low in evaluative-affective consistency but high in evaluative-cognitive consistency (r = .68, p_{diff} < .06). Differences between the latter three stability coefficients were all nonsignificant.

These accessibility and stability data offer preliminary support for our conjecture that low evaluative-cognitive consistency can signify either a genuine attitude based primarily on affect or a weak, possibly vacuous, attitude. Also of interest is the fact that no reliable accessibility or stability difference was observed between $high_{evaluative-cognitive}$–$low_{evaluative-affective}$ attitudes and $low_{evaluative-cognitive}$–$high_{evaluative-affective}$ attitudes. Although the null status of these results makes replication imperative, tentatively they suggest that attitudes whose basis is primarily cognitive may be no more (or less) accessible or temporally stable than attitudes whose basis is primarily affective.

The Attitude-Memory Relation Revisited

As a third test of our emerging analysis of structural consistency we conducted a second attitude memory study. Of prime interest here, we wished to explore the possibility that the congeniality bias observed for low evaluative-cognitive consistency subjects in our first study might have been due to a subset whose attitudes were high in evaluative-affective consistency. After completing our structural consistency measures, subjects were exposed to the same capital punishment belief statements used in the earlier study. As in that study, recall for these statements was assessed after a distractor task (Zimmerman & Chaiken, 1994, Study 2).[15]

---

[15]The results reported here are for subjects who, during the exposure phase, rated their agreement with each belief statement. The remaining subjects rated their familiarity with each statement. As predicted, memory effects for subjects given the latter processing goal were reliably smaller than those obtained for agreement subjects. Because this aspect of the study is not relevant to the present chapter, we ignore it in the text.

Focusing only on evaluative-cognitive consistency, the results replicated those of the earlier experiment. High consistency subjects recalled more incongruent (vs. congruent) belief statements, and low consistency subjects recalled more congruent (vs. incongruent) statements (interaction $p < .05$). Of greater interest are the data we observed when we also blocked subjects on evaluative-affective consistency (high vs. low). The tendency for subjects high in evaluative-cognitive consistency to better recall incongruent belief statements held regardless of evaluative-affective consistency ($Ms = 1.57$ and 2.50 for congruent and incongruent statements). Yet the congruency effect observed for low evaluative-cognitive consistency subjects was indeed restricted to those who were high in evaluative-affective consistency. These subjects recalled appreciably more congruent than incongruent belief statements ($Ms = 3.20$ vs. 1.60). By contrast, and consistent with the vacuity notion, subjects low in both types of structural consistency exhibited no memory bias ($Ms = 1.91$ and 1.91 for congruent and incongruent statements).

Like our accessibility and stability data, these memory data support the idea that attitudes high in either (or both) evaluative-cognitive consistency or evaluative-affective consistency are stronger than attitudes low in both types of consistency. The latter, low–low attitudes failed to predict the valence of subjects' memory for attitude-relevant belief statements, a result consistent with the assumption that such attitudes are either quite weak or vacuous. In contrast, selective recall was appreciable for attitudes high in either or both forms of structural consistency.

The memory data go beyond the accessibility and stability findings in an important way, however. Those data sets revealed little difference between attitudes with presumably strong cognitive support and attitudes with presumably strong affective but little cognitive support. Yet the two types of attitudes predicted opposite patterns of recall: Memory favored counterattitudinal information when attitudes were high in evaluative-cognitive consistency, and proattitudinal information when attitudes were high in evaluative-affective consistency but low in evaluative-cognitive consistency. These results are provocative because they suggest that people may defend the two types of attitudes in different ways.

People with cognitively based attitudes have the ability to defend these attitudes by drawing upon their supportive cognitions in order to bolster their own position and counterargue opposing information. This active resistance mechanism provides a reasonable explanation of the incongruency effect we observed for high evaluative-cognitive consistency subjects. To the extent that these subjects actively attended to and attempted to refute counterattitudinal information, better (immediate) memory for such information would be expected. Although this mediational explanation requires direct testing in subsequent research, it is quite plausible in view of what is currently known about the psychology of attitudes that display high evaluative-cognitive consistency.

Our stability and accessibility data suggest that attitudes summarizing mainly affective associations to the attitude object may be just as resistant to change as those that summarize cognitive associations. Supportive associations of either type, particularly if they are extensive, should dilute the change impact of small-to-moderate amounts of discrepant (cognitive or affective) information (e.g., Anderson, 1968, 1981).[16] Nonetheless, the possessors of affect-based attitudes lack the cognitive resources that would enable them to mount an active defense when challenged by arguments which oppose their attitudes. Such persons may instead turn to more passive defense strategies, such as avoiding counterattitudinal information entirely, paying it scant attention, or summarily rejecting its validity through selective heuristic processing (Chaiken et al., 1989; Liberman & Chaiken, 1992; Giner-Sorolla & Chaiken, 1994; see also Eagly & Chaiken, ch. 16, this volume). At the same time, such persons may bolster their attitudes by invoking validating heuristics (e.g., "most people I know also oppose capital punishment") or by seeking out and paying particular attention to proattitudinal information.

We suggest that the relatively passive resistance mechanism of selective attention produced the congruency effect we observed for low$_{\text{evaluative-cognitive}}$–high$_{\text{evaluative-affective}}$ subjects in our memory study. To the extent that these subjects directed their attention toward proattitudinal belief statements and away from counterattitudinal statements, better memory for proattitudinal information would be expected. Like our interpretation for the high evaluative-cognitive consistency data, this hypothesis also requires direct testing. Nonetheless, together they provide a plausible account of our attitude-memory findings.

Summary

The research we have summarized provides encouraging support for several of our ideas about structural consistency and attitude strength. First, the measurement of evaluative-cognitive consistency and evaluative-affective consistency provides a means of assessing an attitude's congruency with cognitive and affective associations to the attitude object and, quite plausibly, a means of diagnosing the structural bases of people's attitudes. Second, an attitude is strong to the extent that it has clear internal structure, regardless of whether that structure is mainly cognitive, mainly affective, or both cognitive and affective (see also Eagly & Chaiken, ch. 16, this volume). Such attitudes are more accessible, more temporally stable, and more likely to exert selective effects on information processing than attitudes that lack clear structure; very probably, they are also less likely to change in response to persuasive communications. Finally, the specific mechanisms by which people defend their attitudes may depend, in part, on their structural basis. An active process such as counterarguing may be possible mainly in relation to attitudes with a strong cognitive basis. More passive processes such as selective attention and selective heuristic processing may be the more common

---

[16]This statement notwithstanding it may be the case that the two types of attitudes differ in their resistance to more cognitive versus more affective influence attempts. Research on this issue has not yet produced definitive conclusions (e.g., Edwards, 1990; Millar & Millar, 1990).

line of defense in relation to attitudes that enjoy strong affective but weak cognitive support.

IMPLICATIONS FOR ATTITUDE FORMATION

By classifying attitudes along the two structural dimensions of evaluative-cognitive consistency and evaluative-affective consistency we have proposed that, although some attitudes are truly baseless in both dimensions, others have a solid basis in one dimension although they are essentially vacuous in the other. Thus we have argued that measuring both types of consistency may help distinguish attitudes with a primarily cognitive basis from attitudes with a primarily affective basis. If overall evaluation of an object reflects a person's beliefs about the object more faithfully than it reflects the person's emotions or feelings about the object, the attitude (i.e., overall evaluation) is likely to have been derived from the person's cognitions; and if the reverse is true, the attitude is likely to have been derived from the person's affective responses (see also Eagly & Chaiken, 1993).

In research relevant to these possibilities, Millar and Tesser (1986, 1989) manipulated the cognitive versus affective basis of attitudes at the time of their formation, by instructing subjects either to analyze the reasons why they liked or disliked novel puzzles or to merely focus on how they felt about the puzzles. Subjects then indicated their overall evaluation of each puzzle, in addition to listing their reasons for liking or disliking it and their feelings toward it. Millar and Tesser found that attitudes formed under cognitive focus were characterized by a larger number of reasons, and greater evaluative-cognitive consistency, relative to attitudes formed under affective focus. Conversely, attitudes formed under affective focus were characterized by a larger number of feelings and greater evaluative-affective consistency.

These findings indicate that the consistency between overall evaluation and attitude-relevant beliefs and feelings may indeed reflect, not only the structural basis of an attitude, but also the antecedent conditions under which it was formed. For most persons, attitudes toward some objects (e.g., strawberry jam) may tend to be formed affectively, and attitudes toward other objects (e.g., computer disk drives) may tend to be formed cognitively. Yet Millar and Tesser's research suggests, in harmony with research on structural consistency, that individual differences in the basis of attitude formation are also quite likely.

Subsequent research should explore in more depth the validity of structural consistency as an indicator of the manner in which an attitude was formed. In addition, the contribution of affect and cognition to attitude formation deserves to be explored more fully. We suspect that an exclusively affective attitude could have one of at least three possible origins. The attitude may have been learned through emotionally significant experience, especially that occurring early in life. Alternatively, the attitude object may have been linked in a fairly unsophisticated way to another emotionally significant attitude, in the way that negative attitudes toward certain social policies are seen as linked to anti-Black affect in the theory of symbolic racism (e.g., Kinder & Sears, 1981). Yet another possibility is that the person has associated the attitude object with concrete imagery (Fiske, Pratto, & Pavelchak, 1983) which itself arouses affective reactions. For example, an affectively based antiabortion attitude could originate in the revulsion aroused by gruesome images of aborted fetuses.

Conversely, an attitude with an exclusively cognitive basis would most likely have been formed dispassionately, through systematic consideration of the attributes or instrumental consequences associated with the object, or by deduction from a more abstract ideology (see Eagly & Chaiken, ch. 16, this volume). To complete our fourfold classification, an attitude with both a cognitive and affective basis would most likely have been formed through some combination of emotionally significant experience and cognitive elaboration. Finally, although our analysis suggests that attitudes with no apparent basis are structurally weak, it may be premature to interpret them as capricious responses or nonattitudes. Some credence should be given in subsequent research to the possibility that these attitudes are genuine, and that they have been formed though heuristic mechanisms; that is, simple decision rules such as "people agree with people they like," or "majority opinion is correct," which require neither cognitive elaboration nor emotional involvement (see Chaiken et al., 1989; Mackie, 1987; Nemeth, 1986).

ACKNOWLEDGMENTS

Preparation of this chapter was facilitated by a New York University Research Challenge Fund Grant to Shelly Chaiken. We thank the editors and Erik Thompson for their comments on an early draft of the manuscript.

REFERENCES

Abelson, R. P., & Rosenberg, M. J. (1958). Symbolic psycho-logic: A model of attitudinal cognition. *Behavioral Science, 3*, 1–13.

Anderson, N. H. (1968). A simple model for information integration. In R. P. Abelson, E. Aronson, W. J. McGuire, T. M. Newcomb, M. J. Rosenberg, & P. H. Tannenbaum (Eds.), *Theories of cognitive consistency: A sourcebook* (pp. 731–743). Chicago: Rand McNally.

Anderson, N. H. (1981). Integration theory applied to cognitive responses and attitudes. In R. E. Petty, T. M. Ostrom, & T. C. Brock (Eds.), *Cognitive responses in persuasion* (pp. 361–397). Hillsdale, NJ: Lawrence Erlbaum Associates.

Bem, D. J. (1972). Self-perception theory. In L. Berkowitz (Ed.), *Advances in experimental social psychology* (Vol. 6, pp. 1–62). New York: Academic.

Breckler, S. J. (1984). Empirical validation of affect, behavior, and cognition as distinct components of attitude. *Journal of Personality and Social Psychology, 47*, 1191–1205.

Breckler, S. J., & Wiggins, E. C. (1989). Affect versus evaluation in the structure of attitudes. *Journal of Experimental Social Psychology, 25*, 253–271.

Cacioppo, J. T., & Petty, R. E. (1979). Effects of message repetition and position on cognitive response, recall, and persuasion. *Journal of Personality and Social Psychology, 37*, 97–109.

Chaiken, S. (1980). Heuristic versus systematic information processing and the use of source versus message cues in persuasion. *Journal of Personality and Social Psychology, 39*, 752–766.

Chaiken, S. (1982). [Evaluative-cognitive consistency, counterarguing and persuasion]. Unpublished raw data.

Chaiken, S., & Baldwin, M. W. (1981). Affective-cognitive consistency and the effect of salient behavioral information on the self-perception of attitudes. *Journal of Personality and Social Psychology, 41*, 1–12.

Chaiken, S., & Giner-Sorolla, R. (1992). [Structural consistency and accessibility]. Unpublished raw data.

Chaiken, S., Giner-Sorolla, R., & Chen, S. (in press). Beyond accuracy: Defense and impression motives in heuristic and systematic processing. In P. M. Gollwitzer & J. A. Bargh (Eds.), *The psychology of action: Linking motivation and cognition to behavior.* New York: Guilford Press.

Chaiken, S., Liberman, A., & Eagly, A. H. (1989). Heuristic and systematic processing within and beyond the persuasion context. In J. S. Uleman & J. A. Bargh (Eds.), *Unintended thought* (pp. 212–252). New York: Guilford.

Chaiken, S., & Pomerantz, E. M. (1992). [Structural consistency and temporal stability]. Unpublished raw data.

Chaiken, S., & Yates, S. (1985). Affective-cognitive consistency and thought-induced attitude polarization. *Journal of Personality and Social Psychology, 49*, 1470–1481.

Converse, P. E. (1970). Attitudes and non-attitudes: Continuation of a dialogue. In E. R. Tufte (Ed.), *The quantitative analysis of social problems* (pp. 168–189). Reading, MA: Addison-Wesley.

Crowne, D., & Marlowe, D. (1964). *The approval motive.* New York: Wiley.

Doll, J., & Ajzen, I. (1992). Accessibility and stability of predictors in the theory of planned behavior. *Journal of Personality and Social Psychology, 63*, 754–765.

Eagly, A. H., & Chaiken, S. (1993). *The psychology of attitudes.* Fort Worth, TX: Harcourt Brace Jovanovich.

Edwards, K. (1990). The interplay of affect and cognition in attitude formation and change. *Journal of Personality and Social Psychology, 59*, 212–216.

Fazio, R. H. (1986). How do attitudes guide behavior? In R. M. Sorrentino & E. T. Higgins (Eds.), *Handbook of motivation and cognition: Foundations of social behavior* (pp. 204–243). New York: Guilford.

Fazio, R. H. (1989). On the power and functionality of attitudes: The role of attitude accessibility. In A. R. Pratkanis, S. J. Breckler, & A. G. Greenwald (Eds.), *Attitude structure and function* (pp. 153–179). Hillsdale, NJ: Lawrence Erlbaum Associates.

Fazio, R. H., & Zanna, M. P. (1978). Attitudinal qualities relating to the strength of the attitude-behavior relationship. *Journal of Experimental Social Psychology, 14*, 398–408.

Fazio, R. H., & Zanna, M. P. (1981). Direct experience and attitude-behavior consistency. In L. Berkowitz (Ed.), *Advances in experimental social psychology* (Vol. 14, pp. 161–202). New York: Academic.

Festinger, L. (1957). *A theory of cognitive dissonance.* Evanston, IL: Row, Peterson.

Fishbein, M. (1963). An investigation of the relationships between beliefs about an object and the attitude toward that object. *Human Relations, 16*, 233–240.

Fishbein, M., & Ajzen, I. (1975). *Belief, attitude, intention, and behavior: An introduction to theory and research.* Reading, MA: Addison-Wesley.

Fiske, S. T., Pratto, F., & Pavelchak, M. A. (1983). Citizens' images of nuclear war: Content and consequences. *Journal of Social Issues, 39*(1), 41–65.

Giner-Sorolla, R., & Chaiken, S. (1994). *Selective use of heuristic and systematic processing under defense motivation.* Unpublished manuscript, New York University.

Heider, F. (1958). *The psychology of interpersonal relations.* New York: Wiley.

Higgins, E. T. (1989). Knowledge accessibility and activation: Subjectivity and suffering from unconscious sources. In J. S. Uleman & J. A. Bargh (Eds.), *Unintended thought* (pp. 75–123). New York: Guilford.

Houston, D. A., & Fazio, R. H. (1989). Biased processing as a function of attitude accessibility: Making objective judgments subjectively. *Social Cognition, 7,* 51–66.

Jones, E. E., & Aneshansel, J. (1956). The learning and utilization of contravaluant material. *Journal of Abnormal and Social Psychology, 53,* 27–33.

Kinder, D. R., & Sears, D. O. (1981). Prejudice and politics: Symbolic racism versus racial threats to the good life. *Journal of Personality and Social Psychology, 40,* 414–431.

Krosnick, J. A., Boninger, D. S., Chuang, Y. C., Berent, M . K., & Carnot, C. G. (1993). Attitude strength: One construct or many related constructs? *Journal of Personality and Social Psychology, 65,* 1132–1151.

Liberman, A., & Chaiken, S. (1991). Value-conflict and thought-induced attitude change. *Journal of Experimental Social Psychology, 27,* 203–216.

Liberman, A., & Chaiken, S. (1992). Defensive processing of personally relevant health messages. *Personality and Social Psychology Bulletin, 18,* 669–679.

Lord, C. G., Ross, L., & Lepper, M. R. (1979). Biased assimilation and attitude polarization: The effects of prior theories on subsequently considered evidence. *Journal of Personality and Social Psychology, 37,* 2098–2109.

Mackie, D. M. (1987). Systematic and nonsystematic processing of majority and minority persuasive communications. *Journal of Personality and Social Psychology, 53,* 41–52.

Millar, M. G., & Millar, K. U. (1990). Attitude change as a function of attitude type and argument type. *Journal of Personality and Social Psychology, 59,* 217–228.

Millar, M. G., & Tesser, A. (1986). Effects of affective and cognitive focus on the attitude-behavior relation. *Journal of Personality and Social Psychology, 51,* 270–276.

Millar, M. G., & Tesser, A. (1989). The effects of affective-cognitive consistency and thought on the attitude-behavior relation. *Journal of Experimental Social Psychology, 25,* 189–202.

Moreno, K. E., Sheposh, J. P., & Coverdale, G. (1987, August). *Schema and thought as determinants of attitude change.* Paper presented at the 95th annual meeting of the American Psychological Association, New York.

Nemeth, C. J. (1986). Differential contributions of majority and minority influence. *Psychological Review, 93,* 23–32.

Norman, R. (1975). Affective-cognitive consistency, attitudes, conformity, and behavior. *Journal of Personality and Social Psychology, 32,* 83–91.

Pomerantz, E. M., Margolies, D., & Chaiken, S. (1993). *Selective judgment and structural consistency.* Poster presented at the American Psychological Association Meetings, Toronto, Ontario, Canada.

Roberts, J. V. (1985). The attitude-memory relationship after 40 years: A meta-analysis of the literature. *Basic and Applied Social Psychology, 6,* 221–241.

Rokeach, M. (1968). *Beliefs, attitudes, and values.* San Francisco: Jossey-Bass.

Rosenberg, M. J. (1956). Cognitive structure and attitudinal affect. *Journal of Abnormal and Social Psychology, 53,* 367–372.

Rosenberg, M. J. (1960a). An analysis of affective-cognitive consistency. In M. J. Rosenberg, C. I. Hovland, W. J. McGuire, R. P. Abelson, & J. W. Brehm (Eds.), *Attitude organization and change: An analysis of consistency among attitude components* (pp. 15–64). New Haven, CT: Yale University Press.

Rosenberg, M. J. (1960b). Cognitive reorganization in response to the hypnotic reversal of attitudinal affect. *Journal of Personality, 28,* 39–63.

Rosenberg, M. J. (1968). Hedonism, inauthenticity, and other goads toward expansion of a consistency theory. In R. P. Abelson, E. Aronson, W. J. McGuire, T. M. Newcomb, M. J. Rosenberg, & P. H. Tannenbaum (Eds.), *Theories of cognitive consistency: A sourcebook* (pp. 73–111). Chicago: Rand McNally.

Ross, M. (1989). Relation of implicit theories to the construction of personal histories. *Psychological Review, 96,* 341–357.

Salancik, G. R., & Conway, M. (1975). Attitude inferences from salient and relevant cognitive content about behavior. *Journal of Personality and Social Psychology, 32,* 829–840.

Scott, W. A. (1969). Structure of natural cognitions. *Journal of Personality and Social Psychology, 12,* 261–278.

Schlegel, R. P., & DiTecco, D. (1982). Attitudinal structures and the attitude-behavior relation. In M. P. Zanna, E. T. Higgins, & C. P. Herman (Eds.), *Consistency in social behavior: The Ontario symposium* (Vol. 2, pp. 17–49). Hillsdale, NJ: Lawrence Erlbaum Associates.

Tesser, A. (1978). Self-generated attitude change. In L. Berkowitz (Ed.), *Advances in experimental social psychology* (Vol. 11, pp. 289–338). New York: Academic.

Zajonc, R. B. (1968). Cognitive theories in social psychology. In G. Lindzey & E. Aronson (Eds.), *Handbook of social psychology* (2nd ed., Vol. 1, pp. 320–411). Reading, MA: Addison-Wesley.

Zanna, M. P., & Rempel, J. K. (1988). Attitudes: A new look at an old concept. In D. Bar-Tal & A. W. Kruglanski (Eds.), *The social psychology of knowledge* (pp. 315–334). Cambridge, UK: Cambridge University Press.

Zimmerman, J., & Chaiken, S. (1994). *Attitude structure, processing goals, and selective memory.* Unpublished manuscript, New York University.

16

▼▼▼▼▼▼▼

Attitude Strength,
Attitude Structure, and
Resistance to Change

Alice H. Eagly
Purdue University

Shelly Chaiken
New York University

This chapter proposes a conceptualization of attitude strength that links strength to a basic understanding of attitude itself. We therefore begin by giving a definition of attitude, which leads directly to an interpretation of attitude strength as a structural variable. The consequence of attitude strength that we emphasize is resistance to change: Strong attitudes do not readily change. This principle may appear simple, but it camouflages an underlying psychology of some complexity—specifically, a set of mechanisms by which people resist change. We argue that the likelihood that particular mechanisms appear depends not merely on attitude strength, but on the particular structural configuration that underlies an attitude's strength. However, resistance to change is not the only important consequence of attitude strength. Strong attitudes are also relatively persistent over time and predictive of overt behavior, and they exert selective effects on information processing. According to our analysis, these additional consequences are manifestations of strong attitudes' resistance to change rather than independent consequences of strength.

To explain how resistance to change produces these other consequences, we first note that an obvious implication of resistance is that it would foster the temporal stability of attitudes. It is less obvious that attitudes' resistance to change and consequent stability may underlie their superior prediction of behavior (Doll & Ajzen, 1992). If more than a short time intervenes between the assessment of an attitude and the observation of a behavior, instability of the attitude weakens the prediction of the behavior from this attitude because a new attitude—the one held at the moment the behavior is initiated—typically controls the behavior. Finally, consistent with our subsequent analysis, selectivity in information processing is implicated in the very mechanisms by which people avoid changing their attitudes. This chapter thus provides an integrative theory of attitude strength and its several consequences by means of a structural interpretation of strength and the treatment of resistance as strength's critical consequence.

THE STRUCTURAL BASES OF ATTITUDINAL RESISTANCE

Our theory defines attitude strength in terms of the links between an attitude and other aspects of knowledge structures. Our key proposition is that attitudes are strong to the extent that they are well embedded in an existing attitudinal structure. This proposition presupposes a specific definition of attitude itself. This definition is that attitude is a psychological tendency that is expressed by evaluating a particular entity with some degree of favor or disfavor (see Eagly & Chaiken, 1993). Expressed succinctly, attitudes are people's evaluations of *attitude objects*.

Attitudes develop from evaluative responding to an attitude object. Although people may have predispositions to react positively or negatively to a novel attitude object (Tesser, 1993), they do not have an attitude until they first encounter the attitude object and respond evaluatively to it on an affective, cognitive, or behavioral basis. Evaluative responding, whether covert or overt, can produce a psychological tendency to respond with a particular degree of evaluation when subsequently encountering the attitude object. If this response tendency is established, the person can be said to have formed an attitude toward the object. Once an attitude is formed, a mental representation of it would be stored in memory.

The idea that attitudes develop on the basis of evaluative responding implies that an attitude has an internal structure consisting of mental representations of the responses that underlie the attitude. These mental representations may themselves have structural properties of various sorts, as we explain later. Yet, because people form attitudes toward many entities in their environment, the term *structure* also implies relations between attitudes, which produce more global structures encompassing more than one attitude. Both of these aspects of structure—attitudes' internal structure and the molar structures by which attitudes are related to one another—are essential to understanding attitude strength.

An overall evaluation is not all that is stored in memory when attitudes are formed. The experiences that produced the evaluative tendency are also stored. The perceiver would represent these experiences as associations that link the attitude object with the relevant aspects of her or his prior experience. We use the term *intra-attitudinal structure* to refer to this aspect of attitudinal structure.

This internal structure would typically include cognitive content consisting of the perceiver's beliefs about the characteristics of the attitude object. These beliefs may be concrete, perhaps reflecting specific images (e.g., image of a certain forsythia bush in full bloom). But beliefs may also be more abstract, especially when they summarize many experiences (e.g., on a more abstract basis, forsythia might be deemed "extremely colorful").

An attitude's internal structure can also encompass affective and behavioral reactions that were elicited by the attitude object and therefore became associated with it. The affective aspect of attitude structure consists of feelings, moods, emotions, and sympathetic nervous-system activity that people have experienced in relation to an attitude object and subsequently associate with it (e.g., the pleasure elicited by a forsythia in full bloom). Like beliefs, these affects might reflect particular experiences or become more generalized insofar as they summarize responding on multiple occasions. Similarly, the behavioral aspect of intra-attitudinal structure encompasses a person's actions toward the attitude object. Although representations of particular behaviors become associated with attitude objects, behavioral representations may, like cognitions and affects, become generalized on the basis of repeated responding (e.g., cutting forsythia branches for indoor forcing every February).

The entire set of cognitive, affective, and behavioral responses that become associated with an attitude object constitutes its internal structure. These associations would of course differ greatly across persons and attitude objects, not merely in their specific content but in their more abstract characteristics such as the number of associations stored (Eagly, Mladinic, & Otto, 1994; Haddock, Zanna, & Esses, 1993).

The term *structure* also implies relationships between attitudes and thus refers to molar structures that encompass more than one attitude. We have termed these properties of attitudes *inter-attitudinal structure* (Eagly & Chaiken, 1993). Linkages between attitudes may be established on diverse bases. Sometimes logical analyses forge relations between attitudes (e.g., McGuire, 1981). At other times a perceiver may observe a conjunction between two attitude objects. For example, observation of a politician advocating a position on an issue could place in a molar structure attitudes toward the politician and the issue (Heider, 1958; Osgood & Tannenbaum, 1955). Observations of covariation between attitudinal positions could also establish connections between attitudes (e.g., people favorable to animal rights generally support vegetarianism). On these or other bases, attitudes become linked with one another.

These inter-attitudinal structures can be hierarchical in the sense that more abstract and general attitudes encompass more concrete and particular attitudes. For example, one's attitude toward environmentalism is more general than one's related attitudes toward waste recycling or wilderness protection. The more general attitude object can be viewed as a category that contains more specific attitude objects as components and that therefore implies that the specific attitudes have the same valence as the more general attitude. A positive attitude toward environmentalism would thus imply a positive attitude toward specific measures such as recycling.

Intra-attitudinal and inter-attitudinal structure reflect contrasting ways that attitudes are formed. One can form an attitude in an experiential way based on direct or indirect cognitive, affective, or behavioral responding to the attitude object. This intra-attitudinal mode of attitude formation entails storing the information produced by one's responses as mental associations between the attitude object and these responses. By this logic, attitudes represent generalizations from more elementary associations.

Alternatively, one can form an attitude by forging linkages between the attitude object and other attitude objects. These linkages are stored, along with the target attitude itself. Often this mode of attitude formation entails an inference by which a new attitude is a generalization from a more abstract or general attitude that has already been formed. Although most attitudes may have a structure with both intra- and inter-attitudinal aspects, there would be considerable variation in the extent to which attitudes have been formed on one or the other of these bases.[1]

Many other investigators have conceptualized attitude strength in structural terms that are compatible with our analysis. For example, among the intra-attitudinal analyses of strength is Wood's (ch. 11, this volume) concept of working knowledge, which refers to the number of beliefs and behaviors that people are able to retrieve about the attitude object (see also Davidson, ch. 12, this volume).[2] Other psychologists have defined strength in terms of characteristics of intra-attitudinal structure such as the evaluative inconsistency (or ambivalence) of these beliefs (Scott, 1969; Thompson, Zanna, & Griffin, ch. 14, this volume). Also, commitment, a strength variable defined as "the pledging or binding of the individual to behavioral acts" (Kiesler, 1971, p. 30), refers to another aspect of intra-attitudinal structure, namely, the associations between people's attitudes and their overt, often public behaviors in support of that attitude.

Other strength concepts emphasize the evaluative consistency between attitudinal associations and the overall attitude. Evaluative-cognitive consistency refers to the degree of consistency between a person's attitude and the evaluative meaning of his or her beliefs about the attitude object. Similarly, evaluative-affective consistency refers to the consistency between an attitude and the evaluative meaning of the affective reactions experienced in relation to the attitude object. These characteristics of intra-attitudinal structure take into account (respectively) two of the three sets of associations that we have suggested may underlie attitude (and one could easily conceive of a third construct of evaluative-behavioral consistency; Eagly & Chaiken, 1993).

---

[1]A critic might argue that the associations between a target attitude and other attitudes should be viewed merely as beliefs about the attitude object. If, for example, one's attitude toward disarmament is linked to one's values (e.g., world peace), these value linkages could be viewed as beliefs about disarmament. Although such a treatment is found in expectancy-value models of attitude (e.g., Fishbein & Ajzen, 1975; Rosenberg, 1956), for purposes of analyzing resistance to attitude change it is highly instructive to distinguish between associations representing one's own evaluative responding to an attitude object and associations linking the attitude to other attitudes.

[2]Another feature of intra-attitudinal structure, the complexity of the beliefs underlying attitudes (e.g., Linville, 1982; Judd & Lusk, 1984; Tetlock, 1989), has been investigated. However, this structural variable does not fit readily under the rubric of *attitude strength*.

Linkages between attitudes have also been considered in discussions of attitude strength. In particular, this inter-attitudinal aspect of structure has been captured to some extent in the concepts of *embeddedness* (Scott, 1968) and *centrality* (Rokeach, 1968). In addition, some theorists have implied that attitudes' external structure may be hierarchical by emphasizing linkages of attitudes to values, which can be regarded as attitudes toward relatively abstract goals or end states of human existence (Rokeach, 1968, 1973; see Eagly & Chaiken, 1993).

Examples of this hierarchical treatment of attitude strength include Abelson and Prentice's (1989) concept of *value-centrality*, "the degree to which a given belief expresses deeper, more fundamental beliefs" (p. 375). Ostrom and Brock (1968) viewed attitudinal involvement in terms of relations between attitudes and values, and, following this tradition, Johnson and Eagly (1989) proposed the concept of *value-relevant involvement* to refer to a motivational state induced by the linkage of an activated attitude to one's values. Because values are often regarded as core aspects of the self-concept (e.g., Rokeach, 1968), it is not surprising that associations between attitudes and the self have also received emphasis (e.g., Greenwald, 1989; Katz, 1960; M. Sherif & Cantril, 1947).

Although quite a few strength concepts are thus compatible with our structural framework, others' fit is less clear because they have not been formulated in ways that illuminate their structural bases. For example, Krosnick (1990) defined attitude importance as "the degree to which a person is passionately concerned about and personally invested in an attitude" (p. 60), and Abelson (1988) emphasized the conviction or certainty that people have about important attitudes. These strength constructs invoke natural language terms (e.g., conviction) and thus seem to be formulated in terms of metacognitions that people may hold in relation to their strong attitudes (e.g., "this issue is important"). The structural bases of these constructs are unclear and merit investigation.

Fazio's (1986, 1989, ch. 10, this volume) view that *accessibility* is a key aspect (or indicator) of attitude strength is also moot in relation to our framework. His conception of attitude strength stems from his definition of attitude as an association in memory between an object and an evaluation. Yet, this structural treatment does not take into account the aspects of attitude structure that are the bulwarks of our analysis: the internal structure of associations to the attitude object and the external structure of an attitude's links to other attitudes. Indeed, we suggest that accessibility may be a consequence of the embeddedness of an attitude in intra-attitudinal and inter-attitudinal structure; well embedded attitudes may be highly accessible. If so, the consequences of accessibility that Fazio has emphasized (e.g., enhanced attitude-behavior correspondence) could be consequences of attitudes' cognitive, affective, and behavioral associations or attitudes' linkages to other attitudes.

Finally, fans of associative network models may be disappointed that we have not used this terminology to present our structural concepts (see J. R. Anderson, 1983, 1985; J. R. Anderson & Bower, 1974). Network models have been applied to attitudinal structure (e.g., Judd & Krosnick, 1989; see review by Eagly & Chaiken, 1993), and Fazio's (ch. 10, this volume) analysis can be easily cast in network terms. Although our treatment shares some features with this approach, the symbolic language of network models is too general and therefore too limited to encompass the particular structural features of attitudes that are central to our analysis. Such a language would not allow, for example, distinctions between cognitive, affective, and behavioral associations to attitude objects, nor would it effectively express the important differences between intra-attitudinal and inter-attitudinal structure.[3]

ATTITUDINAL STRUCTURE AND RESISTANCE TO CHANGE

Reasonable from several perspectives is the principle that intra-attitudinal structure promotes resistance to change to the extent that this structure is extensive. For example, averaging models of attitudes (e.g., N. H. Anderson, 1981) predict that attitudes are more stable to the extent that they are based on a larger number of beliefs, because new information gained about the attitude object would be averaged with a larger amount of prior information, producing a smaller alteration of the average evaluation.[4] The same logic would hold for the affective and behavioral bases of attitudes. To the extent that an attitude is grounded extensively in prior experience, whether this experience produces cognitive, affective, or behavioral associations or some mix of these, any new input has proportionally smaller impact.

Findings consistent with the general principle that resistance to change is greater to the extent that an attitude has an extensive—or coherent—internal structure are reported in various chapters of this book (e.g., Chaiken, Pomerantz, & Giner-Sorolla, ch. 15, this volume). We therefore mention such findings only briefly and postpone for the moment discussion of the mechanisms through which attitudes' internal structure induces resistance. For example, several studies have shown that providing subjects with information that adds beliefs to their intra-attitudinal structure confers resistance to subsequent communications (e.g.,

---

[3]Considerably less in harmony with our treatment are dimensional models of attitude structure, which feature the assumption that attitudinal structure includes a continuum or dimension (e.g., Judd & Kulik, 1980; Pratkanis, 1989; Sherif, Sherif, & Nebergall, 1965). Although some of these dimensional treatments have implications for attitude strength (e.g., Sherif et al., 1965), this approach has little in common with our own (see Eagly & Chaiken, 1993).

[4]This prediction assumes of course that items of information are separately represented and accessible. Yet associations that have been activated recently and frequently would be especially accessible (e.g., Higgins, 1989). Moreover, under some circumstances, the overall attitude may be retrieved rather than the associations that underlie the attitude (see Eagly & Chaiken, 1993). Yet this prior attitude should be more heavily weighted to the extent that it is based on a large amount of experience with the attitude object (N. H. Anderson, 1981).

Himmelfarb & Youngblood, 1969; Lewan & Stotland, 1961). Consistent with these findings, Wood (1982, ch. 11, this volume) has shown that high levels of working knowledge increase both resistance to counterattitudinal communications and the predictability of behavior from attitudes (see also Davidson, Yantis, Norwood, & Montano, 1985).

Resistance is also facilitated by treatments that enhance or make salient the behavioral aspects of intra-attitudinal structure. Thus, experimentally induced behavioral commitments to attitudinal positions render attitudes resistant to attack (e.g., Halverson & Pallak, 1978; Kiesler, Pallak, & Kanouse, 1968; Pallak, Mueller, Dollar, & Pallak, 1972), as do treatments that merely ask subjects to recall their attitudinally relevant behaviors (Ross, McFarland, Conway, & Zanna, 1983). The resistance effect produced by associations representing one's own behavior is not in principle different from the effect produced by associations that represent beliefs—or associations that represent people's affective experience with attitude objects. Attitudes that have an extensive internal structure should be less easily changed.

Structural variables that reflect the evaluative coherence rather than extensiveness per se of intra-attitudinal structure also predict resistance and related outcomes. In particular, higher levels of evaluative-cognitive consistency predict a variety of strength-related consequences, including resistance to persuasion and high attitude-behavior correspondence (e.g., Norman, 1975; see Chaiken et al., ch. 15, this volume). In addition, higher evaluative-affective consistency and lower levels of ambivalence predict greater attitudinal stability (Bargh, Chaiken, Govender, & Pratto, 1992; Chaiken et al., ch. 15, this volume), and ambivalence lessens attitude-behavior correspondence (e.g., Moore, 1980).

Inter-attitudinal structure can also produce resistance. Why would the fact that an attitude is already embedded in a molar structure dampen change? In general, the answer is that linked attitudes would be under pressure to change if the target attitude changed, as the individual considered the implications of this initial change. Although such reverberating change does occur, inertial forces would counter it.

Connections between attitudes produce resistance to change in a target attitude, according to what might be termed the *domino principle*. This principle, inherent in the image of knocking over one domino in a line of dominoes standing on end, is that change in one element of a structure causes changes in related elements and possibly a chain reaction that would result in a fundamental restructuring of the entire set of interrelated elements. According to our domino theory of attitudinal resistance, when an attitude is linked to other attitudes and change in one element would therefore produce change in linked elements, change is resisted because of the negative implications such widespread attitudinal change would have for the perceiver.

The several components of this theory must be carefully scrutinized. First, the idea that change in one attitude tends to induce changes in other, linked attitudes warrants examination. This idea rests on the venerable assumption that there is a tendency for linked elements of a structure to become evaluatively consistent (e.g., Festinger, 1957; Heider, 1958). From this consistency perspective, attitude change should travel through structures as change in one attitude produces consequences for linked attitudes. Indeed, a moderate amount of research has supported this specific proposition that change can reverberate through attitudinal structures that are composed of linked elements (e.g., Ball-Rokeach, Rokeach, & Grube, 1984; Hendrick & Seyfried, 1974; McGuire, 1960, 1981, 1990; McGuire & McGuire, 1991; Tannenbaum, 1967). However, consistent with our idea that reverberating change is in some sense resisted, this research has also shown that changes in linked attitudes tend to be smaller than changes in the target attitude.[5]

We propose that the very tendency for change to travel through an inter-attitudinal structure acts as an inertial force that prevents the initial change from occurring in the first place (see McGuire, 1981). Yet structural concepts provide no explanation of why changing groups of linked attitudes would be problematic. The rationale is motivational and concerns mental effort as well as unpleasantness and tension. Consider first that mental activity would be required to think through the implications that the initial attitude change has for other, linked attitudes. The more extensive an attitude's internal structure is, the more mental effort would be required. Consistent with Chaiken, Liberman, and Eagly's (1989) least effort and sufficiency principles, such effortful processing is avoided (unless one would anticipate a positive outcome sufficient to justify the effort).[6] Alternatively, an individual could avoid this effort by maintaining or tolerating the inconsistency inherent in having changed one attitude in a molar structure without complementary changes in associated attitudes. However, when the changed attitude and associated attitudes come to mind in the same context, the evaluative inconsistency would be troubling or unpleasant, as cognitive consistency theorists maintained. Because both of these outcomes, extensive mental activity and lingering inconsistency between linked attitudes, are to some extent unpleasant, the initial change would be avoided. Our assumption about unpleasantness is our ultimate rationale for the resistance to change of attitudes with extensive external structure.

---

[5]Decreasing impact may also arise from attitudes' internal structure. Each linked attitude would be to some extent supported by an intra-attitudinal structure composed of associations reflecting the perceiver's prior experience with the linked attitude object. The impact of the changed target attitude would have to compete with the linked attitude's internal structure of supporting associations.

[6]We do not mean to imply an elaborate assessment of the effort that would be required to reconcile a changed attitude with linked attitudes. We suspect that as people begin to think about a change they quickly "run into" a linked attitude (or perhaps several linked attitudes) and that the activation of these linked attitudes provides a rationale for rejecting the initial change. Of course there are no doubt individual differences in the extent to which people are willing to "think through" the implications of changed attitudes (e.g., Cacioppo & Petty, 1982). Another interesting issue is the extent to which people may be consciously aware of the extensiveness of an attitude's implications for linked attitudes or of the effortfulness of the reorientation that a potential change would require.

Very often emphasized in discussions of the dampening effect of inter-attitudinal structure on attitude change is the anchoring of attitudes to values or to the self-concept. For example, Johnson and Eagly (1989) argued that value-relevant involvement should produce resistance to change, a claim consistent with other psychologists' reasoning about the effects of strong attitude-value linkages (e.g., Ostrom & Brock, 1968; Rokeach, 1968). Moreover, M. Sherif and Cantril (1947) maintained that associations between attitudes and valued reference groups are a source of resistance to change. Yet in Sherif and Cantril's writings, the root cause of resistance was protection of the self-concept, a principle that remained important in later treatments of ego-involvement (C. W. Sherif, 1980; C. W. Sherif, Sherif, & Nebergall, 1965).

This repeated emphasis on abstract and general attitudes (e.g., values, positive reference groups, the self) in discussing resistance to change suggests that attitudes that are linked to more abstract attitudes in a hierarchical structure are particularly resistant to change. Our treatment of inter-attitudinal structure supports this reasoning. If a lower level attitude is an implication of a more general attitude, direct attack on the lower level attitude through linking it with negative characteristics would be ineffective, because its support would derive from its relation to the higher level attitude. The higher level attitude would have its own internal structure and typically would be linked by implication to additional lower level attitudes as well. These features would make change in the higher level attitude unlikely. For example, because of the implicational relation between environmental preservation and recycling, it would be difficult to change an environmentalist's attitude toward recycling by pointing out its disadvantages. Change would proceed more readily from higher level to lower level attitudes. If an individual could be convinced that environmental preservation—the abstract attitude object—actually is bad, change in lower level attitudes (e.g., toward recycling) would follow rather directly. Presumably little mental activity would be required to reason in this deductive way from more general to more specific, component attitudes.

Most empirical demonstrations of the general principle that inter-attitudinal structure confers resistance to change have examined attitudes' linkages to more abstract, general attitudes, namely, values, reference groups, and the self. For example, in a demonstration that value linkages dampen attitude change, Ostrom and Brock (1968) had subjects indicate the extent to which various values were reflected in aspects of a topic. Depending on experimental condition, these values were ones that subjects had previously judged as personally important or unimportant. Subsequently, (some) subjects received a counterattitudinal message that was highly discrepant with their attitudes. Subjects in the important-value condition were significantly less influenced by this message than those in the unimportant-value condition. Thus, linking an attitude to important values produced resistance (see also Nelson, 1968). Studies that have merely assessed subjects' preexisting values have yielded compatible results (e.g., Snyder, Mischel, & Lott, 1960; Vaughan & Mangan, 1963).

Links between attitudes and other abstract attitudes can also underlie resistance. In a classic experiment suggesting that links to valued reference groups dampen attitude change, Boy Scouts who highly valued their group membership were less persuaded by a message that was critical of some of the traditional values of scouting than were Scouts who valued their membership less highly (Kelley & Volkart, 1952). Relevant to the claim that ego-involvement produces resistance are experiments that relied on M. Sherif and colleagues' writings for their theoretical perspective. Johnson and Eagly (1989) review of this literature in their meta-analysis of the persuasive effects of various types of involvement found that the type of involvement that the Sherifs discussed (i.e., ego-involvement or value-relevant involvement) did indeed produce resistance to change.

Finally, in another investigation of the principle that linkages to other attitudes produce resistance to change, Rokeach (1968) first classified "beliefs" (i.e., attitudes) into five categories that ranged from extremely central *primitive beliefs* (e.g., beliefs about self constancy) to extremely peripheral *inconsequential beliefs*. Consistent with our analysis, Rokeach argued that more central attitudes are structurally linked with many other attitudes and therefore resist change. To test this hypothesis, Rokeach and collaborators induced change in each of the five classes of attitudes while subjects were in a hypnotic state. This induction had less impact on the target attitudes to the extent that they were more central. Moreover, in accord with the domino principle, Rokeach argued that any changes induced in central attitudes would produce greater change in associated attitudes than would changes induced in more peripheral attitudes. Indeed, the changes induced in subjects' more central attitudes, despite being smaller than the changes induced in peripheral attitudes, produced proportionally larger changes in related attitudes.

ATTITUDE STRUCTURE AND THE PROCESSES BY WHICH CHANGE IS RESISTED

To advance beyond demonstrations that intra- and inter-attitudinal structures produce resistance, investigators need to understand the specific psychological mechanisms that enable people to thwart persuasive efforts. In fact, despite many empirical demonstrations that strong attitudes are not easily changed, relatively little attention has been given to the processes that mediate this resistance. Our structural approach offers some insights into possible mechanisms and may also help explain why strong attitudes often have more pronounced effects on information processing than weaker attitudes do (see Eagly & Chaiken, 1993). Our discussion must necessarily be speculative, given the limited amount of research that has addressed mediating processes.

We first propose that resistance to change can proceed by two contrasting types of reactions—one *active* and the other *passive*. Following the active approach, recipients would attend carefully to attitude-inconsistent information and try to refute it through counterarguing. Following the passive approach, recipients would react to attitude-discrepant information by selectively ignoring it. Ignoring could take place through processes occurring at any of several stages of information processing: Perceivers could fail to expose themselves to the information or fail to attend to it if they were exposed; they could perceive or interpret the information in a biased way or grossly reject its validity; they could have "memory problems" consisting of a failure to store the information or difficulty in retrieving it. Whether active or passive defenses are used in resisting attitude change should be related to the type of structure that supports an attitude.

Intra-Attitudinal Structure

As we have argued, an attitude's internal structure (i.e., the associations that represent one's past experience with the attitude object) provides a counterweight to attitude-discrepant information and in general lessens its persuasiveness. Although such associations should provide resources for a relatively active defense, some types of associations would provide better resources than others. In particular, active resistance would be facilitated by associations containing a large number of beliefs about an attitude object. Consistent with Wood's (ch. 11, this volume) demonstrations, the relatively elaborated belief structure that knowledgeable people possess should allow them to mount an active defense against the counterattitudinal information, provided that these beliefs are accessible. This active defense could entail bolstering one's initial attitude (Abelson, 1959). For example, a prodisarmament individual might counter a message advocating maintenance of military strength by bringing to mind his beliefs about various positive effects of disarmament. In addition, an extensive structure of beliefs should enable an individual to more critically evaluate the validity of a message's arguments by engaging in more effective and extensive counterarguing. Yet under particular circumstances this heightened criticality could make knowledgeable recipients more amenable to attitude change (see Wood, ch. 11, this volume). The factors that might cause knowledgeability to foster change are both situational (i.e., the arguments in the persuasive message are especially compelling) and structural in the inter-attitudinal sense (i.e., the attitude is not linked to other attitudes in a manner that produces inertia; see prior section of chapter).

The organization of the beliefs in one's intra-attitudinal structure, as well as their sheer quantity, would also influence the processes by which people resist changing their strong attitudes. Particularly facilitative of active defense would be an organization in which beliefs are *evaluatively consistent* with attitude (see Chaiken et al., ch. 15, this volume; Rosenberg, 1968). To defend one's attitude actively, one must believe in propositions that support this attitude and not believe in more diverse propositions that could support other attitudinal positions. As noted earlier, research on this structural variable has shown that to the extent that people's beliefs are consistent with their attitudes, they are more resistant to social influence. Relevant to our argument about the active defense that can enable this resistance are findings that consistent persons engage in greater counterarguing of counterattitudinal information (see Chaiken & Yates, 1985; Chaiken et al., ch. 15, this volume). By a similar logic, beliefs that are unambivalent should also facilitate active defenses against persuasive attack.

Associations that are primarily affective would not provide a basis for an active defense vis-à-vis attacking persuasive communications (see Chaiken et al., ch. 15, this volume). If one had mainly affective associations to an attitude object (and few cognitive associations), one would have difficulty in mounting active defenses and therefore by default would have to deal with challenging information in other ways. For example, a person who "loves" another based primarily on affective experience would be unable to counterargue unfavorable information but could preserve the positive attitude by more passive mechanisms. Such responses might involve distorting the information, denying its validity, or not thinking about it. Among additional cognitive mechanisms not relying on a structure of beliefs supporting the attitude is heuristic processing of various cues in the communication situation. Such processing would use simple decision rules, such as "consensus implies correctness" or "experts can be trusted" (Chaiken et al., 1989). To protect their attitudes from change, perceivers would selectively weight cues with negative implications for message validity (e.g., the communicator's lack of expertise, negative audience reactions).

The impact of behavioral associations to an attitude object is more difficult to predict. Like affective associations, they do not provide a basis for counterarguing an attitudinal message. However, one problem in discerning their impact stems from the high probability that they are accompanied by associations of the other types. When engaging in behaviors in relation to an attitude object, one inevitably gains information about its characteristics and often experiences affective reactions as well. Whether active or passive defenses were used might well depend on the extent to which these other associations to the attitude object were primarily cognitive or primarily affective.

In general, the associations that accompany an attitude provide a basis for resisting efforts to change the attitude. The exact mechanisms that allow effective resistance depend on several features of these associations—in particular, on whether they are primarily affective or primarily cognitive and whether they are evaluatively consistent or inconsistent with the overall attitude. Although many of these issues, particularly the implications of affective experience, have seen little development in attitude theory or research, our analysis of intra-attitudinal structure in terms of cognitive, affective, and behavioral associations brings these issues to the fore.

Inter-Attitudinal Structure

The empirical literature we reviewed earlier provides numerous demonstrations that to the extent that target attitudes are well embedded in a structure of other attitudes, they are highly resistant to change, particularly if these other attitudes are quite abstract or general. Yet little empirical attention has been given to the mechanisms that may underlie this resistance.

There has also been little theoretical attention to the processes that mediate people's resistance to changing attitudes that are linked to other attitudes. The major exception to this generalization is social judgment theory, which included the principle that ego-involvement—this theory's contribution to analyzing attitude strength from an inter-attitudinal perspective—amplifies judgmental distortions of persuasive messages (i.e., assimilation and contrast effects; see C. W. Sherif et al., 1965). Given an ego-involving issue, counterattitudinal messages should thus be contrasted more strongly, and greater contrast should produce more negative evaluations of message content, which, in turn, inhibit attitude change. Although empirical evidence that perceptual contrast and biased evaluation mediate resistance to change of ego-involving attitudes is at best mixed, this analysis is deserving of more careful evaluation (see Eagly & Chaiken, 1993; Sarup, Suchner, & Gaylord, 1991). Compatible on the whole with social judgment theory's proposed mechanisms are the processes that Festinger (1957) suggested would be invoked when perceivers were forced to expose themselves to counterattitudinal persuasive messages: inattention to the information, biased perception or miscomprehension of it, and forgetting. Although not proposed specifically in relation to strong attitudes, these processes were characterized by Festinger as *defensive* and as functioning to prevent counterattitudinal information from exerting influence on existing attitudes.

In general agreement with these analyses, we suggest that inter-attitudinal structure would not necessarily promote active, systematic processing of persuasive argumentation. Instead, more passive and avoidant defenses (e.g., contrast, forgetting) would generally be favored. Departing somewhat from this general argument, however, we propose that inter-attitudinal linkages to more abstract attitudes may sometimes provide perceivers with a particular type of active defense against attacks on the target attitude: *deductive counterarguing* that uses the linked abstract concepts to refute the attack. Thus, the linkage to the more abstract attitude could itself be used to justify maintaining the lower level attitude and therefore to negate the attacking arguments. For example, an environmentalist might counter an attack on recycling (as difficult, expensive, etc.) by the deductive argument that recycling is necessary, despite its negative aspects, if we are to preserve the quality of the environment. Invoking the more abstract attitude would obviate the need to counterargue the specific arguments contained in the attack on the lower level attitude. The perceiver in our example could thus keep her attitude toward recycling intact by a deductive counterargument, without bothering to contend with the specific arguments against recycling. Having an elaborated set of beliefs concerning the target attitude would not be a requirement for mounting this sort of active defense through deductive counterarguing.

Linkages of attitudes to very abstract and general attitudes, such as values and core aspects of the self, may not promote this deductive style of active

counterarguing. Such abstract attitudes may have considerable motivational significance but may often not be consciously formulated in terms that allow them
to be readily invoked in deductive counterarguing. For example, a commitment
to empirical social science might be a core aspect of many social psychologists'
identities, but such a broad aspect of one's identity might provide little argumentation against information that, say, attacks the value of social science
research. More avoidant and passive defenses might well be favored, particularly
if the individual lacked an elaborated set of beliefs directly relevant to the
counterattitudinal information. Possible responses would include the avoidant
perceptual and evaluative mechanisms considered by social judgment and dissonance theories.

TECHNIQUES BY WHICH STRONG ATTITUDES
ARE CHANGED

In natural settings there are many efforts to develop techniques to change strong
attitudes. Although it is difficult to change strong attitudes, practitioners of persuasion do not shrink from attempting to change them. Natural settings surely
provide many examples of failures to induce change in strong attitudes, but
sometimes substantial influence occurs. Examples include long-term psychotherapy in which therapists sometimes succeed in inducing major changes in the way
their clients view themselves and their environment. Other examples include
brainwashing and political indoctrination, which has sometimes proven successful
in changing people's political ideologies (Lifton, 1961; Schein, Schneier, &
Barker, 1961). Religious conversion also occurs and can reflect fundamental
change in the way people think about themselves as well as about God and the
nature of the universe (see Batson & Ventis, 1982). Political and religious attitudes
are presumably strong in most people, precisely in the structural terms introduced
in this chapter, and thus the issue of why and how these attitudes are changed
is extremely interesting. Unfortunately there has been little systematic study by
psychologists of the attitudinal aspects of psychotherapy or political and religious
conversion, particularly during the contemporary period. Therefore, our comments are speculative but follow from the structural framework we have presented
in this chapter.

    In terms of the analytical framework of this chapter, techniques that should
be successful in inducing change in strong attitudes can best be understood in
terms of their impact on intra-attitudinal and inter-attitudinal structure. Consider
first change techniques that work through adding substantial intra-attitudinal
structure to people's attitudes—that is, internal structure consistent with the
attitudinal position that the persuader desires to instill. Change techniques that
work through inducing alteration of intra-attitudinal structure should provide
people with a very large amount of new experience with the attitude object. To

the extent that many new associations were added, the attitude abstracted from the new and preexisting associations would be heavily influenced by the new associations, especially given their advantage of recency. Repetition of the new structural elements may be important as well. Thus, massive inputs would be recommended to those interested in changing attitudes that have extensive intra-attitudinal structure, especially inputs that span the range of possible types of associations, from cognitive through affective through behavioral.

From this perspective, it is interesting that well-documented successes in changing strong attitudes have involved bombarding the targeted people with a large amount of information consistent with the desired attitude(s) and, at least sometimes, isolating them from competing influences. Psychotherapy thus often involves frequent contact with a therapist over a relatively long period of time. Religious conversions may involve placing potential converts in a community of religious people who are somewhat isolated from the larger society (Conway & Siegelman, 1978; Lofland, 1977). Similar procedures are evident in ideological conversions such as the brainwashing that some U.S. prisoners of war underwent during the Korean War (Lifton, 1961; Schein et al., 1961). Also interesting in this regard is the case of Patricia Hearst, who underwent an ideological conversion when she was confined by members of a radical group known as the Symbionese Liberation Army (Hearst & Moscow, 1982).

A different approach to changing strong attitudes, explicable in terms of our treatment of inter-attitudinal structure, consists of decoupling an attitude from other attitudes to which it is attached, especially from more abstract attitudes from which it may have been deduced. This approach is consistent with Katz's (1960) analysis of how attitudes that serve a value-expressive function would be changed: The value linkages of the attitude must be addressed. For example, if an individual had favored recycling because of its connection with environmental preservation, an argument that effectively destroyed the link between recycling and environmental protection could be very effective (e.g., the notion that recycling itself requires more energy and resources than using unrecycled materials). Moreover, if the target attitude subsequently became linked to a more general attitude that was inconsistent with it, the target attitude should change toward greater conformity with the general attitude. For example, a person might have a very favorable attitude toward eating meat based in part on his or her belief that consuming meat preserves good health. If the person became convinced that meat eating actually is not particularly healthful, he or she might then link meat eating to another abstract attitude, for example, to environmental protection based on the argument that meat production is an excessively energy-intensive form of producing calories for human consumption. Effective attachment of an attitude to a different abstract attitude could thus change the attitude, perhaps even despite extensive intra-attitudinal support from associations reflecting favorable prior experiences. These more abstract approaches to changing attitudes are worthy of empirical investigation.

In general, strong attitudes *can* be changed, not by ordinary argumentation but by techniques that take into account the structural bases of attitude strength. As we have pointed out, very often massive inputs are needed to change strong attitudes, consistent with the suggestion that attitude strength often has intra-attitudinal sources. In contrast, a much more targeted approach of attacking linkages to abstract values (or other abstract attitudes) can be effective, to the extent that attitude strength has primarily inter-attitudinal sources. In view of our argument that effective persuasive techniques differ for attitudes strong on an intra-attitudinal versus inter-attitudinal basis, a sophisticated assessment of the structure that underlies attitudes could help persuasion campaigns to be effective in inducing change in strong attitudes.

CONCLUSION

In this chapter, we have presented a perspective on attitude structure that regards attitudes as linked to prior experience that is represented in intra-attitudinal structure and as often linked to other attitudes in a molar inter-attitudinal structure. In reviewing some modern and classic work on attitudes, we showed that some treatments of the resistance-inducing effects of attitude strength emphasized attitudes' internal structure. Other treatments implicitly or explicitly emphasized the connections between attitudes. A common and central theme of these treatments of attitude strength is that strong attitudes are not easily changed. Our analysis suggests that the principal reasons why strong attitudes are ordinarily difficult to change can be understood in terms of these attitudes' structural linkages with prior evaluative experience and with other more abstract attitudes.

Our structural treatment of attitude strength has a number of advantages that we have endeavored to explicate in this chapter. In particular, it helps illuminate why strong attitudes are generally difficult to change and sheds some light on other consequences of attitude strength as well. In particular, this analysis explicates the mechanisms by which people avoid changing their attitudes and suggests that selectivity in information processing occurs because it can facilitate resistance to change. In addition, the theory is integrative of quite a few other psychologists' discussions of strength. We thus offer our structural theory of attitude strength in part for its integrative value and invite psychologists to consider this framework as an alternative to the proliferation of overlapping strength-related concepts that characterizes the last decade of research on attitudes.

Our analysis of the relation between attitude strength and resistance to change should help right the balance in attitude theory toward greater attention to resistance. The relative neglect of the processes that mediate resistance to change is somewhat puzzling and perhaps reflects in part a wish to satisfy the desire of consumers of attitude research to know how to change attitudes. Whatever the reasons for concentrating attention on attitude change, full understanding of the

the dynamics of attitudes requires that more equal attention be given to resistance to change.

Giving fuller consideration to resistance demands a small but important alteration in the methods of experimental studies of attitude change. At present, studies typically address the differential effects of treatments and often neglect to examine whether any change has been produced in relation to a baseline representing message recipients' prior attitudes. Indeed, the relative lack of research evidence on whether people's attitudes are changed at all by communications is symptomatic of the broader neglect of the issue of attitudinal resistance.

Finally, we note that an important question in discussions of attitude strength is whether numerous variables that psychologists have invoked in discussions of attitude strength should be reduced to a single construct (Abelson, 1988; Krosnick, Boninger, Chuang, Berent, & Carnot, 1993; Raden, 1985). Our structural analysis suggests that a more complex approach would yield a more differentiated set of predictions. Although our overall prediction is indeed that both intra-attitudinal and inter-attitudinal sources of attitude strength would produce resistance to attitude change, the mechanisms that mediate resistance are somewhat different. Also, as we have shown, the two conceptions of attitude strength have different implications for optimal methods of changing strong attitudes.

ACKNOWLEDGMENTS

This chapter was written while Alice Eagly was a visiting professor at the University of Tuebingen, supported by a grant from the Deutsche Forschungsgemeinschaft. Thanks are extended to the editors and Roger Giner-Sorolla for their comments on earlier versions of this chapter.

REFERENCES

Abelson, R. P. (1959). Modes of resolution of belief dilemmas. *Journal of Conflict Resolution, 3,* 343–352.

Abelson, R. P. (1988). Conviction. *American Psychologist, 43,* 267–275.

Abelson, R. P., & Prentice, D. A. (1989). Beliefs as possessions: A functional perspective. In A. R. Pratkanis, S. J. Breckler, & A. G. Greenwald (Eds.), *Attitude structure and function* (pp. 361–381). Hillsdale, NJ: Lawrence Erlbaum Associates.

Anderson, J. R. (1983). *The architecture of cognition.* Cambridge, MA: Harvard University Press.

Anderson, J. R. (1985). *Cognitive psychology and its implications* (2nd ed.). San Francisco: Freeman.

Anderson, J. R., & Bower, G. H. (1974). A propositional theory of recognition memory. *Memory and Cognition, 2,* 406–412.

Anderson, N. H. (1981). *Foundations of information integration theory.* San Diego, CA: Academic.

Ball-Rokeach, S. J., Rokeach, M., & Grube, J. W. (1984). *The great American values test: Influencing behavior and belief through television.* New York: The Free Press.

Bargh, J. A., Chaiken, S., Govender, R., & Pratto, F. (1992). The generality of the automatic attitude activation effect. *Journal of Personality and Social Psychology, 62,* 893–912.

Batson, C. D., & Ventis, W. L. (1982). *The religious experience: A social-psychological perspective.* New York: Oxford University Press.

Cacioppo, J. T., & Petty, R. E. (1982). The need for cognition. *Journal of Personality and Social Psychology, 42,* 116–131.

Chaiken, S., Liberman, A., & Eagly, A. H. (1989). Heuristic and systematic processing within and beyond the persuasion context. In J. S. Uleman & J. A. Bargh (Eds.), *Unintended thought* (pp. 212–252). New York: Guilford.

Chaiken, S., & Yates, S. (1985). Affective-cognitive consistency and thought-induced attitude polarization. *Journal of Personality and Social Psychology, 49,* 1470–1481.

Conway, F., & Siegelman, J. (1978). *Snapping: America's epidemic of sudden personality change.* New York: Lippincott.

Davidson, A. R., Yantis, S., Norwood, M., & Montano, D. E. (1985). Amount of information about the attitude object and attitude-behavior consistency. *Journal of Personality and Social Psychology, 49,* 1184–1198.

Doll, J., & Ajzen, I. (1992). Accessibility and stability of predictors in the theory of planned behavior. *Journal of Personality and Social Psychology, 63,* 754–765.

Eagly, A. H., & Chaiken, S. (1993). *The psychology of attitudes.* Fort Worth, TX: Harcourt Brace Jovanovich.

Eagly, A. H., Mladinic, A., & Otto, S. (1994). Cognitive and affective bases of attitudes toward social groups and social policies. *Journal of Experimental Social Psychology, 30,* 113–137.

Fazio, R. H. (1986). How do attitudes guide behavior? In R. M. Sorrentino & E. T. Higgins (Eds.), *Handbook of motivation and cognition: Foundations of social behavior* (pp. 204–243). New York: Guilford.

Fazio, R. H. (1989). On the power and functionality of attitudes: The role of attitude accessibility. In A. R. Pratkanis, S. J. Breckler, & A. G. Greenwald (Eds.), *Attitude structure and function* (pp. 153–179). Hillsdale, NJ: Lawrence Erlbaum Associates.

Festinger, L. (1957). *A theory of cognitive dissonance.* Evanston, IL: Row, Peterson.

Fishbein, M., & Ajzen, I. (1975). *Belief, attitude, intention, and behavior: An introduction to theory and research.* Reading, MA: Addison-Wesley.

Greenwald, A. G. (1989). Why attitudes are important: Defining attitude and attitude theory 20 years later. In A. R. Pratkanis, S. J. Breckler, & A. G. Greenwald (Eds.), *Attitude structure and function* (pp. 429–440). Hillsdale, NJ: Lawrence Erlbaum Associates.

Haddock, G., Zanna, M. P., & Esses, V. M. (1993). Assessing the structure of prejudicial attitudes: The case of attitudes toward homosexuals. *Journal of Personality and Social Psychology, 65,* 1105–1118.

Halverson, R. R., & Pallak, M. S. (1978). Commitment, ego-involvement, and resistance to attack. *Journal of Experimental Social Psychology, 14,* 1–12.

Hearst, P. C., & Moscow, A. (1982). *Every secret thing.* Garden City, NY: Doubleday.

Heider, F. (1958). *The psychology of interpersonal relations.* New York: Wiley.

Hendrick, C., & Seyfried, B. A. (1974). Assessing the validity of laboratory-produced attitude change. *Journal of Personality and Social Psychology, 29,* 865–870.

Higgins, E. T. (1989). Knowledge accessibility and activation: Subjectivity and suffering from unconscious sources. In J. S. Uleman & J. A. Bargh (Eds.), *Unintended thought* (pp. 75–123). New York: Guilford.

Himmelfarb, S., & Youngblood, J. (1969). Effects of factual information on creating resistance to emotional appeals. *Psychonomic Science, 14,* 267–270.

Johnson, B. T., & Eagly, A. H. (1989). The effects of involvement on persuasion: A meta-analysis. *Psychological Bulletin, 106,* 290–314.

Judd, C. M., & Krosnick, J. A. (1989). The structural bases of consistency among political attitudes: Effects of political expertise and attitude importance. In A. R. Pratkanis, S. J. Breckler, & A. G.

Greenwald (Eds.), *Attitude structure and function* (pp. 99–128). Hillsdale, NJ: Lawrence Erlbaum Associates.

Judd, C. M., & Kulik, J. A. (1980). Schematic effects of social attitudes on information processing and recall. *Journal of Personality and Social Psychology, 38*, 569–578.

Judd, C. M., & Lusk, C. M. (1984). Knowledge structures and evaluative judgments: Effects of structural variables on judgmental extremity. *Journal of Personality and Social Psychology, 46*, 1193–1207.

Katz, D. (1960). The functional approach to the study of attitudes. *Public Opinion Quarterly, 24*, 163–204.

Kelley, H. H., & Volkart, E. H. (1952). The resistance to change of group-anchored attitudes. *American Sociological Review, 17*, 453–465.

Kiesler, C. A. (1971). *The psychology of commitment: Experiments linking behavior to belief.* San Diego, CA: Academic.

Kiesler, C. A., Pallak, M. S., & Kanouse, D. E. (1968). Interactive effects of commitment and dissonance. *Journal of Personality and Social Psychology, 8*, 331–338.

Krosnick, J. A. (1990). Government policy and citizen passion: A study of issue publics in contemporary America. *Political Behavior, 12*, 59–92.

Krosnick, J. A., Boninger, D. S., Chuang, Y. C., Berent, M. K., & Carnot, C. G. (1993). *Journal of Personality and Social Psychology, 65*, 1132–1151.

Lewan, P. C., & Stotland, E. (1961). The effects of prior information on susceptibility to an emotional appeal. *Journal of Abnormal and Social Psychology, 62*, 450–453.

Lifton, R. J. (1961). *Thought reform and the psychology of totalism: A study of "brainwashing" in China.* New York: Norton.

Linville, P. W. (1982). The complexity-extremity effect and age-based stereotyping. *Journal of Personality and Social Psychology, 42*, 193–211.

Lofland, J. (1977). *Doomsday cult: A study of conversion, proselytization, and maintenance of faith.* New York: Irvington.

McGuire, W. J. (1960). A syllogistic analysis of cognitive relationships. In C. I. Hovland & M. J. Rosenberg (Eds.), *Attitude organization and change: An analysis of consistency among attitude components* (pp. 65–111). New Haven, CT: Yale University Press.

McGuire, W. J. (1981). The probabilogical model of cognitive structure and attitude change. In R. E. Petty, T. M. Ostrom, & T. C. Brock (Eds.), *Cognitive responses in persuasion* (pp. 291–307). Hillsdale, NJ: Lawrence Erlbaum Associates.

McGuire, W. J. (1990). Dynamic operations of thought systems. *American Psychologist, 45*, 504–512.

McGuire, W. J., & McGuire, C. V. (1991). The content, structure, and operation of thought systems. In R. S. Wyer, Jr., & T. K. Srull (Eds.), *Advances in social cognition* (Vol. 4, pp. 1–78). Hillsdale, NJ: Lawrence Erlbaum Associates.

Moore, M. (1980). Validation of the attitude toward any practice scale through the use of ambivalence as a moderator variable. *Educational and Psychological Measurement, 40*, 205–208.

Nelson, C. E. (1968). Anchoring to accepted values as a technique for immunizing beliefs against persuasion. *Journal of Personality and Social Psychology, 9*, 329–334.

Norman, R. (1975). Affective-cognitive consistency, attitudes, conformity, and behavior. *Journal of Personality and Social Psychology, 32*, 83–91.

Osgood, C. E., & Tannenbaum, P. H. (1955). The principle of congruity in the prediction of attitude change. *Psychological Review, 62*, 42–55.

Ostrom, T. M., & Brock, T. C. (1968). A cognitive model of attitudinal involvement. In R. P. Abelson, E. Aronson, W. J. McGuire, T. M. Newcomb, M. J. Rosenberg, & P. H. Tannenbaum (Eds.), *Theories of cognitive consistency: A sourcebook* (pp. 373–383) Chicago: Rand McNally.

Pallak, M. S., Mueller, M., Dollar, K., & Pallak, J. (1972). Effect of commitment on responsiveness to an extreme consonant communication. *Journal of Personality and Social Psychology, 23*, 429–436.

Pratkanis, A. R. (1989). The cognitive representation of attitudes. In A. R. Pratkanis, S. J. Breckler, & A. G. Greenwald (Eds.), *Attitude structure and function* (pp. 71–98). Hillsdale, NJ: Lawrence Erlbaum Associates.

Raden, D. (1985). Strength-related attitude dimensions. *Social Psychology Quarterly, 48,* 312–330.

Rokeach, M. (1968). *Beliefs, attitudes, and values: A theory of organization and change.* San Francisco: Jossey-Bass.

Rokeach, M. (1973). *The nature of human values.* New York: The Free Press.

Rosenberg, M. J. (1956). Cognitive structure and attitudinal affect. *Journal of Abnormal and Social Psychology, 53,* 367–372.

Rosenberg, M. J. (1968). Hedonism, inauthenticity, and other goads toward expansion of a consistency theory. In R. P. Abelson, E. Aronson, W. J. McGuire, T. M. Newcomb, M. J. Rosenberg, & P. H. Tannenbaum (Eds.), *Theories of cognitive consistency: A sourcebook* (pp. 73–111). Chicago: Rand McNally.

Ross, M., McFarland, C., Conway, M., & Zanna, M. P. (1983). Reciprocal relation between attitudes and behavior recall: Committing people to newly formed attitudes. *Journal of Personality and Social Psychology, 45,* 257–267.

Sarup, G., Suchner, R. W., & Gaylord, G. (1991). Contrast effects and attitude change: A test of the two-stage hypothesis of social judgment theory. *Social Psychology Quarterly, 54,* 364–372.

Schein, E. H., Schneier, I., & Barker, C. H. (1961). *Coercive persuasion: A socio-psychological analysis of the "brainwashing" of American civilian prisoners by the Chinese communists.* New York: Norton.

Scott, W. A. (1968). Attitude measurement. In G. Lindzey & E. Aronson (Eds.), *Handbook of social psychology* (2nd ed., Vol. 2, pp. 204–273). Reading, MA: Addison-Wesley.

Scott, W. A. (1969). Structure of natural cognitions. *Journal of Personality and Social Psychology, 12,* 261–278.

Sherif, C. W. (1980). Social values, attitudes, and the involvement of the self. In H. E. Howe, Jr., & M. M. Page (Eds.), *Nebraska Symposium on Motivation, 1979* (Vol. 27, pp. 1–64). Lincoln: University of Nebraska Press.

Sherif, C. W., Sherif, M., & Nebergall, R. E. (1965). *Attitude and attitude change: The social judgment-involvement approach.* Philadelphia: Saunders.

Sherif, M., & Cantril, H. (1947). *The psychology of ego-involvements: Social attitudes and identifications.* New York: Wiley.

Snyder, A. F., Mischel, W., & Lott, B. E. (1960). Value, information, and conformity behavior. *Journal of Personality, 28,* 333–341.

Tannenbaum, P. H. (1967). The congruity principle revisited: Studies in the reduction, induction, and generalization of persuasion. In L. Berkowitz (Ed.), *Advances in experimental social psychology* (Vol. 3, pp. 271–320). San Diego, CA: Academic.

Tesser, A. (1993). The importance of heritability in psychological research: The case of attitudes. *Psychological Review, 100,* 129–142.

Tetlock, P. E. (1989). Structure and function in political belief systems. In A. R. Pratkanis, S. J. Breckler, & A. G. Greenwald (Eds.), *Attitude structure and function* (pp. 129–151). Hillsdale, NJ: Lawrence Erlbaum Associates.

Vaughan, G. M., & Mangan, G. L. (1963). Conformity to group pressure in relation to the value of task material. *Journal of Abnormal and Social Psychology, 66,* 179–183.

Wood, W. (1982). Retrieval of attitude-relevant information from memory: Effects on susceptibility to persuasion and on intrinsic motivation. *Journal of Personality and Social Psychology, 42,* 798–810.

17

▼▼▼▼▼▼▼

Attitude Strength, Attitude Stability, and the Effects of Analyzing Reasons

Maureen Wang Erber
Northeastern Illinois University

Sara D. Hodges
Timothy D. Wilson
University of Virginia

An important part of most definitions of attitudes is that they persist over time. Allport (1935) noted that attitudes "often persist throughout life in the way in which they were fixed in childhood or in youth" (p. 814), whereas Sherif and Cantril (1947) argued that "attitudes, once formed, are more or less enduring states of readiness" (p. 7). Petty and Cacioppo (1981) defined an attitude as "an enduring positive or negative feeling about some person, object, or issue" (p. 7). Consistent with these definitions, there is evidence that attitudes can persist for years or even decades (e.g., Bennett, 1975; G. D. Bishop, Hamilton, & McConahay, 1980; Brown, 1970; Hovland, 1959). Marwell, Aiken, and Demerath (1987), for example, found that the political attitudes of civil rights workers changed little over the course of 20 years. Other kinds of attitudes are also notorious for their resistance to change, such as prejudiced and racist opinions.

Recently, however, a considerable amount of research has been conducted that leads to the opposite conclusion: Attitudes fluctuate over time, and depend on what people happen to be thinking about at any given moment. We have found, for example, that when people are asked to think about why they feel the way they do about an attitude object, they often change their minds about how they feel. We have observed such attitude change when people analyze their reasons toward such diverse things as political candidates (Wilson, Kraft, & Dunn, 1989), dating partners (Wilson, Dunn, Bybee, Hyman, & Rotondo, 1984; Wilson & Kraft, 1993), art posters (Wilson, Lisle, Schooler, Hodges, Klaaren, & LaFleur, 1993), food items (Wilson & Schooler, 1991), vacation pictures

(Wilson et al., 1984), and puzzles (Wilson & Dunn, 1986; for reviews, see Wilson, 1990; Wilson, Dunn, Kraft, & Lisle, 1989; Wilson & Hodges, 1992).

We have been struck by how labile people's attitudes seem to be in our studies. Simply by asking people why they feel the way they do, they change their minds about how they feel, at least temporarily. This finding is consistent with a growing body of research indicating that attitudes are constructed from whatever information happens to be currently accessible. Several authors have suggested that people often have a large, conflicting database relevant to their attitudes on any given topic and that the attitude people have at any given time depends on the subset of these data to which they attend (Feldman & Lynch, 1988; Schwarz & Bless, 1992; Strack & Martin, 1987; Tesser, 1978; Tourangeau & Rasinski, 1988; Wilson & Hodges, 1992; Zaller & Feldman, 1992; Zanna & Rempel, 1988). If so, then attitudes will be unstable to the extent that the information that is accessible at one time implies a different evaluation than the information that is accessible at a later time. We refer to this approach as the *attitudes-as-constructions* model, which assumes that people's attitudes vary in an almost whimsical fashion, depending on the information about the attitude object that happens to come to mind.

This chapter is concerned with the apparent contradiction between the attitudes-as-constructions model and the considerable evidence for attitude stability. The solution that would seem to make the most sense—and which is central to the topic of this book—is that attitude stability depends on attitude strength. Some attitudes are strong and resistant to change, such as those anchored by our basic values and worldviews. Many of these attitudes seem to stay with us for years, like treasured possessions (to use Abelson's, 1986, analogy). Other attitudes are held with much less conviction, and are more likely to change as the person encounters new contexts and new information.

This assumption makes intuitive sense, and is of considerable practical importance. If a presidential candidate learns that a majority of the voters prefer him or her a month before the election, it is critical for the candidate to know how stable these attitudes are. Can he or she be assured that these voters will feel the same way on election day? Many assume that stability depends on how strongly people feel. In a recent exit poll conducted during a presidential primary, for example, voters were asked how certain they were that their choice of candidate was the correct one, with the assumption that people who were certain had strong opinions that were unlikely to change (CBS Evening News, March 17, 1992).

Unfortunately, though, there is a problem with the assumption that attitude stability is predictable from attitude strength: As noted by many of the contributors to this book, attitude strength is not a single construct. Different measures of strength have been found to be remarkably uncorrelated (Abelson, 1988; Krosnick & Abelson, 1991; Krosnick, Boninger, Chuang, Berent, & Carnot, 1993; Raden, 1985; Wilson, Hodges, & Pollack, 1992). In Krosnick and Abelson's (1991) words, different dimensions of attitude strength "are conceptually and empirically separable and may therefore have nonoverlapping effects" (p.

183). It is theoretically possible, of course, that different dimensions of attitude strength could be uncorrelated, but have identical effects on important outcome variables, such as attitude stability. This is what Krosnick and Abelson (1991) concluded in their review: Though uncorrelated, different dimensions have similar effects on attitude-behavior consistency, social perception, and interpersonal attraction. We argue, however, that this is *not* the state of affairs with attitude stability. Different measures of attitude strength are conceptually different, we suggest, and have distinct relationships to attitude stability.

PREDICTING ATTITUDE STABILITY
FROM ATTITUDE STRENGTH

Although we do not have the space to present a thorough review, we give several examples of the kinds of strength measures that have been found to predict attitude stability (for more comprehensive reviews see Cook & Flay, 1978; Krosnick et al., 1993; Petty & Cacioppo, 1986).

Affective–Cognitive Consistency.   One measure of attitude strength is the consistency of people's beliefs and feelings about the issue (Norman, 1975; Rosenberg, 1960, 1968). People who have consistent cognitions and affect presumably have stronger attitudes, whereas those with inconsistent cognitions and affect presumably have weaker, less stable attitudes. To test this assumption, Rosenberg (1968) assessed people's attitudes toward foreign policy and local university issues at 2- to 3-week intervals. The people with the most stable attitudes were those who had consistent affect and cognitions at Time 1.[1]

Conviction.   Abelson (1988) suggested that the best measure of attitude strength is one that he terms "conviction," which has three components: emotional commitment (e.g., how much people think their attitudes express the "real you" and are related to their moral beliefs), cognitive elaboration (e.g., how knowledgeable people are and how long they say they have held their current views), and ego preoccupation (e.g., how important people say the issue is and how often they have thought about it). He found that the more conviction people expressed on four different social issues, the more stable their attitudes were over a 1-month period.

---

[1]As noted by Chaiken, Pomerantz, and Giner-Sorolla (ch. 15, this volume), there has been some confusion in the literature about whether this construct is best referred to as *affective-cognitive consistency* or *evaluative-cognitive consistency*. Chaiken et al. argue persuasively that the latter term is more appropriate, because many studies have actually assessed the consistency between people's overall *evaluation* of an attitude object and their valenced cognitions about that object. We use the term *affective-cognitive consistency* to be consistent with a study of ours we report later, in which we compared people's valenced cognitions with a measure that was, we suggest, more a measure of affect than of people's overall evaluation. (This measure is described in Table 17.1, to be discussed shortly.)

Accessibility. Fazio (1986, 1989) argued that accessible attitudes are more stable than inaccessible attitudes. He defined accessibility as the strength of the association between an attitude object and a person's evaluation of it, as assessed by response time (how long people take to rate their attitude). When this association is strong, people are likely to access their attitude whenever the attitude object is encountered, thus reporting the same attitude over time. When this association is weak, people are less likely to access their attitude, and thus will be more influenced by such contextual variables as social norms, thereby lowering the stability of people's reported attitudes. Consistent with this hypothesis, Fazio and Williams (1986) found that people with accessible attitudes toward the 1984 presidential candidates had more stable attitudes. That is, there was more consistency between their reported attitudes toward the candidates several weeks before the election and whom they reported voting for than there was among people with inaccessible attitudes (see also Bassili, 1993).

Message Elaboration. Petty and Cacioppo's (1986) influential model of persuasion, the Elaboration Likelihood Model, argues that attitudes formed via the central route will be more persistent than those formed via the peripheral route. The central route refers to attitudes that are based on a thoughtful consideration of the issues relevant to the attitude (i.e., to "elaborated" attitudes), whereas the peripheral route refers to attitudes that are based on simple cues about which position is most valid. Petty and Cacioppo (1986) and Petty, Haugtvedt, and Smith (ch. 5, this volume) argue that elaborated attitudes will be more stable because they are more rehearsed; based on more enduring, consistent attitude schemas; and held with greater confidence. An elaborated attitude thus becomes stronger than a nonelaborated one, they argue, and more resistant to persuasion. Consistent with this view, Petty, Cacioppo, Haugtvedt, and Heesacker (cited in Petty & Cacioppo, 1986) found that when people formed elaborated attitudes (via the central route), their attitudes were more likely to persist over a 2-week period than when people formed unelaborated attitudes (via the peripheral route). Similarly, Chaiken (1980) found that attitudes were more likely to persist over a 10-day period if people initially based them on a systematic examination of the issues.

Importance. A number of researchers have found that the more important an attitude is to people, the more stable it is (e.g., Converse, 1964; Hahn, 1970; Krosnick, 1988; Schuman & Presser, 1981). Importance is typically measured by asking people how personally important an issue is to them, or how concerned they are about it (e.g., Krosnick, 1988). Krosnick (1988), for example, found that people's attitudes toward social issues were significantly more stable over several months if they rated these attitudes as important.

Ambivalence. A number of researchers have argued that some attitudes are characterized by ambivalence, defined as having both a positive and a negative evaluation of an attitude object (e.g. Bargh, Chaiken, Govender, & Pratto, 1992;

Kaplan, 1972; Thompson & Zanna, ch. 14, this volume). There is some evidence that ambivalence is associated with attitude instability. Bargh et al. (1992) found a significant correlation between ambivalence and instability, such that the more ambivalent people were, the less stable their attitudes were over a 2-day period. To the extent that people's certainty in their beliefs is equivalent to ambivalence (as suggested by Krosnick & Abelson, 1991), similar evidence has been obtained by Pelham (1991). He measured people's certainty about their self-views, and found that these views were less stable among people with low certainty.

Ego-Involvement. According to social judgment theory, people who are involved in an issue—that is, those for whom the attitude is closely related to their self-identity—will have more stable attitudes (Sherif & Hovland, 1961). Ego-involvement is defined as the magnitude of people's latitude of rejection, which is the number of attitudinal positions people find objectionable, relative to the magnitude of their latitudes of acceptance and noncommitment (the number of attitudinal positions people find acceptable or neutral; Sherif, Kelly, Rodgers, Sarup, & Tittler, 1973). We are unaware of studies that have tested this stability hypothesis directly, though Sherif et al. (1973) found some evidence for a related hypothesis: people involved in an issue were more resistant to change in response to a persuasive communication than were people who were uninvolved.

Knowledge. People vary in how knowledgeable they are about an attitude object, and knowledge may relate to how stable an attitude is. Consistent with this view, Wood, Kallgren, and Priesler (1985) found that attitudes held by knowledgeable people were more stable and resistant to attack (see also Wood, Rhodes, & Biek, ch. 11, this volume).

Behavioral Experience. Fazio and Zanna (1981) demonstrated that attitudes are stronger and more accessible when they are based on direct, behavioral experience with the attitude object, and there is some evidence that such attitudes are more stable over time and more resistant to persuasion attempts (Watts, 1967; Wood, 1982).

Why Are Strong Attitudes Stable?

We have just seen that several different measures of attitude strength predict stability, such that the stronger the attitude, the less likely it is to change over time. Several explanations for this finding have been offered, including the following (for a more detailed discussion of these arguments, see Cook & Flay, 1978; Krosnick, 1988; Petty & Cacioppo, 1986): First, strong attitudes are probably anchored by other beliefs and values, making them more resistant to change. If people were to change their basic religious beliefs, for example, many other attitudes and values linked to these beliefs would have to be changed as well.

Second, people are likely to know more about issues they feel strongly about, making them more resistant to counterarguments. Third, people are likely to associate with others who feel similarly on important issues, and these people help maintain and support these attitudes. Fourth, strong attitudes are often more elaborated and accessible, making it more likely that they will be at the tip of the tongue when people are asked how they feel on different occasions. Fifth, people with strong attitudes are likely to attend to and seek out information relevant to the topic, arming them with still more arguments with which to resist attempts to change their minds (Krosnick et al., 1993). (We should note, however, that this tendency might cut both ways. People who seek out information are also more likely to come across counterattitudinal arguments. People with weak attitudes who do not bother to attend to or seek out relevant information may be less likely to encounter such arguments. We return to this issue later.)

Thus, there are several reasons why strong attitudes are stable attitudes, possibly resolving the dilemma we posed earlier (that there is evidence for both attitude stability and instability). Perhaps the answer is simply that weak attitudes are unstable, whereas strong ones persist over time. As we mentioned earlier, however, a problem with this interpretation is that the different measures of attitude strength we have reviewed tend not to correlate with each other. Thus, there is no single, overall construct of attitude strength that moderates attitude stability. The solution may be that each of the different measures captures a different component of attitude strength, each of which has the same relationship to attitude stability. According to this argument, an attitude can be strong in a number of different ways, but in each case, strength is associated with stability.

Another way of stating this is that the attitudes-as-constructions model we mentioned earlier may apply only to attitudes that are relatively weak. That is, when attitudes are weak, people are more likely to construct them from whatever data happen to be accessible to people. If an attitude is strong in any of several respects it may not have to be constructed each time people encounter the attitude object. Instead, people simply recall how they feel, regardless of what information about the attitude object happens to be accessible.

CAN AN ATTITUDES-AS-CONSTRUCTIONS MODEL ACCOUNT FOR ATTITUDE STABILITY?

It is possible, however, to accommodate attitude stability within a model that views all attitudes as constructions. We suggest that there are two ways that attitudes could be stable within the attitudes-as-constructions model, each of which relates to different dimensions of attitude strength. First, let's assume that attitudes are always constructed on the basis of the information about the attitude object that is most accessible. Let's further assume that one type of datum people often store about an attitude object is how they have previously evaluated it.

When they evaluate the attitude object at a later point in time, this prior evaluation is one piece of information that can be accessed and used to construct a new attitude (Judd & Brauer, ch. 3, this volume). If the prior evaluation is strong and accessible, then it is likely to be weighted heavily, leading to a consistent attitude over time. If it is not, there is a greater likelihood that the information that is accessible at Time 2 will be different from what was accessible at Time 1, producing attitude instability. What influences whether the prior evaluation is accessible? Some of the aspects of attitude strength we reviewed earlier are good bets, such as how much conviction people have, how quickly they respond to attitude questions, how elaborated the prior attitude is, how much behavioral experience people have toward the attitude object, and how important the attitude is. These indices of attitude strength may predict how much people's later evaluation is based on a prior evaluation.

There is a second way in which an attitudes-as-constructions model can accommodate attitude stability. Even if people do not have a strong, accessible prior evaluation on which to base their attitude, their attitude will be stable if they use evaluatively consistent information when constructing their attitudes at different points in time. For example, people might not have a strong, accessible evaluation of a particular political candidate. Each time they form an opinion of the candidate, however, the information that is most accessible is generally positive. At Time 1 they might base their attitude on the fact that the candidate agrees with them on abortion and seems smart, whereas at Time 2 they base their attitude on the fact that the candidate has a viable economic plan and is attractive. Consequently, the attitude they construct is consistently positive from one time to the next.

What determines whether the data that are accessible to people will be evaluatively consistent over time? One determinant may be the consistency of people's overall database about the attitude object. If people's beliefs and feelings are generally consistent, then it does not matter which subset of data people use to construct their attitude—the same evaluation will result. If people have an inconsistent set of beliefs and feelings, there is an increased likelihood that the subset of data used to construct an attitude at Time 2 will imply a different attitude than the subset used at Time 1.

The indices of attitude strength we reviewed earlier, then, may be linked to attitude stability in different ways. Some, such as people's level of conviction, amount of elaboration, and response time can be viewed as measures of how likely a prior evaluation will be used when constructing a new attitude. Others, such as affective-cognitive consistency and ambivalence, may relate more to the consistency of people's database, which predicts how likely people are to use different information when constructing a new attitude.

In the remainder of this chapter we discuss evidence relevant to this classification of strength variables into two general types. We should mention two caveats: First, there is not a great deal of research testing this distinction, thus many of our conclusions will be tentative. Second, we should emphasize that we are not arguing that our scheme is the only way of classifying different measures of attitude strength. Many other schemes, discussed in other chapters in this book, are undoubtedly useful as well. Our distinction has proven to be of some predictive value, however, as we will see.

The data that are most relevant were collected by Wilson et al. (1992). In this study we measured college students' attitudes toward Ronald Reagan on two occasions, separated by several weeks. At an initial laboratory session the participants completed several of the measures of attitude strength we discussed earlier, as listed in Table 17.1. One of these measures was a new one that we devised to provide an additional measure of the consistency of people's database, namely the homogeneity of people's beliefs about the attitude object. As described in Table 17.1, this variable reflects the variance in each individual's valenced beliefs about the attitude object, and is likely to be related to ambivalence. As another measure of the consistency of people's database, we assessed affective-cognitive consistency, using techniques similar to Rosenberg's (1960). It should be noted that these different consistency measures do not have to be correlated. The fact that people have consistent or inconsistent beliefs does not necessarily mean that the average valence of these beliefs is consistent or inconsistent with their affect (see Table 17.1 for a more detailed description of how these variables were measured). As we will see, these two measures were, in fact, uncorrelated with each other.

Several weeks later people took part in what they thought was an unrelated phone survey. As we will soon discuss, some people were first asked to explain why they felt the way they did about President Reagan, to examine the effects of explaining an attitude on attitude stability. Of current concern is the relationship between the different measures of attitude strength and attitude stability in the control condition, where people reported their attitude toward Reagan without analyzing their reasons.

The first question of interest is the relationship between our different measures of attitude strength at Time 1. We performed a principal components factor analysis with a varimax rotation on responses to the different measures, including attitude extremity and amount of media exposure (the number of news stories about Reagan people reported having read or heard; see Table 17.1 for a description of these variables). The measures of knowledge and importance were not included in these analyses, because these variables were part of the measures of cognitive elaboration and ego preoccupation, respectively. On the basis of the eigenvalues, a five-factor solution appeared to fit the data reasonably well (the factor solution is shown in Table 17.2, whereas the correlations between measures are shown in Table 17.3). The first factor corresponds to Abelson's concept of conviction, including his three measures of conviction and the amount of reported behavior relevant to the attitude. The second factor included attitude accessibility, attitude extremity, and, to some extent, ego-involvement. The only variable to load highly on the third factor was our measure of belief homogeneity. Media

TABLE 17.1
Measures of Attitude Strength

Measure	Description
Belief homogeneity	People rated 10 possible accomplishments of the Reagan administration according to (a) how positive or negative each one would be and (b) how much Reagan had achieved each one, both on scales that ranged from −4 to +4. Following Rosenberg (1960), we computed the positivity of subjects' cognitions by multiplying people's responses to (a) and (b) for each item. The homogeneity of people's beliefs was then computed by taking the standard deviation of the 10 belief scores (the products of a × b) for each participant.
Affective-cognitive consistency	Absolute value of the difference between the mean of standardized affect ratings and the mean of standardized cognitive ratings (described above). Affect was measured as suggested by Breckler and Wiggins (1989), by asking people to rate, on semantic differential scales, their "feelings about Ronald Reagan."
Emotional commitment	One of Abelson's (1988) three measures of commitment (e.g., how much people said their attitudes expressed the "real you," and how related they said their attitude was to their moral beliefs).
Cognitive elaboration	One of Abelson's (1988) three measures of commitment (e.g., how knowledgeable people said they were and how long they said they had had their current views).
Ego preoccupation	One of Abelson's (1988) three measures of commitment (e.g., how important people said the topic was to them personally, how often they said they thought about it).
Importance	One of the items on the ego preoccupation scale, asking how important the topic was to them personally.
Knowledge	One of the items on the cognitive elaboration scale, asking how knowledgeable people considered themselves to be.
Accessibility	The speed with which people pressed a "yes" or "no" button when presented with the statement, "President Reagan: Good?" (see Fazio, 1989).
Reported behavior	Sum of five questions about people's past behaviors relevant to the issue (e.g., whether they had ever written a letter to a public official about Reagan).
Ego-involvement	People's latitude of rejection, measured as specified by social judgment theory (Sherif & Hovland, 1961).
Media exposure	The number of news stories about Reagan that people reported reading or hearing in the past year.
Attitude extremity	The distance of people's attitude from the midpoint of the scale

TABLE 17.2
Factor Loadings of Measures of Attitude Strength

Attitude Scale	Loading				
	Factor 1	Factor 2	Factor 3	Factor 4	Factor 5
Factor 1 (32%)					
Cognitive elaboration	.80	.32	.10	.15	.04
Ego preoccupation	.85	.06	.10	.04	−.07
Emotional commitment	.82	.26	−.06	−.03	−.08
Reported behavior	.62	−.13	.04	.13	.30
Factor 2 (12%)					
Response time	.10	.82	−.09	.17	.04
Attitude extremity	.43	.68	−.02	.12	.03
Ego-involvement	−.08	.53	.46	−.43	−.01
Factor 3 (12%)					
Belief homogeneity	.11	−.09	.90	.11	−.04
Factor 4 (10%)					
Media exposure	.12	.22	.11	.87	.05
Factor 5 (9%)					
Affect.-cog. consistency	.02	.07	−.04	.03	.96

Note. The number after each factor represents the percentage of variance accounted for by that factor. All measures were coded such that the higher the value, the greater the consistency of the database or the greater the attitudinal strength. For example, the higher the score on the affective-cognitive consistency measure, the more *consistent* people were, and the higher the score on the response time measure, the *faster* people responded.

exposure had the highest loading on the fourth factor, whereas affective-cognitive consistency was the only variable to load highly on the fifth factor.

We argued earlier that attitude strength measures can be divided into two types: those in which there is a strong evaluation that is likely to be accessible over time (e.g., conviction, response time, importance), and those that reflect the consistency of people's database (belief homogeneity, affective-cognitive consistency). We suggested that this is not the only way in which measures of attitude strength differ, which is borne out by the fact that there was not a neat, two-factor solution, with all of the measures of one type loading highly on one factor, and all the measures of the other type loading highly on the other factor. As found in other, similar investigations, different measures of strength are often uncorrelated, resulting in multifactor solutions (e.g., Krosnick et al., 1993). Consistent with our hypothesized breakdown, however, the measures that we have put in one category (those assessing the accessibility of the evaluation) loaded on different factors than those we have put in the other category (those that assess the consistency of people's database).

The second question of interest is which of our indices of attitude strength predicted attitude stability. To assess stability, we computed the absolute value of the difference between people's standardized attitude responses at Times 1

TABLE 17.3

Correlations Between Measures

Measure	1	2	3	4	5	6	7	8	9	10	11
1. Belief homogeneity											
2. Affect.-cog. consistency	.05										
3. Response time	.01	.03									
4. Knowledge[a]	-.16*	.01	.19**								
5. Ego-involvement	.00	-.04	.08	.08							
6. Cognitive elaboration	-.14	.05	.26**	.88**	.07						
7. Ego preoccupation	-.12	-.02	.16*	.60**	.03	.63**					
8. Emotional commitment	-.04	.01	.22**	.59**	.05	.66**	.63**				
9. Importance[b]	-.09	-.04	.14	.48**	.06	.51**	.85**	.55**			
10. Reported behavior	-.01	.11	.11	.36**	-.03	.37**	.40**	.32**	.34**		
11. Media exposure	-.05	.09	.19*	.31**	-.02	.30**	.20*	.15	.06	.17*	
12. Attitude extremity	-.07	-.01	.43**	.33**	.04	.52**	.30**	.48**	.29**	.23**	.19*

Note. All measures were coded such that the higher the value, the greater the attitude strength. For example, the higher the score on the response time measure, the *faster* people responded, and the higher the score on the affective-cognitive consistency measure, the more *consistent* people were.

[a]The item about knowledge (Line 4) was part of the cognitive elaboration scale (Line 6).

[b]The item about attitude importance (Line 9) was part of the ego preoccupation scale (Line 7).

*p < .05. **p < .01.

TABLE 17.4
Regression of Measures of Attitude Strength on Attitude Stability

Strength Measure	Beta	SE of Beta	t-value
Consistency of people's database			
Affective-cognitive consistency	.44	.12	3.84**
Belief homogeneity	.22	.12	1.87*
Strength and accessibility			
Emotional commitment	.52	.19	2.73**
Cognitive elaboration	.55	.36	1.50
Ego preoccupation	−.23	.26	<1
Response time	−.27	.15	1.81*
Importance	.11	.20	<1
Ego-involvement	−.17	.12	1.44
Reported behavior	−.08	.13	<1
Knowledge	−.44	.30	1.48
Attitude extremity	−.19	.16	1.17
Media exposure	.00	.12	<1

Note. For all variables, a positive beta means that the stronger the attitude, the more stable it was over time.

$*p < .10.$ $**p < .01.$

and 2. We then examined which of the strength variables predicted stability, adjusting for the effects of each of the other variables (using simultaneous regression). The results of this analysis are shown in Table 17.4. As predicted, our measures of the consistency of people's databases were predictive of attitude stability. The more consistent people's affect and cognitions were at Time 1, the more likely they were to hold a similar attitude at Time 2. Similarly, the more homogeneous people's beliefs toward Ronald Reagan were at Time 1, the more likely they were to hold a similar attitude at Time 2.

The results for the other indices of attitude strength were mixed. One of Abelson's measures of conviction—emotional commitment—was strongly related to stability, such that the more committed people were to their attitude at Time 1, the greater the consistency between their Time 1 and Time 2 attitudes. Curiously, however, the notion that strong attitudes are more stable was not borne out on several of the other measures. For example, neither attitude accessibility (as measured by response time) nor attitude knowledge was associated with greater attitude stability; in fact, the direction of these effects was in the opposite direction (though not significantly so).[2] These results are at odds with the studies we reviewed

----

[2]The regression reported in Table 17.4 includes variables (importance, knowledge) that were included as items in some of the other scales (cognitive elaboration, ego preoccupation), possibly resulting in problems of multicollinearity. To address this problem we computed separate regressions that included only the nonredundant measures (i.e., the individual items of knowledge and importance but not the composite measures that included these measures, or only the composite measures without the individual items). Very similar results were found in both of these analyses, and the significance levels of the betas remained virtually unchanged.

earlier that found that many measures of attitude strength correlate positively with attitude stability. These earlier studies, however, tended to include only single measures of strength. Our study is one of the very few that included multiple measures, allowing us to control for the contribution of other measures of attitude strength. It may be that some measures of strength are not associated with stability when the contribution of the other measures are controlled.

We thus have some support for the idea that when it comes to predicting attitude stability, different measures of attitude strength do not operate in the same way. Some measures, we suggest, are best conceived as reflections of the consistency of people's database. In our data set, these measures were associated in the predicted way with attitude stability. Other measures can be viewed as measures of the accessibility of people's evaluation (i.e., the likelihood that a prior evaluation is used to construct a new attitude). Interestingly, when variables such as media exposure, attitude extremity, and the other measures of attitude strength are controlled, many of these measures did not show the expected relationship with attitude stability. Before we make too much of this finding, we should see if it replicates, particularly across attitudes toward a variety of topics. In the meantime, we view these results as providing tentative support for our division of strength variables into two general types: Those that assess the consistency of people's database, which were predictive of attitude stability, and those related generally to the accessibility and strength of people's evaluation, which, surprisingly, were not.

ATTITUDE STRENGTH AS A MODERATOR OF THE EFFECTS OF ANALYZING REASONS

As mentioned earlier, we asked some of the participants in the Wilson et al. (1992) study, before giving their attitude at Time 2, to explain why they felt the way they did about Ronald Reagan. We found, as we have in several other studies, that people who analyzed reasons were significantly more likely to change their attitudes than those who did not (see Hodges & Wilson, 1993, for a more complete discussion of these results). Examining which of our measures of attitude strength moderated this effect may provide further support for our proposed division of strength variables into two types. If the different types of measures are conceptually distinct, then they might moderate the effects of analyzing reasons in different ways. To explore this possibility, we first need to discuss in more detail why analyzing reasons can change people's attitudes.

We suggest that people often do not have perfect access to the reasons behind their attitudes. When they think about why they feel the way they do, the reasons that come to mind are ones that are accessible in memory and sound plausible, but are not always completely accurate (Nisbett & Wilson, 1977). For example, when people think about why they feel the way they do about a particular political candidate, what comes to mind might be that the candidate has different views than they do on labor issues and the necessity of raising taxes. It might be, however, that before people analyzed reasons these factors were relatively unimportant. In fact, people might have had a generally positive reaction to the candidate. After analyzing reasons the negative beliefs become more accessible, and influence people's attitude. That is, people often adopt, at least temporarily, the attitude implied by their reasons. We have found evidence, in several studies, for just this sequence of events (for reviews, see Wilson, 1990; Wilson, Dunn, Kraft, & Lisle, 1989; Wilson & Hodges, 1992).

Even if people do not know exactly why they feel the way they do, it might seem that they would focus only on reasons that were consistent with their initial feelings. Why, for example, would people think of negative attributes of a political candidate, if their initial evaluation was generally positive? This process is more understandable when we view the effects of analyzing reasons in terms of the model of attitudes-as-constructions. If we assume that people construct their attitudes from whatever information is currently accessible, and that analyzing reasons influences the information that is accessible (by focusing people's attention on reasons that sound plausible and are easy to verbalize), then we can see why people base their new attitude on the reasons that come to mind. The question then becomes, when are people likely to bring to mind reasons that are inconsistent with their initial attitude?

Moderating Effects of the Consistency of the Database

One such condition may be the nature of people's attitudinal database. As we have already seen, some attitudes are characterized by consistent beliefs and feelings about the attitude object. Such attitudes are likely to be relatively immune to the effects of analyzing reasons, because even if this kind of introspection focuses people's attention on a subset of their beliefs and feelings, or changes the way in which they weight these different factors, the same evaluation will be implied (i.e., because all of the thoughts and beliefs have the same valence, it does not matter which are used to construct an attitude). Other attitudes are characterized by inconsistent beliefs and/or feelings. This type of attitude, we suggest, is more likely to be changed when people analyze reasons. To the extent that analyzing reasons focuses people's attention on a different subset of these beliefs and feelings, or causes people to weight them differently, a new attitude will result.

This reasoning is consistent with research by Millar and Tesser (1986, 1989; see Tesser, Martin, & Mendolia, ch. 4, this volume). They suggest that thinking about reasons increases the salience of the cognitive component of an attitude. To the extent that a person's original attitude was determined at least in part by the affective component, then focusing on the cognitive component might cause a change in attitude. This would only be the case, however, to the extent that the affective and cognitive components of the attitude are different (i.e., when they imply a different evaluation of the attitude object). If the components were evaluatively consistent, then it would not matter which one determined the attitude. Consistent with this argument, Millar and Tesser (1989) found that the people who were most susceptible to the effects of thinking about reasons were those whose attitudes toward a set of puzzles consisted of inconsistent affective and cognitive components.

Our view is similar, except that we prefer to broaden the view of the data people use to construct their attitudes, and the kinds of inconsistencies that might exist in these data. Millar and Tesser focus on inconsistencies between affect and cognitions. Analyzing reasons might also change people's attitudes, we suggest, if there are inconsistencies among the different cognitions (beliefs) people have about the attitude object, and if analyzing reasons focuses people's attention on a different subset of beliefs than they were using to construct their prior attitude. Thus in our view, people's attitudinal database often consists of a variety of beliefs and feelings, and analyzing reasons can change people's attitudes if there are inconsistencies between or within any of these components.

This prediction can be tested in our survey of attitudes toward Ronald Reagan. It should be recalled that we had two measures of the consistency of people's database: the homogeneity of their valenced beliefs about Ronald Reagan, and the consistency between their beliefs and their affect (see Table 17.1). Because these two measures were uncorrelated ($r = .05$) and loaded on different factors, we divided people into four groups, according to the consistency of their beliefs (belief homogeneity, high vs. low) and the consistency between their affect and cognitions (high vs. low). We then examined the effects of analyzing reasons in each group.[3]

Figure 17.1 displays the stability of people's attitudes in each group, defined here simply as the correlation between people's attitudes at Times 1 and 2. There was a significant three-way interaction on this measure between the reasons manipulation, belief homogeneity, and affective-cognitive consistency. This interaction is best understood by considering the effects of the reasons manipulation in each of the four cells shown in Fig. 17.1. First, as predicted, analyzing reasons had relatively little effect on people who had the most consistent database (see the far left-hand side of Fig. 17.1). Also as predicted, analyzing reasons had more of an effect on people with a moderately inconsistent database, that is, those with homogeneous beliefs but inconsistent affect and cognitions, or those with heterogenous beliefs and consistent affect and cognitions (see the middle cells of Fig. 17.1). In these cells, people who analyzed reasons were significantly more likely to change their attitudes than control subjects, thereby lowering the consistency of their Time 2 attitude with their Time 1 attitude. These results are consistent with the hypothesis (both ours and Millar & Tesser's) that analyzing

---

[3]We also conducted regression analyses treating belief homogeneity and affective-cognitive consistency as continuous variables, and found very similar results to those discussed here.

Time 1, Time 2 Correlation

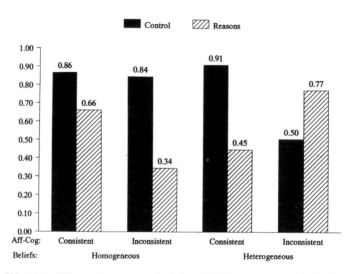

FIG. 17.1.   Effects of reasons manipulation, belief homogeneity, and affective-cognitive consistency on absolute attitude change. The dependent measure is the correlation between Time 1 and Time 2 attitudes, such that the higher the number, the greater the attitude stability.

reasons is most likely to change people's attitudes when there is some inconsistency in people's beliefs and feelings about the attitude object. This inconsistency does not have to be between people's affect and cognitions, as Millar and Tesser suggested. Having inconsistent beliefs seems to be sufficient for analyzing reasons to change people's attitudes.

What about people who had the most inconsistent database, namely those in the far right-hand cell of Fig. 17.1? It appears, on the face of it, that the effects of analyzing reasons here were contrary to our predictions: There was no significant difference in attitude change between those who analyzed reasons and those who did not. In fact, people in the reasons condition actually showed slightly less change over time than those who did not. The story, however, is complicated by the fact that people in this group changed their attitudes a fair amount on their own over time. That is, as we have already seen, people with heterogeneous beliefs and inconsistent affect and cognitions changed their attitudes over time even without analyzing reasons. This is shown clearly in Fig. 17.1, where, among control subjects, those who had heterogeneous beliefs *and* inconsistent affect and cognitions had the least stable attitudes.

Consequently, additional change caused by the reasons manipulation becomes difficult to assess. Consider, for example, a hypothetical subject in the heterogeneous belief-inconsistent affect and cognition cell. Suppose this person's attitude was a 4 on a 6-point scale at Time 1. When contacted at Time 2, his or her attitude has already changed, say, to a 5. If this person does not analyze reasons, then he or she reports a 5, resulting in the relatively low amount of consistency between Time 1 and Time 2 attitudes shown in the control condition at the far right of Fig. 17.1. If this person does analyze reasons at Time 2, suppose that additional attitude change occurred, changing the 5 back to a 4. If so, the measure of change from Time 2 to Time 1 would be $4 - 4 = 0$, falsely indicating that no change had occurred due to analyzing reasons.

One question this interpretation raises is why, if people had already changed their attitudes by the time we asked them to analyze reasons at Time 2, they would change their attitudes back toward their original Time 1 position, instead of adopting an even more extreme attitude (e.g., why our hypothetical subject, who had already changed from a 4 to a 5, did not change to a 6 after analyzing reasons). It may be that people who have highly inconsistent databases are those with ambivalent attitudes, who vacillate between two opposing positions. When we assessed their attitudes again at Time 2, many of these people may have changed from one position to the other. When these people analyzed reasons, however, they might have reexamined the merits of the alternative position, causing a shift back in the direction of their original attitude.

This interpretation is highly speculative, and will of course require further testing. One clear implication from this study, though, is that the effects of a manipulated variable (e.g., analyzing reasons) on attitude stability can be difficult to assess, if people's attitudes have changed on their own. Paradoxically, such a manipulation can push people back to their original attitude, making it look like no change occurred between Times 1 and 2.

Moderating Effects of Other Measures of Attitude Strength

We also examined whether the other measures of attitude strength, such as response time, conviction, and ego-involvement, moderated the effects of analyzing reasons. As reported by Hodges and Wilson (1993), people with inaccessible attitudes, as measured by response time, were more likely to change their attitudes after analyzing reasons than people with accessible attitudes. Interestingly, people with accessible and inaccessible attitudes were equally likely to bring to mind thoughts that were inconsistent with their initial attitudes, when asked to analyze reasons. People with inaccessible attitudes, however, were more likely to infer that their reasons reflected their current attitude, resulting in attitude change. This result is consistent with Fazio, Powell, and Williams' (1989) findings about the effects of situational salience on people's attitudes. Fazio et al. found that people with accessible attitudes were less influenced by the temporary salience of an array of consumer goods. Our findings suggest that people with accessible attitudes will also be less influenced by thoughts that are temporarily salient, namely the reasons they generated about why they felt the way they did.

None of the other measures of attitude strength significantly moderated the effects of analyzing reasons. We also explored several possible higher-order interactions between pairs of strength measures and analyzing reasons, and no significant effects were found. It was particularly surprising that people's reported level of knowledge did not moderate the effects of analyzing reasons, given that it has in some of our previous studies (e.g., Wilson, Kraft, & Dunn, 1989). We should note, however, that the means were in the predicted direction: Unknowledgeable people who analyzed reasons were more likely to change their attitudes than knowledgeable people who analyzed reasons.

IMPLICATIONS AND CONCLUSIONS

We have suggested that one way of classifying different measures of attitude strength is to divide them into two categories: (a) those that assess the consistency of people's database, including measures of affective-cognitive consistency, belief homogeneity, and ambivalence; and (b) those that measure the strength and accessibility of people's general evaluation of the attitude object, including importance, response time, conviction, and message elaboration. We have reported converging evidence for the importance and relevance of the first category. Our measures of the consistency of people's database proved to be independent of other measures of attitude strength (see correlations in Table 17.3), predicted attitude stability (see Table 17.4), and moderated the effects of analyzing reasons on attitude change (see Fig. 17.1).

These findings are consistent with a model that views attitudes as constructions, depending on what information is salient when people consider how they feel (Strack & Martin, 1987; Tesser, 1978; Tourangeau & Rasinski, 1988; Wilson & Hodges, 1992). When people have a consistent database, then their attitudes are likely to remain stable over time, even if they analyze reasons. When there is moderate inconsistency in the database, then analyzing reasons, which can change the information people use to construct an attitude, causes attitude change. When there is a great deal of inconsistency, then attitudes change on their own, even when people do not analyze reasons. The reason for this, we suggest, is that the accessibility of the different contents of people's database is likely to vary over time. If these contents are highly inconsistent with each other, then changes in accessibility will lead to people to construct different attitudes on different occasions.

We acknowledge that our results do not provide direct evidence that people were constructing their attitudes. Our goal was not to test the attitudes-as-constructions model against competing models, but rather to illustrate that it is a useful means of conceptualizing attitude change, and can account for the fact that people's attitudes are often not as stable as traditional views of attitudes suggest (see Tourangeau, Rasinski, & D'Andrade, 1991, for a more direct test of a similar model). We find this model to be particularly helpful in understanding why people change their attitudes after explaining why they feel the way they do, what the limits of this change are, and why attitudes often change on their own, when people do not analyze reasons.

The results for the second category of strength measures were not as straight-forward. Consistent with our hypothesis that these measures are separable from the consistency measures, they did not correlate highly with belief homogeneity or affective-cognitive consistency, and had different effects on attitude stability. The direction of some of the effects of these measures, however, were unexpected. We must await further studies to see how reliable these findings are.

In summary, it is clear, as noted by Raden (1985) and Abelson (1988), that attitude strength is not a unitary construct. Nor is it the case, we suggest, that different measures of strength have similar effects on at least one important outcome variable: attitude stability. Our investigation of attitude stability suggests one way of classifying strength variables into two categories: those that assess the consistency of people's database about the attitude object, and those that measure the strength and accessibility of people's evaluations. Undoubtedly other useful classifications will be discovered in future research. In the meantime, a clear implication is that it would be unwise for researchers to commit themselves prematurely to one or two measures, assuming that they are good proxies for all alternative measures of attitude strength.

ACKNOWLEDGMENTS

The writing of this chapter was supported by a National Science Foundation Graduate Fellowship to Sara Hodges and National Institute of Mental Health Grant MH41841 to Timothy Wilson.

REFERENCES

Abelson, R. P. (1986). Beliefs are like possessions. *Journal for the Theory of Social Behaviour, 16*, 223–250.

Abelson, R. P. (1988). Conviction. *American Psychologist, 43*, 267–275.

Allport, G. W. (1935). Attitudes. In C. Murchison (Ed.), *A handbook of social psychology* (pp. 798–844). Worcester, MA: Clark University Press.

Bargh, J. A., Chaiken, S., Govender, R., & Pratto, F. (1992). The generality of the automatic activation effect. *Journal of Personality and Social Psychology, 62*, 893–912.

Bassili, J. (1993). Response latency versus certainty as indexes of the strength of voting intentions in a CATI survey. *Public Opinion Quarterly, 57*, 54–61.

Bennett, W. L. (1975). *The political mind and the political environment.* Lexington, MA: D.C. Heath.

Bishop, G. D., Hamilton, D. L., & McConahay, J. B. (1980). Attitudes and nonattitudes in the belief systems of mass publics. *The Journal of Social Psychology, 110*, 53–64.

Breckler, S. J., & Wiggins, E. C. (1989). Affect versus evaluation in the structure of attitudes. *Journal of Experimental Social Psychology, 25,* 253–271.

Brown, S. R. (1970). Consistency and the persistence of ideology. *Public Opinion Quarterly, 34,* 60–68.

Chaiken, S. (1980). Heuristic versus systematic information processing and the use of source versus message cues in persuasion. *Journal of Personality and Social Psychology, 39,* 752–756.

Converse, P. E. (1964). The nature of belief systems in mass publics. In D. E. Apter (Ed.), *Ideology and discontent* (pp. 206–261). London: Free Press of Glencoe.

Cook, T. D., & Flay, B. R. (1978). The persistence of experimentally induced attitude change. In L. Berkowitz (Ed.), *Advances in experimental social psychology* (Vol. 11, pp. 1–57). New York: Academic.

Fazio, R. H. (1986). How do attitudes guide behavior? In R. M. Sorrentino & E. T. Higgins (Eds.), *The handbook of motivation and cognition: Foundations of social behavior* (pp. 204–243). New York: Guilford.

Fazio, R. H. (1989). On the power and functionality of attitudes: The role of attitude accessibility. In A. R. Pratkanis, S. J. Breckler, & A. G. Greenwald (Eds.), *Attitude structure and function* (pp. 153–179). Hillsdale, NJ: Lawrence Erlbaum Associates.

Fazio, R. H., Powell, M. C., & Williams, C. J. (1989). The role of attitude accessibility in the attitude-to-behavior process. *Journal of Consumer Research, 16,* 280–288.

Fazio, R. H., & Williams, C. J. (1986). Attitude accessibility as a moderator of the attitude-behavior relation: An investigation of the 1984 presidential election. *Journal of Personality and Social Psychology, 51,* 505–514.

Fazio, R. H., & Zanna, M. P. (1981). Direct experience and attitude-behavior consistency. In L. Berkowitz (Ed.), *Advances in experimental social psychology* (Vol. 14, pp. 161–202). New York: Academic.

Feldman, J. M., & Lynch, J. G. Jr. (1988). Self-generated validity and other effects of measurement on belief, attitude, intention, and behavior. *Journal of Applied Psychology, 73,* 421–435.

Hahn, H. (1970). The political impact of shifting attitudes. *Social Science Quarterly, 51,* 730–742.

Hodges, S. D., & Wilson, T. D. (1993). Effects of analyzing reasons on attitude change: The moderating role of attitude accessibility. *Social Cognition, 11,* 353–366.

Hovland, C. I. (1959). Reconciling conflicting results derived from experimental and survey studies of attitude change. *American Psychologist, 14,* 8–17.

Kaplan, K. (1972). On the ambivalence-indifference problem in attitude theory and measurement: A suggested modification of the semantic differential technique. *Psychological Bulletin, 77,* 361–372.

Krosnick, J. A. (1988). Attitude importance and attitude change. *Journal of Experimental Social Psychology, 24,* 240–255.

Krosnick, J. A., & Abelson, R. P. (1991). The case for measuring attitude strength in surveys. In J. Tanur (Ed.), *Questions about survey questions* (pp. 177–203). New York: Russell Sage Foundation.

Krosnick, J. A., Boninger, D. S., Chuang, Y. C., Berent, M. K., & Carnot, C. G. (1993). Attitude strength: One construct or many related constructs? *Journal of Personality and Social Psychology, 65,* 1132–1151.

Marwell, G., Aiken, M., & Demerath, N. J. (1987). The persistence of political attitudes among 1960s civil rights activists. *Public Opinion Quarterly, 51,* 359–375.

Millar, M. G., & Tesser, A. (1986). Effects of affective and cognitive focus on the attitude-behavior relationship. *Journal of Personality and Social Psychology, 51,* 270–276.

Millar, M. G., & Tesser, A. (1989). The effects of affective-cognitive consistency and thought on the attitude-behavior relation. *Journal of Experimental Social Psychology, 25,* 189–202.

Nisbett, R. E., & Wilson, T. D. (1977). Telling more than we can know: Verbal reports on mental processes. *Psychological Review, 84,* 231–259.

Norman, R. (1975). Affective-cognitive consistency, attitudes, conformity, and behavior. *Journal of Personality and Social Psychology, 32,* 83–91.

Pelham, B. W. (1991). On confidence and consequence: The certainty and importance of self-knowledge. *Journal of Personality and Social Psychology, 60,* 518-530.

Petty, R. E., & Cacioppo, J. T. (1981). *Attitudes and persuasion: Classic and contemporary approaches.* Dubuque, IA: William C. Brown.

Petty, R. E., & Cacioppo, J. T. (1986). *Communication and persuasion: Central and peripheral routes to attitude change.* New York: Springer-Verlag.

Raden, D. (1985). Strength-related attitude dimensions. *Social Psychology Quarterly, 48,* 312-330.

Rosenberg, M. J. (1960). A structural theory of attitude dynamics. *Public Opinion Quarterly, 24,* 319-340.

Rosenberg, M. J. (1968). Hedonism, inauthenticity, and other goals toward expansion of a consistency theory. In R. P. Abelson, E. Aronson, W. J. McGuire, T. M. Newcomb, M. J. Rosenberg, & P. H. Tannenbaum (Eds.), *Theories of consistency: A sourcebook* (pp. 73-111). Chicago: Rand McNally.

Schuman, H., & Presser, S. (1981), *Questions and answers in attitude surveys.* New York: Academic.

Schwarz, N., & Bless, H. (1992). Constructing reality and its alternatives: An inclusion/exclusion model of assimilation and contrast effects in social judgment. In A. Tesser & L. Martin (Eds.), *The construction of social judgment* (pp. 217-245). Hillsdale, NJ: Lawrence Erlbaum Associates.

Sherif, C. W., Kelly, M., Rodgers, H. L. Jr., Sarup, G., & Tittler, B. I. (1973). Personal involvement, social judgment, and action. *Journal of Personality and Social Psychology, 27,* 311-328.

Sherif, M., & Cantril, H. (1947). *The psychology of ego-involvements: Social attitudes and identifications.* New York: Wiley.

Sherif, M., & Hovland, C. I. (1961). *Social judgment: Assimilation and contrast effects in communication and attitude change.* New Haven, CT: Yale University Press.

Strack, F., & Martin, L. L. (1987). Thinking, judging, and communicating: A process account of context effects in attitude surveys. In H. J. Hippler, N. Schwarz, & S. Sudman (Eds.), *Social information processing and survey methodology* (pp. 123-148). New York: Springer-Verlag.

Tesser, A. (1978). Self-generated attitude change. In L. Berkowitz (Ed.), *Advances in experimental social psychology* (Vol. 11, pp. 289-338). New York: Academic.

Tourangeau, R., & Rasinski, K. A. (1988). Cognitive processes underlying context effects in attitude measurement. *Psychological Bulletin, 103,* 299-314.

Tourangeau, R., & Rasinski, K. A., & D'Andrade, R. (1991). Attitude structure and belief accessibility. *Journal of Experimental Social Psychology, 27,* 48-75.

Watts, W. A. (1967). Relative persistence of opinion change induced by active compared to passive participation. *Journal of Personality and Social Psychology, 5,* 4-15.

Wilson, T. D. (1990). Self-persuasion via self-reflection. In J. Olson & M. P. Zanna (Eds.), *Self-inference processes: The Ontario Symposium* (Vol. 6, pp. 43-67). Hillsdale, NJ: Lawrence Erlbaum Associates.

Wilson, T. D., & Dunn, D. S. (1986). Effects of introspection on attitude-behavior consistency: Analyzing reasons versus focusing on feelings. *Journal of Experimental Social Psychology, 22,* 249-263.

Wilson, T. D., Dunn, D. S., Bybee, J. A., Hyman, D. B., & Rotondo, J. A. (1984). Effects of analyzing reasons on attitude-behavior consistency. *Journal of Personality and Social Psychology, 47,* 5-16.

Wilson, T. D., Dunn, D. S., Kraft, D., & Lisle, D. J. (1989). Introspection, attitude change, and attitude-behavior consistency: The disruptive effects of explaining why we feel the way we do. In L. Berkowitz (Ed.), *Advances in experimental social psychology* (Vol. 22, pp. 249-263). San Diego, CA: Academic.

Wilson, T. D., & Hodges, S. D. (1992). Attitudes as temporary constructions. In A. Tesser & L. Martin (Eds.), *The construction of social judgment* (pp. 37-65). Hillsdale, NJ: Lawrence Erlbaum Associates.

Wilson, T. D., Hodges, S. D., & Pollack, S. E. (1992). *Effects of explaining attitudes on attitude stability: Moderating effects of the consistency of people's data base.* Unpublished manuscript, University of Virginia.

Wilson, T. D., & Kraft, D. (1993). Why do I love thee? Effects of repeated introspections on attitudes toward the relationship. *Personality and Social Psychology Bulletin, 19*, 409–418.

Wilson, T. D., Kraft, D., & Dunn, D. S. (1989). The disruptive effects of explaining attitudes: The moderating effect of knowledge about the attitude object. *Journal of Experimental Social Psychology, 25*, 379–400.

Wilson, T. D., Lisle, D., Schooler, J., Hodges, S. D., Klaaren, K. J., & LaFleur, S. J. (1993). Introspecting about reasons can reduce post-choice satisfaction. *Personality and Social Psychology Bulletin, 19*, 331–339.

Wilson, T. D., & Schooler, J. (1991). Thinking too much: Introspection can reduce the quality of preferences and decisions. *Journal of Personality and Social Psychology, 60*, 181–192.

Wood, W. (1982). Retrieval of attitude-relevant information from memory: Effects on susceptibility of persuasion and on intrinsic motivation. *Journal of Personality and Social Psychology, 21*, 73–85.

Wood, W., Kallgren, C. A., & Preisler, R. M. (1985). Access to attitude-relevant information in memory as a determinant of persuasion: The role of message attributes. *Journal of Experimental Social Psychology, 21*, 73–85.

Zaller, J., & Feldman, S. (1992). A simple theory of the survey response: Answering questions versus revealing preferences. *American Journal of Political Science, 36*, 579–616.

Zanna, M. P., & Rempel, J. K. (1988). Attitudes: A new look at an old concept. In D. Bar-Tal & A. W. Kruglanski (Eds.), *The social psychology of knowledge* (pp. 315–334). Cambridge: Cambridge University Press.

18
▼▼▼▼▼▼▼

Measures and Manipulations of Strength-Related Properties of Attitudes: Current Practice and Future Directions

Duane T. Wegener
Yale University

John Downing
Jon A. Krosnick
Richard E. Petty
Ohio State University

As the chapters in this volume illustrate, a variety of properties of attitudes are associated with the strength-related outcomes of persistence, resistance to change, and impact on judgments and behavior. Investigations of strength-related properties of attitudes include studies of the causes and consequences of these properties and the relations among them. Of course, such investigations rely on the ability of researchers to identify, create, or influence strength properties of attitudes.

In this chapter, we discuss a number of methodological considerations in the study of attitude strength. We describe some common measures and manipulations that have been used to study attitude strength, focusing on those constructs highlighted in this volume. We also note potential problems in the current use of the measurement and manipulation approaches, and we propose future directions for research.

GENERAL TECHNIQUES FOR STUDYING ATTITUDE STRENGTH

Three general approaches to studying attitude strength have been used in the literature: manipulation, measurement, and known groups. In the following sections, we describe the use of these general techniques.

Manipulation

Manipulation refers to the random assignment of research participants to groups that differ in some experimental treatment. Such manipulations are generally designed to vary only one particular strength-related construct (e.g., attitude accessibility).

The manipulation approach has often been used in studies of attitude objects about which research participants have had little or no preexperimental experience, perhaps in part because such stimuli allow the greatest amount of experimental control. This technique has also been used on occasion for attitude objects about which people have a great deal of preexperimental experience. In such cases, the effectiveness of the manipulation is often dependent on the preexisting properties of the attitudes. For example, it might be difficult to create differences in the amount of thought associated with an attitude object if people have already thought a great deal about it. It might be much easier to create such differences if the target attitude object is one about which people have not engaged in much prior thinking. In general, researchers dealing with already formed attitudes should be attentive to the initial level of the construct that they wish to modify. If the baseline level is already quite high (e.g., high attitudinal confidence), manipulation could likely reduce this level (i.e., reduce confidence) but it might be difficult to increase it further. The reverse holds if the baseline level of the construct is quite low.

Measurement

Whereas manipulations of variables related to attitude strength are designed to create differences in strength-related dimensions of attitudes, measurement procedures attempt to assess an individual's (or, in some cases, a group's) existing level of the attitude dimension(s) under study. The measurement approach is often used when a study includes attitude objects for which existing dimensions of attitudes are likely to evidence substantial variability, and when manipulation of the desired attitude dimensions might be difficult.

Perhaps because of the conceptual similarities (and relationships) among some of the dimensions of attitudes related to attitude strength, researchers have sometimes measured differing strength dimensions in very similar ways. For example, Aldrich, Sullivan, and Borgida (1989) used 1984 survey data in which people had been asked to rank 14 political issues in order of their importance to "the country as a whole" and "to themselves personally," as an index of *attitude accessibility* (i.e., how easily the topic comes to mind). This measure, however, is very similar to measures of *attitude importance* that have been used by Krosnick and his colleagues (e.g., Krosnick, 1989). Similarly some researchers have studied *direct experience* with smoking using questions such as, "How often do you talk about smoking cigarettes?" (Sherman, Presson, Chassin, Bensenberg, Corty, &

Olshavsky, 1982), which is quite similar to questions used by other researchers to assess accessibility (e.g., Brown, 1974). Thus, if one simply follows the labels that have been given to measures in the past literature, one might use almost identical measures to index conceptually distinct attitude properties. Our goal for this chapter, therefore, is not to review all of the measures (or manipulations) that people have used to investigate the various dimensions of attitudes related to attitude strength. Instead, we attempt to review measures and manipulations that: (a) are relatively distinct from the measures and manipulations of other attitudinal dimensions, and (b) map relatively directly onto the defining features of the attitudinal dimension under study.

Known Groups

The known groups technique examines attitude strength by identifying groups assumed to differ on a particular variable. That is, some characteristic of a group of people serves as a proxy for the variable of interest. In one of the most well-known uses of this technique, the Sherifs and their colleagues studied attitudes that were high versus low in "ego-involvement" by comparing the attitudes of individuals who did and did not belong to particular groups (e.g., by comparing prohibition attitudes of members of the Women's Christian Temperance Union with prohibition attitudes of people not belonging to this group; Hovland, Harvey, & Sherif, 1957; see also Sherif, Sherif, & Nebergall, 1965). In studies of direct experience with attitude objects, known groups have been identified by such indices as where people in the group live (in a study of direct experience with a housing crisis; Regan & Fazio, 1977) and whether or not women in the group have given birth on a prior occasion (in a study of direct experience with breast-feeding; Manstead, Proffitt, & Smart, 1983). The known groups technique has not been used as much as measurement or manipulation in research regarding attitude strength. This is likely due to the fact that groups assumed to differ on one strength dimension are likely to also differ on other dimensions.

Although we focus in this chapter on the techniques of measurement and manipulation, this is not because we view the known groups technique as unimportant. The known groups technique has been used profitably in studies of strength-related properties of attitudes such as direct experience (e.g., Manstead et al., 1983; Regan & Fazio, 1977), personal relevance (e.g., Howard-Pitney, Borgida, & Omoto, 1986; Sivacek & Crano, 1982), and attitude extremity (e.g., Judd & Johnson, 1981). In addition, the known groups technique could prove very useful in applications of research findings regarding attitude strength. For example, there might often be situations in which someone implementing a program would want to identify people who differ in strength-related properties of attitudes even though no opportunity for measurement or manipulation exists. In such cases, the person implementing the program might be able to identify known groups that relate to one or more strength properties.

In the purest form of the known groups technique, measurement of the dimension along which the groups are believed to differ would not take place, but some researchers have included a measurement of the construct to verify that the classification was accurate (e.g., see Howard-Pitney et al., 1986; Judd & Johnson, 1981). When this measurement is done, the known groups technique can function in a way identical to the measurement approach presented in the previous section, in that subjects can be classified on the basis of the measured strength property rather than the group classification.

In contrast to the known groups technique, at least in principle the procedures associated with manipulation and measurement can address the problem of confounding alternative dimensions with the dimension under investigation. In the case of measurement, this is achieved through conducting analyses that statistically control for the impact of any variables associated with the variable of interest that might plausibly be responsible for the observed effects of the variable—assuming that these control variables have been measured. The manipulations approach attempts to avert confounding by carefully creating variance only in the dimension under investigation. Unfortunately, ideal manipulations rarely exist. As a result, researchers often include manipulation checks that attempt to isolate the extent to which the construct of interest has been affected by the manipulation above and beyond the effects of the manipulation on other potentially related constructs. In this way, the manipulation and measurement procedures have much in common and have advantages over the use of a known groups procedure in which no measures of the critical and alternative constructs are taken.

MEASURES AND MANIPULATIONS OF SPECIFIC STRENGTH-RELATED DIMENSIONS

In the following sections, we provide examples of measures and manipulations that have been used to examine strength-related constructs in past empirical research. These examples are not exhaustive. Rather, they are a set of exemplars meant to provide a resource for researchers interested in investigating the attitudinal dimensions related to attitude strength that are featured in this volume. In order to accomplish this, we present measures and manipulations that have been commonly used in the literature and that can be applied across multiple attitude domains. When possible, we present the specific wording of questions assessing the construct associated with attitude strength and/or the response alternatives offered. We also include as much detail as possible regarding the procedures used in manipulations of the construct(s).

Each of the following sections begins with a conceptual definition of the construct and presents samples of measures that have been used in the past. Each entry also contains examples or suggestions for manipulations of the construct, with descriptions of both experimental treatments and control (comparison) conditions. To ease location, the strength-related constructs are presented alphabetically.

Accessibility

Attitude accessibility refers to the ease with which an evaluation comes to mind when one encounters an attitude object (see Fazio, ch. 10, this volume).

Measurement

Response Latency. Researchers often operationalize accessibility as the amount of time between the presentation of an attitude object and the individual's reported evaluation of it (Fazio, Chen, McDonel, & Sherman, 1982). This response latency is typically assessed with a computer that times the delay between presentation of the attitude object and the moment the subject provides an evaluation of the object by pressing a computer key (Fazio, 1986; see Fazio & Williams, 1986, for similar measures using a small microprocessor and a multitrack audio-recorder in the field).

Attitude accessibility has also been measured in computer-assisted telephone interviews. For example, Bassili and Fletcher (1991) had the interviewer press the space bar on a computer keyboard, triggering a computer clock, when he or she uttered the last word in an attitudinal inquiry. A "voice-key" in the computer recorded how long it took the respondent to utter the first sound following the end of the attitudinal inquiry.

To reduce variability in response-time data, one can take the following precautions: instruct research participants to respond as quickly and accurately as possible; include practice trials to familiarize participants with the task; use filler trials so that data adjustments can be made; and use a two-alternative response framework (e.g., yes/no, like/dislike; see Fazio, 1990).

Self-Reports. Although no direct self-report measures of attitude accessibility have been used (e.g., "How easily or quickly does your attitude come to mind when you encounter attitude object X?"), some indirect measures have been developed. For example, one approach to measuring accessibility might be to ask people how often they think or talk about the attitude object. This method assumes that the more accessible the attitude is, the more an individual will report thinking or talking about it. For example, Brown (1974) asked people questions such as: "About how often do you have thoughts about the law?" with response alternatives of "very often," "often," "sometimes," "seldom," and "never."

Manipulation

Experimental Treatments. Manipulations of attitude accessibility typically involve having respondents express the attitude(s) repeatedly. The more often an attitude is expressed, the more accessible it becomes. Consequently, some researchers have asked people to copy their attitudinal responses several times on a number of identical response scales (e.g., Fazio et al., 1982) or to make numerous responses on scales with different evaluative anchors (e.g, like–dislike, good–bad, approve–disapprove). Responses have been made in writing (e.g., Powell & Fazio, 1984), orally (e.g., Bassili & Fletcher, 1991), or via a computer keyboard (e.g., Fazio, 1986).

Comparison Groups. Researchers generally use comparison groups that evaluate the attitude object on fewer occasions than the high accessibility group (e.g., Fazio et al., 1982). Occasionally, in order to control for the number of times that research participants encounter the attitude object, researchers have asked comparison groups to respond to nonevaluative questions regarding the object on as many occasions as the high-accessibility group responds to evaluative questions. Nonevaluative responding (such as noting whether a word has one syllable or not; see Fazio, Sanbonmatsu, Powell, & Kardes, 1986) does not increase attitude accessibility to the same extent as evaluative responding.

Ambivalence

Ambivalence refers to the extent to which one's reactions to an attitude object are evaluatively mixed in that both positive (favorable) and negative (unfavorable) elements are included (see Thompsen, Zanna, & Griffin, ch. 14, this volume).

Measurement

Combining Positive and Negative Reactions. Measures of ambivalence are generally constructed by independently assessing the positive and negative reactions associated with an object and then combining those indices into an ambivalence measure. For example, Hass, Katz, Rizzo, Bailey, and Moore (1992) assessed ambivalence by first asking research participants to fill out a questionnaire that consisted of 10 pro-African-American and 10 anti-African-American statements, each with a 6-point agree–disagree response format (i.e., from 0 = "strongly agree" to 5 = "strongly disagree"). Pro-African-American items included "Many Whites show a real lack of understanding of the problems that Blacks face." Anti-African-American statements included "Black children would do better in school if their parents had better attitudes about learning" (see Katz & Hass, 1988, for the entire set of questions). In order to compute the ambivalence measure, Hass et al. (1992) converted the scores to standard normal (t) scores using the total sample distribution. Then, the ambivalence score was obtained by multiplying the overall pro and anti scores (see Hass, Katz, Rizzo, Bailey, & Eisenstadt, 1991, for a discussion of this computation of ambivalence scores).

Other ways of combining independent assessments of positive and negative reactions to assess ambivalence have also been proposed (see Breckler, in press, for a review). For example, Kaplan (1972) proposed that ambivalence be assessed as "total affect" toward the object (i.e., the sum of positive and negative reactions) minus the "polarity" toward the object (i.e., the absolute value of the difference between the number of positive and negative reactions). If one classifies the category of reaction (positive or negative) that has the smaller number as "conflicting reactions" and classifies the category of reaction that has the largest number as "dominant reactions," then Kaplan's (1972) formulation of ambivalence reduces to ambivalence being a function of only the number of conflicting reactions (i.e., the higher the number of reactions that conflict with other reactions, the higher the level of ambivalence).

In contrast, Thompson et al. (ch. 14, this volume) proposed that increased similarity between positive and negative reactions (i.e., a smaller difference between the number of dominant and conflicting reactions) and increased intensity of those reactions [i.e., a higher average of the number of dominant and conflicting reactions—(dominant + conflicting)/2] increases ambivalence. Thus, in order to construct overall ambivalence indices, Thompson et al. compute the difference between intensity of reactions and similarity of reactions (i.e., to the extent that the number of dominant and conflicting reactions are highly similar, less is subtracted from the intensity portion of the model).

Self-Report. Direct assessments of how mixed or conflicted respondents feel toward the attitude object have also been used as measures of ambivalence. For example, Tourangeau, Rasinski, Bradburn, and D'Andrade (1989) asked respondents the dichotomous question, "Would you say that you are strongly on one side or the other on the <blank> issue, or would you say your feelings are mixed?"

Manipulation

One could manipulate ambivalence by providing research participants with differing proportions of positive versus negative information about an unfamiliar attitude object. For example, Priester and Petty (1993) gave people positive and negative traits about a hypothetical target person. Measures of ambivalence, both self-report and those based on combining separately assessed positive and negative reactions (e.g., Kaplan, 1972), increased as the number of traits that conflicted with one another increased.

Certainty

Certainty refers to the confidence with which an individual holds an attitude: The more confidently an individual believes the attitude to be correct, the more certainty is present (see Gross, Holtz, & Miller, ch. 9, this volume).

Measurement

Certainty has generally been measured using self-reports. For example, Sample and Warland (1973) used a 15-item Likert scale to determine people's attitudes toward student government. After completing the scale, respondents were asked to indicate on a scale of 1 (not certain) to 5 (very certain) how certain they were of each of their 15 responses. The 15 certainty items were then averaged; people with an average of 4 or higher on the certainty scores were considered highly certain, whereas people with an average of less than 4 were considered low in certainty.

Another measure of certainty involves asking respondents to make one overall rating of the certainty of their attitudes. For instance, Fazio and Zanna (1978a) assessed individuals' attitudes toward participating in psychological experiments. After they completed this scale, respondents were then asked "How certain do you feel about your attitude toward volunteering to act as a subject?" on a 9-point scale anchored with 1 = "certain" and 9 = "not certain." Similarly, Fazio and Zanna (1978b) asked research participants to rate their overall certainty in five attitudinal responses on a 7-point scale with 1 = "no confidence at all" and 7 = "extreme confidence." Because some researchers have regarded certainty as the strength of the belief system underlying the attitude, those researchers have measured the certainty of beliefs directly, instead of measuring the certainty of the attitude. Fishbein and Ajzen (1975) used a two-step process to determine the certainty of beliefs. First, beliefs about an attitude object were elicited in a pretest measure, and subsequently people were asked to rate the probabilities that the attributes were actually associated with the object. The greater the probability that an attribute is associated with the object, the more certain the belief.

Manipulation

Experimental Treatment.   Manipulations of certainty involve changing the confidence people have in their attitudes. For example, Fazio and Zanna (1978b) told research participants that the study involved assessment of attitudes and certainty of attitudes toward five different puzzle-type problems. Research participants were then told that "People have been able to devise physiological measures of certainty, and since we want to get as accurate measurements as we can, we decided to couple a self-report measure of attitude with a physiological measure of certainty." Participants were shown the supposed certainty instrument, told that it would measure both heart rate and skin conductance via two electrodes attached on the fingers, and then were notified of its similarity to a lie detector.

The instrument was actually a meter with points demarcated every five units from −100 to +100. Participants were told that the negative end of the scale was the part used for lie detection and that it was not connected for the experiment because people were not expected to lie. The experimenter then explained that the positive half of the scale was the confidence measure—the larger the scale reading, the more confidence an individual had in his or her attitude. Finally, participants were given the attitude scales referring to the 5 problems and were instructed to write down the certainty rating indicated by the certainty instrument next to each of their attitudinal responses. For subjects in the high certainty condition the meter registered a response of approximately 70 for each of the five attitude questions.

Comparison Group. For participants in the low certainty condition of Fazio and Zanna (1978b), the meter indicated an average rating of 20 for each of the attitude questions.

Elaboration

Elaboration is the extent to which an individual has carefully scrutinized and thought about the merits of information relevant to the attitude object (see Petty, Haugtvedt, & Smith, ch. 5, this volume).

Measurement

Thought Listing. A primary tool used in the measurement of elaboration is the thought-listing or "cognitive response" procedure (e.g., Brock, 1967; Green-wald, 1968). In this technique, research participants encounter an attitude object and are then given 2 to 3 minutes to list as many thoughts about the object as possible. For example, Petty and Cacioppo (1977) told research participants that:

> We are now interested in what you were thinking about during the last few minutes. You might have had ideas all favorable to the recommendation, all opposed, all irrelevant . . . or a mixture of the three. Any case is fine; simply list what it was that you were thinking during the last few minutes. The next page contains the form we have prepared for you to use to record your thoughts and ideas. Simply write down the first idea that comes to mind in the first box, the second idea in the second box, etc. . . . You should try to record only those ideas that you were thinking during the last few minutes. Please state your thoughts and ideas as concisely as possible . . . a phrase is sufficient. Ignore spelling, grammar, and punctuation. You will have 2.5 minutes to write your thoughts.

Following listing of the thoughts, either the research participants or independent judges categorize the thoughts into meaningful units (e.g., thoughts favorable, unfavorable, or neutral toward the advocacy of the persuasive message; Cacioppo, Harkins, & Petty, 1981). Some researchers have indexed the amount of elaboration by counting the number of thoughts generated about the attitude object (e.g., Burnkrant & Howard, 1984), with greater elaboration being indicated by a larger number of generated thoughts.

At the group level, a profile of thought favorability might be used to index the extent of thinking, even if the total number of thoughts does not differ across conditions. For example, if the study employs a manipulation of argument quality (e.g., Petty & Cacioppo, 1979b), greater elaboration would be indexed within each condition by a profile of thoughts that better reflects the quality of the issue relevant arguments presented (e.g., a greater proportion of favorable thoughts in response to strong as opposed to weak arguments within a certain level of the variable under study; see Petty & Cacioppo, 1986). Elaboration can also be measured by correlating a favorability index of the thoughts (e.g., subtracting the number of unfavorable thoughts from the number of favorable thoughts and dividing by the total number of thoughts, see Cacioppo et al., 1981) with the favorability of respondents' attitudes. Stronger correlations between thoughts and attitudes indicate that the attitude reflects greater message-relevant thinking (e.g., Chaiken, 1980; Petty & Cacioppo, 1979b).

Argument Quality. Because greater elaboration is associated with greater scrutiny of information relevant to the attitude object, the level of elaboration in a group has also been inferred from the extent to which strong (compelling) reasons in support of a position are more effective at persuading people to support the position than are weak (specious) reasons (Petty, Wells, & Brock, 1976). Argument quality is empirically defined according to the profile of thoughts elicited by the arguments when pretest subjects are instructed to think carefully about the content of the message (i.e., with strong arguments eliciting primarily favorable cognitive responses and weak arguments eliciting primarily unfavorable cognitive responses; see Petty & Cacioppo, 1986).

Self-Reported Cognitive Effort. One of the simplest methods for measuring elaboration is by asking respondents how much effort they expended in processing information relevant to the attitude object. For example, research participants might be asked "How much effort did you put into evaluating the communication?" (see Fukada, 1986; Petty, Harkins, Williams, & Latané, 1977). Alternatively, research participants might be asked the extent to which they generated "many thoughts" or "few thoughts" about a persuasive message (Batra & Ray, 1986).

Individual Differences in Need for Cognition. One might also measure individual differences in the likelihood of elaboration using the Need for Cognition scale (Cacioppo & Petty, 1982). This scale measures the extent to which people enjoy and engage in effortful cognitive endeavors using items such as "Thinking is not my idea of fun." This item is reverse-scored on a scale from 1 ("extremely uncharacteristic of me") to 5 ("extremely characteristic of me"). The most common form of the Need for Cognition scale consists of 18 items (see Cacioppo, Petty, & Kao, 1984), although subsets of the items have also been used with some success in survey research (e.g., Verplanken, 1991).

Manipulation

Experimental Treatments. Perhaps the most direct method for manipulating the amount of elaboration is to instruct research participants to think carefully about the information presented about the attitude object. Instructions of this sort have often been used in pretests of argument quality (see Petty & Cacioppo, 1986). Less direct instructions have also been used. For example, Pratkanis, Greenwald, Leippe, and Baumgardner (1988) asked subjects to "read each paragraph in the article twice. Read each paragraph first for what is said (content). Then read the same paragraph again (before going on to the next), this time paying attention to how it is said (style). As you read, underline the main point of each paragraph" (p. 213). Similar instructions were also used by Gruder, Cook, Hennigan, Flay, Alessis, and Halamaj (1978) and Watts and McGuire (1964).

In addition to instructions to elaborate, there are many variables known to affect the level of elaboration given to persuasive appeals. Many of these are reviewed by Petty et al. (ch. 5, this volume; see also Eagly & Chaiken, 1993; Petty, Priester, & Wegener, 1994). One variable that affects the extent of elaboration in a relatively direct manner is the level of distraction present in the context of the persuasive appeal (with higher levels of distraction corresponding to lower levels of ability to engage in elaborative thought). For example, research participants in Petty et al. (1976; Experiment 2) listened to a persuasive message while they attempted to record the location of Xs that appeared on a screen. In high-distraction conditions, Xs appeared every 5 seconds during the message whereas in the low distraction condition Xs appeared every 15 seconds. Another variable that has influenced the amount of message elaboration is the amount of personal responsibility respondents feel for evaluating the attitude-relevant information. For example, research participants in the high personal responsibility conditions of Petty, Harkins, and Williams (1980; Experiment 2) were told that they were the only person responsible for evaluating an editorial message, whereas low responsibility subjects were told that they were part of a group that was responsible.

Comparison Groups. When direct instructions to think are used to create high levels of elaboration, such conditions might be compared with conditions in which no such instructions are given. Comparison groups for distraction manipulations have included fewer distracting events or no distracting events (Petty et al., 1976). Low levels of personal responsibility have been created by telling research participants that many people share the responsibility of evaluating the message (Petty et al., 1980).

Extremity

Attitude extremity is the degree to which the favorability of an individual's attitude diverges from neutral (i.e., neither favorable nor unfavorable)—the further away from neutral the more extreme, regardless of valence (see Abelson, ch. 2, this volume; Judd & Brauer, ch. 3, this volume; and Tesser, Martin, & Mendolia, ch. 4, this volume).

Measurement

Measures of attitude extremity have generally assessed the amount by which an individual deviates from the midpoint of an attitude scale or scales. For example, Downing, Judd, and Brauer (1992) assessed extremity by calculating an absolute deviation score from the midpoint of a 29-point attitude scale anchored at 1 ("oppose") and 29 ("support") for each of 15 social issues (e.g., abortion rights, animal rights). Similarly, Van der Pligt, Ester, and Van der Lindern (1983) asked participants to report their attitudes toward building more nuclear power stations on a 5-point scale ranging from "strongly opposed" to "strongly in favor." People who responded either "strongly opposed" or "strongly in favor" were classified as holding extreme attitudes toward the object.

Manipulation

Experimental Treatments. Because increasing attitude extremity involves moving attitudes further from the neutral point on a scale, manipulations of attitude extremity might be viewed as producing attitude change. As such, any technique discussed in the attitude change literature (e.g., presenting participants with strong arguments delivered by a credible source, see Petty & Cacioppo, 1986, for a review) could be used to manipulate attitude extremity. However, one might view manipulations that do not provide recipients with any additional information about the object, such as repeated attitude expression, as relatively "pure" manipulations of attitude extremity, though it is possible for individuals to generate new thoughts on the issue even with these "pure" procedures.

Downing et al. (1992) demonstrated that having participants repeatedly express their attitudes on a dichotomous response scale (e.g., bad–good, harmful–beneficial) led to greater extremity in later expressions of attitudes on continuous response scales. In some cases, however, repeated attitudinal expression might not lead to greater extremity (e.g., repeating attitudes on a 9-point bipolar scale might allow respondents to recall the relative extremity of past responses, with commitment pressures leading to no extremity changes in later responses; see Downing et al., 1992).

One could also use mere exposure of the attitude object to make attitudes toward the object more extreme. For relatively novel stimuli (e.g., unfamiliar faces, foreign words, nonsense syllables), mere exposure (i.e., presenting the object to participants repeatedly) generally leads to increased positivity of opinions of the object, even if people who encounter the attitude object(s) do not recognize that they have seen the object(s) before (Kunst-Wilson & Zajonc, 1980; see Bornstein, 1989, for a review). For more meaningful stimuli, however, increased repetition of exposure enhances the dominant cognitive response to the object. For example, attitudes toward negative words (e.g., "hate") become more unfavorable, but attitudes toward positive words (e.g., "love") become more favorable, at least until the point of tedium (see Grush, 1976; Sawyer, 1981).

Similarly, research on mere thought has shown that instructing people to think about an initially likable or dislikable attitude object leads people to view the likable object more favorably and the dislikable object less favorably (Tesser, Martin, & Mendolia, ch. 4, this volume). Research has also indicated, however, that both moderation and polarization of attitudes can result from mere thought. Specifically, polarization (i.e., increased extremity) occurs only if participants have relatively well-integrated and consistent schemas to guide thought, and if participants are motivated to utilize their issue-relevant knowledge (Liberman & Chaiken, 1991; Tesser & Leone, 1977).

Comparison Groups. If persuasive messages are used to create extreme attitudes, then one might provide either no message or an ineffective message (i.e., a message that does not change attitudes) in the control condition (see Petty & Cacioppo, 1986). If one is using repeated attitude expression as a manipulation of extremity, the control group could consist of individuals who either did not complete any scales referring to the attitude object, completed fewer scales than the "extreme" group, or were asked nonevaluative questions about the object (similar to comparison groups used in manipulations of attitude accessibility; see Downing et al., 1992). Similarly, comparison groups for a mere exposure technique could simply encounter the attitude object on fewer occasions than high-exposure groups (Kunst-Wilson & Zajonc, 1980). If one uses mere thought as a manipulation of attitude extremity, the control group might not be instructed to think about the object or might be distracted from doing so (e.g., Sadler & Tesser, 1973).

Importance

Attitude importance refers to a person's perception of the amount of personal importance he or she attaches to an attitude (see Boninger, Krosnick, Berent, & Fabrigar, ch. 7, this volume).

Measurement

Attitude importance has generally been measured using self-reports of concern or caring about the attitude object (see Boninger et al., ch. 7, this volume, for the rationale for asking about the importance of the attitude object rather than the importance of the attitude itself). Researchers have used three basic types of questions to measure perceptions of importance. These include: (a) how important is the attitude object to you personally? (b) how deeply do you care about the attitude object? and (c) how concerned are you about the attitude object? (Krosnick, 1989). For example, Krosnick, Boninger, Chuang, Berent, and Carnot (1993) asked research participants: "How important would you say the issue of capital punishment is to you personally?" accompanied by a 7-point scale from 1 ("Extremely important") to 7 ("Not too important"). Similarly, they asked research participants "How much do you personally care about the issue of capital punishment?" accompanied by a 7-point scale anchored at 1 ("A great deal") and 7 ("Not at all").

Manipulation

Although no research has attempted to convince people that a particular issue should or should not be important to them, some researchers have manipulated the proposed origins of attitude importance. Personal relevance (stemming from self-interest, social identification, or value relevance; cf. Petty, Cacioppo, & Haugtvedt, 1992) has been identified as a proximal cause of attitude importance (Boninger, Krosnick, & Berent, in press). Therefore, manipulations of personal relevance (or of the factors that make up personal relevance) might serve to manipulate attitude importance.

Experimental Treatments.   Consistent with the idea that personal relevance is an origin of attitude importance, manipulations of high personal relevance have also created high levels of perceived personal importance (e.g., Brickner, Harkins, & Ostrom, 1986; Haugtvedt & Wegener, 1994).

Alternatively, Boninger et al. (in press) manipulated importance by using an imagination technique (Anderson, 1983). Research participants in the relevant scenario condition were instructed to imagine themselves in a horrific car accident, and then draw a series of five cartoon pictures depicting the accident and its aftermath. Participants were then asked to draw another sequence of five pictures depicting the same events in a different way. This increased the importance attached to attitudes on traffic safety.

Comparison Groups.   As described in a subsequent section of this chapter, comparison groups for manipulations of personal relevance often consist of topics that are being considered for a distant location or for some time in the future. In experiments that have manipulated importance through imagination scenarios, the comparison group consisted of research participants who imagined a scenario irrelevant to the topic of interest. For example, Boninger et al. (in press) had participants in the irrelevant scenario condition draw a sequence of cartoons about a spring vacation that did not go well.

Knowledge

Knowledge typically refers to the information stored in memory regarding an attitude object. Such information could include beliefs about attributes of the object, memories of one's past behaviors relevant to the object, or memories of feelings associated with the object (see Davidson, ch. 12, this volume; Wood, Rhodes, & Biek, ch. 11, this volume).

Measurement

Knowledge Listing. One method researchers have used for indexing this construct is the knowledge-listing task. For example, subjects are often given a brief period of time (e.g., 2 minutes) to list the characteristics and facts they believe to be true about the attitude object or issue, previous behaviors relevant to the object that they can recall, and so forth (e.g., Wood, Kallgren, & Preisler, 1985; see also Davidson, Yantis, Norwood, & Montano, 1985). Judges can then assess the number of distinct items listed by each respondent (e.g., Wood, 1982).

Quizzes. Other researchers have identified people's levels of knowledge by determining the accuracy of their responses to quizzes about the object or the general domain to which the object belongs. For example, Wilson, Kraft, and Dunn (1989; Experiment 1) asked respondents to answer open-ended factual questions about political candidates (e.g., "Which presidential candidate has been endorsed by the Teamsters Union?") to measure political knowledge. Quizzes utilizing multiple-choice questions have also been used. For example, Sidanius (1988) asked questions such as "What is the name of the major Black opposition group in South Africa? (a) The Congress of Racial Equality, (b) The African Peace and Freedom Congress, (c) South Africans for Freedom, (d) African National Congress, (e) None of the above" (see Sidanius, 1988, pp. 50–51; see also Lusk & Judd, 1988; Zaller, 1990).

Self-Perceptions. Self-reports of how knowledgeable people feel they are about an object have also been used. For instance, Davidson et al. (1985, Study 2) asked subjects to report how well-informed they were about an available flu shot on a 4-point scale ranging from "completely uninformed" to "completely informed" (see also Cacioppo & Petty, 1980). One might also use self-reports to assess how many memories people have that include the attitude object. For example, researchers have asked respondents to estimate the number of behaviors that they have performed toward the attitude object (e.g., Davidson et al., 1985; Fazio & Zanna, 1978a).

Manipulation

Experimental Treatments. Manipulations of knowledge involve presenting research participants with new information about the object or with new experiences of the object. Some manipulations of knowledge have enhanced the sheer amount of general attitude-relevant information that participants encounter. For example, Lewan and Stotland (1961) provided people in the high-knowledge group with information about the attitude object—a European region called Andorra (e.g., the region's geography, language, fiscal systems, etc.; see also Johnson, in press).

Other manipulations of knowledge have attempted to provide more specific information that enables recipients to scrutinize claims made about the object. For example, McMichael (1992) gave people information on the current status of their university (e.g., that currently, 30% of students find a job in their most preferred field immediately after graduation) that enabled them to determine whether a recommendation for the university (e.g., instituting comprehensive exams that would have the effect of making 60% of students find jobs in their most preferred field immediately after graduation) was merited or not.

Manipulations have also given people a greater amount of direct contact with the attitude object. For example, Regan and Fazio (1977; Study 2) gave research participants direct-experience with five puzzles that they were to "get acquainted with" by having participants work the puzzles for approximately 5 minutes (see also Songer-Nocks, 1976). Similar manipulations have been created by asking some research participants to taste a food product (e.g., Berger & Mitchell, 1989; Wu & Shaffer, 1987).

Comparison Groups. Some researchers have used a low-knowledge comparison group that receives information about an object other than the one of interest. For instance, Lewan and Stotland (1961) gave subjects in the low-knowledge condition information about a European region (i.e., Etruria) other than the region of interest. The pieces of information were from the same categories as those given to high-knowledge participants. Other researchers have used a low-knowledge group that receives no information about any object (e.g., McGuire, 1964).

Comparison groups for manipulations of direct experience often involve giving people information that is similar to that provided by the direct contact with the object but that includes no direct contact. For example, in the control group of the Regan and Fazio (1977) experiment, the experimenter orally presented 5 minutes of information about how the puzzles could be solved, including the completed solutions to each puzzle. When manipulations of direct experience involve experiences such as taste of a food product, indirect-experience participants are often given information about the taste and other qualities of the product derived from other participants' self-reports of their direct experiences with the product (e.g., Berger & Mitchell, 1989; Wu & Shaffer, 1987). In these cases, the amount of knowledge is held somewhat comparable, but the basis of the knowledge is varied (i.e., direct vs. indirect experience).

Personal Relevance

Personal relevance refers to the extent to which people believe that a topic or attitude object holds significant consequences for some aspect of their lives (e.g., their outcomes, values, possessions, groups; see Petty & Cacioppo, 1990; Petty et al., 1992). When the attitude topic has personal relevance, people are said to be personally involved with it (see Thomsen, Borgida, & Lavine, ch. 8, this volume). Some research has focused on particular components of personal relevance such as the extent to which the issue is connected to personal outcomes (e.g., in studies of vested interest, see Crano, ch. 6, this volume).

Measurement

Assessments of personal relevance have generally asked how likely the attitude object or issue is to affect the respondent personally, how relevant respondents perceive the issue to be, or how likely it is that a proposal affecting the respondent will be instituted (see Petty & Cacioppo, 1986). For example, Haugtvedt and Wegener (1994) asked research participants to rate their views of the topic of a communication on 11-point scales anchored with 1 ("not personally relevant" and "will not affect me") and 11 ("personally relevant" and "will affect me").

Similarly, in order to assess research participants' perceptions of personal relevance of the topic of instituting senior comprehensive exams, Sivacek and Crano (1982) asked participants to respond to 7-point scales assessing the extent to which respondents agreed with the statement: "It is very likely that I would have to take senior comprehensive exams if they become required as planned" (see also Petty & Cacioppo, 1984). Sivacek and Crano (1982) also used a 7-point scale asking to what extent respondents perceived the recommendation as likely to affect them (i.e., they provided ratings of agreement with the statement: "The issue of whether or not to require senior comprehensive exams at Michigan State University directly affects me").

Manipulation

Experimental Treatments. Manipulations of personal relevance have generally varied what Thomsen et al. (ch. 8, this volume) call self-interest, what Crano (ch. 6, this volume) calls vested-interest, and what Johnson and Eagly (1989) call outcome-involvement. For example, Petty and Cacioppo (1984) presented research participants with a message supposedly from the chairperson of the University Committee on Academic Policy at their university. Participants were informed that the function of the committee was to advise the chancellor on changes in academic policy that should be instituted. High personal relevance was created by further informing participants that the committee was working on academic changes that were to be initiated the next year, whereas low relevance subjects were told that the committee was making recommendations to take effect in 10 years. Similar variations in personal relevance have been created by describing changes as likely to occur either at the research participants' university or at a distant university (e.g., Apsler & Sears, 1968; Haugtvedt & Wegener, 1994; Petty & Cacioppo, 1979b).

Ostrom and Brock (1968) utilized a manipulation of high relevance in which beliefs about the attitude object were manipulated to become related to important values rather than immediate outcomes. That is, research participants first received a message that introduced the participant to a position (i.e., opposing Greenland's admittance into the Pan-American Bank), and were then given statements from the message a second time—each statement from the message being paired with a statement of a value potentially relevant to the message about Greenland's application. Participants were asked to rate the level of appropriateness between the excerpt from the message (i.e., the statement about Greenland) and the value on a 6-point scale from "completely appropriate" to "not at all appropriate." Next, participants were asked to circle a key word in each of the two statements in the pair and to draw a connecting line between them. High as opposed to low personal relevance was created by presenting different sets of value statements in this task. That is, high relevance was created by presenting value statements that had been rated as highly important by an earlier set of respondents.

Personal relevance has also been manipulated through variations of "outcome dependency." These manipulations generally lead research participants to believe that they will be interacting with a target person in some way and that experience with that person will have personal consequences for the research participant. For instance, Omoto and Borgida (1988) created high personal relevance of a target person by leading participants to believe that they were to date the target person for a series of three dates. In a related paradigm, Erber and Fiske (1984) created high personal relevance by instructing participants that a $20 prize would be given to each member of the pair that was able to work together to generate the best educational games for 8-year-olds using some wind-up toys available in the laboratory.

Comparison Groups. For manipulations of personal relevance that inform research participants that some policy will affect them in the near future, comparison groups have generally been told that the policy will either be implemented far in the future or in some other location (e.g., Axsom, Yates, & Chaiken, 1987; Petty & Cacioppo, 1979b). When manipulations of relevance include linking of attitude-relevant statements to important beliefs, the comparison group has been formed by providing value statements for the value-bonding task that have been rated as relatively unimportant by additional respondents (Ostrom & Brock, 1968). For manipulations of personal relevance that involve outcome dependency, the comparison group involves some condition in which the actions of the target person have relatively little effect on rewards and/or punishments to the research participant (e.g., playing a short puzzle game; Omoto & Borgida, 1988).

Structural Consistency

Structural consistency refers to the extent to which an attitude is evaluatively consistent with other attitudes (interattitudinal consistency; see Eagly & Chaiken, ch. 16, this volume), or with the beliefs, affect, or behavior associated with the attitude object (intra-attitudinal consistency: evaluative-cognitive, evaluative-affective, and evaluative-behavioral; see Chaiken, Pomeranz, & Giner-Sorolla, ch. 15, this volume).

Measurement

Intra-Attitudinal Consistency. Measures of intra-attitudinal structure have usually assessed consistency between the overall evaluation and one of the component classes of underlying structure (e.g., evaluative-affective consistency).

Measures of intra-attitudinal consistency have generally included an evaluation (attitude) measure that is either a single index of overall favorability toward the attitude object (e.g., a 9-point scale anchored with very favorable at one end and very unfavorable at the other end with the neutral point explicitly indicated; Norman, 1975) or a set of semantic-differential attitude scales (e.g., 7-point bipolar scales anchored with good vs. bad, positive vs. negative, etc.; e.g., Chaiken & Baldwin, 1981). The affective component of an evaluative-affective consistency measure typically assesses the extent to which the attitude object makes people feel particular affective states (e.g., Breckler & Wiggins, 1989). For example, Crites, Fabrigar, and Petty (1994) assessed research participants' feelings associated with a variety of attitude objects (e.g., snakes, capital punishment) by providing them with a set of semantic-differential affective scales (i.e., 7-point bipolar scales anchored with general emotions that could be associated with objects such as angry vs. relaxed, joy vs. sorrow, etc.; see also Chaiken et al., ch. 15, this volume). An overall evaluative-affective consistency index is formed by rescaling the evaluative and affective components to a common metric (e.g., through standardizing the scores) and computing a difference score between the evaluative and affective component measures (e.g., see Chaiken et al., ch. 15, this volume; Crites et al., 1994).

The cognitive component of an evaluative-cognitive consistency measure typically assesses the extent to which the attitude object possesses traits or attributes that hold favorable or unfavorable evaluative implications. For example, Crites et al. (1994) assessed research participants' cognitions associated with a variety of attitude objects by providing them with a set of semantic-differential cognitive scales (i.e., 7-point bipolar scales anchored with various general attributes of objects such as useful vs. useless, safe vs. unsafe, etc.; see also Erber, Hodges, & Wilson, ch. 17, this volume). The overall evaluative-cognitive consistency index is formed by rescaling the evaluative and cognitive components to a common metric and computing a difference score between the evaluative and cognitive component measures. This procedure parallels the assessment of the evaluative-affective consistency index just described.

Expectancy-value assessments (e.g., Fishbein & Ajzen, 1975) have also been used to assess the cognitive component of evaluative-cognitive consistency, although a parallel affective procedure has not been developed. In the expectancy-value procedure, the goals relevant to the attitude are determined in a pretest. Participants in the primary study rate both the extent to which the attitudinal position helps versus hinders attainment of the goal (instrumentality) and the desirability of goal attainment (value). A sum of the instrumentality × value products represents the cognitive component of evaluative-cognitive consistency (see Chaiken & Baldwin, 1981; Chaiken et al., ch. 15, this volume; Norman, 1975; Rosenberg, 1968). The overall evaluative–cognitive consistency measure could either be formed as previously described or by using the two-step procedure introduced by Rosenberg (1968). That is, research participants can be rank ordered in terms of their evaluation scores and again in terms of their cognitive scores. Then, the absolute value of the discrepancy between each participant's position in these two rankings serves as his or her evaluative-cognitive consistency score (Rosenberg, 1968).

Interattitudinal Consistency. Traditionally, interattitudinal consistency has been evaluated at a group level through correlations among measures of attitudes (with higher correlations presumably indicative of higher levels of consistency; e.g., Converse, 1964). Unfortunately, this measure of between-group differences suffers from at least three distortions due to: (a) between-group differences in measurement error, (b) differences in response variation, and (c) variations in the structural relations that people see among attitudes (i.e., different people might view the same attitudes as relating to one another in different ways; see Judd & Krosnick, 1989, pp. 103–107). In order to avoid these difficulties, one might assess interattitudinal consistency using analyses of covariance structures that correct for the impact of measurement error and response variance (e.g., Judd & Krosnick, 1982). In addition, one might utilize unstandardized regression coefficients that are less affected by response variance, estimate the reliabilities of the variables in each group and disattenuate the unstandardized regression coefficients, and examine only individuals who agree on the implicational relationships among attitude objects (Judd & Krosnick, 1989).

Few individual-level measures exist that assess interattitudinal consistency. In some cases, however, researchers have successfully used self-reports of the implicational links among attitude objects for this purpose. For example, Judd, Drake, Downing, and Krosnick (1991) asked research participants "If you knew where someone stood on Issue A, how confident would you be in predicting where he or she stood on Issue B?" The response options on a 7-point scale were anchored at "very confident" (1) and "not at all confident" (7).

Manipulation

Experimental Treatments. Although little work manipulating intra-attitudinal structure has taken place, there are at least a couple of methods that one might consider for doing so. For example, it has been proposed that mere thought

(Tesser, 1978) increases the consistency of stored knowledge underlying the attitude. That is, although some relatively well-integrated knowledge structure is required for the mere thought-polarization effect (e.g., Tesser & Leone, 1977), the knowledge base underlying the attitude becomes even more organized and consistent through mere thought about the object (see also McGuire, 1960a, 1960b). One might even be able to accomplish this within the categories of knowledge potentially underlying the attitude. For example, one could identify people who hold primarily affectively or cognitively based attitudes (e.g., Millar & Millar, 1990) and enhance consistency of the affective or cognitive base underlying the evaluation by having individuals think about the affective or cognitive bases of their attitudes.

Alternatively, one might attempt to manipulate intra-attitudinal structure by providing people with information about a novel attitude object that is either evaluatively consistent or inconsistent. A variety of possibilities exist. The information could be consistent or inconsistent with the attitude toward the object (i.e., creating differences in evaluative-affective or evaluative-cognitive consistency). In such a case, however, the new information about the object would have to be incorporated into the person's knowledge structure underlying the attitude without changing the attitude (or else people might end up with differences in attitude valence but no difference in intra-attitudinal consistency).

Consistency or inconsistency of intra-attitudinal structure could also be either within or across dimensions of information. For example, one might present research participants with affective information followed by evaluatively consistent or inconsistent cognitive information (creating differences in affective-cognitive consistency) or by evaluatively consistent or inconsistent affective information (creating differences in consistency of affective information). Importantly, in cases where both affective and cognitive information are presented, the order in which the information is received might create differences in the underlying base of the attitude, which has important consequences for which kinds of persuasive attempts successfully change the attitude (see Edwards, 1990; Millar & Millar, 1990).

Research attempting to manipulate interattitudinal structure has also been sparse. In a recent study, however, Judd and Downing (1990) asked people to repeatedly think about the relationships between pairs of attitude positions. That is, research participants were told that each screen of a computer program would present a question (e.g., "If you knew that someone favored 'Star Wars,' do you think they would favor or oppose capital punishment?") and that their job was to answer each question as quickly and accurately as possible. Presumably, the greater the number of repetitions of such responses, the greater the strength of the relations among attitudes (i.e., the higher the interattitudinal consistency).

Comparison Groups. If one were using mere thought to increase intra-attitudinal consistency, the comparison group would consist of individuals who either were not asked to think about the attitude object or were distracted from doing so (e.g., Sadler & Tesser, 1973). If one were to present information about novel attitude objects, the low-consistency group would receive information that is evaluatively inconsistent (cf., section on ambivalence). When researchers use repetition of thought about implicational relationships as a manipulation of interattitudinal consistency, the comparison group might be asked to think of each pair of attitudes few or no times.

INFERENCES BASED ON MEASURES AND MANIPULATIONS

Advances in the study of attitude strength depend on the ability of researchers to adequately identify, create, or influence dimensions of attitudes related to their strength. An equally important aspect of studies of attitude strength is the inferences that people make regarding the role of specific strength-related dimensions. That is, most of the attitude strength literature consists of measures or manipulations of a focal dimension that is found to relate to some hypothesized strength-related outcome. Upon finding this result, researchers often draw conclusions about the role of the specific dimension in affecting the strength-related outcome.

If research on attitude strength is to advance, however, it is necessary for researchers in the field to scrutinize the inferences that are made based on our current manipulations and measures. Perhaps the most important aspect of scrutinizing current conclusions regards potential confounds in manipulations and measures of strength-related attitude dimensions. In the following sections, we discuss the implications of this problem for manipulation and measurement procedures, and we present classes of future research that might improve our understanding of the manipulations and measures currently in use.

Measurement

Controlling for Confounds

It is always possible that measures of one attitude dimension covary with measures of other constructs. If so, confounded constructs could be responsible for an observed relation between the construct of interest and some strength-related outcome(s). To address this concern, in a complete measurement procedure, one would want to assess not only the dimension(s) of interest but also any competing variable(s) that might be responsible for the relation(s) between the dimension(s) of interest and the dependent measure. For example, consider a researcher who wishes to study the impact of attitude accessibility per se on attitude persistence using the measurement technique but realizes that differing amounts of thought given to the issue might also be responsible for the association between accessibility and persistence. Such a researcher should measure not only attitude accessibility and persistence but also amount of thought given to the issue. By taking these additional measures, the researcher can statistically control for the competing dimension (i.e., amount of thought) and thus better estimate the unique impact of the attitudinal property being studied (i.e., attitude accessibility).

In many cases, however, researchers include only measures of the focal dimension of interest (with no measures of alternative variables that might be responsible for the effects of interest in the study). In such cases, one cannot be sure that associations between the measured dimension and the outcome of interest are not due to an unmeasured third variable. This is not to say that one could reasonably expect researchers to measure *all* constructs potentially responsible for the effects of the variable under study—often the relations among these variables are not yet known, or practical considerations keep one from including the large number of measures that would be required to exhaust the range of variables potentially at work. Yet, researchers using the measurement approach should keep in mind that a relationship between a measured dimension and an outcome of interest could be due to an unmeasured third variable.

Importantly, when one measures dimensions of attitudes associated with attitude strength, the most likely dimensions to covary with such measures (and the most likely to provide potentially competing explanations of the data) are other dimensions of attitudes related to strength. Thus, if one attempts to investigate the *unique* impact of some strength-related dimension, measures of other strength-related properties are often the crucial constructs that must be statistically partialled in tests of the hypothesis under study. If this is not done, one might reach conclusions about one attitude dimension that are actually due to another attitude dimension.

Comparability of Measures

In developing measures of attitudinal dimensions related to strength, researchers must make both conceptual and methodological decisions. For instance, researchers must consider (and often define) the conceptual nature of the construct they wish to measure. At times, however, the nature of the construct might be broad enough to include measures that tap into aspects of the construct that might or might not cohere conceptually. Consider the construct of attitude-relevant knowledge. A variety of measures of knowledge have been proposed and used in the literature (e.g., knowledge listing, quizzes, self-reports). Do these varied measures index the same construct? To be sure, the measures are all related to and likely index differences in attitude-relevant knowledge. It might be, however, that aspects of these measures map onto classes of knowledge that have demonstrably different strength-related consequences.

Knowledge listing tasks are generally focused on information about the specific attitude object, whereas knowledge quizzes are often about a class of information that is related but not directly associated with the attitude object.

Also, quizzes tend to focus on the assessment of "accurate" information, whereas knowledge listings index the amount of information associated with an object whether accurate or not. Thus, although the two measures might be generally related, one can easily conceive of instances in which the two measures diverge (e.g., when one has a great deal of accurate general political knowledge but knows little or nothing about a particular political issue). One can imagine a variety of ways in which mechanisms associated with these two measures of knowledge might also differ. For example, subjective knowledge about a particular object might provide counterarguments to a persuasive appeal about the object (which could encourage resistance to change), whereas accurate knowledge about a domain of expertise related to the object (but not directly connected to the object) might or might not provide counterarguments to a persuasive appeal about the object. On the other hand, general knowledge might be more closely tied to resistance due to inter-attitudinal consistency pressures (see Eagly & Chaiken, ch. 16, this volume) than is object-specific knowledge.

Of course, similar issues arise for any attitudinal dimensions measured through self-reports of perceptions of the attitudinal dimension versus measures directed at quantifying the actual amount of the dimension. In the case of attitude-relevant knowledge, the actual information that people have associated with the object might have important meaning above and beyond the simple perception of having a large amount of knowledge, and the mere perception of being informed might sometimes have an impact beyond one's actual knowledge on an issue. Similar differences might be realized for other attitude dimensions such as perceived ambivalence versus the actual existence of conflicting reactions toward the attitude object, or perceived accessibility rather than the actual time it takes to retrieve one's attitude.

Manipulation

The informative value of a manipulation is determined at least in part by the purity of that manipulation. That is, a manipulation of a strength-related dimension is most informative to the extent that it creates differences only in the conceptual construct under investigation rather than in related constructs that potentially affect the outcome measure(s) in the study.[1] If a manipulation creates differences in more than one property of the attitude, the results of that study can only be interpreted as they relate to all of the dimensions affected by the

---

[1]In this context, it is important to note that random assignment serves only to equate groups on dimensions that have not been impacted by the manipulation. For example, consider an experiment in which attitude accessibility is examined using a manipulation that creates differences in attitude accessibility and direct experience. In such a case, random assignment equates the groups on factors other than direct experience and attitude accessibility, but differences in direct experience might be responsible for the results even though the manipulation was aimed at creating differences only in attitude accessibility.

manipulation.[2] Importantly, in studies of attitude strength, other strength-related properties of attitudes are the primary dimensions that might have been altered by manipulations of the focal attitude property.

Because manipulations of dimensions of attitude strength, like all manipulations, might affect more variables than is intended, evaluation of such studies should include some thought about related properties of attitudes that might also have been affected by the manipulation. If multiple properties of the attitude are likely affected by a given manipulation, scrutiny must be given to the extent to which the various attitude properties provide conflicting explanations for the effect(s) of the manipulation.

There are a variety of ways in which the effects of a manipulation might be investigated. One that has been used is for the researcher to collect manipulation checks that assess induced differences in the construct of interest. Collection of measures of the focal construct alone are not sufficient for assessing the purity of the manipulation, however. One would also need to measure other constructs that might be affected by the manipulation and that might be responsible for the observed relation between the manipulated variable and the dependent variable. Through use of such procedures, either relatively pure manipulations of the construct of interest might be developed or differences in related constructs might be statistically controlled in order to assess the unique role of the construct of interest. In this way, manipulation procedures can also involve the same steps that are necessary in optimal use of the measurement procedure.

Thus, one of the important refinements for future research on attitude strength is to investigate the extent to which manipulations used in such studies affect more than the primary construct assumed to be associated with the manipulation. As one example of this, consider research on repeated attitude expression. As noted in the earlier sections on attitude accessibility and extremity, each of these constructs can be affected by repeated expression of the attitude (at least under certain conditions). Thus, it is important to note that researchers typically have been careful to separate accessibility from extremity effects (see Fazio, ch. 10, this volume).

Recent research suggests, however, that manipulations of repeated expression can create differences in other strength-related constructs as well. For example, Roese and Olson (1994) found that differences in attitude accessibility (as a result of repeated attitude expression) led to differences in respondents' perceptions of importance of the attitude topic. It might be that differences in attitude

---

[2]Of course, across a number of experiments, a researcher might use different manipulations that each vary the dimension of interest along with some other dimension (e.g., one manipulation that varies accessibility and direct experience, one that varies accessibility and amount of elaboration, one that varies accessibility and attitude extremity, etc.). To the extent that the same results are obtained using these varied manipulations, one might argue that differences in attitude accessibility constitute the most parsimonious explanation of the results (especially if the dimensions confounded with accessibility would not each also reasonably produce the same result).

importance as a result of repeated attitude expression have consequences related to attitude strength. For example, if people seek out and process information more, to the extent that the topic of the information is perceived as more important or relevant, then increases in repeated expression might bring about increases in elaboration. Consistent with this possibility, Priester, Fabrigar, Wegener, and Petty (1994) found that higher levels of repeated attitude expression on the topic of vegetarianism led to higher levels of processing of a later persuasive message on the topic (as evidenced by greater persuasion when strong as opposed to weak arguments were presented in favor of vegetarianism). Regardless of whether perceived importance or relevance is identified as a mediator of this effect, the results of this study suggest that results of repeated expression manipulations might be due in part to differences in elaboration elicited by the repeated expression. Thus, it appears that the manipulation of repeated attitude expression might be related to a variety of strength-related properties of attitudes (i.e., accessibility, extremity, importance, and elaboration).

One potential next step for this research is to investigate the extent to which the various attitudinal dimensions might be responsible for the effects of repeated expression manipulations. For example, researchers might take measures of the attitudinal dimensions in order to index the unique impact of each dimension statistically controlling for the others. Alternatively, researchers might add manipulations that selectively eliminate differences in one or more of the dimensions in order to investigate the contributions of that dimension (e.g., engaging in repeated attitude expression concurrent with a distraction task or not in order to affect the level of spontaneous elaboration of attitude-relevant knowledge that occurs during the repeated expression procedure).

Similar procedures might prove useful for investigating the qualities of manipulations of many of the strength-related dimensions of attitudes. For example, manipulations that increase the amount of general attitude-relevant knowledge that a person possesses have been shown to increase the amount of elaboration given to new information about the attitude object (e.g., see Johnson, in press; Lewan & Stotland, 1961). Because the knowledge given to research participants is often not directly related to the subsequent information (e.g., in a persuasive message), the increase in elaboration could be because of an increase in curiosity about the object or an increase in perceived importance of the object. Are the strength-related effects of these manipulations due to knowledge or due to elaboration? Such questions are likely to be addressed in future research.

Are Measures and Manipulations Interchangeable?

For most of the dimensions of attitudes related to strength, both measures and manipulations have been developed in the literature. These measures and manipulations are often discussed in terms of the same underlying constructs (and are named as such, as in the current chapter). Thus, it would appear that researchers assume that the measures of a strength-related dimension are tapping into the same fundamental construct that is being influenced by manipulations of that strength-related dimension. In many cases, this is probably accurate. One way to refine and improve our studies of attitude strength, however, is to investigate instances in which measures and manipulations might tap somewhat different constructs (and thus might lead to differing strength-related effects).

Consider, for example, measures and manipulations of attitude accessibility. Manipulations of attitude accessibility through repeated attitude expression have been associated with many of the same effects as measures of attitude accessibility through response latency (see Fazio, ch. 10, this volume). Are the two necessarily interchangeable, however? Response latency measures of attitude accessibility are likely to index differences in the ease with which an evaluation of an object comes to mind, but might also be likely to index other properties of an attitude. This is because a variety of dimensions of attitudes might be associated with how often an attitude comes to mind. For example, if people view the attitude object as interesting or relevant to them, it would stand to reason that they would think about the object more often and to a greater extent (e.g., Rennier, 1988). Thus, for example, attitudes measured as high in accessibility could be those attitudes perceived as more important (Krosnick, 1989) and for which more thought has occurred. Other factors might also affect how often the attitude comes to mind (e.g., how much knowledge people have about the object, how interested they are in the object, how many links exist between the attitude object and other pieces of information, etc). Therefore, it is possible that attitudes measured as high in accessibility also tend to be high on a variety of other strength-related properties of attitudes.

If this is the case, one might imagine some cases in which results associated with measures of response latency would differ from those associated with manipulations of attitude accessibility. Consider resistance to counterpersuasion, for example. Results from a variety of studies suggest that increases in resistance are due at least in part to increases in counterarguing of the counterpersuasive appeals (e.g., Haugtvedt & Petty, 1992; Haugtvedt & Wegener, 1994; McGuire, 1964). Without the ability to counterargue the threatening appeal, favorable responses to the appeal are likely to dominate and produce persuasion. Thus, if measures of differences in attitude accessibility also gauge differences in variables that are associated with the availability of counterarguments (e.g., attitude-relevant knowledge or level of elaboration given to the attitude object), measures of accessibility might be more likely to be associated with resistance to counterpersuasion (e.g., Bassili & Fletcher, 1991; Fazio, ch. 10, this volume) than would manipulations of accessibility per se. Importantly, if such differences were found, they would be because of differences in the fundamental constructs being tapped by the measures and manipulations.

Similar issues could be raised concerning measures and manipulations of other strength-related dimensions of attitudes. For example, manipulations of knowledge that do not provide information relevant to claims about the merits of the attitude object are unlikely to produce differences in ability to counterargue persuasive appeals, whereas listing measures of knowledge might often be associated with (and could be coded for) ability to scrutinize persuasive appeals.

CONCLUSION

Many advances have been made investigating the dimensions of attitudes related to attitude strength, yet many important questions remain unresolved. Among the most important of these questions are how our measures and manipulations of strength-related dimensions relate to the constructs we mean to study. At times, single manipulations or measures might affect or assess multiple constructs related to attitude strength. To the extent that this is the case, inferences regarding the unique contributions of each strength-related dimension await procedures that experimentally or statistically control for the confounded dimensions.

In some cases, however, researchers must decide whether their interest is in understanding the unique contribution that one dimension makes to variance in some outcome, or in understanding mediation. That is, in some instances, the crucial role of a strength-related dimension of an attitude is to create differences in another strength-related attitude dimension. In such cases, differences in the two dimensions might not be considered alternative explanations (i.e., confounds) but rather as one dimension mediating the effects of the other dimension. When this occurs, conceptual and empirical advances might be necessary in order to specify the ordering of effects that ultimately result in the strength-related outcomes of interest. Various chapters in this book have offered speculations about some possible causal orderings. Within any such mediational studies, however, the issues raised in this chapter concerning appropriate use of (and inferences based on) manipulation and measurement will be pertinent. Future advances in the study of attitude strength will depend on refinement of current manipulations and measures and will also depend on development of new manipulations and measures that isolate the particular attitudinal dimensions that result in strength-related outcomes.

ACKNOWLEDGMENTS

Preparation of this chapter was supported by an NSF grant to Richard E. Petty (BNS 9021647) and an NSF grant to Jon A. Krosnick (BNS 8920430).

REFERENCES

Aldrich, J. H., Sullivan, J. L., & Borgida, E. (1989). Foreign affairs and issue voting: Do presidential candidates "waltz before a blind audience"? *American Political Science Review, 83*, 123–142.
Anderson, C. A. (1983). Imagination and expectation: The effect of imagining behavioral scripts on personal intentions. *Journal of Personality and Social Psychology, 45*, 293–305.

Apsler, R., & Sears, D. O. (1968). Warning, personal involvement, and attitude change. *Journal of Personality and Social Psychology, 9,* 162–166.

Axsom, D., Yates, S., & Chaiken, S. (1987). Audience response as a heuristic cue in persuasion. *Journal of Personality and Social Psychology, 53,* 30–40.

Bassili, J. N., & Fletcher, J. F. (1991). Response-time measurement in survey research: A method for CATI and a new look at nonattitudes. *Public Opinion Quarterly, 55,* 331–346.

Batra, R., & Ray, M. (1986). Situational effects of advertising repetition: The moderating influence of motivation, ability, and opportunity to respond. *Journal of Consumer Research, 12,* 432–445.

Berger, I. E., & Mitchell, A. A. (1989). The effect of advertising on attitude accessibility, attitude confidence, and the attitude-behavior relationship. *Journal of Consumer Research, 16,* 269–279.

Boninger, D. S., Krosnick, J. A., & Berent, M. K. (in press). The origins of attitude importance: Self-interest, social identification, and value-relevance. *Journal of Personality and Social Psychology.*

Bornstein, R. F. (1989). Exposure and affect: Overview and meta-analysis of research, 1968–1987. *Psychological Bulletin, 106,* 265–289.

Breckler, S. J. (in press). A comparison of numerical indexes for measuring attitudinal ambivalence. *Educational and Psychological Measurement.*

Breckler, S. J., & Wiggins, E. C. (1989). Affect versus evaluation in the structure of attitudes. *Journal of Experimental Social Psychology, 25,* 253–271.

Brickner, M. A., Harkins, S. G., & Ostrom, T. M. (1986). Effects of personal involvement: Thought-provoking implications for social loafing. *Journal of Personality and Social Psychology, 51,* 763–769.

Brock, T. C. (1967). Communication discrepancy and intent to persuade as determinants of counterargument production. *Journal of Experimental Social Psychology, 3,* 296–309.

Brown, R. (1974). Further comment on the risky shift. *American Psychologist, 29,* 468–470.

Burnkrant, R. E., & Howard, D. J. (1984). Effects of the use of introductory rhetorical questions versus statements on information processing. *Journal of Personality and Social Psychology, 47,* 1218–1230.

Cacioppo, J. T., Harkins, S. G., & Petty, R. E. (1981). The nature of attitudes and cognitive responses and their relationships to behavior. In R. E. Petty, T. M. Ostrom, & T. C. Brock (Eds.), *Cognitive responses in persuasion* (pp. 31–54). Hillsdale, NJ: Lawrence Erlbaum Associates.

Cacioppo, J. T., & Petty, R. E. (1980). Sex differences in influenceability: Toward specifying the underlying processes. *Personality and Social Psychology Bulletin, 6,* 651–656.

Cacioppo, J. T., & Petty, R. E. (1982). The need for cognition. *Journal of Personality and Social Psychology, 42,* 116–131.

Cacioppo, J. T., Petty, R. E., & Kao, C. (1984). The efficient assessment of need for cognition. *Journal of Personality Assessment, 48,* 306–307.

Chaiken, S. (1980). Heuristic versus systematic information processing and the use of source versus message cues in persuasion. *Journal of Personality and Social Psychology, 39,* 752–756.

Chaiken, S., & Baldwin, M. W. (1981). Affective-cognitive consistency and the effect of salient behavioral information on the self-perception of attitudes. *Journal of Personality and Social Psychology, 41,* 1–12.

Converse, P. E. (1964). The nature of belief systems in mass publics. In D. E. Apter (Ed.), *Ideology and discontent* (pp. 206–261). New York: The Free Press.

Crites, S., Fabrigar, L., & Petty, R. E. (1994). Measuring the affective and cognitive properties of attitudes: Conceptual and methodological issues. *Personality and Social Psychology Bulletin, 20,* 619–634.

Davidson, A. R., Yantis, S., Norwood, M., & Montano, D. E. (1985). Amount of information about the attitude object and attitude-behavior consistency. *Journal of Personality and Social Psychology, 49,* 1184–1198.

Downing, J. W., Judd, C. M., & Brauer, M. (1992). Effects of repeated expressions on attitude extremity. *Journal of Personality and Social Psychology, 63,* 17–29.

Eagly, A. H., & Chaiken, S. (1993). *The psychology of attitudes.* New York: Harcourt Brace Jovanovich.

Edwards, K. (1990). The interplay of affect and cognition in attitude formation and change. *Journal of Personality and Social Psychology, 59,* 202–216.

Erber, R., & Fiske, S. T. (1984). Outcome dependency and attention to inconsistent information. *Journal of Personality and Social Psychology, 47,* 709–726.

Fazio, R. H. (1986). How do attitudes guide behavior? In R. M. Sorrentino & E. T. Higgins (Eds.), *The handbook of motivation and cognition* (pp. 204–243). New York: Guilford.

Fazio, R. H. (1990). A practical guide to the use of response latency in social psychological research. In C. Hendrick & M. S. Clark (Eds.), *Review of personality and social psychology* (Vol. 11, pp. 74–97). Newbury Park, CA: Sage.

Fazio, R. H., Chen, J., McDonel, E. C., & Sherman, S. J. (1982). Attitude accessibility, attitude-behavior consistency, and the strength of the object-evaluation association. *Journal of Experimental Social Psychology, 18,* 339–357.

Fazio, R. H., Sanbonmatsu, D. M., Powell, M. C., & Kardes, F. R. (1986). On the automatic activation of attitudes. *Journal of Personality and Social Psychology, 50,* 229–238.

Fazio, R. H., & Williams, C. J. (1986). Attitude accessibility as a moderator of the attitude-perception and attitude-behavior relations: An investigation of the 1984 presidential election. *Journal of Personality and Social Psychology, 51,* 505–514.

Fazio, R. H., & Zanna, M. P. (1978a). Attitudinal qualities relating to the strength of the attitude-behavior relationship. *Journal of Experimental Social Psychology, 14,* 398–408.

Fazio, R. H., & Zanna, M. P. (1978b). On the predictive validity of attitudes: The role of direct experience and confidence. *Journal of Personality, 46,* 228–243.

Fishbein, M., & Ajzen, I. (1975). *Belief, attitude, intention, and behavior: An introduction to theory and research.* Reading, MA: Addison-Wesley.

Fukada, H. (1986). Psychological processes mediating the persuasion inhibiting effect of forewarning in fear arousing communication. *Psychological Reports, 58,* 87–90.

Greenwald, A. G. (1968). Cognitive learning, cognitive response to persuasion, and attitude change. In A. G. Greenwald, T. C. Brock, & T. M. Ostrom (Eds.), *Psychological foundations of attitudes* (pp. 148–170). New York: Academic.

Gruder, C. L., Cook, T. D., Hennigan, K. M., Flay, B. R., Alessis, C., & Halamaj, J. (1978). Empirical tests of the absolute sleeper effect predicted from the discounting cue hypothesis. *Journal of Personality and Social Psychology, 36,* 1061–1074.

Grush, J. E. (1976). Attitude formation and mere exposure phenomena: A nonartificial explanation of empirical findings. *Journal of Personality and Social Psychology, 33,* 281–290.

Hass, R. G., Katz, I., Rizzo, N., Bailey, J., & Eisenstadt, D. (1991). Cross-racial appraisal as related to attitude ambivalence and cognitive complexity. *Personality and Social Psychology Bulletin, 17,* 83–92.

Hass, R. G., Katz, I., Rizzo, N., Bailey, J., & Moore, L. (1992). When racial ambivalence evokes negative affect: Using a disguised measure of mood. *Personality and Social Psychology Bulletin, 18,* 786–797.

Haugtvedt, C. P., & Petty, R. E. (1992). Personality and persuasion: Need for cognition moderates the persistence and resistance of attitude changes. *Journal of Personality and Social Psychology, 63,* 308–319.

Haugtvedt, C. P., & Wegener, D. T. (1994). Message order effects in persuasion: An attitude strength perspective. *Journal of Consumer Research, 21,* 205–218.

Howard-Pitney, B., Borgida, E., & Omoto, A. M. (1986). Personal involvement: An examination of processing differences. *Social Cognition, 4,* 39–57.

Hovland, C. I., Harvey, O. J., & Sherif, M. (1957). Assimilation and contrast effects in reactions to communication and attitude change. *Journal of Abnormal and Social Psychology, 55,* 244–252.

Johnson, B. T. (in press). The effects of involvement, argument strength, and topic knowledge on persuasion. *Journal of Experimental Social Psychology.*

Johnson, B. T., & Eagly, A. H. (1989). The effects of involvement on persuasion: A meta-analysis. *Psychological Bulletin, 106,* 290–314.

Judd, C. M., & Johnson, J. T. (1981). Attitudes, polarization, and diagnosticity: Exploring the effects of affect. *Journal of Personality and Social Psychology, 41,* 25–36.

Judd, C. M., & Downing, J. W. (1990). Political expertise and the development of attitude consistency. *Social Cognition, 8,* 104–124.

Judd, C. M., Drake, R. A., Downing, J. W., & Krosnick, J. A. (1991). Some dynamic properties of attitude structures: Context-induced response facilitation and polarization. *Journal of Personality and Social Psychology, 60,* 193–202.

Judd, C. M., & Krosnick, J. A. (1982). Attitude centrality, organization, and measurement. *Journal of Personality and Social Psychology, 42,* 436–447.

Judd, C. M., & Krosnick, J. A. (1989). The structural bases of consistency among political attitudes: Effects of political expertise and attitude importance. In A. R. Pratkanis, S. J. Breckler, & A. G. Greenwald (Eds.), *Attitude structure and function* (pp. 99–128). Hillsdale, NJ: Lawrence Erlbaum Associates.

Kaplan, K. J. (1972). On the ambivalence-indifference problem in attitude theory and measurement: A suggested modification of the semantic differential techniques. *Psychological Bulletin, 77,* 361–372.

Katz, I., & Hass, R. G. (1988). Racial ambivalence and American value conflict: Correlational and priming studies of dual cognitive structures. *Journal of Personality and Social Psychology, 55,* 893–905.

Krosnick, J. A. (1989). Attitude importance and attitude accessibility. *Personality and Social Psychology Bulletin, 15,* 297–308.

Krosnick, J. A., Boninger, D. S., Chuang, Y. C., Berent, M. K., & Carnot, C. G. (1993). Attitude strength: One construct or many related constructs? *Journal of Personality and Social Psychology, 65,* 1132–1151.

Kunst-Wilson, W. R., & Zajonc, R. B. (1980). Affective discrimination of stimuli that cannot be recognized. *Science, 207,* 557–558.

Lewan, P. C., & Stotland, E. (1961). The effects of prior information on susceptibility to an emotional appeal. *Journal of Abnormal and Social Psychology, 62,* 450–453.

Liberman, A., & Chaiken, S. (1991). Value conflict and thought-induced attitude change. *Journal of Experimental Social Psychology, 27,* 203–216.

Lusk, C. M., & Judd, C. M. (1988). Political expertise and the structural mediators of candidate evaluations. *Journal of Experimental Social Psychology, 24,* 105–126.

Manstead, A. S. R., Proffitt, C., & Smart, J. L. (1983). Predicting and understanding mothers' infant-feeding intentions and behavior: Testing the theory of reasoned action. *Journal of Personality and Social Psychology, 44,* 657–671.

McGuire, W. J. (1960a). Cognitive consistency and attitude change. *Journal of Abnormal and Social Psychology, 60,* 345–353.

McGuire, W. J. (1960b). A syllogistic analysis of cognitive relationships. In C. I. Hovland & M. J. Rosenberg (Eds.), *Attitude organization and change: An analysis of consistency among attitude components* (pp. 65–111). New Haven, CT: Yale University Press.

McGuire, W. J. (1964). Inducing resistance to persuasion: Some contemporary approaches. In L. Berkowitz (Ed.), *Advances in experimental social psychology* (Vol. 1, pp. 191–229). San Diego, CA: Academic Press.

McMichael, S. (1992). *Knowledge can both increase and decrease persuasion: An analysis within the Elaboration Likelihood Model.* Unpublished master's thesis, Ohio State University, Columbus.

Millar, M. G., & Millar, K. U. (1990). Attitude change as a function of attitude type and argument type. *Journal of Personality and Social Psychology, 59,* 217–228.

Norman, R. (1975). Affective-cognitive consistency, attitudes, conformity, and behavior. *Journal of Personality and Social Psychology, 32,* 83–91.

Omoto, A. M., & Borgida, E. (1988). Guess who might be coming to dinner?: Personal involvement and racial stereotyping. *Journal of Experimental Social Psychology. 24*, 571–593.

Ostrom, T. M., & Brock, T. C. (1968). A cognitive model of attitudinal involvement. In R. P. Abelson, E. Aronson, W. J. McGuire, T. M. Newcomb, M. J. Rosenberg, & P. H. Tannenbaum (Eds.), *Theories of cognitive consistency: A sourcebook* (pp. 373–383). Chicago: Rand McNally.

Petty, R. E., & Cacioppo, J. T. (1977). Forewarning, cognitive responding, and resistance to persuasion. *Journal of Personality and Social Psychology, 35*, 645–655.

Petty, R. E., & Cacioppo, J. T. (1979a). Effects of forewarning of persuasive intent and involvement on cognitive responses. *Personality and Social Psychology Bulletin, 5*, 173–176.

Petty, R. E., & Cacioppo, J. T. (1979b). Issue involvement can increase or decrease persuasion by enhancing message-relevant cognitive responses. *Journal of Personality and Social Psychology, 37*, 1915–1926.

Petty, R. E., & Cacioppo, J. T. (1984). The effects of involvement on responses to argument quantity and quality: Central and peripheral routes to persuasion. *Journal of Personality and Social Psychology, 46*, 69–81.

Petty, R. E., & Cacioppo, J. T. (1986). *Communication and persuasion: Central and peripheral routes to attitude change.* New York: Springer-Verlag.

Petty, R. E., & Cacioppo, J. T. (1990). Involvement and persuasion: Tradition versus integration. *Psychological Bulletin, 107*, 367–374.

Petty, R. E., Cacioppo, J. T., & Haugtvedt, C. (1992). Involvement and persuasion: An appreciative look at the Sherifs' contribution to the study of self-relevance and attitude change. In D. Granberg & G. Sarup (Eds.), *Social judgment and intergroup relations: Essays in honor of Muzafer Sherif* (pp. 147–174). New York: Springer-Verlag.

Petty, R. E., Harkins, S. G., & Williams, K. D. (1980). The effects of group diffusion of cognitive effort on attitudes: An information processing view. *Journal of Personality and Social Psychology, 38*, 81–92.

Petty, R. E., Harkins, S. G., Williams, K. D., & Latané, B. (1977). The effects of group size on cognitive effort and evaluation. *Personality and Social Psychology Bulletin, 3*, 579–582.

Petty, R. E., Priester, J. R., & Wegener, D. T. (1994). Cognitive processes in attitude change. In R. S. Wyer & T. K. Srull (Eds.), *Handbook of social cognition (2nd Edition)* (Vol. 2, pp. 69–142). Hillsdale, NJ: Lawrence Erlbaum Associates.

Petty, R. E., Wells, G. L., & Brock, T. C. (1976). Distraction can enhance or reduce yielding to propaganda: Thought disruption versus effort justification. *Journal of Personality and Social Psychology, 34*, 874–884.

Powell, M. C., & Fazio, R. H. (1984). Attitude accessibility as a function of repeated attitudinal expression. *Personality and Social Psychology Bulletin, 10*, 139–148.

Pratkanis, A. R., Greenwald, A. G., Leippe, M. R., & Baumgardner, M. H. (1988). In search of reliable persuasion effects: III. The sleeper effect is dead. Long live the sleeper effect. *Journal of Personality and Social Psychology, 54*, 203–218.

Priester, J. R., Fabrigar, L. R., Wegener, D. T., & Petty, R. E. (1994, May). *Message elaboration as a function of manipulated attitude accessibility.* Paper presented at the annual meeting of the Midwestern Psychological Association, Chicago, IL.

Priester, J. R., & Petty, R. E. (1993, May). *The nature of attitudinal ambivalence: An experimental investigation.* Paper presented at the annual meeting of the Midwestern Psychological Association, Chicago, IL.

Regan, D. T., & Fazio, R. H. (1977). On the consistency between attitudes and behavior: Look to the method of attitude formation. *Journal of Experimental Social Psychology, 13*, 28–45.

Rennier, G. A. (1988). *The strength of the object-evaluation association, the attitude-behavior relationship, and the elaboration likelihood model of persuasion.* Unpublished doctoral dissertation, University of Missouri, Columbia.

Roese, N. J., & Olson, J. M. (1994). Attitude importance as a function of repeated attitude expression. *Journal of Experimental Social Psychology, 30*, 39–51.

Rosenberg, M. (1968). Hedonism, inauthenticity, and other goads toward expansion of a consistency theory. In R. P. Abelson, E. Aronson, W. J. McGuire, T. M. Newcomb, M. J. Rosenberg, & P. H. Tannenbaum (Eds.) *Theories of cognitive consistency: A sourcebook* (pp. 73–111). Chicago: Rand McNally.

Sadler, O., & Tesser, A. (1973). Some effects of salience and time upon interpersonal hostility and attraction during social isolation. *Sociometry, 36*, 99–112.

Sample, J., & Warland, R. (1973). Attitudes and the prediction of behavior. *Social Forces, 51*, 292–304.

Sawyer, A. G. (1981). Repetition, cognitive responses, and persuasion. In R. E. Petty, T. M. Ostrom, & T. C. Brock (Eds.), *Cognitive responses in persuasion* (pp. 237–261). Hillsdale, NJ: Lawrence Erlbaum Associates.

Sherif, C., Sherif, M., & Nebergall, R. (1965). *Attitude and attitude change: The social judgment-involvement approach*. Philadelphia: Saunders.

Sherman, S. J., Presson, C. C., Chassin, L., Bensenberg, M., Corty, E., & Olshavsky, R. W. (1982). Smoking intentions in adolescents: Direct experience and predictability. *Personality and Social Psychology Bulletin, 8*, 376–383.

Sidanius, J. (1988). Political sophistication and political deviance: A structural equation examination of context theory. *Journal of Personality and Social Psychology, 55*, 37–51.

Sivacek, J., & Crano, W. D. (1982). Vested interest as a moderator of attitude-behavior consistency. *Journal of Personality and Social Psychology, 43*, 210–221.

Songer-Nocks, E. (1976). Situational factors affecting the weighting of predictor components in the Fishbein Model. *Journal of Experimental Social Psychology, 12*, 56–69.

Tesser, A. (1978). Self-generated attitude change. In L. Berkowitz (Ed.), *Advances in experimental social psychology* (Vol. 11, pp. 289–338). San Diego, CA: Academic.

Tesser, A., & Leone, C. (1977). Cognitive schemas and thought as a determinant of attitude change. *Journal of Experimental Social Psychology, 13*, 340–356.

Tourangeau, R., Rasinski, K. A., Bradburn, N., & D'Andrade, R. (1989). Belief accessibility and context effects in attitude measurement. *Journal of Experimental Social Psychology, 25*, 401–421.

Van der Pligt, J., Ester, P., & Van der Lindern, J. (1983). Attitude extremity, consensus and diagnosticity. *European Journal of Social Psychology, 13*, 437–439.

Verplanken, B. (1991). Persuasive communication of risk information: A test of cue versus message processing effects in a field experiment. *Personality and Social Psychology Bulletin, 17*, 188–193.

Watts, W. A., & McGuire, W. J. (1964). Persistence of induced opinion change and retention of the inducing message contents. *Journal of Abnormal and Social Psychology, 68*, 233–241.

Wilson, T. D., Kraft, D., & Dunn, D. S. (1989). The disruptive effects of explaining attitudes: The moderating effect of knowledge about the attitude object. *Journal of Experimental Social Psychology, 25*, 379–400.

Wood, W. (1982). Retrieval of attitude-relevant information from memory: Effects on susceptibility to persuasion and on intrinsic motivation. *Journal of Personality and Social Psychology, 42*, 798–810.

Wood, W., Kallgren, C. A., & Preisler, R. M. (1985). Access to attitude-relevant information in memory as a determinant of persuasion: The role of message attributes. *Journal of Experimental Social Psychology, 21*, 73–85.

Wu, C., & Shaffer, D. R. (1987). Susceptibility to persuasive appeals as a function of source credibility and prior experience with the attitude object. *Journal of Personality and Social Psychology, 52*, 677–688.

Zaller, J. (1990). Political awareness, elite opinion leadership, and the mass survey response. *Social Cognition, 8*, 125–153.

Author Index

Subject Index